INTERACTIVE COMPUTER GRAPHICS

Functional, Procedural and Device-Level Methods

INTERNATIONAL COMPUTER SCIENCE SERIES

Consulting Editors   **A D McGettrick**   University of Strathclyde
                             J van Leeuwen   University of Utrecht

SELECTED TITLES IN THE SERIES

Comparative Programming Languages   *L B Wilson and R G Clark*

Distributed Systems: Concepts and Design   *G Coulouris and J Dollimore*

C Programming in a UNIX Environment   *J Kay and R Kummerfeld*

Numerical Methods with FORTRAN 77: A Practical Introduction   *L V Atkinson, P J Harley and J D Hudson*

Software Engineering (3rd Edn)   *I Sommerville*

High-Level Languages and their Compilers   *D Watson*

Programming in Ada (3rd Edn)   *J G P Barnes*

Elements of Functional Programming   *C Reade*

Software Development with Modula-2   *D Budgen*

Programming for Artificial Intelligence: Methods, Tools and Applications
W Kreutzer and B J McKenzie

Common Lisp Programming for Artificial Intelligence   *T Hasemer and J Domingue*

TITLES OF RELATED INTEREST

Parallel Processing for Computer Vision and Display   *P Dew, R Earnshaw and T Heywood* (Eds)

Fundamentals of Interactive Computer Graphics   *J Foley and A van Dam*

Computer Graphics: Systems and Concepts   *R Salmon and M Slater*

Fundamentals of Three-Dimensional Computer Graphics   *A Watt*

SIGGRAPH Conference Proceedings   *ACM Press*

INTERACTIVE COMPUTER GRAPHICS

Functional, Procedural and Device-Level Methods

Peter Burger
Duncan Gillies
Imperial College of Science, Technology and Medicine

Addison-Wesley Publishing Company

Wokingham, England · Reading, Massachusetts · Menlo Park, California
New York · Don Mills, Ontario · Amsterdam · Bonn
Sydney · Singapore · Tokyo · Madrid · San Juan

The programs presented in this book have been included for their instructional
value. They have been tested with care but are not guaranteed for any particular
purpose. The publisher does not offer any warranties or representations, nor does
it accept any liabilities with respect to the programs.

Many of the designations used by manufacturers and sellers to distinguish their
products are claimed as trademarks. Addison-Wesley has made every attempt to
supply trademark information about manufacturers and their products mentioned
in this book. A list of the trademark designations and their owners appears on
page xvi.

Cover designed by Marshall Henrichs
and printed by The Riverside Printing Co. (Reading) Ltd.
Illustrations by Chartwell Illustrators.
Typeset by CRB Typesetting Services, Ely, Cambs.
Printed in Great Britain by The Bath Press, Avon.

First printed 1989.   Reprinted 1990.

British Library Cataloguing in Publication Data
Gillies, Duncan
   Interactive computer graphics: functional, procedural and device-level
   methods.
   1. Computer systems. Graphic displays
   I. Title   II. Burger, Peter
   006.6

   ISBN 0-201-17439-1

Library of Congress Cataloguing in Publication Data
Gillies, Duncan.
   Interactive computer graphics / Duncan Gillies, Peter Burger.
      p.   cm.
   Bibliography: p.
   Includes index.
   ISBN 0-201-17439-1
   1. Computer graphics.   I. Burger, Peter.   II. Title.
T385.G53 1989
006.6--dc19
                                                        88-15766
                                                            CIP

Preface

Rationale for the book

The curious reader looking at this book for the first time will probably be wondering why we wrote a new book on interactive computer graphics when there are at present a large number of books available on the market. Our first impetus for writing this book came in 1985 when we first taught a final year Honours Computer Science course consisting entirely of computer graphics topics. We found that it was difficult to recommend to the students one book containing all the material we wanted to cover. Moreover, it became rapidly clear that the subject of computer graphics is particularly prone to partial treatment by most authors. Some authors provide an excellent theoretical foundation, but fall short on practical methods, whereas others provide solutions, sometimes in the form of programs, but give little insight into how they were obtained.

It is now well established that software engineers need to use different levels of abstraction to describe problems. Graphics programmers are no exception to this rule, and, as the title of this book indicates, we distinguish between three levels of abstraction: the **functional**, **procedural** and **device** levels. Initial specifications require abstract, high-level tools capable of expressing the whole problem succinctly. Over the last few years, computer scientists have used formal mathematical methods to define specifications. More recently, functional languages have been developed to provide a direct implementation of this highest level. At this time, however, these implementations are inefficient and as yet unsuitable for many problems. Nevertheless, description at the functional level remains an important technique for providing an overall understanding of solutions to complex problems. Practical software engineers will need to describe their system procedurally, in the form of algorithms. Imperative languages now provide excellent design support for implementation at the procedural level and are suitable for solving a wide variety of problems. However, there are cases where the properties of the actual hardware devices cannot be ignored. These are often problems involving user inter-action or other time-dependent constraints. Thus, software engineers may need to utilize device features, such as specific register addresses, in their programs.

In interactive computer graphics, there are well-developed functional, procedural and device-level descriptions. In many cases, they cannot be separated from each other, and a full understanding of each is essential in mastering the difficulties of this very complex field. The following example will illuminate this claim.

Drawing a three-dimensional scene containing opaque solid bodies is a very common and important preoccupation of computer graphics researchers and is based on the determination of the portions of object surfaces visible to the viewer. This is appropriately called the **visible surface determination problem**. In its more abstract form, the problem can be expressed functionally through Cartesian geometry, or by means of vector algebra. These descriptions are well understood and can provide designers with a high degree of confidence that their algorithms are correct. However, any picture that we wish to generate will have a finite resolution. Thus, vertices cannot be represented as infinitely small points, nor edges as infinitely thin lines. There are many details hidden by the abstract, functional level that must be considered before a picture can be drawn. In the past 25 years, literally hundreds of algorithms have been devised, or reinvented, and optimized for solving the visible surface problem at the procedural level. It is unlikely that further gain will accrue from refining the procedural methods. Instead, recent attention has been paid to the graphics devices themselves. In the past five years, technology and graphics hardware advances have provided a special hardware solution called the **z-buffer**, which will probably replace most software-based algorithms in the future. Consequently, to fully understand the visible surface problem, and indeed many other topics of computer graphics, it is essential to deal with all three levels.

In formulating the functional level descriptions in this book, we have made extensive use of vector algebra. The comprehensive treatment of geometrical relationships by vectors may be new to many readers, and may at first seem difficult. However, there are major advantages in this approach. Vector algebra, being more abstract than Cartesian geometry, allows considerable simplification to be made to the analysis of a problem. The reader who is familiar with Cartesian methods can verify this fact by glancing at the derivations for the specularly reflected vector on page 309 or the refractively transmitted vector on page 391 or the texture mapping of a quadrilateral on page 412. Compared with the derivations provided by other authors using Cartesian space, these are simple, concise and elegant. The importance of vector algebra as a simple tool for describing geometry can be seen clearly when dealing with three-dimensional problems. These are notoriously difficult to visualize and consequently prone to errors.

Vector algebra allows a uniform treatment of two- and three-dimensional space, and provides a simple yet highly expressive notation for three-dimensional problems. Thus, its use allows programmers to formalize and prove their algorithms before expressing them procedurally. This gives them a higher degree of confidence that their solutions are correct. After having used vector methods extensively for the past four years, we are fully convinced of the advantages they provide for describing geometrical relationships. Vector equations have proved almost invaluable in several areas, particularly ray tracing, spline surfaces and texture mapping.

There are many excellent books on vector methods currently available. However, these are not related to the specific problem of computer graphics. Conversely, many computer graphics authors have shied away from the more mathematically difficult topics, or have collected the mathematical derivations of computer graphics subjects in a separate book. Where they have used vector algebra, it has usually been for notational convenience, rather than as a tool for analysis or argument. Selecting vector algebra as our fundamental mathematical tool, we have found that it is possible to keep the complexity of derivations down and still treat the topics in a rigorous manner.

Turning to the procedural level, we find that, as ultimately a picture will be drawn with reference to the X–Y co-ordinates of the screen or printed page, the most appropriate mathematical tool is Cartesian geometry. This proves to be most convenient, since a mapping between vector space and Cartesian space is easy to achieve in practice. Thus, graphics programmers can analyze their problem extensively in vector space and, having arrived at the simplest solution, can translate it into Cartesian geometry for implementation.

Although the interface between the functional and procedural levels is easy to manipulate, procedural methods are far from simple. We have often made this discovery through generating the illustrations for this book. We believe that it is only possible to teach a computing subject at a deep level of understanding by actually implementing one's algorithms. Time and time again we have found that it is not a trivial matter to implement graphics algorithms. Often, the exceptional cases make a seemingly straightforward algorithm very difficult or even useless to implement. Many workers in computer graphics do not actually generate their own pictures, and the pictures used in the majority of textbooks have not been generated by the authors. We believe that is is only possible to present the procedural level correctly by implementing all the algorithms. We have followed this principle, even to the extent that our colour plates, with one exception, have been exclusively generated by us or by our students. The one exception is the complete CIE chromaticity diagram, which, as we show in Chapter 7, cannot be generated by computer. Complex computer-generated pictures take hours of both programmer and computer time. However, we believe that the effort invested is worthwhile.

We have found numerous occasions where the obvious procedural solutions contain subtle difficulties that no previous authors have reported; for example, the need to preserve the vertical direction in picture transformations to avoid turning objects upside-down, which we describe beginning on page 182.

Lastly, by generating our own pictures we have been forced to think carefully about the device level. This is particularly so in our case, since we have been using low-cost hardware, and it has been essential to program it in a way that utilizes it to the full.

Our answer to the original question of 'Why did we write yet another book on interactive graphics' may now be summarized. We wanted to present a comprehensive coverage of the material based on the three hierarchical levels. We believe that this treatment is theoretically well founded and of immediate practical use, and that by relating the functional description to the device level we have provided an effective methodology for graphics program design.

How the book can be used

This book is primarily aimed at the final year undergraduate or graduate student of computer science or engineering taking a comprehensive, advanced course in computer graphics. However, it includes much more material than one could hope to cover in a term of lectures, and can serve as a reference book on computer graphics for postgraduates working in industry or in research.

We have assumed that the reader is familiar with mathematics up to elementary calculus and has studied physics at the high school and secondary school level. During the teaching of this material, we have found that our students' elementary knowledge of vectors and matrices was sometimes insufficient for their effective use in graphics. Once the concepts of position and direction vectors and vector equations are better understood by the student, progress becomes easier. For this reason, an appendix summarizing these methods has been included.

During the writing of the book, we spent many hours trying to find relevant information in other books and papers. Often, descriptions were given without many of the important and relevant details, so that when we were ready to implement a graphics procedure, we still had to spend time working out the details. Thus, we decided to direct this book both to the student who wants to find out about computer graphics and to those who want to go further and implement some of the algorithms. We strongly believe that neither computer source code nor mathematical equations should be used by themselves to demonstrate principles. This tends to mix up the functional and procedural levels and leads to confusion. We have therefore adopted a compromise in describing the interface between the functional and procedural levels by using a rather flexible pseudo-code of our own. The main idea of using pseudo-code is to hide details that are readily understood by the implementer. We believe that a programmer familiar with any conventional high-level language should be able to translate these algorithms into computer code. On the other hand, the student who does not wish to get involved with programming should be able to understand the important algorithmic aspects from the pseudo-code descriptions. Some authors have gone further to provide actual programs in their books. The justification for doing this is usually to make the book more practical. However, we believe that it has the opposite effect. It encourages readers to take the lazy course of typing in the code without fully understanding it. This is poor programming practice and if applied to large systems will be the source of many errors and considerable wasted time.

It is our belief that a rigorous basis for any aspect of science and engineering is essential. All the same, we realize that there are many readers with a flair for graphics and programming who find mathematical argument difficult. Consequently, we have tried to add enough verbal explanations to the derivations so that those who do not like algebra can still follow the line of reasoning without actually working out the equations themselves. However, as with all other algebraic proofs or procedures, a fuller understanding will only come from actually doing the algebra.

To assist teachers who may wish to base a course on this book, we have provided practise material for students at the end of each chapter. These are of three kinds: exercises, problems and projects. Exercises are the most elementary and are intended to assist the student in memorizing the important aspects of each chapter. The next level are called problems. We would normally set similar problems for a supervised tutorial period, where the students may require occasional hints and advice on the solution. Lastly, we have provided suggestions for projects. These are of greater scope, requiring program design and implementation, and could form the basis of a whole term's practical work.

Organization of the book

In organizing the book, we have taken care to order the material in a coherent manner without forward references. However, we have also tried to ensure that as many of the topics as possible are self-sufficient and do not depend on material covered in an earlier part of the book. Thus, the book can be used selectively. Some topics have received extensive treatment which may not be of interest to all readers and may be left out. The inclusion of material was not always governed by the breadth of its applicability. Sometimes topics were included because they are not available elsewhere, and this enhances the reference aspect of this book.

The first five chapters would be normally covered by most courses on computer graphics.

Chapter 1 lays the foundation of our treatment of the whole subject and its division into the three hierarchical levels. It also describes the device level in sufficient detail to understand how pictures are generated by a computer. Hardware devices are not discussed again until Chapter 10.

Chapter 2 deals with graphics systems and provides an overview of the currently popular GKS standard. It may seem that some of the material relating to devices is redundant, but it is very important to demonstrate that devices must be described at both the hardware and systems levels. An often neglected but very essential part of all graphics systems, the graphics database, is also extensively discussed. This chapter introduces the concept of device-independent graphics, which is applied in most modern graphics systems.

Chapter 3 discusses how pictures may be generated for raster scan devices from a geometrical description of data. The extensive treatment on second-order curve generation may be skipped without endangering the understanding of the rest of the book. Simulation of half-toning is a useful technique for users of cheap computer systems who are provided only with a bi-level display device.

Chapter 4 is an important chapter since it introduces the vector methods that are extensively used in the rest of the book. This is the chapter where the analytical foundations of our derivations are described. Readers unfamiliar with vector algebra should study it alongside the appendix, which contains the operations and rules of vector and matrix algebra. In this chapter, we also apply vectors to visualizing and analyzing geometrical relationships in three-dimensional space. The simple method of constructing a straight line from a starting point (position vector) and a direction (direction vector) finds many uses in the subsequent chapters of the book.

Chapter 5 introduces the classical three-dimensional graphics problem of displaying solid opaque objects. It is an important chapter for the understanding of techniques used in traditional computer graphics and also for the many applications of vector equations to be found in it. Anyone who would like to have an understanding of the problems and techniques that interactive graphics program designers face should study Chapter 5 thoroughly.

Chapters 6 to 10 are more specialized than the preceding ones. They all cover important topics but it may not be necessary to study them in great depth. It is our belief that no chapter should be completely skipped, although some may be reviewed rather than studied in detail. It is difficult to ascribe an order of importance to them since it will be determined by the particular interests of the students or teachers. Chapter 10, which discusses computer hardware, should definitely be included in a modern course because at this time more and more graphics solutions are emigrating to the hardware.

Chapters 6 and 8 contain a great deal of algebra. Nevertheless, it is important to demonstrate how spline curves are constructed. The idea of a blending function is a fundamental concept that should not be ignored. Ray tracing is also an important technique and it should be possible to cover the principles of ray tracing without the details of the algebra if desired. Sections on ray tracing a CSG tree may be skipped without affecting the coverage of other parts of the book; however, the concept of a CSG model should be at least reviewed in a comprehensive computer graphics course.

Chapters 7 and 9 are concerned with providing realistic computer-generated pictures and should be of interest to students who would like to generate their own. The illustrations accompanying this book provide proof that, with quite affordable equipment and some patience, interesting pictures can be generated.

We have chosen not to provide a comprehensive list of publications on computer graphics. Several other books and review articles contain such lists, which may be of little use to the undergraduate student who will not have time to pursue the subject further. Researchers in computer graphics will normally compile their own lists. Instead, we have referred to some classic papers whose contents have stood the test of time and to a few modern papers that provide further treatment of aspects we have not included. We believe that these references provide specialist backup for interested readers and a minimal set from which a research student could begin to work in computer graphics.

Supplement

An *Instructor's Guide* is available from the publisher, containing: selected solutions to exercises and problems; some useful and practical algorithms used by the authors; and teaching hints for the instructor.

Acknowledgements

We are indebted to many of our students who made suggestions, criticized our notes and provided encouragement in developing the material for this book. We have been particularly fortunate to be able to participate in the International Association for the Exchange of Students for Technical Experience (IAESTE) scheme. Under its auspices, we have been able to employ summer vacation students from around the world who have helped us with the programming, and have made their own individual contributions to the book. In particular, we would like to thank Zoltan Fekete from Hungary, Lina Karam from Lebanon, Mofana Mphaka from Lesotho and Anna Stickler from Austria. Our own students have also made extensive contributions. It would be impossible to write a comprehensive list of those who have influenced our thinking, either through argument or through the results of their project work. However, Roger Sayle deserves particular mention for his work on the generation of the ray-traced colour plates, including the cover illustration. Lastly, we would like to thank our employer, Imperial College of Science, Technology and Medicine, who gave us the intellectual freedom to design and teach courses on computer graphics, and the time to write this book.

Peter Burger
Duncan Gillies
April 1989

Contents

1

Device-Level Graphics

Computers and graphics devices are the basic components of both computer graphics and image-processing systems. Graphics systems usually generate their own images, while those of image-processing systems are captured by a video camera. Interactive computer graphics systems allow user interaction and can be described at three hierarchical system levels: device, procedural and functional. The role of the operating system and the graphics database within this system structure are also very important. It is essential to make a clear distinction between the physical devices and the device level. The operation and basic functionality of both output and input devices are discussed in this chapter. Current interest is focused on raster-type output devices; however, vector-generating and hardcopy devices are also integral parts of graphics systems. Graphical input device types are many and varied. The keyboard and the mouse, which are the two most common ones, are discussed in detail in this chapter. Others, such as digital tablets, digitizers and video cameras are also worth studying. Building on the physical devices, the device level presents an interface to applications with which the input and output functions are activated. The device level consists of enquiry, output and input functions. A small but sufficient set of these three types of device functions can be defined for a simple interactive graphics system.

1.1   INTRODUCTION

The term **computer graphics** is often associated with flying images of space vehicles, transparent glass-like crystal balls bouncing almost weightlessly on a computer screen or with fierce-looking aliens trying to outwit and kill an innocent-looking person on the screen in an arcade game. And, indeed, at least in terms of computer time and man-years of effort, these computer graphics activities have been the most prominent in the recent past. There is a measure of fascination in creating the appearance of a solid object on the screen of a computer solely by the execution of a list of computer instructions. Figure 1.1 shows an example of a computer-generated image. In this case, it is a solid cup made of some imaginary material and illuminated by two light sources. The surface properties of the cup, its orientation and size, and the number and position of light sources are of course all controlled by the computer program. Nevertheless, the cup looks real and solid. This image was generated by very simple means – a personal computer or PC and a simple graphics system – and required very little computer time. More elaborate computer-generated scenes, such as the ones generated for Hollywood, require the resources of larger and more expensive computers.

Figure 1.1
Computer-generated picture of a three-dimensional solid surface of revolution. Two light sources are used and parameters are set so that the object seems to be made of a shiny material.

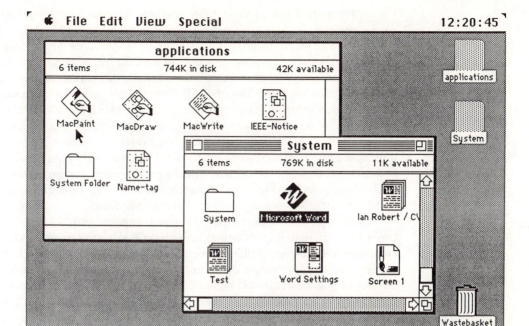

Figure 1.2

The screen of an Apple MacIntosh computer shows graphical man–machine interface. The mouse marker is shown as an arrow under the icon named MacPaint. The icon named Microsoft Word has been selected for action and is shown in reverse video.

Figure 1.3

Photograph of a mouse which is a versatile graphical input device. Being low cost, it revolutionized the man–machine interface of many modern computer systems.

But there is more to computer graphics than the creation of realistic scenes. Figure 1.2 shows the computer screen of an Apple Macintosh Plus computer. The graphical images on the screen, called **icons**, are created and manipulated by graphics programs and are used for communication between the user and the computer. A pointing device, the **mouse**, which can be pushed around the table (Figure 1.3), controls the position of the arrow shown at the top left of Figure 1.2 just under the icon named **MacPaint**. By pointing to an icon and depressing the button on the mouse input device, the user can select a particular application program for execution. This form of graphical communication using both graphical input and output devices has revolutionized the man–machine interface of modern computers and will probably become the most significant contribution of computer graphics to man's powerful set of computer tools in the near future.

Another very important area where computer graphics plays a central role is engineering design. **Computer-aided engineering (CAE)** and **computer-aided design (CAD)** are being extensively used in a large number of areas, including aerospace, automotive engineering, boat building, civil engineering and electronics. Figure 1.4 shows a digital circuit diagram as it would appear on a computer screen, with a small area of the overall circuit enlarged. The ability of such CAE programs to roam around large, dense and complicated diagrams and selectively display parts of the design at any level of magnification is just one example of the versatility that can be achieved by computer graphics in the design process (see Colour Plates 1 and 2).

Yet another and equally important area where computer graphics techniques are used is business. In Figure 1.5, two typical graphical representations (bars and pie chart) of business data are shown.

It would be possible to continue this listing of application areas of computer graphics for a long time. However, the examples given so far give a good indication of the wide range of application areas in practice.

Complementary to computer graphics is the important related field of image processing. The term **image processing** is used to describe those computer-processing activities that deal with real images – that is, images captured by a camera and converted to numerical data. For example, Figure 1.6 shows an internal view of the human colon. Superimposed on this image are computer-generated contour lines, which are of importance to the clinician. Applications of image processing include medical imaging and automatic diagnosis of medical images, robotic vision, automatic satellite surveillance and many more.

In general, computer graphics covers the generation and manipulation of graphics scenes (pictures) by a digital computer. The origin of the pictures distinguishes computer graphics from image processing. Image processing is mainly concerned with the manipulation of real video images obtained by a camera. For computer graphics, on the other hand, it is more usual for the pictures to be defined either by numerical data or by

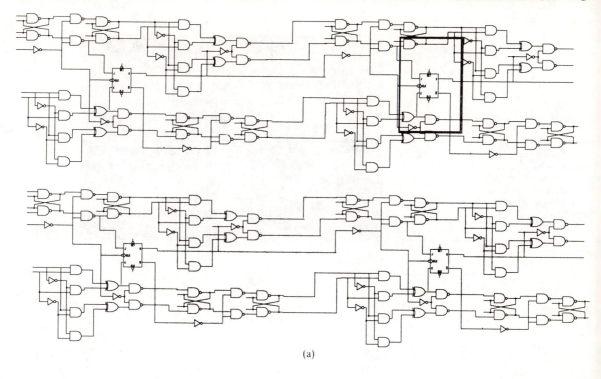

(a)

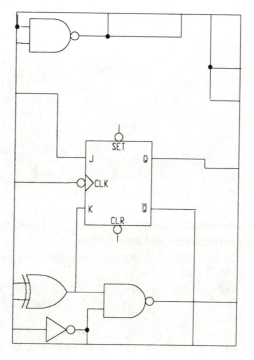

(b)

Figure 1.4

Example of graphical output for a CAD program to help in the construction of complex digital circuit diagrams. The inset shows a magnified or 'zoomed in' area of the circuit. Graphical means are most effective for presenting complex systems that have large amounts of detail.

Figure 1.5
Graphical presentation has become the preferred way of dealing with business data. Standard bar and pie charts are shown in this computer-generated picture. Normally, the diagrams would use colour to provide a more easily readable chart. In modern business systems, these charts can be automatically generated from data contained in spread sheets.

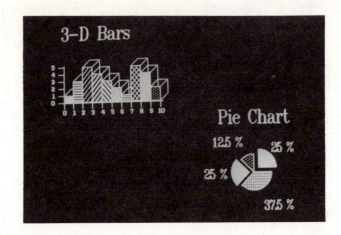

Figure 1.6
A large number of medical diagnostic techniques use both image processing and computer graphics to provide valuable information to the physician. Superimposed on an image from an endoscope, patches of dark areas are outlined by subdivided rectangular regions.

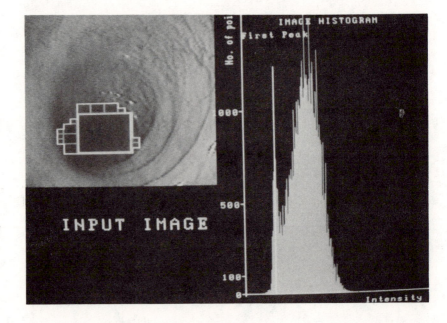

algorithms. Thus, the practitioners of computer graphics create visual images never before seen by human eyes. Some of the important activities of computer graphics, several of which were described earlier, are:

- business charts,
- desk-top publishing,
- graphic user interfaces,
- computer-assisted teaching,
- industrial training,
- scientific plots,
- modelling and simulation,
- computer-aided design,
- drafting,
- movies,
- computer games,
- advertising,
- television logos.

whereas the major activities in the closely related field of image processing include:

- picture enhancement,
- segmentation,
- feature detection,
- pattern recognition,
- three-dimensional reconstruction,
- model construction.

Since video images must be quantized for computer storage, images representing real scenes must also be expressed as digital data before they can be processed. Hence, when these images are displayed and manipulated by a computer, areas of computer graphics overlap areas of image processing.

Interactive computer graphics is mainly concerned with the generation and manipulation of graphics scenes in real time with human control or interaction. Since the ultimate evaluation of a graphical image can be done only by a person viewing the image, all computer graphics activities could be considered interactive. Unfortunately, *real time* often means waiting minutes or hours for a completed picture. The requirements for effective real-time processing in computer graphics place a significant burden on even the largest and fastest computers.

The generation and control of computer images requires knowledge in many fields of computing, from the detailed knowledge of graphics hardware to the presently active research areas of functional and object-oriented programming. Before discussing the details of how graphical images are generated by a computer, let us look first at the hierarchical nature of computer systems designed for picture generation.

1.2   INTERACTIVE COMPUTER GRAPHICS SYSTEMS

The purpose of computer graphics is to generate and manipulate graphics scenes. As was mentioned in the last section, even if the final result is a static picture, it is impossible to work with computer graphics without an interactive facility, since the only way the results can be evaluated is by looking at it. Therefore, an interactive facility will always be assumed in these discussions of graphics systems. Three levels of an interactive computer graphics system can be distinguished, as shown in Figure 1.7.

Figure 1.7

A graphics system can be divided into three hierarchical levels as shown. When designing such a system, it is important to remember that the ultimate performance depends on all three levels and how well they relate to each other.

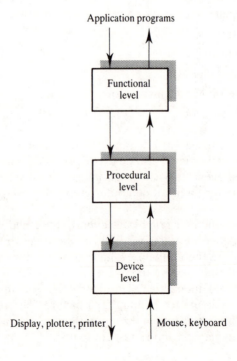

(1)   the **functional level**,

(2)   the **procedural level**,

(3)   the **device level**.

The highest level is the functional level. Here, commands are expressed in terms of graphics requirements. Informally, these requirements can be specified in terms such as: 'draw a chart from given data', 'draw the perspective view of a building or a city', 'generate the changing scene visible through the window of a helicopter', and so on. In practice, however, formal notations are needed for expressing such concepts; indeed, there are specific application packages, and even special graphics languages, that have been developed for special applications.

The lowest level is the device level. This is the level where the actual scenes are generated. Physical graphics devices, often referred to as **hardware**, are naturally classified into two groups, **input** and **output devices**, where the point of reference is the computer. Input devices provide data to the computer whereas output devices generate the graphics scenes from data stored or generated by the computer.

Input devices fall into two classes: those that are manipulated by the user – for example, pointer devices like the mouse, light pen and digitizing tablet; and those that convert real images into digital data – for example, video cameras and optical scanners. Output devices can also be classified into two types. One type is used interactively and is referred to here as a **display device**. The other type produces hardcopy output and includes devices such as pen plotters, matrix printers, laser printers, ink jet printers, typesetting equipment and microfilm printers. Although attention will be focused on the interactive type of output device, the effective use of hardcopy devices is also a difficult and important aspect of computer graphics. The authors were painfully reminded of the importance of hardcopy output by the problems they faced in providing illustrations for this book.

It is important to make a distinction between what is called the device level and the physical devices themselves. For example, the actual electrical signals that produce a bright dot on the screen may be very far removed from the computer instruction (possibly given in a higher-level language) that initiates this action. The term 'device level' is defined therefore as the collection of facilities (callable from a computer program) that are fixed for a given computer graphics system. In practice, the device level includes the actual physical input and output devices, the device driver programs and the operating system facilities that serve the graphics devices.

Many of the practical difficulties that graphics programmers face originate from the huge variety and scope of device-level functions. Graphics devices of today are often highly complex and may themselves contain complex multiprocessing system software, large memory systems

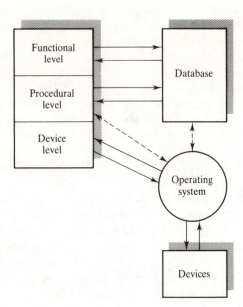

Figure 1.8

The database and the operating system play important roles in graphics systems. This schematic diagram indicates how the three system levels and the other parts of the computer system are connected.

and parallel or pipelined data processors. Because of the interactive nature of the system, the speed of processing is an important consideration for graphics software designers and this speed is greatly influenced by the utilization of device-level facilities. However, it is very difficult to discuss these problems in general terms, exactly because of the large variety of device-level functionality found in different systems. What is important at this point is the recognition that in every system there will be a device-level boundary that is defined by a set of fixed device-level functions. These may include simple drawing functions like drawing a line or a circle, or filling an area with a particular colour or shades of colours. With the rapid advances of very-large-scale integration (VLSI) graphics processors, more and more graphics facilities are being included in the device level, thereby drawing the functional and device levels closer and closer together.

Whatever is left between the functional and the device levels – that is, the interface between these two – is called the procedural level. This level includes special algorithms that solve computer graphics problems efficiently and procedures that utilize these algorithms. Frequently, particular features of the device level play an important role in inventing new graphics algorithms, while new functional languages influence the creation of new algorithms from the top level. Another very important element of this interface level is the graphics database (see Figure 1.8). The structure of the graphics database also greatly influences the efficiency of the algorithms and the complexity of the graphics procedures.

In addition to the three levels of a graphics system and the database, the operating system of the computer also plays an important role in providing communication between the elements of the system and the user. As many graphics programmers will have experienced, it is very difficult to deal with only one of the components of a graphics system in isolation, since the overall speed of generation and the quality of the pictures depend on all of these components. Figure 1.8 is a schematic diagram of a graphics system showing the components and their functional interconnection.

Let us now adopt a *bottom-up* approach and look at the characteristics of a simple device level. This will introduce the fundamentals of graphics devices, which is probably the part of computer graphics that is least familiar to most readers.

1.3   GRAPHICAL OUTPUT DEVICES

The evaluation of the quality of a picture has to be performed ultimately by the eyes, which form an extremely sensitive and complex system. There are millions of light-sensitive rods and cones in the human retina that enable the eyes to work at a wide range of picture intensities, colours and lighting conditions. It is generally accepted that all visible colours may be produced by the linear sum of three primary colours: blue, which has a short wavelength; green, which has a medium wavelength; and red, which has a long wavelength. Accepting this principle, it follows that the quality of a picture may be characterized by its resolution and contrast. **Resolution** specifies the smallest picture area that can be characterized by a specific colour intensity and **contrast** specifies the range of intensities the picture contains.

The resolution of a photograph, for example, is measured in dots per inch in both the horizontal and vertical dimensions, or dots per square inch. The resolution of a high-quality printed photograph is limited by the **graininess** of the picture. Under large magnification, a picture appears as a collection of small irregular areas, each with uniform intensity. The equivalent resolution may be as high as 4000 dots per inch (or 16 million dots per square inch). The resolution of a high-quality colour transparency may be much higher.

Turning to television broadcasting, the resolution of a television picture is determined by the mechanics of picture production. The cathode ray tube (CRT) works on the principle that red, blue and green dots embedded in the television screen become fluorescent when they are struck by an electron beam. This beam is scanned one horizontal line at a time (see Figure 1.9) and 575 visible lines make up a picture. Thus, the vertical resolution depends on the size of the television screen. A screen measuring 7 inches in height and approximately 12 inches diagonally will

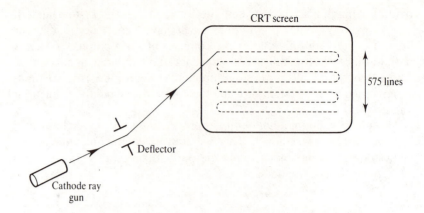

Figure 1.9

Schematic diagram of a CRT or raster-type output device. In practice, the 575 lines are displayed by interlacing, which means that only every other line is displayed by one complete sweep of the electron beam. The remaining lines are displayed in the successive frame, which is displaced down by one line width.

have a resolution of 82 dots per inch, $^{1}/_{50}$th of a high-resolution photograph. The older, monochrome television systems work with analogue signals, which means that their horizontal resolution cannot be expressed exactly. The horizontal resolution of today's colour television pictures can be estimated around 750 dots per full picture or approximately 75 dots per inch for a screen having a 12-inch diagonal. The contrast produced by a cathode ray tube varies continuously but with a limited range, since the maximum brightness is limited by the luminescence of the cathode ray tube. Electrical control circuits in this case can be used to set both the brightness and the contrast of the picture.

The contrast of a simple black and white printed picture can range from completely black to completely white, with the absolute range of intensities being a function of the illumination used to view the picture. It is very difficult to quantize the contrast of a printed photograph, since each grain of a picture can exhibit a continuous spectrum of intensities between black and white; it is only possible to tell whether a picture is of high contrast or low contrast.

The black and white illustrations in this book are interesting examples of graphical picture production. The picture shown in Figure 1.10 gives the appearance of variable contrast, but in fact it was generated by black ink only – the picture is made up of small picture elements that are either totally white or totally black. Thus, this picture is made up of bi-level picture elements, but due to the high resolution of the picture, approximately 1000 dots per inch, the individual dots cannot be resolved and continuous tones are seen instead. The inset, which shows a small area of the picture magnified 50 times, shows the true nature of this printing process.

Computer-generated pictures, by their nature, must be quantized both in resolution and contrast, since the information is stored digitally. The ultimate resolution of the produced picture depends on the computer's

Figure 1.10
A monochrome photograph reproduced by half-toning. The photograph shows 180 Queensgate, London, designed by the celebrated Victorian architect Norman Shaw and built in 1883. It was demolished in 1965 to make way for the present 180 Queensgate which houses the Department of Computing at Imperial College. The photograph was taken by Sidney Newbery around 1950. The black and white picture gives the impression of continuously varying brightness. However, it is produced by controlling the ratio of white to black areas, according to the required brightness of the picture. The inset shows a portion of the picture enlarged 50 times. Reproduced courtesy of Imperial College Archives.

memory size, the program that generates the picture and the physical limitations of the graphical output device.

Most current display devices use television-type display monitors which are used in a point-plotting mode, as shown schematically in Figure 1.11. The simplest of these output devices produces black and white images. In these devices, the smallest picture element, called a **pixel**, can be either turned on (bright) or turned off (dark). The resolution of the

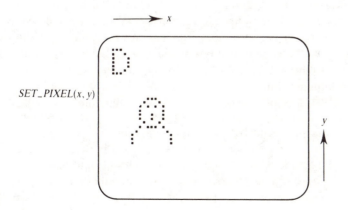

SET_PIXEL(*x*, *y*)

Figure 1.11
Simple graphical output devices allow small picture elements called pixels to be turned ON or OFF. A specific number of ON pixels produce an acceptable approximation to a line drawing.

Table 1.1 Colour mapping of the EGA graphics device shows that only 16 colours can be displayed at any one time. Any 1 of the 16 colours may be selected from a palette of 64 different colours.

Logical Colour Number	Actual Colour Number	Colour
0	0	Black
1	13	Light blue
2	8	Red
.	.	.
.	.	.
.	.	.
15	63	White

simplest of graphics terminals is around 30 pixels per inch (300×200 pixels), but better quality graphics displays have a total of 512×512 or approximately 250000 pixels over an 8×8 square inch area. The highest resolution graphics terminals belong to graphics workstations which today can contain as many as 4 million (2000×2000) pixels over an area having 15 to 20 inches on one side. However, the resolution in such cases is still only around 150 dots per inch, which is only $1/25$th of a high-quality photograph.

More complex graphics display terminals can also control the brightness and sometimes the colour of each pixel. The simplest of these can produce a small number of fixed colours. The popular enhanced graphics adaptor (EGA) for the IBM PC/AT and their compatibles can display 16 different colours at any one time. This means that for each pixel, four bits are specified, which select one of the 16 possible colours. Since the EGA has a resolution of 640×350 pixels, the total number of stored bits for the display reaches almost 900000, which amounts to 112 kbytes.

Another characteristic feature of coloured display terminals is their colour **palettes**. The colour palette contains all the possible colour shades that the terminal can produce, which is often a larger set than can be displayed on the screen at any one time. The EGA has a palette of 64 different colours out of which only 16 can be displayed at any one time. The four bits stored for each pixel specify the colour number. A colour-mapping scheme then specifies the actual colours, in the range 0 to 63, assigned to each colour number. This colour mapping is shown in Table 1.1. Colours produced by this colour-mapping scheme are called **logical colours**, since there is no direct correspondence between the colour number and the actual colour characteristics, such as brightness.

The best display systems can provide true-shaded images by controlling the brightness at each pixel. Shaded colours are provided by the

Table 1.2 A shaded display allows the selection of red, green and blue (RGB) intensities for any one of a large number of displayable colours. The RGB intensities allow the selection of both colour (hue) and brightness. Usually, the number of displayable colours at any one time is much smaller than the number of physically possible shades (the palette).

Logical Colour Number	Red Intensity	Blue Intensity	Green Intensity	Colour
0	0	0	0	Black
1	255	0	0	Red
2	0	255	255	Light yellow
3	200	100	100	Orange
4	100	100	100	Gray
.	.	.	.	.
.	.	.	.	.
.	.	.	.	.
255	255	255	255	White

individual brightness of the three primary colours, which may be set under program control. The physical range of displayable brightness, from black to white, is determined by the physical characteristics of the display device, but the number of distinct brightness levels is determined by the number of bits stored for each pixel. The largest number of bits used in practice is 24 (eight bits per primary colour), which allows 256 brightness levels for each primary colour or a total number of over 16 million colour shades. This is a much larger number than the eye can distinguish within the limited range of colours that any practical display can produce. This large number of colours requires a very large number of stored bytes; for a 1000 × 1000 pixel system 24 million bytes are required.

In many moderately priced graphics systems the number of displayable colours is reduced by the utilization of a colour-mapping scheme similar to that described earlier. In this case, as shown in Table 1.2, three primary colour intensities are associated with each colour number. In a frequently used hardware arrangement there are 256 different colours, logical colours in this case, and each one may be selected from a palette of 16 million. It is also possible to use the same colour terminal for different gray levels (equal intensities being used for each of the three primary colours), in which case the colour number (0 to 255) can be directly associated with the gray (monochrome) brightness levels.

So far, the discussion has concentrated on **raster**-type display devices; that is, devices controlled by the intensity values of a matrix of picture elements or pixels. Some years ago, **vector-plotting** display devices, which produce complex line drawings, were also popular. The basic display element of these devices is a line segment, which may be specified by its starting position, length and orientation angle with respect to, for example, the horizontal. Since the hardware takes care of the actual line segment generation, the drawing of a long line segment may be much faster with this type of device than with a raster-type display device, which, for a long line, requires the 'turning on' of a large number of pixels. Nevertheless, because of the difficulties involved in producing areas with filled or shaded colours with vector-plotting devices, and the rapidly decreasing cost of large semiconductor memories used in high-resolution raster devices, such devices have been almost completely replaced by raster-type systems.

As mentioned earlier, computer graphics systems often provide hardcopy facilities in addition to interactive display devices. Computer-drawn diagrams or pictures are usually generated by pen plotters, or dot matrix, ink jet or laser printers. The common characteristic of almost all computer hardcopy devices is that they cannot vary the brightness level of a printed dot. The appearance of different gray levels or shaded colours may be produced by the variation of the density of printed dots. This requires the so-called dithering technique, which will be discussed in Chapter 3.

Plotters are often vector-drawing devices that accept straight line segments as primitives. Most modern plotters work *digitally*. This means that all line segments are specified by distances in the x and y directions which are integer multiples of the smallest step size of the plotter. The step size defines the plotter's resolution which for a good quality plotter is around 300 increments per inch (approximately 0.003 inch step size). Some pen plotters allow the changing of pens under program control and thus allow the drawing of lines with variable thickness and colour. Colour Plate 1 shows a multi-coloured VLSI circuit diagram printed using a six-pen plotter.

Dot matrix, ink jet and laser printers behave similarly to raster-scanning devices and have a fixed resolution. Their horizontal and vertical resolutions may not be the same. Dot matrix printers print 7 to 12 scan lines at a time at resolutions of 70 to 200 dots per inch. Laser printers are the newest type of dot matrix printer. They have a resolution of 300 dots per inch and provide excellent quality black and white images.

Finally, let us look at one fundamental problem of interactive computer graphics which is the direct result of the structures of its output devices. A medium resolution, raster colour display will have $512 \times 512 \times 18$ bits (six bits per primary colour), or approximately 600 000 bytes, of information. If real-time graphics is required, then the display must be updated at least 25 times per second. This requires the computation of 15 million bytes per second to refresh the full screen. Even if the calculations are trivial, which they may not be, this is a monumental task. Computer instruction speeds may be of the order of 10 million instructions per second. If we need, say, 10 instructions per pixel, which is a very optimistic estimate, a picture would be generated in 15 s. Current advances in the VLSI design of graphics processors are constantly improving the performance of specialized graphics workstations such that the graphical transformation by translation, rotation or scaling of geometric objects constructed with thousands of small coloured and shaded polygons can be viewed in real time.

1.4   GRAPHICAL INPUT DEVICES

Since most modern computer graphics facilities provide interactive processing, graphics input devices have become important components of these systems. The traditional computer keyboard is still an integral part of most systems and is required for typing in numerical data, commands, components, file names and so on. In addition to the keyboard, the so-called **pointing device** or **locator** has also become an essential component. The most frequently used pointing device is the mouse, which was introduced earlier in the chapter (see Figure 1.3). The mouse is an extremely versatile device and, because of its simple physical construction and reliable operation, it is inexpensive as well. It is placed on the desk top and may be moved around. Its push button(s) may be pressed at the same time. The mouse provides motion and direction indications to the computer through a small ball in its base, which rolls when it is moved. It becomes a pointing device when a visible marker appears on the screen and moves in the same direction as the mouse. It is both interesting and important to examine the various ways a mouse can be used as a graphics input device because this will demonstrate some of the issues involved in the separation of the device and procedural levels and the effect this has on interactive processing.

It is possible to provide either hardware or system software that connects the mouse input to the visible marker on the screen which, according to the definition of the device level given earlier, defines a single pointing device (see Figure 1.12). The device driver maintains a current absolute screen position (pixel row and column numbers) which is where the marker is displayed. When the mouse is moved, its motion indicator generates an interrupt, which is transmitted to the device driver. The driver updates the marker position according to the direction of motion, erases the marker shown at the old position and redisplays the marker at the new position. These are not trivial tasks and the graphics user is relieved of them. The application programmer has a function available which, when called, returns the current screen position of the marker and the status of the push button(s). But, the convenience for the user is paid for by the lack of flexibility.

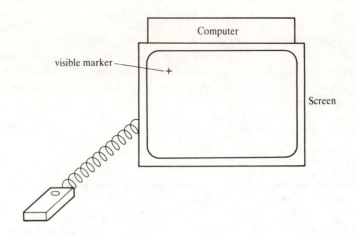

Figure 1.12

The physical movement of the mouse produces a corresponding movement of a visible marker (for example a cross, an arrow or a stylized hand) on the screen. The display may be updated by hardware or could be under software control. Functionally, the input and output components together define a single pointing device.

An effective way of communicating with the user of an interactive graphics program is to change the size, shape, colour or function of the visible marker of a pointing device. The shape, size or colour of the visible marker could communicate what information the program requires from the user or what type of command it is currently executing. Highlighting a menu item, for example, by changing the colour or type of the characters is an effective way of communicating to the user the currently active menu entry, which is selected by pointing at it with the mouse. All these actions require the separation of the input function, which is motion detection, and the output function, which is the provision of a visible marker for the pointing device. Complete flexibility can only be achieved if both input and output processes are under the control of the application program and not the device driver.

Another physical limitation introduced by the one-device mouse driver is due to the finite resolution of the screen. Since the position is defined by the visible marker shown, the resolution of the numerical input data is limited by the resolution of the screen, which may be much less than the physical resolution of the mouse. By separating the input and output functions, this physical limitation is eliminated. For example, it is quite feasible when constructing a mechanical drawing to specify the co-ordinate positions to five or six digits accuracy, while screen pixels limit the visible marker resolution to three digits. In cases like this, the visible marker of the mouse has to be separated from its input function, which may be easily achieved, since there is no need for a one to one correspondence between the mouse units and the pixels on the screen.

These factors partially explain the rapid acceptance and success of the mouse over the older, more traditional pointing devices, such as the light pen or touch-sensitive screen. Both the light pen and the touch-sensitive screen, where the pointing device is the user's finger, are connected inherently to the screen and, as has been shown, are severely

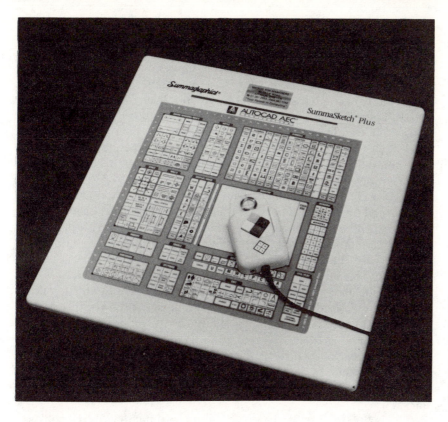

Figure 1.13
The graphic tablet shown in this photograph provides a very high resolution pointing device which is particularly useful for CAD and CAE applications. With a plastic overlay sheet, the device is customized for specific application programs.

limited by it. There is even an ergonomic problem associated with pointing directly at the screen: it is normally placed at eye level and the arm gets rapidly tired.

A more expensive and more precise version of the separate input and visible marker arrangement uses the so-called **graphic tablet** input device (see Figure 1.13). As can be seen from the figure, the ordinary desk top is replaced by a specially constructed flat surface, which can indicate the absolute position of a pen-like marker touching the tablet or a mouse-like device sliding on the top of the tablet. Pressing the pen-like device replaces the pushing of the button on the mouse. One advantage of the graphic tablet is that it simulates the ordinary drawing activity with a pen or pencil; consequently, it can be preferred by artists working with computers. The other advantage of this device is that the tablet may be overlaid by a thin sheet of plastic with special areas drawn on it which are labelled and assigned to specific computer functions. The resolution of the drawings on this sheet is far greater than the resolution of the screen and a very large number of functions can be made available to the user simultaneously. This arrangement has become standard for complex CAD and CAE applications. It is obvious that the tablet, as an input device, is independent of a visible marker, since it provides an absolute position independently of the resolution of the screen. Its disadvantage is its higher cost and the additional space required.

There are a large number of other input devices, like the joy-stick, the tracker ball, and levers and dials, but they do not add any new functionality to graphical input and are disappearing from use. As has been seen, graphical input consists of either an absolute two-dimensional position, an indication of the direction of motion of a pointing device or the pressing of various buttons. The use of a physical input device for indicating a three-dimensional position or motion is a difficult problem and has not been solved satisfactorily at the present.

In addition to input devices for interactive control, input devices are also needed for the collection and transmission of graphical data from the outside world to the computer. Specialized mechanical measuring devices exist that can provide precise three-dimensional position information. Such a device may be used to enter the dimensions of an object into the computer. This process is called **digitization**. For surfaces that are reasonably smooth, the principle of triangulation can be used to obtain a three-dimensional description. Modern scanning devices used for this purpose use a low-powered laser beam focused into a straight horizontal line. This line is projected on to the object to be measured. If viewed from an oblique angle, the line appears distorted. Its distance from a reference point can be used as a measure of depth. Thus, a depth can be obtained for a series of sample points along the line and the process repeated for a series of scan lines.

Finally, the video camera, as a graphics input device, can convert a real graphics scene into pixel intensities or, in the case of a colour camera, into the intensities of the three primary colours. In this case, three-dimensional scenes are reduced to two spatial dimensions by photographic projection.

1.5 GRAPHICS DEVICE LEVEL

To clarify further the use of graphics output and input devices in a computer system, this section describes the procedures available to a computer program. The collection of all the available procedures defines the graphics device-level boundary.

For the purpose of this discussion, the following minimum hardware configuration is assumed: a digital computer with one graphics terminal, possibly one hardcopy graphics output device, an ASCII keyboard and one pointing device – for example, a mouse with at least one button. The hardcopy device, if it exists, is assumed to be used only to produce a hardcopy version of what is displayed on the viewing screen; therefore, it will not be considered as a separate output device.

In addition to the required input and output functions, the system will also require **enquiry functions**, which provide the application programmer with hardware-specific information. Since the generated pictures are viewed, they must have a reasonable size and resolution. Furthermore, to relate pixel numbers to real distances, the characteristics of the viewing screen must be known.

1.5.1   Enquiry functions

For a simple bi-level raster device the following enquiry function facility must be provided:

$$GET\_RASTER\_DEVICE\_CONSTANTS(\textbf{var } XPixels, YPixels : \textbf{integer};$$
$$\textbf{var } XSize, YSize : \textbf{real})$$

Note here that the conventions of the Pascal language have been used to indicate that the values of the **var** parameters are returned by the system after the call of the function. The pixels are numbered in the horizontal direction from 0 to $XPixels - 1$, in the vertical direction from 0 to $YPixels - 1$ and the pixel origin is assumed to be at the lower left corner of the screen. The variables $XSize$ and $YSize$ give the size of the viewing surface in inches. This information is required to compute the aspect ratio of the display device. The **aspect ratio** of any viewing surface is the ratio of its horizontal length to its vertical height. In dealing with the device level of computer graphics, it is important that this is measured in pixels so that a correction can be made before drawing to ensure that a square remains square and a circle a circle, regardless of the device that is being used. For this purpose, the aspect ratio is defined to be:

$$AspectRatio = \left(\frac{XPixels}{XSize}\right) \Big/ \left(\frac{YPixels}{YSize}\right)$$

in units of horizontal pixels to vertical pixels. The calculation of the aspect correction should be done by the device driver. Although a real multiply is required, the precision of the calculation is not great, and a few shifts and adds will normally suffice. An example will make this definition clearer. The IBM EGA display has a resolution of 640 horizontal and 350 vertical pixels. It is usually displayed on a 12-inch monitor in which the horizontal size is 10 inches and the vertical 7 inches. The aspect ratio in terms of length is therefore 10/7. There are 64 pixels per horizontal inch and 50 pixels per vertical inch. This gives an aspect ratio of 64/50 = 1.28 horizontal to vertical pixels. Thus, a square of vertical side 10 pixels will have a horizontal side of 13 pixels.

If a vector device, rather than a raster device, is used for output a similar enquiry function defines the size of the screen both in inches and as an integer number of the smallest increments of a vector. In addition, the maximum length of a vector may be limited to a size smaller than the entire screen:

GET_VECTOR_DEVICE_CONSTANTS(**var** *XIncrs, YIncrs* : **integer**;
var *MaxXSize, MaxYSize* : **integer**;
var *Xsize, YSize* : **real**)

If the display can produce colours, then the number of simultaneously displayable colours is a system constant. If it can display shaded colours, then the available intensity levels in the three primary colours are also defined by the hardware. The enquiry function for colours can be defined as:

GET_COLOUR_CONSTANTS(**var** *NumberOfColours* : **integer**;
var *MaxRedIntensity, MaxGreenIntensity,*
MaxBlueIntensity : **integer**)

Since effective man–machine communication requires the simultaneous display of both graphics and text, the size of characters in terms of the number of pixels is also required by the application programmer. In simple systems, only one character size is available. However, others may provide a choice of sizes. The enquiry function:

GET_CHARACTER_SIZE(**var** *XSize, YSize* : **real**)

returns the current character box size. This defines a rectangular area which covers the displayed character and the space around it when consecutive characters are displayed. If a display is capable of generating a number of character sizes, then the enquiry function returns the size of the currently active character size.

It may also be useful to relate the input functions of the mouse with its physical motion. The mouse supplies the number of steps it has been moved in both the x and y directions, while the enquiry function:

GET_MOUSE_RESOLUTION(**var** *XStep, YStep* : **real**)

returns the actual physical distance moved when a step is recorded by the mouse.

1.5.2 Output functions

This section presents a short summary of the ouput functions of a simple graphics system based on raster and non-raster devices. It is important to remember that the specific details of these functions are unimportant. The functions as presented here are unlikely to appear in any application language exactly as stated. Again, Pascal language conventions have been used to specify functionality in a concise manner.

Raster devices

The most common forms for the output functions of a simple bi-level raster device are:

> SET_PIXEL(*XPixel*, *YPixel* : **integer**)
>
> CLEAR_PIXEL(*XPixel*, *YPixel* : **integer**)

where the values for variables *XPixel* and *YPixel* must be within the ranges specified by the enquiry function. To be able to use effective interactive techniques for graphics programs, even in the case of such a simple bi-level device, either the 'reading' or the complementing of the pixel intensity is also required. The complementing of the pixel value is often referred to as the EXCLUSIVE OR (XOR) function. In this case, it can be defined as:

> COMPLEMENT_PIXEL(*XPixel*, *YPixel* : **integer**)

On a bi-level device, the *COMPLEMENT_PIXEL* procedure turns the pixel intensity ON if it was OFF and OFF if it was ON. It therefore computes and displays the XOR function with binary 1. The displaying and moving of a visible marker that could, for example, be a pointer controlled by the mouse, may be executed with this function. When the marker is displayed, its pixels are set to white on a black background and black on a white background. The XOR function may also be used to erase the marker and restore the display, since XORing the same pixel twice resets it to its original state. Note that simply setting or clearing the pixels may not produce the desired effect; moreover, it will destroy information on the screen.

If the XOR function is not provided by the device level, then a *READ* procedure must be used. This function can be defined as:

> READ_PIXEL_VALUE(*XPixel*, *YPixel* : **integer**;
>
>   **var** *PixelValue* : **integer**)

where an integer value is used for the output variable *PixelValue*, which in the monochrome case may be set to 0 for OFF and to 1 for ON. Obviously, if the *READ_PIXEL_VALUE* function is available, then the complementing of the pixel can be executed by the software. After reading the pixel value, it can be set or cleared according to the complement of its value. It is interesting to note that some graphics systems fail to provide either of these functions to the programmer, in which case it is not possible to provide many important interactive functions under direct program control.

Raster devices with logical colour output may have a similar set of output functions with the definition of a *FOREGROUND* and a *BACKGROUND* colour. The *SET_PIXEL* function sets the pixel colour to the foreground colour, while the *CLEAR_PIXEL* function sets it equal to the background colour. In this case, two additional functions are needed:

> *SET_FOREGROUND_COLOUR*(*ColourNumber* : **integer**)
>
> *SET_BACKGROUND_COLOUR*(*ColourNumber* : **integer**)

Strictly speaking, these two functions are not output functions, since they do not directly produce output. Rather, they change the characteristics of the output device. Borrowing the terminology of currently used graphics systems, these two functions change the **attributes** of the output functions. The concept of attributes is very important for efficient graphics processing because it significantly reduces the required number of parameters in graphics procedures. Although attributes will be discussed in detail in Chapter 2, the concept is introduced here as attributes are also important elements of the device level. Their role is comparable to that of global variables in computer programs.

As many graphics display devices are designed with drawing attributes, a set of procedures needs to be defined to manipulate them. The simple bi-level device requires only two functions, one controlling the drawing attribute:

> *SET_DISPLAY_MODE*(*DisplayMode* : **integer**)

and the other the setting of a pixel value:

> *DISPLAY_PIXEL*(*XPixel, YPixel* : **integer**)

The function *SET_DISPLAY_MODE* is used to choose the mode in which the pixels are to be altered. For all subsequent calls, *DISPLAY_PIXEL* will use that drawing mode. It will therefore be the equivalent function to *SET_PIXEL*, *CLEAR_PIXEL* or *COMPLEMENT_PIXEL*, depending on which mode has been set. The advantage of using attributes is that once they are set, they remain set and affect all output functions in a similar way. For example, more advanced graphics displays provide additional drawing functions, such as:

> *DRAW_LINE*(*XStart, YStart, XEnd, YEnd* : **integer**)
>
> *DRAW_CIRCLE*(*Centre, Radius* : **integer**)
>
> *DRAW_ELLIPSE*(*Centre, MajorAxis, MinorAxis* : **integer**)

in which case all drawing functions are executed according to the current value of the *DisplayMode* variable.

Display devices that can produce shaded colours can also have a drawing colour attribute that is similar to the foreground colour for logical colours. As seen earlier, shaded colours are also defined by a colour mapping. In this case, the *COMPLEMENT_PIXEL* function operates on the logical colour number. To produce the correct results, colours with complement colour numbers should be mapped to complement colour values. For example, if in an eight-bit system the colour number 64 (binary 01000000) represents green, then its complement colour, which is colour number 191 (binary 10111111), should be mapped to colour yellow. The reason why yellow is considered to be the complement of green will be discussed in Chapter 7.

To be able to produce textual information, many graphics display devices provide a character output function of the form:

DRAW_TEXT(*XStart, YStart* : **integer**; *CharacterString* : **text**)

where the variables *XStart* and *Ystart* define the lower left corner pixel of the displayed character string. Attributes in this case could specify character size and style.

When a display with shaded colours is used, the colour-mapping table stores what is in effect a large set of device attributes. The table entries specify three primary colour intensities for each logical colour. A procedure is supplied that allows the setting up of the colour table and has the form:

SET_COLOUR_TABLE(*ColourNumber* : **integer**;
　　　　　　　　 RedIntensity, GreenIntensity,
　　　　　　　　 BlueIntensity : **integer**)

In the case where the mouse is provided with a device-generated visible marker on the screen, it is convenient to be able to control the displaying of this marker. Two simple functions could control this attribute of the mouse:

SHOW_MOUSE_MARKER( )
HIDE_MOUSE_MARKER( )

Non-raster devices

For non-raster output devices some of the output functions have different functional forms. This section gives a short summary of the output functions for the two most common non-raster types of output device: vector displays and the matrix printer.

A vector display device is similar to a pen plotter. The fundamental drawing function is a straight line while the drawing attribute is whether

---

Algorithm 1.1

Dot matrix printer control.

for each scan line **do**
begin
{ Initialize and start scan motion }
for *NByte* = 1 **to** *LastByte* **do**
SEND_BYTE_TO_PRINTER(ByteArray[NByte]);
{ Advance paper }
end

---

the pen is UP (not drawing) or DOWN (drawing). These may be incorporated into two output functions:

$$MOVE\_PEN\_ABSOLUTE(XPosition, YPosition : \textbf{integer};$$
$$PenStatus : \textbf{integer})$$
$$MOVE\_PEN\_RELATIVE(DeltaX, DeltaY : \textbf{integer};$$
$$PenStatus : \textbf{integer})$$

The co-ordinates are expressed in terms of the smallest increment the plotter (or vector display) can draw. Another form of output function for vector displays can be:

$$DRAW\_VECTOR(Length, Angle : \textbf{real}; BeamStatus : \textbf{integer})$$

which is similar to the *MOVE_PEN_RELATIVE* function but is defined in inches and degrees. The output function of the *Turtle Graphics* system is similar to this *DRAW_VECTOR* function. The drawing functions may be separated from the attribute set functions, which are the lifting or lowering of the pen or the turning ON or turning OFF of the electron beam.

Dot matrix printers (both black and white and coloured ink jet printers) or laser printers can also be used for producing graphical output. In fact, the resulting diagram is similar to that of a raster device, since the drawing mechanism produces a rectangular matrix of dots on paper. However, the output functions differ because the individual dots of the device cannot be randomly addressed. Frequently, the start of a scan line is specified, after which a number of bytes corresponding to the ON or OFF values of the picture have to be sent to the printer. A typical algorithm for the control of a matrix printer is shown in pseudo code in Algorithm 1.1.

Many display devices are provided with an automatic *dump* facility that can be activated by a simple function call:

DUMP_SCREEN( )

to produce a hardcopy equivalent of the displayed graphics scene on a matrix printer.

1.5.3 Input functions

Computer input devices are more difficult to control than output devices because they provide two kinds of input. Firstly, there is data, such as the position of the mouse or the ASCII character most recently typed. Secondly, there is event information, such as whether a button has been pushed. In non-interactive programs, events are hidden from the programmer. For example, in Pascal the traditional *READ* input function returns characters to the calling program only if a line has been entered and the ENTER (or carriage return) key has been pressed. Thus, events are controlled by the operating system and input functions return control to the calling program only when data is available. Borrowing again from current graphics systems terminology, this mode of input control is called the **request mode**.

It is not possible to design effective interactive graphics programs with only the request mode of input. Even in a simple system there are three kinds of input: keyboard, mouse as a pointing device and the mouse push button. If the program were to issue a request type of call to the keyboard, for example, there would be no way to acknowledge the moving of the mouse or the pressing of the mouse button before a key was typed. Such a situation would provide a very restrictive user interface. One simple solution is to provide input functions that always return control to the calling program, but also indicate the current device status or, alternatively, that input has not been entered since the last function call. This mode of operation is called **sample mode** control.

The mouse is a good example of a device that needs to be sampled for interaction purposes. For example, if we are controlling the position of a visible marker, we sample the mouse and, if it has moved, the current marker is erased and redrawn at the new position. This loop continues until it is terminated by another form of input – for example, a push on the mouse button. To achieve this kind of interaction, the following function is needed:

SAMPLE_MOUSE(**var** *XPosition*, *YPosition* : **integer**;
                          var *Button* : **integer**)

While the input function *SAMPLE_MOUSE* works well for mouse-like devices, a similar function is not particularly suitable for the keyboard.

The pressing of a key is a discrete event, unlike the mouse co-ordinates, which represent the state of the mouse. As mentioned before, the simplest form of the keyboard input function operates in request mode and is of the form:

KEYBOARD_INPUT(**var** *Key* : **char**)

When a call is made to this routine, the system waits until a key is pressed, after which it returns the ASCII code of the pressed key. To be able to use this function in an interactive environment, a *CLEAR_KEYBOARD* function is also required, which throws away all previous inputs to the keyboard before the time of the call.

For true interactive processing, a keyboard input routine in sample mode is needed. To use sample mode, it is necessary to introduce a keyboard buffer that stores the codes of the keys pressed in order. For the simplest case, a one-character buffer could be used. However, for most applications a much larger buffer is required, allowing a type-ahead facility:

SAMPLE_KEYBOARD_BUFFER(**var** *Buffer* : **text**;
var *NCharacters* : **integer**)

This procedure returns the current contents of the keyboard buffer together with the number of valid characters and has the side effect of clearing the device buffer as well.

Note that in both cases the event information is still hidden by the operating system. A keyboard event in the simplest case constitutes the pressing of any key. To handle events at the device level, an interrupt facility is required which allows program control to be transferred immediately after the event has occurred.

Another way of processing mouse events is to use the following *MOUSE_EVENT* routine:

MOUSE_EVENT(**var** *XPosition, YPosition* : **array** [1..*EvMax*] **of integer**;
var *NumberOfEvents* : **integer**)

The variable *NumberOfEvents* is returned to indicate how many mouse events, if any, have occurred, while the arrays store the positions. The *MOUSE_EVENT* function illustrates the difference between sample and event mode. If the *SAMPLE_MOUSE* function is used, the *XPosition* and *YPosition* variables indicate the position of the mouse and the *Button* variable the button status (1 = pushed, 0 = released) at the time of the procedure call. If the system is sluggish, it is possible to miss the exact time when the button is pressed and the *SAMPLE_MOUSE* procedure would rarely indicate button action. However, often the information required is the mouse position at the time when the button was pushed. This is obtained with the *MOUSE_EVENT* procedure.

This completes the list of simple input functions that demonstrate the fundamental device-level requirements for an interactive graphics system. Obviously, in a practical graphics system a much larger number of functions will be available.

1.5.4   Other functions

Before discussing how the device level may be interfaced to the next higher, program level, this section presents a few examples of systems programs that are often necessary for the overall control of the systems hardware. Normally, two general functions are needed: one to start the system, the other to return the system to its normal (often, non-graphic) operating mode. These function calls are required because most terminals work either in graphics or in ASCII mode. If the graphics system does not reset the terminal to its ASCII mode after it has terminated, then it will be impossible to interact with the operating system. Two functions are added to the device level:

> *START_GRAPHICS_SYSTEM*()
> *CLOSE_DOWN_GRAPHICS_SYSTEM*()

It is convenient to use the initializing function, *START_GRAPHICS _SYSTEM*, to set up a complete set of default attribute values that define the simplest mode of operating the system. In this case, the writing mode, the initial mouse position and the initial colour intensities in the colour table should be set. The screen should be cleared and the input status of the keyboard and mouse cleared. It is also convenient to provide *RESET* functions for the devices; for example:

> *RESET_DISPLAY*()
> *RESET_KEYBOARD*()
> *RESET_MOUSE*()
> *RESET_PRINTER*()

These six additional functions finally complete a convenient set of simple functions at the device level. In Chapter 10, which examines more advanced hardware devices, a more complex and powerful set of device functions will be discovered.

With the understanding of how graphics devices work and with the given set of device-level functions, any application software package may be constructed. For each such application, a set of higher-level functions will be designed and the graphics database created. Redesigning these higher-level functions every time new application software is written is nothing else but constantly reinventing the wheel. This can be avoided by using an integrated graphics package, the so-called graphics kernel, which includes all common higher-level functions. The advantage of having such a kernel and the development of standard kernels will be the subject of the next chapter.

Exercises

1.1 What is the difference between computer graphics and image processing? Find at least three practical examples for which both image-processing and computer graphics techniques are required.

1.2 Give definitions of the terms 'graphics device' and 'graphics device level' and discuss how they are different for a specific example of an input and an output device.

1.3 Define the procedural level of a graphics system. Discuss how the procedural level is influenced by the structure of the database. Where would you draw the boundary between the procedural and the functional levels? Give a specific example which shows how the three levels of a graphics system are related.

1.4 Discuss the advantages and disadvantages of providing a single device function for a mouse and its visible marker as compared to using separate input and output functions.

1.5 What types of information are provided by graphics device enquiry functions and why are they needed by the application programmer?

1.6 Discuss how graphical attributes are used for output functions. Give specific examples for a set of output functions for a bi-level raster device with and without using drawing attributes.

1.7 Discuss how the Request, sample and event types of interaction operate for a keyboard. Explain why it is necessary to provide a *CLEAR_KEYBOARD* function for interactive programs if only the request mode of operation is available.

Problems

1.8 Convert Figure 1.8 into a data-flow diagram and show the types of data passed between the graphics software, the database and the operating system.

1.9 Convert Figure 1.8 into a structure chart and show the hierarchical structure of the six functional elements. Indicate the types of function calls and data passed between the connected elements using pseudo code.

1.10 Derive an expression that determines the number of bytes of storage required for the frame buffer of a colour display with given resolution and contrast.

1.11 A vector-type display can handle up to 500 vectors with average length of two inches and refresh rate of 50 times per second. The same performance is required from a raster-type device which has 1000×1000 pixels and an 8-inch square screen. Estimate the maximum time allowed for the SET_PIXEL procedure to obtain this performance.

1.12 Assume that a software generated mouse marker is within a $10 \times 10 = 100$ pixels area of the screen. Estimate the computer instruction speeds you require to be able to update the mouse marker in a tight software loop within 0.1 second (a good interactive speed). Assume some reasonable ratio of memory access and purely data processing instructions. Do these calculations for the cases when an XOR pixel function is available, and when only a READ_PIXEL function is used. Assume that the raster memory read cycle is the same as the computer's memory read cycle.

1.13 Discuss the difference to the user of a graphics system between the operating system providing a MOUSE_EVENT procedure using hardware interrupts, and the software simulation of the same functionality with a SAMPLE_MOUSE type of procedure.

Project

1.14 Define a minimum set of software callable hardware functions for a keyboard, mouse with one button, and a simple bi-level raster display and, using pseudo code, write a set of procedures for a convenient graphics device level.

2 Graphics Systems and Standards

Building upon the device level, the Graphical Kernel System (GKS) level helps the application programmer to achieve portability. Portability can be provided by device, language, system and programmer independence. Device independence is achieved by normalization, language independence by the definition of functionality in a language-independent form (using pseudo code, for example). System and programmer independence are of concern to the computer manufacturers and universities. Another important aspect of the graphics kernel is the graphical database. In this chapter, the components of a kernel are described using many elements of GKS and PHIGS standards as examples. Device normalization, logical output and input device functions, and the use of a large number of graphics system attributes help in the realization of portable graphics software. Important logical input and output function types are provided by GKS which define a basic graphics system. Extensions should also be considered for a more general graphics facility. The three input modes, request, sample and event, are closely related to the operation of interactive input devices which were discussed in Chapter 1. The division of a picture into subpictures with the application of geometric transformations (translation, rotation, scaling) is demonstrated through the graphical construction of the cross-section of a gear wheel. Subpictures can be defined by both segmented and hierarchical data structures. The segmented picture structure of GKS is presented in detail in this chapter, and the hierarchical structure of PHIGS is demonstrated as well. For graphical databases, the separation of numerical and topological data is highly beneficial. Savings in both space and execution time can be achieved with careful analysis and design of the database.

2.1 INTRODUCTION

Chapter 1 examined how graphics devices work and presented a collection of procedures that defined a very simple graphics device level. In theory, it would be possible to write any graphics application program using no more than these procedures. In practice, however, this would be very wasteful. It would be similar to using machine or assembly language for writing a complex computer program. Just as higher-level computer languages like FORTRAN, Pascal, LISP and PROLOG were developed for helping complex program development, graphics systems have evolved for helping graphics application programmers. Unfortunately, the general acceptance of specific graphics systems has faced many difficulties.

Since graphics processing must include physical devices as well as special (graphical) databases, it is necessary to specify more than just a higher-level language; an interface to this higher-level language is required. This is the reason why the term **graphics system** is used. It defines a complete integrated system consisting of graphics devices, procedures, graphics databases and, possibly, some application packages. There are two often opposing requirements for a modern graphics system. From the application programmer's point of view, the most important requirement is **portability**. From the user's (and manufacturer's) point of view, the deciding factors are often **speed**, and **functionality**, which can be achieved only with a **flexible** system. Flexibility means that the system should allow the programmer to manipulate very low-level functions, in addition to providing solutions to routine problems. A good illustration of flexibility in computer languages is the emerging 'standard' C language. This contains a substantial number of higher-level features, such as abstract data types, but also allows the programmer to manipulate the computer's registers. It is no accident that C is becoming the favourite language for graphics-related programs. A similar combination of high-and low-level functionality is required for a successful graphics system, but the wide range of operational characteristics of available graphics devices and processors prevents the development of a standard that could serve both these functions for all systems.

The aim of this chapter is to discuss computer graphics in a hardware- and software-independent manner with the focus on functionality, rather than detailed descriptions of all aspects of the established Graphical Kernel System (GKS) and emerging GKS-3D, PHIGS or X-Window standards. The emphasis is mainly on those ideas that seem to work well in current systems and which will probably form part of the next generation of graphics standards. The terminology used is that of the presently popular graphics systems (in particular, GKS), thereby providing a degree of programmer independence to those who will be working with these systems.

2.2   REQUIREMENTS OF GRAPHICS SYSTEMS

2.2.1   Portability

Since there is currently a proliferation of terminals, graphics displays, computers and operating systems, it is imperative that application programmers should be able to design graphics-based applications without any specific computer system or hardware in mind, so that their work can be easily ported to any other physical system. Standardization at the functional level is the key to portability and standards have been devised with the specific intention of achieving this. The route to portability is to provide independence of aspects of the computer system, such as device independence, language independence, computer independence and programmer independence. The ways in which independence may be achieved in those four fields will now be discussed.

Device independence

Device independence means that an application package will operate with a large variety of device types. Display devices of different size, resolution or technology, or graphical input devices of a large variety, may be connected to a complex graphics system. Therefore, in this context, device independence means that a displayed picture can be sent to several hard-copy devices – a pen plotter, a matrix printer, a laser writer – such that the produced pictures will correspond to the displayed picture as closely as the physical characteristics of the output devices allow. The solution to device independence is through *logical* input and output devices. Logical devices used by the application software are serviced by the actual physical devices of the computer system at execution time. The problems associated with this mapping of logical devices into physical ones will be discussed in Sections 2.6 and 2.7.

In addition to working towards standardized logical devices, *de facto* physical device standards evolve because of the popularity of particular manufacturers' products. Examples of *de facto* standards are the Tektronix 4010/4014 terminal protocol for vector display devices, the IBM EGA hardware configuration for raster graphics systems, the PostScript language for laser printers and the Microsoft mouse for graphical input. Each has its own protocol for passing messages between the device and the computer. Unfortunately, these standards exist by virtue of the large volume of sales of the associated product and not necessarily of their own virtues.

At the functional level, device independence is resolved by providing a normalized device co-ordinate system for the programmer to work with. This removes the need for working in plotter inches or pixel numbers.

Language independence

Language independence is achieved by defining the graphical functionality of a system in a language-independent manner. This means that graphics capabilities are defined by user facilities rather than fixed procedures. These facilities are implemented by an integrated set of procedures coded in a suitable language for a particular system. In addition to the generic system procedures, a **language binding** is provided to a large number of application languages, such as FORTRAN, Pascal and PROLOG, so that the graphics functions appear to the programmer as ordinary library functions.

Computer independence

The most important goal of professional societies supporting international standards is the acceptance of these standards by major manufacturers. Once a standard like GKS is adopted, it is their hope that all new computers will support it. However, while standards improve portability, they restrict the efficient utilization of new hardware or advances in operating system facilities. Moreover, because it takes a long time to agree on an international standard, the standards are often based on old technology. This is a serious problem, especially in a rapidly changing field like computer graphics where new developments like parallel or vector processing have become very important in the design of modern, high-speed systems. Some manufacturers solve this problem by providing extensions to the standard, while others ignore it altogether.

Programmer independence

Programmer independence means that programmers use the same standards for all their application programs and reject the temptation to use convenient but non-standard extensions. This is an important concern of educators and, consequently, must be the concern of this textbook. The decision as to which standard should be taught and how strictly this standard should be adhered to is a difficult problem. Staunch supporters of standards would like to see all education kept within the bounds of established standards. In contrast, others would argue that higher education should be concerned with fundamental principles, which never change, and not current practices, which may be out of date by the time a student graduates.

Fortunately, advances in the computer field are evolutionary. This means that popular languages and systems come and go but useful advances and innovations remain an integral part of future systems. The first widely used graphics system, **CORE**, introduced normalized device co-ordinates and transformation matrices and solved the problems associated with device-independent, two-dimensional graphical output. The next system to emerge, GKS, incorporated the good features of CORE, produced input device normalizations, developed effective ways of dealing with a large number of global system variables (or attributes) and provided an elementary graphics database. Since GKS still proved too difficult to use for highly interactive or three-dimensional applications, new systems like **PHIGS (Programmer's Hierarchical Interactive Graphics System)** and GKS-3D have been developed.

A problem with comprehensive graphics systems like GKS is that it may be well suited for large and complex systems, but it has a prohibitively large overhead for small interactive systems, such as personal computers. *De facto* system standards, like the **Graphics Environment Manager (GEM)**, have developed which, interestingly enough, contain many similar features to GKS, but incorporate many of the operating system's functions in addition to graphics. All the large graphics systems mentioned so far solved device-independent graphics for images, although they did not pay much attention to the use of graphics for the user interface. There is no doubt that it is possible to design a menu- or icon-driven user interface within GKS, but it is not easy. If the only requirement is pop-up menus and icons, it seems foolish to carry along all the overheads that GKS requires. Therefore, other systems, like X-Windows and GEM have implemented good graphical user interfaces and are becoming *de facto* standards. In the X-Windows system, it is also possible to draw lines, circles, fill shapes, output text and so on in a device-independent manner. Some users will no doubt advocate that the X-Windows system should be used as the overall new standard.

2.2.2 Flexibility

Nowhere is flexibility more important than in interactive graphics systems. The computational demands of interactive (real-time) picture generation are so large that the most critical parts of the software must be coded in an efficient language (often in assembly language). Low-level languages can take advantage of specific hardware features of the available graphics devices. At the same time, what 'looks right' to the viewer can depend on the specific display device used, and software modification is required for the generation of high quality and realistic pictures. Unfortunately, champions of strict standards are reluctant to provide flexibility and this fact makes it difficult for sophisticated users to accept strict standards.

2.3 GRAPHICAL KERNEL SYSTEM

As the name of the **Graphical Kernel System (GKS)** standard indicates, the 'standard' portion of the graphics system is neither a complete operating system nor a complete graphics software package. Rather, it lies at the heart of the graphics system, directing and controlling all communications between devices, users and the database. This part is referred to here as the **graphics kernel (GK)**, indicating that it is very close to the GKS standard, but is based on the required functionality and does not constitute a strict standard.

The graphics kernel incorporates the most commonly used graphics functions into the operating system through system calls or a collection of linkable library object programs. Standards try to define an inclusive set of these functions, but obviously any given set will be insufficient (or awkward) for some applications or may contain many unused functions for others. To define functionality, it is necessary to describe what each function does and what user parameters it requires. In the following descriptions, not much attention is paid to the order or types of these parameters, since the details of the function-calling sequences are language dependent. Moreover, a programmer will always need to consult the appropriate manual for these details.

Another aspect of the graphics kernel is the graphics database. The database must be an integral part of the kernel, especially in the case of hierarchical picture structures where a complex picture is built from a combination of small picture elements, The global variables of the graphics system, like drawing attributes and current graphics transformation constants, can also be considered as part of the database.

Finally, no matter how device independent the graphics kernel is, it must, ultimately, direct graphical output to physical output devices and collect user-supplied data from input devices. To separate the use of a graphics device in the graphics kernel from its physical implementation, the concept of a logical workstation has been developed.

2.3.1 Concept of a logical workstation

The **logical workstation** identifies a logical system unit containing at least one viewing surface (graphical output) and any number of input devices. This use of the word *workstation* should not be confused with that of current equipment manufacturers, who often use it to describe a physical device, which is one specific instance of a logical workstation. The terms **engineering workstation** and **graphics workstation** refer to specific configurations of selected physical components. A logical workstation can be a simple terminal, a large printer, a digitizer or a comprehensive engineering workstation containing one viewing or plotting surface and several input devices, such as a light pen, a mouse, a graphic tablet, dials or a keyboard.

In GKS, the interaction between a user and the system must occur through an active workstation. A task to be carried out may not require anything of the user other than the typing of a set of parameters at a keyboard; on the other hand, full graphical interaction may be required. The activation of logical workstations allows the processing of many devices in parallel. For example, the user of GKS will specify which workstation the creations are to be sent to and the effect should be the same regardless of the device, so that a set of commands that draw a picture on a terminal screen will also print that picture on a flatbed plotter or create that picture as a microfilm slide. The same type of normalization is carried out for input devices. The details of the normalization operations will be discussed in a later section.

Before a workstation can be activated, it has to be made known to the system by the *OPEN_WORKSTATION* operation. Along with its inverse operation, two functions are defined:

> *OPEN_WORKSTATION*(*WorkstationIdentifier* : **integer**; ... other parameters ...)
>
> *CLOSE_WORKSTATION*(*WorkstationIdentifier* : **integer**)

There is a similarity between these functions and the operating system functions *OPEN_FILE* and *CLOSE_FILE*. These functions are required to limit the overhead of maintaining input/output (I/O) drivers and buffers by keeping only those drivers that are actually used by the application programs in the system. The parameters of the *OPEN_WORKSTATION* function are device and system dependent. Consequently, the workstation identifier, which is usually an integer, will select a particular physical device, which will cause problems of portability. For example, consider how the selection of the pen plotter may be achieved and what will happen if the system does not have a pen plotter when the *OPEN_WORKSTATION* function is called. In fact, such problems are not so different from those associated with operating systems. Device identification can be achieved by assigning integer values to globally recognized names, such as *PenPlotter*, *CADWorkstation* and so on. The status of workstations and system errors can in general be found out by calling built-in enquiry functions. Enquiry functions are not only important at the device level, but at all levels of interactive graphics systems. In this case, they could be used to find out the configuration of the system, the available hardware components or the operating status of specific hardware devices. For example, the following function:

> *ENQUIRE_WORKSTATION_STATUS*(*WorkstationIdentifier* : **integer**;
> **var** *Status* : **integer**)

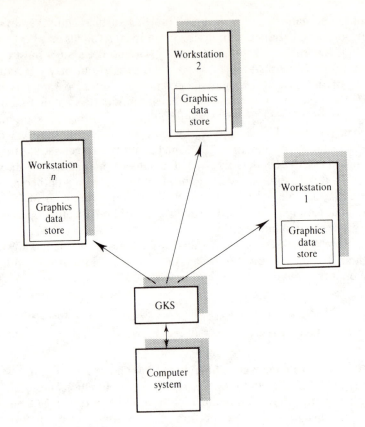

Figure 2.1

The organization of a GKS-based graphics system with logical workstations and their associated graphical data storage elements.

could return the status of the workstation indicating whether the selected workstation exists, is operational or active and so on.

Once a workstation is included in the system it can be made active (or passive) by the functions:

ACTIVATE_WORKSTATION(*WorkstationIdentifier* : **integer**)

DEACTIVATE_WORKSTATION(*WorkstationIdentifier* : **integer**)

The graphics functions executed by the program affect all active workstations, thereby permitting many graphics devices to work in parallel. The concept of a workstation, as defined by GKS, is unusual in the sense that the kernel does not have a central graphics data store. The graphics primitive functions, like the drawing of a line or the displaying of some text, are sent to the workstation(s) where they are stored. Each workstation must have a local storage (at least functionally) to store its complete operational state. (State here includes all drawing output primitives, drawing attributes and so on.) By activating and deactivating selected workstations, the same GKS list of output functions may result in different

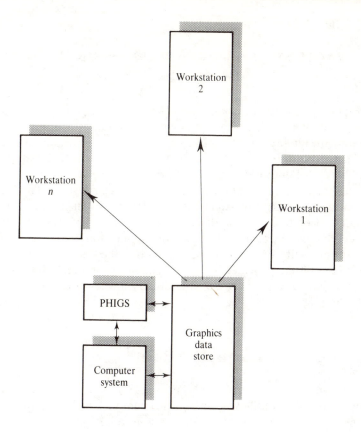

Figure 2.2
The organization of a PHIGS-based graphics system where there is only one central graphical data storage which is serving all workstations.

visible output on different workstations. This arrangement is shown schematically in Figure 2.1.

An alternative arrangement, shown in Figure 2.2, uses a centralized graphics data store. Here, the workstations can be selectively enabled or disabled, but there is only one copy of the graphics data from which all displayed versions are derived. In this case, the graphics functions manipulate the database, rather than the workstations. This alternative functional arrangement is more suitable for interactive systems using graphical modelling and is supported by PHIGS.

It is the aim of the graphics kernel to treat all workstations uniformly; however, this aim is only partially achieved. The difficulty lies in the fundamental difference between interactive devices like terminals and non-interactive output devices such as printers. The problem that cannot be avoided by the concept of a GKS type logical workstation is **picture regeneration**. In an efficient interactive graphics system, especially if it is used for animation, small portions of a complex graphics scene need to be changed while the majority of the picture components remain the same.

Some of the GKS functions can provide only global operations, such as:

CLEAR_WORKSTATION(*WorkstationIdentifier* : **integer**)

REGENERATE_WORKSTATION(*WorkstationIdentifier* : **integer**)

which operate on large drawing areas. Since updating a large area of the display screen may take a very long time, this mode of operation may be completely unsuitable for interactive applications. In addition to this problem, the regeneration of pictures needs to be controlled differently for different types of output devices. GKS provides some complicated ways of controlling picture regeneration, but these will not be described here as the aim is not to discuss any system in detail but to call attention to the difficulties encountered in standardizing grossly different types of physical devices. Whatever system is chosen by the application programmer, these considerations will cause problems, especially if the system is highly interactive. In the system provided by PHIGS, updating of interactive terminals is automatically executed, so that the display always correctly shows the state of the graphics database.

2.3.2   Device normalization

Device normalization is an area where GKS is very successful and all graphics kernels should have a similar mechanism by which various input and output devices can be handled without referring to their physical characteristics. All viewing surfaces are defined by two-dimensional square areas with floating-point co-ordinate values from [0, 0] (lower left-hand corner) to [1.0, 1.0] (upper right-hand corner). Co-ordinates in this system are referred to as **normalized device co-ordinates**. For each device in the system, there will be a procedure, which is part of the device driver, which will translate the normalized device co-ordinates into the physical device units, such as pixel addresses or plotter increments.

Graphical data are normally specified by the user in a co-ordinate system with convenient physical units for a specific application – for example, light years for the astronomer or microns for the VLSI designer. This real-world physical co-ordinate system is called the **world co-ordinate system**. All interactions between the data and the user occur in world co-ordinates specified in some particular physical units. The mapping of world co-ordinates into normalized device co-ordinates is achieved by a **normalization transformation**.

As the graphical data usually extends well beyond what can be shown at any one time, the normalization transformation requires that the part of the scene to be viewed is defined by the co-ordinates of a rectangular **window** which, as shown in Figure 2.3, is defined within the world

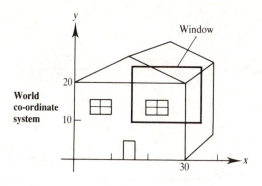

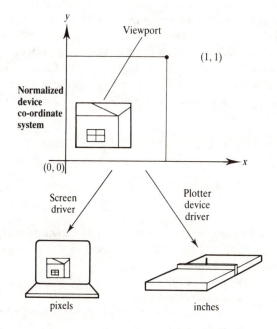

Figure 2.3

The normalization transformation is defined by both window and viewport co-ordinates. The window is defined in terms of user or world co-ordinates, while the viewport is given in normalized device co-ordinates.

co-ordinate system. All graphical entities outside the defined window are ignored by the system and are said to be **clipped**.

The graphical scene inside the window is mapped on to a rectangular viewing area that may be smaller than the entire viewing surface. This rectangular area is called a **viewport** and is defined in normalized device co-ordinates. A window–viewport pair defines a mapping which is the normalization transformation. If a device is selected, and a window and viewport are selected, then a complete transformation can be defined. For example, for a raster device, the complete transformation can be expressed by the following equations:

$$XPixel = (XResolution - 1)$$

$$\times \left(ViewportXMin + \frac{(ViewportXMax - ViewportXMin)(X - WindowXMin)}{(WindowXMax - WindowXMin)} \right)$$

$$YPixel = (YResolution - 1)$$

$$\times \left(ViewportYMin + \frac{(ViewportYMax - ViewportYMin)(Y - WindowYMin)}{(WindowYMax - WindowYMin)} \right)$$

where *XPixel* and *YPixel* are the integer pixel co-ordinates that can be directly used with the *SET_PIXEL* device function, $[X, Y]$ is a point in the world co-ordinate system, *XResolution* and *YResolution* are the number of pixels for the entire viewing surface in the x and y direction, respectively, and the other eight real values define the window and viewport. As mentioned before, the window variables are given in world co-ordinates and the viewport variables in normalized co-ordinates. This complete drawing transformation acts like a drawing attribute for all the drawing primitives in a program. It could be neatly expressed as one procedure, such as:

PICTURE_TRANSFORMATION(*DeviceType* : **integer**;
WindowXMin, *WindowYMin* : **real**;
WindowXMax, *WindowYMax* : **real**;
ViewportXMin, *ViewportYMin* : **real**;
ViewportXMax, *ViewportYMax* : **real**)

Usually, the selection of device, window and viewport variables is done separately, even though all of them must be specified to produce a meaningful drawing transformation.

If the viewport is fixed in size, it is possible to effectively zoom into and out of the graphics scene by changing the size of the window. However, if different aspect ratios are used for the window and the viewport, the horizontal and vertical directions will be scaled differently and the original drawing will be distorted. The problem of avoiding distortion due to aspect ratio changes is a device-dependent one. Some systems define the normalized device co-ordinates [0.0, 0.0] and [1.0, 1.0] as the extreme corners of the largest square that can be fitted on to the viewing surface. Thus, correct results will be achieved if the window and the viewport are defined with the same aspect ratio. However, other systems use co-ordinates for the extreme points of the viewing surface and, since this is not in general square, a correction must be applied to one of the viewport dimensions to achieve the desired result.

By using a number of window–viewport pairs, the viewing surface can be divided into a number of independent rectangular areas where different portions of the user's graphics data can be shown. This is commonly done when menu selection of a number of icons is offered, either in side menus or in pop-up menus. As far as output is concerned, only one viewport can be active at any one time, but as far as the positional input of a pointing device is concerned, it may be placed inside any one of the viewports shown on the screen. To handle the input, GKS allows the definition of a large number of viewport–window pairs by the functions:

SET_WINDOW(*WindowIdentifier* : **integer**; *XMin, XMax, YMin, YMax* : **real**)

SET_VIEWPORT(*ViewportIdentifier* : **integer**; *XMin, XMax, YMin, YMax* : **real**)

where each normalization transformation is identified by an integer number and is activated by the function:

SELECT_NORMALIZATION_TRANSFORMATION(*Identifier* : **integer**)

This is similar to setting an attribute of the workstation. The kernel saves all defined window–viewport co-ordinates in a list and will use the value of the variable *Identifier* in the *SELECT_NORMALIZATION_ TRANSFORMATION* function. The bulk of the data is stored within the workstation, while the different normalization transformations can be activated by the passing of a single integer variable to the system. Once a normalization transformation has been selected, all output functions will occur within the active viewport and will be clipped by it.

The input functions return the value of the current normalization transformation as a parameter. For the mouse, the function will be similar to the device-level function *SAMPLE_MOUSE*( ), which can now be represented as:

SAMPLE_MOUSE(**var** *NormalizationTransformation* : **integer**;
var *XPosition, YPosition* : **real**)

where the returned values for the position of the mouse, *XPosition* and *YPosition*, can be given in normalized co-ordinates, in the range of [0, 0] to [1, 1], and the value of the parameter *NormalizationTransformation* defines the mapping from normalized device co-ordinates to world co-ordinates. To calculate the values in user co-ordinates, an enquiry function is required, which returns the window and viewport co-ordinates of any defined normalization transformation. Alternatively, an input function can be designed, which returns the input position either in the world co-ordinate system or in normalized device co-ordinates, according to a switch set by the programmer.

By convention, normalization transformation 0 is defined as the entire screen using the window–viewport pair:

SET_WINDOW(0, 0, 1, 0, 1)

SET_VIEWPORT(0, 0, 1, 0, 1)

It cannot be redefined and this transformation number is returned on an input sample when the visible marker is outside all defined viewports, or if no viewports were defined at all. By default, normalization transformation 0 is made active when a workstation is activated.

In systems where overlapping viewports are allowed, priorities must be established which define the respective depth of overlapping viewports – that is, which viewport obscures other viewports. As the lower normalization transformation numbers have higher priority by default, the default normalization transformation (with value 0) has the highest priority initially. Priorities may be changed by the function:

SET_VIEWPORT_INPUT_PRIORITY(*NormTran*1, *NormTran*2 : **integer**; *WhichWay* : **order**)

where the variable *WhichWay* can have one of the values *higher* or *lower*. This function sets the priority of the first normalization transformation with respect to the second.

With these definitions and functions, device normalization has been solved and device independence has been achieved. However, like everything else, a price has to be paid for this convenience – a possible decrease in efficiency and speed. The device normalization method used by GKS assumes that co-ordinates are defined as floating-point numbers and these have to be converted to pixel numbers whenever the display is updated. In a large, non-interactive system, the fact that manipulating integer numbers may be much faster, and the data may require much less storage, may be unimportant; however, for a highly interactive program running on a personal computer, efficiency may be very important. It is appropriate then that the GEM system defines its user co-ordinate space as integers in the range [0, 0] to [32767, 32767]. Of course, only a small portion of this user space is visible on the screen which, for the EGA system, can be expressed by pixel co-ordinates [0, 0] to [639, 349].

2.3.3 Output functions

The purpose of the graphics kernel output functions is to minimize the amount of programming steps necessary to display and manipulate a complex graphics scene. The simplest type of picture is made up of lines, so this section starts by describing a set of output primitives to handle line drawings. Output primitives for producing coloured and shaded areas, markers for supporting graphs and charts, and text are also described.

Line-drawing primitives

The simplest form of a line drawing is a **polyline**, which is defined by a number of points connected by straight-line segments. The output function necessary to display such a connected set of lines may be described as:

> DRAW_POLYLINE(*SetOfPoints*)

where *SetOfPoints* is some type of data structure, such as an array or list, which contains the co-ordinates of the points. The GKS standard defines a much more restricted use of this function, namely:

> POLYLINE(*NPoints* : **integer**; *XArray*, *YArray* : **array of real**)

where *XArray* and *YArray* store the *x* and *y* user co-ordinates for the connected points. Thus, GKS restricts the data structure to be real arrays.

Since some graphics data consists of disconnected line segments, rather than polylines, a similar output function for line segments can also be provided. This has no equivalent in GKS but could be defined by the function:

> DRAW_LINE_SEGMENTS(*SetOfLineSegments*)

where a line segment is defined by a pair of points. A set of line segments is more general than a polyline, but when a polyline is represented as a set of line segments, redundant points are included in the data.

A line drawing can be further generalized by allowing other shapes to be drawn, such as circles, ellipses, circular or elliptical arcs and interpolated curves, in which case an even higher-level drawing function can be defined:

> DRAW_LINE_DRAWING(*SetOfLineDrawingPrimitives*)

Here, the set of primitives may contain any defined shapes – polylines, line segments, circles and so on. GKS does not provide for such a high-level drawing function, neither do most currently used graphics systems. But, such a convenient high-level functionality would be expected in a well-designed object-oriented system.

Since the parameters of the line-drawing functions only provide geometric information, a mechanism is needed to define the type and the colour of the lines used for drawing. It has already been mentioned that a number of drawing attributes can be defined for a graphical output function. GKS handles attributes by assigning them to the system state as global variables. To be able to handle such 'invisible' system components, two types of functions are required:

(1)   *SET_ATTRIBUTE* functions,
(2)   *ENQUIRE_ATTRIBUTE* functions.

The *enquire*-type functions are needed because the user may want to temporarily change some of the attributes in the middle of a complex program and later restore them to their original values. GKS defines a large number of both *SET* and *ENQUIRY* functions. For example, the *POLYLINE* drawing function has the following attributes:

> *Style* (solid, dotted, dashed),
>
> *LineWidth*,
>
> *Colour*,
>
> *Brightness*.

Often, attributes are collected into a global table of values, called a **bundle**. Each bundle of attributes is identified by an integer number called a **bundle index**. To change a set of attributes for the *POLYLINE* function, the following GKS procedure is used:

> *SET_POLYLINE_INDEX*(*BundleIndex* : **integer**)

This method is consistent with the way in which the normalization transformation is handled. The system stores all predefined attribute bundles and then maintains a set of global variables, which define the current set of attribute values. If the *BundleIndex* is not set, then default values are provided to all attributes that define the simplest working conditions. In the case of the line attributes, a set of reasonable default conditions could be *Solid* for *Style*, one-pixel wide for *LineWidth*, white for *Colour* (over dark background) and normal for *Brightness*. Since the line styles, brightness levels and other line-drawing characteristics usually depend on the capability of the hardware, the attributes are often device dependent.

Area-filling primitives

In addition to line drawings, many graphical output devices are capable of producing coloured and shaded areas, the simplest of which are polygons (bordered by straight lines). The following GKS primitive **paints** a polygon with a predefined pattern and colour:

> *FILL_AREA*(*NPoints* : **integer**; *XArray*, *YArray* : **array of real**)

The parameters have the same meaning as those of the *POLYLINE* procedure, but the line segments are not drawn – only the area of the polygon defined by the line segments is filled. The pattern, colour and other characteristics are defined by area fill attributes; for example:

Style (solid, cross-hatch, shaded pattern),

Colour,

Brightness.

The functionality of the *FILL_AREA*( ) primitive output function is very restrictive since only solid polygons can be handled. Areas delineated by other shapes, such as circular arcs and interpolated curves, are not included in the GKS standard. Also, areas that contain holes cannot be used. A more generalized output primitive would have the form:

FILL_AREAS(*SetOfPrimitiveAreas*)

where the primitive areas include a wider set than simple polygons. A specific area-filling (or shading) problem occurs for three-dimensional objects constructed from planar polygonal facets. It is expected that the three-dimensional standards will include such area-shading primitives.

There is a GKS area-filling primitive called *CELL_ARRAY* that is specifically designed for raster devices. It may be defined in user co-ordinates by the following function:

CELL_ARRAY(*XMin, YMin, XMax, YMax* : **real**; *Dx, Dy* : **real**; *Colour* : **array** [0..*XPixels* − 1, 0..*YPixels* − 1] **of integer**)

where a rectangular area is defined by the variables *XMin*, *YMin*, *XMax* and *YMax* in world co-ordinates and is divided into a number of small rectangular areas with sides *Dx* and *Dy*. Each small rectangular area is filled with the colour given in the two-dimensional array *Colour*. Using the *CELL_ARRAY* function, displays can be manipulated at the pixel level. Obviously, the physical characteristics of the raster device, which are the number of pixels in the horizontal and vertical direction, the aspect ratio of the pixels and the number of available colours, have to be known before this function can be applied. Therefore, an *ENQUIRE_DEVICE_ CHARACTERISTICS* function will have to be a part of the system.

Markers

For some applications, it is necessary to plot or mark a set of points, rather than to draw lines between them. Marks are usually small crosses, circles, squares or solid dots. This output function supports business charts, scientific graphs and the like. In GKS, the *POLYMARKER* procedure is defined for this purpose:

POLYMARKER(*NPoints* : **integer**; *XArray, YArray* : **array of real**)

Attributes are also associated with the polymarker, such as:

Style (the type of marker used),

Size,

Colour,

Brightness.

The *POLYMARKER* primitive is not as general as the line-drawing or area-filling primitives. Its appearance in the graphics kernel level originates from the requirement of using charts and graphs. In fact, higher-level primitives that draw a scientific graph, a business bar chart or pie chart are defined in many graphics systems that support business-oriented data-processing functions.

Text output

Text output is essential to all graphics applications. Text can be used to annotate a diagram, label a viewport or as entries in a menu that controls some man–machine interaction. Modern graphics interfaces often use a pointing device for user interaction, rather than requiring the user to type commands. Text output is so important that it is included in the device level. The features provided at the kernel level allow the handling of character strings, instead of individual characters, and provide a large number of text attributes to control the size, colour, intensity and the direction of the displayed text. The output primitive in GKS is similar to the device function:

TEXT(*XPosition*, *YPosition* : **real**; *String* : **text**)

Text attributes are:

Style (type of font, bold, italic),

Size,

Colour,

Intensity,

Alignment (left-justified, right-justified, centred)

Direction (angle in degrees).

With these output functions, a reasonably complete set of output primitives has been specified for a two-dimensional graphics kernel. It is more difficult to specify primitives for three-dimensional scenes, especially since the generation of graphics for three-dimensional objects has not yet been discussed (see Chapter 4).

2.3.4   Input functions

Standardization of input functions, like the standardization of output functions, presents problems, since there are a wide variety of different types of input device that may be used. Device independence means that the same software should run and perform well on a variety of systems, which may have a large number of different types of hardware input devices. The solution is to develop the software using logical classes of input and to map the classes of input functions to actual devices at execution time. Logical input devices correspond to operations that the user may require and they can be implemented by several hardware device types. In addition to the type of data expected from the input device, there is also a mode of operation that can be specified for a logical device.

Logical input types

There are four generally useful logical input device types defined by GKS; namely, *LOCATOR*, *VALUATOR*, *CHOICE* and *STRING*. They may be implemented on a number of devices.

A **locator** device provides the x and y values of a point in a two-dimensional Cartesian co-ordinate system. It may be most easily created by means of cross-hairs on the screen or a visible marker. The values are controlled by a variety of devices, including the mouse, special cursor control keys on the terminal, a roller ball or a joystick. As discussed before, the *LOCATOR* input function returns the normalization transformation number applicable to the selected point, in addition to the x and y co-ordinates, and thus defines the selected window–viewport co-ordinates.

A **valuator** device provides a single value. In many cases, a designer may wish to have the size of some object varied continually – for example, to choose a size for a pin to fit a hole that has already been drawn. This value may be read from a dial, some form of shaft encoder or may be typed in as a number.

A **choice** device provides an integer number as an indication of one item selected from a number of items. As part of a graphics system, a number of predefined choices may be provided for, say, defining the type of shading used. This can be provided by means of a panel with several buttons, special function keys on the terminal or menus displayed on the screen.

A **string** device is for the purposes of inputting text to be printed on a drawing. At present, there is no good substitute for the terminal keyboard; however, a microphone and voice-recognition system may become a realistic input device in the future.

GKS also provides two more input functions that are closely related to the structure of GKS and may have to be modified for a different graphics system. These are the pick and stroke devices.

The input function of a **pick** device is based on the picture structure of GKS, which uses picture segments as small identifiable picture elements. This input device picks out one segment of a graphics scene. The user of a complex graphics system will frequently need to pick small objects, or perhaps parts of a large picture. This may be done by any device that is capable of pointing. A mouse with a visible marker, a marker on a graphic tablet, a light pen or a touch-sensitive screen are convenient physical pick devices. The picture element must be visibly identified. This may be done by lines of enhanced intensity, different colours or different line types. Logically, the *PICK* function returns an identifier that points to a GKS segment.

Since GKS is built around the *POLYLINE* as its most important output function, a special **stroke** input function type is defined for the entering of a polyline. The stroke type of input device provides a list of straight-line segments as input data. In many instances, a designer may wish to input a series of lines making up the outline of an object. This can of course be provided by a locator device, but for greater convenience the stroke is provided. Typically, a designer will use a digitizing tablet. This is used in the following way: the pointer is moved to the start of the first line, a button is pushed and then the pointer is moved to subsequent line endpoints, pressing the button each time to enter the points.

While typical examples for these device types have been given, a logical input device is defined independently of its physical implementation. It is quite conceivable to run a GKS-based application package with only a keyboard as an input device and with many different logical input device types. The special arrow keys can serve to move a pointer on the screen, values can be typed as numbers and function keys can be used for choice inputs.

Input modes

For any type of logical input device, a mode of operation may also be specified. Three modes of input are defined in GKS: request, sample and event. These three modes are the same as those discussed at the device level. In GKS, they are related to logical input devices to cover the most frequently required input configurations. It should be noted that while the GKS standard defines these three modes, many present implementations do not provide the most complex of the three, the event mode of operation. System control for the three modes of operation is shown schematically in Figure 2.4.

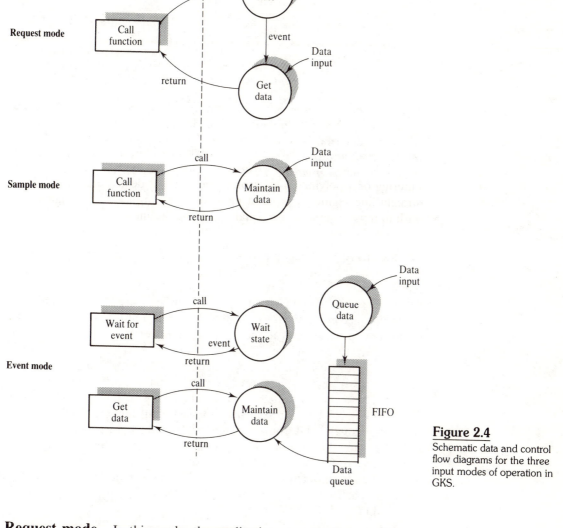

Figure 2.4
Schematic data and control flow diagrams for the three input modes of operation in GKS.

Request mode   In this mode, the application program requests input, after which the GKS-based system does not return control to the program until the input becomes available. This is similar to the way in which a high-level language reads input data from a terminal. If the user specifies that the mouse position is to be read in request mode then control returns to the application program only after the operator has pushed a button on the mouse. Three examples of logical input functions operating in the request mode are as follows:

$$REQUEST\_LOCATOR(WorkstationIdentifier : \textbf{integer}; InputDeviceIdentifier : \textbf{integer};$$
$$\textbf{var } Status : \textbf{boolean};$$
$$\textbf{var } NormalizationTransformation : \textbf{integer};$$
$$\textbf{var } XPosition, YPosition : \textbf{real})$$

$$REQUEST\_VALUATOR(WorkstationIdentifier : \textbf{integer}; InputDeviceIdentifier : \textbf{integer};$$
$$\textbf{var } Status : \textbf{boolean}; \textbf{var } Value : \textbf{real})$$

$$REQUEST\_STRING(WorkstationIdentifier : \textbf{integer}; InputDeviceIdentifier : \textbf{integer};$$
$$\textbf{var } Status : \textbf{boolean}; \textbf{var } NumberOfCharacters : \textbf{integer};$$
$$\textbf{var } Characters : \textbf{text})$$

As can be seen, a unique input function with a specified calling sequence is defined for each logical input type. GKS has six such functions. The *Status* parameter determines whether the input is valid and provides a rudimentary error indication – pressing the BREAK key on the keyboard, for example. The *NormalizationTransformation* variable indicates the active viewport for the locator input action. The other variables are described by their names. The other three input functions are similar to the ones shown here and are applied to the choice, stroke, and pick input types.

Sample mode   In sample mode, the program requests and receives an input value without waiting. This mode may be used for continuously readable devices. For example, the graphics display driver of an airplane would continuously read the current orientation of the aircraft and update the display accordingly. Any change of value is redrawn immediately, or as soon as the program can attend to the updating of the display. Chapter 1 has already discussed the unsuitability of the keyboard as a sampled device. However, to use it to implement, say, the *SAMPLE_LOCATOR* function, a keyboard driver has to be written that will continually read and process the keyboard buffer. A problem arises with this implementation when no key has been pressed since the last input request. Some systems return the ASCII NUL (binary 0) in this case, which means that the NUL character cannot be used for any other purpose – a possible inconvenience that could interfere with the portability of the software.

The actual functions operating in the sample mode have exactly the same form as their request counterpart except that the term *REQUEST* is replaced by *SAMPLE*. Hence:

$$SAMPLE\_CHOICE(WorkstationIdentifier : \textbf{integer}; InputDeviceIdentifier : \textbf{integer};$$
$$\textbf{var } Status : \textbf{boolean}; \textbf{var } Choice : \textbf{integer})$$

and similar procedures for the other classes of logical input are used.

Event mode   Like sample mode, the event mode of operation is appropriate only for certain types of device. The keyboard is ideal, since it is essentially event driven. A dial reading a value is more suitable for sampling. If such a device were to be used in event mode, an event could be defined as the time instant when the input value changes. This could cause an unwieldy number of events to be generated, which would lead to a sluggish system. As was seen at the device level, events are placed in a queue at the time they occur. The application program can find out the status of the queue (empty or full) and, on request, can empty the queue on a first-in, first-out basis (FIFO queue).

The GKS standard handles the event mode by two types of input function. The first queries the system to find out whether an event has occurred. There is only one queue per workstation and the function has the form:

$AWAIT\_EVENT(TimeOut$: **integer**; $WorkstationIdentifier$: **integer**;
$\quad\quad$ **var** $DeviceClass$: **devicetype**; **var** $DeviceNumber$: **integer**)

This function normally operates in request mode; that is, it waits until an event has occurred before returning control to the calling program. If a small value is provided for the $TimeOut$ variable, control is returned after the specified number of milliseconds, even if an event did not occur. The returned value for the $DeviceClass$ variable specifies one of the six input device types in the case where an event occurred or a special $NotValid$ indicator if the waiting time exceeded the $TimeOut$ value. It can be seen that programming difficulties would occur when there are a large number of input devices operating in event mode. The $AWAIT\_EVENT$ function only indicates the first event that may belong to any one of the devices, whereas the application software may be interested in only one particular input device.

When the application program knows that an event has occurred, it can take it out of the queue with the GET input function, which has a unique form for each input type. Three examples are as follows:

$GET\_LOCATOR($**var** $NormalizationTransformation$: **integer**;
$\quad\quad$ **var** $XPosition, YPosition$: **real**)
$GET\_VALUATOR($**var** $Value$: **real**)
$GET\_STRING($**var** $NumberOfCharacters$: **integer**; **var** $Characters$: **text**)

The setting of the input mode in GKS has to be done for each type of input device and for each active workstation, unless the request mode, which is the default mode for all input devices, is required. The function that sets the input mode has the form:

$SET\_MODE\_FOR\_LOCATOR(WorkstationIdentifier$: **integer**;
$\quad\quad$ $InputDeviceIdentifier$: **integer**;
$\quad\quad$ $Mode$: **inputmode**; $Echo$: **boolean**)

There are six separate functions for setting the input mode for each device type. The *Echo* variable is used in GKS to activate a visible indication of input action. This could show highlighting, rubber banding, control of the mouse marker and so on. In most GKS systems, the actions supplied by the *Echo* facility are hardware dependent.

Mixed modes   In general, many different modes of operation can occur simultaneously. For example, a frequently needed interactive program that positions an object interactively may be expressed by the following pseudocode:

```
{ Draw object at initial position }
{ Set pointer position at initial position }
repeat
   if the help button is pressed
   then set help request flag
   else begin
        { Sample pointer position }
        if position is in valid area of screen
        then begin
             { Erase object at old position }
             { Draw object at new position }
             end
        end
until pointer button pressed or help button pressed
if pointer button pressed
then record the position of the object in the database
```

In this program, both the sample and the event modes operate simultaneously. The event mode, with zero *TimeOut*, is used to check the help button and the pointer button, while the sample mode is used to read the pointer position. In addition, a good interactive feature, the HELP facility, is available at all times – this could be activated, for example, by pressing a special key on the keyboard. It is fair to say that it would not be very easy to reproduce this program using facilities of the GKS standard only.

2.3.5   Multiprocessing in graphics systems

In a complex graphics system, such as one based on the GKS type of kernel, a number of workstations may be opened and be active simultaneously. It is assumed that graphics data is stored in each workstation. The workstation data is changed when the workstation is updated, but it cannot be assumed that the visible portion of the workstation reflects the changes automatically. In many cases, this requires a large number of complex operations, while in other cases it is impossible to execute the required changes. In the case of a plotter, for example, if part of the drawing has already occurred, it cannot be changed.

Indeed, by looking at the functions performed by an interactive workstation, it can be seen that there must be input processes accepting data from the input devices, as well as an output process refreshing the screen. The data must be stored in such a way that it can be accessed by all active processes without conflict. In expensive workstations, multiple processors are used for many of these functions. On the other hand, if only a simple terminal is connected to a GKS system, which has no storage capability except a simple frame buffer, then all the functions the workstation cannot perform must be done by the GKS system software.

There is a GKS facility called *DEFERRING_PICTURE_CHANGES* that tries to help in the operation of vastly different types of output device. A **deferral mode** may be set and updating of the display may be done *ASAP* (as soon as possible), *BNIL* (before the next interaction with a local input device), *BNIG* (before the next interaction with any input device) or *ASTI* (at some other time). The GKS facility *UPDATE_WORKSTATION* is used to update the workstation immediately. Obviously, this is not the place to delve into the details of these very complicated software features, but it is important to realize the difficulties that may arise when direct control of the interactive nature of input and output devices is given up to all-knowing and all-powerful workstations.

2.4   GRAPHICAL USER INTERFACE

The emergence of graphical interfaces revolutionized the methods of man–machine interaction used in modern computers. In fact, this is the area of computing where graphics will have both the greatest impact and affect the largest number of users. Two hardware components are needed for an effective graphics user interface: a graphics screen and a pointing device. Recently, the mouse, which has already been described in Chapter 1, became the *de facto* standard input device. Graphics screens with resolutions as low as 640×200 have been used for acceptable graphical interaction between user and the computer. A resolution of 1000×700 for a 12-inch screen should be sufficient for the most advanced applications.

While GKS concentrates on simple drawing and input primitives only, other kernels also provide primitive functions for the graphical user interactions. Obviously, there is a great advantage in integrating the tools of graphics interaction with other graphics primitives. However, since GKS itself is a very large system, integrating it with another system like GEM or X-Window may be very difficult.

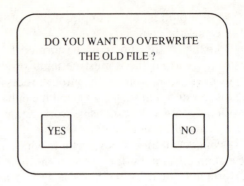

Figure 2.5
A dialogue box may be used in request mode for a simple graphical user interface facility. The box appears on the screen and the system waits until the mouse marker is placed in one of the answer areas and its button is pressed. After interaction, the dialogue box is removed from the screen.

To demonstrate the use of graphics interaction tools, the primitive *DIALOGUE_BOX* will be used. A typical dialogue box is shown in Figure 2.5. The dialogue box may be invoked by the following function:

ACTIVATE_DIALOGUE_BOX(*BoxSpecifier* : ↑ *BoxDataStructure*;
XPosition, *YPosition*, *Size* : **real**;
var *Choice* : **integer**)

The parameter ↑ *BoxSpecifier* points to a graphics data structure, or a list that may contain any drawing primitives. Through a primitive like *CELL_ARRAY*, icons may be created. The primitive *TEXT* is used for the required messages. The *ACTIVATE_DIALOGUE_BOX* function works in request mode. Once the function is invoked, the program transfers control to the system; control will not return to the program until the user has indicated a choice by pointing with the mouse to one of the answer areas and clicking the button. Normally, the dialogue box disappears on completion of the dialogue box function and the screen is restored to its original state.

If the user interaction functions are incorporated within the graphics system, then the display position and box size parameters could refer to the currently active viewport and could be given in normalized device co-ordinates. In a system where true multiprocessing is implemented, different viewports may be active at the same time, and so multiple dialogue boxes could appear, each waiting for user interaction. It is quite feasible to provide dialogue boxes for every input device type in the system. One may be used to collect textual information, such as answers to questions issued by the application program, and another to return a value.

One of the important aspects of this graphical interface facility is that it can use all the power of the graphics system, possibly even animation. The other important aspect of this example is that the *ACTIVATE_DIALOGUE_BOX* function creates a temporary input device that, in functional terms, behaves just like any other logical input device.

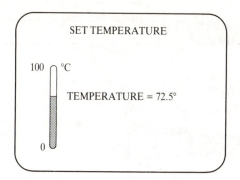

SET TEMPERATURE

Figure 2.6
A scrollbar graphical interface facility may be used in sample mode to specify a value. The slide shows values between 0 and 100 °C. The current setting is 72.5 °C. Whenever the mouse marker is placed on the slide and the button is pressed, the setting is changed.

There are other interface facilities that work in the sample or event mode. For example, the facility called *SCROLLBAR*, illustrated in Figure 2.6, presents a slide region that may be adjusted using the mouse. A function call:

$$ACTIVATE\_SCROLLBAR(\ Scrollbar\_Identifier : \textbf{integer};$$
$$Scrollbar\_Specifier : \uparrow ScrollbarDataStructure;$$
$$XPosition, YPosition, Size : \textbf{real})$$

draws the scrollbar box and sets it up as a logical input device operating in sample mode. The function:

$$SAMPLE\_SCROLLBAR(Scrollbar\_Identifier : \textbf{integer}; \textbf{var}\ Value : \textbf{real})$$

could then be used to read the value shown on the screen. The function:

$$DEACTIVATE\_SCROLLBAR(Scrollbar\_Identifier : \textbf{integer})$$

is used to remove the scrollbar input function and its visual representation from the system.

A similar action box may be designed for event-mode input operation. For example, a so-called pop-up menu system may be activated by a similar interactive facility which can provide the display shown in Figure 2.7. The order of the selection of the different menu items may be significant and could be determined from a queued input event list normally associated with event-mode operation. Similar *ACTIVATE* and *DEACTIVATE* functions could be used along with an input function that returns the first item in the event queue.

From these simple examples, it can be seen how a well-designed graphics kernel can relieve the application programmer of a large number of routine programming tasks while, at the same time, providing an effective, well-organised and helpful graphics user interface.

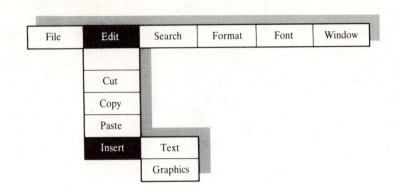

Figure 2.7
A pop-down menu shows a hierarchical structure of commands which may be activated by successive pointing with the mouse and clicking with its button. The selections may be saved in an event queue and subsequently interrogated by the application program.

2.5 SUBPICTURES AND GRAPHICAL TRANSFORMATIONS

It would be difficult to construct a complex picture from the *POLYLINE* primitive, even if the picture contained only straight lines. A picture that has no other structure than lines cannot be manipulated very efficiently, since a logical entity within the picture cannot be considered as a subpicture. In a way, subpictures are similar to subprograms, such as functions and procedures, in a computer program. Like subprograms, there are two advantages in using subpictures. Firstly, if the duplication of the subpicture is required, then the new occurrence of the subpicture may be copied from the old one. Secondly, a given subpicture may be associated with a logical entity and a complex scene may be divided up to yield a collection of simple scenes. Furthermore, it is easier to handle, modify or correct a collection of simple scenes than a complex scene.

What makes subpictures even more useful is the graphical transformations that may be applied to them. To demonstrate this use of subpictures and transformations, only two-dimensional space will be used. A more detailed treatment of three-dimensional transformations will be given in Chapter 4.

There are three basic transformations in two-dimensional graphics:

(1) **Translation**, a simple move in the *x*–*y* plane.

(2) **Rotation**, by a given angle with respect to a specified point in the *x*–*y* plane, usually the origin.

(3) **Scaling**, in both *x* and *y* directions and with respect to a specified point in the same plane.

These transformations can be used to modify simple subpictures to construct complex pictures. There are two ways in which a complex picture may be constructed from simpler picture elements. The intuitive way is to think of subpictures as entities. However, it is also possible to construct a picture with a strictly linear structure by inserting suitably transformed elements of other picture sections. This process is called **substantiation** and the picture elements are called **segments** in GKS. In a way, segments are similar to macros in a low-level programming language. The difference between subpictures and segments can be paralleled with the difference between procedures, which are self-consistent programming units, and macros, which are templates for substitution. The construction of a picture from subpictures will be demonstrated by a simple example: the drawing of the cross-section of a gear wheel.

2.5.1.   Construction of a drawing

A gear wheel is made up of 30 teeth drawn around a thin cylinder. The gear can be created easily by defining a tooth as a primitive element and then having it drawn in 30 different places. The functions needed to construct this drawing will be introduced without regard to their implementation, since this exercise is more of a conceptual treatment, rather than a detailed description using a graphics system. The problem will be discussed informally at first, without reference to GKS or other kernels, and then the implementations will be considered in more detail.

The first step is to define the picture, named *Tooth* in this case, by a function called *DEFINE_PICTURE*:

```
DEFINE_PICTURE(Tooth)
    X[1] := 0; X[2] := 0.2; X[3] := 0.6; X[4] := 0.6; X[5] := 0.2; X[6] := 0;
    Y[1] := 0; Y[2] := 0.2; Y[3] := 0.2; Y[4] := 0.8; Y[5] := 0.8; Y[6] := 1;
    POLYLINE(6, X, Y);
    END_DEFINITION(Tooth);
```

Having defined the picture *Tooth*, it can be viewed by invoking the output function called *DRAW_PICTURE*:

```
DRAW_PICTURE(Tooth)
```

which produces the drawing shown in Figure 2.8(a).

The next step is to scale this subpicture. A new function, called *SCALE_PICTURE*, is used which is similar to the *DEFINE_PICTURE* routine in the sense that it defines a new picture as a scaled version of the original one. Scaling is executed by the specified constants in X and Y with respect to the origin [0, 0]. Since 30 teeth have to fit around the circumference of a circle, this *Tooth* must be scaled so that its width is equal to $2R \sin (6°)$, where the radius is defined as R. It is assumed here that the SIN and COS functions are given in terms of degrees. To preserve the

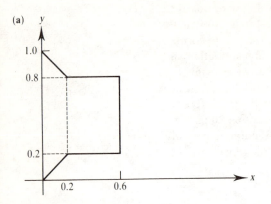

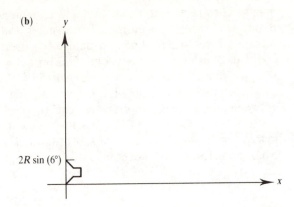

Figure 2.8
(a) The line drawing of the cross-section of a normalized gear tooth is defined by one polyline with five line segments. (b) The scaled version of the tooth of which 30 teeth will fit around a circle of radius R.

same aspect ratio, the scaling must be the same in both the X and Y directions. The following sequence of instructions:

```
DEFINE_PICTURE(ScaledTooth)
    SCALE_PICTURE(Tooth, 2*R*SIN(6), 2*R*SIN(6))
END_DEFINITION(ScaledTooth);
DRAW_PICTURE(ScaledTooth);
```

results in the picture shown in Figure 2.8(b).

The next transformation is to place the origin at the centre of the gear and to draw one tooth at its correct position. This requires translation. The translation in the X direction is equal to $R\cos(6°)$ and in the Y direction is equal to $-R\sin(6°)$. A new function is required for translation. The sequence of instructions is:

```
DEFINE_PICTURE(CorrectTooth)
    TRANSLATE_PICTURE(ScaledTooth, R*COS(6), -R*SIN(6))
END_DEFINITION(CorrectTooth);
DRAW_PICTURE(CorrectTooth);
```

and the produced drawing is shown in Figure 2.8(c).

Finally, rotations are needed to draw the entire gear wheel. Each rotation is through an angle of $360/30 = 12°$. The **for** loop will be used to construct the gear, otherwise it would be necessary to invoke the rotated tooth 30 times. The hole in the middle is defined with a radius of $R/12$ and

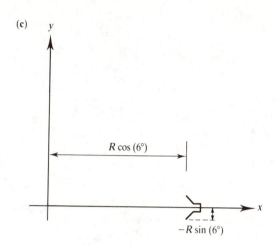

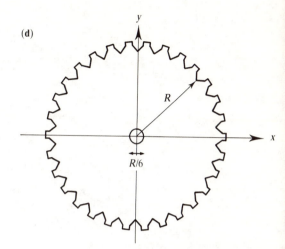

Figure 2.8
(c) The translated version of the scaled gear tooth is in position and the centre of the gear is at the origin.
(d) The final picture of the cross-section of the gear is generated by repeated rotations of the correctly placed scaled tooth using 12° for each rotation. The centre of the gear is drawn by a circle-drawing primitive.

a new function *CIRCLE* is used to draw it:

```
DEFINE_PICTURE(Gear)
  for j := 0 to 29 do
  begin
    Angle := j*12;
    ROTATE_PICTURE(CorrectTooth, Angle);
  end;
  CIRCLE(0, 0, R/12)
END_DEFINITION(Gear);
DRAW_PICTURE(Gear);
```

The drawing of *Gear* is shown in Figure 2.8(d).

This example illustrates how a complex picture can be built up in a hierarchical manner using the subpicture as a simple element. In fact, the picture *Gear* may be represented by a structure that differs from a simple tree-like data structure by the introduction of transformations, a special element of graphical data structures. This data structure is shown schematically in Figure 2.9. Without worrying about the details of implementation here, it can be seen how a complex picture can be made up of primitives (lines, circles, arcs), subpictures and transformations.

2.5.2 Segments

The GKS standard will be used to demonstrate the details of a segmented data structure. The mechanism for creating a segment in GKS uses the *OPEN_SEGMENT* and the *CLOSE_SEGMENT* primitives. A segment is

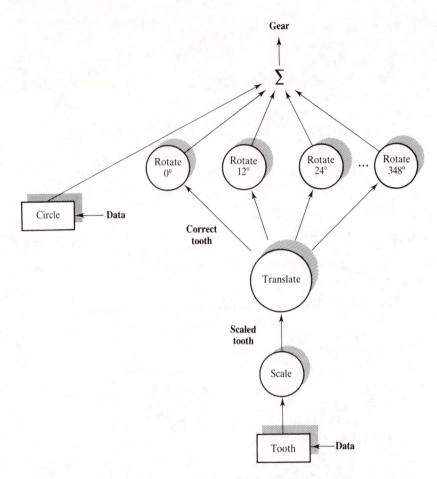

Figure 2.9

This schematic diagram shows how the gear is produced from the repeated application of the generic tooth data and the circle-drawing primitive. Various gear sizes with varying numbers of teeth may be produced with the same picture-constructing structure.

identified by a simple integer number. An example of a GKS program that defines a segment similar to the subpicture *Tooth* is as follows:

```
var XTooth, YTooth : array [1..6] of real;
    XTooth[1] := 0; XTooth[2] := 0.2; XTooth[3] := 0.6;
    XTooth[4] := 0.6; XTooth[5] := 0.2; XTooth[6] := 0;
    YTooth[1] := 0; YTooth[2] := 0.2; YTooth[3] := 0.2;
    YTooth[4] := 0.8; YTooth[5] := 0.8; YTooth[6] := 1.0;
OPEN_SEGMENT(Tooth)
    SET_POLYLINE_INDEX(Default);
    POLYLINE(6, XTooth, YTooth);
CLOSE_SEGMENT;
```

Note that the *CLOSE_SEGMENT* function does not require a parameter, since in this linear, non-hierarchical data structure only one segment may be open at any one time. According to GKS conventions, the segment is sent to all currently active workstations.

The usefulness of a segment definition is that the created segment has attributes that can be set by other primitive GKS functions. There are four attributes for segments and the four functions that change these attributes are:

SET_SEGMENT_TRANSFORMATION(*SegmentIdentifier* : **integer**;
Matrix : **TransformationMatrix**)
SET_SEGMENT_VISIBILITY(*SegmentIdentifier* : **integer**; *Visible* : **boolean**)
SET_SEGMENT_HIGHLIGHTING(*SegmentIdentifier* : **integer**; *Highlighted* : **boolean**)
SET_SEGMENT_PRIORITY(*SegmentIdentifier* : **integer**; *Priority* : **real**)

The variable *Matrix* in the *SET_SEGMENT_TRANSFORMATION* function contains constants for all three types of graphical transformation (translation, rotation and scaling). Two types of GKS procedures convert simple graphical transformations into matrix elements. One sets the matrix elements:

SET_TRANSFORMATION_MATRIX(**var** *Matrix* : **TransformationMatrix**; ...
transformation details ...)

and the other creates a new transformation matrix, from a current one, to which new transformations are applied:

ACCUMULATE_TRANSFORMATION_MATRIX(*OldMatrix* : **TransformationMatrix**;
var *NewMatrix* :
TransformationMatrix;
... transformation details ...)

Changing a segment's transformation matrix without complete picture regeneration may cause unexpected problems in GKS systems not designed for interactive applications.

The *VISIBILITY* attribute allows the blanking out of segments, the *HIGHLIGHTING* attribute invokes some hardware-defined highlighting scheme (brighter lines, different colour, blinking) and the *PRIORITY* attribute determines which segment is closer to the viewer. These attributes have to be defined before a segment is opened, so that the correct picture is generated (or defaults used). However, once the picture is drawn, the attributes can be changed and they can be used, for example, to highlight different segments of a picture interactively or make them visible/invisible under program control. Unfortunately, the problem of regeneration arises here which is hardware dependent. Functionally, at least, an interactive workstation should always display a segment with its correct attributes.

Difficulties arising with segments that exist on workstations rather than in some central store has created the need for an alternative graphics system. PHIGS is such a system which, as mentioned before, executes picture generation interactively from a central, hierarchically structured picture store.

If segments are to be used as subpictures, the list of primitives must be stored somewhere. To avoid adding new types of system components to GKS, the designers have provided one special workstation per system, called the **workstation-independent segment storage (WISS)**, whose sole role is to store picture segments. Thus, when the WISS workstation is active and a segment is defined, a copy of the segment is retained in the WISS. Retrieval of the segment from the WISS can be done in three ways. The most useful GKS function inserts the segment list into the current picture, which may be a segment itself, after applying specified picture transformations through a transformation matrix. The following GKS primitive is used:

INSERT_SEGMENT(*SegmentIdentifier* : **integer**; *Matrix* : **TransformationMatrix**)

where the transformations defined by *Matrix* are applied to the segment primitives before they are inserted into the GKS list of primitives. This function appears to create a hierarchical picture structure but, in fact, only the primitives of the segment are copied into the currently active workstations. Furthermore, the original segment structure disappears even if a segment is open when the *INSERT_SEGMENT* function is invoked. The best way of demonstrating this is by the example of the *Gear* picture.

The GKS primitives required to produce the picture of *Gear* on a workstation are:

```
DEACTIVATE_WORKSTATION(MyWorkstation);
ACTIVATE_WORKSTATION(Wiss);
OPEN_SEGMENT(1);
   POLYLINE(6, XGear, YGear);
CLOSE_SEGMENT;
SET_TRANSFORMATION_MATRIX(Matrix1, ... scale by 2 * R * SIN(6), R * SIN(6),
                               translate by R * COS(6), −R * SIN(6) ...);
OPEN_SEGMENT(2);
  for j := 0 to 29 do
  begin
    Angle := j * 12;
    INSERT_SEGMENT(1, Matrix1);
    ACCUMULATE_TRANSFORMATION_MATRIX(Matrix1, ... rotate by Angle
                                                  ...);
  end;
CLOSE_SEGMENT;
DEACTIVATE(Wiss);
ACTIVATE_WORKSTATION(MyWorkstation);
INSERT_SEGMENT(2, IdentityMatrix);
```

In this particular example, the segment structure of *Gear* is lost on *MyWorkstation* because no segment is open when the primitives of segment 2 are transferred. The variable *IdentityMatrix* refers to a transformation matrix that does not alter the drawing primitives. Note that it is also possible to open a new segment (segment 3, for example) and define *Gear* as a segment on *MyWorkstation* as well by using the *Insert_Segment* function.

It is important to call the reader's attention to the fact that the graphical data is duplicated in all active workstations and not 'pointed' to. Hence, if the segment in the WISS is subsequently redefined or deleted, this will have no visible effect on the other workstations into which the segment primitives were previously copied.

2.5.3   Hierarchical data structures

In this section, we examine how picture structures may be translated into an organized hierarchical database. As shown in Figure 2.10, a picture may be constructed from subpictures, which themselves may be constructed from simpler ones. The concept of attributes (visibility, priority, colour, intensity, style) may also be used for subpictures as they were used for primitives such as lines, areas, markers and text. Between each hierarchical level, there is a graphical transformation facility, in addition to a possible attribute change facility. In these structures, graphical data, pointers to other data structures and transformation directives are stored. As far as attributes are concerned, the concept of **inheritance** can be used. This means that the attributes are inherited from parents (higher-level pictures), as opposed to being locally defined.

In a complex graphics system, the graphics database should be an integral part of the graphics processor subsystem. The graphics processor includes both hardware processors and complex graphics software. In GKS, however, this is not the case, since the database is invisible and processing inherently invokes data storage. What happens in an application package that uses GKS, for example, is that the package has its own database and processing facilities, and the processing is translated to GKS at the lowest level. This introduces inefficiencies, since a direct approach to hardware processing could take better advantage of the structure of the database. This can be demonstrated by the following simple example.

To write a building architecture walk-through system, the inside of a building may be defined by a collection of co-ordinates that specify rooms, corridors, staircases and so on. Each picture element, like a room, a door, a window, a corridor or a staircase, may consist of ten to hundreds of line segments. If the building is viewed from the inside of a room, then it is only possible to see those lines belonging to other rooms that can be seen

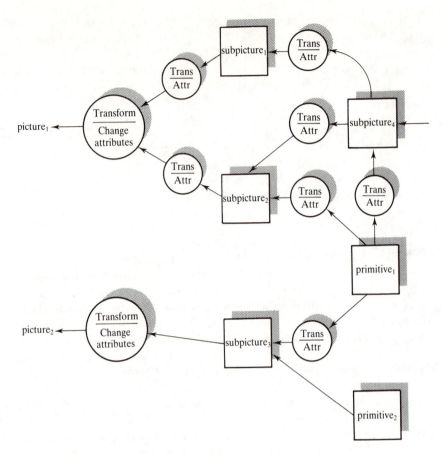

Figure 2.10

The hierarchical structure of a graphical database allows the construction of a picture or subpicture from primitives or other subpictures. When a subpicture (or primitive) is used, its shape can be altered by geometrical transformations and its appearance by the transformation of its attributes.

through open doors or windows. Hence, the topological information as to which rooms are adjacent to other rooms could prune the number of lines that have to be considered. To use GKS with a data structure like this, a translation is necessary from visible lines to polylines, which may be very time consuming.

This example demonstrates the important distinction between numerical and topological data. The following example further illustrates the distinction between these two types of data.

Consider the definition of a unit cube placed at the origin of a three-dimensional Cartesian co-ordinate system. To define the cube, six facets have to be specified. This data can be specified as six quadruplets of $[x, y, z]$ co-ordinates specifying six planar polygons (square sheets), as shown in Table 2.1. If the co-ordinates were transformed in this representation, the computations would take three times longer than necessary,

Table 2.1 Definition of a cube using one database.

Facet	Vertex(1)	Vertex(2)	Vertex(3)	Vertex(4)
1	0,0,0	0,1,0	1,1,0	1,0,0
2	0,0,1	0,1,1	1,1,1	1,0,1
3	0,0,0	0,0,1	1,0,1	1,0,0
4	0,1,0	0,1,1	1,1,1	1,1,0
5	0,0,0	0,0,1	0,1,1	0,1,0
6	1,0,0	1,0,1	1,1,1	1,1,0

since each vertex is represented three times. Moreover, even with the redundant vertex data present, it would take considerable searching time to determine which two facets meet at a given edge or which three facets meet at a given vertex, since the database is lacking any topological information.

The same definition can be represented using two separate databases, as shown in Table 2.2. The numerical database stores the coordinates of the eight vertices. The topological data defines edges and facets in a hierarchical structure. The search for a common edge between two facets is much faster in the topological database, since there are only

Table 2.2 Definition of a cube using two databases.

(Numerical Data)			(Topological Data)		
Vertex	Data	Edge	(Which vertices?)	Facet	(Which edges?)
1	0,0,0	1	1,2	1	1,2,3,4
2	0,0,1	2	2,6	2	5,6,7,8
3	0,1,0	3	6,5	3	1,10,5,9
4	0,1,1	4	5,1	4	3,11,7,12
5	1,0,0	5	3,4	5	4,9,8,12
6	1,0,1	6	4,8	6	2,10,6,11
7	1,1,0	7	8,7		
8	1,1,1	8	7,3		
		9	1,3		
		10	2,4		
		11	6,8		
		12	5,7		

four integer numbers for each facet stored, instead of 12 real co-ordinate values. Furthermore, when graphical transformations are applied, only the numerical database is transformed, thereby avoiding redundant numerical computations. Other topological information, such as which side of a facet is the inner and which the outer, can also be usefully added to the graphics database.

These simple examples of a graphical data structure demonstrate that the organisation of data is an important factor in the efficient handling of graphical information. Both the device and the kernel levels influence the efficiency of the overall graphics system. In the following chapters, the procedural and functional levels will be studied in more detail; however, the roles of these lower levels should never be forgotten. Ultimately, any system is limited by its slowest component.

Exercises

2.1 Discuss the difficulties with designing portable graphics systems. Explain why portability and flexibility are opposing requirements. Suggest a means by which both can be achieved satisfactorily.

2.2 What is the meaning of the term 'kernel' in GKS?

2.3 Describe the difference between GKS and PHIGS type of graphics systems. List specific advantages and disadvantages of one system compared to the other.

2.4 What parameter values must be known in order to translate a mouse marker position given by pixel numbers to the horizontal and vertical distances measured in the user's co-ordinate system? Derive an expression for this calculation.

2.5 In a graphics system there are two active viewports. In the first viewport the entire user space is shown. With a mouse whose input position is defined by pixel numbers, a rectangle is selected in the first viewport. The inside area of the rectangle drawn in the first viewport is mapped to the second viewport where a zoomed-in portion of the user space is displayed. Using pseudo code, show all required calculations if the graphics scene in the first viewport is constructed only from line segments.

2.6 List and define a minimum set of GKS-type output functions for a graphics system that has 16 logical colours. Compile a single list of drawing attributes assuming that only one list is used for all output functions.

2.7 Demonstrate that the device level and the kernel level are different by describing specific features of the kernel level that do not have their equivalent representation at the device level.

2.8 Explain why it is more difficult to handle input than output functions in a device-independent manner.

2.9 In GKS there are four useful logical input types and three modes of operation. Combining modes and types gives 12 different specific data transfer functions. Identify the hardware device that is most suited for each of the 12 input transfers. (For example, text input in event mode is best served by an ASCII keyboard.)

2.10 Define input functions for a mouse having two push buttons and working as a simple pointing device in request, sample and event modes. Show calling sequences and find an appropriate practical example for each mode of operation.

2.11 Show that the event mode is a desirable feature by describing the required operational characteristics of a practical graphics system for which the lack of the event mode of operation would create severe difficulties for an application programmer.

2.12 Compare segmented and hierarchical picture databases and discuss their respective advantages and disadvantages. Why can the WISS not be considered as a central data store in GKS?

Problems

2.13 A square in user co-ordinates is defined by the corners:

$$[-5, 5], [5, 5], [5, 15], [-5, 15]$$

Determine the pixel co-ordinate values for the corners of the square for a 1024 × 1024 pixels viewing surface and draw the visible portions of the square with respect to the whole viewing surface when the following normalization transformations are used:

(a) *SET_WINDOW*(1, 0, 1, 0, 1)
     SET_VIEWPORT(1, 0.5, 1.0, 0.5, 1.0)

(b) *SET_WINDOW*(2, −30, 30, −20, 40)
     SET_VIEWPORT(2, 0.1, 0.5, 0.5, 0.9)

(c) *SET_WINDOW*(3, −10, 10, 10, 20)
     SET_VIEWPORT(3, 0, 1.0, 0, 0.5)

(d) *SET_WINDOW*(4, −100, 100, −100, 100)
  SET_VIEWPORT(4, 0, 0.4, 0, 0.2)

2.14 Using the smallest number of GKS primitives possible create the drawing of the full house shown in Figure 2.3.

2.15 You have to implement the GKS *VALUATOR*, *CHOICE* and *STRING* input types using only the keyboard. For each of the facilities provided, define the GKS system level procedures, the user interface and the global variable space required for implementing the GKS input primitives when:

(a) Only request mode is allowed.

(b) Request and sample modes are allowed.

(c) All three input modes are allowed.

2.16 Describe in detail the effect of the GKS operations on the WISS database when the program shown on page 66 is executed.

2.17 Design the data structure and a set of procedures in pseudo code that provide the WISS facility in a GKS system. Design the procedure that executes the *INSERT_SEGMENT* facility.

2.18 Design the data structure for a hierarchical graphics database consisting of lines, circular arcs and text in a specific higher-level language (Pascal, MODULA, C). Write the access procedures, including the modification and enquiry functions for attributes and transformations.

2.19 Using your favourite programming language, implement a general dialogue box facility using device level functions only. Show in detail how this facility could be included in some available application software.

2.20 Using GKS-type facilities, implement a scrollbar graphical interaction facility. Describe how multiple scrollbars may be kept active in a GKS system.

2.21 In the computer representation of the inside of a building, an array of three-dimensional points is used to hold the numerical data. These points represent the corner co-ordinates of walls, doors and windows. Show how you would set up a topological database for a walk-through system. Pay attention to the efficiency of finding the relevant walls, open doors and windows when a person is located in a given room and looks in a particular direction.

Projects

2.22 Using GKS-like drawing primitives, design a package for the drawing of scientific graphs from a set of [x, y] data points. Include functions for labelling the axis, connecting points, positioning markers and legends, and scaling.

2.23 Assume that a convenient device level has been provided for a simple display, keyboard and mouse system. Outline the required procedures for implementing the basic line and text drawing, input and enquiry functions of GKS. From the design of these procedures, define the most convenient device level for your system.

3

Fundamental Algorithms for Raster Graphics

Raster algorithms are the most fundamental algorithms that any graphics programmer will be called upon to write, and for this reason their efficient implementation is important. This chapter discusses in some detail how the most useful primitives may be drawn. These are straight lines and polygons, and second-order curves. The most widely applicable method is the differential drawing algorithm; however, consideration is also given to parametric and scan line methods. In some applications, the graphics programmer will need to draw not only the boundaries of closed curves and polygons, but also to fill them in. Two distinct types of filling algorithms are described. Seed filling only uses information already on the screen, while scan line filling uses a functional description of the boundary of the primitive to be filled, and will produce a much faster algorithm.

Devices for which it is possible to set the pixels to a range of illumination values allow line drawing to be improved visually by smoothing out the jagged appearance of some lines. This is called anti-aliasing and can be done by either modifying the fundamental algorithms themselves or by postprocessing the picture. The latter method is treated in detail, introducing an important mathematical method called convolution, which will be encountered later in the book.

Most graphics printers and simple video terminals can only draw pixels in two colours. Several methods are described for reproducing shaded images on these systems. These algorithms are fundamentally important in the field of printing and typesetting by computer.

3.1 INTRODUCTION

A raster device is one where the screen is divided into a number of discrete dots or pixels that can be set to some intensity value. In the last 10 years, the raster device has displaced the high-resolution vector tubes in all but a few applications. This was initially due to the cost advantage gained by mass production. However, graphics systems were quick to exploit the particular property that pixels can be addressed individually, and consequently any area of the picture can be altered without affecting the remainder. This is in contrast to the storage tube, where it is necessary to redraw the entire picture every time an alteration is to be made. One important application of this feature is the implementation of pop-up windows and moving icons, which are the basis of the modern approach to the control of interactive systems.

Due to two features of current raster technology, vector tubes have survived. These are the comparatively low resolution of raster devices, which ultimately limits the detail that can be seen on one screen, and the relatively long time taken to update large areas of the screen. Increasing the resolution represents a possible solution to the first problem, but at the expense of the second. However, the degree to which the resolution can be raised is limited by cost. As resolution is increased, the number of pixels goes up according to a square law, and the cost of the associated hardware and memory accelerates in cost to the point where vector tubes become viable alternatives.

Vector tubes use low-persistence phosphor, which continues to emit light for only a short time after it has been excited by the beam. As there is no frame buffer, the display data is stored in its geometric form, usually as a list of vectors specified by their magnitude and direction. The amount of information displayed by a vector tube is limited by the sum of the lengths of all the displayed line segments. Since the lines are refreshed in real time, if the number of line segments becomes too large, the display will start to flicker. Because the data are in geometric form, transformations (translation, rotation, scaling) and zooming effects can be performed instantaneously (within one refresh cycle). These systems are confined to specialist applications, such as molecular modelling, where line drawings are acceptable.

From a computational viewpoint, the main advantage of raster images is that they can be represented directly in memory. Each pixel is allocated a number of bits, determining the number of distinct intensity levels with which gray shades or colours can be represented. For example, a system with four bits per pixel will be able to set that pixel to $2^4 = 16$ distinct intensity levels. A system with only one bit per pixel can only support pixels being either ON or OFF and is termed **bi-level**. At the lowest level, a picture is represented as a square array of intensities, which is called a **frame**. In the following treatment, it is assumed that each raster device has at least one frame buffer; that is, a block of memory that can be written directly by the processor and which can be displayed on the screen. Many modern systems have several such buffers.

The frame, or raster, representation is completely different from the geometric descriptions that a programmer would naturally use to describe the procedural level of graphics. Hence, a transformation is required between the two representations. This is called **rasterization** or **scan conversion**. Since rasterization is a sampling process, it is clear that information is lost when it is carried out, which causes two problems. The first is the appearance of unpleasant effects in the final image, such as straight lines appearing jagged. The second is that the transformation is irreversible. It is very difficult, or even impossible, in general to construct a geometric description from a raster representation. Thus, operations such as scaling and rotation cannot be carried out on a raster representation of the image without introducing further distortion.

Any modern raster graphics device will present a simple interface to the systems programmer. The most comprehensive systems will provide many functions – for example, terminals that interpret GKS commands in the hardware. Mid-priced systems will provide a number of graphics primitives for drawing lines, polygons and other objects, and will allow a range of intensities for individual pixels, specified in bits per pixel. The cheapest systems will only provide a bi-level display and a rudimentary interface. The minimum that will be provided is the ability to set, clear and complement the intensity values of individual pixels.

This chapter begins by concentrating on these cheaper systems, discussing the fundamental algorithms for drawing lines and conic sections, filling polygons and representing shaded images. Since other, higher-level routines will frequently call these fundamental procedures, the performance of the system will depend on how efficiently the fundamental algorithms are implemented. Thus, they illustrate both the procedural and computational aspects of graphics.

For the purposes of these algorithms, it is assumed that the pixel on the bottom left-hand side of the screen is the origin and that pixels are spaced at unit intervals. Thus, each pixel is addressed by integer co-ordinates. Normally, the frame buffer will be mapped in the memory space of the system that drives it. If this is so, a computation must be made of the correct memory address before any pixel can be changed. More complex systems will compute the address in the associated hardware. In both cases, addressing the raster will represent an overhead, which must be minimized in the implementation of the fundamental algorithms. As the computation of the raster address is machine dependent, it will not be considered further here, except to observe that table lookup can often be employed to increase speed at the cost of memory. Since a pixel occupies an area of the screen, the convention that the co-ordinate represents the centre of that area will be adopted.

Algorithm 3.1

First octant differential line generator.

```
Differential := (y₂ − y₁)/(x₂ − x₁);
x := x₁; y := y₁;
SET_PIXEL(x, y);
Error := 0;
while x < x₂ do
begin
    Error := Error + Differential;
    if Error >= 1/2
    then begin
            y := y + 1;
            Error := Error − 1;
        end;
    x := x + 1;
    SET_PIXEL(x, y);
end (* while *);
```

3.2 LINE DRAWINGS

The simplest example of a general class of differential algorithms is that used to draw representations of straight lines on a raster screen (see Algorithm 3.1). The principle is illustrated in Figure 3.1 for the first Cartesian octant; that is, where the slope of the line is between 0 and 1. The line is drawn between co-ordinate points $[x_1, y_1]$ and $[x_2, y_2]$. The basis is to step through the x ordinates from x_1 to x_2, where x_1 is less than x_2, and calculate the error made by not drawing the line at its exact position. At each point, a decision is taken as to which of the two pixels that bound the real position of the line at that x ordinate is the closest, and then this pixel is set to ON. Zero error, is assumed at point $[x_1, y_1]$ meaning that the line passes through the initial point. The change in error, when moving from one pixel to the next, can be simply computed by adding the differential to the current error value. In the case of a line, the differential is equal to the constant $(y_2 − y_1)/(x_2 − x_1)$. If the error is larger than 0.5, then the y value of the ON pixel is incremented by one and the error is decreased by one. The procedure terminates when the pixel at location $[x_2, y_2]$ is turned ON.

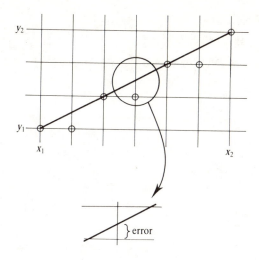

Key

⊕   Illuminated pixels

+   Dark pixels

Figure 3.1

The differential line-drawing method for the first octant. The error value shown is computed and used to decide which pixel is closest to the true line. The closest pixel is illuminated.

As Algorithm 3.1 is one of the most fundamental algorithms, it is necessary to consider its implementation in further detail in order to optimize its speed. The pixel co-ordinates will be represented by integer quantities. As the algorithm stands, the differential must be represented as a real quantity, and as a consequence the error will also be real. Some gain in speed, particularly on cheaper systems, can be made by arranging for these quantities to be represented by integers. Since:

$$\text{Differential} = \frac{\Delta y}{\Delta x} = \frac{y_2 - y_1}{x_2 - x_1}$$

and Δx and Δy are pixel distances, therefore they can be represented by integers. Thus, if the differential is multiplied by Δx, then it too can be represented by an integer. Furthermore, since the error is found by accumulating the differential, it will also be an integer quantity, ranging between 0 and Δx. The decision as to which pixel is nearer can be made by comparing it to Δx **div** 2. When this is computed in assembler code, the value of Δx **div** 2 will need to occupy a register during the computation, or worse still reside in memory. Thus, the comparison operation will require a

Algorithm 3.2

First octant integer differential line generator.

```
Δx := x₂ − x₁;
Δy := y₂ − y₁;
Error := −(Δx div 2);
x := x₁; y := y₁;
SET_PIXEL(x, y);
while x < x₂ do
begin
    Error := Error + Δy;
    if Error >= 0
    then begin
            y := y + 1;
            Error := Error − Δx;
        end;
    x := x + 1;
    SET_PIXEL(x, y);
end (* while *);
```

whole register comparison, or possibly a fetch from memory on small systems. Gains in speed could therefore be achieved if the comparison could be made with zero, which requires only that a condition flag be tested. This can be arranged by initializing the error to $-(\Delta x \text{ div } 2)$. The error will now range from $-(\Delta x \text{ div } 2)$ to $+(\Delta x \text{ div } 2)$, with the comparison point being zero. These changes yield a computationally efficient algorithm, first published by Bresenham (1965), which is shown in Algorithm 3.2.

Algorithm 3.2 solves the problem for the first Cartesian octant. Similar algorithms can be described for the other octants, noting that for slopes greater than 1 or less than -1, it is necessary to step through the y ordinates, computing the error in the x ordinate. Figure 3.2 illustrates this point. Clearly, there is a symmetry between octant 1 and octant 5. For any line in octant 5, it is only necessary to swap the endpoints and then use the algorithm for octant 1. This swap can also be performed outside the main loop with very little computational overhead. Extending this symmetry, it follows that an algorithm need only be devised for four of the octants; therefore, no further consideration needs to be given to octants 4, 5, 6 and

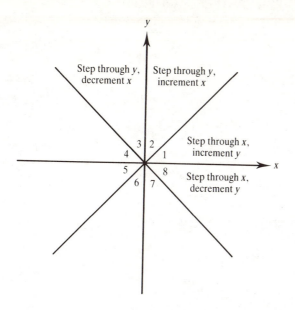

Step through y,
decrement x

Step through y,
increment x

3 2
4   1

Step through x,
increment y

5   8
6 7

Step through x,
decrement y

Figure 3.2

The Cartesian octants. The method for implementing a differential algorithm of octants 1, 2, 3 and 8 is indicated. For high-speed implementation, a different block of code is required for octants 2 and 3.

7. A further small adjustment enables octants 1 and 8 to be handled with the same code; that is, to set up a register with the incremental change to y, either 1 or -1, before executing the loop. This can be done without any computational cost, since a register-to-register add takes the same time as a register increment. A similar method can be used so that octants 2 and 3 can also be computed by the same code.

It is tempting to further adjust the code so that octant 2 can be computed by the same code as octant 1. This could be achieved by swapping the x and y values on initializing, and then swapping them back just before setting the pixel. However, this is undesirable because it requires the introduction of a test into the main loop, just before a pixel is set. This is an overhead carried for every pixel in the line and is consequently very expensive in time. The duplication of the code for the first and second octants is a trivial overhead in memory utilization, in even the smallest system.

Thus, a complete line generator can be constructed as shown in Algorithms 3.3.

It is interesting to observe that intersecting lines drawn by the differential method could cross, yet have no common pixel, and hence no intersection in the frame buffer. This fact need not worry the graphics programmer, who will generally be working at the functional or procedural level. However, for low-level line intersection algorithms, possibly intended for hardware implementation, these cases must be catered for, and a selection of one of the four closest pixels to the real intersection must be made.

Algorithm 3.3

Complete integer differential line generator.

```
Δx := x₂ − x₁;
Δy := y₂ − y₁;
if abs(Δx) > abs(Δy)
then begin
        if Δx < 0
        then begin
                SWAP(x₂, x₁);
                SWAP(y₂, y₁);
            end;
        if y₂ > y₁
        then YIncrement := 1
        else YIncrement := −1;
        { Compute the first octant algorithm }
    end
else begin
        (* abs(Δx) < abs(Δy) *)
        if Δy < 0
        then begin
                SWAP(x₂, x₁);
                SWAP(y₂, y₁);
            end;
        if x₂ > x₁
        then XIncrement := 1
        else XIncrement := −1;
        { Compute the second octant algorithm }
    end
```

3.3   POLYGON FILLING

The next class of algorithms to be considered is that used to fill a bounded region of the raster screen with a given pattern or uniform colour. In the case of a uniform filling colour, all pixels in the specified area will be set to the same value. Polygon filling is a simple case of the general problem of filling a bounded area on the screen.

Fundamentally, there are two ways in which to define a closed area to be filled:

(1)   First, the bounded area can be geometrically defined. In general, the area may be defined by curves (circular arcs, polynomials, splines), but for the purposes of explanation a closed polygon consisting of straight line edges will be used.

(2)   The second way of defining a closed area is by setting the pixels that lie on the boundary of the area to a specified intensity or colour.

In the first case, the information about the boundary of the area remains intact by the filling process. In the second case, if the colour or intensity used to fill the inside of the area is the same as that of the boundary, the boundaries may disappear and the filling process becomes irreversible. If the filling and boundary colours are different, the boundary pixels will retain their identity.

The next section presents area-filling algorithms for polygons defined by straight edges. Later in the chapter, filling algorithms based on the intensities of the border pixels will be discussed.

3.3.1   Scan line filling

The first type of filling algorithm that will be considered is an example of a class of algorithms that is based on the idea of computing the intersections of the object being drawn with a horizontal (or vertical) line, known as the **scan line**. The scan line normally corresponds to a row of pixels. The principle of the algorithm is illustrated in Figure 3.3, which shows a polygon to be filled with a typical scan line. The intersections with the polygon edges divide the scan line into a number of spans, in this case five.

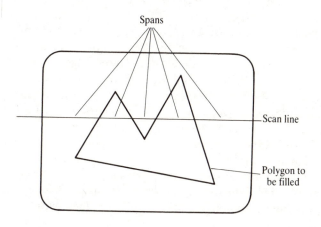

Spans

Scan line

Polygon to be filled

Figure 3.3
Polygon filling by line scan. Each horizontal row of pixels is divided into a number of spans by the edges of the polygon to be filled. These spans are alternatively inside then outside the polygon. In this case, the polygon is wholly contained within the window and so alternate spans to the right of the first intersection have their pixels illuminated.

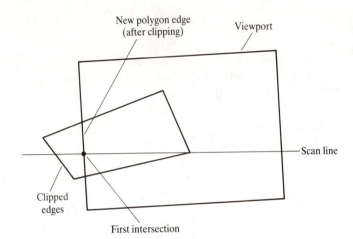

Figure 3.4

Filling a clipped polygon. If the clipped edges are removed from the polygon description and replaced by the viewport edges that clip them, the algorithm may be carried out as for the unclipped polygon shown in Figure 3.3.

To fill the polygon, all the pixels that are contained in the polygon need to be set to ON, or to the filling colour value in the case of multi-level or colour displays. Note that if all the pixels on one span are contained, then those on adjacent spans are not, and vice versa.

A problem arises in determining which spans are contained, if the polygon is clipped by the viewport. If the polygon edges are passed to the filling algorithm as a list of clipped lines, then there will be insufficient information to decide, in general, which areas are inside and which are outside the polygon. It is therefore assumed that in cases where a polygon is not contained entirely inside the viewport, parts of the viewport border become edges of the polygon. Consequently, the representation passed to the filling algorithm includes, in its border line segment list, those parts of the viewport border that define the boundary of the polygon. This situation is illustrated in Figure 3.4. Thus, it can be assumed, without loss of generality, that the first contained span will be to the right of the leftmost intersection with a polygon edge.

Although at the procedural level it is convenient to think of computing the algorithm by stepping through the scan lines, calculating the intersection of each scan line with each polygon edge is not the fastest implementation. It is better to step through the polygon edges, computing the intersections of each polygon edge with the scan lines, and saving the intersection points in a data structure. The increased speed is the result of the optimized Bresenham or differential line-drawing algorithm which can be applied to the area-filling process. When all edges have been processed, the algorithm traverses the data structure by scan line, filling all pixels between intersections, as described earlier.

One possible data structure that can be used for scan line filling is shown in Figure 3.5. It consists of a list of scan lines, with each scan line

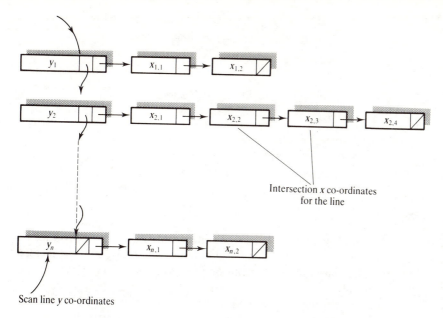

Intersection x co-ordinates
for the line

Scan line y co-ordinates

Figure 3.5
A data structure for filling
polygons by the scan line
method. Each y ordinate
defines the position of a scan
line. Each adjacent pair of x
ordinates represents a span on
the scan line.

record having a pointer to the head of a list of pixel x co-ordinates representing the intersections of the polygon edges with that scan line. The x co-ordinates must be in order of increasing x values. This data structure can be built by first checking through the polygon endpoints to find the maximum and minimum values of y. Using these the scan line list can be constructed.

At the starting point of the edge, which is at vertex $[x_1, y_1]$, the x and y values of the intersection are known and the intersection value ($x = x_1$) is added to the horizontal scan line located at $y = y_1$. Following Bresenham's algorithm, whenever the value of y is changed, a new intersection point is added to a neighbouring scan line – for the first intersection point, y is equal to $y_1 + 1$ or $y_1 - 1$. The process is continued until y becomes equal to y_2, the y value at the second vertex of the edge. As mentioned before, the intersection values are inserted into the list, keeping it ordered at all times.

This method should provide exactly one intersection for each edge and for each scan line that crosses it. However, care is needed here because a straight line may be represented by more than one pixel on one scan line in the raster image. Figure 3.6 shows the pixels that should be set by the differential line-drawing algorithm for two edges. The described algorithm selects the crossing points identified by crosses. As shown, the line-filling algorithm can miss several pixels on the right side of the edge on the right. If the same intensities are used for filling and borders, the filled polygon would have different boundaries to an unfilled one in this case.

Figure 3.6

Using the differential line-drawing algorithm, the black boundary pixels are found. The leftmost of these, indicated by the crosses, are selected as the intersection point between the edge and the scan line. This, however, will not give the most accurate result on the right-hand boundary. The problem can be solved by drawing the boundary lines in the required filling colour.

Key

○ Boundary pixels

✷ Pixels calculated as intersection points

● Pixels set by the line-filling algorithm

The simplest way to ensure that line drawing and filling produce the same shapes is to treat them separately. While the intersections are calculated, the differential algorithm can be used to set the boundary pixels to the required fill value.

Having built the data structure, it is traversed scan line by scan line. Since the intersection values are in order, and it is known that the first contained span is to the right of the first intersection on the list, all that is needed is to set all the pixels between each adjacent pair of x co-ordinates to the fill value for each scan line. The complete algorithm is as shown in Algorithm 3.4.

Some variants have been proposed to this basic idea, which may be appropriate in certain hardware configurations. For example, some bi-level terminals have operations that can be carried out on all pixels to the right of a certain point in the horizontal scan line. For such terminals, a simple algorithm is given in Algorithm 3.5. The final step in this algorithm is required since, depending on the convention adopted, either the left-or the right-hand boundaries will not be drawn. Note that the order in which the spans are complemented does not matter, since the complementing operations will set the correct pixels to ON after all the edges of the polygon have been processed. This simple algorithm has the added advantage that it is not necessary to build a data structure for the intersections.

The algorithms presented so far have been area-filling routines for straight-line boundaries and constant-filling values. For arbitrary curvilinear boundaries and fill patterns, some modifications are required. The calculations of spans for each scan line can be similarly performed for general curvilinear boundaries, in which case there is an obvious advantage in defining the curves by differential algorithms – differential algorithms for ellipses will be shown in the next section. Once the intersections are known and are sorted, the spans are defined and the area filling with arbitrary fill patterns can proceed similarly to Algorithm 3.4. Repeated patterns can be created by the application of the $MOD()$ function. The

Algorithm 3.4

Scan line polygon fill.

Data Structure:

ScanLinePointer = ↑ *Scanline*;
XpixelPointer = ↑ *PixelList*;
Scanline = **record**

        Ypixel : 0..*Yresolution* − 1;
        NextScanline : *ScanlinePointer*;
        List : *XpixelPointer*;
    end;
PixelList = **record**

        Xpixel : 0..*Xresolution* − 1;
        NextIntersection : *XpixelPointer*;
    end;

Process:

{ Remove any horizontal lines from the polygon data }
{ Search the polygon edge endpoints to find *ymax* and *ymin* }
{ Create an ordered list of scan lines }
for each polygon edge **do**
   for *scanline* := *ystart* **to** *yfinish* **do**
   begin
     { Find all *Xpixels* that would be set on the scan line by the differential line-drawing algorithm }
     { Add the first *x* address in order on the list for the scan line }
     { Set the other pixels (if any) to the desired fill value }
   end;
for each scan line in the data structure **do**
begin
   { Set on all pixels between adjacent spans }
   { Dispose of the list entries }
end;

pattern may be defined as a function of x and y pixel co-ordinate values, say $PATTERN(x, y)$ where x ranges from 0 to $XPattern - 1$ and y from 0 to $YPattern - 1$. If filling is required at co-ordinates $XCross$ and $YScan$, then the value used to set the pixel is given by:

$$PATTERN(MOD(XCross, XPattern), MOD(YScan, YPattern))$$

Algorithm 3.5

Complementary scan line polygon fill algorithm.

for each edge of the polygon **do**
for each scan line it intersects with **do**
begin
    { Find the first x value that would be set on the scan line by the differential line-drawing algorithm }
    { Complement all pixels to the right of that point }
end;
{ Use the differential line-drawing algorithm to draw the boundary }

3.3.2   Seed filling

A second type of algorithm, called **seed filling**, is used to fill areas defined by pixels on the screen which form a bounded region. The principal difference between the scan line and seed fill algorithms is the level at which the data is represented. Seed fill algorithms use information in the frame buffer, rather than a functional description of the area to be filled. These are appropriate for cases when the lines defining the polygon do not belong to an internal data structure. This occurs when the polygon results from the intersection of rasterized lines that are entered individually or belong to different polygons. This is often found in programs that support the graphic arts and architecture. Seed filling works for a closed area of any shape; therefore, there is no advantage in limiting the discussions to polygons in this case.

As mentioned before, the results of this type of area filling depend on the respective values of the boundary pixels and the values used for filling. For a bi-level output device, some or all of the original boundary will be lost. As shown in Figure 3.7, if we start with two intersecting polygons and fill all three internal areas, there is no way to recover the shape of the inside area from the resulting solid filled shape.

The basic idea behind seed filling is simple. Starting with a known contained point called the seed, the algorithm sets it to the fill value and then tests its neighbours. Each one of the neighbouring pixels that is neither a boundary point nor has been set is set and its neighbours are tested. The process can be best described by the recursive Algorithm 3.6.

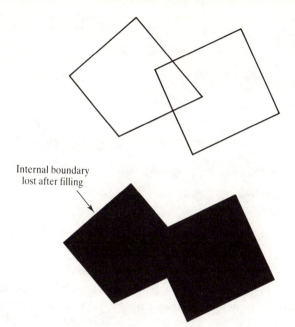

Internal boundary
lost after filling

Figure 3.7
Seed filling may be irreversible.
If the three areas bounded by
the intersection of the two
polygons are filled, then the
internal boundaries are lost.
This is not the case in scan line
filling.

Algorithm 3.6

Recursive seed fill.

procedure *SEED_FILL*(*x*, *y* : **integer**)

if (*PIXEL_VALUE*(*x*, *y*) < > *BoundaryValue*) **and** (*PIXEL_VALUE*(*x*, *y*) < > *FillValue*)
then begin
        SET_PIXEL(*x*, *y*, *FillValue*);
        SEED_FILL(*x* + 1, *y*);
        SEED_FILL(*x* − 1, *y*);
        SEED_FILL(*x*, *y* + 1);
        SEED_FILL(*x*, *y* − 1);
    end
end;

(* To start the seed filling, execute the procedure call: *)
SEED_FILL(*XSeed*, *YSeed*);

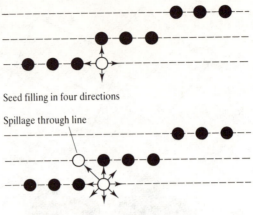

Seed filling in four directions

Spillage through line

Seed filling with diagonal directions

Figure 3.8

If the boundary lines are drawn using the differential line-drawing algorithm, then seed filling may proceed only in the vertical and horizontal directions. If the diagonal directions are used, the seed will spill through the boundary and then continue unchecked.

Note that the variables *FillValue* and *BoundaryValue* are global to the recursion. For completeness, they could be included in the procedure parameters, but they have been left out in this case for simplicity. In the case of a bi-level device, the fill value and the boundary value will be the same. Problems may arise, however, at the boundary of the screen ($x = 0$ or $x = XPixels - 1$). Either tests for the screen boundaries must be included in the algorithm, or it must be ensured that the area to be filled is completely surrounded by pixels set to *BoundaryValue*.

It has been suggested by some authors that the algorithm can be modified so that the recursive calls are made on the diagonally adjacent pixels. This, however, does not improve the efficiency, and moreover it restricts the boundary types that can be used. For example, it would no longer work with boundaries formed by lines drawn with the differential algorithm. This problem is illustrated in Figure 3.8. Here, a seed fill algorithm spills through the boundary from where it can carry on unchecked.

In Algorithm 3.6, the frame buffer is addressed directly using only a function to read the value of the pixels and a known boundary value defining the area. For interactive drawing systems, the seed pixel can be identified by a locator device. For bi-level devices, there is no problem in defining the boundary value, since it must be the complement of the value of the seed pixel; otherwise, the procedure would terminate without doing anything. For coloured systems, on the other hand, a boundary value must be identified. If this is done by the user identifying a pixel value, again usually with a locator, then the technique is called **boundary filling**. Alternatively, the algorithm could be implemented such that any pixel value not equal to the seed value is considered a boundary. This method is referred to as **flood filling**.

Algorithm 3.7

Flood filling with user-defined stack.

```
FloodValue := PIXEL_VALUE(XSeed, YSeed);
PUSH(XSeed); PUSH(YSeed);
while stack not empty do
begin
  POP(y); POP(x);
  SET_PIXEL(x, y, FillValue);
  if PIXEL_VALUE(x + 1, y) = FloodValue
  then begin
         PUSH(x + 1); PUSH(y)
       end
  if PIXEL_VALUE(x - 1, y) = FloodValue
  then begin
         PUSH(x - 1); PUSH(y)
       end
  if PIXEL_VALUE(x, y + 1) = FloodValue
  then begin
         PUSH(x); PUSH(y + 1)
       end
  if PIXEL_VALUE(x, y - 1) = FloodValue
  then begin
         PUSH(x); PUSH(y - 1)
       end
end
```

The recursive implementation carries with it large overheads in memory size and computation speed. At each pixel to be set, it is necessary to address the raster to read its four neighbours. Hence, five raster locations are read per pixel. Moreover, the recursive procedure creates a large number of stack frames, especially in cases where a large area is to be filled on a high-resolution system. For these reasons, it may be necessary to implement the algorithm at a low level to gain a speed advantage. In such cases, the stacking, which is carried out automatically by the recursive algorithm, must be implemented explicitly. This is done in Algorithm 3.7, where a flood fill is used.

Unfortunately, Algorithm 3.7 suffers from the same inefficiencies as Algorithm 3.6, since each pixel to be set causes four stacking operations

Algorithm 3.8

Directed recursive seed fill for a bi-level device.

procedure $SEED_FILL_LEFT(x, y : $ **integer**$)$;

if $(PIXEL\_VALUE(x, y) <> BoundaryValue)$
then begin
      $SET\_PIXEL(x, y, FillValue)$;
      $SEED\_FILL\_LEFT(x - 1, y)$;
      $SEED\_FILL\_ABOVE(x, y + 1)$;
      $SEED\_FILL\_BELOW(x, y - 1)$;
   end

Similarly:

procedure $SEED_FILL_RIGHT(x, y : $ **integer**$)$;
procedure $SEED_FILL_ABOVE(x, y : $ **integer**$)$;
procedure $SEED_FILL_BELOW(x, y : $ **integer**$)$;

and requires five frame buffer read operations. In practice, when implemented in a high-level language such as Pascal, this method can prove to be slower than the recursive procedure due to the overheads associated with the user-defined stack, which would be greater than those of the Pascal running system. However, it is possible to improve the performance of the algorithm at the expense of making it more complex. The simplest way this can be done is to make use of the fact that the last pixel set is known. Algorithm 3.8 is a modified version of Algorithm 3.6 that uses four different recursive procedures. In this Algorithm, $SEED\_FILL\_LEFT$ is called whenever it is desired to move left from the pixel that has just been set. Hence, it need not contain a call to $SEED\_FILL\_RIGHT$, since that pixel has already been set. By this means, the number of raster addresses to be read per pixel is reduced from five to four, with a corresponding gain in speed.

More efficiency can be gained by an algorithm similar to the scan line algorithm which proceeds along lines in the horizontal or vertical direction until the boundary is encountered. To demonstrate this method, the algorithm that uses horizontal scan lines will be considered (Algorithm 3.9). While filling proceeds on one scan line, the adjacent scan lines have to be tested in order to introduce new seeds for the filling to continue.

Algorithm 3.9

Ordered seed fill.

PUSH(XSeed); PUSH(YSeed);
repeat
    UpSeedFound := false;
    DownSeedFound := false;
    POP(y); POP(x);
    $x_{left} := x - 1; y_{left} := y;$
    LeftUpSeedFound := PIXEL_VALUE(x, y + 1) <> BoundaryValue;
    LeftDownSeedFound := PIXEL_VALUE(x, y − 1) <> BoundaryValue;
    while *PIXEL_VALUE(x, y) <> BoundaryValue* **do**
    begin
        SET_PIXEL(x, y, FillValue);
        if *PIXEL_VALUE(x, y + 1) <> BoundaryValue*
        then if not *UpSeedFound*
            then begin
                    PUSH(x); PUSH(y + 1);
                    UpSeedFound := true;
                end
        else *UpSeedFound := false;*
        if *PIXEL_VALUE(x, y − 1) <> BoundaryValue*
        then if not *DownSeedFound*
            then begin
                    PUSH(x); PUSH(y − 1);
                    DownSeedFound := true;
                end
        else *DownSeedFound := false;*
        x := x + 1;
    end;
    while *PIXEL_VALUE(x_{left}, y_{left}) <> BoundaryValue* **do**
    begin
        { Process the line moving left from x_{left}, y_{left} using flags *LeftUpSeedFound* and *LeftDownSeedFound* }
    end;
until stack is empty;

Since only one seed should be generated for each span, two Boolean variables called *UpSeedFound* and *DownSeedFound* are defined. They indicate whether a seed has been introduced in the upper or lower neighbouring scan lines, respectively. The *UpSeedFound* and *DownSeedFound* variables are reset to *false* when a boundary pixel is detected at one of the

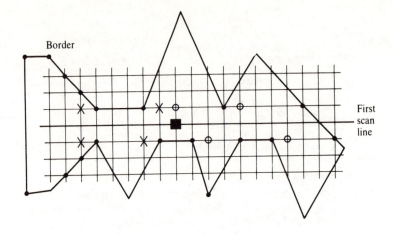

Figure 3.9
If seed filling is performed line by line, it is necessary to generate seeds in the lines above and below to cope with non-convex polygons. The extra seeds generated when moving to the right are marked with 'o'. Those generated moving to the left are marked with '×'.

Key

■ First seed

○ Seeds generated by scanning to the right

× Seeds generated by scanning to the left

two neighbouring scan lines. In this way, isolated areas are not missed, as shown in Figure 3.9.

In Algorithm 3.9, the frame store only has to be read three times for each pixel set; therefore, it is the fastest of the implementations discussed. Moreover, the stack space required is much smaller, being only twice the number of distinct spans in the most disjointed scan line. However, it is still likely to be less efficient than the scan line algorithm, since no account has been taken of the structure of the polygon to be filled.

3.4 CONIC SECTION GENERATION

So far, this chapter has only considered drawing lines or polygons bounded by straight-line segments. However, in general, it is necessary to draw other curves, and of these the most useful class are those of second order. These may be represented as planar sections of a cone. Three methods are widely used, the choice depending on the application and the form in which the data is presented. This section only considers the generation of ellipses, since they give a good illustration of the methods. The algorithms presented may be very simply adapted to circles, which are degenerate cases of ellipses. With small modifications, the same methods can also be used to generate hyperbolas and parabolas, although these curves are not so frequently encountered in two-dimensional graphics applications.

3.4.1 Parametric ellipse generation

Ellipses centred on the origin and symmetric about the Cartesian axes are described by a pair of parametric equations:

$$x = a \cos(\theta)$$
$$y = b \sin(\theta)$$

As the parameter θ varies between 0 and 2π radians, so the locus of $[x, y]$ describes an ellipse of axis lengths a and b. If $a = b$, the locus is a circle. In general, it is necessary to draw ellipses at any angle of orientation and at any position. A more complex formulation, which centres the ellipse at $[x_c, y_c]$ with an angle ϕ between the axis of length a and the x axis, is needed:

$$x = a \cos(\theta) \cos(\phi) - b \sin(\theta) \sin(\phi) + x_c$$
$$y = a \cos(\theta) \sin(\phi) + b \sin(\theta) \cos(\phi) + y_c$$

The derivation of this formulation is done by applying a rotation and a translation to the equations for an ellipse placed symmetrically about the origin. A method by which this may be done is described in Chapter 4. Since the angle ϕ is fixed while the ellipse is being drawn, the formulation reduces to:

$$x = A \cos(\theta) - B \sin(\theta) + x_c \tag{3.1}$$
$$y = C \cos(\theta) + D \sin(\theta) + y_c \tag{3.2}$$

where the values of A, B, C and D may be computed during initialization.

As is shown by Equations (3.1) and (3.2), the centre of the ellipse $[x_c, y_c]$ appears only in the last term of the equations. Therefore, it is possible, without loss of generality, to consider only the case of ellipses centred at the origin, with the extra additions being performed after all other calculations. For maximum efficiency, the addition of the $[x_c, y_c]$ offset will be done using device co-ordinates, which are small integer quantities.

The algorithm proceeds by drawing a straight-line approximation to the ellipse. Single points are found at equal intervals of the parameter and then joined using the differential line-drawing algorithm. Speed can be enhanced here if a table is used to store precomputed values for the *Cos* and *Sin* functions. Using degrees rather than radians in the algorithm gives a convenient and, for most applications, a sufficiently accurate way of quantizing the angles. Obviously, to be more precise, 0.1 or 0.01 degree intervals may be used. Only one table is needed, which, in Algorithm 3.10, is chosen as the *SinTable*. Some further savings in space may be made in the storage by making use of the fact that $\sin(\theta) = -\sin(\theta - \pi)$ and

Algorithm 3.10

Parametric ellipse generation.

$CosPhi := SinTable[\phi + 90];$
$SinPhi := SinTable[\phi];$
$A := a * CosPhi; B := b * SinPhi;$
$C := a * SinPhi; D := b * CosPhi;$
$x_0 := A + x_c; y_0 := C + y_c;$
$Increment := 360 \textbf{ div } NoOfLineSegments;$
$\theta := 0;$
$\textbf{for } j := 1 \textbf{ to } NoOfLineSegments \textbf{ do}$
$\textbf{begin}$
  $\theta := \theta + Increment;$
  $CosTheta := SinTable[\theta + 90];$
  $SinTheta := SinTable[\theta];$
  $x_1 := A * CosTheta - B * SinTheta + x_c$
  $y_1 := C * CosTheta + D * SinTheta + y_c$
  $DRAW\_LINE(x_0, y_0, x_1, y_1);$
  $x_0 := x_1; y_0 := y_1;$
$\textbf{end}$

$\sin(\theta) = \sin(\pi - \theta)$. Thus, only entries for the range 0 to $\pi/2$ (0 to 90°) are required. However, this saving is made at a small computational cost required to determine the range of the angle and adjust the sign accordingly.

In all cases of ellipse generation, a major saving in computation time may be made by exploiting the inherent symmetry of the ellipse. Referring to Figure 3.10, two sets of points are calculated simultaneously, starting at parameter values separated by π radians. Computing $[x_1, y_1]$ first, the symmetry gives:

$$x_0 - x_1 = xs_1 - xs_0$$
$$y_0 - y_1 = ys_1 - ys_0$$

Thus, $[xs_1, ys_1]$ is computed with only two additions.

One major failing of this parametric formulation occurs when the ratio of the major to minor axis of the ellipse is large. In places where the curvature is great, a large number of line segments is needed to give a correct representation. For the other parts, fewer segments will suffice.

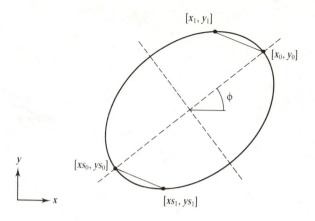

Figure 3.10
The symmetry of the ellipse can be used to reduce the drawing time. Since $([x_0, y_0] - [x_1, y_1])$ is equal to $- ([xs_0, yx_0] - [xs_1, ys_1])$ only one-half of the points need to be computed from the parametric equations.

Hence, if the number of segments is fixed in the algorithm, it will always be possible to find an ellipse where discontinuities become obvious. One possible solution is to change the algorithm so that it uses a non-linear distribution of parameter points.

When computing this algorithm at the raster level, some attention is needed to achieve the correct aspect ratio. If the pixels are square – that is, a horizontal line of n adjacent pixels is the same length on the screen as a vertical line of n adjacent pixels – then there is no difficulty. The values of a, b, x_c and y_c are simply passed to the ellipse generator in pixel units. However, if the pixels are not square, then the simplest technique is to pass the parameters in units of the smaller pixel separation. On cheap systems, this is usually in the horizontal direction. After computation of a co-ordinate, the ordinate with the larger pixel separation is corrected by dividing it by the appropriate aspect factor. In practice, this divide only requires a few shift and add operations to achieve sufficient accuracy.

As before, integer values can be used by simply scaling all quantities up, including the cosine and sine tables, before the computation and down again before drawing. These scalings should normally be by powers of 2 so that they may be computed by shifting.

3.4.2 Scan line ellipse generation

Although simple, the table lookup method does not match well with raster graphics hardware, which plots points rather than draws lines. Consequently, two other approaches have been tried. The first of these, which is equally applicable to filling ellipses as well as drawing the outlines, is illustrated by Figure 3.11.

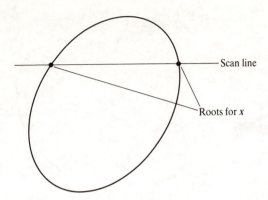

Scan line

Roots for x

Figure 3.11

The scan line method of ellipse generation. For a fixed value of y, the equation for the rotated ellipse reduces to a quadratic in x.

For this method, the appropriate formulation of the ellipse equation is the Cartesian; namely:

$$\frac{x^2}{a^2} + \frac{y^2}{b^2} = 1$$

For an ellipse whose major axis is at an angle ϕ to the x axis, the following substitution is made:

$$x \leftarrow x \cos(\phi) - y \sin(\phi)$$
$$y \leftarrow x \sin(\phi) + y \cos(\phi)$$

giving:

$$\frac{[x \cos(\phi) - y \sin(\phi)]^2}{a^2} + \frac{[x \sin(\phi) + y \cos(\phi)]^2}{b^2} = 1$$

As before, a transformation of the origin can be handled by simply adding $[x_c, y_c]$ to the final results in device co-ordinates.

On initialization, the fact that ϕ is a constant is used to make the further substitutions:

$$P = \frac{\cos(\phi)}{a}$$

$$Q = \frac{\sin(\phi)}{b}$$

Now, y has a constant value for each scan line, so for the ith line this can be written:

$$R = \frac{-y_i \sin(\phi)}{a}$$

$$S = \frac{y_i \cos(\phi)}{b}$$

where $y = y_i$, which gives a quadratic in x:

$$(Px + R)^2 + (Qx + S)^2 = 1$$

which rearranges to:

$$x = \frac{-(PR + QS) \pm \sqrt{P^2 + Q^2 - (PS - QR)^2}}{P^2 + Q^2}$$

This equation looks rather unpromising from a computational viewpoint. However, it should be noted that many of the constants can be precomputed. For example:

$$P^2 + Q^2 = \frac{\cos^2(\phi)}{a^2} + \frac{\sin^2(\phi)}{b^2}$$

and this is a constant independent of the scan line being computed. If all the parts that can be precomputed are isolated, an equation of the form:

$$x = K_1 + K_2 y_i \pm \sqrt{(K_3 y_i^2 + K_4)} \qquad (3.3)$$

results, which requires only three multiplies and a square root.

This equation need only be computed for scan lines that intersect the ellipse. The bounding cases can be found from the points where the square root in Equation (3.3) evaluates to zero. This condition is given by the equation:

$$y = \pm \sqrt{(b^2 \cos^2(\phi) + a^2 \sin^2(\phi))} \qquad (3.4)$$

For an accurate drawing, the two x roots need to be evaluated for every scan line between the two roots of Equation (3.4). However, as before, symmetry can be used to simplify the situation. The available symmetry is about the centre of the ellipse, as illustrated in Figure 3.12. This reduces the number of computations by two, so that the number of iterations required is a quarter of the total number of pixels to be set. Algorithm 3.11 exploits this symmetry.

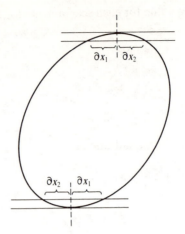

Figure 3.12

Symmetry in the scan line ellipse algorithm. The algorithm should first find the top and bottom of the ellipse. Using the symmetry indicated, only one-half of the scan lines need to be computed from the Cartesian equations.

Algorithm 3.11

Scan line ellipse generator.

{ Compute the top and bottom pixels, [$XTop$, $YTop$] and [$XBottom$, $YBottom$] }
$XTopLeft_1 := XTop$; $XTopRight_1 := XTop$; $XBottomLeft_1 := XBottom$; $XBottomRight_1 := XBottom$;
$YTop_1 := YTop$; $YBottom_1 := YBottom$;
$Axis := YBottom + YTop$;
{ Set up y co-ordinates of the lines to be drawn in array $Lines$ }
for $j := 1$ **to** $LinesUsed$ **do**
begin
    $YTop := Lines[j]$;
    $COMPUTE\_ROOTS(YTop, XTopLeft, XTopRight)$;
    $YBottom := Axis - YTop$;   (* Compute symmetric cases *)
    $XBottomLeft := XBottomLeft_1 + XTopRight_1 - XTopRight$;
    $XBottomRight := XBottomRight_1 + XTopLeft_1 - XTopLeft$;
    $DRAW\_LINE([XTopLeft_1, YTop_1], [XTopLeft, YTop])$;
    $DRAW\_LINE([XTopRight_1, YTop_1], [XTopRight, YTop])$;
    $DRAW\_LINE([XBottomLeft_1, YBottom_1], [XBottomLeft, YBottom])$;
    $DRAW\_LINE([XBottomRight_1, YBottom_1], [XBottomRight, YBottom])$;
    $XBottomLeft_1 := XBottomLeft$; $XBottomRight_1 := XBottomRight$; $XTopLeft_1 := XTopLeft$;
    $XTopRight_1 := XTopRight$;
    $YBottom_1 := YBottom$; $YTop_1 := YTop$;
end

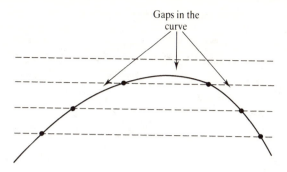

Gaps in the
curve

Figure 3.13
At places where the slope of
the ellipse is near to zero, the
scan line algorithm leaves gaps
between adjacent pixels.

Care must be taken with this method when the slope of the ellipse is close to zero. At these points, the drawing begins to look discontinuous, as shown in Figure 3.13. The problem can be cured by checking when the difference between adjacent scan line roots is greater than one pixel and filling the empty space along the scan lines. Another possibility would be to detect the places where the slope of the tangent to the ellipse is in the range ± 1 and then use vertical scan lines as is illustrated in Figure 3.14. This method will produce an accurate drawing but requires additional computation, since the total number of scan lines is increased.

To identify the points where the slope is 1, it is simplest to use the parametric formulation and find the corresponding four values of θ, as shown in Figure 3.15. For the non-rotated ellipse:

$$\frac{dy}{dx} = \frac{y'}{x'} = \frac{-b \cos(\theta)}{a \sin(\theta)} = \frac{-b}{a \tan(\theta)}$$

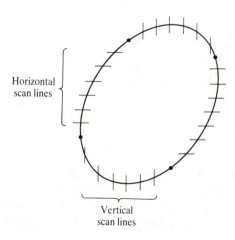

Horizontal
scan lines

Vertical
scan lines

Figure 3.14
A complete ellipse could be
drawn by using vertical scan
lines where the slope is less
than one. However, this
method destroys the symmetry
and will thus take longer to
compute.

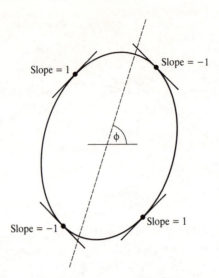

Figure 3.15
Finding the points on the ellipse where the slope is ± 1 divides it into four regions.

if this is equated to 1 and -1, the desired slopes are obtained. For the rotated case, the tangents are rotated through the same angle as the ellipse. Thus, if a tangent to the ellipse has an angle χ to the x-axis in the unrotated case, then after rotating the ellipse by an angle ϕ, the angle of the tangent to the x-axis will be $\chi + \phi$. When this is equated to 1, it gives:

$$\tan(\chi + \phi) = 1$$

$$\chi = \arctan(1) - \phi = \frac{\pi}{4} - \phi$$

Thus, to find the required points, the slope in a non-rotated ellipse is equated with $\arctan(\pi/4 - \phi)$. Thus, the points are given by:

$$\tan(\theta_1) = \frac{-b}{a \arctan(\pi/4 - \phi)}$$

$$\tan(\theta_2) = \frac{-b}{a \arctan(-\pi/4 - \phi)}$$

(3.5)

and by symmetry:

$$\theta_3 = \pi + \theta_1 \quad \text{and} \quad \theta_4 = \pi + \theta_2$$

The values of θ_1, θ_2, θ_3 and θ_4 can be then used to compute pixel co-ordinates from which the scan line algorithm can proceed.

A faster algorithm can be achieved by only computing a small number of selected scan lines and interpolating these with straight-line

Figure 3.16
Using linear interpolation to
speed up the drawing of an
ellipse by the scan line method
can produce disturbing
discontinuities where the slope
of the ellipse is close to zero.

segments. However, care is required in selecting the scan lines, since a linear choice produces an unrealistic image for a small number of lines. This point is illustrated in Figure 3.16. More scan lines are required where the slope is near zero and less when it is large. The use of a fixed algorithm for this purpose will introduce a negligible overhead in computation and will allow a further reduction in the number of scan lines computed. For example, to compute nine lines, a suitable distribution would be to compute the first four spaced at n lines apart, the next three at $2n$ and the last two at $3n$. This would cover an area of $16n$ lines, and so for a particular case, n can be found using only shifts.

Algorithm 3.11 can be easily optimized. For example, many assignments can be saved by duplicating the code within the loop and by treating the last scan line as a special case.

The scan line method is the most appropriate algorithm for drawing filled ellipses. The algorithm simply computes every scan line and draws a line between the two roots found, using whatever pixel attribute is required.

3.4.3 Differential ellipse generation

The differential ellipse generator works in an identical manner to the differential line-drawing algorithm. In other words, from any one point on the curve, the next point is computed by adding a factor proportional to the slope. In the case of the straight line, the slope is a fixed constant; however, for an ellipse, it will change from pixel to pixel and must be recomputed every time. Some loss of accuracy always occurs in this case due to the fact that the the differential is computed by a finite approximation.

This section develops the method using the parametric formulation of the non-rotated ellipse. The next section discusses how the algorithm may be adapted for raster application.

Starting with the first differentials:

$$x = a \cos(\theta) \qquad x' = -a \sin(\theta)$$
$$y = b \sin(\theta) \qquad y' = b \cos(\theta)$$

The trigonometric functions can be eliminated to give:

$$x' = -\frac{a}{b}y$$

$$y' = \frac{b}{a}x$$

To make these equations discrete, the following substitutions are made:

$$x' = \frac{dx}{d\theta} = \frac{\Delta x}{\Delta \theta}$$

and similarly for y' yielding:

$$\Delta x = -\frac{a}{b}y\,\Delta\theta$$

$$\Delta y = \frac{b}{a}x\,\Delta\theta$$

(3.6)

The simplest way to compute a differential is by a forward difference and using this method, the following substitutions are made:

$$\Delta x = x_{i+1} - x_i \quad \text{at} \quad [x_i, y_i]$$
$$\Delta y = y_{i+1} - y_i \quad \text{at} \quad [x_i, y_i]$$

Using this approximation, a difference equation formulation is found:

$$x_{i+1} = x_i - \frac{a}{b}y_i\,\Delta\theta$$

$$y_{i+1} = y_i + \frac{b}{a}x_i\,\Delta\theta$$

This, however, does not provide an ideal algorithm, since the increment needs to be very small before a sufficiently accurate computation of the differential is achieved. In particular, it is possible to show that this algorithm will never draw a closed curve due to the fact that the differential is taken in a forward direction. This problem can be avoided by using the symmetry of the ellipse and joining up four segments. However, if this is done, there will be discontinuous derivatives where the four pieces join.

Algorithm 3.12

First-order ellipse generator.

```
x := 0; y := b; Δθ := 8 * ARCTAN(1)/NoOfSegments;
k₁ := (1 − Δθ * Δθ/4); k₂ := (1 + Δθ * Δθ/4);
for j := 1 to NoOfSegments do
begin
    x₁ := (k₁ * x − y * a * Δθ/b)/k₂
    y₁ := (k₁ * y + x * b * Δθ/a)/k₂
    DRAW_LINE(x, y, x₁, y₁);
    x := x₁; y := y₁;
end;
```

A better solution to the problem is to use a central difference in the formulation. Thus:

$$\Delta x = x_{i+1} - x_i \quad \text{at} \quad \left[\frac{(x_i + x_{i+1})}{2}, \frac{(y_i + y_{i+1})}{2}\right]$$

$$\Delta y = y_{i+1} - y_i \quad \text{at} \quad \left[\frac{(x_i + x_{i+1})}{2}, \frac{(y_i + y_{i+1})}{2}\right]$$

Making these substitutions into Equation (3.6) gives:

$$x_{i+1} - x_i = -\frac{a}{b} \Delta\theta \frac{y_i + y_{i+1}}{2}$$

$$y_{i+1} - y_i = \frac{b}{a} \Delta\theta \frac{x_i + x_{i+1}}{2}$$

Before an algorithm can be devised, it is necessary to rearrange these equations such that x_{i+1} and y_{i+1} are expressed in terms of x_i and y_i. This yields the following equations:

$$x_{i+1}(4 + \Delta\theta^2) = x_i(4 - \Delta\theta^2) - 4\frac{a}{b}\Delta\theta y_i$$

$$y_{i+1}(4 + \Delta\theta^2) = y_i(4 - \Delta\theta^2) + 4\frac{b}{a}\Delta\theta x_i$$

These equations are used in Algorithm 3.12.

Algorithm 3.12 would be optimized in its final implementation by precomputation of the constants. All that is required in the loop is four multiplies and two additions, which makes the algorithm very fast.

An alternative method of formulating the differential algorithm is to use the second differential rather than the first. To compute a discrete approximation to the second differential, three points need to be used:

$$x' = \frac{x_i - x_{i-1}}{\Delta\theta} \quad \text{between } x_i \text{ and } x_{i-1}$$

$$= \frac{x_{i+1} - x_i}{\Delta\theta} \quad \text{between } x_{i+1} \text{ and } x_i$$

so:

$$x'' = \frac{1}{\Delta\theta} \frac{x_{i+1} - x_i - x_i + x_{i-1}}{\Delta\theta} \quad \text{at } x_i$$

$$= \frac{x_{i+1} - 2x_i + x_{i-1}}{\Delta\theta^2}$$

This method gives a central difference for the second differential automatically. The second differential of the ellipse is:

$$x'' = -a\cos(\theta) = -x \quad \text{and} \quad y'' = -b\sin(\theta) = -y$$

Substituting for the second differential gives:

$$-x_i\Delta\theta^2 = x_{i+1} - 2x_i + x_{i-1}$$

resulting in difference equation:

$$x_{i+1} = (2 - \Delta\theta^2)x_i - x_{i-1}$$

and similarly:

$$y_{i+1} = (2 - \Delta\theta^2)y_i - y_{i-1}$$

It is surprising to note that the a and b values do not appear in these difference equations and, moreover, the x and y equations are independent. The effect of parameters a and b is captured in the initial conditions and these are obtained from the first-order Equation (3.6) yielding the second-order algorithm (see Algorithm 3.13).

Algorithm 3.13 always produces a closed curve, although for large values of $\Delta\theta$ some skew can be observed in it.

Algorithm 3.13

Second-order differential ellipse generator.

```
x₀ := 0; y₀ := b; Δθ := 8 * ARCTAN(1)/NoOfSegments;
Δ2θ := Δθ * Δθ;
x₁ := x₀ − (a/b) * Δθ * y₀;
y₁ := y₀ + (b/a) * Δθ * x₀;
DRAW_LINE(x₀, y₀, x₁, y₁);
for j := 1 to NoOfSegments − 1 do
begin
  x₂ := (2 − Δ2θ) * x₁ − x₀;
  y₂ := (2 − Δ2θ) * y₁ − y₀;
  DRAW_LINE(x₁, y₁, x₂, y₂);
  x₀ := x₁; x₁ := x₂; y₀ := y₁; y₁ := y₂;
end;
```

So far, only ellipses centred on the origin and with the major axis parallel to a Cartesian axis have been considered, in which case there is symmetry about the major and minor axes, which can be exploited to reduce the computation time. Ellipses at an angle to the axes can be dealt with by starting with the rotated parametric representation, which is given in Equations (3.1) and (3.2). Again, it is not necessary to consider the translation of the centre to $[x_c, y_c]$, as this can be treated as an extra addition in the final stages of the algorithm. Indeed, it is advantageous to remove the term from the equations, since a constant offset will magnify any error in the differentials.

Differentiating with respect to θ gives:

$$x' = -A \sin(\theta) - B \cos(\theta)$$
$$y' = -C \sin(\theta) + D \cos(\theta)$$

$$x'' = -A \cos(\theta) + B \sin(\theta) = -x$$
$$y'' = -C \cos(\theta) - D \sin(\theta) = -y$$

Rather surprisingly, the same difference equations as before are obtained. And, again, a, b and ϕ do not appear in the difference equation but are found in the initial conditions, which may be computed from the first derivative case. To do this, the ellipse equations need to be inverted to give:

$$a \cos(\theta) = x \cos(\phi) + y \sin(\phi)$$
$$b \sin(\theta) = -x \sin(\phi) + y \cos(\phi)$$

which can be used to eliminate the parameter θ from the first differential. Substituting for $\cos(\theta)$ and $\sin(\theta)$ yields a pair of equations of the form:

$$x' = k_1 x + k_2 y + k_3$$
$$y' = k_4 x + k_5 y + k_6$$

which, when converted to a difference equation, will give a value for the second point on the curve.

3.4.4 Rasterization of the differential ellipse generator

Adapting the algorithm to make it suitable for low-level raster implementation is largely a matter of eliminating the parameter $\Delta\theta$ from the difference equations. This then gives equations in Δx and Δy, and these quantities can be associated with the distance between two pixels. First, however, it is necessary to divide the ellipse into four sections, corresponding to the quadrant division of the differential line-drawing algorithm. The regions are bounded by the points where the slope of the ellipse is 1 or -1. This is done as previously described using Equation (3.5). As shown in Figure 3.14, the algorithm will step up through the x pixels in the first region, computing the error in y; in region 2, the algorithm will step up through the y pixels, calculating the error in x; and so on. The first-order difference equation must be used, since using equal increments in one of the axes introduces a zero in the second-order formulation.

The regions are processed in order. For region 1, the algorithm steps downwards through the x pixels. The difference equation is therefore simplified in that:

$$x' = k_1 x_i + k_2 y_i + k_3 = -\frac{1}{\Delta\theta}$$

$$y' = k_4 x_i + k_5 y_i + k_6 = \frac{y_{i+1} - y_i}{\Delta\theta} = \frac{e_i}{\Delta\theta}$$

where e_i means the error increment at y_i. Thus, eliminating $\Delta\theta$ gives:

$$e_i = \frac{k_1 x_i + k_2 y_i + k_3}{k_4 x_i + k_5 y_i + k_6}$$

In the same way as for the differential line generator, the error is accumulated; when it goes above $\frac{1}{2}$ or below $-\frac{1}{2}$, the y pixel is changed. Notice that the top and bottom of the product are computed incrementally, so that account of the constant differences in x can be taken. Thus:

$$T_{i+1} = T_i - \frac{k_4}{k_5} + e_i$$

$$B_{i+1} = B_i - \frac{k_1}{k_5} + \frac{k_2}{k_5} e_i$$

and:

$$e_{i+1} = \frac{T_{i+1}}{B_{i+1}}$$

which requires one multiply and one divide per pixel. Symmetry is again available in the same way as the scan line algorithm. Thus, depending on the computation of the square root in Equation (3.3), the speed of this method will be comparable to the scan line method.

3.4.5 Generalizing the differential method to other curves

A generalization of the differential method to cope with smooth curves of other degrees has been suggested by van Aken and Novak (1985). The idea is a simple extension of the differential line-drawing algorithm. As before, the algorithm proceeds from pixel to pixel and, after setting a pixel, makes a decision as to which pixel is the next to be set.

If the equation is expressed in a functional form, that is:

$$f(x, y) = 0$$

the value of the term $f(x_c, y_c)$ can be used as an indicator of how close the curve passes to the pixel at $[x_c, y_c]$: the lower the modulus of the term, the nearer the pixel. Thus, a simple algorithm, at any pixel, is to compute the value of $|f(x_c, y_c)|$ for all potential successor pixels and then to select the lowest. However, if the function f is non-linear, this heuristic may not give very accurate results. In such a case, a better method is to use the midpoints of the pixels.

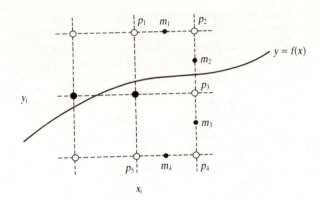

Figure 3.17

The midpoints between pixels can be used to determine which pixel is closest to the line. The midpoint pair that intersects the line bounds the closest pixel.

The principle of the general algorithm is shown in Figure 3.17, where p_1, p_2, p_3, p_4 and p_5 are the pixels and m_1, $m2$, $m3$ and $m4$ are the midpoints. The decision that has to be made now is which pair of adjacent midpoints lie on opposite sides of the true curve. This can be determined by examining the signs of the terms $f(x_m, y_m)$ for each midpoint, since points on opposite sides of the curve will yield opposite signs. In the case of Figure 3.16, m_1 and m_2 will have different signs from m_3 and m_4; thus, m_2 to m_3 can be identified as the crossing point, and so p_3 is the nearest pixel. The method as stated requires that there are no discontinuities in the curve and that it does not loop back over itself.

Great savings can be made if it is possible to estimate which pair of pixels the curve will pass between – in this example, it is p_2 and p_3. In such cases, it is only necessary to compute the value of $f(x_m, y_m)$ at the midpoint of these two and then use its sign to determine which of the two pixels is the closer. The relation between the sign of the term and the side of the curve can be found from one other point, but in many cases it may be a constant for all the pixels on the curve. In the case of the differential line generator, the octant to which the line belongs is precomputed, and this will uniquely determine which pair of pixels should be considered at every point in the algorithm. Thus, in essence the differential line generator can be seen as a special case of this general method, with the computation of the term replaced by the incremental error computation. Similarly, in the case of the ellipse, a preprocessing step was used to divide the ellipse into regions bounded by the places where the differential was ±1, and in each of these regions the choice of successor pixels was again made uniquely.

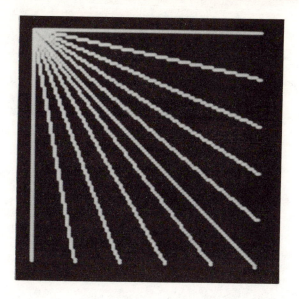

Figure 3.18
Alias effects in straight lines.
The alias is worst where the line
approaches the vertical or
horizontal.

3.5   ANTI-ALIASING

A well-known effect of the Bresenham algorithm, and other similar methods used for drawing lines on raster terminals, is the jagged staircase appearance of lines at certain angles, shown in Figure 3.18. This is the effect of presenting a discrete (sampled) approximation of a continuous function and is caused by the presence of what is called an alias frequency. As the samples are increased, by using a higher-resolution screen, so the effect is reduced. All methods of anti-aliasing require that the pixel intensity be varied, and hence are not suitable for bi-level devices. The greater the number of available bit planes, the greater the number of discrete intensity levels, and the more effective the algorithm.

One approach to the problem is to modify the fundamental algorithms themselves in order to utilize the different intensity levels available at each pixel. Consider, for example, the Bresenham algorithm. It is simple to modify this algorithm so that, as the error factor increases, the intensity of one pixel is reduced and the intensity of the adjacent one is increased. For a terminal with $Imax$ distinct levels of intensity for each pixel, and so the number of bit planes = $\log_2(Imax)$, Algorithm 3.14 may be used.

Algorithm 3.14

Differential line-drawing algorithm with anti-aliasing.

```
Error := 0;
SET_PIXEL(x, y, Imax);
while x < XFinal do
begin
  Error := Error + Δy;
  if Error >= Δx
  then begin
         y := y + 1;
         Error := Error − Δx;
      end;
  x := x + 1;
  Ipix := Error * Imax/Δx;
  SET_PIXEL(x, y, Imax − Ipix);
  SET_PIXEL(x, y + 1, Ipix);
end (* while *);
```

Algorithm 3.14 can be optimized for speed of computation by the same method described for the ordinary differential line-drawing algorithm. In practice, it may need further adjustment if a line of even intensity is to be produced. The problem is that if adjacent pixels are lit to half-intensity, the eye will perceive them as being dimmer than a single pixel lit to full intensity. Hence, some correction is required to the values of $Ipix$ and $Imax - Ipix$. This correction will depend on the value computed for $Ipix$, being maximum when $Ipix = Imax/2$, at which point the two illuminated pixels will be of equal intensity. A simple multiplicative correction can be applied using:

$$1 + k\left(1 - \left|1 - \frac{2\,Ipix}{Imax}\right|\right)$$

Figure 3.19 shows examples drawn with various values of k. The value of the constant k can be chosen to produce the best results in a particular application.

So far, in these discussions of line and curve drawing, the width of a line has not been considered. However, the problem of achieving an equal intensity along a single anti-aliased line arises because lines of different

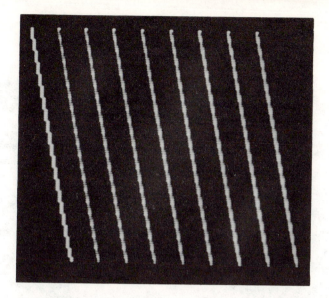

Figure 3.19
Lines produced by anti-aliasing using a modified Bresenham's algorithm. The line on the left is not anti-aliased. The remaining lines are drawn with the value of the constant k increasing from 0.0 to 0.7 from left to right.

intensites are perceived as having different widths. The differential algorithms presented have assumed that the real line to be drawn was infinitely thin, the actual drawing being done with single pixels. In the case of a straight line, it is clear to see that there are more pixels per unit length in a horizontal line than in a line at 45° to the axes. This fact can be used to provide a measure of 'thickness' for a line drawn on the raster screen. If the minimum line width in a raster representation is defined to be exactly one pixel wide, which occurs when the line is drawn in the horizontal or vertical direction, then the line thickness can be defined as:

$$\frac{\text{number of pixels per unit length}}{\text{number of pixels per unit length of a horizontal line}}$$

The effective minimum width of a rasterized line drawn at an angle will always be smaller than the horizontal or vertical case. Because of variations in effective thickness along the line, it is very difficult to achieve good results with anti-aliasing thin lines.

Apart from the case of modifying fundamental algorithms, it is usual to anti-alias by postprocessing an already rasterized picture; that is, the normal fundamental algorithms are used to generate a raster image file (a file specifying the intensities of each pixel on the screen), which is then processed to produce an anti-aliased image that can be displayed. This method has the advantage that the fundamental generation algorithms can be kept simple. Postprocessing can work well with filled polygons and thick lines, but is less successful with thin line drawings. Figure 3.20 shows an

(a)

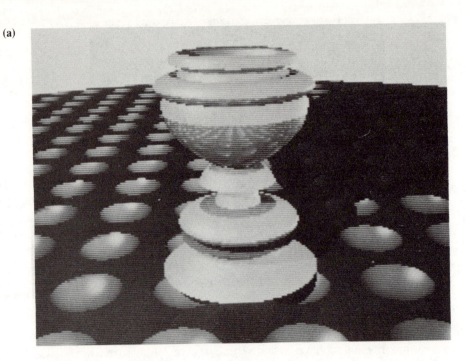

(b)

(c)

(d)

Figure 3.20
Anti-aliasing by postprocessing.
(a) shows a picture generated
at low resolution. (b) has been
anti-aliased once using a 3×3
convolution filter. (c) has been
anti-aliased twice, and (d) three
times. The effect is progressive
de-focusing which removes not
only the alias effects, but also
the fine details, such as the
reflections in the chalice. This
figure should be compared with
Figure 1.1, where anti-aliasing
has been done by computing
four super-samples per pixel.

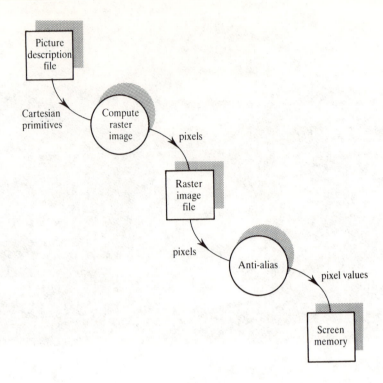

Figure 3.21
Anti-aliasing by postprocessing.

original and an anti-aliased computer-generated image for which the postprocessing method was used. The order in which the picture data is processed is shown schematically in Figure 3.21.

Two methods have been suggested for postprocessing, which differ mainly in detail. They are called **supersampling** and **filtering** and are discussed in the following sections.

3.5.1   Super-sampling

The super-sampling algorithm makes use of the property that alias effects decrease with resolution. The algorithm that generates the picture is executed for higher resolution than the output device can handle. For example, given a terminal with four bit planes, the screen image could be generated as if the pixel resolution was multiplied by four in both the horizontal and vertical directions. Thus, all the raster addresses in the input primitives are multiplied by four. Now, the computed (high-resolution) image has to be mapped on to the real screen. The simplest way of doing this is to add up the values of the 16 computed pixels that map on to each real pixel to get an intensity value. If the high-resolution image

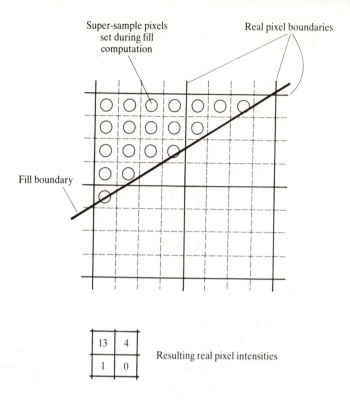

Super-sample pixels
set during fill
computation

Real pixel boundaries

Fill boundary

13	4
1	0

Resulting real pixel intensities

Figure 3.22

Anti-aliasing by super-sampling.
Each pixel is assumed to cover
a rectangular area of the
screen. The real pixels are
subdivided into a number of
super-sample pixels. For any
one real pixel area, the pixel
illumination is set proportional
to the number of super-sample
pixels illuminated in that area.

intensities are computed as bi-level (0 or 1), the following simple mapping
between the computed bi-level intensity value and the pixel value can be
used:

$$PixelValue = \textbf{round}\left(\frac{15 \sum BiLevelValues}{16}\right)$$

where the **round** function evaluates an integer closest to its real argument.
Figure 3.22 illustrates the approach for the boundary of a filled area.

Although super-sampling will work reasonably well when processing
boundaries of fill areas, it does not prove satisfactory in cases where thin
lines are drawn. This problem is illustrated by Figure 3.23. Here, it can be
seen that only four of the super-samples in a block of sixteen corresponding
to a real pixel will be set; thus, the intensity of the whole line will be too
low. Moreover, in the case shown, the alias effects will still be seen in the
final image. A further disadvantage of super-sampling is that the computation of the higher-resolution image will take longer.

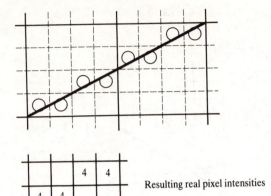

Resulting real pixel intensities

Figure 3.23
Super-sampling a thin line will
not anti-alias it correctly.

3.5.2 Filtering

In this technique, either a bi-or multi-level image is generated at normal resolution. The generated image is processed in a way that averages the pixel intensities in each small area of the screen. The value of a pixel in the anti-aliased image is computed as the weighted sum of its immediate neighbours, with the weight inversely related to distance. A common way of doing this is to use the nine neighbouring pixels and weights:

$\frac{1}{36}$	$\frac{1}{9}$	$\frac{1}{36}$
$\frac{1}{9}$	$\frac{4}{9}$	$\frac{1}{9}$
$\frac{1}{36}$	$\frac{1}{9}$	$\frac{1}{36}$

The sum of the weights is equal to 1, which leads to the expression:

$$O(x, y) = \frac{1}{36}I[x - 1, y + 1] + \frac{1}{9}I[x, y + 1] + \frac{1}{36}I[x + 1, y + 1]$$

$$+ \frac{1}{9}I[x - 1, y] + \frac{4}{9}I[x, y] + \frac{1}{9}I[x + 1, y]$$

$$+ \frac{1}{36}I[x - 1, y - 1] + \frac{1}{9}I[x, y - 1] + \frac{1}{36}I[x + 1, y - 1]$$

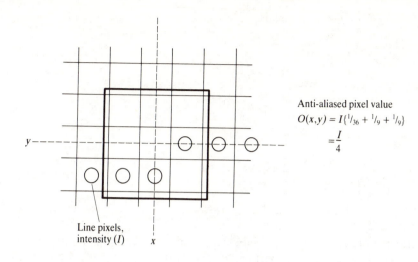

Anti-aliased pixel value
$$O(x,y) = I\{^1/_{36} + {^1/_9} + {^1/_9}\}$$
$$= \frac{I}{4}$$

Line pixels,
intensity (I) x

Figure 3.24

Computing the anti-aliased
value of a pixel using a 3 × 3
convolution mask.

which simplifies to:

$$O(x, y) = \frac{4}{9}I(x, y)$$

$$+ \frac{1}{9}\Big(I[x - 1, y] + I[x + 1, y] + I[x, y - 1] + I[x, y + 1]\Big)$$

$$+ \frac{1}{36}\Big(I[x - 1, y - 1] + I[x + 1, y - 1] + I[x - 1, y + 1]$$

$$+ I[x + 1, y + 1]\Big)$$

where $O(x, y)$ is the anti-aliased pixel value for point $[x, y]$, and $I(x, y)$ is
the raw pixel value.

Note that some scaling may be necessary to utilize the full intensity
range of the display. Note also that as the image function does not have to
be bi-level in this formulation, the technique can be applied to a shaded
image. Figure 3.24 shows the technique applied to a line computed by a bi-
level display algorithm.

The effect of using a simple 3 × 3 filter will depend on the resolution of the screen. For higher resolutions, the effect will be less pronounced, so several applications of the filter may be necessary to produce
the desired effect. The alternative solution is to use a broader mask, say
5 × 5 or 7 × 7.

Note that a super-sampled image can also be filtered to produce a
lower-resolution actual image. In fact, the method just described could be

considered a degenerate example in which the filter used is:

$\dfrac{1}{16}$	$\dfrac{1}{16}$	$\dfrac{1}{16}$	$\dfrac{1}{16}$
$\dfrac{1}{16}$	$\dfrac{1}{16}$	$\dfrac{1}{16}$	$\dfrac{1}{16}$
$\dfrac{1}{16}$	$\dfrac{1}{16}$	$\dfrac{1}{16}$	$\dfrac{1}{16}$
$\dfrac{1}{16}$	$\dfrac{1}{16}$	$\dfrac{1}{16}$	$\dfrac{1}{16}$

Different filters could of course be used in mapping a super-sampled image into a real pixel array. In particular, a function that falls off with distance will give good results.

3.5.3 Convolution

The techniques just described are examples of an important mathematical technique known as **convolution**. As this will be encountered later in the book, a more general definition will be given here.

Briefly, convolution defines a way of combining two functions. For cases encountered in computer graphics, the functions are discrete; so, for two dimensions, the convolution of two functions f and I is defined as:

$$C(p, q) = \sum_{x=0}^{XRes-1} \sum_{y=0}^{YRes-1} I(x, y) f(p-x, q-y)$$

where $I(x, y)$ is the discrete function defining the pixel values, $f(u, v)$ is a function called a filter and $[0..XRes - 1, 0..YRes - 1]$ is the range over which $I(x, y)$ is non-zero. The filter function in the example of Section 3.5.2 is defined by the following expressions:

$$
\begin{aligned}
f(u, v) = 4/9 \quad &\text{if} \quad u = v = 0 \\
1/9 \quad &\text{if} \quad (u = 0 \text{ and } |v| = 1) \text{ or } (v = 0 \text{ and } |u| = 1) \\
1/36 \quad &\text{if} \quad |u| = |v| = 1 \\
0 \quad &\text{if} \quad |u| > 1 \text{ or } |v| > 1
\end{aligned}
$$

and $C(p, q)$ is the anti-aliased value for pixel $[p, q]$.

Note that problems arise for p and q values at the borders; namely, when $q = 0$, $q = XRes - 1$, $p = 0$ or $p = YRes - 1$. It was assumed that the picture intensity function $I(x, y)$ was equal to zero outside the proper ranges of x and y. If there are discontinuities at the borders of the picture – a solid white border, for example – then they will be anti-aliased. Using the defined filter, which also drops to zero for $|u| > 1$ or $|v| > 1$, a simple trick can be used by adding two extra rows and columns to the picture and setting the values for these extra pixels to give the desired results. The sum now becomes:

$$C(p, q) = \sum_{x=-1}^{XRes} \sum_{y=-1}^{YRes} I(x, y) f(p-x, q-y)$$

p and q are computed again in the range $[0..XRes - 1]$ and $[0..YRes - 1]$. For filters with larger ranges, more rows and columns must be added for the same correction of the anti-aliasing effects at the border.

3.6 GENERATION OF SHADED PICTURES ON BI-LEVEL DEVICES

As has been seen, many raster-type display and hardcopy devices are bi-level, meaning that only two intensities are possible for each pixel. If the frame buffer contains a '1', then the pixel on the screen is illuminated, resulting in a light dot. Printers will usually produce a dark dot for the same value. Alternatively, a frame buffer entry of '0' will produce a dark pixel on the screen, but a light dot on the printed page. Devices that can only produce a few colours can be considered bi-level for each colour. None of these devices can produce pictures with continuous gray tones or shaded colours. However, it is possible to create the effect of shading with bi-level pixel values by varying the ratio of black to white pixels in each small area of the screen. Due to the limited resolving power of the eye, it sees a continuous intensity at normal viewing.

A similar technique has been used in the printing industry for centuries. It is called the **half-toning technique** and uses dots of ink whose sizes or density vary according to the required local intensity function. The dot is placed in the middle of the pixel area and the ratio of the black dot area to the pixel area is inversely proportional to the required intensity. Figure 1.10 shows a black and white photograph with continuous gray levels but, of course, it appears in this book as a half-tone. The enlarged portion of the picture clearly shows that the shading is produced by the local variation of the ratio of black to white surfaces. If the diameter of the ink dot can vary continuously, this technique would produce continuous half-tone levels.

Unfortunately, a computer display device cannot change the size of its electron beam, nor a matrix printer the size of its printed dot. Therefore, continuous half-tones cannot be produced on these devices using the same technique. For a bi-level display device, the only possible way of producing shaded pictures is to vary the ratio of the number of pixels turned ON (intensity = 1) to the number turned OFF (intensity = 0) as a function of position.

The quality of a digitized picture stored in computer memory may be expressed by its number of points or pixels and the number of discreet intensity levels it has at each pixel. The pixels are usually arranged on a rectangular mesh and the picture data can be expressed as an array of integers ranging from 0 to a maximum intensity value:

$$PictureData[0..XPicture, 0..YPicture] : 0..MaxPictureIntensity$$

The digitized data for the photograph shown in Figure 1.10 has approximately 300×300 or $90\,000$ pixels and 256 distinct intensity levels (*MaxPictureIntensity* = 255). The display or printing device has similar characteristics, which can also be expressed as two-dimensional data. In the case of memory-mapped displays, this represents the frame buffer:

$$DeviceData[0..XDevice, 0..YDevice] : 0..MaxDeviceIntensity$$

where for a bi-level device *MaxDeviceIntensity* has the value of 1. Of course, *XResolution* = *XDevice* + 1 and *YResolution* = *YDevice* + 1. The successful mapping of picture data to device data is the topic of this section.

3.6.1 Simulation of half-tones

The simplest method of generating apparent shading with a bi-level device is to divide the display area into a number of small areas and to turn a number of pixels ON in each area according to the local picture intensity. If the small area has a simple rectangular shape of $N \times M$ pixels, as shown in Figure 3.25, the number of intensities range from 0, all pixels OFF, to $N \times M$, all pixels illuminated.

The division of the display surface into small areas determines the effective resolution of the displayed picture, since in each small area only one picture intensity value is assumed. If the resolution of the picture data is higher than the displayed resolution, then an average of the picture data intensities can be taken in each small area.

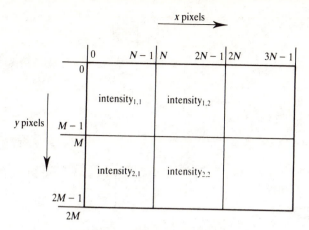

Figure 3.25

To simulate gray levels with a bi-level device, a rectangular area of N × M pixels is assigned a brightness level which determines the number of pixels to be turned ON within the small rectangular area.

If the resolution of the display device is expressed by the number of pixels in both the x and y directions as $XDevice \times YDevice$, then with $N \times M$ pixels in each display area, the displayed picture resolution is:

$$PictureResolution = \left(\frac{XDevice}{N}\right)\left(\frac{YDevice}{M}\right)$$

The displayed intensity can be normalized and expressed as a real number:

$$DisplayIntensity = \frac{NumberOfPixelsOn}{PixelsPerArea}$$

which has the range of 0 to 1. A similar normalization transforms *PictureData* into a real number, with *PictureIntensity* also having a range of 0 to 1:

$$PictureIntensity = \frac{PictureData}{MaxPictureIntensity}$$

From the known *PictureIntensity*, the required number of illuminated pixels can be easily calculated and may be expressed as a function:

```
function PIXELS_ON(N, M : integer; Intensity : real) : integer;
begin
  if (Intensity < 1.0)
    then PIXELS_ON := trunc(Intensity * (N * M + 1))
    else PIXELS_ON := N * M;
end
```

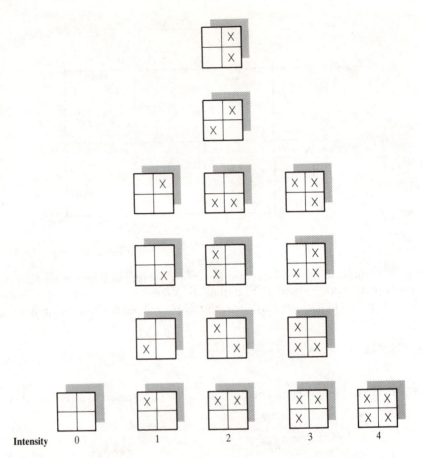

Figure 3.26

In a 2 × 2 pixel area, the number of intensity levels is equal to five. For intensities 1 to 3, there are a number of ways the ON pixels can be arranged. The different ON pixel arrangements may produce very different half-toning effects.

From this simple function, the number of pixels is known, but for the intermediate intensities the positions of the illuminated pixels are still undefined. For example, with a 2 × 2 pixels area, five intensity levels are possible. As shown in Figure 3.26, there are a number of possible patterns that can be used for each intermediate intensity. Obviously, the number of possible patterns for larger numbers of pixels grows rapidly. Unfortunately, the simple idea that, for a given intensity level, the same pattern of illuminated pixels can be used throughout a picture does not give the best results. The problem of selecting a particular pattern for a given intensity and picture position has been extensively researched, but there is no general technique that provides satisfactory results in all cases. The difficulty lies in uniform repeated patterns, such as streaks, that can be produced with this half-toning technique when large areas of the picture have slowly varying (or constant) picture intensities. This problem of unwanted streaks is exaggerated by the nature of the human eye, which accentuates sudden changes in intensity values.

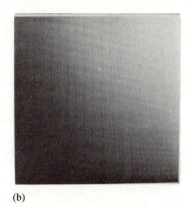

(a)

(b)

(c)

(d)

Figure 3.27

Four test patterns to be used for comparing various half-toning techniques. The first one has sudden intensity changes. The intensity for the second is a linear function of distance and can be expressed by the normalized intensity function $(x + y)/2$. The third is governed by a square law and is characterized by $(x^2 + y^2)/2$. The fourth is a digitized version of the photograh shown in Figure 1.10.

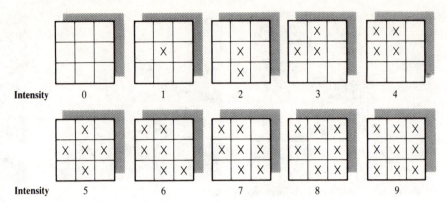

Figure 3.28

Half-toning patterns used for a
3 × 3 pixel area.

The commonly used simulated half-toning techniques are illustrated using the three test patterns shown in Figure 3.27 and the photograph shown in Figure 1.10. The first pattern is divided into nine areas of constant intensity and the intensities are arranged in such a way that dark areas border light areas. This pattern can be used to test the shading method's ability to simulate large constant areas and sudden jumps in picture intensity. The second and third patterns change intensities as continuous functions. The contour curves of equal intensities are straight lines in pattern 2. Thus:

$$PictureIntensity_2(x, y) = \frac{x + y}{2}$$

where x and y are given in normalized device co-ordinates with range $0..1$. For pattern number 3, circles of constant intensity are used; hence:

$$PictureIntensity_3(x, y) = \frac{x^2 + y^2}{2}$$

where, again, x and y are the normalized horizontal and vertical co-ordinates.

The first step is to generate results choosing the same pattern for each given intensity, regardless of its position in the picture. In this case, a 3 × 3 area will be used so that 10 intensity levels can be represented. The arrangement of illuminated pixels is shown in Figure 3.28. The illuminated pixels are placed as close to the middle of the small picture area as possible to simulate the effect of varying dot sizes.

A general half-toning algorithm requires parameters that define the resolution of the display and the size of the half-toning matrix. It also requires data for the illuminated pixel patterns for each intensity value. A suitable set of parameters are:

NRows: number of small areas in the vertical direction
NColumns: number of small areas in the horizontal direction
XPixels: number of pixels horizontally in each small area
YPixels: number of pixels vertically in each small area

The following Boolean matrix defines the illuminated pixel patterns:

OnPixelPatterns[0..*XPixels* * *YPixels*, 0..*XPixels* − 1, 0..*YPixels* − 1]

The function *PIXELS_ON*, defined earlier, transforms a normalized intensity value (range 0 to 1.0) to an integer number that specifies the number of pixels that must be turned ON in each small area. Using this function and the described test patterns at a given normalized position [x, y] gives:

PIXELS_ON(*XPixels*, *YPixels*, *PictureIntensity*(x, y)) : **integer**

Finally, it is assumed that the display pixels are turned ON by the function:

SET_PIXEL(*XPixel*, *YPixel*)

The normalized [x, y] positions are calculated at the middle of the small rectangular (or square) areas. These conventions are adopted in Algorithm 3.15.

The four test patterns printed with this simulated half-tone technique are shown in Figure 3.29. Seventy 3 × 3 areas are used in both the x and y directions, giving a total of 210 × 210 = 44 100 pixels. The results are not very satisfactory. The first test pattern shows unpleasant irregularities where the surface should be smooth. The second and third test patterns clearly show the finite number of distinct intensity levels. There are 10 levels, since a 3 × 3 area was chosen. The distinct jumps in intensity levels will be reduced if an area larger than 3 × 3 is selected for the half-tone simulation. The fourth test pattern seems to be the most successful because, psychologically, if the eyes can recognize a meaningful scene, they are more likely to skip over small irregular details.

An improvement in the simulated half-toning results may be obtained by selecting the pattern of illuminated pixels as a function of the x and y co-ordinates of its centre in the image. This method uses different patterns of illuminated pixels at neighbouring areas, even if the picture intensities are the same. It is a form of **texture mapping** in the sense that in a small local area, a selected texture or regular pattern of pixels is

Algorithm 3.15

Simulation of half-toning.

```
DisplayRow := 0;
for YRow := 0 to Nrows − 1 do
begin
  Y := (0.5 + YRow)/Nrows;
  DisplayColumn := 0;
  for XCol := 0 to NColumns − 1 do
  begin
    X := (0.5 + XRow)/NColumns;
    for XPix := 0 to XPixels − 1 do
      for YPix := 0 to YPixels − 1 do
      begin
        NPix := PIXELS_ON(XPixels, YPixels, PictureIntensity(X, Y));
        if (OnPixelPatterns[NPix, XPix, YPix])
        then SET_PIXEL(DisplayColumn + Xpix, DisplayRow + Ypix);
      end;
      DisplayColumn := DisplayColumn + XPixels;
  end;
  DisplayRow := DisplayRow + YPixels;
end;
```

displayed. Pattern selection is a difficult algorithmic problem, but some hardware devices, such as the laser printer, can produce smooth textures. Figure 3.30 shows the same test patterns produced by a laser printer. The results are much more pleasing.

The figures presented here were generated using approximately 100 dots per inch resolution to accentuate the visible effects of these shading techniques. A high-quality phototypesetting system may have as many as 2000 dots per inch resolution, in which case either texture mapping or continuous half-toning can solve the shading problem.

3.6.2 Ordered dithering

The term **dithering** was originally applied to the method used to reduce the effect of sharp edges when intensities jumped from one discrete value to another. This was accomplished by adding small random intensities, called **dithering noise**, to the picture intensities at each point. The technique of

(a)

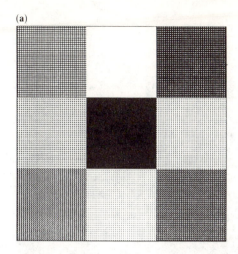

(b)

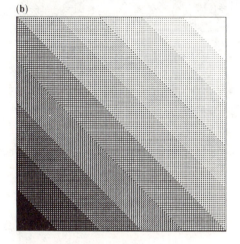

(c)

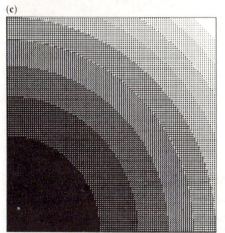

(d)

Figure 3.29

Four test patterns consisting of three simple intensity functions and a photograph are reproduced on a bi-level device by simulated half-toning. The patterns of pixels are shown in Figure 3.28. The limitation of using only 10 intensity levels is clearly visible.

(a)

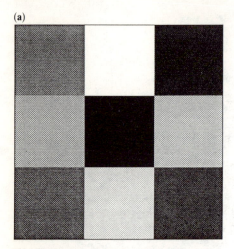

(b)

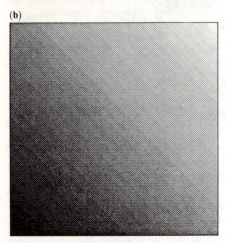

(c)

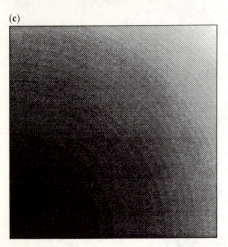

(d)

Figure 3.30

The four test patterns are reproduced by texture mapping using a laser printer.

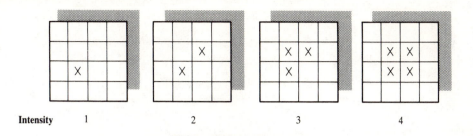

Intensity   1   2   3   4

Figure 3.31

The dithering matrix contains integer numbers that indicate the order in which the pixels are turned ON for successive intensity values. The matrix and the associated pixel patterns are shown for four intensities.

Dithering matrix

ordered dithering uses intensities in a matrix, which is laid down on the picture in a periodic manner analagous to the way the half-toning matrix was laid down in Figure 3.26. A very simple algorithm has been based on this technique to solve the shading problem with bi-level devices. It is similar to simulated half-toning.

A dithering mask is produced by numbering each of its dots, starting from 1. The order of the numbers is chosen to avoid, as far as possible, undesirable patterns in the final picture. A dither mask using four successive intensities together with the corresponding half-toning patterns is shown in Figure 3.31.

The dithering algorithm uses the integer numbers in the mask to represent the order in which the dots are added to the patterns. The dithering matrices for 3×3, 4×4 and 5×5 areas are shown in Figure 3.32. For any given scaled picture intensity (the scaled intensity is equal to $N * M * PictureIntensity$, which is in the range of 0 to 16 for the 4×4 case), the pattern of illuminated pixels can be easily deduced from this matrix, since the pixel is turned ON if the integer number stored in the matrix is smaller than or equal to the scaled picture intensity.

The 4×4 matrix will be used here to demonstrate this technique. The matrix is laid down periodically over the picture surface as shown in Figure 3.25. At each pixel position, the intensity of the picture at each of the 16 pixels is compared to the integer numbers stored in the matrix and the pixel is illuminated if the intensity is greater than or equal to this number. This method differs from simulated half-toning in that picture intensities are used at each pixel, while for half-toning, an average intensity

(a)

3	7	5
6	1	2
9	4	8

(b)

1	9	3	11
13	5	15	7
4	12	2	10
16	8	14	6

(c)

22	11	18	15	24
16	3	7	5	10
21	6	1	2	19
13	9	4	8	14
25	17	20	12	23

Figure 3.32
The dithering matrix for 3×3, 4×4 and 5×5 pixel areas.

is used over the entire rectangular area. The same parameters will be used here as for simulated half-toning. The dither matrix is given by:

$$DitherMatrix[0..XPixels - 1, 0..YPixels - 1]$$

The algorithm for ordered dithering (Algorithm 3.16) is particularly simple since the **mod**( ) function can be used to determine the index numbers in the dithering matrix from the pixel numbers. The results are shown in Figure 3.33. These show that an improvement has been gained for test patterns 2 and 3, due to the increased number of intensity levels, but this algorithm has been unable to eliminate the unwanted streaks.

(a)

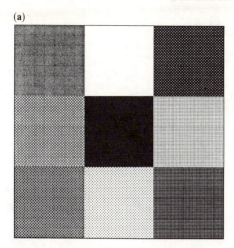

(b)

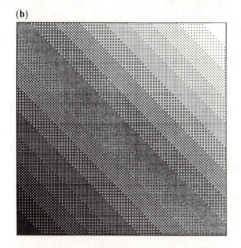

(c)

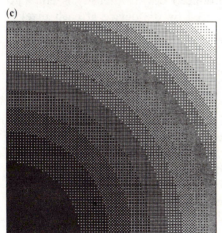

(d)

Figure 3.33

The four test patterns reproduced by dithering using the 4 × 4 pixel dithering matrix shown in Figure 3.32.

Algorithm 3.16

Ordered dithering.

$MaxXPixels := NCols * XPixels$;
$MaxYPixels := NRows * YPixels$;
for $YPicturePix := 0$ **to** $(MaxYPixels - 1)$ **do**
begin
  $YPix := YPicturePix$ **mod** $YPixels$;
  $Y := 0.5 + YPicturePix/MaxYPixels$;
  for $XPicturePix := 0$ **to** $(MaxXPixels - 1)$ **do**
  begin
    $XPix := XPicturePix$ **mod** $XPixels$;
    $X := 0.5 + XPicturePix/MaxXPixels$;
    if $(DitherMatrix[Xpix, Ypix] <= PIXELS\_ON(XPixels, YPixels, PictureIntensity(X, Y)))$
    then $SET\_PIXEL(XPicturePix, YPicturePix)$;
  end;
end;

3.6.3   Error-distribution algorithms

A theoretically much more appealing and generally much more applicable shading algorithm can be deduced from the examination of the error caused at each device pixel. If the measured normalized picture intensity is equal to *PictureIntensity* and the produced device intensity is equal to *DeviceIntensity*, then the error produced by the device at each pixel is equal to:

$$Error = PictureIntensity - DeviceIntensity$$

In this formulation, there is no restriction on the number of intensity levels the picture or the device may have. If a device has a number of intensity levels, the *DeviceIntensity* closest to the required *PictureIntensity* is selected and the error is minimized. The idea behind the error-distribution algorithm is to distribute the measured error among neighbouring pixels that have not yet been displayed so that the decision to turn a pixel ON will be modified by this error. The average displayed intensity should be corrected to the required intensity over the immediate neighbourhood of the displayed pixel.

Algorithm 3.17

Simple error distribution.

AccumulatedError := 0;
for each pixel of the picture in some order **do**
begin
   { Determine the *DeviceIntensity* that minimizes the *Error* and calculate the *Error* by the following
     expression }
   Error := (*PictureIntensity* + *AccumulatedError*) − *DeviceIntensity*;
   { Turn on the pixel with the found *DeviceIntensity* }
   AccumulatedError := *Error*;
end

The variables of this method are the selection of the neighbourhood over which the error is distributed and the order in which the pixels are scanned. The simplest algorithm considers only one pixel at a time and can be expressed as shown in Algorithm 3.17.

For a bi-level device, the pixels will be turned ON if the value of (*PictureIntensity* + *AccumulatedError*) is larger than 0.5, since in this case

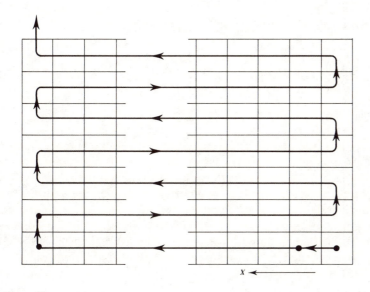

x ←————————

Figure 3.34

A simple continuous path for the error-distribution algorithm.

(a)

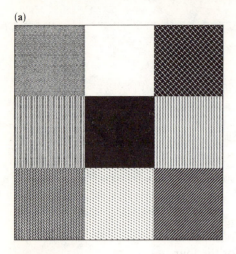

(b)

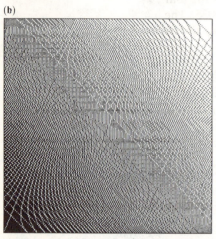

(c)

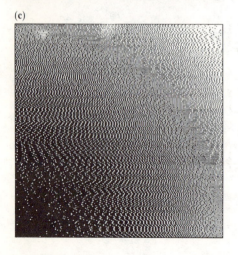

(d)

Figure 3.35

The four test patterns reproduced by a bi-level device using the error-distribution algorithm and the simple continuous path shown in Figure 3.34.

DeviceIntensity can only have values of 0 and 1. Intuitively, it can be seen that this algorithm makes sense because at very low intensities, say *PictureIntensity* = 0.1, no pixels will be turned on for five times, until the *AccumulatedError* reaches 0.5. Then, when it is turned ON, the *AccumulatedError* becomes equal to −0.5 and from then on only every tenth pixel will be turned ON.

For this simple case, the only variable in the method is the order in which the picture is scanned. It is intuitively obvious that any local error should be distributed in the neighbourhood of the pixel, hence the picture has to be scanned in a continuous path (following a pixel by a neighbouring pixel). Many different types of continuous curves may be constructed, and the consideration of the different paths would lead to complexities that are beyond the scope of this book. One simple path is shown in Figure 3.34. This scans the picture in the horizontal direction, alternating from left to right to right to left to follow a continuous curve. The results for the four test patterns using this simple algorithm are shown in Figure 3.35. The results in this case are quite pleasing. Other *space-filling* curves may also be used. A well-known and geometrically interesting one is Hilbert's space-filling curve, which is described by Griffith (1987).

A variation of this simple algorithm is attributed to Floyd and Steinberg (1975). Instead of accumulating the error for each successive pixel, the error is distributed in the neighbourhood of the pixel. Floyd and Steinberg used a 2 × 2 square area. The scanning of the picture must be done in such a way that, within the four squares, three pixels have not yet been processed. The distributed fraction of the error is made inversely proportional to the distance between the centre points of the pixels. In the case of a 2 × 2 square, the ratios closely approximate ³⁄₈ for neighbouring pixels and ¹⁄₄ for pixels touching at the corners only. This is shown in Figure 3.36. Normally, this algorithm is presented by scanning the picture from

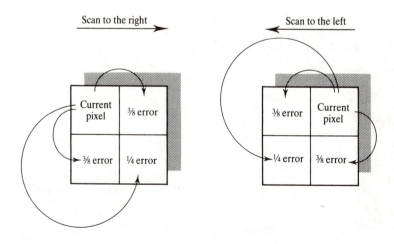

Figure 3.36

Error distribution within a neighbourhood of four pixels as used by the technique of Floyd–Steinberg.

(a)

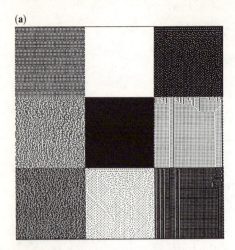

(b)

(c)

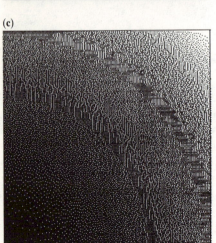

(d)

Figure 3.37
The four test patterns
reproduced by the Floyd–
Steinberg error-distribution
algorithm.

Algorithm 3.18

Floyd–Steinberg error-distribution algorithm.

{ Set *AccumulatedError*[*XPixel*, *YPixel*] to zero for all pixels used }
for each pixel of the picture scanning right or left **do**
begin
   { Determine the *DeviceIntensity* that minimizes the *Error* and calculate the *Error* by the following
expression }
   Error := *PictureIntensity*[*XPixel*, *YPixel*] + *AccumulatedError*[*XPixel*, *YPixel*] − *DeviceIntensity*;
   { Turn on the pixel with the found *DeviceIntensity* }
   if scanning to the right
   then begin
     AccumulatedError[*XPixel* + 1, *YPixel*] := *AccumulatedError*[*XPixel* + 1, *YPixel*] + (3/8) ∗ *Error*;
     AccumulatedError[*XPixel*, *YPixel* + 1] := *AccumulatedError*[*Xpixel*, *YPixel* + 1] + (3/8) ∗ *Error*;
     AccumulatedError[*XPixel* + 1, *YPixel* + 1] := *AccumulatedError*[*Xpixel* + 1, *YPixel* + 1]
                            + (1/4) ∗ *Error*;
       end
   else begin
     AccumulatedError[*XPixel* − 1, *YPixel*] := *AccumulatedError*[*Xpixel* − 1, *YPixel*] + (3/8) ∗ *Error*;
     AccumulatedError[*XPixel*, *YPixel* + 1] := *AccumulatedError*[*Xpixel*, *YPixel* + 1] + (3/8) ∗ *Error*;
     AccumulatedError[*XPixel* − 1, *YPixel* + 1] := *AccumulatedError*[*XPixel* − 1, *YPixel* + 1]
                            + (1/4) ∗ *Error*;
       end;
  end;

left to right only. It is also possible to keep a continuous curve by scanning alternately from left to right and then right to left. The latter path has been used to generate the test patterns shown in Figure 3.37.

Algorithm 3.17 can be easily modified for this method by using a matrix for the *AccumulatedError*, which stores a real value for each pixel (Algorithm 3.18). The ranges of the indices for the *AccumulatedError* matrix must be set large enough so that out-of-range errors will not occur at the borders of the picture. Algorithm 3.18 has been described in terms of a two-dimensional *AccumulatedError* matrix because it is easily modifiable for different scanning paths and for the distribution of errors in larger than 2 × 2 matrices. For this special 2 × 2 case, only a one-dimensional array is required, to keep the accumulated errors for the next line to be scanned.

The best results can be expected from the error-distribution algorithm when intensity variations are reasonably continuous and the picture intensities are approaching a constant around the borders. The worst effects will occur at large intensity changes, as seen in test pattern 1.

3.6.4 Dithering for producing colour shades

A coloured monitor that can produce a large number of colour shades is expensive. Colour hardcopy devices like ink jet printers can usually produce eight different colours (including white and black). When coloured illuminated solid objects are displayed, the shading of these objects with a few colours will show disturbing bands of colours, which will not look very realistic. The dithering of two different colours at the boundaries of these bands will produce the impression of a continuous change from one colour to another.

Using the limited number of colours provided by an inkjet printer, dithering can provide a much larger number of apparent colour shades. The addition of black and white dots can even change the brightness of the apparent colour. Unfortunately, it is very difficult to develop a comprehensive and scientific method for dithering in general and the difficulties become much more severe when colour is used. This is an important research and development area for the application minded and the artistically inclined.

Exercises

3.1 A line is to be drawn on the screen from pixel [7, 7] to pixel [2, 5]. Which octant does it belong to? If line generators are available for octants 1, 2, 3 and 8, which one would be used to draw it? What is the differential? What is the maximum error when the line is drawn.

3.2 Write an explanation of the term 'differential algorithm'.

3.3 Algorithm 3.6 is used to fill the square with corners at pixel co-ordinates [3, 6] and [7, 11]. The first seed is pixel is [5, 8]. In what order are the pixels set?

3.4 Modify Algorithm 3.7 to perform a boundary-filling algorithm that preserves the boundary.

3.5 Write implementations for the procedures *SEED_FILL_RIGHT*, *SEED_FILL_ABOVE* and *SEED_FILL_BELOW* mentioned in Algorithm 3.8.

3.6 Modify Algorithm 3.8 to cope with devices that can display more than two colours.

3.7 Simplify Algorithm 3.10 to produce a parametric circle generator.

3.8 Three adjacent, equally spaced points on an ellipse have co-ordinates $P_1 = [10, 10]$, $P_2 = [10.5, 9.5]$ and $P_3 = [10.9, 9.1]$. For point P_2, estimate the first differential using (a) the forward difference and (b) the central difference; the second differential using the central difference when $\Delta\theta = 0.02$.

3.9 A line is drawn on a raster screen using a differential line-drawing algorithm. In the rectangular area with corners at pixel co-ordinates $[10, 5]$ and $[14, 7]$, the following pixels are set to *Imax*: $[10, 5]$, $[11, 5]$, $[12, 6]$, $[13, 6]$, $[14, 6]$. All other pixels in the area are set to zero. The picture is then anti-aliased using the filter described in Section 3.5.2. If *Imax* = 255, calculate the anti-aliased pixel values for pixels $[11, 6]$, $[12, 6]$ and $[13, 6]$.

3.10 A picture has been calculated for display on a workstation with eight bit planes. Thus, pixels are assigned values in the range $[0..255]$. It is moved to a bi-level device and drawn using the 4×4 ordered dithering matrix shown in Figure 3.32. Draw the pixel patterns produced for pixels in the original image with the following intensities: 20, 169 and 241.

Problems

3.11 Write a pseudo code description of the differential line-drawing algorithm for the third Cartesian octant in the form required by Algorithm 3.3. Do not use real arithmetic.

3.12 How many multiplication operations and how many square root operations are required to compute each scan line of an efficient line scan circle generator?

3.13 Write the pseudo code for the rasterized differential ellipse generator.

3.14 Write the pseudo code for a general-purpose curve-drawing algorithm using a function call $f(x, y)$ to evaluate the left-hand side of the curve equation $f(x, y) = 0$. Devise an implementation of $f(x, y)$ that will develop this into a package for drawing polynomial curves of the form:

$$y = a_0 + a_1x + a_2x^2 + a_3x^3 \ldots$$

3.15 Estimate how many more arithmetic operations are required to draw a line of length n pixels using the anti-aliased, rather than the ordinary, form of Bresenham's algorithm. Is it possible that on a 512×512 resolution screen a postprocessing convolution algorithm would be a faster way of anti-aliasing a line drawing?

3.16 The standard convolution mask requires the use of a divide by 9 for its computation. Can you devise one, or more, 3×3 masks in which the division could be done by shifting, to increase the efficiency of computation. Discuss the likely effect of using your mask compared to the standard.

3.17 It is not very efficient to compute a convolution for anti-aliasing on a pixel-by-pixel basis, since this requires the same multiplications to be carried out several times. Devise an efficient algorithm to compute a convolution of a raster image with the standard 3×3 anti-aliasing mask assuming that, in addition to the frame buffer, you have sufficient memory to hold additional frames. Modify the algorithm to use as little extra memory as possible.

3.18 Modify Algorithm 3.18 so that the picture is scanned following the Hilbert space-filling curve.

Projects

3.19 Implement Bresenham's algorithm with anti-aliasing on a system with eight bit planes. Investigate the best way of scaling the pixel intensities to give lines of apparent equal intensity in all directions. Compare the result with lines anti-aliased by postprocessing using the standard convolution filter and with the filters devised as a solution to Exercise 3.16, taking note of the computation time and visual effect of each method.

3.20 Run-length encoding is a useful way to reduce the size of files storing pictures. In addition to the picture data, some control bytes are added to the file, which use the following format:

Bit 0–6: A positive integer, N, in the range $[0..127]$.

If bit 7 is 0, then the next byte in the file is a data byte to be repeated $N + 3$ times. It is followed by the next control byte.

If bit 7 is 1, then the next N bytes in the file are normal data bytes.

Write programs for run-length encoding files. Assume that the pixel bytes are in the range [0..255] and that they are ordered in the file starting from pixel address [0, 0]. Adjacent bytes are normally adjacent pixels on a horizontal line ordered in the positive x direction. The lines are ordered in the positive y direction. You should provide procedures that will take the input from either an unencoded file of bytes or one pixel at a time from a program generating a picture. You should also provide a program to decode a file, returning the next data pixel in order. Your system should include some header information, such as the screen resolution and physical size.

4 Analysis of Two- and Three-Dimensional Space

Vector methods are the basis of understanding and analyzing objects and scenes in two and three dimensions. The most applicable results of vector algebra are presented here and will form the foundations of the algorithmic methods used in subsequent chapters of the book. The representation of lines, line segments, planes and triangles is considered in some detail, as these are the primitive elements from which many scenes can be composed.

The intersections between lines and planes and between two planes are described, since these form an important part of the calculation of the visible parts of a scene to be drawn. For similar reasons, the problem of containment is discussed. In its simplest form, this is the calculation of whether a point is contained within a polygon or, in the 3D case, a polyhedron. Another containment problem, clipping, determines which segments of a line are contained within a polygon or polyhedron.

It is important for graphics systems to be able to draw a scene from any point in space and to be able to move objects to given positions and orientations in the scene. These transformations are most readily done by matrix methods, which are discussed in detail. Finally, the concept of projection from three to two dimensions is discussed. Two methods of projection onto a plane, parallel and perspective, are considered in detail.

4.1   INTRODUCTION

In general, people find it easy to comprehend two-dimensional (2D) diagrams but often have difficulties in visualizing or constructing two-dimensional representations of three-dimensional (3D) scenes. Obviously, it is of great importance to be able to represent and manipulate 3D objects in graphics systems, although, of course, the final graphical representation is always 2D. For example, an architectural practice will need to store a complete 3D model of a proposed building and to draw its 2D projected image from a wide variety of different viewpoints. Similar applications are found in the engineering industry where computer-aided engineering (CAE) and computer-aided design (CAD) are extensively used (see Chapter 1).

Despite the importance of 3D modelling, procedural methods have developed very little, and international standards organizations have yet to agree on a 3D graphics kernel, even after several years of trying. The difficulties encountered in characterizing the procedural level demonstrate that it is essential for any serious user of graphics to approach problems in three dimensions at the functional level. Fortunately, a very well-developed functional level is provided by vector and matrix algebra, from which simple methods for describing the geometry of 3D can be devised. Another advantage of the functional, or vector algebraic, approach is that it works equally well for two and three dimensions, so that both can be treated at the same time. In fact, 3D problems can be illustrated in 2D space, while the relationships expressed by vectors and matrices can be easily extended to three dimensions without difficulty. The use of vectors for 3D picture construction is a departure from the purely Cartesian representations used in many previous graphics text-books. The authors firmly believe that the ability to 'see' vector relationships in space is both a powerful tool and an effective way of acquiring the ability to visualize and interpret geometrical relationships in three dimensions. The appendix at the back of the book gives a short review of vectors and vector algebra.

Ultimately, all the algorithms will be expressed in Cartesian space, since all current graphics terminals work in Cartesian geometry. The transfer from vector to Cartesian space can be viewed as a change of description from the functional to the procedural and, in keeping with all good software design practice, should be delayed until the last possible moment. Current rapid hardware developments in the field of computer graphics also point to the importance of the functional level, since it is not inconceivable that within a short time hardware systems that can operate directly at the functional level of 3D interactive computer graphics will be available.

4.2   VECTORS AND CARTESIAN SPACE

In its usual representation, the Cartesian components of a vector represent distances along the three principal axes; hence, a vector can be moved to any starting point and it remains the same. Looking at the same movement but from the vector's point of view, it can be seen that the vector also remains the same, or is invariant, if the origin of the co-ordinate system is translated. A vector that is invariant under translation is called a **direction vector**.

The simplest graphics element is a **point**. In Cartesian space, it is defined by distances from the origin along the three principal axes. As a point is also represented by an *n*-tuple, it can be considered as an instance of a vector (having two or three components, depending on the dimension of the space). It is a vector of fixed position whose starting point is at the origin. This type of vector is called a **position vector**. It is easy to show that if the origin of a co-ordinate system is changed, then the components of a position vector also change. In fact, as shown in Figure 4.1, there is a change of the origin to **O′**. In the new co-ordinate system, the position vector **P** changes to **P′**, where:

$$\mathbf{P'} = \mathbf{P} - \mathbf{O'}$$

Thus, a translation of the origin can be expressed as the subtraction of two vectors. This vector equation holds for both 2D and 3D space.

Whenever a vector expression is used to define some geometric relationship, it is essential that the type of the vectors – position or direction – is clearly shown. Therefore, upper-case letters will be used for

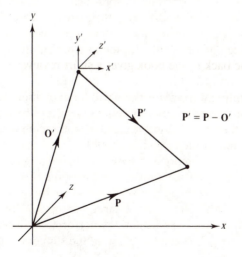

$$\mathbf{P'} = \mathbf{P} - \mathbf{O'}$$

Figure 4.1

Position vectors differ from direction vectors in that they are not invariant to a shift of origin. Translation of the origin by vector **O′** is equivalent to subtracting **O′** from all position vectors.

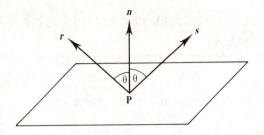

Figure 4.2
Calculation of a reflected
vector. The fact that **s**, **n** and **r**
can be drawn lying in one
plane gives a simple
relationship to solve for **r**.

position vectors and lower-case ones for direction vectors. Similarly, as
described in the appendix, it is useful to identify vectors whose magnitude
is equal to 1; hence, these will be denoted by *italic* script. The magnitude of
a vector **d** is denoted as $|\mathbf{d}|$, so the unit vector in the direction of **d** is given
by:

$$d = \frac{\mathbf{d}}{|\mathbf{d}|}$$

A direction vector has been used here because unit vectors are often used
to define a direction in 3D space. The interpretation of a position vector of
unit length, say, *D* or $\mathbf{D}/|\mathbf{D}|$ is much more restrictive and defines the surface
of a sphere with unit length radius centred at the origin. The difference
between position and direction vectors disappears when the functional
description is changed to the procedural one, since computationally all
vectors are treated equally as arrays having two or three components.

Before proceeding with 3D geometric entities such as lines and
planes, a graphics problem and its solution will be described to demonstrate the usefulness of the vector approach. As shown in Figure 4.2, a
point on a 3D mirror-like surface with Cartesian co-ordinates $P[x, y, z]$
reflects a ray of light. Knowing the direction of the surface normal and the
location of the light source, the problem is to calculate the direction of the
reflected light. By the laws of optics, this problem can be described by
three direction (unit) vectors: *s*, the direction of the light source as viewed
from point **P**; *n*, the normal to the surface; and *r*, the reflection vector. If
the three vectors are translated to point $P[x, y, z]$, the three vectors lie in
one plane and the angle between *s* and *n* (the incident angle) is equal to
that between *r* and *n* (the reflection angle).

These are 3D vectors and considerable algebra is required to find
the components of *r* in Cartesian space. Since the three vectors are in one
plane, the problem reduces to two dimensions in vector space. Without
loss of generality, the plane of the three vectors can be rotated into the
plane of the paper and the calculations performed entirely in two dimensions. From Figure 4.2, it can be seen that the sum of the unit vectors *r* and

s produces a vector along the normal. As the length of the vector is unknown, this is written:

$$r + s = \alpha n \tag{4.1}$$

where α is a scalar parameter. Since the dot product of two unit vectors is equal to the cosine of the angle between them:

$$r \cdot n = s \cdot n \tag{4.2}$$

which expresses the equality of the incident and reflection angles. Taking the dot product of both sides of Equation (4.1) with n, and with $|n| = 1$ gives:

$$\alpha = r \cdot n + s \cdot n = 2(s \cdot n)$$

and, finally, the result:

$$r = 2(s \cdot n)n - s$$

This is a simple vector equation and the Cartesian components of r can be easily expressed as:

$$r_c = 2(s_x n_x + s_y n_y + s_z n_z)n_c - s_c$$

where x, y or z are substituted in place of the subscript c.

This problem demonstrates the compactness of the vector description and the easy translation of the resulting vector equations into Cartesian form. It also should help in the visualization of the 3D problem we have just solved. It would be much more difficult to solve this problem by purely algebraic methods.

4.3   VECTOR LINE EQUATION

The last section showed that the subtraction of two position vectors is equivalent to the translation of the Cartesian co-ordinate system. This section now considers the addition of a direction vector to a position vector.

If the vector **d** is multiplied by a scalar, it will not change its direction. Only its magnitude changes, so a general sum can be written:

$$\mathbf{L} = \mathbf{P} + \mu\mathbf{d} \tag{4.3}$$

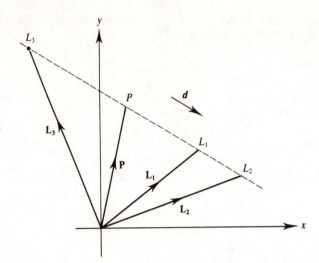

Figure 4.3
The vector line equation. A line is defined as the locus of a position vector **P** + μ**d** as μ is varied. Different values of μ give the different position vectors, **L₁**, **L₂**, **L₃**, which all lie on the line.

The result is a position vector and the locus of **L** as μ changes is a straight line. This is shown for the 2D case in Figure 4.3. For μ = 2, 3 and −3, the position vectors are **L₁**, **L₂** and **L₃** which define the three Cartesian points L_1, L_2 and L_3 lying on a straight line that goes through point P and has the direction specified by vector **d**. The vector **P** is sometimes called the base vector. This vector formulation is called the **parametric line equation**, since the vector **L** depends on the value of the scalar parameter μ. The convention adopted here is to use μ and ν for scalar parameters. Equation (4.3) demonstrates the method that will be used here to describe lines, curves, surfaces and 3D objects by means of vectors. The collection of all points described by a varying position vector defines the geometric entity which in this case is equal to $L[x, y, z]$, a straight line.

It is instructive to relate the parametric equation to the usual Cartesian representation of a straight line as a linear function $y = f(x)$. Two dimensions will be used for a simpler description of the straight line whose Cartesian co-ordinates can be expressed from Equation (4.3) by the following two equations:

$$x = P_x + \mu d_x$$
$$y = Py + \mu d_y$$

(4.4)

where the point L with co-ordinates $[x, y]$ is any point on the straight line. μ can be eliminated from the two equations, as long as $d_x \neq 0$, to give:

$$y = \left[P_y - \left(\frac{d_y}{d_x} \right) P_x \right] + \left(\frac{d_y}{d_x} \right) x$$

which is the same as the well-known form of the straight line equation $y = mx + c$, where m specifies the slope of the line and is equal to (d_y/d_x). A more general formulation of the same equation is:

$$Ax + By + C = 0$$

where, in this case:

$$A = d_y$$
$$B = -d_x$$
$$C = d_x P_y - d_y P_x$$

This form of the equation will be referred to as the Cartesian form, or sometimes the functional form, since it can be written as $f(x, y) = 0$.

It is worth noting that the direction vector $\mathbf{d} = [d_x, d_y]$ is perpendicular to the normal to the line, which can be defined by the normal direction vector, $\mathbf{n}$:

$$\mathbf{n} = [d_y, -d_x]$$

The magnitude of $\mathbf{n}$ is equal to the magnitude of $\mathbf{d}$. It can be verified from the definition of the dot product that $\mathbf{n} \cdot \mathbf{d} = 0$. The line equation can also be found by substituting, into the dot product, a general vector along the line for the direction vector $\mathbf{d}$. If:

$$\mathbf{d} = \mathbf{L} - \mathbf{P_1}$$

where $\mathbf{L}$ is a general point on the line and $\mathbf{P_1}$ is some known fixed point on the line:

$$(\mathbf{L} - \mathbf{P_1}) \cdot \mathbf{n} = 0$$

Thus, a straight line is defined by a point $\mathbf{P_1}$ on the line and a direction vector $\mathbf{n}$, which is normal to the line.

The graphical interpretation can be easily seen from the vector equation. Figure 4.3 clearly indicates the geometric construction of a line by vectors, without the need to express it with co-ordinate values. There are many advantages to the vector description. First of all, the vector equation for a line, Equation (4.3), is the same in three dimensions. The analytical function for a line in three dimensions is, in contrast, rather awkward and must be expressed by two linear equations. Secondly, all lines may be expressed by the vector equation. However, the line $x = $ constant cannot be clearly expressed in the analytical form $y = f(x)$, although it will work for the general equation $Ax + By + C = 0$. Thirdly, more information is immediately apparent from the vector equation than the analytical function. The equation describes the locus of a point as the scalar constant μ varies. If $\mu = 0$, then the point is exactly at the given point $\mathbf{P_1}$; if $\mu > 0$ then the point L on the line is on one side, while with $\mu < 0$ it is on the other side of point $\mathbf{P_1}$.

Finally, the two or three Cartesian equations derived from the vector equation express the line in its parametric form, as shown in Equation (4.4). Here, the scalar μ is the parameter and, for any value of μ, the equations evaluate to the co-ordinate of a point on the line. This formulation is very useful for generating the line on a raster type of display device.

4.4 LINE SEGMENTS

Another important advantage of the vector representation is that line segments may be easily defined from two points. This allows a direct transfer between the functional description and its implementation, which, as was seen in Chapter 3, is frequently concerned with drawing line segments between two points on the raster screen.

A line segment is defined by two points, P_1 and P_2, or two position vectors, $\mathbf{P_1}$ and $\mathbf{P_2}$. As shown in Figure 4.4, a direction vector $\mathbf{d}$ may be formed by subtracting vector $\mathbf{P_2}$ from $\mathbf{P_1}$:

$$\mathbf{d} = \mathbf{P_2} - \mathbf{P_1} \tag{4.5}$$

Figure 4.4

The vector line equation may be written using two position vectors as the locus of $\mathbf{P_1} + \mu(\mathbf{P_2} - \mathbf{P_1})$ as μ varies. In this form, the value of μ indicates which segment of the line the computed point lies on.

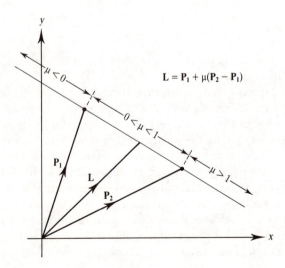

Note in passing that **d** can be treated as a proper direction vector, since if the origin of the co-ordinate system is moved to the point defined by position vector **O′**, then the vector in the new co-ordinate system is equal to:

$$\mathbf{d'} = \mathbf{P'_2} - \mathbf{P'_1} = (\mathbf{P_2} - \mathbf{O'}) - (\mathbf{P_1} - \mathbf{O'}) = \mathbf{P_2} - \mathbf{P_1} = \mathbf{d}$$

and hence it is invariant to translation.

Now, substituting Equation (4.5) into the vector line equation gives the equation for the line in the form:

$$\mathbf{L} = \mathbf{P_1} + \mu(\mathbf{P_2} - \mathbf{P_1}) \tag{4.6}$$

which is a vector equation for the straight line that goes through two points P_1 and P_2. Moreover, the value of the scalar constant μ indicates the section of the line where **L** is located. In computer graphics, the interest is usually in the segment of the line between P_1 and P_2. This can be easily tested by examining the value of μ:

If $0 \leqslant \mu \leqslant 1$, then the point is on the line segment between P_1 and P_2

If $\mu < 0$, then the point lies outside the line segment P_1 to P_2 on the side of point P_1

If $\mu > 1$, then the point lies outside the line segment P_1 to P_2 on the side of point P_2

In fact, any subrange of the possible values of parameter μ will define a line segment, but normally the range of interest is $[0..1]$.

These properties of the vector equation of a line segment can be used when the intersection of two line segments in two dimensions is to be found. There is, of course, a clear distinction between infinitely extended lines in two dimensions that always cross if they are not parallel and line segments that cross only if the crossing point lies within both line segments. For example, consider two line segments, the first extending from point P_{11} to P_{12} and the second from P_{21} to P_{22}. Their line equations are:

$$\mathbf{L_1} = \mathbf{P_{11}} + \mu(\mathbf{P_{12}} - \mathbf{P_{11}})$$
$$\mathbf{L_2} = \mathbf{P_{21}} + v(\mathbf{P_{22}} - \mathbf{P_{21}})$$

and the intersection of the two line segments is expressed by the vector equation $\mathbf{L_1} = \mathbf{L_2}$, or:

$$\mathbf{P_{11}} + \mu(\mathbf{P_{12}} - \mathbf{P_{11}}) = \mathbf{P_{21}} + v(\mathbf{P_{22}} - \mathbf{P_{21}})$$

which can be written as two equations, one for each Cartesian ordinate:

$$x_{11} + \mu(x_{12} - x_{11}) = x_{21} + v(x_{22} - x_{21})$$
$$y_{11} + \mu(y_{12} - y_{11}) = y_{21} + v(y_{22} - y_{21})$$

These two linear equations in two unknowns can be solved for scalar values μ and ν, as long as the two line segments are not parallel. The conditions for the two line segments to intersect are given by:

$$0 < \mu < 1 \quad \text{and} \quad 0 < \nu < 1$$

If either of these two conditions is not true, then the two line segments do not intersect.

4.4.1 Containment

There is a simple 2D graphical algorithm that uses the intersection of line segments to determine whether an arbitrary point P lies inside or outside a given polygon. As shown in Figure 4.5, the polygon is defined by a number of line segments extending from point P_i to P_{i+1} with $i = 1, 2, 3, ..., N$. The polygon has N sides and, for convenience, the vertex P_{N+1} has been defined to be the same as P_1. For any given point $P = [x, y]$, the **containment** of this point by the polygon can be determined by Algorithm 4.1, which counts the intersections between the polygon edges and a horizontal line segment:

$$\mathbf{H} = \mathbf{P} + \mu \boldsymbol{i} \qquad \mu > 0$$

where $\boldsymbol{i}$ is the unit vector in the x direction.

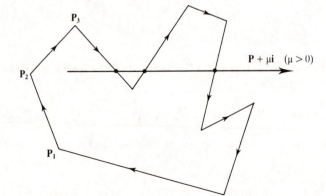

Figure 4.5
The ray containment test. To tell whether a point is contained within a polygon, we draw a line from it in one direction to infinity and count the number of times it intersects the polygon edges. If the count is odd, then the point is contained. If it is even, then the point is outside.

Algorithm 4.1

Ray containment test.

NoOfCrossings := 0;
for k := 1 **to** N **do**
begin
    { Solve the equation $\mathbf{P_k} + v(\mathbf{P_{k+1}} - \mathbf{P_k}) = \mathbf{P} + \mu i$ for μ and v }
    if ($\mu > 0$ **and** $0 <= v < 1$)
    then *NoOfCrossings* := *NoOfCrossings* + 1
end;
Contained = ODD(NoOfCrossings);

At the procedural level, there are some special cases that cause difficulties. These occur if the horizontal line crosses one or more vertices of the polygon. The difficulties are demonstrated in 2D in Figure 4.6. It is assumed that the test point lies on the horizontal line shown in Figure 4.6. To get the correct results, vertex V_1 should be regarded as providing no intersection (or providing two intersections), while vertices V_2, V_3 and V_4 provide one intersection each. If just the edges are processed, all vertices would be handled the same way, and therefore it would be difficult to distinguish between them procedurally. One way of solving this problem is to detect the condition when **H** passes through one or more vertices and provide special testing for these cases. The rules are not difficult and are given in Algorithm 4.2, which assumes that neighbouring edges are not collinear. This algorithm might not work for $k = 1$ or $k = N$ unless $\mathbf{P_{N+2}}$ is set equal to $\mathbf{P_2}$ and $\mathbf{P_0}$ to $\mathbf{P_N}$.

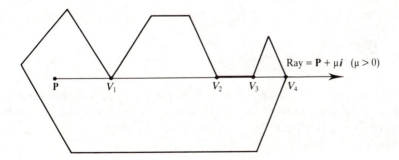

Ray = $\mathbf{P} + \mu i$ ($\mu > 0$)

Figure 4.6

Special cases for the ray containment test. If the ray cuts a vertex, then a special computation is required. V_1 should be counted as two intersections, while V_2, V_3 and V_4 should be counted as one intersection.

Algorithm 4.2

Special cases of the ray containment test.

if the horizontal piercing ray crosses vertex P_k **and** does not cross vertex P_{k-1}
then begin
    if the horizontal piercing ray crosses vertex P_{k+1}
    then $L := k + 2$
    else $L := k + 1$;
    if $\text{sign}(y_L - P_y) <> \text{sign}(y_{k-1} - P_y)$
    then $NoOfCrossing := NoOfCrossing + 1$
end;

4.5 PLANES

In 3D space, a plane may be defined by any three non-collinear points, P_1, P_2 and P_3. The equation for a position vector $\mathbf{P}$, which defines a point lying on the plane, is given by:

$$\mathbf{P} = \mathbf{P_1} + \mu(\mathbf{P_2} - \mathbf{P_1}) + \nu(\mathbf{P_3} - \mathbf{P_1}) \tag{4.7}$$

The fact that the locus of $\mathbf{P}$ as μ and ν vary is a plane follows directly from the fact that this equation is linear in three dimensions. Hence, the surface it describes must be a plane. Secondly, it is clear that the points defined by $\mathbf{P_1}$, $\mathbf{P_2}$ and $\mathbf{P_3}$ must lie in the plane, since they are simply the points given by the conditions:

If $\mu = 0$ and $\nu = 0$, then $\mathbf{P} = \mathbf{P_1}$
If $\mu = 1$ and $\nu = 0$, then $\mathbf{P} = \mathbf{P_2}$
If $\mu = 0$ and $\nu = 1$, then $\mathbf{P} = \mathbf{P_3}$

Fixing one of the parameters causes the equation to degenerate into a line equation. For example, setting μ to zero gives the equation for the line joining P_1 to P_3, while setting ν to zero gives the line joining P_1 to P_2. This is illustrated in Figure 4.7.

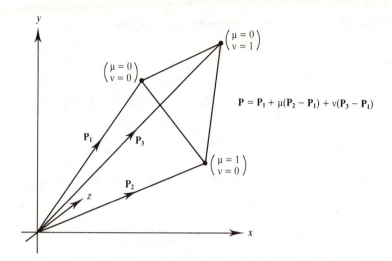

$$\mathbf{P} = \mathbf{P}_1 + \mu(\mathbf{P}_2 - \mathbf{P}_1) + \nu(\mathbf{P}_3 - \mathbf{P}_1)$$

Figure 4.7
The vector plane equation. If a plane is defined in terms of three position vectors, then the values of the parameters μ and ν provide information about where on the plane the point lies. For example, if $\mu = 0$, then the point lies on the line joining P_1 and P_3.

In the same way that a parameter subrange defines a line segment in Equation (4.6), so a subrange applied to μ and ν in Equation (4.7) defines a bounded area of the plane. The boundary is a parallelogram, which may be shown simply by considering the four loci formed, by fixing each parameter in turn to its maximum and minimum values.

Another useful subrange on μ and ν is defined by the following three inequalities:

$$\mu > 0, \quad \nu > 0 \quad \text{and} \quad \mu + \nu < 1$$

The locus defined by $\mathbf{P}$ restricted by these conditions is bounded by the triangle P_1, P_2 and P_3, as shown in Figure 4.7. Thus, these conditions may be used to determine whether the intersection point between a line and a plane is within a given triangle. This property is important for dealing with objects defined by triangular facets.

Lastly, Equation (4.7) can be broken into three linear equations in x, y and z, from which μ and ν may be eliminated and a functional form, $Ax + By + Cz + D = 0$, found. It will be shown later that the coefficients A, B and C define the normal to the plane and that the fourth parameter D can be calculated from the normal and a known point in the plane.

There is a second way in which the equation of a plane can be formulated from vectors. Using the fact that the dot product of orthogonal vectors is zero, if $\mathbf{n}$ is a direction vector that is normal to the plane and $\mathbf{p}$ is any direction vector in the plane, it follows that:

$$\mathbf{n} \cdot \mathbf{p} = 0 \tag{4.8}$$

This formulation may be associated with a Cartesian representation by setting the direction vector **p** equal to:

$$\mathbf{p} = \mathbf{P} - \mathbf{P_1}$$

where $\mathbf{P_1}$ is the position vector of a fixed point and $\mathbf{P} = [x, y, z]$ is the position vector of a general point in the plane. Thus:

$$\mathbf{n} \cdot (\mathbf{P} - \mathbf{P_1}) = 0$$

Since the dot product is associative over addition, this equation can be rewritten:

$$\mathbf{n} \cdot \mathbf{P} = \mathbf{n} \cdot \mathbf{P_1}$$

This is the vector equation for a plane defined by a point $\mathbf{P_1}$ and the normal to the plane is **n**. The dot product $\mathbf{n} \cdot \mathbf{P_1}$ is equal to a scalar constant, say s, and the equation of the plane becomes:

$$\mathbf{n} \cdot \mathbf{P} = s \tag{4.9}$$

Expanding the dot product, using a general point $\mathbf{P} = [x, y, z]$, yields the familiar Cartesian equation of a plane:

$$n_x x + n_y y + n_z z - s = 0$$

Using the more familiar form, $Ax + By + Cz + D = 0$, gives:

$$A = n_x; \quad B = n_y; \quad C = n_z; \quad D = -\mathbf{P_1} \cdot \mathbf{n}$$

In cases where a normal vector to a plane is not known, but two non-parallel vectors in the plane, **p** and **q**, are known, use can be made of the following cross-products:

$$\mathbf{n} = \mathbf{p} \times \mathbf{q} = -\mathbf{q} \times \mathbf{p}$$

since **n** is orthogonal to both **p** and **q**.

For three points in the plane, the normal direction can be determined from the position vectors extending to the given points:

$$\mathbf{n} = (\mathbf{P_1} - \mathbf{P_2}) \times (\mathbf{P_1} - \mathbf{P_3}) \tag{4.10}$$

Substituting Equation (4.10) into Equation (4.8) gives the other formulation of the vector equation for a plane:

$$[(\mathbf{P_1} - \mathbf{P_2}) \times (\mathbf{P_1} - \mathbf{P_3})] \cdot (\mathbf{P_1} - \mathbf{P}) = 0 \tag{4.11}$$

Algorithm 4.3

The plane equation.

The following type definitions are assumed:

type *ordinate* = (x, y, z);
        vector = **array** [*ordinate*] **of real**;

var *i* : *ordinate*;
        v_1, v_2, P_1, P_2, P_3 : *vector*;

(* From the given position vectors compute two vectors that lie on the plane. Assign them to v_1 and v_2 *)

for $i := x$ **to** z **do**
begin
    $v_1[i] := P_1[i] - P_2[i]$;
    $v_2[i] := P_1[i] - P_3[i]$;
end;

(* Compute the cross-product of v_1 and v_2. This will be a normal vector to the plane *)

$a := v_1[y] * v_2[z] - v_1[z] * v_2[y]$;
$b := v_1[z] * v_2[x] - v_1[x] * v_2[z]$;
$c := v_1[x] * v_2[y] - v_1[y] * v_2[x]$;

(* Calculate the constant d *)

$d := - (a * P_2[x] + b * P_2[y] + c * P_2[z])$;

(* The functional form of the plane equation is $a * x + b * y + c * z + d = 0$ *)

where, as before, the points defined by the locus of position vector **P** describe the plane.

The ease with which a vector description can be converted into a procedure is illustrated by Algorithm 4.3. This simply converts a vector form of the equation, specified by the three points P_1, P_2 and P_3 as given in Equation (4.7), into the functional form of a linear equation.

The direction of the normal in Equation (4.8) and Equation (4.9) is immaterial. An examination of the algorithm will show that by substituting $[-a, -b, -c]$ for $[a, b, c]$, the sign of d is changed and the same equation results. However, in many cases it is important to distinguish which direction the normal vector to the plane points. One particular case is where an object is defined as a set of bounded planes, called **facets**. For a variety of purposes, it is essential to determine whether the normal is inward, pointing to the object interior, or outward. The difference between the two is only a matter of sign, which can be achieved by executing the cross-product in reverse order:

$$\mathbf{n} = \mathbf{p} \times \mathbf{q} = -\mathbf{q} \times \mathbf{p}$$

This is equivalent to switching the data for the two position vectors $\mathbf{P_2}$ and $\mathbf{P_3}$ in Equation (4.11). Thus, it is possible to arrange the data for the vertices in the correct numerical order, in which case the vector expression for the normal to the plane will always yield the same type of normal, the inward normal being the common choice. In cases where only the Cartesian equation of the plane is required, the type of the normal is not important.

4.5.1 Co-planar vectors

Frequently, it is necessary to manipulate vectors constrained to lie in a given plane. When these vectors are direction vectors, they can be freely translated; thus, it can be assumed, without loss of generality, that the direction vectors all start at a fixed position in the plane. The same can be said for position vectors, if the origin of the co-ordinate system is moved to the plane.

An important result that has a bearing on this discussion, in that it allows some simplification in this case, is obtained by making the following substitutions in Equation (4.7):

$$\mathbf{p} = \mathbf{P} - \mathbf{P_1}$$
$$\mathbf{q} = \mathbf{P_2} - \mathbf{P_1}$$
$$\mathbf{r} = \mathbf{P_3} - \mathbf{P_1}$$

yielding:

$$\mathbf{p} = \mu\mathbf{q} + \nu\mathbf{r} \qquad (4.12)$$

Note that, as discussed in Section 4.4, $\mathbf{p}$, $\mathbf{q}$ and $\mathbf{r}$ can be treated as direction vectors, since they are invariant to translation. Furthermore, since no restriction was placed on the choice of P_1, P_2 or P_3, other than they are not collinear, q and r may be considered any two non-parallel vectors that may be constrained to lie in the plane described by Equation (4.7). Also, as P is a variable, it follows that p can be considered as a general vector direction that can also be made to lie in the same plane. Equation (4.12) is useful in the analysis of planes and in many instances will help in avoiding the use of either the cross-product or Cartesian space in making assertions about vectors that are co-planar.

It should be noted that, in the general case, since direction vectors are invariant to position, any two non-parallel vectors will define, not one, but a family of parallel planes. A third vector is considered to be co-planar with them if it is also parallel to this family of planes, in which case it can be written as a linear combination of the first two, as in Equation (4.12). One particular plane can be chosen by specifying a starting point for the direction vectors. A simpler definition results if only those planes including the origin $[0, 0, 0]$ are considered. In this case, direction vectors become position vectors, so two non-parallel position vectors define a plane and the endpoint of the position vector defined as the linear combination of these two vectors also lies in the same plane.

4.6 PROPERTIES OF LINES AND PLANES

With vector equations specifying lines and planes, it is comparatively easy to express the intersection of lines and planes, which are some of the most frequent calculations required in computer graphics.

4.6.1 Space subdivision

Given a plane, $n \cdot P = s$, it is frequently necessary to determine whether or not a number of points described by position vectors, P_1, P_2, P_3, lie on the same side of the plane. This may be done simply by examination of the sign of the term:

$$n \cdot (P_i - P_0) \tag{4.13}$$

where P_0 is the position vector of a point in the plane different from P_i.

Figure 4.8

A plane can be defined by its normal vector. The sense of the normal vector is arbitrary, but once it is fixed it can be used to determine which side of a plane a point P_i lies. P_i is joined to any point P_0 on the plane. If the angle it makes with the normal is acute, it is on the side to which the normal points, and vice versa.

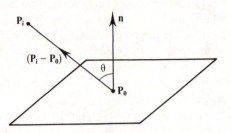

Turning to the definition of the dot product, which is given in the appendix, Equation (4.13) can be rewritten as:

$$|\mathbf{n}|\,|\mathbf{P_i} - \mathbf{P_0}|\cos(\theta)$$

where θ is the angle between $|\mathbf{n}|$ and $\mathbf{P_i} - \mathbf{P_0}$. It is clear that the sign of the term depends on the angle θ:

If $\quad \dfrac{-\pi}{2} < \theta < \dfrac{\pi}{2}\quad$ the result will be positive

If $\quad\quad \theta = \dfrac{\pi}{2}\quad$ the result will be zero

If $\quad\quad \theta > \dfrac{\pi}{2}\quad$ the result will be negative

Hence, referring to Figure 4.8, it can be seen that if the angle is acute – that is, the sign of the term is positive – then the point P_i lies on one side of the plane. In particular, on the side of the plane into which the normal vector $\mathbf{n}$ points, if the angle is obtuse, and thus the sign is negative, then P_i is on the opposite side to which the normal points. Thus, if the sign of Equation (4.13) is the same for each point under test, then all the points will lie on the same side of the plane.

4.6.2 Intersection of a line and a plane

Taking the vector equation of a plane:

$$\mathbf{n} \bullet \mathbf{P} = s \tag{4.14}$$

and recalling that a line has equation:

$$\mathbf{P} = \mathbf{P_1} + \mu\mathbf{d} \tag{4.15}$$

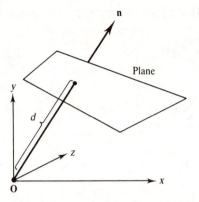

Figure 4.9
The distance of a plane from
the origin can be found from
the equation of the line through
the origin in the direction of the
normal vector to the plane. It
has equation $\mathbf{L} = \mu\mathbf{n}$.

it follows that the point of intersection can be obtained simply by substituting the value of **P** in Equation (4.15) into Equation (4.14) giving:

$$\mathbf{n} \cdot (\mathbf{P_1} + \mu\mathbf{d}) = s$$

Then, expanding the equation gives:

$$\mu = \frac{s - \mathbf{n} \cdot \mathbf{P_1}}{\mathbf{n} \cdot \mathbf{d}}$$

The value of μ can be computed and substituted into the equation of the line to determine the components of **P**.

Note that the distance of a plane from the origin can be found from the line normal to the plane that goes through the origin $\mathbf{O} = [0, 0, 0]$ (see Figure 4.9). The zero vector $[0, 0, 0]$ can be used as a position vector, but has no significance as a direction vector, since its direction is undefined. The plane is defined by:

$$\mathbf{n} \cdot \mathbf{P} = s \tag{4.16}$$

and the line normal to the plane that goes through the origin is given by:

$$\mathbf{P} = \mathbf{O} + \mu\mathbf{n} = \mu\mathbf{n} \tag{4.17}$$

Eliminating **P** by substituting Equation (4.17) into Equation (4.16) gives:

$$\mu\mathbf{n} \cdot \mathbf{n} = s$$

and:

$$\mu = \frac{s}{\mathbf{n} \cdot \mathbf{n}} = \frac{s}{|\mathbf{n}|^2}$$

Thus, substituting this value of μ back into Equation (4.17), the point of intersection is expressed by the position vector:

$$\mathbf{P} = \left(\frac{s}{|\mathbf{n}|^2}\right)\mathbf{n}$$

The distance from the origin to the point of intersection is equal to the magnitude of position vector $\mathbf{P}$, or:

$$|\mathbf{P}| = \left(\frac{s}{|\mathbf{n}|^2}\right)|\mathbf{n}| = \frac{s}{|\mathbf{n}|}$$

If the normal $\mathbf{n}$ in the plane equation, $(\mathbf{n} \cdot \mathbf{P} = s)$, is a unit vector, then the distance is simply equal to s. This gives the vector equation of a plane that is normal to a given direction vector $\mathbf{n}$ and is a given distance away from the origin. Clearly, the equation $\mathbf{n} \cdot \mathbf{P} = 0$ defines a plane that goes through the origin.

4.6.3 Line of intersection of two planes

Here, the cross-product is most useful. Suppose two different planes are given by the equations:

$$\mathbf{n}_1 \cdot \mathbf{P} = s_1$$
$$\mathbf{n}_2 \cdot \mathbf{P} = s_2$$

where $\mathbf{n}_1$ and $\mathbf{n}_2$ are the normal vectors. It can be seen immediately that the line of intersection of the two planes must be orthogonal to both normal directions – that is, it must lie in both the planes. From this, it follows directly that the vector product:

$$\mathbf{d} = \mathbf{n}_1 \times \mathbf{n}_2$$

specifies the direction of the line of intersection, as shown in Figure 4.10. It thus remains to find a point on the line. Calling the position vector associated with this point, $\mathbf{L}_1$, a vector equation of the line of intersection is given by:

$$\mathbf{L} = \mathbf{L}_1 + \mu(\mathbf{n}_1 \times \mathbf{n}_2)$$

Since the point L_1 is on the line, the two plane equations must be simultaneously satisfied:

$$\mathbf{n}_1 \cdot \mathbf{L}_1 = s_1 \quad \text{and} \quad \mathbf{n}_2 \cdot \mathbf{L}_1 = s_2 \tag{4.18}$$

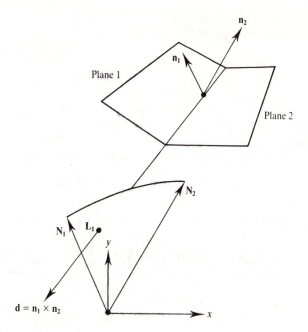

Figure 4.10
The line of intersection of two planes has a direction perpendicular to their normal vectors. The calculation of a position vector on the line is done on the plane through the origin which is parallel to the directions of $\mathbf{n_1}$ and $\mathbf{n_2}$.

As there is an infinite number of possible solutions for $\mathbf{L_1}$ that will satisfy these two equations, an arbitrary choice must be made. One such point can be found by defining two position vectors, $\mathbf{N_1}$ and $\mathbf{N_2}$, simply as:

$$\mathbf{N_1} = \mathbf{n_1} \quad \text{and} \quad \mathbf{N_2} = \mathbf{n_2}$$

and place the point $\mathbf{L_1}$ in the plane spanned by the two vectors $\mathbf{N_1}$ and $\mathbf{N_2}$. This is demonstrated in Figure 4.10. The plane will cross the origin and since, it is perpendicular to the line of intersection, $\mathbf{L}$, the point $\mathbf{L_1}$ will always exist. Therefore:

$$\mathbf{L_1} = \alpha\mathbf{N_1} + \beta\mathbf{N_2} = \alpha\mathbf{n_1} + \beta\mathbf{n_2} \qquad (4.19)$$

where α and β are scalar quantities. To solve for values that yield a vector satisfying Equation (4.18), dot products are taken of both sides of Equation (4.19) with the normal vectors:

$$\mathbf{L_1} \cdot \mathbf{n_1} = \alpha|\mathbf{n_1}|^2 + \beta\mathbf{n_1} \cdot \mathbf{n_2} = s_1$$
$$\mathbf{L_1} \cdot \mathbf{n_2} = \alpha\mathbf{n_1} \cdot \mathbf{n_2} + \beta|\mathbf{n_2}|^2 = s_2$$

Since $\mathbf{n}_1$ and $\mathbf{n}_2$ are not parallel, these equations can be solved for the scalar values α and β by conventional Gaussian elimination to give:

$$\alpha = \frac{s_2 \mathbf{n}_1 \cdot \mathbf{n}_2 - s_1 |\mathbf{n}_2|^2}{(\mathbf{n}_1 \cdot \mathbf{n}_2)^2 - |\mathbf{n}_1|^2 |\mathbf{n}_2|^2}$$

$$\beta = \frac{s_1 \mathbf{n}_1 \cdot \mathbf{n}_2 - s_2 |\mathbf{n}_1|^2}{(\mathbf{n}_1 \cdot \mathbf{n}_2)^2 - |\mathbf{n}_1|^2 |\mathbf{n}_2|^2}$$

Having values for α and β, the components of the position vector $\mathbf{L}_1$ can be calculated and the line of intersection for two planes obtained:

$$\mathbf{L} = \mathbf{L}_1 + \mu(\mathbf{n}_1 \times \mathbf{n}_2)$$

4.7   ALGORITHMS FOR 3D VOLUMES

In graphics applications, it is frequently necessary to deal with objects defined by a set of planar facets that normally form a polyhedron. The typical algorithms required for such objects are, firstly, those that decide whether a point is contained within a volume and, secondly, what span of a line is contained within a solid object for the purposes of clipping.

4.7.1   Containment within a convex volume

A convex object can be defined as one for which a line joining any two points on the surface is completely contained within the object. The simplest way of representing a convex object is as the volume bounded by three or more plane equations. If the planes are represented by their inner normal with respect to the object being represented, together with the constant in Equation (4.9), then the containment of a given point within the object can be simply tested by the method outlined in Section 4.6 for determining space subdivision. Algorithm 4.4 tests for containment by checking the point against every plane. If the point is on the inner side of all planes, it is contained.

Algorithm 4.4 would normally be implemented using a conditional loop, rather than a **for** loop, since testing can terminate as soon as the point is found to be on the outside of any plane. The point $\mathbf{P}_0$ can be found by substituting simple values, such as zero, for two of the ordinates into the plane equation and solving for the third.

Frequently, however, convex objects are represented by lists of edges, which define bounded planar facets, rather than as a set of plane equations. In these cases, if the edge vectors are defined in a consistent

Algorithm 4.4

Containment within a convex object defined by planes.

Contained := **true**;
for each plane bounding the object **do**
begin
　{ Choose a point $\mathbf{P_0}$ on the plane }
　if $\mathbf{n} \cdot (\mathbf{P} - \mathbf{P_0}) < 0$
　then *Contained* := **false**;
end

sense, then it will be possible to derive the inner normal from the cross-product of two adjacent edges. However, this will not always be the case, so an alternative algorithm is required. The principle remains the same; that is, the point is tested with each facet in turn, using the normal, and one of the vertices for the point $\mathbf{P_0}$. Then, the normal direction is tested by using a point that is known to be contained. From the definition of a convex object, it is known that any other vertex, not on the plane being tested, will be satisfactory. In practice, the two tests are combined as shown in Algorithm 4.5.

Algorithm 4.5

Containment within a convex object defined by vertices.

Contained := **true**;
for each plane bounding the object **do**
begin
　{ Choose three vertices $\mathbf{V_1}, \mathbf{V_2}, \mathbf{V_3}$ on the plane }
　{ Compute the normal $\mathbf{n} = (\mathbf{V_1} - \mathbf{V_2}) \times (\mathbf{V_1} - \mathbf{V_3})$ }
　{ Choose a vertex $\mathbf{V_i}$ on any other plane }
　if $SIGN(\mathbf{n} \cdot (\mathbf{P} - \mathbf{V_1})) <> SIGN(\mathbf{n} \cdot (\mathbf{P} - \mathbf{V_i}))$
　then *Contained* := **false**;
end

Algorithm 4.6

Clipping to a convex volume.

```
Clipped := false;
FaceNo := 1;
repeat
   if OUTSIDE(P₁, Face[FaceNo]) and OUTSIDE(P₂, Face[FaceNo])
   then Clipped := true;
   if not OUTSIDE(P₁, Face[FaceNo]) and OUTSIDE(P₂, Face[FaceNo])
   then P₂ := INTERSECTION(P₁, P₂, Face[FaceNo]);
   if OUTSIDE(P₁, Face[FaceNo]) and not OUTSIDE(P₂, Face[FaceNo])
   then P₁ := INTERSECTION(P₁, P₂, Face[FaceNo]);
   FaceNo := FaceNo + 1;
until Clipped or (FaceNo > NoOfFaces);
```

A comparison of Algorithms 4.4 and 4.5 illustrates that the storage of the inner surface normal for the faces of a 3D object will save computer time and will simplify the procedures to be constructed.

4.7.2 Clipping to a convex volume

Algorithm 4.6, attributed to Cyrus and Beck, is a simple extension of Algorithm 4.4. The method is to check both endpoints of the line against each plane defining the object. If both points are on the inside of any one plane, then no further action is required and the algorithm proceeds to the next plane. If both points are outside any one plane, then the line is completely clipped. If one point is outside, and one inside, then the intersection of the line and the plane is found, which replaces the outside endpoint.

Given a line joining P_1 and P_2 and a convex object bounded by planar facets whose representation is stored in the array *Face*, Algorithm 4.6 finds the line segment lying completely within the volume. Use is made of a procedure *OUTSIDE*, which is an implementation of Algorithm 4.5, and a procedure *INTERSECTION*, which could be implemented following the method outlined in Section 4.6.

Algorithm 4.7

Containment within a concave volume.

{ Choose a ray $\mathbf{P} + \mu k$ from the test point }
NoOfIntersections := 0;
for each facet **do**
begin
   { Compute μ for the intersection of the ray and the plane of the facet }
   if $\mu > 0$
   then begin
       { Compute the co-ordinate of the intersection }
       { Test its $[x, y]$ for containment within the polygon formed by the $[x, y]$ components of the
         vertices defining the facet }
       if contained within the polygon
       then *NoOfIntersections* := *NoOfIntersections* + 1;
     end
end;
Contained := *ODD*(*NoOfIntersections*);

4.7.3   Non-convex objects

Non-convex objects can be highly complex and can contain holes. Consequently, the simple testing based on inner normal is no longer applicable in these cases. Often, complicated shapes and surfaces are approximated with a large number of small planar facets, in which case the calculations for the containment of a point or the clipping of a line become relatively simple, although time consuming.

The containment of a point $\mathbf{P}$ can be calculated by a 3D version of the piercing test, which is given in Algorithm 4.7. It is very similar to the 2D case described in Algorithm 4.1. A ray emanating from the point under test is chosen. Each planar facet bounding the object is checked to see if it has an intersection with the ray. The total number of intersections is counted and if odd, the point is contained. The test with each facet is in two parts. The first is to establish whether the ray intersects the plane in which the facet under test lies. The second is to determine whether the intersection is within the bounded area defining the facet, which is the same as the 2D containment algorithm.

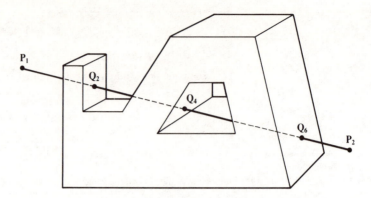

Figure 4.11

Clipping a line to a non-convex polyhedron.

As the ray travelling in the positive z direction has been chosen here ($k = [0, 0, 1]$), the test to see if the intersection on a given plane is within the bounds of the facet can be done in two dimensions, with the projection of the vertices of the facet on to the x–y plane. This is an example of orthographic projection, which will be discussed in greater detail in Section 4.9. Note that for objects defined by triangular facets, the containment within the face may be easily found using the method outlined at the start of Section 4.5.

The clipping of a line segment by a non-convex object may slice the line into many segments which alternately are inside and outside the volume. This is illustrated by Figure 4.11, which features the clipping of a line segment by a non-convex object with a hole in it. Those line segments that are outside the volume will be referred to as *visible*. The clipping of the line joining the points $\mathbf{P_1}$ and $\mathbf{P_2}$ is done by taking the ray:

$$\mathbf{L} = \mathbf{P_1} + \mu(\mathbf{P_2} - \mathbf{P_1}) \qquad \mu >= 0$$

and finding all the intersection points between it and the polygonal facets using, in principle, the method outlined in Algorithm 4.7. The intersection points found are stored as a sorted list of values of μ. This ordered set of intersection points is labelled by $\mathbf{Q_1}, \mathbf{Q_2}, ..., \mathbf{Q_N}$ in Figure 4.11. If N, the number of intersections, is odd, $\mathbf{P_1}$ is within the volume and is not visible, otherwise it is visible. This determines the visibility of the first segment, which extends from $\mathbf{P_1}$ to $\mathbf{Q_1}$. Then, all other intersections are considered in increasing order of μ for which $\mu \leqslant 1$ and they are alternately visible and non-visible.

Although simple in concept, the algorithm is difficult to implement, since it contains many problems at the procedural level. These are the problems associated with the piercing ray intersecting vertices or being parts of edges, shown in Figure 4.6. In the 3D case, the ray may lie in the plane of a facet as well.

4.7.4   Division of an arbitrary object into convex parts

Another method that deals with non-convex objects breaks a concave volume into several convex ones, after which each convex sub-object may be tested separately. To do this, the plane of each facet is considered in turn and a test is made to see which side of it the other vertices of the polyhedron lie. If they all lie on the same side of the plane, then the polyhedron is convex with respect to this plane. If not, the object is divided into two or more sub-objects by slicing it along the plane and collecting together the vertices with the same sign. This task is difficult to achieve at the procedural level. However, its outline is as follows. The first step is to determine how many sub-objects the original object has been divided into. This can be done by checking the connectivity of the vertices. A matrix is set up containing a row and a column for each vertex on one side of the plane. This will contain a 1 at every place where the row vertex is directly connected to the column vertex. In the transitive closure of this matrix, vertices connected by any path have non-zero entries and so can be easily extracted. The transitive closure of matrix $\mathbf{B}$ with dimension n is defined as $\mathbf{B}^n$. There are algorithms that compute this more efficiently than evaluation of the products. To simplify the procedure, it only continues if the cutting plane has sliced the object into exactly two sub-objects; that is, when the vertices can be divided into two sets such that their transitive closure matrices contain no zero entries. It can be shown that there will be at least one such plane for any concave object.

The next step is to identify those edges that cross the cutting plane and to compute the intersection points. This may be done using the algorithm for the intersection of a line and a plane. Since it is known which edge belongs to which polygon in the original object, the resulting points can be joined with edges. Use can also be made of the fact that the new boundary formed will be the same for objects on both sides of the cutting plane. This then gives enough information to construct a description of two sub-objects, which together occupy the same space as the original volume.

Once an object has been divided into two sub-objects, the algorithm is re-entered with those sub-objects. It proceeds until all sub-objects are found to be convex.

4.7.5   Triangulation

Previous sections have shown that for general objects, the containment calculations for arbitrarily shaped polygons can be very complex and time consuming. One approach to this problem is to divide all planar surfaces into triangles, since a triangle is always convex and, as was shown in

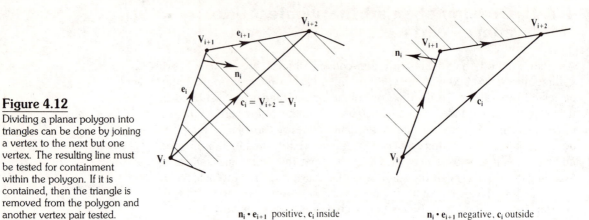

Figure 4.12
Dividing a planar polygon into triangles can be done by joining a vertex to the next but one vertex. The resulting line must be tested for containment within the polygon. If it is contained, then the triangle is removed from the polygon and another vertex pair tested.

Section 4.5, the containment test for a triangle is very simple. The division of an arbitrary polygon into triangles is called **triangulation**.

Triangulation is a well-studied problem in computational geometry. A simple algorithm for a polygon that contains no holes is to search around the border of a polygon until two adjacent edges are found for which the line that completes the triangle lies within the polygon. An N-sided polygon is represented by an ordered set of vertices $V_1, V_2, \ldots, V_N$, where for convenience $V_{N+1} = V_1$. The edge vectors are given by:

$$e_i = V_{i+1} - V_i$$

which are also ordered consistently in the clockwise direction. It is assumed that the inner normal n_i of each edge e_i is known. The direction vector, which completes the triangle, is given by:

$$c_i = e_{i+1} - e_i = V_{i+2} - V_i$$

A simple check eliminates cases where parts of a line lie outside the polygon. This may be done by testing the inner surface normal of one edge with the edge vector of the other edge, as shown in Figure 4.12. If the value of $n_i \cdot e_{i+1}$ is negative, at least part of the line lies outside the polygon. If the dot product is positive, then at least part of the line c_i lies within the polygon and must be tested further for intersection with the other edges. If there is no such intersection, then the three vertices are taken as one triangle, the algorithm is re-entered and V_{i+1} is removed from the vertex list.

This simple algorithm decomposes an arbitrary polygon into triangles without regard to size or shape, or computational efficiency. It will not deal with polygons that have holes in them. These may be eliminated by relatively simple preprocessing. More complex algorithms have recently been presented by Chazelle and Incerpi [1984] and Fournier and Montuno [1984].

4.8   CO-ORDINATE TRANSFORMATIONS

Many applications require the graphical transformation of objects in Cartesian space. The three basic transformations are:

(1)   translation,

(2)   scaling,

(3)   rotation.

It has been demonstrated by Euler that any object can be placed anywhere in Cartesian space by means of linear translation and rotation about the principal axes. For graphics, it is also convenient to be able to change the size of an object, and so scaling is included as well. The most convenient way of treating co-ordinate transformations is to set up matrices containing the parameters of the transformations and to use matrix multiplications to reduce a series of transformations to a combined, single transformation matrix. A review of matrix algebra is given in the appendix.

To treat all three transformations in a uniform manner, it is necessary to use an additional component in the vectors and increase the dimensions of the matrices. For 3D space, four-dimensional vectors are used, which have four so-called **homogeneous co-ordinates**. The four components of a homogeneous vector are reduced to three dimensions by the following normalization operation:

$$[x, y, z, h] \rightarrow \left[\frac{x}{h}, \frac{y}{h}, \frac{z}{h} \right]$$

Any position or direction vector in Cartesian space may be written in this four-ordinate form as $[x, y, z, 1]$. Four-by-four transformation matrices will be set up in such a way that a vector $[x, y, z, 1]$ postmultiplied by any transformation matrix made up from the basic operations will result in a new vector with components $[x', y', z', 1]$. Thus, as far as transformations are concerned, the fourth dimension will normally remain 1. All useful graphical transformations may be broken down into products of the three basic transformations.

4.8.1 Translation

Translation of a point may be executed by the postmultiplication of the transformation matrix, T, where:

$$T = \begin{bmatrix} 1 & 0 & 0 & 0 \\ 0 & 1 & 0 & 0 \\ 0 & 0 & 1 & 0 \\ t_x & t_y & t_z & 1 \end{bmatrix}$$

thus:

$$[x, y, z, 1] \bullet \mathbf{T} = [x + t_x, y + t_y, z + t_z, 1]$$

This transformation, when applied to all points of the object, will move the object by the magnitude and direction of vector $[t_x, t_y, t_z]$. The inverse of this matrix is found by substituting $-t_x$ for t_x, $-t_y$ for t_y and $-t_z$ for t_z. No translation is achieved by translation values $[0, 0, 0]$ which, when substituted into the translation matrix, give the four-dimensional identity matrix $\mathbf{I}$. Note that translation cannot be achieved by using a three-by-three matrix multiplication with a 3D vector. This is the most important reason for using homogeneous co-ordinates, since they allow composite transformations to be handled by one matrix.

Care must be taken when applying translation to vector formulations, since, as already mentioned, direction vectors are invariant to position and so should not be translated. In contrast, position vectors are fixed and must be translated.

4.8.2 Scaling

Scaling means the scaling of the Cartesian space by multiplying each co-ordinate value with scaling constants $[s_x, s_y, s_z]$. The scaling transformation matrix is given by:

$$S = \begin{bmatrix} s_x & 0 & 0 & 0 \\ 0 & s_y & 0 & 0 \\ 0 & 0 & s_z & 0 \\ 0 & 0 & 0 & 1 \end{bmatrix}$$

so that:

$$[x, y, z, 1] \cdot S = [s_x x, s_y y, s_z z, 1]$$

When this transformation is applied to all points of an object, the object normally changes both its size and location. Only objects centred on the origin will remain in the same position. The scaling transformation matrix, S, is executed with reference to the origin and only the origin remains at the same place. All other points change their positions, unless all the scaling constants have a value of 1. The inverse of the scaling matrix can be obtained by substituting $1/s_x$ for s_x, $1/s_y$ for s_y and $1/s_z$ for s_z. The identity matrix results if $s_x = s_y = s_z = 1$.

Scaling may also be done with reference to a given point $\mathbf{P_0} = [x_0, y_0, z_0]$, which may be at the centre of the object. This is equivalent to a combined transformation of translation of the point $\mathbf{P_0}$ to the origin, scaling and then translation again to restore $\mathbf{P_0}$ to its original position. The three transformations in the correct order, left to right, can be expressed by three matrices:

$$\begin{bmatrix} 1 & 0 & 0 & 0 \\ 0 & 1 & 0 & 0 \\ 0 & 0 & 1 & 0 \\ -x_0 & -y_0 & -z_0 & 1 \end{bmatrix} \cdot \begin{bmatrix} s_x & 0 & 0 & 0 \\ 0 & s_y & 0 & 0 \\ 0 & 0 & s_z & 0 \\ 0 & 0 & 0 & 1 \end{bmatrix} \cdot \begin{bmatrix} 1 & 0 & 0 & 0 \\ 0 & 1 & 0 & 0 \\ 0 & 0 & 1 & 0 \\ x_0 & y_0 & z_0 & 1 \end{bmatrix}$$

which may be multiplied out to yield the single matrix:

$$\begin{bmatrix} s_x & 0 & 0 & 0 \\ 0 & s_y & 0 & 0 \\ 0 & 0 & s_z & 0 \\ x_0(1 - s_x) & y_0(1 - s_y) & z_0(1 - s_z) & 1 \end{bmatrix}$$

Looking at the matrix for the scaling of an object centred on a point $\mathbf{P_0}$ illustrates an important point; that is, that the order in which the transformations are applied must be carefully observed. The combined transformation matrix can be written as the product of three elementary ones:

$$S_p = T \cdot S_o \cdot T^{-1}$$

If the order of the transformations were irrelevant, it would be possible to swap, for example, the first two to yield:

$$S_p = S_o \cdot T \cdot T^{-1}$$
$$= S_o \cdot I$$
$$= S_o$$

which is clearly false. Similar *reductio ad absurdum* arguments can be used to show that, in general, a different result is obtained by exchanging the order of any pair of transformation matrices.

4.8.3 Rotation

In the case of rotation, it is necessary to specify an axis. For the 2D case, rotations are carried out about the origin, which is equivalent to a rotation about the z axis in a 3D system. There are three different matrices for rotation about the three Cartesian axes, which represent the simplest cases of rotation matrices. Rotation around the x axis with angle θ is expressed by the matrix:

$$R_x = \begin{bmatrix} 1 & 0 & 0 & 0 \\ 0 & \cos(\theta) & \sin(\theta) & 0 \\ 0 & -\sin(\theta) & \cos(\theta) & 0 \\ 0 & 0 & 0 & 1 \end{bmatrix}$$

Rotation around the y axis by angle θ is given by:

$$R_y = \begin{bmatrix} \cos(\theta) & 0 & -\sin(\theta) & 0 \\ 0 & 1 & 0 & 0 \\ \sin(\theta) & 0 & \cos(\theta) & 0 \\ 0 & 0 & 0 & 1 \end{bmatrix}$$

and rotation around the z axis is given by:

$$R_z = \begin{bmatrix} \cos(\theta) & \sin(\theta) & 0 & 0 \\ -\sin(\theta) & \cos(\theta) & 0 & 0 \\ 0 & 0 & 1 & 0 \\ 0 & 0 & 0 & 1 \end{bmatrix}$$

The inversions of these matrices can be found by substituting $-\theta$ for θ. With $\theta = 0$, the identity matrices are obtained.

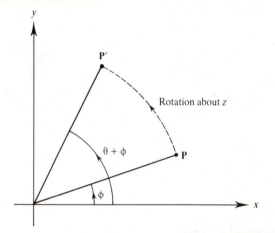

Rotation about z

Figure 4.13
Derivation of the rotation matrix. The rotation is viewed from the negative z axis and is in an anti-clockwise direction.

The 2D matrix for rotating about the origin may be obtained by removing the fourth row and column from the matrix R_z:

$$[x, y, 1]_{\text{rotated}} = [x, y, 1] \begin{bmatrix} \cos(\theta) & \sin(\theta) & 0 \\ -\sin(\theta) & \cos(\theta) & 0 \\ 0 & 0 & 1 \end{bmatrix}$$

Some care is required here regarding the signs. The formulation given obeys the conventions of a left-handed co-ordinate system. That is, if the x and y axes are drawn in the conventional 2D way, with the positive y axis pointing upwards and the positive x axis to the right, then the positive z axis points into the page. In this case, rotation is in a clockwise direction when viewed from the positive side of the axis.

Figure 4.13 shows a point **P** in the x–y plane viewed from the negative z axis. An anti-clockwise rotation of θ applied to it about the z axis, which is equivalent to a clockwise rotation viewed from the positive z axis, will transform it into **P**′:

$$P'_x = |\mathbf{P}| \cos(\theta + \phi)$$
$$= |\mathbf{P}| \cos(\phi) \cos(\theta) - |\mathbf{P}| \sin(\phi) \sin(\theta)$$
$$= P_x \cos(\theta) - P_y \sin(\theta)$$
$$P'_y = |\mathbf{P}| \sin(\theta + \phi)$$
$$= |\mathbf{P}| \cos(\phi) \sin(\theta) + |\mathbf{P}| \sin(\phi) \cos(\theta)$$
$$= P_x \sin(\theta) + P_y \cos(\theta)$$

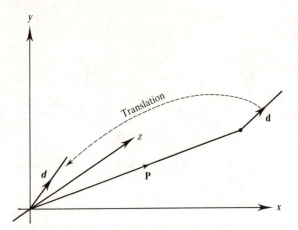

Figure 4.14

Rotation about a general line. The first step is to transform all points so that the line about which the rotation is to take place passes through the origin.

Since rotation is about the z axis, it is clear that $P'_z = P_z$. Hence, the transformation can be written in matrix form:

$$\mathbf{P'} = \mathbf{P} \cdot \begin{bmatrix} \cos(\theta) & \sin(\theta) & 0 & 0 \\ -\sin(\theta) & \cos(\theta) & 0 & 0 \\ 0 & 0 & 1 & 0 \\ 0 & 0 & 0 & 1 \end{bmatrix}$$

as required.

4.8.4 Rotation about a general line

Suppose that an object is to be rotated along the line:

$$\mathbf{L} = \mathbf{P} + \mu\mathbf{d}$$

where $\mathbf{P}$ is the position vector of a point on the line and $\mathbf{d}$ is a direction vector along the line. The first step is to move the point $\mathbf{P}$ to the origin, using the matrix:

$$A = \begin{bmatrix} 1 & 0 & 0 & 0 \\ 0 & 1 & 0 & 0 \\ 0 & 0 & 1 & 0 \\ -P_x & -P_y & -P_z & 1 \end{bmatrix}$$

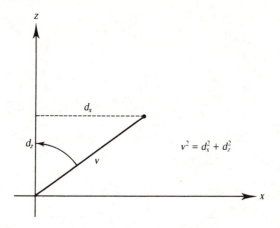

$$v^2 = d_x^2 + d_z^2$$

Figure 4.15

To rotate about a general line through the origin, the points are first transformed so that the line about which the rotation is to take place lies in the plane $x = 0$.

This is shown in Figure 4.14. Next, a rotation is made about the y axis so that **d** lies in the plane $x = 0$. A view of the line from the positive y direction is shown in Figure 4.15. Using the fact that **d** is defined by the distances along the ordinates $[d_x, d_y, d_z]$ and using the notation:

$$v^2 = d_x^2 + d_z^2$$

the rotation matrix is given by:

$$B = \begin{bmatrix} \dfrac{d_z}{v} & 0 & \dfrac{d_x}{v} & 0 \\ 0 & 1 & 0 & 0 \\ -\dfrac{d_x}{v} & 0 & \dfrac{d_z}{v} & 0 \\ 0 & 0 & 0 & 1 \end{bmatrix}$$

Note that the computation of the cos and sin functions has been avoided for this rotation by use of the direction cosines.

Figure 4.16 illustrates the position after this transformation. Note that the y ordinate is still d_y, since rotation about the y axis will not change it. Application of Pythagoras's theorem gives the new z ordinate, which is the value v that was computed previously. From this position, to get the direction vector lying along the z axis, a further rotation is needed. This time it is about the x axis:

$$C = \begin{bmatrix} 1 & 0 & 0 & 0 \\ 0 & \dfrac{v}{|\mathbf{d}|} & \dfrac{d_y}{|\mathbf{d}|} & 0 \\ 0 & -\dfrac{d_y}{|\mathbf{d}|} & \dfrac{v}{|\mathbf{d}|} & 0 \\ 0 & 0 & 0 & 1 \end{bmatrix}$$

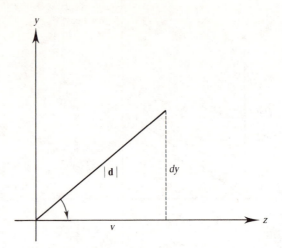

Figure 4.16
To rotate about a general line
on the plane $x = 0$, the points
are first transformed so that the
rotation is about the z axis. This
rotation may be carried out by
a standard transformation
matrix.

The rotation about the z axis is:

$$R = \begin{bmatrix} \cos(\theta) & \sin(\theta) & 0 & 0 \\ -\sin(\theta) & \cos(\theta) & 0 & 0 \\ 0 & 0 & 1 & 0 \\ 0 & 0 & 0 & 1 \end{bmatrix}$$

With the previous transforms, a general direction vector **d** was lined up with the z axis. So, taking the inverses, a complete transformation matrix is obtained:

$$T = A \cdot B \cdot C \cdot R \cdot C^{-1} \cdot B^{-1} \cdot A^{-1}$$

and, for each point that is to be rotated about the line, the transformed point is:

$$\mathbf{P'} = \mathbf{P} \cdot T$$

Again, these calculations for the overall transformation matrix T demonstrate the very important principle that the order in which the matrices are multiplied is critical.

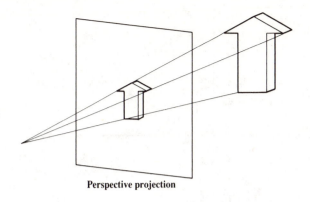

Perspective projection

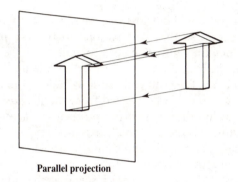

Parallel projection

Figure 4.17
In perspective projection, all the projectors meet at one point. In parallel projection, they meet at infinity.

4.9   PROJECTION

Projection is a transformation that reduces the dimensionality of space. Graphical projections reduce 3D space to two dimensions and allow the viewing of 3D scenes on a 2D display surface. Since most displays use planar viewing surfaces, the most commonly used projection surface is a plane. This will be referred to as the **plane of projection**, or the **viewing surface**.

Projection, just like all other transformations, is performed point by point. Straight lines, called **projectors**, are drawn through the points in 3D space and the projected point becomes the intersection between the projector and the plane of projection. The two most common projections are **parallel** and **perspective projections** (see Figure 4.17). For parallel projections, the projectors are all parallel to each other and they are defined by a

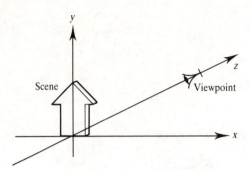

Figure 4.18
To view a general scene, it is necessary to specify a plane of projection and a direction of view.

direction vector **d**. For perspective projections, all projectors pass through one point, called the **centre of projection**, which will be designated by the position vector **C**.

It is possible, without loss of generality, to fix the direction of the plane of projection so that it is parallel to the x–y plane (the z axis is normal to the plane). If the plane of projection of a scene is not parallel to the x–y plane, then rotations can be used to line up the projection plane with the x–y plane. This will considerably reduce the algebra. Also, as a convention, the scene will be viewed from the negative towards the positive z direction; in other words, the projectors starting at the object are always drawn towards the negative z axis.

As already shown, difficulties may arise when the functional level is translated to the procedural level. One instance of this occurs with viewing transformations. Consider a graphics scene at the origin which is viewed from the centre of projection at **C** = [0, 0, 10] (see Figure 4.18). According to the required viewing transformation, the scene must be first translated by the vector [0, 0, −10], which produces the conditions shown in Figure 4.19. Now, the scene must be rotated by 180° so that the viewing vector is

Figure 4.19
By convention, perspective projection is done on to a plane parallel to the x–y plane, with the viewpoint at the origin. A simple translation of the object of Figure 4.18 along the z axis is required to place the viewpoint at the origin.

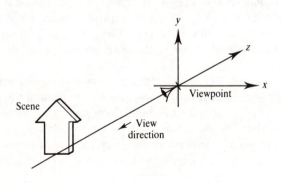

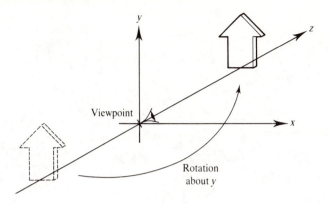

Figure 4.20
The conventional direction of view is along the positive z axis. If a rotation of 180° about the y axis is applied to the scene of Figure 4.19, the correct result is obtained.

directed towards the positive z axis. There are two ways of performing this rotation. If it is made around the y axis, the scene shown in Figure 4.20 results. Alternatively, rotation around the x axis, results in Figure 4.21. Here, the viewed scene is turned upside down. To restore the image, a further rotation of 180° is required around the z axis. At the procedural level, there is no method by which one rotation should be preferred to the other; thus, an inverted image may result. To avoid this problem, a test vector must be stored with the picture data. It points upwards before the transformations and is tested afterwards. This example gives a good indication of the practical difficulties encountered when implementing the graphics functional level, even for simple problems.

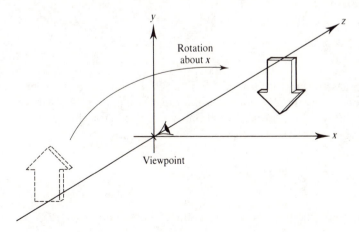

Figure 4.21
If a rotation of 180° about the x axis is applied to the scene of Figure 4.19, a mathematically correct solution is obtained; however, the picture is drawn upside down.

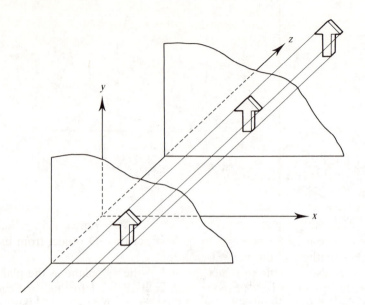

Figure 4.22

The size of an object in orthographic projection is independent of its distance from the plane of projection.

4.9.1 Orthographic projection

The simplest projection is a parallel projection for which the projectors are perpendicular to the plane of projection. As shown in Figure 4.22, the plane of projection may be translated along the projectors without any change in the projection image. The simplest is to fix the plane at the origin and translate the scene so that all objects are in the positive half-space. The projected points in the $z = 0$ plane with projectors in the direction of:

$$\mathbf{d} = -\mathbf{k}$$

where $\mathbf{k}$ is the unit vector in the z direction, will have the same x and y components as the 3D points, while the z component is set to zero. This can be shown by the line equation of the projector that goes through a given point $\mathbf{P} = [P_x, P_y, P_z]$:

$$\mathbf{L} = \mathbf{P} + \mu\mathbf{d} = [P_x, P_y, (P_z - \mu)]$$

which intersects the $z = 0$ plane at the projected point $[P_x, P_y, 0]$.

The same transformation may be expressed by a transformation matrix, R_z for parallel projection with projectors in the z direction:

$$R_z = \begin{bmatrix} 1 & 0 & 0 & 0 \\ 0 & 1 & 0 & 0 \\ 0 & 0 & 0 & 0 \\ 0 & 0 & 0 & 1 \end{bmatrix}$$

Observe that the elements in the third row and third column of this matrix are all zero. This yields a zero determinant, which is the condition for a singular matrix. This is reasonable because the projection transformation maps points in 3D space on to a 2D surface. The transformation has no inverse, since it is not possible to reconstruct the 3D object from its 2D projection without additional information.

It is also possible to select the y–z or the x–z plane as the plane of projection, in which case similar matrices are used for the orthogonal projection:

$$R_x = \begin{bmatrix} 0 & 0 & 0 & 0 \\ 0 & 1 & 0 & 0 \\ 0 & 0 & 1 & 0 \\ 0 & 0 & 0 & 1 \end{bmatrix} \qquad R_y = \begin{bmatrix} 1 & 0 & 0 & 0 \\ 0 & 0 & 0 & 0 \\ 0 & 0 & 1 & 0 \\ 0 & 0 & 0 & 1 \end{bmatrix}$$

Orthographic projection is a familiar form of representation in architectural plan and elevation drawings and in mechanical drawings.

4.9.2   Oblique projection

If parallel projectors that are not perpendicular to the plane of projection are chosen, an oblique projection is obtained. The plane of projection is chosen to be the $z = 0$ plane and the projectors are defined by a direction vector $\mathbf{d} = [d_x, d_y, d_z]$ where $d_z \neq 0$. The projector drawn from a given point $\mathbf{P_0}$ is defined by the vector equation:

$$\mathbf{L} = \mathbf{P_0} - \mu\mathbf{d}$$

and the projected point, where $z = 0$, is given by the value of μ:

$$\mu = \frac{z_0}{d_z}$$

Substituting this value into the equation of the projector gives the following values for the x and y co-ordinates of the projected point, $\mathbf{P_0'}$:

$$x_0' = x_0 - z_0\left(\frac{d_x}{d_z}\right) \quad \text{and} \quad y_0' = y_0 - z_0\left(\frac{d_y}{d_z}\right)$$

and the transformation matrix for an oblique projection is equal to:

$$R_o = \begin{bmatrix} 1 & 0 & 0 & 0 \\ 0 & 1 & 0 & 0 \\ -\dfrac{d_x}{d_z} & -\dfrac{d_y}{d_z} & 0 & 0 \\ 0 & 0 & 0 & 1 \end{bmatrix}$$

4.9.3 Perspective projection

Perspective projection uses projectors that all go through a fixed point, the centre of projection, which is sometimes referred to as the eye or viewpoint. The centre of projection is normally placed on the opposite side of the plane of projection from the object being projected. Thus, perspective projection works like a pin-hole camera, which forces the light rays to go through one single point. The difference in the case of the camera is that the image is behind the centre of projection; therefore, it is inverted.

To simplify the algebra, the first step is to apply a translation of the scene so that the centre of projection is at the origin. Then, rotations are applied until the plane of projection becomes parallel to the x–y axis. This arrangement is shown in Figure 4.23. All projectors go through the origin; therefore, the vector equation of a projector that goes through point $\mathbf{P_0} = [x_0, y_0, z_0]$ is given by:

$$\mathbf{L} = \mu\mathbf{P_0}$$

The projection plane must be placed between the point and the origin and is assumed to be at a distance f from the origin. The equation of this plane is $z = f$ and, solving the vector equation for μ, gives:

$$\mu = \frac{f}{z_0}$$

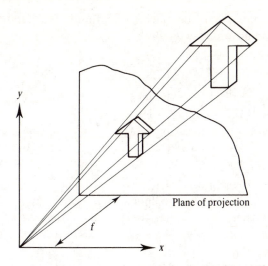

Figure 4.23
A perspective projection is normally computed with the centre of projection at the origin and the viewing plane given by $z = f$, where f is a positive constant. The size of the image depends on the value of f.

which, when substituted into the equation of the projector, gives the co-ordinates of the projected point, $\mathbf{P'_0}$:

$$x'_0 = \frac{fx_0}{z_0} \quad \text{and} \quad y'_0 = \frac{fy_0}{z_0}$$

The perspective transformation becomes particularly simple when the distance f is equal to 1, when the co-ordinates of the projected point are equal to the x and y co-ordinates of each point divided by the z co-ordinate. The same result can be derived by drawing the projector in two dimensions and using similar triangles. The matrix representation of a perspective transformation is given by:

$$R_p = \begin{bmatrix} 1 & 0 & 0 & 0 \\ 0 & 1 & 0 & 0 \\ 0 & 0 & 1 & \dfrac{1}{f} \\ 0 & 0 & 0 & 0 \end{bmatrix}$$

This is the first time that the fourth column of the transformation matrix has been different from the column vector $[0, 0, 0, 1]^{\mathrm{T}}$. In fact, the elements in the fourth column may be used for general perspective projections. Taking the centre of projection as the origin and having the plane of projection aligned with the x–y axis makes this form of the matrix particularly simple. It can be shown that this is the correct matrix by applying it to the position vector $\mathbf{P_0}$:

$$[x_0, y_0, z_0, 1] \cdot \begin{bmatrix} 1 & 0 & 0 & 0 \\ 0 & 1 & 0 & 0 \\ 0 & 0 & 1 & \dfrac{1}{f} \\ 0 & 0 & 0 & 0 \end{bmatrix} = \left[x_0, y_0, z_0, \dfrac{z_0}{f} \right]$$

According to the rules of homogeneous co-ordinates, 3D co-ordinates are obtained by normalizing the four-dimensional vector (multiply its components by f/z_0), giving $[fx_0/z_0, fy_0/z_0, f, 1]$, which is the correct answer.

4.9.4 Vanishing points

Artists and architects have been constructing perspective views on a 2D surface without referring to three dimensions by using **vanishing points**. They rely on the ways in which a perspective projection handles parallel lines. There are two rules:

(1)   The perspective projection of parallel lines is also parallel if the lines are parallel to the plane of projection.

(2)   The perspective projection of parallel lines all pass through one point in the plane of projection if the lines are not parallel to the plane of projection.

Using three vanishing points, the perspective projection of a house is shown in Figure 4.24. The rectangular volume of the house has four families of parallel lines. The vertical lines are parallel to the plane of projection ($z = f$) and, therefore, remain parallel and vertical. The lines along the length of the house meet at one vanishing point at the right, while the lines along the width of the house meet at the other vanishing point. The two visible edges of the roof's gable end meet at a third vanishing point, which is outside of the area of the diagram.

The vanishing point produced by the perspective projection of a family of parallel lines can be calculated by the vector equation of lines that are all parallel to a direction vector $\mathbf{h}$:

$\mathbf{L} = \mathbf{P} + \mu\mathbf{h}$

where each parallel line is defined by a point in three dimensions, $\mathbf{P}$. To find the vanishing point for the projected lines, the perspective projection

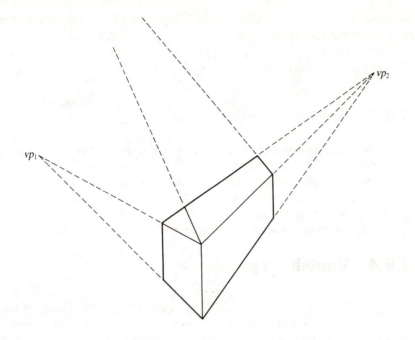

Figure 4.24
Architects use vanishing points to draw parallel lines in perspective projection. All lines that are parallel in a 3D scene will meet at a unique point in the perspective projection of that scene or will be parallel, as is the case with the vertical lines shown here.

of a point on the line is found by calculating the z component of any point on the line:

$$L_z = P_z + \mu h_z$$

and from this the x and y co-ordinates of the projected points:

$$L'_x = \frac{fL_x}{L_z} = \frac{f(P_x + \mu h_x)}{P_z + \mu h_z}$$

$$L'_y = \frac{fL_y}{L_z} = \frac{f(P_y + \mu h_y)}{P_z + \mu h_z}$$

The vanishing point in 3D space, where parallel lines meet, is at infinity. This point is found by taking the limit:

$$\mu \rightarrow \text{infinity}$$

which yields:

$$L'_x = \frac{fh_x}{h_z}$$

$$L'_y = \frac{fh_y}{h_z}$$

Both these expressions are independent of the point **P**, which specifies the location of the line in 3D space. Hence, as long as $h_z \neq 0$ (the line is not parallel to the x–y plane), all lines parallel to the direction vector **h** will meet at the vanishing point $[fh_x/h_z, fh_y/h_z]$.

4.9.5 Back projection

Many graphics algorithms are designed in image space; that is, they deal with the projected 2D image. A projection of a line segment is a line segment in two dimensions. When a point is specified on the projected image, often, we would like to find the 3D co-ordinates of the point. This is done using back projection.

Suppose a line segment is specified by the following two points in 3D space:

$$\mathbf{P_1} = [x_1, y_1, z_1] \quad \text{and} \quad \mathbf{P_2} = [x_2, y_2, z_2]$$

The projected line segment is given by points $\mathbf{P_1'}$ and $\mathbf{P_2'}$, which can be considered as 2D position vectors, or 3D vectors with their z components set equal to f. Unfortunately, it is futile to try to solve the vector/matrix equation using the projection matrix because, ultimately, the transformation matrix would have to be inverted and, as is known, the matrix is singular. On the other hand, it is possible to calculate the intersection between a projector passing through a point $\mathbf{P'}$ with the original 3D line segment. The projected point is given by:

$$\mathbf{P'} = \mathbf{P_1'} + \rho(\mathbf{P_2'} - \mathbf{P_1'})$$

The equation for the projector that passes through the origin is given by:

$$\mathbf{L} = v\mathbf{P'}$$

and the equation for the intersection point is given by:

$$v\left[\mathbf{P_1'} + \rho(\mathbf{P_2'} - \mathbf{P_1'})\right] = \mathbf{P_1} + \mu(\mathbf{P_2} - \mathbf{P_1})$$

The equation may be expressed in terms of $\mathbf{P_1}$ and $\mathbf{P_2}$:

$$vf\left[\frac{\mathbf{P_1}}{z_1} + \rho\left(\frac{\mathbf{P_2}}{z_2} - \frac{\mathbf{P_1}}{z_1}\right)\right] = \mathbf{P_1} + \mu(\mathbf{P_2} - \mathbf{P_1})$$

From the z component of this vector equation, the following is obtained:

$$vf = z_1 + \mu(z_2 - z_1)$$

Substituting this value into either the x or y component of the vector equation and, after some considerable algebraic manipulations, μ is obtained as a function of ρ:

$$\mu = \frac{\rho z_1}{z_2 + \rho(z_1 - z_2)}$$

which is independent of the location of the plane of projection $(z = f)$ and the x or the y co-ordinates of the end points of the line segment. This equation can be tested with the points $\mathbf{P}_1$, when both μ and ρ are equal to 0, and $\mathbf{P}_2$, when both μ and ρ are equal to 1. A more compact way of expressing this relationship is:

$$\mu = \frac{1}{1 + \left(\frac{z_2}{z_1}\right)\left(\frac{1}{\rho} - 1\right)}$$

The half-point of the projected line segment $(\rho = \frac{1}{2})$ is back projected to the half-point of the original line segment $(\mu = \frac{1}{2})$ only if $z_1 = z_2$.

This chapter presented the properties of 2D and 3D space using the tools of vector and matrix algebra. Vector equations provide a compact and often easily visualized functional description for graphics problems. They can be easily translated to Cartesian co-ordinates and so to reliable algebraic procedures. Direction vectors and the functionality of variable position vectors are used for the representation of lines, surfaces and objects in the rest of this book.

Exercises

4.1 Find the unit direction vector in the direction of the line joining point $\mathbf{P_0} = [-1, 5]$ to $\mathbf{P_1} = [3, 2]$.

4.2 Find the coefficients (A, B, C) of the Cartesian line equation $Ax + By + C = 0$ for the line joining points $\mathbf{P_0}$ and $\mathbf{P_1}$ defined in Exercise 4.1.

4.3 A 2D line is defined by points $\mathbf{P_1} = [1, 4]$ and $\mathbf{P_2} = [4, 1]$ in the form shown in Equation (4.6). Calculate the value of the parameter μ for the points $[0, 5]$, $[3, 2]$ and $[6, -1]$, checking that the points do lie on the line.

4.4 Calculate the intersection point, if any, between the line segments joining the points $[-1, 0]$ to $[1.5, 1]$ and $[2, 0]$ to $[1, 3]$.

4.5 A plane is defined by three points $[1, 0, -1]$, $[2, 5, 3]$ and $[3, -1, 2]$. Calculate the coefficients (A, B, C, D) of its Cartesian equation $Ax + By + Cz + D = 0$.

4.6 Find the shortest distance of the plane of Exercise 4.5 from the origin.

4.7 Find the line of intersection of the two planes that pass through the origin and have normal vectors $[1, 2, 5]$ and $[3, -1, 2]$.

4.8 Calculate the transformation matrix that rotates points through $90°$ about the line through the origin in the direction $[1, 1, 1]$.

4.9 If the centre of projection is at the origin and the plane of projection is $z = 5$, what homogeneous co-ordinate results by projection of the point $[3, 5, 20]$ using the matrix $\mathbf{R_p}$ of Section 4.9.3. What is the corresponding Cartesian co-ordinate?

4.10 For the arrangement of Exercise 4.9, what is the vanishing point for the family of lines parallel to the direction $[2, 3, -1]$?

Problems

4.11 Given two points $\mathbf{P_1}$ and $\mathbf{P_2}$ in 2D space, determine the vector equation for the line that bisects the line segment between $\mathbf{P_1}$ and $\mathbf{P_2}$ and is perpendicular to it. Express the constants A, B, and C of the line equation $Ax + By + C = 0$ in terms of the known ordinates x_1, y_1, x_2 and y_2.

4.12 Given three points $\mathbf{P_1}$, $\mathbf{P_2}$ and $\mathbf{P_3}$ in 2D space, determine the vector equation of the line that goes through point $\mathbf{P_1}$ and bisects the angle between the two lines connecting points $\mathbf{P_1}$ to $\mathbf{P_2}$ and $\mathbf{P_1}$ to $\mathbf{P_3}$. Determine the Cartesian line equation constants A, B, and C.

4.13 A line in 2D space can be defined by one position vector, say $\mathbf{P}$, by stating that the line goes though the endpoint of the position vector and is perpendicular to it. Determine vector equations for the intersection of two lines defined by two position vectors $\mathbf{P_1}$ and $\mathbf{P_2}$. Calculate the intersection ordinates in terms of the ordinates of the position vectors.

4.14 Derive a vector equation in 2D space for a line that is given by a direction vector $\mathbf{d}$, a position vector $\mathbf{P_0}$ and a distance s. The line is parallel to $\mathbf{d}$ and is s distance away from point $\mathbf{P_0}$. (There are two such lines.)

4.15 Given three points $\mathbf{P_1}$, $\mathbf{P_2}$ and $\mathbf{P_3}$ in 2D space, determine the centre point $\mathbf{C}$ and the radius r of a circle passing through the three points by using vector equations.

4.16 Extend Exercise 4.4 to 3D space by finding the equation of a plane with $\mathbf{d}$ as its normal and with s as the shortest distance away from the 3D point $\mathbf{P_0}$.

4.17 Points contained within a rotated rectangle in 2D space can be defined by one of its vertices, say $\mathbf{V_1}$, and two perpendicular unit vectors, b and w, with the following equation:

$$\mathbf{R} = \mathbf{V_1} + \alpha b + \beta w$$

and two inequalities:

$$0 \leqslant \alpha \leqslant B \quad \text{and} \quad 0 \leqslant \beta \leqslant W$$

The rectangle has length B and width W. Given a point $\mathbf{P}$ in 2D space, devise a vector method to determine whether the point is contained within the rectangle.

4.18 Extend the method of Problem 4.17 to three dimensions. In this case, a line is given by a point P_0 and a unit direction vector d:

$$\mathbf{P} = \mathbf{P_0} + \mu d$$

and the vector equation determines whether the intersection point between the line and the plane of the rectangle is contained within the rectangle. From the vector equation, determine the necessary calculations to make this test.

4.19 A plane can be defined in 3D space by one position vector, say $\mathbf{P}$, by stating that the plane goes through the endpoint of the vector and is perpendicular to it. Express the intersection of this plane and a general line that goes through the origin; namely, d where d is a known unit direction vector. Show how the Cartesian ordinates are calculated for this intersection point.

4.20 Calculate the components of the transformation matrix that rotates a general unit direction vector d into the direction of the $+z$ axis. Check your result by multiplying the d vector with the matrix that should give the vector $[0, 0, 1]$.

4.21 Determine the algorithm for the special cases in the 3D ray piercing test.

4.22 A general non-convex viewport is given by a list of edges or a polyline (in normalized device co-ordinates). Construct an algorithm that calculates the combined viewport of two intersecting viewports. The algorithm produces a list of n edges where n is zero if the viewports are disjoint. The new edge list is equal to the list of one of the two viewports when it is contained entirely within the other. Make sure that your algorithm works for all cases.

4.23 Under what conditions can the order of rotation and scaling be interchanged?

4.24 Derive equations for the general perspective projection problem when the centre of projection is given by the position vector $\mathbf{C}$ and the plane of projection by the unit direction vector d so that the equation for the plane of projection is:

$$(\mathbf{P} - (\mathbf{C} + fd)) \cdot d = 0$$

The x axis in the projection plane can be indicated by x', which is in the plane that contains the x axis of the fixed co-ordinate system and passes through the point $\mathbf{C} + fd$. Suggest the calculations required to determine the projected point x_0' and y_0' of a general point $\mathbf{P_0}$. Use vector equations to solve this problem.

4.25 Repeat Problem 4.24 by first calculating the components of the matrix that performs the defined general perspective projection.

4.26 Derive the equation given for the back projection in Section 4.9 and express ρ as a function of μ.

Project

4.27 Design and implement a preprocessor program that accepts vectors and matrices as well as the following operators: add, subtract, dot product, cross-product, modulus, transpose, vector/matrix multiply, matrix/matrix multiply, matrix inversion, calculation of the determinant. The output of the program should be an executable source code in your favourite language.

5

Picture Generation Using Solid Polyhedra

The description of a solid volume as space bounded by a large number of planar polygonal facets is a popular method in computer graphics applications, especially in computer-aided design and engineering. Planar polygons produce straight line edges and point vertices when the 3D scene is projected on to the 2D plane of the display. Solid objects can be specified as a list of 3D vertex co-ordinates and topological data that defines how edges are connected between vertices and how facets are bounded by edges. The problems of generating the projected image include the transformation and projection of edges, their clipping to a 2D viewport and the determination of those portions of the objects that are visible (or hidden) by the objects themselves. If lines are used to draw the projected picture, then hidden line elimination algorithms are employed; these are described for both the simple case of a single convex object and for a general scene containing a number of arbitrarily shaped objects. If the surface-rendering capabilities of a raster scan device are used, then the pictures are generated by visible surface algorithms. These involve the determination, for each pixel on the display, the object surface visible for the viewer at that pixel. The z-buffer, the scan line and the area subdivision algorithms for solving the visible surface problem, are discussed in detail. Since there may be millions of pixels and thousands of facets, methods must be found that improve the efficiency of visible surface algorithms. Bounding volumes, sorting and exploiting coherence are all well-known practical techniques which are outlined.

5.1 INTRODUCTION

A common requirement of computer graphics systems is the display of graphic scenes consisting of a collection of 3D solid objects. For some applications of this type, a graphics system must effectively simulate a video camera. Thus, calculated and displayed picture colours and intensities should have a good approximation to the real video image, as seen by the camera. Other applications may be less demanding on this aspect of realism. For example, engineering drawings may require representations such as cross-sections, cut-out views and orthographic or perspective projections. Many aspects of this picture-generation problem have to be solved before an acceptable representation of the scene can be viewed on a graphics display device. Firstly, numerical representations of the objects must be chosen. Secondly, illumination of the scene and light reflection models for the surfaces of the objects have to be devised. Thirdly, the viewing functions, such as the viewing position, the viewing angle and the methods of projection, must be decided upon. These different aspects will be examined in this and subsequent chapters. This chapter concentrates particularly on the problem of determining which parts of a complex picture are visible from the viewer's point of view.

The problem of determining the visible parts of a complex scene is often referred to as the **hidden line** or **hidden surface** problem in computer graphics, for historical reasons. The earliest computer-generated pictures of objects were line drawings, since at that time the fastest display devices were vector-generating displays. Objects were represented by straight-line edges and the problem became the calculation of those portions of these edges that were visible (or hidden) to the viewer. Groups of edges of the same object defined planar facets, which could hide other edges or sections of edges positioned behind them. Many algorithms have been proposed for the removal (or the non-drawing) of hidden portions of edges. The approaches used have been governed by the type of output device (line drawing or raster scan), the data structure and by the author's ingenuity. The famous review article, 'Characterisation of Ten Hidden Surface Algorithms' by Sutherland, Sproull and Schumaker (1974) covers many aspects of the early work.

The replacement of vector displays with raster scan display devices, which can produce shaded colour intensities at each pixel, shifted the interest from the elimination of *hidden edges* to the determination of *visible surfaces*. In this case, the major problem became the selection of the object which contributes its surface illumination value to a given pixel on the display screen. More recent developments have meant that the use of straight edges and facets to represent solid objects could be replaced with geometrical descriptions of solids constructed from spheres, cylinders, cones and other mathematically defined continuous shapes, for which the visible surface determination is critically important.

As a closely related problem to visible lines, clipping in two dimensions will be discussed first. Next, picture generation will be examined by the viewing problem; that is, the problem of specifying which parts of the objects appear and how their exact locations on the screen are determined. Finally, the determination of the visible portions will be outlined. Obviously, the topic of hidden lines and visible surfaces is a very extensive one. So, to avoid getting lost in the details of various algorithms, determining the hidden edges of solid faceted objects will be demonstrated by using two algorithms. The first is a simple method that can be applied to a single convex object. The second handles a completely general multi-object scene, but it may be too slow for a large number of objects. Later, when the determination of visible surfaces is discussed, other classes of algorithms, which are practical and highly efficient for the generation of complex graphics scenes, will be discussed. Not all possible algorithms will be discussed; rather, the ones that have stood the test of time and remained practical over the years are emphasized. These are algorithms that are still in use, are applicable to raster scan displays, or are easily implementable by VLSI devices.

5.2   CLIPPING IN TWO DIMENSIONS

An important problem to be solved in the development of hidden line or visible surface algorithms is to determine which sections of a line are contained within an arbitrary polygon in 2D space. The objective is to determine the visibility of a distant line, which may be covered by a facet when they are projected into two dimensions. This problem amounts to a simple case of hidden line elimination, sometimes called a covering problem, and is solved by drawing those sections of the line that are outside the polygon. However, if this problem is viewed by looking through the polygon, which forms the boundary of a window or a viewport, then the problem is a clipping one. In this case, those portions of the line that are contained within the polygon are drawn. In terms of the algorithms involved, the problems are essentially the same.

5.2.1   Clipping to areas bounded by closed general polygons

To solve the problem in general, it is necessary to consider concave polygons, rather than the simpler case of convex or rectangular polygons. General polygons can easily result from the projection of facets of concave

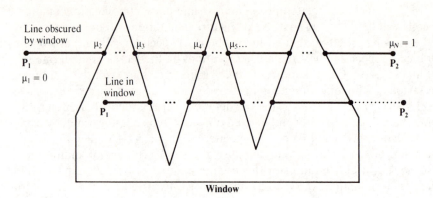

Figure 5.1

Clipping of a line with a convex polygon produces an ordered set of scalar parameter values (μ_i) which determine alternating visible and hidden line segments.

polyhedra. Moreover, systems that allow multiple windows on one screen are becoming common, and overlapping windows will generate clipping boundaries that may be concave.

The solution to the general problem consists of two parts. The first requires the intersection between the line to be clipped and all the boundary lines of the polygon. These calculations involve the intersection of line segments, which has already been discussed in Section 4.4. For each intersection found, the parameter value μ_i is saved. This defines the intersection point on the line as:

$$\mathbf{P_i} = \mathbf{P_1} + \mu_i(\mathbf{P_2} - \mathbf{P_1})$$

When all intersections have been found, the μ_i values are sorted into ascending order.

The second part is to determine the visibility. A test is carried out to see if the endpoint $\mu = 0$ is contained within the polygon. This may be done using the ray test described in Section 4.4. If it is, then the contained spans of the line are given by $\{0, \mu_1\}, \{\mu_2, \mu_3\}, \{\mu_4, \mu_5\}, \ldots$. The values of $\mu_1, \mu_2, \ldots$, are the ordered intersection points, as shown in Figure 5.1. If the point $\mu = 0$ is not contained within the polygon, the contained spans are given by $\{\mu_1, \mu_2\}, \{\mu_3, \mu_4\}, \ldots$. Thus, the algorithm is very similar to the scan line polygon-filling algorithm already considered (see Chapter 3).

Section 4.4 dealt with the special case of when the testing ray was parallel to the x axis and passed through one or more vertices. A similar situation is encountered here, except that the testing ray, which is the clipped line, can have a general direction. The test at the vertices must be made whether the neighbouring vertices lie on the same or different sides of the line. This is a simple test because the general equation of the line:

$$Ax + By + C = 0$$

Algorithm 5.1

Clipping to a concave polygon.

```
{ Sort the polygon vertices into order }
{ Eliminate the common vertex from adjacent edges which are collinear }
for i = 0 to NoOfEdges do
begin
    { Find the intersection of the edge [Vi, Vi+1] with the line to be clipped [P1, P2] }
    (* μ is the parameter value of the intersection with [P1, P2] *)
    (* ν is the parameter value of the intersection with [Vi, Vi+1] *)
    if 0 < μ < 1
    then begin
            if 0 < ν < 1
            then add μ to the intersection list
            else if ν = 0
                    then if DIFFERENT_SIDES(Vi−1, Vi+1)
                            then add μ to the intersection list
        end
            (* Do not test for the special case ν = 1 since it will also appear on the next edge as ν = 0 *)
end;
{ Sort the intersection list into ascending order of μ }
if CONTAINED(P1, Polygon)
then add μ = 0 at the head of the intersection list
{ Draw alternate spans of μ on the list }
```

can be used. It can be shown that $A = y_1 - y_2$, $B = x_2 - x_1$, and $C = x_1y_2 - y_1x_2$ where $\mathbf{P_1} = [x_1, y_1]$ and $\mathbf{P_2} = [x_2, y_2]$. If the clipped line passes through vertex $\mathbf{V_i}$, and not $\mathbf{V_{i-1}}$ and $\mathbf{V_{i+1}}$, then the following test determines whether the vertex should be counted as a crossing point:

$$\mathbf{sign}(Ax_{i-1} + By_{i-1} + C) \neq \mathbf{sign}(Ax_{i+1} + By_{i+1} + C)$$

If the line passes through $\mathbf{V_{i-1}}$ or $\mathbf{V_{i+1}}$ as well, then a test is made for $\mathbf{V_{i-2}}$ or $\mathbf{V_{i+2}}$, but not for both. The visibility of those spans of the line that overlap the edges of the polygon may not be calculated correctly with this method, but by assuming that the line is always clipped by the border of the polygon, the borders can be drawn after the line has been drawn. These calculations are very similar to those shown in Section 4.4. The clipping algorithm is summarized in Algorithm 5.1.

Algorithm 5.1 may be simply extended to cover other special cases, such as polygons containing holes, that can be decomposed into separate clipping and covering problems. Problems resulting from multiple windows overlapping can be similarly decomposed.

5.2.2   Clipping to rectangular windows

A special case of the clipping and covering algorithm occurs when the polygon is rectangular. This is common for windowing applications, but rare in cases where the polygon results from the projection of a facet in 3D space. The most common algorithm is the one attributed to Sutherland and Cohen. Here, the lines bounding the window are extended to infinity to divide the Cartesian space into nine regions, as illustrated in Figure 5.2. Each region is labelled with a four-bit binary number, or code, which is derived as follows:

> bit 3 is set in the region above the window
>
> bit 2 is set in the region below the window
>
> bit 1 is set in the region right of the window
>
> bit 0 is set in the region left of the window

The two endpoints of the line to be clipped are identified as belonging to two respective regions, with binary codes C_1 and C_2. A simple test is performed on the region codes:

> **if** (C_1 **bitwise AND** C_2) $\neq 0$, **then** the line is totally invisible
>
> **if** (C_1 **bitwise OR** C_2) $= 0$, **then** the line is totally visible

If neither of these conditions is met, then further processing is necessary. This is done by computing the intersection of the line and one of the line segments bounding the window. If an intersection is found, then the algorithm is called recursively, with the intersection point replacing the original. The line segment may be selected by examining the code of the area where the point to be replaced lies:

> If bit 3 set, then compute the intersection with the top of the window
>
> If bit 2 set, then compute the intersection with the bottom
>
> . . .

The intersections can be calculated from the window boundaries, $x = $ constant or $y = $ constant, which specify one of the co-ordinates. The other co-ordinate may be computed using the parametric line equation.

An alternative way of finding the intersections when clipping to a rectangular window is known as **midpoint subdivision**. This algorithm is

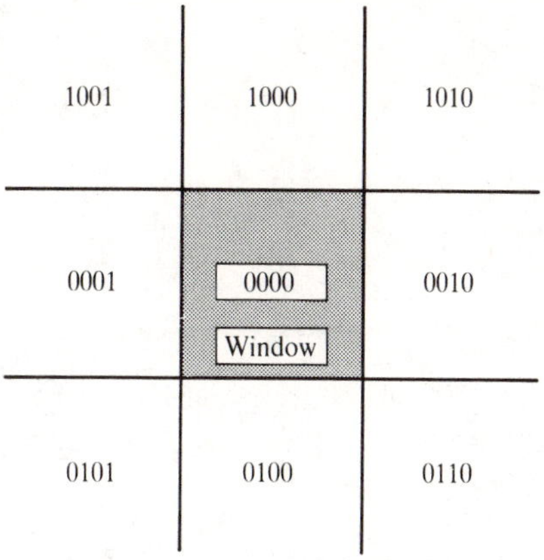

```
1001          1000          1010


0001         | 0000 |       0010
             | Window |

0101          0100          0110
```

Figure 5.2
When a line segment is clipped by a rectangular window, a simple logical operation on two binary codes derived from the location of the endpoints determines total visibility or invisibility. The binary codes are assigned according to the location of the endpoints.

basically a binary search, which can be easily implemented in hardware. The search starts with the two endpoints being on opposite sides of the x = constant or y = constant borders. The sum of the two endpoint co-ordinates is halved (one add and one left shift for each co-ordinate) and then the midpoint is tested. Depending on the side of the border on which the midpoint lies, one of the endpoints is replaced by the midpoint and the search continues until the intersection point is found. The improvements in the speed of hardware for arithmetic operations, as well as their decreasing cost, have made this method largely redundant.

The implementation of clipping to rectangular windows is now so important in the creation of multiple window systems that it is likely to become a hardware feature of future graphics workstations. However, it is included here because it may still be important to the graphics programmer in optimizing hidden line problems. For a concave polygon, with many edges, the general Algorithm 5.1 requires the computation of many intersections. If a complex polygon is to be tested with many different lines, it may prove beneficial to place a rectangular bounding box around it and then use Sutherland–Cohen clipping to eliminate lines that can have no intersection, before proceeding to the main part of the algorithm.

5.3 SOLID OBJECTS DEFINED BY PLANAR POLYGONAL FACETS

This section considers solid objects defined by planar polygonal facets. The numerical representation of solid-faceted objects is relatively simple – a convenient representation of these objects was discussed in Chapter 2 and

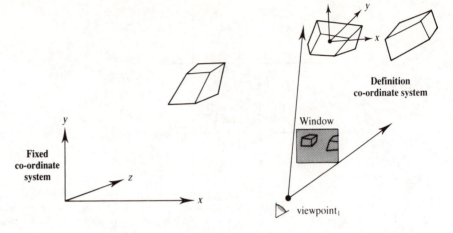

Figure 5.3
Similar types of object in a 3D
scene can be handled by one
fixed or viewing co-ordinate
and several definition
co-ordinate systems. An
instance of an object is defined
by translation, rotation and
scaling transformations while
numerical data such as vertex
co-ordinates are given in the
definition co-ordinate system.

will be used in subsequent discussions. The numerical data (real numbers) consists of a list of vertices for each object. The topological data (pointers) describes which vertices form edges and which edges form facets. A list of outside normals will also be added to the numerical data. If such a list is not available, the vector product of two edges belonging to the facet defines the normal vector, and a test like those described in Chapter 4 will identify the outward sense. Alternatively, the order of the edges can be chosen in such a way that the cross-product between two successive edges always generates the outside normal vector.

The viewing and displaying of the objects involves 3D transformations, scaling, clipping and projections. The vertices are defined in the world or user co-ordinate system (see Chapter 3), which may have real spatial dimensions such as inches, miles and so on. In cases where there are several instances of the same object type in a scene, it is convenient to define one fixed world co-ordinate system, in which the whole scene resides, and a special **definition** co-ordinate system for each object type. This means that each object has its vertices defined with respect to its individual co-ordinate system. An instance of any object may be created by using scaling and rotation operations with respect to its definition co-ordinate system, followed by a translation within the fixed world co-ordinate system (see Figure 5.3). The position of the viewer, the direction in which the viewer looks at the scene and the viewing angles are defined within the fixed world co-ordinate system. Since a window is needed for translating user co-ordinates to normalized device co-ordinates, a projection plane, sometimes called a **front clipping plane**, is also used. The size of the window and its distance from the viewer are defined in user co-ordinates. Sometimes, a **back clipping plane** is also included. Objects beyond the back clipping plane become invisible, saving computation time.

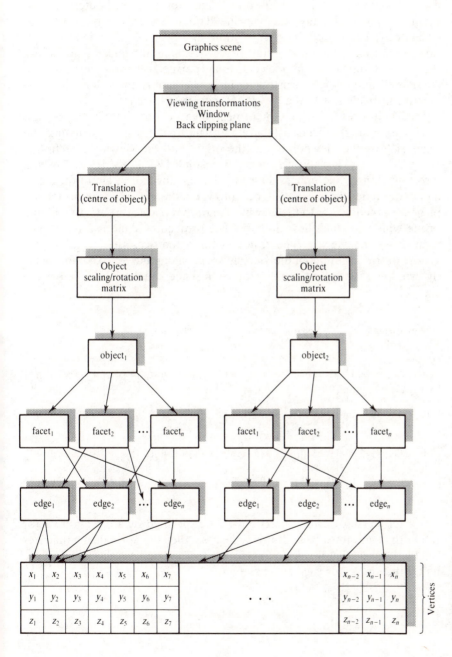

Figure 5.4

The structure of the graphical database is hierarchical. At the bottom is the 3D numerical data for the vertices specified in the definition co-ordinate system. On top of the vertices, the topological instructions prescribe how vertices produce edges and edges form facets. Further up there are object transformations while at the top a single viewing transformation is used for all objects.

Figure 5.4 shows the structure of the database. At the bottom, there is a list of 3D points that define the vertices of the object in its own definition co-ordinate system. The topological data defines the object by describing how the edges and facets are formed. For each object, a scaling and a rotation matrix allow the object to be transformed. The position of each object is given in world co-ordinates for the fixed reference co-ordinate system. Finally, the viewing data refers to the reference co-ordinate system as well. Transformations and projections define the relationship between the object data (the vertices) and the image data (where the vertices appear to the viewer). Only perspective projections will be considered here, since an orthographic projection is equivalent to a perspective projection with the viewpoint moved far away.

The process by which the projected vertices of a graphics scene are calculated is summarized in Figure 5.5. The first step is to normalize the scene so that the viewpoint is at the origin and the viewing direction is along the z axis. Let the viewer be at position $[V_x, V_y, V_z]$, viewing in a direction along a line that, when rotated by an angle of θ_x about the x axis and by θ_y about the y axis, will point towards the $+z$ axis. The projection plane is perpendicular to the viewing vector that passes through the middle of the window, which has width W. The projection plane is a distance F away from the viewer. The transformation matrices that translate the viewer to the origin, align the viewing vector along the $+z$ axis, normalize the window size and make the projection plane equal to the $z = 1$ plane are:

Move viewer to origin	Rotate around the X axis	Rotate around the Y axis	Scale

$$
\begin{bmatrix} 1 & 0 & 0 & 0 \\ 0 & 1 & 0 & 1 \\ 0 & 0 & 1 & 0 \\ -V_x & -V_y & -V_z & 1 \end{bmatrix} \cdot
\begin{bmatrix} 1 & 0 & 0 & 0 \\ 0 & \cos(\theta_x) & -\sin(\theta_x) & 0 \\ 0 & \sin(\theta_x) & \cos(\theta_x) & 0 \\ 0 & 0 & 0 & 1 \end{bmatrix} \cdot
\begin{bmatrix} \cos(\theta_y) & 0 & \sin(\theta_y) & 0 \\ 0 & 1 & 0 & 0 \\ -\sin(\theta_y) & 0 & \cos(\theta_y) & 0 \\ 0 & 0 & 0 & 1 \end{bmatrix} \cdot
\begin{bmatrix} \frac{1}{W} & 0 & 0 & 0 \\ 0 & \frac{1}{W} & 0 & 0 \\ 0 & 0 & \frac{1}{F} & 0 \\ 0 & 0 & 0 & 1 \end{bmatrix}
$$

Often, the viewing direction will be specified by a direction vector rather than viewing angles. If this is the case, then the normalizing matrices can be derived from the direction cosines as described in Section 4.8. If the unit direction vector is given as d, then:

$$
\theta_x = -\arctan\left(\frac{d_y}{d_z}\right)
$$

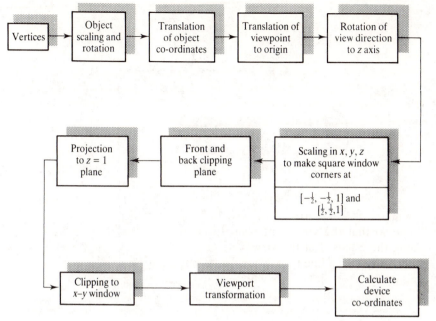

Figure 5.5
The viewing pipeline for wire-frame models shows the required calculations that convert vertex co-ordinates to pixel numbers. The calculations include projection, object transformations, clipping and normalization transformations.

or:

$$\sin(\theta_x) = -\frac{d_y}{v} \quad \text{and} \quad \cos(\theta_x) = \frac{d_z}{v}$$

where:

$$v = \sqrt{(d_y^2 + d_z^2)}$$

Similarly:

$$\theta_y = \arctan\left(\frac{d_x}{v}\right)$$

and:

$$\sin(\theta_y) = d_x \quad \text{and} \quad \cos(\theta_y) = v$$

After multiplication, the four matrices produce one combined viewing transformation matrix. Since separate translations, rotations and scalings are allowed for each object, these transformation matrices can be

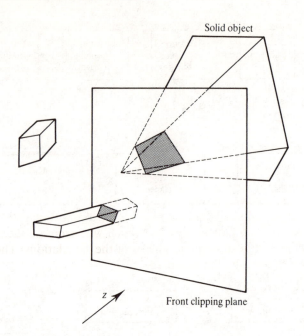

Solid object

z

Front clipping plane

Figure 5.6
Objects partially clipped by the
front clipping plane create new
vertices, edges and even facets
which have to be computed
and included in the object
database.

multiplied with the viewing matrix to produce one combined transformation matrix per object. This combined matrix is then used to calculate the normalized vertex co-ordinates for each object. Assuming a square window is being used, it will have corner co-ordinates $[\frac{1}{2}, \frac{1}{2}, 1]$ and $[-\frac{1}{2}, -\frac{1}{2}, 1]$.

The next operation is clipping with respect to the front clipping plane. In many cases, the scenes will be arranged such that all the objects fall behind the front clipping plane. However, for certain applications, such as systems that produce the impression of walking through a building, objects in front of the clipping plane cannot be avoided. When considering clipping in three dimensions, it is important to distinguish totally clipped objects, in this case those that lie completely in front of the clipping plane, and partially clipped objects that are intersected by the clipping plane. Objects in the normalized scene can be classified according to the z co-ordinate. Since the front clipping plane has equation $z = 1$, totally clipped objects have all z co-ordinates less than 1 and partially clipped objects will have some z co-ordinates less than 1. To determine the class of an object, it is only necessary to find and test the maximum and minimum z co-ordinate of its vertices.

Any totally clipped object may be removed from the scene. For partially clipped objects, there are two possible approaches. The simplest is to remove them from the scene. This strategy will give reasonable results in cases where the scene consists of a large number of small objects. The second approach is to find the intersection of the clipped objects with the front clipping plane. Since solid objects are being considered, the intersection with the plane $z = 1$ will create new facets and modify existing ones, as shown in Figure 5.6. This may produce the desired visual result in, for example, engineering applications or architectural visualization programs. For complex objects, the calculation of these new or changed facets may be very complicated. It is worth noting that in cases where the intersection with the front clipping plane is outside the viewing window, no further clipping calculations are required, since the object will be correctly clipped to the window.

Having ensured that all objects are located on the far side of the projection plane, it is now possible to proceed with either projection or further clipping operations. If clipping is to be performed first, then a 3D viewing volume must be used. This is bounded by four side planes and, if defined, the back clipping plane. At this stage, it is normal only to test for, and eliminate, totally clipped objects, which will decrease the number of operations during the subsequent phases of the calculations. The rules for eliminating an object by the side planes are:

$$\frac{2x_i}{W} \geqslant z_i \quad \text{for all } i = 1, 2, 3, \ldots \text{ or}$$

$$\frac{2x_i}{W} \leqslant -z_i \quad \text{for all } i = 1, 2, 3, \ldots \text{ or}$$

$$\frac{2y_i}{W} \geqslant -z_i \quad \text{for all } i = 1, 2, 3, \ldots \text{ or}$$

$$\frac{2y_i}{W} \leqslant -z_i \quad \text{for all } i = 1, 2, 3, \ldots \text{ or}$$

where W, the side of the window, is equal to 1 in the normalized scene. If all vertices satisfy any one of the four criteria, then the object is completely invisible. The first two conditions are illustrated in Figure 5.7, which shows the x–z plane. It works for a square window with width W and unit distance from the viewpoint. Different width and height constants will appear in the conditions for non-square windows.

Clipping by the back plane is done simply by comparing the z value of the vertices with the z value of the back plane. Note that the back clipping plane can be moved to infinity; that is, not considered at all.

If projection is carried out without 3D clipping, there is a risk of processing a large number of vertices that will not appear in the final picture. With the viewpoint at the origin and the projection plane at $z = 1$, the projected points can be calculated by dividing the x and y co-ordinates of each vertex by the z co-ordinate. This yields a list of 2D $[x, y]$ co-ordinates for the projected vertices. After projection, the problem is reduced to two dimensions and clipping is done simply for the window in this case, $[-W/2, -W/2]$ to $[W/2, W/2]$). It is true that in the normalized scene $W = 1$, but for more general applications of these clipping tests, W

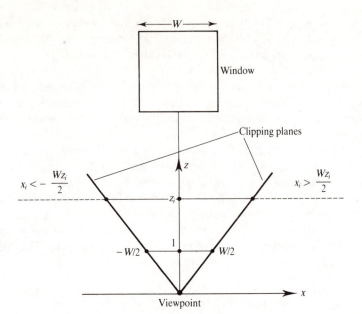

Figure 5.7
3D clipping by the side planes can be demonstrated in the x–z plane where a point outside the window satisfies one of the conditions $x_i < -Wz_i/2$ or $x_i > Wz_i/2$. Similar tests are made for y_i in the y–z plane.

may be different than 1 and therefore it is retained in the following expressions. A device-level algorithm, such as the Sutherland–Cohen algorithm described in Section 5.2, may be used for clipping. However, it may be advantageous first to apply some conditions, which find totally invisible objects:

$$Px_i \geq \frac{W}{2} \quad \text{for all } i = 1, 2, 3, \dots \textbf{ or}$$

$$Px_i \leq -\frac{W}{2} \quad \text{for all } i = 1, 2, 3, \dots \textbf{ or}$$

$$Py_i \geq \frac{W}{2} \quad \text{for all } i = 1, 2, 3, \dots \textbf{ or}$$

$$Py_i \leq -\frac{W}{2} \quad \text{for all } i = 1, 2, 3, \dots \textbf{ or}$$

where Px_i and Py_i are the projected x and y co-ordinates of the vertices. A min–max bounding box for the projected object may also be determined when computing the projection. This is the smallest rectangle containing the object. In this case, the totally invisible test reduces to:

$$\left(MinX > \frac{W}{2}\right) \text{ or } \left(MaxX < -\frac{W}{2}\right) \text{ or } \left(MinY > \frac{W}{2}\right) \text{ or } \left(MaxY < -\frac{W}{2}\right)$$

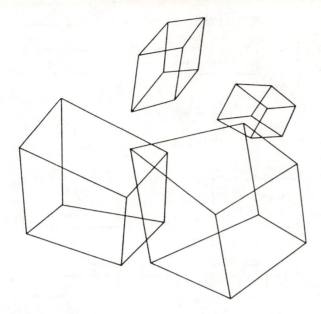

Figure 5.8
In the projected image of wire-frame models, there are different possible interpretations for the shapes and orientation of the objects. The correct shapes may be deduced from the same image if the hidden line segments are eliminated.

The calculations so far have produced a list of projected vertices and topological information that orders these vertices into objects, facets and edges. If a line drawing of all the edges is being produced, which is called the **wire-frame model**, then only two tasks are left: the clipping of lines with respect to the normalized window and the transformation of the normalized points to device co-ordinates. Clipping, as discussed before, involves the determination of the intersection points between the edges and the window sides. Note that it is still possible, during these clipping operations, to find that some edges are entirely outside the window. Device co-ordinates are determined according to an optional viewport and the scaling constants for the device. The technique is described in detail in Section 2.4.

The calculations from user co-ordinates to device co-ordinates are shown in Figure 5.5 in the form of a viewing pipeline. The pipeline is an important way of achieving parallel processing in graphics and will be discussed in Chapter 10 in the context of advanced graphics hardware structures. The main interest in the viewing pipeline, for the purposes of this book, is its functionality, not computing efficiency; therefore, the details of the calculations that should be optimized during implementation are not considered. Usually, the optimization of the calculations will be hardware dependent. The wire-frame model of a scene consisting of a few objects is shown in Figure 5.8.

If a picture with solid objects is required, then the visibility of each object must be determined before clipping and displaying can take place.

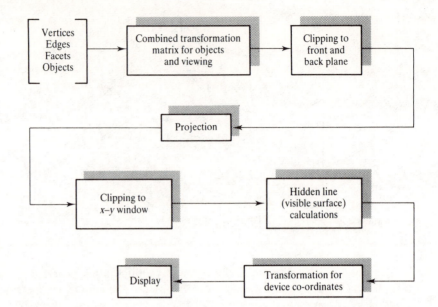

Figure 5.9
This viewing pipeline shows the calculations required to produce the projected image of solid objects with the elimination of hidden lines or surfaces.

This is known as the hidden line or visible surface calculations. A viewing pipeline for the generation of a graphics scene with solid objects is shown in Figure 5.9. The results of these calculations will be a list of visible lines (edges or portions of edges) and a list of visible surfaces (facets or portions of facets). All the information is given in two dimensions as the edges and surfaces have already been projected. The clipping of both edges and facets will be done with reference to the 2D window $[-W/2, -W/2]$, $[W/2, W/2]$ before the co-ordinates are transformed to device co-ordinates. Figure 5.10 shows a scene where there are different

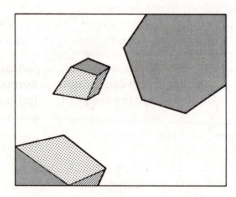

Figure 5.10
When the facets of solid objects are projected and viewed through a window, segments of the window sides become effectively edges for facets which are clipped by the window.

shaded patterns on the surfaces of the solid objects. This figure demonstrates that the window edges do clip some of the projected facets.

Having discussed transformations and clipping, the only task in the viewing pipeline of Figure 5.9 that has not been described yet is the hidden line and/or visible surface calculations. These will be the topics of the following sections.

5.4 VISIBLE EDGES OF A SINGLE CONVEX OBJECT WITH PLANAR FACETS

This section begins its treatment of the hidden line elimination problem by considering the simplest case: a single convex object. The convex property of a solid object ensures that any straight line connecting two points on the surface of the object lies on the surface or entirely within the object. It can be shown that a convex object with planar facets and straight-line edges can be constructed by the intersection of infinite planes that are co-planar with the facets. Each infinite plane divides space into two half-spaces: in one-half space, called the **inside**, lies the object; the other half-space, called the **outside**, is empty. The solid object is formed by the intersection of all the inside half-spaces.

The convex property ensures that, for a single solid convex object, a facet is either totally visible or totally invisible (hidden). This is an important simplification for the hidden line elimination problem. Facets that point their outside surfaces towards the viewer are visible and all edges belonging to these facets are also visible. Those facets that face away from the viewer are not visible, since they are hidden by the object itself, and are called **self-hidden**. Note that an edge may belong to both a visible and a self-hidden facet, in which case it is visible. This is one reason why it is more convenient to look for the visible surfaces rather than to try to eliminate the hidden ones.

If the outside normal direction vectors of the facets have been included in the database then the test for visibility is particularly simple. As shown in Figure 5.11, the angle between the outside normal and the vector drawn from a vertex of the facet to the centre of projection is always acute for a visible facet. The sign of the dot product for an acute angle is always positive; therefore, the facet with vertex $[V_x, V_y, V_z]$ and outside normal direction vector $[n_x, n_y, n_z]$ is visible if:

$$\mathbf{V} \cdot \mathbf{n} = V_x n_x + V_y n_y + V_z n_z < 0$$

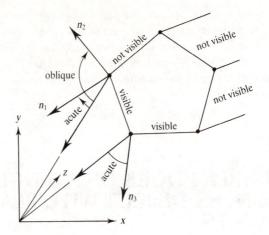

Figure 5.11

Self-hidden facets can be found by the cosine of the angle between the outside normal vector to the surface and a direction vector connecting a point on the surface to the centre of projection. Oblique angles indicate self-hidden facets.

because the direction vector from the vertex to the origin is $[-V_x, -V_y, -V_z]$.

Note also that the limiting case – when the dot product is equal to zero and the viewing vector from the vertex to the origin is co-planar with the facet – has not been included here because for a convex solid object these edges always join visible facets that ensure the visibility of the common edge. Algorithm 5.2 uses this test to produce a list of visible edges. The redundancy test in this algorithm ensures that common edges of visible facets are not added twice to the list. The usefulness of this test will depend on the application; in some cases, it will not be worthwhile to implement such a test. If the test is not implemented, then some edges will be drawn twice.

In cases where the outside normal vector is not available, it has to be calculated. As already shown, the normal direction vector may be calculated by the cross-product of two direction vectors that lie along two edges of the facet. If three vertices of the facet are given by position vectors $\mathbf{V_1}$, $\mathbf{V_2}$ and $\mathbf{V_3}$, then the normal vector may be calculated by the cross-product:

$$\mathbf{n} = (\mathbf{V_1} - \mathbf{V_2}) \times (\mathbf{V_1} - \mathbf{V_3})$$

but, in general, it is not known whether this is the inside or the outside normal.

It is possible to determine whether the normal is inside or outside if the co-ordinates of a point located inside the convex object are known. In defining the database, a definition co-ordinate system was used for each type of object. If the origin of this co-ordinate system was placed inside the convex object, then its corresponding point in the fixed world co-ordinate system can be taken as a contained point. If this is not the case, then taking

Algorithm 5.2

Elimination of self-hidden facets and edges.

```
{ Mark all edges as untested }
{ Set visible edge list to empty }
for all facets do
begin
   if the dot product is less than zero
   then begin
           { Add each untested edge that belongs to this facet to the list }
           { Mark each such edge as tested }
        end
end
```

the average of the co-ordinates of all vertices belonging to a convex object yields a point that must lie inside the object. Thus, the position vector $\mathbf{A}$ of a contained point can be calculated using the following equation:

$$\mathbf{A} = \frac{1}{n} \sum_{i=1}^{n} \mathbf{V_i}$$

where n is the number of vertices. The direction vector that points from the internal point towards a vertex on the facet, by definition, points towards the outside of the object (see Figure 5.12). Therefore, its dot product with the normal vector will be positive if the normal vector is itself pointing towards the outside. The test is then:

if $\mathbf{n} \bullet (\mathbf{V_1} - \mathbf{A}) > 0$
then $\mathbf{n}$ is the outside normal
else $-\mathbf{n}$ is the outside normal

Once the outside normal is known, Algorithm 5.2 can be applied to produce a list of visible edges.

It may seem that the algorithm for single convex objects is not of much use, since most realistic scenes consist of many objects and, in general, convexity cannot be enforced. But, it can be shown that self-hidden facets cannot be visible in multi-object scenes and, furthermore, that they cannot even hide other edges. Therefore, such facets may be

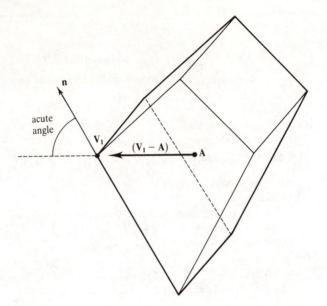

Figure 5.12
Knowing an internal point of the solid object, the sign of the dot product of the normal to the plane of the facet and a direction vector connecting the internal point to a vertex on the facet determines the sense of the normal. For outside normals, the dot product is positive.

eliminated from the hidden line calculations even for the general multi-object case. This calculation may therefore be inserted in the viewing pipeline, before the general hidden line algorithm is applied, to reduce the number of facets to be tested, thereby increasing the computation speed.

5.5   VISIBLE EDGES FOR A GENERAL SCENE

This section discusses an algorithm that produces the visible projected edges of a general scene consisting of solid-faceted non-convex objects. The basic algorithm is presented first; then, possible ways of improving its efficiency are discussed.

5.5.1   The basic algorithm

The main problem is that facets may obscure only portions of edges and may break up edges into a number of visible and hidden segments. Thus, the algorithm is divided into two parts. First, a list of edge segments that are either totally visible or totally hidden has to be produced. Second, the visibility for each edge segment must be determined. The algorithm is shown as Algorithm 5.3.

Algorithm 5.3

Visible edges for a general scene.

{ Eliminate self-hidden facets }
{ Project all potentially visible edges and clip them to the window }
for each projected edge **do**
begin
   { Initialize a list of crossing points for this edge to contain only the two endpoints of the edge }
   for all other edges not belonging to the same facet **do**
   begin
      { Calculate the crossing points of the two edges }
      if the crossing point is within both projected edge segments
      then begin
          { Add this crossing point to the list retaining an ordered list of the parameters μ_i }
        end
   end
end;

(* All the projected edges have now been divided into a number of segments *)

for each edge segment **do**
begin
   { Calculate the 2D co-ordinates of the midpoint of the projected edge segment **M** and, by back
   projection, determine the corresponding point on the edge, **B** }
      for each facet that does not include this edge **do**
      if the z co-ordinate of the facet at the projected co-ordinates $[M'_x, M'_y]$ is less than B_z
      then delete this edge segment from the list
end

Most calculations included in Algorithm 5.3 have already been described, but a short description of the required procedures will be given. The algorithm starts in the projected image space with a list of 2D line segments, from which those that are self-hidden or clipped by the window have been eliminated. Each line segment may be specified by its two projected vertices; **L1**$_i$ and **L2**$_i$, where the values of variable **i** ranges from 1 to the number of edges. Each edge also belongs to a given facet. A collection of edge segments is defined for each edge by the two vertices and an ordered list of scalars, $\mu_{i,k}$. At the start, there are two values for $\mu_{i,k}$; namely:

$$\mu_{i,1} = 0 \quad \text{and} \quad \mu_{i,2} = 1$$

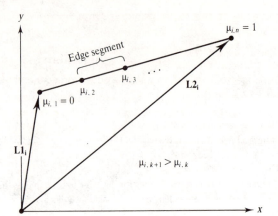

Figure 5.13

Intersection between projected edges divides each edge into an ordered list of projected edge segments which are either totally visible or totally hidden. The ordered values of parameter $\mu_{i,k}$ for each edge define the segments.

which define the entire edge as one line segment in the parametric representation of the line:

$$\mathbf{L_i} = \mathbf{L1_i} + \mu_{i,k}(\mathbf{L2_i} - \mathbf{L1_i})$$

The intersection is calculated between this edge and all other edges not belonging to the same facet. For normal solids, each edge will belong to two facets. For a more general scene, which may include infinitely thin opaque sheets, edges may belong to only one facet.

These calculations involve the intersection of 2D line segments, described in Section 4.4. Edges belonging to the same facet either do not intersect this edge or intersect it only at one end, $\mu = 0$ or $\mu = 1$; therefore, they are not tested. If a true intersection point is found, then its μ value is inserted into the list in such a way that:

$$\mu_{i,k} < \mu_{i,k+1}$$

Thus, the list becomes an ordered list of edge segments, as shown in Figure 5.13. When all edges have been processed, the result is a list of edge segments with endpoints in two dimensions:

$$\mathbf{L1_{i,k}} = \mathbf{L1_i} + \mu_{i,k}(\mathbf{L2_i} - \mathbf{L1_i})$$
$$\mathbf{L2_{i,k}} = \mathbf{L1_i} + \mu_{i,k+1}(\mathbf{L2_i} - \mathbf{L1_i})$$

where k ranges from 1 to the number of edge segments for each edge and, as before, i ranges from 1 to the number of original edges. Note that in the case where there is only one line segment, $\mathbf{L1_{i,1}}$ becomes $\mathbf{L1_i}$ and $\mathbf{L2_{i,2}}$ becomes $\mathbf{L2_i}$.

The first part of the algorithm has thus produced a list of edge segments that are either totally visible or totally hidden, since visibility can change only at a projected crossing point. The second part of the algorithm must determine the visibility of each edge segment. It is possible to determine whether an edge segment is hidden by another facet by examining one point on it. The midpoint is chosen here, in preference to the endpoint, since it will not be necessary to consider the limiting case of facets that touch the projected edge segment. The midpoint of the projected edge segment is defined by the parameter value:

$$\lambda_{i,k} = \frac{1}{2}\left(\mu_{i,k} + \mu_{i,k+1}\right)$$

This parameter value defines a point on the projected edge segment and also a point on the original edge by back projection, which is a process described in Chapter 4. The co-ordinates of the midpoint of the projected edge segment will be denoted:

$$\mathbf{M} = [M_x, M_y, 1]$$

while the back-projected midpoint will be denoted:

$$\mathbf{B} = [B_x, B_y, B_z]$$

Since **M** is the midpoint of the projected edge segment, it can be shown that:

$$B_z = \frac{2V1_z V2_z}{V1_z + V2_z}$$

where the endpoints of the edge segment are:

$$\mathbf{V1} = [V1_x, V1_y, V1_z] \quad \text{and} \quad \mathbf{V2} = [V2_x, V2_y, V2_z]$$

As shown in Figure 5.14, a ray is cast from the origin through the midpoint **M** that also passes through the point **B**. This line is the viewing vector, which can be expressed by the position vector **W**:

$$\mathbf{W} = \alpha\mathbf{B}$$

using the scalar quantity α. The next step is to determine the point of intersection between this viewing vector **W** and each facet not containing the edge under test. Taking any one vertex of the facet, say **V0**, and the

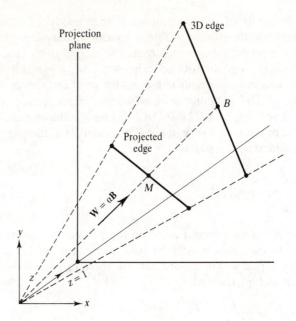

Figure 5.14
The midpoint of the projected edge segment designated by position vector **M** is back projected to the 3D edge resulting in point **B**. The viewing ray passing through point **B** (or **M**) can be used to test whether facets hide this edge segment from the viewer.

normal direction vector **n** of its plane, and assuming the intersection with the plane is at $\mathbf{W} = \alpha_1\mathbf{B}$, then it follows that:

$$(\mathbf{W} - \mathbf{V0}) \bullet \mathbf{n} = 0$$

which gives a simple linear equation for α_1:

$$(\alpha_1 B_x - V0_x)n_x + (\alpha_1 B_y - V0_y)n_y + (\alpha_1 B_z - V0_z)n_z = 0$$

If α_1 is larger than 1, then the facet is behind the back-projected midpoint and the facet cannot hide the edge segment. If α_1 is less than $1/B_z$, then the intersection with the facet is in front of the front clipping plane and it can be ignored. In both of these cases, no further calculations are necessary. On the other hand, if the value for α is within these two limits, then a containment test must be made to find out whether the intersection with the plane of the facet is located within the facet. The ray containment test, described in Chapter 4, can be used for this purpose. Its description will not be repeated here, but note that the projected edges have already been calculated, and therefore the containment test can be made in two dimensions. The facet is described by its two dimensional projected edges and the containment test is made for the midpoint **M**. If the point is contained, then the edge segment is hidden, it can be dropped and the **for** loops exited. If the midpoint is not contained, then another facet must be examined till all facets have been checked.

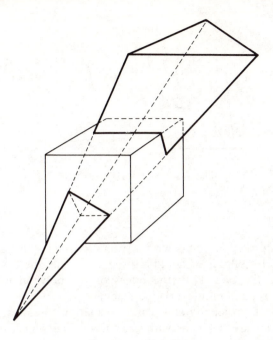

Figure 5.15
When objects are allowed to penetrate each other, new edges are created at the intersection of facets. The vertices belonging to these new edges must be precalculated and added to the object database before the visible surface or hidden line calculations are made.

While the algorithm may seem long and complicated, it is constructed from well-defined and tested procedures and it is completely general. There are two special classes of solid objects that have to be handled differently from ordinary solids. The first is the limiting case of infinitely thin opaque sheets, which may be included into the facet list without loss of generality. The only special treatment required for infinitely thin sheets is that the self-hidden test for them is ignored. Since both sides of a sheet are visible, it can never be self-hidden.

The other special case is penetrating objects. When two objects penetrate each other, as shown in Figure 5.15, edges appear that are not part of the original object database. Such a scene must be preprocessed, the additional edges determined and added to the database. Note that the additional edges do not produce additional facets, since they are on the existing surfaces of the solid objects. Once all these additional edges are included in the database, Algorithm 5.3 can be applied.

There are also special cases where the algorithm may go wrong. For example, in the 2D intersection calculations when straight-line edges are processed, the calculations will break down if two edges are parallel to each other. As long as the projected edges do not exactly overlap, parallel edges will not produce intersection points, but overlapping edges will. Hence, projected edges that overlap but belong to different facets must be identified and their intersection points included in the list of intersections. As shown in Figure 5.16, the correct way of handling overlapping edges is

Figure 5.16

Special cases occur when edges belonging to different facets appear collinear in the projected image. Intersection calculations between these edges break down. The diagram shows that, for correct handling of these special cases, the containment test for facets must include the edges. In the final drawing, the crossing point characterized by μ_1 is visible while that for μ_2 is hidden.

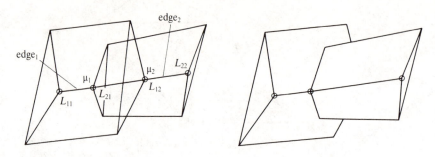

to include intersection points with a scalar constant – in this case, μ_1 for $edge_1$ and μ_2 for $edge_2$. It should also be noted that the containment test must include the boundary (the edge) of the polygon for the correct visibility determination of overlapping edges.

The back-projection and plane calculations break down for edges and facets that are collinear with the viewing ray. Such edges may be ignored since they appear as single points in the image plane. Facets that are collinear with the viewing rays appear as single lines and will require special handling. The algorithms for these special cases are similar to those used for collinear edges shown in Figure 5.16.

5.5.2 Questions of efficiency

Before discussing the more interesting problems associated with visible surfaces and raster scan output devices, it is worthwhile examining the execution speed of the general algorithm designed for determining the visible edges of a complex scene and to look for possible ways of making improvements. It is important to emphasize that the output of this algorithm is a list of line segments in normalized co-ordinates and its execution speed is not affected by the output device, only by the size of the database.

For a large database containing thousands of edges and facets, there are two critical areas of the algorithm. The first is the calculation of edge segments, where execution time is proportional to the square of the number of edges. Fortunately, this calculation only has to be done in two dimensions. There are two methods by which the execution time may be significantly reduced. The first uses **bounding rectangles** for the line segments, the second uses **sorting**.

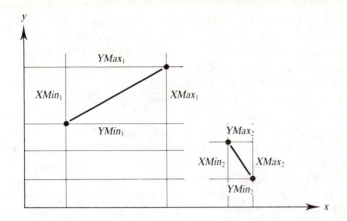

Figure 5.17
Bounding rectangles for 2D edge segments allow the rapid determination of the possibility of valid crossing points between segments. The calculations require comparisons and logical operations only.

A bounding rectangle may be defined for a 2D line by the minimum and maximum x and y co-ordinates of its endpoints, as shown in Figure 5.17. Two line segments can only cross if the following condition is true:

$$(XMax_1 > XMin_2) \textbf{ and } (XMax_2 > XMin_1) \textbf{ and } (YMax_1 > YMin_2) \textbf{ and } (YMax_2 > YMin_1)$$

This test requires only comparisons and will eliminate the calculation of the crossing point for a large number of segments. It becomes even more valuable if the line segments are sorted. For example, suppose a list is created containing the line segments in increasing order of their *XMin* values. If these line segments are processed in order, then testing can terminate when $XMin_2$ exceeds $XMax_1$ of the line segment under test. All succeeding line segments will also fail the test and will not have to be tested at all. Similar tests will work for $XMin_1$, $YMin_2$ and $YMin_1$.

The other critical procedure whose execution time depends on the product of the number of line segments and facets is the containment test. This test is done in two dimensions and a similar method of bounding rectangles and sorting will decrease the execution times. For facets, it is also possible to include a z or depth bounding with values *ZMax* and *ZMin*, thus creating a bounding box in three dimensions. If these bounding boxes are sorted according to their *ZMin* or *ZMax* values and a test made for the intersection between the back-projected ray and the facets in depth order, then the number of facets tested is likely to be reduced. **Depth sorting** and **depth bounding** will always be important aspects of visibility tests.

The general algorithm presented for solving the visible line segment problem will in fact work for all shapes. It works mainly in the image plane – that is, in 2D space. Many other algorithms have been published in the literature, some of which work mainly in object space, and some of which provide better efficiency by restricting the type of objects that can be used, for example, to convex objects or objects without holes. The algorithm due to Roberts (1964) is one example. It was the first algorithm published that solved the hidden line problem for all cases of interest. However, many of the details of this, and similar algorithms, are no longer relevant in the context of the modern raster scan devices.

It is worth mentioning briefly how a general algorithm for visible edge segments that works totally in object (3D) space can be devised. Each potentially visible line segment is checked against every opaque facet. The visible parts of each line segment in three dimensions is found by 3D clipping. As long as each individual facet is convex, any line segment can be divided by one facet into at most three parts – two visible and one hidden. The 3D clipping can be done with planes that pass through the origin (the viewpoint) and the edges of each facet. Triangular facets will provide the easiest algorithm. To construct an algorithm for completely general shapes is very difficult and will not be attempted here.

5.6   VISIBLE SURFACE ALGORITHMS FOR RASTER SCAN DEVICES

In cases where the display device is controlled by a frame buffer containing the intensity values for $N \times M$ pixels, methods other than those using visible line segments can be used for handling the task of representing a complex scene with solid objects. For example, it is possible to use hidden line algorithms first and then draw the list of visible line segments on the raster scan device using Bresenham's or similar algorithms. However, with raster technology, it is possible to display different surfaces using different colours or intensities. This section discusses the efficient determination of the intensity values of each pixel of the frame buffer from the geometrical data of objects, facets, edges and vertices. Some of the algorithms developed here can be applied to hidden edges as well.

5.6.1   Painter's algorithm

The simplest of the algorithms, the so-called painter's algorithm, will be considered first. Since the objects under question can be described as a collection of opaque facets, each facet may be assigned a given colour shade. The next step is to **paint** each facet on the display screen, beginning with the facet furthest away from the viewer and proceeding with facets in decreasing order of their depth or z co-ordinate values. The algorithm may be expressed as shown in Algorithm 5.4.

Algorithm 5.4

Painter's algorithm.

{ Set all pixels to the background shade intensities }
{ Eliminate self-hidden and clipped facets }
{ Sort the remaining facets in descending order of their depth, or z co-ordinate }
for each facet on the sorted list **do**
begin
   { Project the facet on to the screen }
   { Set each pixel covered by the facet to the shade of the facet }
end

Note that the painter's algorithm uses object space for sorting and image space for filling. Although simple, it does not work for a general case, only for two-and-a-half dimensional scenes, which means that all objects are single opaque facets parallel to the x–y plane but with different z (depth) values. Such scenes do occur in practice. One good example is VLSI circuit diagrams.

If the facets are truly 3D, then tests must be made to determine overlapping facets. Even so, it is possible to arrange objects, as shown in Figure 5.18, so that they cannot be rendered by the painter's algorithm, since none of the objects is clearly at the front. It is possible to set up

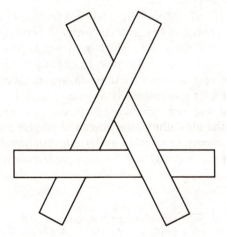

Figure 5.18

Three objects for which the painter's algorithm fails, because it is not possible to arrange the objects in a strict order of their depth.

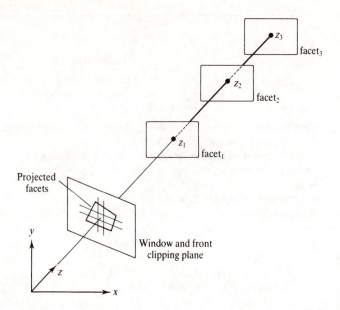

Figure 5.19
The z-buffer visible surface algorithm compares the z co-ordinates of intersection points between a viewing ray and facets. It determines the pixel RGB intensities according to the facet closest to the viewer.

increasingly more complex tests to determine the depth relationship between facets. If these fail to determine the ordering, then the facets must be subdivided into suitable subfacets. These complications make the painter's algorithm impractical for general application. However, this simple algorithm clearly demonstrates the difference between hidden line and visible surface calculations. The following sections describe more practical visible surface algorithms.

5.6.2 *z*-buffer algorithm

A modified painter's algorithm that works for the most general case uses a **z-buffer** in which a real number is stored for each pixel co-ordinate. Figure 5.19 demonstrates this algorithm, which is shown in Algorithm 5.5.

Algorithm 5.5 is one of the most frequently used algorithms at the present. The main reason is that it can be easily implemented in hardware, especially if the facets are restricted to simple shapes, such as triangles. Chapter 4 showed that any complicated shape can be broken into a set of triangles. The projected facet in this case is a triangle for which there is a very simple containment test – this was described in Section 4.5. The buffer is easily implemented in RAM and the back projection is calculated by the solution of the equation:

$$z = \frac{C}{1 - Ap_x - Bp_y}$$

Algorithm 5.5

z-buffer algorithm.

{ Set all pixels to the background shade intensities and all elements in the *z*-buffer to the largest real number it can hold }
{ Eliminate self-hidden and clipped facets }
for each remaining facet **do**
begin
    { Project the facet on to the screen }
    for each pixel value covered by this facet **do**
    begin
        { Back project the pixel co-ordinates to the facet and determine the *z* co-ordinate of the point on the facet }
        if the *z* co-ordinate is smaller than the value in the *z*-buffer
        then begin
            { Replace the value in the buffer with the calculated *z* co-ordinate }
            { Set the pixel intensities to the shade of this facet }
        end
    end
end

---

where p_x and p_y are the co-ordinates of the pixel and the equation for the plane of the facet is:

$$z = Ax + By + C$$

The *z*-buffer algorithm effectively sorts the facets pixel by pixel. Whenever a facet is found that is closer to the viewer than the one found previously, the intensity of the pixel is reset. There are serious problems of program size and efficiency if the algorithm is to be implemented by software. The *z*-buffer itself may have to be very large if the *z* co-ordinates of the objects have to be calculated accurately. Sorting the facets by the *ZMin* of their 3D bounding boxes, for example, and processing them from front to back helps to eliminate most of the resetting of the pixel intensities and ensures that most operations are comparisons that fail, since the pixel is set to its correct intensity early in the process. A test of the *ZMin* value to the current *z*-buffer value can be used to eliminate the back projection. The *z*-buffer becomes a useful software technique when it is combined with the scan line algorithm, which is described in the next section.

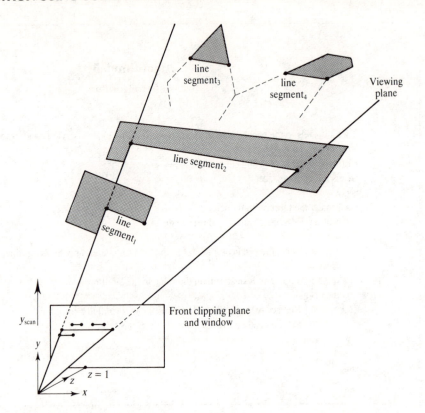

Figure 5.20
The scan line algorithm considers only one horizontal line in the viewing window at a time. The viewing plane cuts some of the facets producing lines that are projected and become 2D line segments with their y ordinate value equal to y_{scan}.

5.6.3   Scan line algorithms for determining visible surfaces

The z-buffer algorithm proceeds by processing each facet in turn. Its execution time is proportional to the number of facets and the average number of pixels the facets cover. Scan line algorithms process each pixel in turn and the execution time is proportional to the number of pixels on the display screen. When the objects cover a very small area of the display surface, the scanning by objects is more efficient; however, if the objects cover most of the viewing surface, then scanning by pixels could be more advantageous. As will be seen shortly, sorting is also important for these algorithms.

Scan line algorithms process the picture one row of pixels at a time. This corresponds, in world co-ordinates, to a small band of y values. The y co-ordinate at the middle of the band is defined as y_{scan}. As shown in Figure 5.20, a plane can be drawn through the viewpoint and the scan line, which will normally cut some of the facets. The intersection between this plane and the facets generates a list of 3D line segments that will be

Algorithm 5.6

Scan line algorithm with a z-buffer.

{ Eliminate self-hidden and clipped facets }
for each scan line **do**
begin
  { Set all pixels in this row to the background shade }
  { Set the z-buffer for each pixel on the line to its maximum value }
  for each facet **do**
  begin
    { Determine the intersection of the facet with a plane that passes through the origin and the scan line }
    { Project the intersection points on to the scan line }
    for each pixel value covered by the projected line **do**
    begin
      { Find the z co-ordinate of the point on the facet by back projection }
      if the z co-ordinate is smaller than the value in the z-buffer
      then begin
          { Replace the value in the buffer with value z }
          { Set the pixel intensities to the shade of this facet }
        end
    end
  end
end

projected into segments of the scan line $y = y_{\text{scan}}$. For each of these, an x_{min} and an x_{max} value may be found.

The version of the scan line algorithm shown in Algorithm 5.6 is in its simplest form – that is, when all facets are assumed to be convex. This means that one facet produces only one line segment when it is cut by the viewing plane. It uses a z-buffer that only needs to contain sufficient entries for one line of pixels.

Superficially, there is not much difference between Algorithms 5.5 and 5.6, but the implementation details of the scan line algorithm has many advantages. First of all, the z-buffer covers only a row of pixels and is reduced to a reasonable size. Second, the containment and back-projection calculations are done for lines, not planar polygons. In fact, since the distances between pixels are constant, once the z value is known for the facet for one pixel, the z value for the next pixel can be easily calculated by one addition. If the plane equation of the facet is $z = Ax + By + C$, then the difference between two z values for two neighbouring pixels is equal to $A \Delta x$, where Δx is the distance between two pixels.

A great improvement in the efficiency of this algorithm may be obtained if ordered lists of the facets and the line segments, called **spans**, are maintained as the pixels are processed. Clearly, if the facets are ordered by their z value for a given pixel, as shown in Figure 5.19, then no z-buffer is required. The pixel shade is determined by the first facet in the list. The maintenance of such an ordered list as the algorithm proceeds from pixel to pixel can be done efficiently by making use of **spatial coherence**. In this particular case, spatial coherence results from the fact that the depth order of facets does not usually change very much between adjacent pixels. Moreover, the places where it does change on a given scan line can be easily identified, and it is only at these places that it is necessary to recompute the pixel intensity value.

At the heart of this algorithm lies the maintenance of an **active list**, which contains only those facets that are actually intersected by the plane through the current scan line. Spatial coherence can be exploited here, since the scan lines are processed in order. Hence, for each new scan line, only a few new facets are added, and a few others are dropped from the list. For this purpose, facets are characterized by their minimum and maximum projected y values, which determine when they become active and when they are no longer needed. When, in Algorithm 5.6, processing is only done for the active facets, a considerable saving in time can be made.

Coherence between adjacent pixels along the scan line can be exploited by using an active line segment or span list. For a given scan line, each facet in the active list can be characterized by its projected minimum and maximum x values. These values represent the only places where visibility can change along the line. Algorithm 5.7 employs both these coherence properties to improve the speed. Note that the algorithm works almost entirely in the image space. Note also that separate active and passive lists for facets and spans are introduced to clarify the use of spatial coherence. A more efficient implementation would only use one list, with an active portion of it indicated by pointers.

In this algorithm, the use of ordered active lists has been emphasized while the problems associated with calculating the z co-ordinates of the intersected line segments have been ignored. At the edges of the solid objects, the line segments belonging to different facets will meet and will have the same z value. This may require special processing in a practical algorithm.

5.6.4   Area subdivision algorithms

An ingenious method of solving the visible surface problems is the use of subdivision of area. It was originally introduced by Warnock (1968, 1969).

Algorithm 5.7

Scan line algorithms with active lists.

{ Eliminate self-hidden and clipped facets }
{ Project all remaining facets on to the image plane }
{ Calculate the *YMax* and *YMin* values for each projected facet }
{ Sort the facets into descending order of *YMax* and add them to a passive facet list }
for each facet on the passive list **do**
  if *YMax* > *TopScanLine*
  then remove the facet from the passive list and add it to the active list that is ordered by *YMin*;
CurrentColour := *BackgroundColour*;
for *YScan* := *TopScanLine* **to** *BottomScanLine* **do**
begin
  for each facet on the active list **do**
    if *YMin* > *YScan*
  then remove the facet from the active list;
  for each facet on the passive list **do**
    if *YMax* > *YScan*
  then remove the facet from the passive list and add it to the active list that is ordered by *YMin*;

  for each facet on the active list **do**
  begin
    { Calculate the intersections between the projected edges and the scan line }
    { Calculate *XMax* and *XMin* of each span of the scan line covered by the facet }
    { Sort each span on to a passive span list in ascending order of *XMin* }
  end

  for each span on the passive span list **do**
    if *XMin* < *LeftmostPixel*
  then remove the span from the ordered span list and add it in order of *XMax* to the active span list
  for *XPixel* := *LeftmostPixel* **to** *RightmostPixel* **do**
  begin
    for each span on the active span list **do**
      if *XMax* < *XPixel*
    then remove the span from the active span list;
    for each span on the passive span list **do**
      if *XMin* < *Xpixel*
    then remove the span from the passive span list and add it in order of *XMax* to the active span list
    if the active span list has changed
    then compute the *CurrentPixelIntensity* by finding the closest facet covering the pixel;
    SET_PIXEL(*XPixel*, *YPixel*, *CurrentPixelIntensity*);
  end (* for all *XPixels* *)
end (* for all scan lines *)

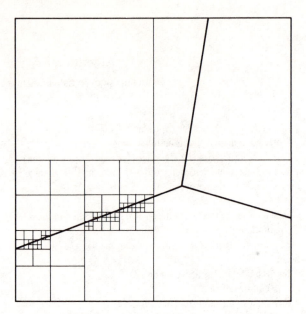

Figure 5.21
Warnock's area subdivision
algorithm recursively divides
each square area into four
equal squares until no edges
appear in a subdivided area.
An area with no edges inside it
can be filled with the
appropriate shaded pixel values
determined by one facet only.

The idea behind it is the recognition that if, in a defined area of the screen, only one surface is visible, then the area can be filled with the visible attributes of the surface, which are calculated only once.

To find areas where only one surface is visible, a recursive division method is applied. If, in an area of the display, more than one surface is visible – that is, at least one edge appears – then the area can be divided into two or four smaller areas and the test for a single surface made again. The tests are made recursively until all areas are small enough so that they contain only single surfaces. The algorithm is demonstrated with a simple example in Figure 5.21, where the scene is a corner of a room with three differently shaded surfaces. The division halves both the width and the height of the original window to yield four subwindows. The upper left subwindow contains no edges and will not be subdivided any further. Some more subdivisions are indicated in the lower left corner of the window.

The area subdivision algorithm works mainly in image space and it can only be used for raster scan devices, since the subdivisions must terminate even if there are a large number of edges. For raster scan display devices, an area equal to one pixel cannot be divided any further; thus, when this ultimate limit is reached, the subdivision must stop. The only time that calculations must be done in object space is when an undivided area is found and two or more facets are projected to the same area. This is illustrated in Figure 5.22 which shows two objects. Within the shaded area there are no projected edges in the image plane, but there are four facets that could determine the final pixel intensities. In such cases, depth sorting of the surfaces is still necessary.

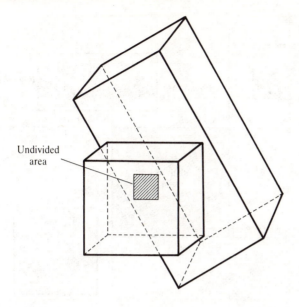

Figure 5.22
When the area subdivision algorithm is used for these two objects, the indicated small area has no projected edges within it; however, there are four facets behind the area. The closest facet must be found before the area can be filled with the correct pixel intensities.

For each undivided area, the intensities are determined for all the pixels by one calculation; so, for cases where the area is large, a large saving in time is made. The depth test is only made once for the whole area, unlike the z-buffer algorithm which makes the test for each pixel. The time saving is large if the projected facets are large. Thus, Warnock's algorithm works best when there is significant **area coherence** in the scene; that is, when a large majority of pixel intensities are the same as those of their neighbours. The simplest statement of the algorithm in its recursive form is shown in Algorithm 5.8.

For Algorithm 5.8 to work efficiently, simple tests must be devised for determining whether a rectangular area contains a simple scene or not. The minimum and maximum x and y values for each facet define a bounding rectangle that can be used for this purpose. A simple scene is found by two criteria. The first is demonstrated in Figure 5.23, which shows facets that are totally disjoint from the rectangular area. The criterion for this test is:

$$(BoundXMin > EndXPixel) \textbf{ or } (BoundXMax < StartXPixel) \textbf{ or}$$
$$(BoundYMin > EndYPixel) \textbf{ or } (BoundYMax < StartYPixel)$$

where $BoundXMin$, $BoundXMax$, . . . , are the co-ordinates of the projected bounding rectangle of the facet. The second criterion, demonstrated in Figure 5.24, is that at least one bounding rectangle completely surrounds the scene and all other facets appearing in the scene are further away from

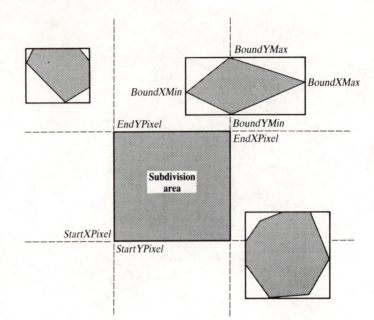

Figure 5.23
Simple comparison tests can be made for projected facets to determine whether they could contribute edges to a subdivided area. Co-ordinates of the bounding rectangle for the facet can be compared to the co-ordinates of the subdivided area and topologically disjoint facets eliminated.

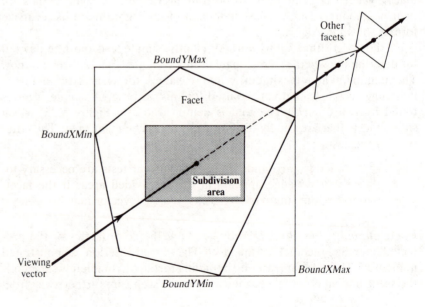

Figure 5.24
Comparison tests can be made to determine whether a bounding rectangle can completely surround a subdivision area. The tests for the bounding rectangle normally take much less time than the calculations of the intersection points between the edges and the area boundaries.

Algorithm 5.8

Recursive area subdivision algorithm.

```
procedure Warnock(StartXPixel, StartYPixel, EndXPixel, EndYPixel);
    begin
        if ((StartXPixel <> EndXPixel) or (StartYPixel <> EndYPixel))
            and there is at least one edge within the rectangular scene
        then begin
                MiddleX := (StartXPixel + EndXPixel) div 2;
                MiddleY := (StartYPixel + EndYPixel) div 2;
                Warnock(StartXPixel, StartYPixel, MiddleX, MiddleY);
                Warnock(MiddleX, StartYPixel, EndXPixel, MiddleY);
                Warnock(StartXPixel, MiddleY, MiddleX, EndYPixel);
                Warnock(MiddleX, MiddleY, EndXPixel, EndYPixel)
            end
        else begin
                { Sort all facets appearing in this scene with respect to their depth }
                { Fill the entire rectangular scene with the shade of the closest facet to the viewer }
            end
    end (* the Warnock procedure *)
    { Eliminate self-hidden and clipped facets }
    { Project all remaining facets on to the image plane }
    Warnock(0, 0, MaxXPixels, MaxYPixels)
```

the viewer than the surrounding facet. The test for a surrounding facet based on the minimum and maximum values are:

$(BoundXMin < StartxPixel)$ **and** $(BoundXMax > EndXPixel)$ **and**
$(BoundYMin < StartYPixel)$ **and** $(BoundYMax > EndYPixel)$

Unfortunately, the test for the bounding rectangle does not ensure that the facet also completely surrounds the scene. Further tests are necessary to make certain that no edge appears in the subdivided area. If the facet completely covers the subdivided area, then a view vector may be used to test the depths of the other facets. In the case where all other facets appearing in this area are further away from the viewer than the covering facet, then, regardless of whether they intersect the area or not, they are totally hidden and the intensity for all the pixels has been found. These tests are shown in Algorithm 5.9.

Algorithm 5.9

Tests for simple subdivided areas.

ShadeOfArea := *BackgroundColour*;
SceneStatus := *Simple*;
{ Set *ZFacet* to a number larger than the largest *z* value of any object }
{ Set the viewing vector at the middle of the subdivided area }
for all projected facets **do**
begin
   if the facet is not disjoint from the scene
   then begin
        if the facet completely covers the area
        then begin
            if the *z* value of the facet pierced by the viewing vector is smaller than *ZFacet*
            then begin
                ZFacet := *Z*;
                SceneStatus := *Simple*;
                ShadeOfArea := *ShadeOfFacet*;
                { Save the constants *A*, *B* and *C* which express the equation of the plane
                    z = *Ax* + *By* + *C* for the current facet }
                end
            end (* the **if** for a completely covered area *)
        else begin
            if the *z* value of any vertex or edge inside the subdivided area is smaller than the *z* value
                of the covering facet calculated by the saved *A*, *B*, and *C* constants
            then begin
                ZFacet := *Z*;
                SceneStatus := **not** *Simple*;
                { Set the viewing vector to the point where the *z* value was calculated }
            end
        end (* the case when at least one edge or vertex is inside the subdivided area *)
     end (* for all non-disjoint facets *)
end; (* the **for** loop for all facets *)
if (*SceneStatus* = *Simple*)
then { Fill area with *ShadeOfArea* }

                The idea behind Warnock's algorithm is simple, but the implementation is not without difficulties. As shown in Figure 5.21, there are many subdivisions around edges and if the subdivisions are continued down to a single pixel level for a large number of pixels, then a large amount of computation has been done in addition to the depth test for each pixel. A modified version of the Warnock algorithm can be constructed to stop the subdivision when only one edge appears in the subdivided area. If the edge is visible, then the filling of the area is made with two shades, after the edge has been drawn. Similarly, a simple vertex may be allowed in the subdivided area, although the filling of such an area becomes more complex. These modifications may improve the performance of the algorithm in many cases, but the special conditions destroy its elegance and simplicity.

Another idea is to divide the screen area according to the locations of the edges, rather than by simple distance halving. This may lead to efficient algorithms for simple objects, but could cause many complications for complex scenes. Nevertheless, a whole class of new algorithms could be developed from the principle of area coherence.

Warnock's algorithm will compete with the scan line or z-buffer algorithms in many situations. Similarly, the modified painter's algorithm could work fastest for special cases. These comparisons are valid if the hidden line or visible surface algorithms are executed by software. With the decreasing costs of hardware components these comparisons may be futile, since within the foreseeable future it will be possible to use hardware processors for visible surface calculations, for which the z-buffer algorithm is the most likely one to be used.

Exercises

5.1 Describe the difference between visible surface and visible line algorithms as applied to raster displays and planar faceted objects.

5.2 Explain why some clipping and hidden line elimination algorithms solve essentially the same problem. Can clipping be related to visible surface algorithms as well?

5.3 The projected image of a line segment with endpoints [2, 2, 2] and [12, 15, 3] is obscured by a triangular window with apexes [3, 1], [2, 4] and [4, 4]. Calculate the visible line segments produced. Perspective projection is used with the centre of projection at the origin and the projection plane at $z = 1$.

5.4 Set up a database for objects defined by a list of triangular facets and show all the required calculations for the new edge segments produced by the object and the front clipping plane at $z = 1$.

5.5   For a general perspective projection, the centre of projection is at the origin and the centre of the viewing window is at the point [1, 3, 5]. The plane of projection is perpendicular to the direction vector [1, 3, 5]. Calculate the geometrical transformation matrix that transforms the centre of the window to the point [0, 0, 1] and lines up the plane of the window parallel to the x–y plane.

5.6   Discuss why totally and partially clipped objects are treated differently by viewing pipelines that use 3D clipping.

5.7   A triangular facet of a convex object with vertices [1, 2, 3], [2, 2, 1], and [2, 3, 2] is viewed from different directions. The centre of projection is always on the z axis ($x = 0$ and $y = 0$). Find those z values for which the facet appears to be self-hidden if it is known that the point [5, 5, 5] is inside the object.

5.8   Design an algorithm that detects and handles properly those edges whose projection overlaps each other. Assume that the projected co-ordinates are given as integers.

5.9   Draw a sketch of a 3D scene for which the painter's algorithm does not work and show the projected scene, using different colours for the objects, to demonstrate the error caused by the algorithm.

Problems

5.10   The centre of two square-shaped windows is the same and is at point [0.5, 0.5] in normalized device co-ordinates. Edges are viewed through the larger window with sides 0.3 but obscured by the smaller one which has sides of 0.1. Develop binary codes and simple bitwise binary operations similar to the Sutherland–Cohen algorithm which determine either the total visibility or the total invisibility of a line segment.

5.11   When rectangular windows partially overlap each other, very complicated window shapes may be created. However, it is possible to divide even the most complicated shape into a number of small rectangular windows. Assume that a rectangular window, window$_1$ [x_{11}, y_{11}, x_{12}, y_{12}], is overlayed with a second window, window$_2$ [x_{21}, y_{21}, x_{22}, y_{22}], such that the new window can be defined by the area:

within window$_1$ but not within window$_2$

Design an algorithm that returns the co-ordinates of a number of rectangles (the minimum number is zero, the maximum is four) whose union gives the new window. Discuss how these may be used for general clipping of a line.

5.12 Change the algorithm of Exercise 5.11 by assuming that the total visible surface is defined by the normalized device coordinates [0, 0, 1, 1] and the new window is defined by its complement. This means that any complex window may be defined by the union of a number of rectangles that define the areas outside the window. Note that the original rectangular window will be defined by four rectangles. Discuss how the clipping of a general line could be executed in this system.

5.13 Design an algorithm that clips a general polygon by a rectangular window. The clipping may produce a number of polygons (or none at all), for which some of the edges will be parts of the clipping window borders. The original polygon is defined by vertices V_i with i in the range 0 to N and $V_N = V_0$. The vertices are arranged in such a way that if you walk from V_i to V_{i+1}, the inside of the polygon is on your right. The window is defined by co-ordinates $[x_1, y_1, x_2, y_2]$. Ensure that the order of the vertices for the new polygon(s) is maintained in the order for the original polygon.

5.14 Multiply the viewing, projection and normalization transformation matrices and determine the components of a single matrix that produces pixel co-ordinates from projected 3D points viewed in a general direction.

5.15 In a graphics system, each convex object is defined with respect to its own fixed co-ordinate system, whose origin is placed at the object's centre of gravity, **CG**. Prove that if the **CG** of the convex object is on the z axis (co-ordinates $[0, 0, z_{CG}]$), then the visibility of any one of its facets can be determined by calculating the intersection of the plane of the facet with the z axis and testing whether it is between the origin and z_{CG}. Design an algorithm based on this test to determine whether a facet of a convex object placed anywhere in the system is self-hidden. Which definition of the plane equation is most suitable for this algorithm?

5.16 A graphics scene consists of a large number of solid rectangular objects, which may have been derived from bounding boxes. Compare the number of calculations required to:

(a)   Eliminate objects by 3D clipping first and then project the vertices.

(b)   Transform all the vertices, using one matrix calculation, first and then clip in 2D using the viewport and the vertices in pixel co-ordinates.

Estimate the ratio of totally to partially clipped objects at which the two methods would take approximately the same amount of time. Make some reasonable assumptions about instruction times for integer and floating-point arithmetic, comparison, memory read and store instructions.

5.17 Design a data structure for solid-faceted objects that could minimize the computation required by the general visible edge algorithm described in Section 5.5. Try to optimize the time needed to find out which facets belong to (or do not belong to) an edge and which edges belong to a facet. Using your data structure, design an algorithm that treats penetrating objects correctly.

5.18 Design the algorithm for 3D clipping of edges by triangular facets. Show in detail all the calculations necessary to implement the algorithm. Incorporate as many time-saving features as you can – for example bounding boxes, sorting. Compare the required calculations in 3D and those suggested by the general algorithm in Section 5.5. Can you identify situations when one would be definitely preferable to the other?

5.19 It is possible to define a 2D line by the bounding rectangle co-ordinates x_{min}, y_{min}, x_{max}, y_{max} and a Boolean flag that indicates whether the two points on the line are $[x_{min}, y_{min}]$ and $[x_{max}, y_{max}]$ or $[x_{min}, y_{max}]$ and $[x_{max}, y_{min}]$. Discuss the advantages and disadvantages of this line description for the hidden/visible edge problem. The same idea can be extended to 3D by using the bounding box co-ordinates and two flags. Discuss the effect of graphical transformations on this data representation.

5.20 A graphics scene consists of a very large number of coloured, square-shaped, infinitely thin sheets. Each sheet is one unit square and has a unique colour. For each one of the situations below, design an optimized algorithm that solves the visible surface problem by setting all pixels of the viewing screen to the correct colour.

(a)   The edges of the sheets are parallel either to the x or the y axis, respectively, and the position of each sheet is defined by the co-ordinates of the midpoint $[x_0, y_0, z_0]$.

(b)   The sheets are parallel to the x–y plane. The position of each sheet is defined by its midpoint and the angle between one of its edges and the x axis.

(c)   The sheets can have any orientation. The position of each sheet is defined by the position of its midpoint and three angles of rotation.

5.21 Modify Algorithm 5.6 so that it can process general non-convex polygons. Discuss how the sorting and the active/passive lists would have to be changed for the most efficient processing of your algorithm.

5.22 A 3D graphics scene has a very large number of randomly positioned solid objects with average projected areas of 100×100 or a total of $10\,000$ pixels. The viewport is a 1000×1000 pixel square area. Assume uniform distribution of the objects. Compare the efficiency of the z-buffer algorithm and the scan line algorithm, with and without sorting and active/passive lists, by estimating the total execution time required to process N objects. Assume that all machine instruction execution times, regardless of whether they involve integer or real arithmetic, registers or memory, are the same. Estimate the asymptotic function of execution time for each processing method for very large N values.

5.23 Design an algorithm to determine whether, within a subdivided rectangular area of the screen, a projected convex polygon has no edges, one edge but no vertices, one vertex or more than one vertex. Try to optimize your algorithm for speed. How would you change your algorithm to process non-convex polygons?

Projects

5.24 Obviously, there are a large number of projects that implement the various algorithms described in this chapter. The most worthwhile project, from an educational point of view, would be to compare the difficulties in implementing the various algorithms and their running time for a large number of objects. For comparisons, it is probably all right to consider cubes aligned with the x–y–z axis, although their size, number and distribution (uniform or clustered) should be varied. This database reduces most of the calculations to two dimensions if orthographic projection is used. Depending on time and resources, perspective projection should also be tested. More adventurous students could try randomly rotated cubes, which introduce many complications in all the algorithms.

5.25 Implement Warnock's area subdivision algorithm for triangular facets. Produce three versions: one that looks for no edges in a subdivided area; one that allows one edge but no vertex; and one that allows one vertex and its associated edges only. Test your algorithms using perspective projection of equilateral triangles with random size whose planes are parallel to the x–y axis, where one of their edges is parallel to the x axis and are at a random distance away from the origin. Use a reasonably small window area, perhaps 64×64 pixels.

5.26 Design a walk-through architectural program for the inside of a building consisting of rooms with simple rectangular doors and windows. All rooms have the same ceiling height, vertical walls and rectangular floors. Use 3D clipping instead of visible surface or visible line algorithms.

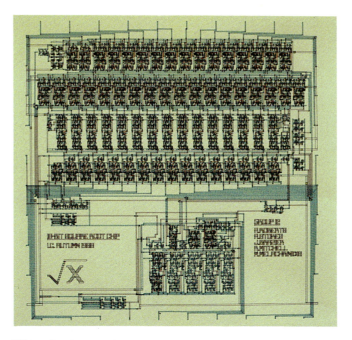

Plate 1 The VLSI circuit of a square root chip designed by students at Imperial College. This final print was made using a Hewlett Packard six-pen plotter.

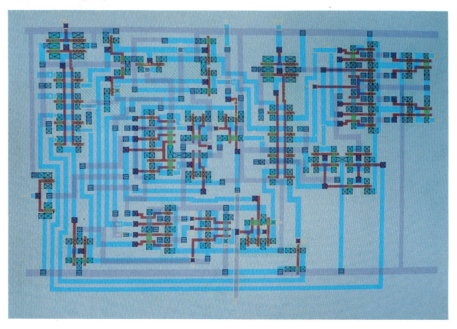

Plate 2 Part of a VLSI circuit design being created using a graphics editor on a Sun Workstation.

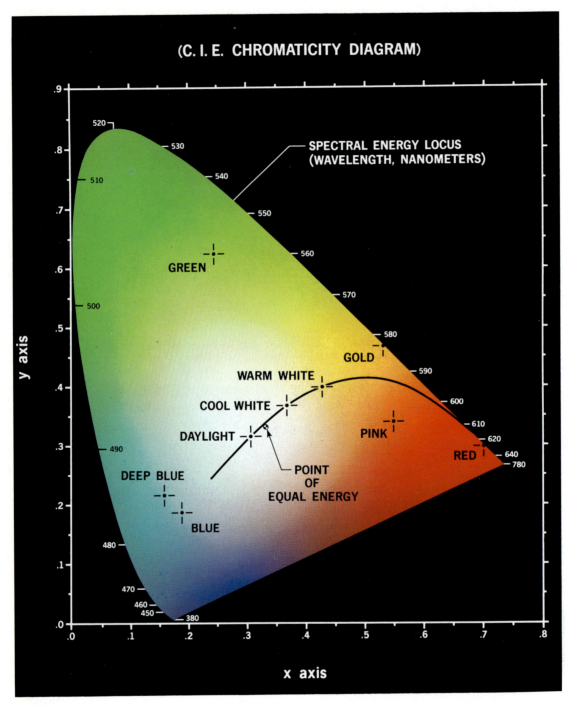

Plate 3 The complete CIE colour diagram. (Courtesy of International Lighting Department, General Electric Company, USA.)

Plate 4 The colours that can be produced using the RGB model with a typical television monitor.

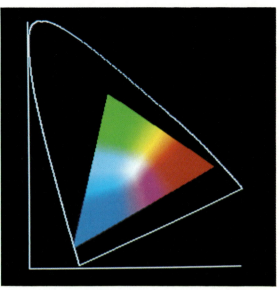

Plate 5 The relation between the CIE diagram and the colours that can be realized using a typical television monitor.

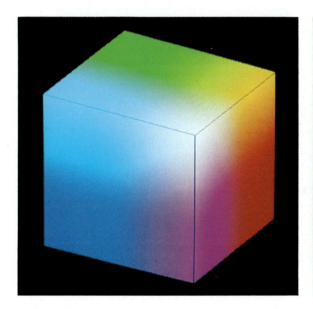

Plate 6 The complete RGB space drawn as a three-dimensional cube. The hidden vertex appears black.

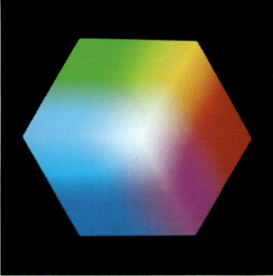

Plate 7 The colour hexagon.

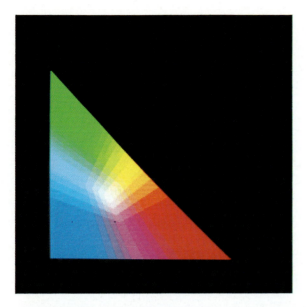

Plate 8   The effect of colour quantization on the colours realizable by a typical monitor. The picture uses the same data as Plate 4, but instead of displaying it with 24 bits of intensity data per pixel, it has been quantized into eight bits using the octree quantization algorithm described in Chapter 7.

Plate 9   The effect of colour quantization on a typical graphics scene. This picture uses the same data as Plate 14. Here it is displayed using eight bits per pixel after octree quantization. Comparing this picture with Plate 14, some loss of quality will be observed. In particular colour contours can be seen in the sky and on the chalice.

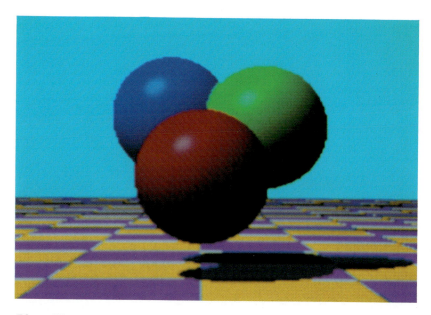

Plate 10 This picture was generated using low resolution (200 by 200 pixels). Alias effects can be seen around the edges of the spheres. The chess board pattern on the floor will be seen to break up in the distance. This is again an alias effect.

Plate 11 This picture uses the same resolution as Plate 10, but has been anti-aliased by using six supersamples per pixel. The result is generally satisfactory.

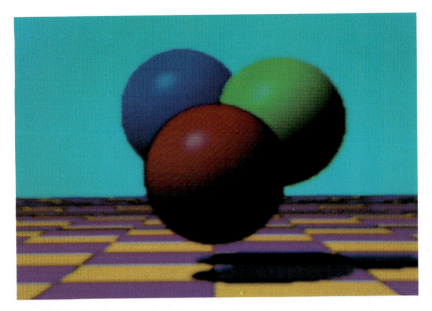

Plate 12   The same picture as Plates 10 and 11, but this time the anti-aliasing has been done by convolution. Notice that although the convolution has reduced the alias effect at the edge of the spheres, it has not removed the problem with the chess board pattern.

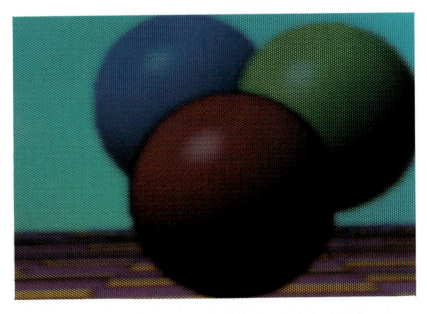

Plate 13   This picture shows a detail of Plate 10 after anti-aliasing using three passes of a 3 by 3 convolution filter. The alias on the chess board is still visible, and bands of false colours are beginning to appear at the boundaries.

Plate 14 Ray tracing a solid of revolution. Three levels of reflection have been computed in this picture.

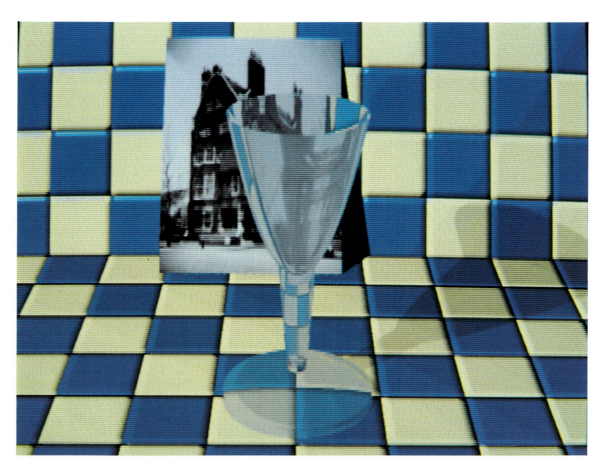

Plate 15 Ray tracing a transparent solid of revolution. Five levels of reflection and two of refraction have been used. Notice that the use of a texture map, used in this case to create a photograph, can provide a lot of detail for very little computational cost.

Plate 16 An example of recursive texture mapping. This picture has been quantized into eight bits per pixel with no deterioration in quality.

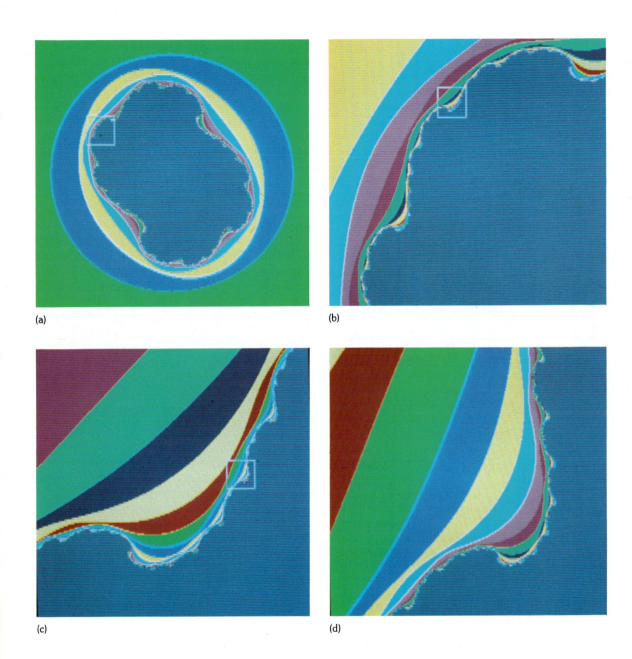

(a)

(b)

(c)

(d)

Plate 17 Plots of Mandelbrodt's function with λ = 0.5 + 0.5j. In each case a gray area is made up of the pixels that remain bounded. Each band of colour requires one more iteration of the function before its pixels will diverge. The whole argand diagram from [−2, − 2.5j] to [3,2.5j] is shown in (a). Each successive picture is an amplification of the small white square in the previous picture. However far we go, the picture retains the same features. The boundary is infinitely long.

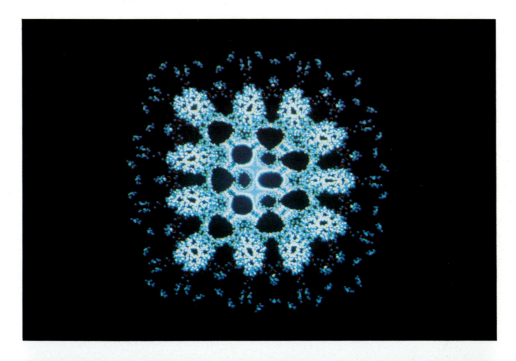

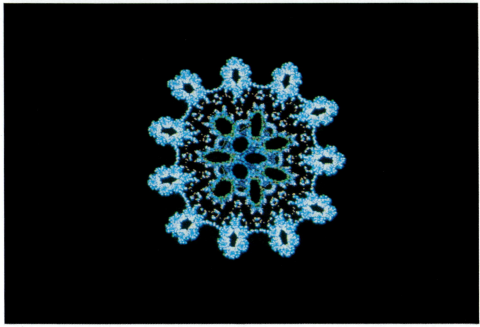

Plate 18 Chaotic functions are those which when iterated never converge or diverge. Plotting the iterations can result in some delicate and beautiful patterns.

Plate 19 This picture was generated using a camera lens model. The apperture was set to f5.6, and the focus adjusted so that the point of sharpest focus is at the front of the picture. The rubic cube is slightly out of focus, and the background scene with the lamp, picture and wallpaper is further out of focus. It was necessary to anti-alias the picture by supersampling after the focusing had been computed in order to remove severe alias effects caused when the circle of confusion was approximately one pixel in diameter.

6 Spline Curves and Surfaces

Splines provide a very useful way of generating smooth curves and surfaces from a small number of control points, thus saving space in the database at the expense of increased computation time in drawing the scene. They also provide an effective way of modelling irregular-shaped objects.

Using parametric representations, spline curves may be formulated in two or three dimensions. Curves that pass close to the control points without actually going through them are the simplest to compute. Belonging to this class are the Bezier curves and surfaces, and the *B*-splines, both of which are widely used in graphics systems. At the expense of additional computation time, the *B*-splines can be made to pass through the knots. Different interpolating splines can be computed using cubic patches or polynomial approximation. These each have different characteristics and therefore produce different effects.

Surfaces may be approximated by similar methods to those used for curves. Drawing them poses the problem of removal of hidden lines. If the surfaces are broken into triangular facets, then the hidden line algorithms of the previous chapter can be applied. A faster algorithm for doing this is the floating horizon, and in many cases reasonable surfaces can be drawn using it.

Depending on the drawing algorithm chosen, one set of knots can be used to produce a wide variety of different surfaces. Several important ways of drawing a surface based on a single set of knots are discussed and their results compared.

6.1   INTRODUCTION

So far, only polyhedral models of 3D objects have been considered. These use a set of points joined by straight-line segments to form planar facets. If a smooth surface is to be represented by this method, a large number of facets must be used to ensure that discontinuities are not observed. This causes a large increase in the size of the resulting database, which was a major problem when CAD systems were introduced for the design of cars and aircraft. For this reason, most of the pioneering work for its solution was done by these industries.

An alternative to using planar facets made up of straight-line segments is to store a small set of points, called **knots**, and some function of those points from which a smooth curve or surface can be generated. This saves space in the database at the cost of extra computation at run time. The resulting curves are called **splines**. The name *spline* comes from boat building where planks of wood were formed into shape by bending them round pegs hammered into the ground. Originally, it was the pegs that were called splines, although the word is now used to describe the smooth curve itself.

There are two ways in which spline curves and surfaces can be constructed. The first is called **interpolation**, in which the curve or surface passes through each knot. The designer specifies a representative selection of points lying on the surface of the object that he wishes to draw. In the second method, called **approximation**, the curve does not necessarily pass through the knots, but passes close to them. In practice, approximation is easier to compute and can be used effectively in many cases. One example is in the design of car body shapes, where designers' decisions are governed by style and fashion. On the other hand, interpolation is essential in the drawing of high-tolerance components, such as those found in a car engine.

Most of the treatment in this chapter will be concerned with algorithms for drawing spline curves, which are the loci of single points in 2D or 3D space. Surfaces are most readily drawn as two orthogonal sets of spline curves, although it is possible to represent them in the computer as a function of two independent variables.

The position vector representation of points in 2D or 3D space will be used throughout the analysis of splines. $N + 1$ knots are defined by the position vectors $\mathbf{P_0}, \mathbf{P_1}, ..., \mathbf{P_N}$. Normally, the parametric representation of spline curves will be used, where any point on the curve, $\mathbf{P}$, is expressed by a function:

$$\mathbf{P}(\mu) = f(\mu, \mathbf{P_0}, \mathbf{P_1}, ..., \mathbf{P_N})$$

As μ varies, the locus of $\mathbf{P}$ is the spline curve. As in the formulation of the line equation, the segment of the curve to be drawn is usually defined by

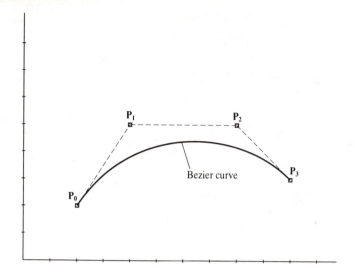

Figure 6.1
The Bezier curve through four
knots. Only the endpoints are
interpolated, and the slope of
the curve at each endpoint is
equal to the line joining the
endpoint to its neighbour.

the subrange $[0..1]$ of μ. The position of **P** at the values $\mu = 0$ and $\mu = 1$ will define the endpoints of the spline. Surfaces will be formulated in the same way, but will require two parameters, μ and v, which will also normally be in the range $[0..1]$.

6.2   BEZIER CURVES

One of the simplest ways of approximating a curve was made popular by Bezier in the context of car body design. It was based on a mathematical formulation by Casteljau.

   A typical Bezier curve is shown in Figure 6.1. Here, four knots P_0, P_1, P_2 and P_3 are shown. The main properties of all Bezier curves is that they go through the end knots and that the slope at each endpoint is the same as that of the line joining the end knot to its immediate neighbour. The curve may be thought of as having its ends *clamped* at the slope of the end lines while each point exercises a *pull* on the direction of the curve, which is proportional to its distance. The convention adopted here and elsewhere is to use a total of $N + 1$ knots, labelled from 0 to N.

6.2.1   Casteljau's algorithm

Computation of the Bezier curve may be done using a simple recursive algorithm, originated by Casteljau, which is best illustrated by means of a

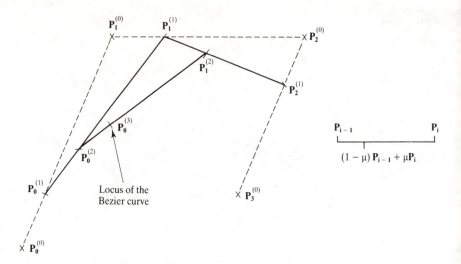

Figure 6.2
Casteljau's construction of the Bezier curve. Each line is subdivided in the same proportion and the division points of adjacent lines are joined. The process is continued until only one point remains, which is the locus of the Bezier curve.

geometric construction. First of all, the knots are joined by line segments. Then, a value of μ is selected in the range $[0..1]$ and points are marked off on each line segment corresponding to the parametric distance μ chosen. This gives a new set of points, one less in number than the original knots. These are joined by line segments and a new set of points is marked on these segments at the same parametric distance μ. The construction continues until a single point is obtained, and this point is the locus of the Bezier curve as μ varies between 0 and 1. An illustration is given in Figure 6.2. As before, a subscript is used to label the knots from 0 to N. In addition, a bracketed superscript is used to indicate which set of construction lines the point was generated from. Hence, for a point on any line segment:

$$\mathbf{P}_i^{(j)} = \mathbf{P}_i^{(j-1)} + \mu(\mathbf{P}_{i+1}^{(j-1)} - \mathbf{P}_i^{(j-1)})$$

which can be written in the more useful form for splines:

$$\mathbf{P}_i^{(j)} = (1 - \mu)\mathbf{P}_i^{(j-1)} + \mu\mathbf{P}_{i+1}^{(j-1)} \qquad (6.1)$$

For a given μ value, N sets of lines have to be constructed and the point $\mathbf{P}_0^{(N)}$ will lie on the Bezier curve. The knots $\mathbf{P}_i$ are expressed by the zero-order points:

$$\mathbf{P}_i = \mathbf{P}_i^{(0)}$$

Algorithm 6.1

Recursive Bezier curve generator.

type *ordinate* = [*x, y, z*];
      point = **array** [*ordinate*] **of real**;
      construction_points = **array** [0..*n*, 0..*n*] **of** *point*;

function *Casteljau* (**var P** : *construction_points*; *i, j* : **integer**; μ : **real**) : *point*;
begin
  if *j* = 1
  then *Casteljau* := (1 − μ) ∗ **P[i, 0]** + μ ∗ **P[i+1, 0]**
  else *Casteljau* := (1 − μ) ∗ *Casteljau*(**P**, *i, j* − 1, μ)+ μ ∗ *Casteljau*(**P**, *i* + 1, *j* − 1, μ)
end;

(∗ The curve can be drawn with the following section of code, which draws a straight line approximation.
  The number of line segments drawn is stored in the variable *NoOfSegments* ∗)

var *Locus* : *point*;

MOVE_TO(*P*[0][*x*], *P*[0][*y*]);
for *k* := 1 **to** *NoOfSegments* **do**
begin
  μ = *k*/*NoOfSegments*;
  Locus := *Casteljau*(*KnotArray*, 0, *N*, μ);
  DRAW_TO(*Locus*[*x*], *Locus*[*y*]);
end;

This geometric construction has been encapsulated in Algorithm 6.1, in which the function returns a type *point*, and vector by scalar multiplication is indicated by ∗.

6.2.2 Blending

It was stated earlier that the knots seem to exert a 'pull' on the Bezier curve. Another way to say the same thing is to consider that the locus of the curve consists of a *blend* of its knots. This can be clearly seen when the

Casteljau algorithm is applied to the degenerate case of two knots. The result is the parametric line equation:

$$\mathbf{P} = (1 - \mu)\mathbf{P}_0^{(0)} + \mu\mathbf{P}_1^{(0)}$$

where the two position vectors are being linearly blended to produce a third. The parameter μ may be thought of as measuring the distance along the line.

Expanding the Casteljau equation for $\mathbf{P}^{(2)}$ gives:

$$\begin{aligned}
\mathbf{P}_0^{(2)} &= (1 - \mu)\mathbf{P}_0^{(1)} + \mu\mathbf{P}_1^{(1)} \\
&= (1 - \mu)((1 - \mu)\mathbf{P}_0^{(0)} + \mu\mathbf{P}_1^{(0)}) + \mu((1 - \mu)\mathbf{P}_1^{(0)} + \mu\mathbf{P}_2^{(0)}) \\
&= (1 - \mu)^2\mathbf{P}_0^{(0)} + 2\mu(1 - \mu)\mathbf{P}_1^{(0)} + \mu^2\mathbf{P}_2^{(0)}
\end{aligned}$$

which is now a blend of three points. On examining the coefficients:

$$\begin{aligned}
w_2(\mu) &= \mu^2 \\
w_1(\mu) &= 2\mu(1 - \mu) \\
w_0(\mu) &= (1 - \mu)^2
\end{aligned}$$

which are plotted in Figure 6.3, it can be seen that each has its maximum value at a different value of μ. w_0 is maximum where $\mu = 0$, so at this point, $\mathbf{P}_0^{(0)}$ has the most influence. When $\mu = \frac{1}{2}$, then the knot $\mathbf{P}_1^{(0)}$ has twice the weight of the other two knots, and so the curve is pulled towards it. At all values of μ, the weights will sum to 1; that is:

$$w_0(\mu) + w_1(\mu) + w_2(\mu) = 1$$

This very important property of blending curves ensures that a uniform blend is achieved at all values of μ.

The reader may care to verify that by expanding the recursion equation for the next order, $\mathbf{P}_0^{(3)}$, the resulting blend has four coefficients:

$$\mathbf{P}_0^{(3)} = (1 - \mu)^3\mathbf{P}_0^{(0)} + 3\mu(1 - \mu)^2\mathbf{P}_1^{(0)} + 3\mu^2(1 - \mu)\mathbf{P}_2^{(0)} + \mu^3\mathbf{P}_4^{(0)}$$

and as the process is continued, the familiar binomial expansion appears. Thus, a general iterative form of the Bezier curve can be written:

$$\mathbf{P}(\mu) = \sum_{i=0}^{N} \mathbf{P}_i W(N, i, \mu)$$

where W is called the **Bernstein blending function**, where

$$W(N, i, \mu) = [^N C_i]\mu^i(1 - \mu)^{N-i} \text{ and } [^N C_i] = N!/(i!(N - i)!).$$

As usual, there are $N + 1$ knots in total.

(a)

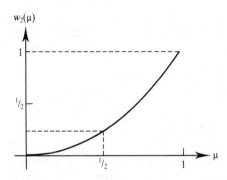

(b)

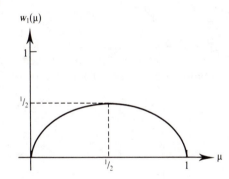

(c)

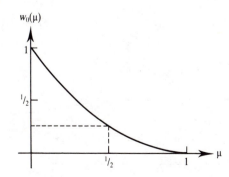

Figure 6.3
Second-order blending curves.
For any value of μ the three
curves sum to 1.

As with the vector line equation, there is a similar division of the Bezier curve into segments of importance, defined by:

$$\mu = 0, \qquad P(0) = P_0$$
$$\mu = 1, \qquad P(1) = P_N$$
$$0 < \mu < 1, \qquad P(\mu) = \text{some blend of all } P_i$$

The iterative equation for the Bezier curve can be computed slightly more efficiently in terms of space than the recursive form, although in the 2D case this is not likely to be significant, since it is rare to use Bezier curves for more than a few points. Care must be taken to avoid overflow when computing the Bernstein functions. Note that, since vector equations are used, there is no difference between the formulation of the Bezier curve in two and three dimensions.

The iterative solution, although slower and less elegant, generalizes to surface construction more easily, and so tends to be used in preference. To represent surfaces, two parameters are needed. The equation may be written:

$$P(\mu, v) = \sum_{i=0}^{N} \sum_{j=0}^{M} P_{i,j} W(N, i, \mu) W(M, j, v)$$

Here, a grid of knots regularly placed is being used to give an approximation to the surface being represented. There will be $(N + 1) \times (M + 1)$ of them in total.

Figure 6.4

The Bezier curve through six knots. It has the effect of smoothing out irregularities.

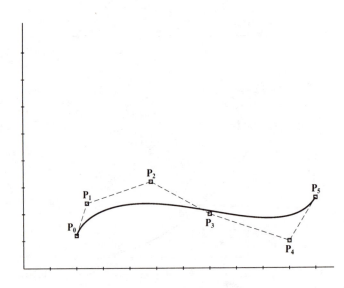

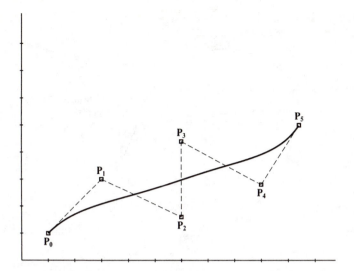

Figure 6.5

The lack of local control in Bezier curves can sometimes produce unwanted effects. Here the zig-zag shape of the knots has been completely smoothed out by the Bezier curve.

6.2.3 Characteristics of Bezier curves

As previously mentioned, Bezier curves have their end gradient clamped to the slope of the end line segments and, between the ends, they blend the positions of all the points. These features give the Bezier curve its characteristic shape, as shown in Figures 6.1 and 6.2. A similar predictable result is shown in Figure 6.4. Since all points are included, it will be noted that the blend has the effect of smoothing out local features. This lack of

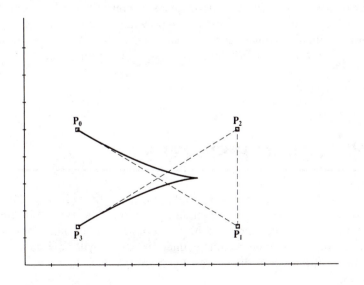

Figure 6.6

Bezier curves can sometimes display discontinuities. Here, for a very simple knot set, a cusp is produced. Generally speaking, such effects are undesirable, but can occur in a way that is difficult to predict.

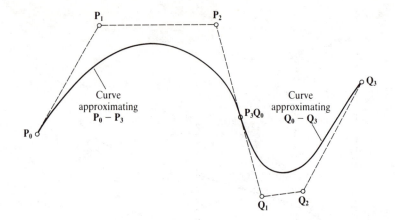

Figure 6.7
Fine detail can be modelled by Bezier curves by breaking the required shape into small pieces and approximating each with a separate Bezier curve. The fact that the slope at the endpoints follows the linear interpolation of the knots can be used to join the pieces continuously. P_2, P_3 and Q_1 lie on a straight line, thus the slope of each Bezier curve at P_3 is the same, and a continuous curve is created.

locality can give unintended results. For example, Figure 6.5 shows a set of knots disposed in a zig-zag pattern. The Bezier curve smoothes out this pattern completely as shown.

A second problem with Bezier curves is the presence of discontinuities in the resulting curve. These can occur when there is some looping in the curve, even in simple cases, such as the example shown in Figure 6.6.

The problem of lack of local control can be offset to some degree by generating a curve from a number of small pieces. This can be done easily since, as already noted, the gradient at the endpoint of a Bezier curve is the same as the gradient of the line joining the first and second (or penultimate and last) knots. Thus, a continuous curve can be created by ensuring that the last two knots of one section are co-linear with the first two knots of the succeeding section. An example is given in Figure 6.7. This technique is rather tedious to use, so in circumstances where local control is required, together with the convenience of using more than a few knots, Bezier curves are not used. The *B*-splines are adopted in preference.

6.3 CUBIC *B*-SPLINES

In principal, the *B*-splines are similar to the Bezier curves. The main difference is in the choice of blending function. The Bernstein blending function takes all knots into account, except at the endpoints. By contrast, the third-order *B*-spline blending function, which will now be discussed, only takes into account the nearest knots, at the most four.

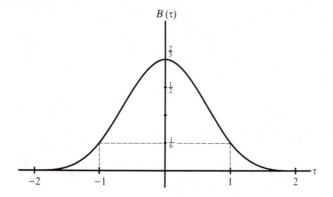

$B(\tau)$

Figure 6.8
The *B*-spline blending curve is a symmetric bell shape.

Figure 6.8 shows the third-order *B*-spline blending function. It has a characteristic bell shape and falls to zero for $|\tau| > 2$. It is a piecewise curve and may be written using five equations:

$$
\begin{aligned}
B(\tau) &= \frac{1}{6}\left(2 + \tau\right)^3 & -2 \leqslant \tau \leqslant -1 \\
&= \frac{1}{6}\left(4 - 6\tau^2 - 3\tau^3\right) & -1 \leqslant \tau \leqslant 0 \\
&= \frac{1}{6}\left(4 - 6\tau^2 + 3\tau^3\right) & 0 \leqslant \tau \leqslant 1 \\
&= \frac{1}{6}\left(2 - \tau\right)^3 & 1 \leqslant \tau \leqslant 2 \\
&= 0 & 2 \leqslant |\tau|
\end{aligned}
$$

(6.2)

These are sometimes written as individual cubic polynomials, which are defined on the interval $[0..1]$:

$$
\begin{aligned}
b_{-2}(\gamma) &= \frac{1}{6}\gamma^3 \\
b_{-1}(\gamma) &= \frac{1}{6}\left(1 + 3\gamma + 3\gamma^2 - 3\gamma^3\right) \\
b_0(\gamma) &= \frac{1}{6}\left(4 - 6\gamma^2 + 3\gamma^3\right) \\
b_1(\gamma) &= \frac{1}{6}\left(1 - 3\gamma + 3\gamma^2 - \gamma^3\right)
\end{aligned}
$$

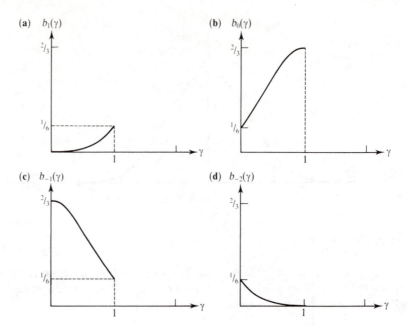

Figure 6.9

The third-order *B*-spline blending curve is made up of four pieces, each defined by a cubic equation. As with the second-order blending curves (Figure 6.3), for any value of γ the four values of *b*(γ) sum to 1.

These individual cubic functions of γ are shown in Figure 6.9 in the range 0 to 1. They are combined as follows to give the five equations describing $B(\tau)$:

$$\begin{aligned}
B(\tau) = b_{-2}(\tau + 2) &\qquad -2 \leqslant \tau \leqslant -1 \\
b_{-1}(\tau + 1) &\qquad -1 \leqslant \tau \leqslant 0 \\
b_0(\tau) &\qquad 0 \leqslant \tau \leqslant 1 \\
b_1(\tau - 1) &\qquad 1 \leqslant \tau \leqslant 2 \\
0 &\qquad 2 \leqslant |\tau|
\end{aligned}$$

The third-order curve has three important properties:

(1)   It is symmetrical about $\tau = 0$, thus $B(-\tau) = B(\tau)$.

(2)   Its first and second derivatives are continuous at the places where the pieces join ($\tau = \pm 2, \pm 1, 0$).

(3)   For any given value of γ, it has the very important property that:

$$b_{-2}(\gamma) + b_{-1}(\gamma) + b_0(\gamma) + b_1(\gamma) = 1$$

or, relating this to the actual blending function:

$$B(\tau - 2) + B(\tau - 1) + B(\tau) + B(\tau + 1) = 1 \qquad 0 < \tau \leqslant 1$$

The third condition ensures that if all knots are the same, $P_i = P_0$, then the spline is also equal to P_0 for all values of μ. All practical splines must satisfy this condition, which has been satisfied for all splines studied so far.

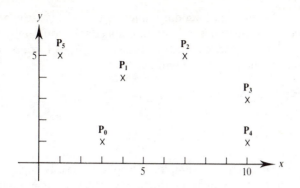

(a)

Figure 6.10
Spline curves are normally constructed using knots defined in Cartesian space. These may be placed without restriction and, as in this example, loops can be used.

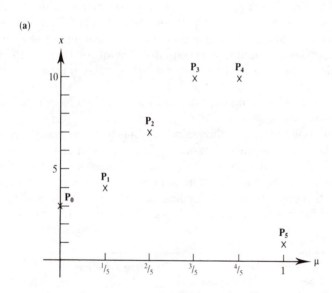

(b)

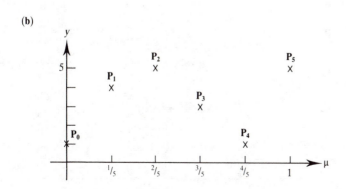

Figure 6.11
The spline functions are defined in parametric space. Here, each knot is taken to lie at equal intervals of the parameter (μ). The knots of Figure 6.10 are shown here plotted at equal intervals of μ in the range [0..1].

To use the *B*-spline blending function effectively, it is necessary to adopt the convention that the knots are spaced at equal intervals of the parameter. Thus, for the knot $\mathbf{P_i}$ out of a set of $N + 1$ knots, the corresponding value of the parameter will be:

$$\mu = \frac{i}{N} \qquad\qquad (6.3)$$

This will be clarified by an example. If a spline curve is being constructed from the six knots shown in Figure 6.10, in Cartesian space, then each knot may be plotted against the parameter, in parameter space, as shown in Figure 6.11. It is easy to see that any set of knots could be plotted at equal intervals of the parameter μ in a similar fashion.

The blending function may now be associated with the curve by letting the inter-knot distance equal one unit of τ. The effect of making this choice is that, when computing a point on the curve for a given value of μ, exactly four knots are always taken into account, or three in the limiting case. This can be seen by drawing the blending curve on the same horizontal axis as the plot of *x* against μ. Figure 6.12 shows the curve placed with its centre at $\mu = \frac{1}{2}$. Wherever it is drawn, its non-zero part will cover at most four knots.

To draw the spline, the locus [*x*, *y*] has to be computed as μ varies. Each ordinate is computed separately. Taking *x* as an example, for a given value of μ, the blending curve is aligned with the plot of the *x* ordinates of the knots against μ. This was done in Figure 6.12 for $\mu = \frac{1}{2}$. At each knot position, the value from the blending curve at that point is read and the knot's *x* value is multiplied by it. Hence, for Figure 6.12, the values are:

Knot	*x* Co-ordinate	Blending Function Value	*x* B
$\mathbf{P_0}$	3	0	0
$\mathbf{P_1}$	4	$\dfrac{1}{48}$	$\dfrac{4}{48}$
$\mathbf{P_2}$	7	$\dfrac{23}{48}$	$\dfrac{161}{48}$
$\mathbf{P_3}$	10	$\dfrac{23}{48}$	$\dfrac{230}{48}$
$\mathbf{P_4}$	10	$\dfrac{1}{48}$	$\dfrac{10}{48}$
$\mathbf{P_5}$	1	0	0

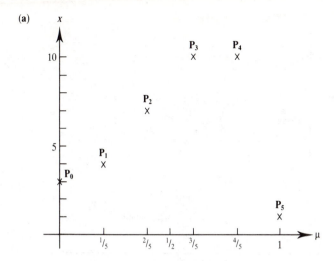

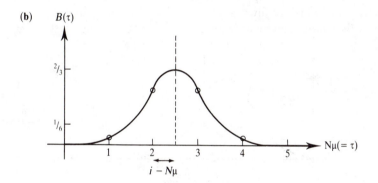

Figure 6.12
The blending curve is applied to calculate points on the spline curve. To calculate the point at $\mu = 1/2$, the centre of the curve is placed at $\mu = 1/2$. The scale of the curve is adjusted so that the inter-knot distance is one unit of τ in Figure 6.8. For each knot, a weight is read off the blending curve.

Summing the final column gives a value of 405/48, which is the value of the *x* ordinate for the point where $\mu = 1/2$. The *y* ordinate is found in the same way.

This method produces a blend of the four knots closest to the position on the curve being computed, the weights depending on the distance. This ensures the required locality properties. It can be summarized by the following single equation:

$$\mathbf{P}(\mu) = \sum_{i=0}^{N} \mathbf{P}_i B(i - N\mu)$$

The term $i - N\mu$ is often a cause of confusion. It is used to compute the distance of each knot from the centre of the blending curve so that its weight can be found. Referring again to Figure 6.12, it can be seen that the

(a)

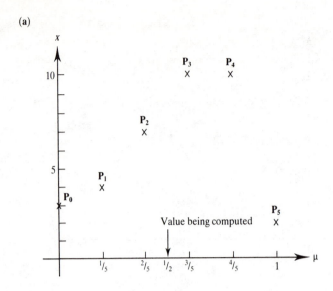

(b)

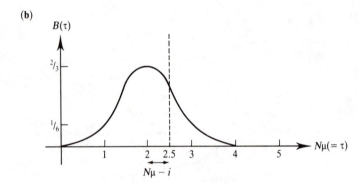

Figure 6.13

An alternative way to compute the spline is to calculate the weight of each knot in turn. For knot $\mathbf{P_2}$, the blending curve centre is placed at $\mu = 2/5$ and the weight for $\mathbf{P_2}$ at $\mu = 1/2$ can be read off.

centre of the curve is placed at the point where $\mu = \frac{1}{2}$ and $N\mu = 2.5$. Thus, the distance to, for example, knot 2 is $-\frac{1}{2}$ and the value of the blending function, as defined in Equation (6.2), is $B(-\frac{1}{2})$.

An alternative way to view the process of computing the spline locus for a given value of μ is to find the weight for each knot by placing the blending curve with its centre at the knot and read the value of the function at the point $N\mu$. Thus, in Figure 6.13, the blending curve would be placed with centre over, say, knot 2 ($N\mu = 2$) and the distance found to the point where $N\mu = 2.5$. This would give a weight of $B(\frac{1}{2})$ for knot 2. Since, as already noted, the B function is symmetric, $B(\tau) = B(-\tau)$, and thus the same weight is obtained. Visualizing the computation this way, it is convenient to write the spline equation in the form:

$$\mathbf{P}(\mu) = \sum_{i=0}^{N} \mathbf{P}_i B(N\mu - i) \tag{6.4}$$

which is the normal form in which it appears in most other texts. If the value is computed at the point where $\mu = j/N$ – that is, the point where the curve is locally closest to knot $\mathbf{P_j}$ – then Equation (6.4) reduces to:

$$\mathbf{P}(\mu) = \sum_{i=0}^{N} \mathbf{P_i} B(j - i)$$

The sum can be expanded to give:

$$\mathbf{P}\left(\frac{j}{N}\right) = \mathbf{P_0}B(j) + \mathbf{P_1}B(j-1) + \ldots + \mathbf{P_{j-2}}B(2) + \mathbf{P_{j-1}}B(1) + \mathbf{P_j}B(0)$$
$$+ \mathbf{P_{j+1}}B(-1) + \mathbf{P_{j+2}}B(-2) + \ldots + \mathbf{P_n}B(j - N)$$

Referring to the definition of the blending function, its value falls to zero for arguments greater than 2 or less than -2. Hence, all but three terms are zero, yielding:

$$\mathbf{P}\left(\frac{j}{N}\right) = \mathbf{P_{j-1}}B(1) + \mathbf{P_j}B(0) + \mathbf{P_{j+1}}B(-1)$$
$$= \frac{1}{6}\mathbf{P_{j-1}} + \frac{2}{3}\mathbf{P_j} + \frac{1}{6}\mathbf{P_{j+1}}$$

For cases where the value of the parameter μ corresponds to a knot position, the blending equation is always of this form. For other values of μ there are four terms.

The *B*-spline defined in Equation (6.4) is another example of convolution. It is the one-dimensional equivalent of the formulation given in Chapter 3 for the anti-aliasing of a raster image. Thus, the effect of Equation (6.4) may be visualized as the bell-shaped curve sliding over the plot of the knots in parameter space, in an analogous way to which the 3×3 mask is slid over the raster image to achieve the blend. The main difference comes from the fact that μ is a continuous variable. Hence, it is possible to compute a value of the locus of the spline at any point, not just at discrete positions of the pixels.

This way of computing the spline produces good results in the middle of the curve, but unfortunately it does not give a good result at the ends. This can be seen by substituting the values $\mu = 0$ and $\mu = 1$ into Equation (6.4), yielding:

$$\mathbf{P}(0) = \frac{2}{3}\mathbf{P_0} + \frac{1}{6}\mathbf{P_1} \neq \mathbf{P_0}$$
$$\mathbf{P}(1) = \frac{2}{3}\mathbf{P_N} + \frac{1}{6}\mathbf{P_{N-1}} \neq \mathbf{P_N}$$

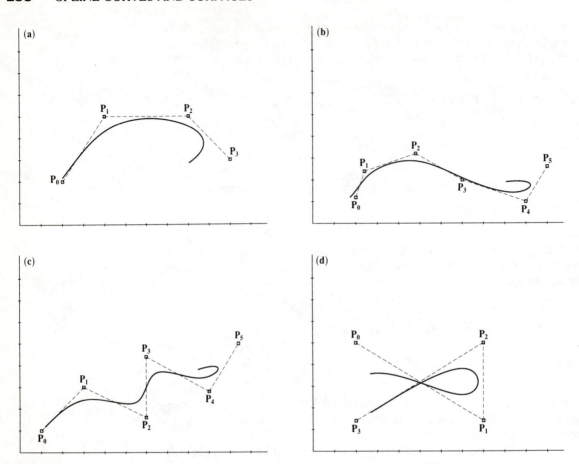

Figure 6.14

B-spline curves with a free end condition. The knot sets used are the same as for the Bezier curves. Although the curves give good results near the middle, there is very little that can be said about the ends.

which shows that, in general, the curve will not go through the end points. In fact, very little can be said about what it does do! Figure 6.14 shows the effect of Equation (6.4) on the same sets of knots used to illustrate the Bezier curves.

Several methods of dealing with this problem have been tried. One simple way is to introduce multiple endpoints. For example, the endpoints can be doubled up by rewriting the spline equations as:

$$\mathbf{P} = \sum_{i=-1}^{N+1} \mathbf{P}_i B(N\mu - i)$$

where:

$$\mathbf{P}_{-1} = \mathbf{P}_0 \quad \text{and} \quad \mathbf{P}_{N+1} = \mathbf{P}_N$$

so there are still only $N + 1$ different knots in all.

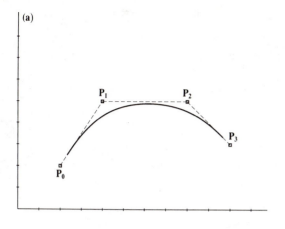

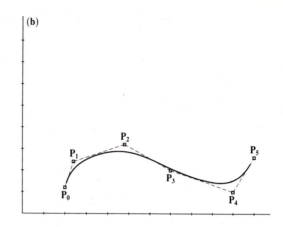

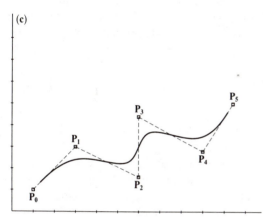

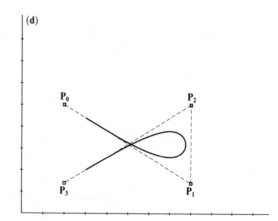

Figure 6.15
A simple method of making the *B*-spline curves behave better at the ends is to duplicate the endpoints. The results are an improvement, but the splines still do not interpolate the endpoints.

Introducing double knots anywhere in a *B*-spline has the effect of pulling the curve strongly towards the position of the double knot, which is a useful technique in some cases. The effect of doubled endpoints on the test set of knots is shown in Figure 6.15. The curve still does not go through the endpoints, although it is pulled to them rather more than before.

One way of getting the spline to go through a given knot is to triplicate it. This will be apparent from Equation (6.4). However, this will in general cause discontinuities in the curve. In the case of the endpoints, this would not be a problem in many cases.

A better way of getting the correct effect at the end of the curve is to introduce **phantom** endpoints, whose value constrains the curve to pass through P_0 or P_N. As with the double endpoints, these phantom points are denoted as P_{-1} and P_{N+1}, which gives:

$$P(\mu) = \sum_{i=-1}^{N+1} P_i B(N\mu - i)$$

$$(6.5)$$

If the curve is to pass through the knot $\mathbf{P_0}$:

$$P(0) = \frac{1}{6}\mathbf{P_{-1}} + \frac{2}{3}\mathbf{P_0} + \frac{1}{6}\mathbf{P_1} = \mathbf{P_0}$$

and, therefore:

$$\mathbf{P_{-1}} = 2\mathbf{P_0} - \mathbf{P_1} \qquad\qquad (6.6)$$

Similarly, at the other end it is easy to show that:

$$\mathbf{P_{N+1}} = 2\mathbf{P_N} - \mathbf{P_{N-1}} \qquad\qquad (6.7)$$

This method has the additional advantage that the slope at the ends follows the gradient of the line joining the end knots, a property that can be verified by differentiating Equation (6.5) with respect to μ, and noting that:

$$\frac{dy}{dx} = \frac{\dfrac{dy}{d\mu}}{\dfrac{dx}{d\mu}}$$

Equation (6.5), with the phantom points defined by Equation (6.6) and Equation (6.7) gives, at last, a usable form of the *B*-spline. Figure 6.16 illustrates its characteristic shape when applied to the four knot sets that were used to illustrate the behaviour of Bezier curves. Figure 6.16 should be compared with Figures 6.1, 6.4, 6.5, 6.6, 6.14 and 6.15.

6.3.1   Interpolation using *B*-splines

B-splines may be used to interpolate data points instead of simply passing close to them. The method is somewhat similar to the trick of introducing phantom points given in the last section. Instead of using the actual knots, $\mathbf{P_i}$, in the spline equation a complete set of phantom, or **parametric knots**, $\mathbf{A_i}$, is computed and used. These knots are chosen so that the spline curve interpolates the real *geometric* knots.

This section considers the case where $N + 1$ geometric knots are to be interpolated. As usual, they will be denoted $\mathbf{P_0}$ to $\mathbf{P_N}$. In this formulation, $N + 3$ parametric knots will be used, denoted $\mathbf{A_{-1}}$ to $\mathbf{A_{N+1}}$. The extra two knots are to allow flexibility setting the gradient at the ends of the spline, which will be a useful feature in piecing together several sections of curve without introducing discontinuities.

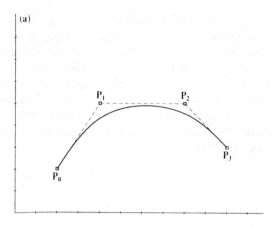

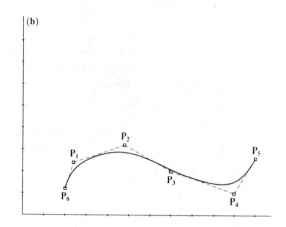

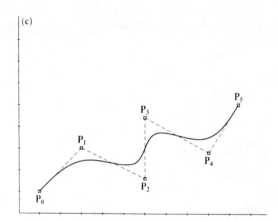

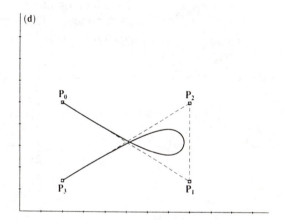

Figure 6.16
Using phantom endpoints the
third-order *B*-spline curves give
predictable results and preserve
local properties. Like the Bezier
curves, the slope at the
endpoints is the same as the
linear interpolant.

The equation of the interpolating spline is:

$$\mathbf{P}(\mu) = \sum_{i=-1}^{N+1} B(N\mu - i)\mathbf{A_i} \tag{6.8}$$

but before it can be used, a set of values must be computed for $\mathbf{A_i}$. To do
this, use is made of the fact that the geometric knots appear at equal
intervals of the parameter μ ($\mu = 0$, $1/N$, $2/N$, ..., 1). So, by substituting the
geometric knots on the right-hand side of Equation (6.8) with the corresponding μ in the left-hand side, a set of equations is obtained:

$$\mathbf{P}\left(\frac{j}{N}\right) = \mathbf{P_j} = \frac{1}{6}\mathbf{A_{j-1}} + \frac{2}{3}\mathbf{A_j} + \frac{1}{6}\mathbf{A_{j+1}}$$

There is one of these for each geometric knot, yielding $N + 1$ equations. However, there are $(N + 3)$ unknown values of $\mathbf{A_i}$. The other two equations come from placing a further constraint on the ends of the curve, which in this case will be to fix the gradient at the ends. This is known as a **clamped end condition** and can be used to determine the shape at the ends of a spline, or to piece together two splines without introducing a discontinuity. The gradients at the ends will be denoted by the direction vectors $\mathbf{g_0}$ and $\mathbf{g_N}$. To compute them, the spline equation (6.8) needs to be differentiated with respect to μ. This yields:

$$\mathbf{P'}(\mu) = N \sum_{i=-1}^{N+1} B'(N\mu - i)\mathbf{A_i} \tag{6.9}$$

To obtain a solution, the B function must be differentiated with respect to its parameter. This can be done by differentiating the individual pieces given in Equation (6.2):

$$
\begin{aligned}
B'(\tau) &= \frac{1}{2}\left(2 + \tau\right)^2 & -2 \leq \tau \leq -1 \\
&= \frac{1}{2}\left(-4\tau - 3\tau^2\right) & -1 \leq \tau \leq 0 \\
&= \frac{1}{2}\left(-4\tau + 3\tau^2\right) & 0 \leq \tau \leq 1 \\
&= -\frac{1}{2}\left(2 - \tau\right)^2 & 1 \leq \tau \leq 2 \\
&= 0 & 2 \leq |\tau|
\end{aligned}
$$

Figure 6.17 plots this differential function over its non-zero range. This now enables an expression to be written for the gradient at the endpoints, by substituting the values $\mu = 0$ and $\mu = 1$ into Equation (6.9), giving:

$$\mathbf{P'}(0) = \mathbf{g_0} = N\left[\mathbf{A_{-1}}B'(1) + \mathbf{A_0}B'(0) + \mathbf{A_1}B'(-1)\right]$$

$$= \frac{N}{2}\left(\mathbf{A_1} - \mathbf{A_{-1}}\right)$$

and similarly:

$$\mathbf{P'}(1) = \mathbf{g_N} = \frac{N}{2}\left(\mathbf{A_{N+1}} - \mathbf{A_{N-1}}\right) \tag{6.10}$$

Since the gradient at the ends is an input, or alternatively can be set to some default value such as the forward difference, enough equations are

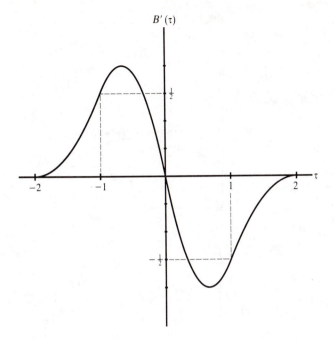

$B'(\tau)$

Figure 6.17
The first differential of the third-order *B*-spline blending curve of Figure 6.8. It consists of four pieces defined by second-order functions which are the derivatives of the cubic functions making up the blending curve shown in Figure 6.9.

now available to solve for the parametric knots A_i. The equations may be neatly summarized by writing them in matrix form $M \cdot A = V$ as follows:

$$
\begin{bmatrix}
-\dfrac{N}{2} & 0 & \dfrac{N}{2} & 0 & 0 & 0 & \cdots & 0 & 0 & 0 \\[2mm]
\dfrac{1}{6} & \dfrac{2}{3} & \dfrac{1}{6} & 0 & 0 & 0 & \cdots & 0 & 0 & 0 \\[2mm]
0 & \dfrac{1}{6} & \dfrac{2}{3} & \dfrac{1}{6} & 0 & 0 & \cdots & 0 & 0 & 0 \\[2mm]
0 & 0 & \dfrac{1}{6} & \dfrac{2}{3} & \dfrac{1}{6} & 0 & \cdots & 0 & 0 & 0 \\[2mm]
\cdot & \cdot & \cdot & \cdot & \cdot & \cdot & & \cdot & \cdot & \cdot \\
\cdot & \cdot & \cdot & \cdot & \cdot & \cdot & & \cdot & \cdot & \cdot \\
\cdot & & & & & & & & & \\
0 & 0 & 0 & 0 & 0 & & \cdots & \dfrac{2}{3} & \dfrac{1}{6} & 0 \\[2mm]
0 & 0 & 0 & 0 & 0 & & \cdots & \dfrac{1}{6} & \dfrac{2}{3} & \dfrac{1}{6} \\[2mm]
0 & 0 & 0 & 0 & 0 & & \cdots & -\dfrac{N}{2} & 0 & \dfrac{N}{2}
\end{bmatrix}
\cdot
\begin{bmatrix}
A_{-1} \\[2mm]
A_0 \\[2mm]
A_1 \\[2mm]
A_2 \\[2mm]
\cdot \\
\cdot \\
\cdot \\
A_{N-1} \\[2mm]
A_N \\[2mm]
A_{N+1}
\end{bmatrix}
=
\begin{bmatrix}
g_0 \\[2mm]
P_0 \\[2mm]
P_1 \\[2mm]
P_2 \\[2mm]
\cdot \\
\cdot \\
\cdot \\
P_{N-1} \\[2mm]
P_N \\[2mm]
g_N
\end{bmatrix}
$$

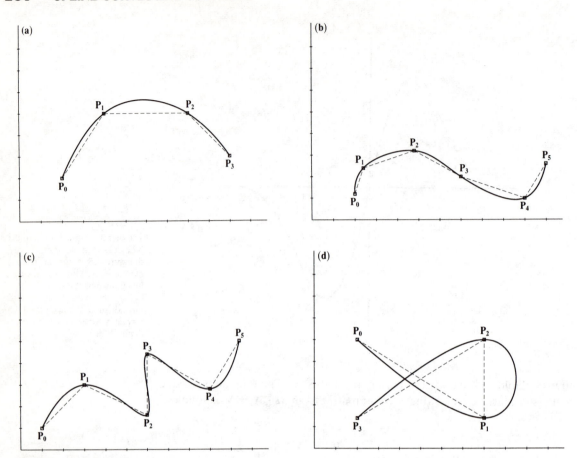

Figure 6.18
Full interpolation using
B-splines. The gradients at the
ends have been set to produce
the required results.

where the vector **A** contains the phantom knots, **V** contains the geometric knots and the gradients at the end, and *M* is a matrix that depends only on the number of knots, *N*.

The solution can be found, for example, by Gaussian elimination. Since the matrix does not depend on the values of the knots, a more direct method is to invert the matrix, which can be precalculated for a number of *N* values. If the inverted matrix for a given *N* is available, then the values of the phantom knots may be calculated by matrix/vector multiplication:

$$\mathbf{A} = M^{-1} \cdot \mathbf{V}$$

The *B*-spline interpolants for the test set of knots are shown in Figure 6.18.

6.4   RECURSIVE *B*-SPLINES

So far, this chapter has only considered the case of the third-order *B*-spline curve; that is, splines constructed from a blending function that is defined by cubic polynomials. Attention has been focused on the cubic blending function because it gives good results in the majority of cases, and with the use of tension and skew the designer can normally obtain whatever shape curve is required. However, it is possible to construct splines using other order blending functions, and this provides an alternative way of altering the local detail in the spline.

The *B*-spline blending function given in Equation (6.2) is just one of a family of blending functions that may be conveniently defined by a recursive computational procedure:

$$B^{(0)}(\tau) = 1 \quad \text{if} \quad 0 \le \tau \le 1$$
$$= 0 \quad \text{otherwise}$$

and:

$$B^{(j)}(\tau) = \frac{1}{j+1}\left(\tau B^{(j-1)}(\tau) + (j + 1 - \tau)B^{(j-1)}(\tau - 1)\right) \tag{6.11}$$

As before, $(N + 1)$ knots are used, labelled from 0 to N, and they are spaced at equal intervals of the parameter μ, which is in the range $[0..1]$. The superscript j is the order of the blending curve. One important difference to the previous definition is that the blending curves are defined with $\tau = 0$ being the point where the curve first becomes non-zero. This is the point equivalent to $\tau = -2$ in the formulation of Equation (6.2), which is the same as $B^{(3)}(\tau + 2)$ in the formulation of Equation (6.11). As before, the parameter τ is taken to be equivalent to $N\mu$ in Equation (6.11).

By expanding the recursion, it can be shown that the parameter range over which Equation (6.11) is non-zero is:

$$0 < \tau < j + 1$$

So, the curve positioned centrally on the origin is given by:

$$B^{(j)}\left(\tau + \frac{(j+1)}{2}\right)$$

and, as before, it can be centred at a given value of μ by using:

$$\tau = N\mu - i$$

Thus, the spline equation for the j'th order blending function is:

$$\mathbf{P}(\mu) = \sum_{i=0}^{N} \mathbf{P_i} B^{(j)}\left(N\mu - i + \frac{(j+1)}{2}\right) \tag{6.12}$$

To relate this formulation to the one given in Section 6.3, the first- and third-order blending curves will be considered. To obtain the first-order blending curve, $j = 1$ is substituted into Equation (6.11) to give:

$$B^{(1)}(\tau) = \tau B^{(0)}(\tau) + (2 - \tau)B^{(0)}(\tau - 1)$$

Substituting $j = 1$ into Equation (6.12) gives:

$$\mathbf{P}(\mu) = \sum_{i=0}^{N} \mathbf{P_i} B^{(1)}(N\mu - i + 1) \tag{6.13}$$

Now, consider the spline values in the neighbourhood of two adjacent knots, say $\mathbf{P_K}$ and $\mathbf{P_{K+1}}$. In particular, consider the parameter values between $N\mu = K$ and $N\mu = K + 1$. A normalized variable, γ can be used here, which is defined by:

$$\gamma = N\mu - K$$

with the range of interest being $0 < \gamma < 1$. The four terms of the sum in Equation (6.13) for which the index is near to the two selected knots are:

$$\mathbf{P_{K-1}} B^{(1)}(N\mu - K + 2) + \mathbf{P_K} B^{(1)}(N\mu - K + 1) + \mathbf{P_{K+1}} B^{(1)}(N\mu - K)$$
$$+ \mathbf{P_{K+2}} B^{(1)}(N\mu - K - 1)$$

and all other terms are zero. Substituting the normalized variable $\gamma = N\mu - K$ into the first-order B functions, they can be expressed by the zero-order functions as:

$$B^{(1)}(N\mu - K + 2) = B^{(1)}(\gamma + 2)$$
$$= (\gamma + 2)B^{(0)}(\gamma + 2) + (-\gamma)B^{(0)}(\gamma + 1)$$
$$B^{(1)}(N\mu - K + 1) = B^{(1)}(\gamma + 1)$$
$$= (\gamma + 1)B^{(0)}(\gamma + 1) + (1 - \gamma)B^{(0)}(\gamma)$$
$$B^{(1)}(N\mu - K) \quad = B^{(1)}(\gamma)$$
$$= (\gamma)B^{(0)}(\gamma) + (2 - \gamma)B^{(0)}(\gamma - 1)$$
$$B^{(1)}(N\mu - K - 1) = B^{(1)}(\gamma - 1)$$
$$= (\gamma - 1)B^{(0)}(\gamma - 1) + (3 - \gamma)B^{(0)}(\gamma - 2) \tag{6.14}$$

Because of the nature of the $B^{(0)}$ function, and since $0 < \gamma < 1$, the only non-zero instances of the $B^{(0)}$ functions in Equation (6.14) are those containing variable γ by itself. Hence:

$$B^{(1)}(\gamma + 2) = B^{(1)}(\gamma - 1) = 0$$
$$B^{(1)}(\gamma + 1) = (1 - \gamma)$$
$$B^{(1)}(\gamma) = \gamma$$

and the spline equation is given by:

$$\mathbf{P}(\mu) = (1 - \gamma)\mathbf{P_K} + \gamma\,\mathbf{P_{K+1}} \qquad 0 < \gamma < 1$$

which, since $\gamma = N\mu - K$, can also be written in terms of μ as:

$$\mathbf{P}(\mu) = [1 - (N\mu - K)]\mathbf{P_K} + [N\mu - K]\mathbf{P_{K+1}} \qquad K < N\mu < K + 1$$

which is the vector line equation and confirms that blending with the function $B^{(1)}$ is equivalent to linear interpolation of the knots.

Turning to the third-order function, it is easy to demonstrate the equivalence of the recursive formulation to the piecewise Equation (6.2). Remembering the fact that $B(\tau)$ is equivalent to $B^{(3)}(\tau + 2)$, the expansion of the blending curve is:

$$\begin{aligned} B^{(3)}(\tau + 2) = (1/6)[\ (\tau + 2)^3 B^{(0)}(\tau + 2) + (4 - 6\tau^2 - 3\tau^3)B^{(0)}(\tau + 1) \\ + (4 - 6\tau^2 + 3\tau^3)B^{(0)}(\tau) + (2 - \tau)^3 B^{(0)}(\tau - 1)] \end{aligned}$$

Thus, the $B^{(0)}$ functions effectively piece the curve together in the correct way.

Figure 6.19 shows a plot of $B^{(j)}(\tau)$ as j increases. It can be seen that the same bell shape gets progressively flatter and flatter and, as a consequence, the degree of local control is reduced. At the same time, more and more knots influence the spline at each point. As the order increases, so does the continuity in the spline. If $B^{(0)}$ functions are used, then the result is a discontinuous set of points, the original knots, as can be easily verified by substituting $j = 0$ in Equation (6.12). If the $B^{(1)}$ functions are used, linear interpolation is obtained; thus, the curve is continuous, but discontinuous in all derivatives. If $B^{(2)}$ is used, then first-order continuity is gained as well. $B^{(3)}$ gives second-order continuity, and so on.

It might possibly be expected that the *B*-spline approaches the Bezier curve when the order of the recursive function is increased. This is only partially true. For N knots, the highest order function producing a practically useful spline is given by $j = N$, since this gives the non-zero range of $(N + 1)$ in the normalized variable τ. This means that all the knots contribute to the spline value, so it should be similar to the Bezier curve.

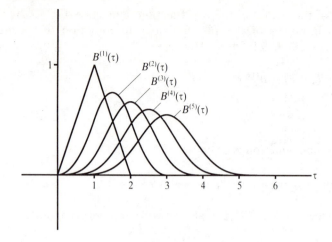

Figure 6.19
The family of *B*-spline blending curves. $B^{(1)}$ produces linear interpolation. The second-order curve is made up from the three pieces shown in Figure 6.3. The third-order curve is the familiar blending function of Figure 6.8. Using higher-order blending curves produces smoother curves which take less account of local detail.

It is true that by setting $j = N$ all knots are included in the spline calculation, but this occurs at the midpoint of the curve. At the endpoints, since the blending function is shifted to the knot position, only half of the function overlaps the knots and only half of the knots contribute to the spline value. This clearly demonstrates the difference in the techniques of *B*-splines and Bezier curves. Bezier curves are well defined at the endpoints of the spline, *B*-splines are not. It is also true that with the correct choice of phantom knots and a high-order of blending function, the *B*-spline curve can be made to approximate the Bezier curve.

6.5 β-SPLINES

B-splines have proved popular due to the predictable results that they give the designer and the high speed with which they can be computed. However, there are cases where they can exhibit undesirable properties, or where they do not represent the designer's intentions. These cases can be dealt with by using a different shaped blending curve. The effect on the shape of a curve that can be created by changing the blending function has been extensively studied. One important class of such functions with similar properties to the *B* functions, use the so-called β blending functions. This section considers the third-order case.

The β functions are represented in the same piecewise manner as the *B* function (Equation (6.2)), but two extra parameters are used. These are called **tension** and **skew**, represented by symbols t and s, whose values determine the exact shape of the curve. When $t = 0$ (no tension) and $s = 1$

(no skew), the equations are reduced to the *B*-spline blending functions. Positive values of tension ($t > 0$) increase the amplitudes of the two middle segments of the third-order curve with respect to the first and last segments. Increasing skew values ($s > 1$) increases the amplitudes of the two segments on the right with respect to the two segments on the left. Decreasing values of skew ($0 < s < 1$) increases the amplitude of the left side of the curve. The segments for the β-spline given by Barsky (1983) are:

$$\beta(\tau) = \frac{2}{\delta}(2 + \tau)^3 \qquad\qquad -2 \leq \tau \leq -1$$

$$= \frac{1}{\delta}\Big[(t + 4s + 4s^2) - 6(1 - s^2)\tau - 3(2 + t + 2s)\tau^2$$

$$- 2(1 + t + s + s^2)\tau^3\Big] \qquad -1 \leq \tau \leq 0$$

$$= \frac{1}{\delta}\Big[(t + 4s + 4s^2) - 6(s - s^3)\tau - 3(t + 2s^2 + 2s^3)\tau^2$$

$$+ 2(t + s + s^2 + s^3)\tau^3\Big] \qquad 0 \leq \tau \leq 1$$

$$= \frac{2}{\delta}s^3(2 - \tau)^3 \qquad\qquad 1 \leq \tau \leq 2$$

$$= 0 \qquad\qquad 2 \leq |\tau|$$

where:

$$\delta = t + 2s^3 + 4s^2 + 4s + 2$$

The effect of the tension parameter will be considered first. With $s = 1$ (no skew) the blending function remains symmetrical and can be easily compared to the *B*-spline. The segments are given by:

$$\beta(\tau) = \frac{2}{(12 + t)}(2 + \tau)^3 \qquad\qquad -2 \leq \tau \leq -1$$

$$= \frac{1}{(12 + t)}\Big[(8 + t) - 3(4 + t)\tau^2 - 2(3 + t)\tau^3\Big] \qquad -1 \leq \tau \leq 0$$

$$= \frac{1}{(12 + t)}\Big[(8 + t) - 3(4 + t)\tau^2 + 2(3 + t)\tau^3\Big] \qquad 0 \leq \tau \leq 1$$

$$= \frac{2}{(12 + t)}(2 - \tau)^3 \qquad\qquad 1 \leq \tau \leq 2$$

$$= 0 \qquad\qquad \text{otherwise}$$

The blending function is still symmetrical with respect to $\tau = 0$, so that $\beta(-\tau) = \beta(\tau)$. With increasing t, the two middle sections become larger

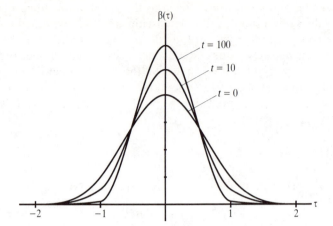

Figure 6.20

The effect of increasing tension on the third-order blending curve. As tension is increased, a taller thinner curve is produced, giving more weight to the points close to the centre.

with respect to the two side section. With very large t values, the two side sections become very small and the middle sections approach the functions:

$$\beta(\tau) = 1 - 3\tau^2 - 2\tau^3 \qquad -1 \leqslant \tau \leqslant 0$$
$$= 1 - 3\tau^2 + 2\tau^3 \qquad 0 \leqslant \tau \leqslant 1$$

which does satisfy the spline condition $\beta(\tau - 1) + \beta(\tau) = 1 \; (0 \leqslant \tau \leqslant 1)$ and is a continuous function with continuous first and second derivatives at $\tau = 0$. Its first derivative is continuous at $|\tau| = 1$, but has discontinuous second derivatives.

The effect of changing the tension on the blending curve is illustrated in Figure 6.20. An increase produces a taller, thinner curve, which in effect draws the curve closer to the middle knots. The effect on the zig-zag knot set is shown in Figure 6.21. As the tension is increased, the spline tends towards a linear interpolation of the knots. The idea of tension coming from the notion that the pull exerted on the curve by the knots is increasing.

The curve shown in Figure 6.21 uses phantom endpoints to produce a clamped end condition. Calculating the phantom points in a manner analogous to the cubic B-spline curve gives:

$$\mathbf{P}_{-1} = \frac{[(1 - \beta(0))\mathbf{P}_0 - \beta(-1)\mathbf{P}_1]}{\beta(1)} \quad \text{and} \quad \mathbf{P}_{N+1} = \frac{[(1 - \beta(0))\mathbf{P}_N - \beta(1)\mathbf{P}_{N-1}]}{\beta(-1)}$$

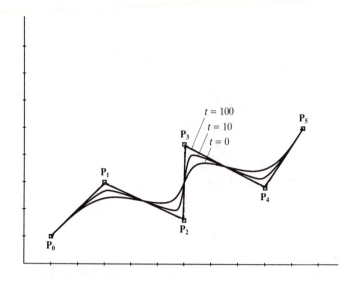

Figure 6.21
The effect of increasing tension is to pull the spline closer to the knots. If a very high tension is used, the resulting spline is close to linear interpolation.

Consider now the use of skew with no tension ($t = 0$). The following equations are obtained:

$$\beta(\tau) = \frac{1}{(1 + 2s + 2s^2 + s^3)}(2 + \tau)^3 \qquad\qquad -2 \leqslant \tau \leqslant -1$$

$$= \frac{1}{(1 + 2s + 2s^2 + s^3)}\big[2s(1 + s) - 3(1 - s^2)\tau$$
$$\qquad\qquad - 3(1 + s)\tau^2 - (1 + s + s^2)\tau^3\big] \qquad -1 \leqslant \tau \leqslant 0$$

$$= \frac{1}{(1 + 2s + 2s^2 + s^3)}\big[2s(1 + s) - 3s(1 - s^2)\tau$$
$$\qquad\qquad - 3s^2(1 + s)\tau^2 + s(1 + s + s^2)\tau^3\big] \qquad 0 \leqslant \tau \leqslant 1$$

$$= \frac{s^3}{(1 + 2s + 2s^2 + s^3)}(2 - \tau)^3 \qquad\qquad 1 \leqslant \tau \leqslant 2$$

$$= 0 \qquad\qquad 2 \leqslant |\tau|$$

Thus, when $s > 1$, the segments on the right get larger. For very large s values, only the two right segments survive, so that:

$$\beta(\tau) = 3\tau - 3\tau^2 + \tau^3 \qquad 0 \leqslant \tau \leqslant 1$$
$$= (2 - \tau)^3 \qquad\qquad 1 \leqslant \tau \leqslant 2$$

which is a continuous function, but has discontinuous first and second derivatives at $\tau = 0$ and $\tau = 1$.

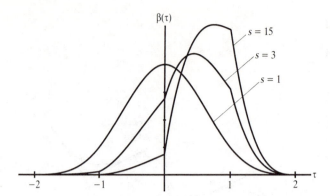

Figure 6.22

The effect of skewing a curve.
The skewed blending function
is no longer continuous in the
first derivative.

The effect of changing the bias, or skew, on the blending function is shown in Figure 6.22. It introduces discontinuous derivatives and asymmetry into the blending function. The effect on a simple set of knots is shown in Figure 6.23. The effect of skew does not correspond to any easily describable property in design, and so tends to be used less than tension.

Mathematically, the β-splines behave in the same way as the *B*-splines. Thus, the same techniques that have been discussed for correcting the ends of the *B*-splines may equally be applied to the β-splines. Similarly, β-spline interpolation of the knots may be performed.

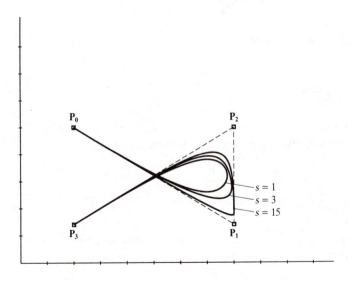

Figure 6.23

Making the blending curve
skew pulls the curve towards
the knots with higher index
numbers.

6.6   POLYNOMIAL INTERPOLATION

This chapter has concentrated extensively on the *B*-splines and β-Splines because they have properties that make them suitable for virtually every application in CAD and graphics. However, there are many other spline techniques used for specific purposes. In the simplest case, a set of $N + 1$ points can be interpolated by a polynomial of degree N. This may be seen by writing the equation in the form:

$$x(\mu) = K_N\mu^N + K_{N-1}\mu^{N-1} + \dots + K_1\mu + K_0 \tag{6.15}$$

where the K_i are unknown constant coefficients. A set of values must be found for these coefficients to make the spline curve interpolate the knots. Substituting in the values of the parameter μ, which correspond to the knots, $N + 1$ linear equations are obtained in the coefficients K_i, which can be solved by Gaussian elimination. Similar equations can be found defining the locus of y and z. Polynomials of this form are limited to small numbers of knots, since the use of high-degree polynomials causes instabilities, which appear as sinusoidal ripples in the resulting curve. For this reason, it is rare to use polynomials of degree greater than three.

The solution using Gaussian elimination is expensive in computer time and can be avoided by using the spline equation written in the form of a Lagrange polynomial, which, using Cartesian space, has equation:

$$y = \sum_{i=0}^{N} y_i L_i(x) \tag{6.16}$$

where:

$$L_i(x) = \frac{(x - x_0)(x - x_1) \dots (x - x_{i-1})(x - x_{i+1}) \dots (x - x_N)}{(x_i - x_0) \dots (x_i - x_{i-1})(x_i - x_{i+1}) \dots (x_i - x_N)}$$

Thus, the degree of the polynomial is one less than the number of points to be interpolated. Putting $N = 1$ for example, yields two points. It is easily seen that Equation (6.16) reduces to that of a straight line. The Cartesian form of this equation has been presented, since it is clear to see how it interpolates the knots. However, it is of limited usefulness, as will be explained shortly. A parametric form of this equation can be derived by substituting points **P** for the y values and a parameter μ for the x values:

$$\mathbf{P}(\mu) = \sum_{i=0}^{i=N} \mathbf{P_i}L_i(\mu)$$

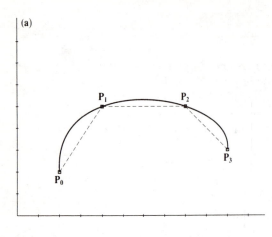

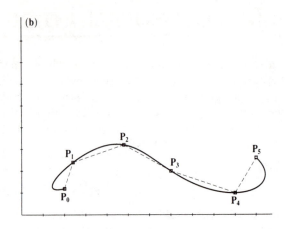

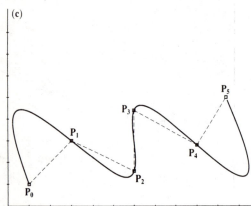

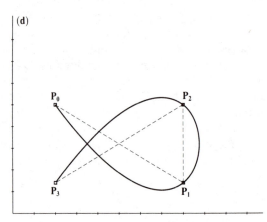

Figure 6.24

Using polynomial interpolation such as Lagrange polynomials works satisfactorily for low numbers of knots, which have low-order interpolants (a) and (d). However, as the number of knots is increased, there is a tendency for unwanted sinusoidal ripples to appear, as shown in (b) and particularly (c).

where:

$$L_i(\mu) = \frac{(N\mu)(N\mu - 1)(N\mu - 2)\dots(N\mu - i + 1)(N\mu - i - 1)\dots(N\mu - N + 2)(N\mu - N + 1)(N\mu - N)}{(i)(i - 1)(i - 2)\dots(1)(-1)\dots(i - N + 2)(i - N + 1)(i - N)}$$

If $N\mu = K$, a knot position, then

$$L_i(K/N) = 0 \text{ for all } i \neq K$$
and $L_i(K/N) = 1$ for $i = K$.

To illustrate the use of polynomial interpolation, the same knot sets used in Figure 6.18 to illustrate the use of B-spline interpolation, are interpolated using Lagrange polynomials in Figure 6.24. Notice how the method works well for up to four knots, but instabilities can be seen in the examples with six knots.

Parametric equations give a direct method by which a polynomial interpolating spline can be determined going through any number of points in two or three dimensions. But, what does this really mean in the

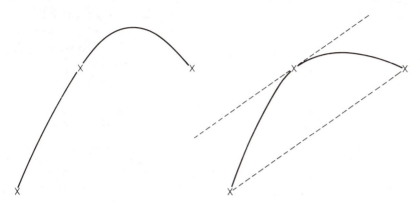

$$y = c_0 + c_1x + c_2x^2 \qquad\qquad x = a_0 + a_1\mu + a_2\mu^2$$
$$y = b_0 + b_1\mu + b_2\mu^2$$

Figure 6.25
For any three points, we can interpolate in Cartesian space using a second-order polynomial. There is only one solution for c_0, c_1 and c_2. If, alternatively, we use a parametric representation, we still have only one possible solution for a_0, a_1, a_2, b_0, b_1 and b_2, and we obtain a different curve.

Cartesian space or in the functional representation of $y = f(x)$? The second-order parametric curve can go through any three points and it has six coefficients; namely:

$$x = a_0 + a_1\mu + a_2\mu^2$$
$$y = b_0 + b_1\mu + b_2\mu^2$$

In two dimensions, the six coefficients can be uniquely determined from the six components of the three points $\mathbf{P_0}$, $\mathbf{P_1}$ and $\mathbf{P_2}$. The second-order Cartesian polynomial $y = f(x)$ has only three coefficients:

$$y = c_0 + c_1x + c_2x^2$$

and it can also go through any given three points $[x_i, y_i]$ for $i = 0, 1, 2$. The difference between the two curves is demonstrated in Figure 6.25 for a particular selection of three points. Depending on the choice of the points, the two formulations can produce very different types of curve.

The difference is in the formulation of the second-order curve $y = f(x)$, since in general the second-order function should be represented in its implicit form $f(x, y) = 0$. This function has six coefficients; however, it can be normalized by dividing each term by any non-zero coefficient, leaving only five of them independent. Assuming that the constant term is not zero, the general second-order function can therefore be written as:

$$1 + c_1x + c_2y + c_3x^2 + c_4y^2 + c_5xy = 0$$

The five coefficients cannot be determined from interpolating through three points. Two more conditions are required. On the other hand, from the six coefficients of the parametric curve, the five coefficients of the general function $f(x, y)$ can be uniquely determined, which means that the parametric curve selects one particular general function from an infinite number of possible curves. Without going too deeply into the mathematical aspects of these second-order polynomials, it is possible to show that one of the additional conditions the parametric curve satisfies is that its derivative at the middle point is equal to the central difference, or:

$$\frac{dy}{dx} = \frac{y_2 - y_0}{x_2 - x_0} \quad \text{at } x = x_1$$

The difference between the parametric representation of curves in two dimensions and their Cartesian equivalents has been discussed here because the parametric representation is often readily accepted without the realization that it may provide surprising results in the x–y space. Even in the second-order case, a parametric representation that looks like a simple parabola may provide any conic section when the $y = f(x)$ function is drawn. When the order is increased beyond two, the number of coefficients for the general $f(x, y) = 0$ function rapidly increases and it becomes more and more difficult to find a meaningful relationship between the parametric and Cartesian representations.

6.6.1 Blending of second-order splines

As has been seen in the case of the recursive B-splines, the lower the order of the spline, the closer to a piecewise linear approximation is the resulting curve. Hence, second-order formulations have the advantage that they cannot exhibit ripples, since these are properties of third and higher orders. Two second-order splines may be blended together to form a third-order spline. This may be viewed as if the zero-order blending function were of the second order in μ and one step of recursion would produce the next, or third, order polynomials.

A simple interpolation technique that uses the blending of second-order polynomials was proposed by Overhauser. This is sometimes referred to as parabolic blending, although this is a misnomer because the second-order polynomials could be any conic section. A second-order polynomial in the parameter variable μ can be used to interpolate three points in 2D or 3D space. The aim here is to produce a spline between knot $\mathbf{P_i}$ and $\mathbf{P_{i+1}}$, using the normalized variable $\tau = N\mu - i$ with the range of τ between 0 and 1. As shown in Figure 6.26, taking four points $\mathbf{P_{i-1}}, \mathbf{P_i}, \mathbf{P_{i+1}}$, and $\mathbf{P_{i+2}}$, the curve interpolating the centre two points, $\mathbf{P_i}$ and $\mathbf{P_{i+1}}$, can be found by blending the two second-order polynomials in τ defined by the

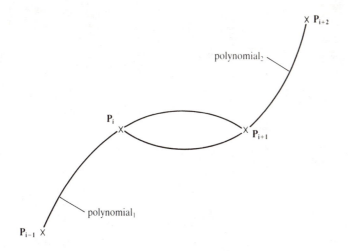

Figure 6.26
Interpolation can be done by blending two polynomials of second order. Between points P_i and P_{i+1} the curve is a linear blend of polynomial$_1$ and polynomial$_2$. This is called the Overhauser spline.

outer three points, P_{i-1}, P_i, P_{i+1} and P_i, P_{i+1}, P_{i+2}. The coefficients can be found by Lagrange polynomials as:

$$\frac{1}{2}\tau(\tau - 1)P_{i-1} - (\tau + 1)(\tau - 1)P_i + \frac{1}{2}\tau(\tau + 1)P_{i+1} \qquad \text{polynomial}_1$$

$$\frac{1}{2}(\tau - 1)(\tau - 2)P_i - \tau(\tau - 2)P_{i+1} + \frac{1}{2}\tau(\tau - 1)P_{i+2} \qquad \text{polynomial}_2$$

The locus between points P_i and P_{i+1} is a blend of the two conic curves. Since the variable τ takes on values between 0 and 1, the two parametric curves can be blended by the spline:

$$P(\tau) = (1 - \tau)\, \text{polynomial}_1 + \tau\, \text{polynomial}_2$$

which will go through the two endpoints and will approximate the first polynomial near $\tau = 0$ and the second around $\tau = 1$. The combined equations give:

$$P(\tau) = P_i + \frac{1}{2}(P_{i+1} - P_{i-1})\tau + \frac{1}{2}(-P_{i+2} + 4P_{i+1} - 5P_i + 2P_{i-1})\tau^2$$

$$+ \frac{1}{2}(P_{i+2} - 3P_{i+1} + 3P_i - P_{i-1})\tau^3$$

To show what conditions this spline equation satisfies, in addition to passing through two points, the derivative $P'(\tau) = dP(\tau)/d\tau$ is taken and

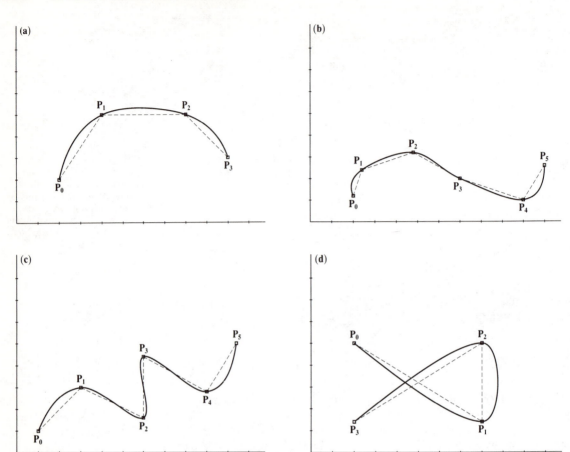

Figure 6.27

Interpolation using the Overhauser method. A linear blend of two second-order curves gives a third-order interpolant, and therefore the results are not dissimilar to those produced using the third-order *B*-spline.

evaluated at the knot positions $\tau = 0$ and $\tau = 1$:

$$\mathbf{P}'(0) = \frac{1}{2}(\mathbf{P}_{i+1} - \mathbf{P}_{i-1})$$

$$\mathbf{P}'(1) = \frac{1}{2}(\mathbf{P}_{i+2} - \mathbf{P}_i)$$

These differentials are equal to the central difference around knots $\mathbf{P}_i$ and $\mathbf{P}_{i+1}$. This can be seen in the 2D case when:

$$\frac{dy}{dx} = y' = \frac{\dfrac{dy}{d\tau}}{\dfrac{dx}{d\tau}}$$

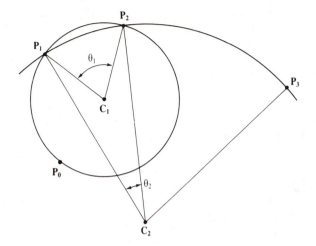

Figure 6.28

Interpolation can be done by blending circles. The circle through P_0, P_1 and P_2 has centre C_1 and radius r_1. The circle through P_1, P_2 and P_3 has centre C_2 and radius r_2. Between P_1 and P_2 an interpolant can be produced by taking successive circles with centres and radii interpolating C_1, C_2 and r_1, r_2, and angles interpolating θ_1 and θ_2.

and:

$$y'(0) = \frac{y_{i+1} - y_{i-1}}{x_{i+1} - x_{i-1}}$$

$$y'(1) = \frac{y_{i+2} - y_i}{x_{i+2} - x_i}$$

The effect of interpolating the test set of knots using polynomial blending is shown in Figure 6.27.

Blending of second-order polynomials can also be done for Cartesian functions $f(x, y) = 0$. For example, the blending of second-order splines can be applied to circular arcs. A circle can be drawn between any three points; hence, for two successive sets, an interpolation for the middle knots can be found by linearly interpolating the centre and radii of the two circles. As shown in Figure 6.28, four points P_0 to P_3 are considered in relation to one circle with centre C_1 passing through points P_0, P_1, P_2 and another circle with centre C_2 passing through points P_1, P_2, P_3. The two direction vectors are:

$$r_1 = P_1 - C_1$$
$$r_2 = P_1 - C_2$$

The circle can be expressed by the vector/matrix equation:

$$P_{\text{circle}} = C_i + r_i \cdot R(\theta)$$

where R is the 2D rotation matrix. If the angle between P_1 and P_2 for the first circle is equal to θ_1 and that for the second circle is θ_2, then the blended spline can be expressed by the following vector/matrix equation:

$$\mathbf{P}(\tau) = (1 - \tau)\mathbf{C_1} + \mathbf{r_1} \cdot R((1 - \tau)\theta_1) + \tau\mathbf{C_2} + \mathbf{r_2} \cdot R(\tau\,\theta_2)$$

Care is required in processing cases where the sign of the radius changes; that is, when the centre crosses the spline.

6.6.2   Cubic splines

The most common technique using cubic splines is to join the knots in pairs with a separate spline patch in between each. Taking two knots $\mathbf{P_i}$ and $\mathbf{P_{i+1}}$ and a parameter τ, which varies between 0 and 1 between them, the spline equation can be expressed as:

$$\mathbf{P}(\tau) = \mathbf{K_3}\tau^3 + \mathbf{K_2}\tau^2 + \mathbf{K_1}\tau + \mathbf{K_0}$$

To determine the spline, the values of the coefficients $\mathbf{K}$ must be found. To simplify the treatment, only one ordinate, the x value, will be considered. The values for y and z can be found in an analogous way.

The equation for the x co-ordinate of the spline patch is:

$$x = K_3\tau^3 + K_2\tau^2 + K_1\tau + K_0 \tag{6.17}$$

Substituting the actual values at the knots, $[x_i, 0]$ and $[x_{i+1}, 1]$, into Equation (6.17) gives two linear equations with four unknowns (K_0 to K_3). This means there is an infinite number of possible solutions will go through the knots. However, it must be ensured that each piece of the curve will join smoothly with the piece drawn through the previous two knots. This can be achieved by ensuring that, at each knot, the first differential of the two curves that meet is the same. The first differential of the spline is:

$$x' = 3K_3\tau^2 + 2K_2\tau + K_1 \tag{6.18}$$

A further equation is obtained by substituting the value of knot $[x_i, 0]$ into Equation (6.18) and equating the value of x' with that found for the previous section. In the case of the first section, a value for the gradient can be fixed by the designer.

Note that there are four constants for each patch and that the equation of continuity allows the calculation of the first derivative of the second patch, if the first derivative of the first patch is known. Similarly, the third patch can be processed from the known values for the second patch, and so on. Hence, the coefficients of the patches are coupled by the continuity condition. But, there are still only three equations for each patch, so another condition is needed in order to solve for the four coefficients.

The fourth equation can be found in a number of ways. It is frequently proposed that to get the best smoothness in the final curve, not only the first differential, but also the second should be continuous at the knots. The second differential is given by:

$$x'' = 6K_3\tau + 2K_2$$

The first and second derivatives of the first patch at the first knot are still not fixed and so they can be freely chosen. From these and the two interpolating conditions, all four coefficients of the first patch can be calculated. The coefficients determine the first-and second-order differentials at the second knot and, equating these, the coefficients of the second patch can be determined. The procedure continues until all four coefficients for all patches are determined.

There are, however, two problems with using second-order continuity. Firstly, the gradient at the end of the last section cannot be controlled; and, secondly, and more seriously, the computation always moves in a forward direction. This can cause instabilities in the form of sinusoidal oscillations, which are amplified as the computation proceeds, and therefore are more likely to appear as the number of knots increases. It is also possible to fix the first derivatives at the ends of the curve, similarly to Bezier curves, but then the coupling of coefficients will make it necessary to invert a large matrix and oscillations can still develop in the inside of the curve when a large number of knots are used.

A better solution is, therefore, to drop the second-order continuity criterion and derive the third and fourth equations by fixing the values of the gradient at both ends of the patch. In this way, the patches are decoupled and the four coefficients can be calculated independently for each patch. Using the central difference gives:

$$\frac{dx}{d\tau} = x'(\tau) = \frac{x_{i+1} - x_{i-1}}{\tau_{i+1} - \tau_{i-1}} = \frac{x_{i+1} - x_{i-1}}{2} \qquad \text{at } x_i$$

This, in effect, reproduces the interpolation method suggested by Overhauser, which was described in the last section.

The foregoing equation can be used to calculate a gradient at each knot, except the first and last. The gradient at the endpoints is either supplied by a forward (or backward) difference, as it is for the Bezier curves, or a choice can be made by the designer such that the curve can be joined in the correct way to another part of the drawing. Thus, for each adjacent pair of x values plotted against the parameter τ, $[x_i, 0]$, $[x_{i+1}, 1]$, the values can be substituted into Equations (6.17) and (6.18) to obtain four equations for the four unknown coefficients. Using this method, a set of linear equations can be written for the coefficients of a section. Since

$\tau = 0$ at point $\mathbf{P_i}$ and $\tau = 1$ at $\mathbf{P_{i+1}}$, the following simple matrix formulation is obtained:

$$
\begin{bmatrix}
0 & 0 & 0 & 1 \\
1 & 1 & 1 & 1 \\
0 & 0 & 1 & 0 \\
3 & 2 & 1 & 0
\end{bmatrix}
\cdot
\begin{bmatrix}
K_3 \\
K_2 \\
K_1 \\
K_0
\end{bmatrix}
=
\begin{bmatrix}
x_i \\
x_{i+1} \\
x'_i \\
x'_{i+1}
\end{bmatrix}
$$

This is a constant non-singular matrix, which can therefore be inverted, giving:

$$
\begin{bmatrix}
K_3 \\
K_2 \\
K_1 \\
K_0
\end{bmatrix}
=
\begin{bmatrix}
2 & -2 & 1 & 1 \\
-3 & 3 & -2 & -1 \\
0 & 0 & 1 & 0 \\
1 & 0 & 0 & 0
\end{bmatrix}
\cdot
\begin{bmatrix}
x_i \\
x_{i+1} \\
x'_i \\
x'_{i+1}
\end{bmatrix}
$$

The calculation of the coefficients does not specify the method by which the differentials at the knot positions are determined. If the central difference formula is used, then the calculations reduce to the following 4×4 matrix/vector multiplication:

$$
\begin{bmatrix}
K_3 \\
\\
K_2 \\
\\
K_1 \\
\\
K_0
\end{bmatrix}
=
\begin{bmatrix}
-\dfrac{1}{2} & \dfrac{3}{2} & -\dfrac{3}{2} & \dfrac{1}{2} \\
1 & -\dfrac{5}{2} & 2 & -\dfrac{1}{2} \\
-\dfrac{1}{2} & 0 & \dfrac{1}{2} & 0 \\
0 & 1 & 0 & 0
\end{bmatrix}
\cdot
\begin{bmatrix}
x_{i-1} \\
\\
x_i \\
\\
x_{i+1} \\
\\
x_{i+2}
\end{bmatrix}
$$

Similar equations can be derived for y and z, and from these a simple algorithm for determining the coefficients and drawing the spline for each section.

An alternative to specifying the gradient at the end knots is to use a second-order spline between the first and last knot pairs. This will have just three unknown coefficients, and therefore no gradient need be specified for the first and last knots.

6.7   SURFACE REPRESENTATIONS

Surfaces may be modelled using similar techniques to those already described, but with two parameters that are treated as orthogonal. As before, a blend of a set of knots will be considered, which can be regarded as being laid out in a rectangular array, or tensor. For a B-spline surface, the B blending functions are used, yielding the tensor product equation for the locus of the approximating surface:

$$
\mathbf{P}(\mu, \nu) = [\mathbf{B}(N\mu), \mathbf{B}(N\mu - 1), \dots \mathbf{B}(N\mu - N)] \cdot
\begin{bmatrix}
\mathbf{P}_{0,0} & \mathbf{P}_{0,1} & \cdots & \mathbf{P}_{0,M} \\
\mathbf{P}_{1,0} & \mathbf{P}_{1,1} & \cdots & \mathbf{P}_{1,M} \\
\cdot & \cdot & & \cdot \\
\cdot & \cdot & & \cdot \\
\cdot & \cdot & & \cdot \\
\mathbf{P}_{N,0} & \mathbf{P}_{N,1} & \cdots & \mathbf{P}_{N,M}
\end{bmatrix}
\cdot
\begin{bmatrix}
\mathbf{B}(M\nu) \\
\mathbf{B}(M\nu - 1) \\
\cdot \\
\cdot \\
\cdot \\
\mathbf{B}(M\nu - M)
\end{bmatrix}
$$

The tensor formulation may also be written as a double sum:

$$
\mathbf{P}(\mu, \nu) = \sum_{i=0}^{N} \sum_{j=0}^{M} \mathbf{P}_{i,j} B(N\mu - i) B(M\nu - j) \tag{6.19}
$$

Note that, as with the B-spline curves, a blending function can be visualized applied to the matrix of knot vectors. This time, however, the blending function is a 2D surface, resulting from the product of the two B functions. The spline will have 16 non-zero terms in general, but only nine will be non-zero if the μ and ν values indicate a knot position, $\mu = i/N$ and $\nu = j/M$. It is convenient to use a matrix/vector product to indicate the required calculations of the spline value for the knot positions:

$$
\mathbf{P}\!\left(\frac{i}{M}, \frac{j}{N}\right) = \begin{bmatrix} \dfrac{1}{6}, \dfrac{2}{3}, \dfrac{1}{6} \end{bmatrix} \cdot
\begin{bmatrix}
\mathbf{P}_{i-1,j-1} & \mathbf{P}_{i-1,j} & \mathbf{P}_{i-1,j+1} \\
\mathbf{P}_{i,j-1} & \mathbf{P}_{i,j} & \mathbf{P}_{i,j+1} \\
\mathbf{P}_{i+1,j-1} & \mathbf{P}_{i+1,j} & \mathbf{P}_{i+1,j+1}
\end{bmatrix}
\cdot
\begin{bmatrix}
\dfrac{1}{6} \\
\dfrac{2}{3} \\
\dfrac{1}{6}
\end{bmatrix}
$$

which gives:

$$
\mathbf{P}\!\left(\frac{i}{N}, \frac{j}{M}\right) = \frac{1}{36}(\mathbf{P}_{i-1,j-1} + \mathbf{P}_{i-1,j+1} + \mathbf{P}_{i+1,j-1} + \mathbf{P}_{i+1,j+1})
$$

$$
+ \frac{1}{9}(\mathbf{P}_{i-1,j} + \mathbf{P}_{i+1,j} + \mathbf{P}_{i,j-1} + \mathbf{P}_{i,j+1})
$$

$$
+ \frac{4}{9}\mathbf{P}_{i,j} \tag{6.20}
$$

The edge points cause the same problems as the endpoints in the one-dimensional case. The surface will follow the position of the knots away from the edges, but there is little that can be said about the locus at the edges, and particularly at the corners.

To control the surface at the edge, similar methods to B-spline curves can be applied. Corresponding to the double endpoint method, two extra rows and columns are needed which duplicate all the edge knots. The tensor thus becomes:

$$
\begin{array}{cccccc}
\mathbf{P}_{-1,-1} & \mathbf{P}_{-1,0} & \mathbf{P}_{-1,1} & \cdots & \mathbf{P}_{-1,M} & \mathbf{P}_{-1,M+1} \\[6pt]
\mathbf{P}_{0,-1} & \mathbf{P}_{0,0} & \mathbf{P}_{0,1} & \cdots & \mathbf{P}_{0,M} & \mathbf{P}_{0,M+1} \\[6pt]
\mathbf{P}_{1,-1} & \mathbf{P}_{1,0} & \cdots & \cdots & \cdots & \mathbf{P}_{1,M+1} \\[6pt]
 & & \textbf{Geometric knots} & & & \\[6pt]
\cdots & \cdots & \cdots & \cdots & \cdots & \cdots \\[6pt]
\mathbf{P}_{N,-1} & \mathbf{P}_{N,0} & \cdots & \cdots & \mathbf{P}_{N,M} & \mathbf{P}_{N,M+1} \\[6pt]
\mathbf{P}_{N+1,-1} & \cdots & \cdots & \cdots & \cdots & \mathbf{P}_{N+1,M+1}
\end{array}
$$

The double endpoint method sets the values in the two extra rows and columns to be the same as their adjacent row or column; that is:

$$\mathbf{P}_{-1,j} = \mathbf{P}_{0,j} \qquad \mathbf{P}_{N+1,j} = \mathbf{P}_{N,j} \qquad \mathbf{P}_{i,-1} = \mathbf{P}_{i,0} \qquad \mathbf{P}_{i,M+1} = \mathbf{P}_{i,M}$$

In this case, Equation (6.20) is applied at the corner knot position, $\mathbf{P}_{0,0}$, and after substituting the doubled end values for the column $j = -1$ and row $i = -1$, the following is obtained:

$$\mathbf{P}(0, 0) = \mathbf{P}_{0,0} = \frac{1}{36}(\mathbf{P}_{-1,-1} + \mathbf{P}_{0,1} + \mathbf{P}_{1,0} + \mathbf{P}_{1,1})$$
$$+ \frac{1}{9}(\mathbf{P}_{0,0} + \mathbf{P}_{1,0} + \mathbf{P}_{0,0} + \mathbf{P}_{0,1}) + \frac{4}{9}\mathbf{P}_{0,0}$$

from which $\mathbf{P}_{-1,-1}$ can be expressed as:

$$\mathbf{P}_{-1,-1} = 12\mathbf{P}_{0,0} - 5\mathbf{P}_{0,1} - 5\mathbf{P}_{1,0} - \mathbf{P}_{1,1}$$

This equation allows a phantom point value to be computed for $\mathbf{P}_{-1,-1}$ which will cause the surface to go through the corner point $\mathbf{P}_{0,0}$. Similar expressions for $\mathbf{P}_{-1,M+1}$, $\mathbf{P}_{N+1,-1}$ and $\mathbf{P}_{N+1,M+1}$ will force the surface to go through the four corner knots. Because of the doubling of the knots, the surface will follow the edge knots more closely, but still will not go through them. A surface with the corners clamped is shown in Figure 6.29.

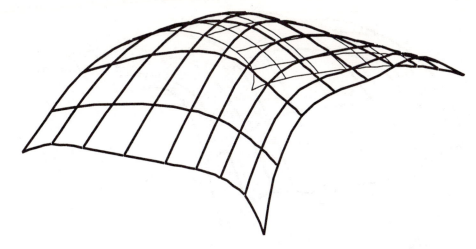

Figure 6.29
A surface representation where
the four corners have been
constrained to fit the corner
points.

As for the one-dimensional case, a number of phantom knots can be used to interpolate all the edge knots. We can use $2(N + 1 + M + 1) + 4$ phantom knots $\mathbf{A}_{-1,j}$, $\mathbf{A}_{N+1,j}$, $\mathbf{A}_{i,-1}$, and $\mathbf{A}_{i,M+1}$ which completely surround the surface and have $2(N + 1 + M + 1)$ equations for the real knots at the edges. This will leave four more conditions on the gradients, which can be set, for example, at the four corners. Since a surface is being considered here, the derivatives will be expressed as partial derivatives with respect to the parameters μ and ν and there will be two such derivatives at the corners. For example, using central differences, the two partial derivatives at the corner $\mathbf{P}_{0,0}$ are:

$$\frac{\partial \mathbf{P}}{\partial \mu} = \frac{N}{2}(\mathbf{P}_{1,0} - \mathbf{P}_{-1,0})$$

$$\frac{\partial \mathbf{P}}{\partial \nu} = \frac{M}{2}(\mathbf{P}_{0,1} - \mathbf{P}_{0,-1})$$

Figure 6.30 shows a surface that interpolates the edges. It uses the same knots as the surface of Figure 6.29. Note that the detail on the edge contours is greatly increased, but away from the edges the surface is the same as Figure 6.29.

6.7.1 Tubes

A special case of spline surfaces is tubes, where the cross-section may vary in any chosen way. To model these, the extra rows and columns in the

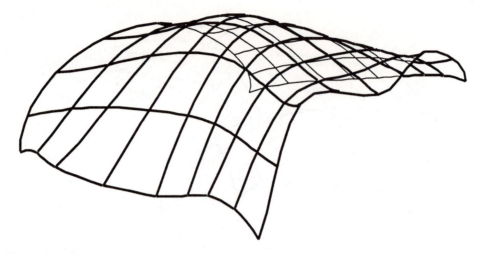

Figure 6.30

A surface using the same knots as in Figure 6.28. The edges have been made to interpolate the knots. Note that there is more detail around the edges than in Figure 6.29, but away from the edges the surfaces are substantially the same.

tensor are used. Three extra columns are needed this time, which are wrapped around so that:

$$\mathbf{P}_{i,-1} = \mathbf{P}_{i,M} \qquad \mathbf{P}_{i,M+1} = \mathbf{P}_{i,0} \qquad \mathbf{P}_{i,M+2} = \mathbf{P}_{i,1}$$

The two extra rows are treated as before:

$$\mathbf{P}_{-1,j} = \mathbf{P}_{0,j} \quad \text{and} \quad \mathbf{P}_{N+1,j} = \mathbf{P}_{N,j}$$

This means that the elements of the tensor now are:

$\mathbf{P}_{0,M}$	$\mathbf{P}_{0,0}$	$\mathbf{P}_{0,1}$	$\cdots$	$\mathbf{P}_{0,M}$	$\mathbf{P}_{0,0}$	$\mathbf{P}_{0,1}$
$\mathbf{P}_{0,M}$	$\mathbf{P}_{0,0}$	$\mathbf{P}_{0,1}$	$\cdots$	$\mathbf{P}_{0,M}$	$\mathbf{P}_{0,0}$	$\mathbf{P}_{0,1}$
$\mathbf{P}_{1,M}$	$\mathbf{P}_{1,0}$	$\cdots$	$\cdots$	$\cdots$	$\mathbf{P}_{1,0}$	$\mathbf{P}_{1,1}$
$\cdots$	$\cdots$	$\cdots$	$\cdots$ **Geometric knots**	$\cdots$	$\cdots$	$\cdots$
$\mathbf{P}_{N,M}$	$\mathbf{P}_{N,0}$	$\cdots$	$\cdots$	$\mathbf{P}_{N,M}$	$\mathbf{P}_{N,0}$	$\mathbf{P}_{N,1}$
$\mathbf{P}_{N,M}$	$\cdots$	$\cdots$	$\cdots$	$\cdots$	$\mathbf{P}_{N,0}$	$\mathbf{P}_{N,1}$

If the surface is now completed over the normal range of knots, the value of the locus is the same at each end of the rows. This will result in a tube surface that comes near to the knots without actually interpolating them. Note, again, that this method relies on the property of the third-order *B*-spline that the evaluation of the spline at a knot position involves only the knot and its two immediate neighbours. The knots of Figures 6.29 and 6.30 are used to draw the tube of Figure 6.31.

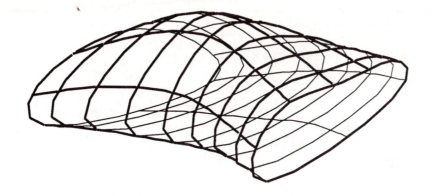

Figure 6.31
A surface drawn with the same knots used in Figures 6.29 and 6.30, but with the end conditions arranged to form a tube.

6.7.2 Drawing surfaces

Producing the appearance of a realistic surface on a computer-generated image involves the calculation of light intensities as they appear to the viewer at each pixel. (This problem will be discussed further in the next two chapters.) However, several techniques are available by which it is possible to produce a line-drawing representation of a surface.

One of the techniques is called **lofting**, a term originating from the aircraft industry. As with all 3D pictures, it is necessary to select a viewpoint, a view surface and a projection method. Having done this, lofting a surface consists of drawing a series of contours, keeping one of the parameters constant for each contour. For example, keeping the μ parameter constant, say 0, the contour is divided into K equal intervals, giving $K + 1$ points in 3D:

$$x_k = x\left(0, \frac{k}{K}\right)$$

$$y_k = y\left(0, \frac{k}{K}\right) \qquad k = 0, 1, 2, ..., K$$

$$z_k = z\left(0, \frac{k}{K}\right)$$

where x, y and z are the three Cartesian components of the surface spline $\mathbf{P}(\mu, v)$. Projecting these points and then connecting them produces one contour curve. Then, by plotting the curves for μ values of $1/N$, $2/N$, ..., 1, the surface contours may be drawn. Algorithm 6.2 draws this set of curves.

The set of contours for constant μ for the test set of knots is shown in Figure 6.32. The clamped corner condition has been used. The contours

Algorithm 6.2

Lofting in μ.

```
for j := 0 to N do
begin
  μ := j/N;
  for k := 0 to NoOfLineSegments do
  begin
    v := k/NoOfLineSegments;
    Locus := PROJECTION(P(μ, v));
    if k = 0
    then MOVE_TO(locus[x], locus[y])
    else DRAW_TO(locus[x], locus[y]):
  end
end;
```

created by fixing ν to a set of values are shown in Figure 6.33. Notice that neither the μ nor the ν contours are readily interpreted on their own. The best visual appearance is achieved when both sets of contours are drawn, as shown in Figure 6.29.

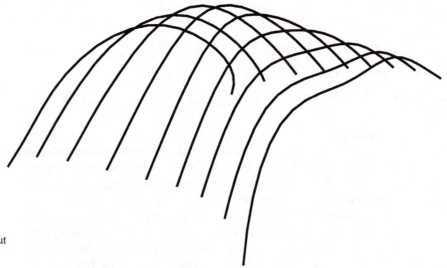

Figure 6.32

The surface of Figure 6.29 but only contours of constant μ have been drawn.

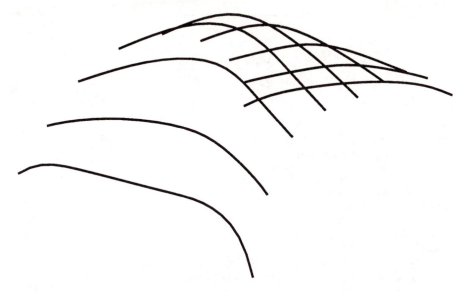

Figure 6.33
The surface of Figure 6.29 but only contours of constant v have been drawn.

Difficulties arise because this is basically a wire-frame representation and without hidden line elimination, the different contour curves could overlap each other badly. The general hidden line algorithm can be used in this case, since the quadrilateral areas bounded by the line segments can be triangulated and the triangles considered as opaque planar facets.

In the case where the knots are placed on a regular grid of x and z values:

$$x_i = \frac{i}{N} \quad \text{and} \quad z_j = \frac{j}{M} \qquad i = 0, 1, 2, ..., N \quad \text{and} \quad j = 0, 1, 2, ..., M$$

a method called the **floating-horizon** algorithm can be used, which does a simplified hidden line elimination. This algorithm is based on the special location of the viewpoint and it also places some limitations on the surface characteristics for which the hidden line elimination method will produce the correct results. It is based on the drawing of the small edges connecting the grid points on the surface in order of their depth priority. Not all possible surfaces will be drawn correctly at each grid position, but the algorithm presented here will work in most cases and provide satisfactory results. The only alternative is to solve the complete hidden line elimination problem, which will require much more computation time.

It is assumed, as usual, that the viewpoint is at the origin $[0, 0, 0]$ and that the view is in the z direction. The y axis is taken to be vertical. Points on the surface will be connected with straight lines, just as for

Algorithm 6.3

Floating horizon algorithm for surface $y = f(x,z)$.

```
var
  MaxBuffer : array [0..XPixels] of integer;
  MinBuffer : array [0..XPixels] of integer;

  { Set every element of MaxBuffer to 0 }
  { Set every element of MinBuffer to the largest integer }
  for j := 0 to NoOfμSegments do
  begin
    for i := 0 to NoOfvSegments − 1 do
    begin
      Point₁ = PROJECT_SURFACE_POINT(i/NoOfvSegments, y, j/NoOfμSegments);
      Point₂ = PROJECT_SURFACE_POINT((i + 1)/NoOfvSegments, y, j/NoOfμSegments);
      HIDDEN_BRESENHAM(Point₁, Point₂);
    end;
    if (j < NoOfμSegments) then
    for i := 0 to NoOfvSegments do
    begin
      Point₁ = PROJECT_SURFACE_POINT(i/NoOfvSegments, y, j/NoOfμSegments);
      Point₂ = PROJECT_SURFACE_POINT(i/NoOfvSegments, y, (j + 1)/NoOfμSegments);
      HIDDEN_BRESENHAM(Point₁, Point,₂);
    end;
  end;

procedure HIDDEN_BRESENHAM(Point₁, Point₂);
begin
(* Do a Bresenham algorithm between points Point₁ and Point₂ with the following modification *)

  for each pixel [X, Y] to be set do
  begin
    if (MaxBuffer[X] < Y) then
    begin
      MaxBuffer[X] := Y;
      SET_PIXEL(X, Y);
    end;
    if (MinBuffer[X] > Y) then
    begin
      MinBuffer[X] := Y;
      SET_PIXEL(X, Y);
    end
  end
end;
```

lofting, and a grid generated. It is assumed in general that the depth of $[x, y, z_1]$ is less than $[x, y, z_2]$ if $z_1 < z_2$. The contours are drawn with increasing z values.

For Figures 6.29, 6.30 and 6.31, the hidden lines were detected using the floating horizon method and are drawn fainter than the visible lines. The knots are arranged so that the contours of constant μ are approximately ordered in z. They were drawn in order of increasing μ. The contours of constant v were drawn not as full contours, but in pieces. After drawing the contour for μ_i, the segments for each constant v contour falling between the μ_i and μ_{i+1} contours were drawn, then the contour for μ_{i+1} was drawn.

Since for most reasonably behaved surfaces the line segments are drawn according to their depth priority, two buffers are used to maintain the maximum and minimum y values for each given vertical pixel number (similar to the scan-line z-buffer technique). Algorithm 6.3 summarizes the method, but it is not optimized for speed.

6.7.3   Interpolation with *B*-spline surfaces

To interpolate the points fully, a process of solution of linear equations is again possible. The real knots $\mathbf{P}_{i,j}$ are replaced in the matrix by parametric knots $\mathbf{A}_{i,j}$.

Substituting a real knot value gives Equation (6.20), which can also be written in the following expanded form:

$$\mathbf{P}_{i,j} = \frac{1}{36}\mathbf{A}_{i-1,j-1} + \frac{1}{9}\mathbf{A}_{i-1,j} + \frac{1}{36}\mathbf{A}_{i-1,j+1}$$
$$+ \frac{1}{9}\mathbf{A}_{i,j-1} + \frac{4}{9}\mathbf{A}_{i,j} + \frac{1}{9}\mathbf{A}_{i,j+1}$$
$$+ \frac{1}{36}\mathbf{A}_{i+1,j-1} + \frac{1}{9}\mathbf{A}_{i+1,j} + \frac{1}{36}\mathbf{A}_{i+1,j+1}$$

The coefficients result from the product of the B functions and there are $(N + 1) \times (M + 1)$ such equations.

To express the clamped end condition, the two extra rows and columns of parametric knots are used:

$$\mathbf{A}_{-1,j} \quad \mathbf{A}_{i,-1} \quad \mathbf{A}_{i,M+1} \quad \text{and} \quad \mathbf{A}_{N+1,j}$$

The gradient of the surface must be specified with respect to μ at the top and bottom edges, where top and bottom refer to the way the tensor has been arranged in Equation (6.19), and at the left and right edges with respect to v.

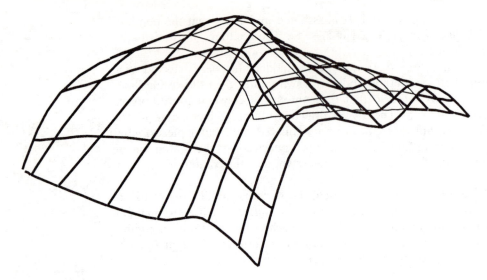

Figure 6.34

The surface of Figures 6.29 to 6.33 drawn interpolating the knots fully. Note that there is much more detail in the contours than on any other figure. The different gradient condition along the bottom edge gives it a different shape from Figure 6.30.

To find the gradient with respect to μ, the partial derivative of the tensor Equation (6.19) with respect to μ must be taken. This only affects the blending functions in μ, $B(N\mu - i)$, which are replaced by their derivatives $NB'(N\mu - i)$. Thus, at the edge points where $\mu = 0$, for example $\mathbf{P_{0,j}}$, the gradient is:

$$\frac{\partial \mathbf{P}}{\partial \mu} = \frac{N}{2}\left[\frac{1}{6}\mathbf{A}_{1,j-1} + \frac{2}{3}\mathbf{A}_{1,j} + \frac{1}{6}\mathbf{A}_{1,j+1}\right]$$
$$- \frac{N}{2}\left[\frac{1}{6}\mathbf{A}_{-1,j-1} + \frac{2}{3}\mathbf{A}_{-1,j} + \frac{1}{6}\mathbf{A}_{-1,j+1}\right] \quad \text{at } \mu = 0, \nu = \frac{j}{M}$$

The other partial derivatives are evaluated in the same way, giving a set of $2(M + 1)$ equations at the top and bottom edges and $2(N + 1)$ equations at the left and right edges. The edge gradients may be chosen by the designer or set to a default such as the forward difference. In total, a system of $(N + 3) \times (M + 3) - 4$ linear equations are obtained, which may be solved by means of Gaussian elimination. Since there is a total of $(N + 3) \times (M + 3)$ phantom knots, there is no need to solve for the four corners of the $\mathbf{A}_{i,j}$ matrix and they may be set to zero. The interpolated surface for the test knots is shown in Figure 6.34, using the floating horizon algorithm.

For $10 \times 10 = 100$ knots, a 144×144 matrix has to be inverted or a system of 140 linear equations solved. It is true that once the matrix is inverted for a given N and M, direct vector/matrix multiplications are only required to calculate the $(N + 3) \times (M+3) - 4$ phantom coefficients; therefore, this method can be practical even for a large number of knots.

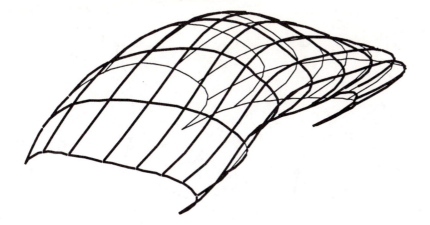

Figure 6.35
The surface of Figures 6.29 to 6.34 drawn with free edges. Away from the edges it is the same as Figure 6.28; however, near the edges it is completely unpredictable, as in the case of the spline curves. The hidden lines have been identified by the floating horizon algorithm and have been drawn faint. Note how the algorithm produces a ragged result where the surface curves about an axis that is far from horizontal, as at the right-hand edge.

This is becoming true especially today, when modern engineering work-stations are equipped with very large floating-point processing power. Alternatively, an approximate solution can be obtained using the Jacobi method. Since, in each equation, the term with the largest coefficient is the real knot $P_{i,j}$, the convergence of this method is very fast. This makes it especially suitable for small computers and real-time applications.

It is interesting to note the diversity of shapes produced by the different edge conditions applied to the same set of knots. The full inter-polant, Figure 6.34, shows the most detail, whereas the clamped corner surface, Figure 6.29, smoothes out the irregularities. The free-edge condition surface, Figure 6.35, gives unpredictable behaviour at the edges, analogous to the free-end spline curve. The floating horizon algorithm gives its worst result on the right-hand side of this surface, where it curves back underneath itself.

6.7.4 Patches

Another method for interpolating a large surface, perhaps with thousands of knots, while using a moderately priced system is to use surface patches. As shown in Figure 6.36, each surface patch only interpolates a very few knots (normally four) and then is joined to its neighbours in a continuous fashion. This technique is similar to cubic patches for spline curves, which were discussed in Section 6.6.

The patches are joined in such a way that continuity with the neighbouring patches is assured, at least to the first order (continuous gradients). In this case, only the first-order differentials must be matched with respect to the parameters at each knot. It can, for example, be

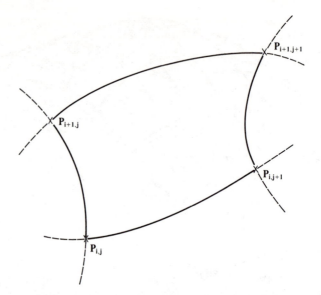

Figure 6.36
A spline patch is a surface interpolating four knots. The technique of breaking a knot set into separate patches and interpolating each independently has been a popular way to reduce the complexity of the computation of a surface interpolant. With higher-speed computers and cheap memories it is becoming less important.

assumed that the gradients are known at each of the four knot positions of the patch by evaluating central differences. Hence, the two gradients at knot $\mathbf{P}_{i,j}$ are:

$$g_{i,j} = \frac{\partial \mathbf{P}}{\partial \mu} = \frac{N}{2}(\mathbf{P}_{i+1,j} - \mathbf{P}_{i-1,j}) \qquad \text{at } \mu = \frac{i}{N}, \ v = \frac{j}{M}$$

and:

$$h_{i,j} = \frac{\partial \mathbf{P}}{\partial v} = \frac{M}{2}(\mathbf{P}_{i,j+1} - \mathbf{P}_{i,j-1}) \qquad \text{at } \mu = \frac{i}{N}, \ v = \frac{j}{M}$$

and there are six more at the other three knots. By using 16 phantom knots, $\mathbf{A}_{i-1,j-1}$ to $\mathbf{A}_{i+2,j+2}$, but setting the corner knots to zero as before:

$$\mathbf{A}_{i-1,j-1} = \mathbf{A}_{i-1,j+2} = \mathbf{A}_{i+2,j-1} = \mathbf{A}_{i+2,j+2} = 0$$

12 unknown knots result. Four equations are given by the value of the spline at the knot positions:

$$\mathbf{P}\left(\frac{i}{N}, \frac{j}{M}\right) = \frac{1}{36}[\mathbf{P}_{i-1,j-1} + \mathbf{P}_{i-1,j+1} + \mathbf{P}_{i+1,j-1} + \mathbf{P}_{i+1,j+1}]$$

$$+ \frac{1}{9}[\mathbf{P}_{i,j-1} + \mathbf{P}_{i,j+1} + \mathbf{P}_{i-1,j} + \mathbf{P}_{i+1,j}] + \frac{4}{9}\mathbf{P}_{i,j}$$

With the eight equations given by the gradients, this gives the necessary 12 equations. If a matrix of the phantom knot co-ordinates, using column vectors for $A_{i,j}$, is defined as:

$$A = [A_{i-1,j}, A_{i-1,j+1}, A_{i,j-1}, A_{i,j}, A_{i,j+1}, A_{i,j+2}, A_{i+1,j-1}, A_{i+1,j},$$
$$A_{i+1,j+1}, A_{i+1,j+2}, A_{i+2,j}, A_{i+2,j+1}]$$

and a matrix of the geometric knots and gradients as:

$$C = [g_{i,j}, g_{i,j+1}, h_{i,j}, P_{i,j}, P_{i,j+1}, h_{i,j+1}, h_{i+1,j}, P_{i+1,j}, P_{i+1,j+1},$$
$$h_{i+1,j+1}, g_{i+1,j}, g_{i+1,j+1}]$$

then the matrix equation is:

$$C = A \cdot M$$

where the matrix M is equal to:

$$
\begin{bmatrix}
-\dfrac{N}{2} & 0 & 0 & \dfrac{1}{9} & \dfrac{1}{36} & 0 & 0 & 0 & 0 & 0 & 0 & 0 \\[2mm]
0 & -\dfrac{N}{2} & 0 & \dfrac{1}{36} & \dfrac{1}{9} & 0 & 0 & 0 & 0 & 0 & 0 & 0 \\[2mm]
0 & 0 & -\dfrac{M}{2} & \dfrac{1}{9} & 0 & 0 & 0 & \dfrac{1}{36} & 0 & 0 & 0 & 0 \\[2mm]
0 & 0 & 0 & \dfrac{4}{9} & \dfrac{1}{9} & -\dfrac{M}{2} & 0 & \dfrac{1}{9} & \dfrac{1}{36} & 0 & -\dfrac{N}{2} & 0 \\[2mm]
0 & 0 & \dfrac{M}{2} & \dfrac{1}{9} & \dfrac{4}{9} & 0 & 0 & \dfrac{1}{36} & \dfrac{1}{9} & 0 & 0 & -\dfrac{N}{2} \\[2mm]
0 & 0 & 0 & 0 & \dfrac{1}{9} & \dfrac{M}{2} & 0 & 0 & \dfrac{1}{36} & 0 & 0 & 0 \\[2mm]
0 & 0 & 0 & \dfrac{1}{36} & 0 & 0 & -\dfrac{M}{2} & \dfrac{1}{9} & 0 & 0 & 0 & 0 \\[2mm]
\dfrac{N}{2} & 0 & 0 & \dfrac{1}{9} & \dfrac{1}{36} & 0 & 0 & \dfrac{4}{9} & \dfrac{1}{9} & -\dfrac{M}{2} & 0 & 0 \\[2mm]
0 & \dfrac{N}{2} & 0 & \dfrac{1}{36} & \dfrac{1}{9} & 0 & \dfrac{M}{2} & \dfrac{1}{9} & \dfrac{4}{9} & 0 & 0 & 0 \\[2mm]
0 & 0 & 0 & 0 & \dfrac{1}{36} & 0 & 0 & \dfrac{1}{36} & \dfrac{1}{9} & \dfrac{M}{2} & 0 & 0 \\[2mm]
0 & 0 & 0 & 0 & 0 & 0 & 0 & \dfrac{1}{9} & \dfrac{1}{36} & 0 & \dfrac{N}{2} & 0 \\[2mm]
0 & 0 & 0 & 0 & 0 & 0 & 0 & \dfrac{1}{36} & \dfrac{1}{9} & 0 & 0 & \dfrac{N}{2}
\end{bmatrix}
$$

If matrix M is inverted, the coefficients $A_{i,j}$ can be calculated by the matrix multiplication:

$$A = C \bullet M^{-1}$$

An alternative approach is to reduce the problem to the solution of four curves. For example, if the value of μ is fixed to give the ith row and the tensor product is multiplied out, then a set of four linear equations are generated that have to be solved for the positions of the two phantom knots, which will be part of a contour drawn at fixed μ. This method does not give an equation for the surface; rather, it has to be solved for four curve equations. So, when drawing the surface, if more contours are required than there are knots, further interpolation between the contours through the knots is required. The simplest way of doing this is by means of linear interpolation, a method known as the Coons patch.

If a parameter substitution is made such that over the patch being computed both parameters are in the range [0..1], then for the case in question the following substitutions are made:

$$\tau = N \bullet \mu - i$$
$$\zeta = M \bullet v - j$$

Then the patch in its bi-variate form is:

$$P(\tau, \zeta) = [B(\tau + 1), B(\tau), B(\tau - 1), B(\tau - 2)] \bullet \begin{bmatrix} A_{-1,-1} & A_{-1,0} & A_{-1,1} & A_{-1,2} \\ A_{0,-1} & A_{0,0} & A_{0,1} & A_{0,2} \\ A_{1,-1} & A_{1,0} & A_{1,1} & A_{1,2} \\ A_{2,-1} & A_{2,0} & A_{2,1} & A_{2,2} \end{bmatrix} \bullet \begin{bmatrix} B(\zeta + 1) \\ B(\zeta) \\ B(\zeta - 1) \\ B(\zeta - 2) \end{bmatrix}$$

Simplifying this by taking the case of $\zeta = 0$, one of four uni-variate functions bounding the patch is obtained:

$$P(\tau, 0) = [B(\tau + 1), B(\tau), B(\tau - 1), B(\tau - 2)] \bullet \begin{bmatrix} \frac{1}{6}A_{-1,-1} + \frac{2}{3}A_{-1,0} + \frac{1}{6}A_{-1,1} \\ \frac{1}{6}A_{0,-1} + \frac{2}{3}A_{0,0} + \frac{1}{6}A_{0,1} \\ \frac{1}{6}A_{1,-1} + \frac{2}{3}A_{1,0} + \frac{1}{6}A_{1,1} \\ \frac{1}{6}A_{2,-1} + \frac{2}{3}A_{2,0} + \frac{1}{6}A_{2,1} \end{bmatrix}$$

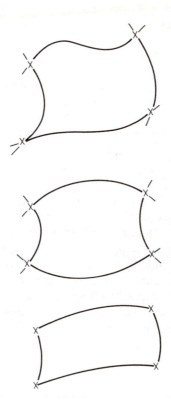

Figure 6.37
Spline patches can produce a
wide variety of effects
depending on the differentials
at the edges. They are normally
pieced together in a way that
preserves continuity of the first
derivative at the edges.

If a further simplification is made to the notation, by using the substitution:

$$\mathbf{A}_i = \frac{1}{6}\mathbf{A}_{i,-1} + \frac{2}{3}\mathbf{A}_{i,0} + \frac{1}{6}\mathbf{A}_{i,1}$$

then the equation of a uni-variate B spline through two knots is given by:

$$\mathbf{P}(\tau, 0) = \sum_{i=-1}^{2} \mathbf{A}_i B(\tau - i) \qquad \text{for } \tau = 0 \quad \text{and} \quad \tau = 1 \qquad \textbf{(6.21)}$$

Values for the constants $\mathbf{A}_i$ can be computed by substituting the values $\tau = 0$ and $\tau = 1$ in Equation (6.21) to obtain two equations for the knot positions. By differentiating Equation (6.21) and substituting the same values, two equations for the gradient given on page 292 are obtained. Thus, a solution for the $\mathbf{A}_i$ can be found for each ordinate (x, y and z component).

The patch is bounded by four such uni-variate functions:

$$\mathbf{P}(\tau, 0), \quad \mathbf{P}(\tau, 1), \quad \mathbf{P}(0, \zeta) \quad \text{and} \quad \mathbf{P}(1, \ \zeta)$$

The interpolation between these four functions is treated as linear in parameter space, hence:

$$\begin{aligned}
\mathbf{P}(\tau, \zeta) = \ &\mathbf{P}(\tau, 0)(1 - \zeta) + \mathbf{P}(\tau, 1)\zeta + \mathbf{P}(0, \zeta)(1 - \tau) \\
&+ \mathbf{P}(1, \zeta)\tau - \mathbf{P}(0, 0)(1 - \tau)(1 - \zeta) - \mathbf{P}(0, 1)(1 - \tau)\zeta \\
&- \mathbf{P}(1, 0) \, \tau \, (1 - \zeta) - \mathbf{P}(1, 1) \, \tau\zeta
\end{aligned}$$

which can be seen to interpolate the corners correctly. The patch method works well in most cases, as Figure 6.37 illustrates.

Throughout this treatment of spline surfaces, the third-order *B* blending function has been used. The treatment, however, applies equally well to other blending functions. Tension and skew may be applied, in an analogous way to the curve case, by using the β function. Similarly, substitution of the Bernstein blending function into the tensor product yields the Bezier surface. As is the case for curves, the Bezier surfaces cannot be made to interpolate the knots in a usable way.

Exercises

6.1 A 2D set of knots has the *x–y* co-ordinates [0, 0], [1, 5], [3, 1], [6, 2], [8, 6] and [5, 7]. For values of the parameter $\mu = \frac{1}{3}$ and $\mu = \frac{2}{3}$, use the Casteljau algorithm to construct geometrically the points on the Bezier curve.

6.2 For the knots given in Exercise 6.1, calculate the points on the Bezier curve for $\mu = \frac{1}{3}$ and $\mu = \frac{2}{3}$ using the Bernstein blending function. Check that the results are the same as those for Exercise 6.1.

6.3 Calculate the value of $B(\tau)$ for $\tau = -1.5, -0.5, 0.5$ and 1.5. Check that the sum of the four results is 1.

6.4 Use your results of Exercise 6.3 to calculate the point given by $\mu = \frac{1}{2}$ on the *B*-spline curve approximating the knots of Exercise 6.1.

6.5 Calculate the points for which $\mu = 0, \frac{1}{5}, \frac{4}{5}$ and 1 on the free-end *B*-spline curve approximating the knots of Exercise 6.1. Use these points to sketch the spline curve.

6.6 Calculate the phantom endpoints required to make a *B*-spline curve on the knots of Exercise 6.1 go through the endpoints.

6.7 Explain the difference between the terms parametric knots and geometric knots.

6.8 Explain what is meant by a clamped end condition. Does the phantom endpoint method for *B*-spline curves impose a clamped end condition?

6.9 Calculate the coefficients of the interpolating polynomial $y = ax^2 + bx + c$ that will pass through the points $\mathbf{P_0} = [0, 3]$, $\mathbf{P_1} = [-2, 0]$ and $\mathbf{P_2} = [2, 3]$. Sketch its shape.

6.10 Calculate the coefficients of the parametric interpolating polynomial $y = a_y\mu^2 + b_y\mu + c_y$ and $x = a_x\mu^2 + b_x\mu + c_x$ that pass through the three points defined in Exercise 6.9. Sketch the shape of the resulting curve. Note that $\mu = 0$ at $\mathbf{P_0}$, $\mu = \frac{1}{2}$ at $\mathbf{P_1}$ and $\mu = 1$ at $\mathbf{P_2}$.

Problems

6.11 Prove that for four knots, the Casteljau recursive construction of the Bezier curves gives the same results as the Bernstein blending function.

6.12 Use mathematical induction to prove that the Casteljau recursive construction gives the same result as the Bernstein blending formulation for any number of knots. (*Difficult*)

6.13 A blending curve is to be constructed from three individual quadratic splines of the form:

$$B(\tau) = a\tau^2 + b\tau + c$$

The curve is to pass through the points $\mathbf{P_0} = [-\frac{3}{2}, 0]$, $\mathbf{P_1} = [-\frac{1}{2}, \frac{1}{2}]$, $\mathbf{P_2} = [\frac{1}{2}, \frac{1}{2}]$ and $\mathbf{P_3} = [\frac{3}{2}, 0]$. The first differential is to be continuous where the pieces join, and is to be equal to 0 at $\mathbf{P_0}$. Compute the coefficients a, b and c for the three pieces. Verify that the slope at $\mathbf{P_3} = 0$. Check that your curve is the same shape as $B^{(2)}$.

6.14 A spline surface is represented by a tensor product as explained in Section 6.7. If $N = 7$, $M = 9$, $\mu = 0.3$ and $v = 0.6$, which of the knots $\mathbf{P_{i,j}}$ have non-zero coefficients? What are the coefficients?

6.15 For the surface of Problem 6.14, which knots appear in the sum to find the gradient with respect to v at the point $\mu = 0.3$, $v = 0.6$, and what are their coefficients?

6.16 Devise a general algorithm to find the 16 knots that have non-zero coefficients for a given μ, v in the tensor formulation of the spline surface.

Projects

6.17 Carry out an investigation of the effect of the use of different blending functions on *B*-spline curves. Write a system to set up 2D knot sets and calculate the approximating splines with blending curves of any order. Investigate how to make the curves interpolate the endpoints for high-order blending functions. Find out how the results compare with those obtained by varying the tension in the third-order spline, and how the high-order splines compare with the Bezier curve approximation.

6.18 Write a system to investigate the effects of the different end conditions on the drawing of a *B*-spline surface. The conditions to be investigated should include free edges, interpolated corners, interpolated edges, the interpolating surface and tubes. The system should have the provision to input a set of knots, and should use the floating horizon algorithm to eliminate hidden lines.

7 Illumination and Colour Models for Solid Objects

To produce a realistic computer-generated representation of solid opaque objects, a light reflection model of surfaces has to be defined. The two simplest models use diffuse and specular reflections which approximate reasonably well the light-reflecting properties of matt and shiny surfaces. The reflected light intensity can be calculated at the surface from the incident light direction, the direction of the surface normal and the position of the viewer. Rendering is a combination of laws based on optics and the heuristic selection of features or functions that produce acceptable visual results. In this chapter continuous surfaces are approximated by a large number of planar facets. The appearance of continuously varying intensities may be achieved by calculating intensities at the vertices of the facets and by interpolating over their area. Two major methods – Gouraud and Phong shadings – are described. The rendering of objects is further developed by introducing colour. A connection between visually observable and physically defined colours is made by the presentation of the chromaticity or CIE diagram. Other useful colour models, such as the RGB cube, the HSV and the HLS models are also discussed. The chapter closes with a short discussion on colour quantization, which attempts to solve the problem of reproducing a picture made up of a large number of colour shades on a monitor that has only a limited number of available colours.

7.1   INTRODUCTION

Most people are accustomed to viewing scenes on a 2D television screen and readily accept that what they see is a true representation of the original 3D objects placed in front of the camera. However, this acceptance is based on the fact that the camera reproduces a real scene reasonably well, and that cues such as object occlusion can be used to establish the 3D interpretation. The task of defining a relationship between the 3D scene and the pixel intensities on the television screen is a very difficult one. The same problem is encountered when a realistic 3D graphics scene is generated from geometric and illumination data. The process of creating realistic graphics scenes from geometric data is called **rendering** in computer graphics. This chapter discusses this extremely complicated problem in two stages. First, it examines how solid surfaces reflect monochromatic light. Then, it discusses how realistic coloured images may be created.

7.2   RENDERING OF ILLUMINATED SOLID OBJECTS

In Figure 7.1, a simple illumination model is shown which assumes a linear relationship between the incident and reflected intensities of light at the illuminated surface. The surface of the object is treated as a collection of small planar surfaces, each having a well-defined outside normal direction

Figure 7.1

The simplest illumination model assumes a linear relationship between incident light intensity and surface brightness. The total illumination is calculated as the sum of contributions from individual light sources.

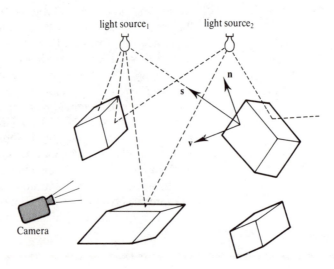

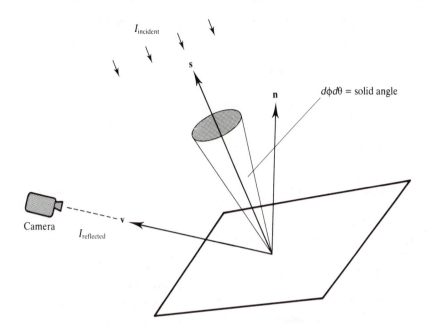

$I_{incident}$

s

n

$d\phi d\theta$ = solid angle

Camera

$I_{reflected}$

v

Figure 7.2
The reflectivity function determines the light reflected due to the incident light within a differential solid angle and is a function of the incident light direction, the viewing position, the surface normal and the reflecting characteristics of the surface.

vector **n**. Assuming that one pixel in the final image corresponds to just one such small surface element, the intensity of the pixel is determined by the light intensity reflected from that surface in the direction of the camera. This viewing direction is denoted by the vector **v**. Since the surface may be illuminated from a large number of directions with varied light intensities, the combined reflected light intensity in this model may be calculated as the sum of the individual reflected intensities due to each light source. The individual reflected intensities are a function of the surface normal, the viewing vector **v**, the direction of the light source, denoted **s**, and the intensity of the light source.

To calculate the exact reflected light intensity at a point, it is necessary to integrate the incident light intensity function, I, multiplied by the **reflectivity function** of the surface, R, over a half-spherical volume:

$$\text{Pixel intensity} = \int R(\mathbf{s}, \mathbf{n}, \mathbf{v}) I(\phi, \theta) \, d\phi d\theta$$

where $d\phi d\theta$ is the differential solid angle. As illustrated in Figure 7.2, the reflectivity function determines the fraction of the light reflected from the surface in the specific direction given by the viewing vector **v**.

This volume integral formulation is, however, of limited use when rendering a computer graphics scene. If a scene contains a large number of

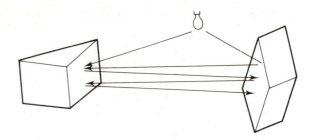

Figure 7.3
In the real world, light bounces back and forth between objects bounded by highly reflecting surfaces. It is not possible to calculate accurately such multiple reflections for a general scene containing a large number of objects.

objects, then light would be bouncing back and forth between objects, as illustrated in Figure 7.3. At each point where a light ray strikes a matt-surfaced object, rays would be reflected in all directions. So, even if there are only a few point sources of light, there will be an infinite number of reflected rays. These could be approximated by discrete samples, but, even so, the computer time required to calculate such multiple reflections accurately becomes excessive. Moreover, these computations would need to be made for each pixel, and high-quality systems contain millions of pixels!

Psychological factors also play a very important role in the successful rendering of objects. Human vision is highly complex and is sensitive to small variations. Computer-generated pictures based on physical laws often do not look real at all, partly because the laws are only approximations and partly because of other effects such as non-linearities in the display device. Taking into consideration all these factors, it becomes apparent that rendering is not a simple science. Illumination models must be simple, calculations fast and, ultimately, special tricks must be used to make the final result acceptable to the viewer. Many of these aspects of rendering are discussed in the following pages.

7.3 CALCULATING REFLECTED LIGHT INTENSITIES

An object that does not produce light itself may absorb, reflect or transmit light when it is illuminated by other light sources. This is what gives an object its visible characteristics. The way in which an object is seen depends on the number, position and properties of the light sources, the light absorbed, transmitted or reflected, and the respective positions of the light sources, the object and the viewer.

An object can be illuminated by a number of different types of light sources. Mathematically, the two simplest types are the point source and

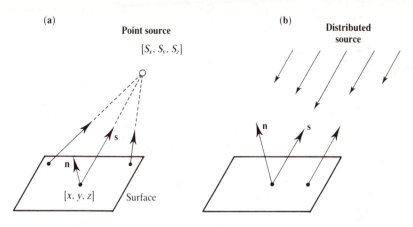

Figure 7.4
Two types of idealized light source are used for simple rendering of graphics scenes. The incident light direction for a point light source can be calculated from the light source position and the point on the surface. The incident light direction for a distributed source is constant.

the uniformly distributed light source. (The latter corresponds to a point source at infinity.) For both of these sources, the direction of the incident light can be easily determined. In the first case, as shown in Figure 7.4, the incident light direction is given by the direction of the vector connecting the surface element to the light source. In the second case, the incident light direction is a constant. Uniform illumination can be approximated by moving the light source far away from the object, when the incident light vectors become almost parallel to each other. In the subsequent discussions, it is assumed that illumination is from one of these ideal light sources.

The simplest physical description of light reflective surfaces considers only two types; namely, **diffuse** and **specular** reflections. Diffuse reflection is a characteristic of matt surfaces, while specular reflection occurs at the surface of shiny objects. Most objects produce both diffuse and specular reflections to some degree.

7.3.1 Diffuse reflection

The physical explanation for diffuse reflection is that light is absorbed by a thin layer under the surface and then re-radiated. This physical process has two major characteristics:

(1)   Light is reflected uniformly in all directions and therefore the reflected light intensity is independent of the position of the viewer.

(2)   The reflectivity is a function of wavelength or colour, which is important when considering the rendering of coloured objects.

As already mentioned in Section 7.2, the reflected light intensity in this simple model is proportional to the incident light energy. As shown in

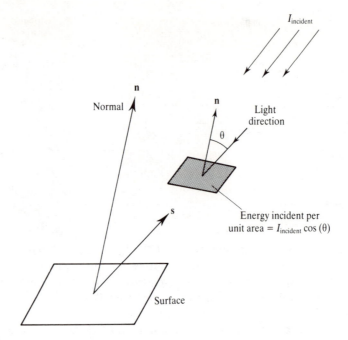

Figure 7.5

The energy per unit area incident to a small surface area is proportional to the cosine of the angle between the incident light direction and the normal to the surface.

Figure 7.5, the incident light energy per unit area depends on the the cosine of the angle between the incident light direction and the outside normal to the surface. Thus, the reflected light intensity can be calculated by the equation:

$$I_{\text{reflected}} = I_{\text{incident}} R_{\text{diff}} \cos(\theta) \tag{7.1}$$

which is known as **Lambert's cosine law**. R_{diff} is the reflectivity for diffuse reflection and θ is the angle between the incident light and the normal vector to the surface. If a direction vector from the surface of the object to the light source is called **s** and the outside normal to the surface is **n**, then the same equation may be expressed by the dot product of these two vectors. The resulting new equation is:

$$I_{\text{reflected}} = I_{\text{incident}} R_{\text{diff}} (s \cdot n) \tag{7.2}$$

where unit vectors $s = \mathbf{s}/|\mathbf{s}|$ and $n = \mathbf{n}/|\mathbf{n}|$ are used for the light and the normal vector directions. Note that if a point light source is used, then *s* can be calculated from the difference of the position vectors pointing to the surface and the light source; if a uniform light source is used, then the unit vector *s* is a known constant. Two cubes with surfaces producing purely

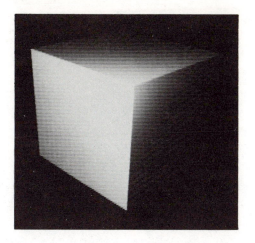 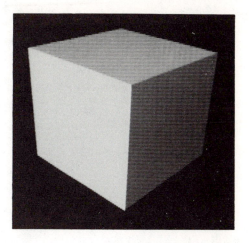

diffuse reflection and which are illuminated by a point and a distributed light source are rendered in Figure 7.6 using Equation (7.2).

Figure 7.6
Two cubes with surfaces producing purely diffuse reflection are illuminated with a point and distributed light source.

7.3.2 Specular reflection

A mirror is a perfect specular reflector that reflects incident light in one direction only. As shown in Figure 7.7, the unit direction vector pointing towards the light, *s*, the unit surface normal, *n*, and the unit direction vector of the reflected light, *r*, are all in one plane with the angle, θ, between *s* and *n* being equal to the angle between *n* and *r*. A point source illuminating such a perfect mirror produces light at one point only, while the rest of the surface remains completely dark. A uniform source produces uniform intensity. This will be observed when viewing the reflection of the sky or the moon in a mirror.

Most shiny surfaces are not perfect mirrors, which means that the light intensity may be much larger in the direction of *r* than in other

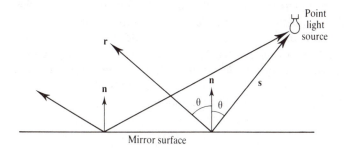

Figure 7.7
For highly specular or mirror-like surfaces, the angle between the incident light direction and the surface normal is equal to the angle between the reflected light ray and the normal. The incident, reflected and the normal vectors are all in one plane.

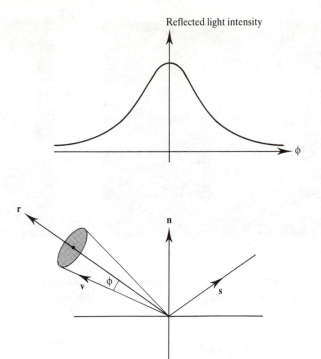

Figure 7.8
For ordinary shiny surfaces the majority of the reflected light travels in the direction of the reflection vector and decreases rapidly in directions away from the reflection vector. Equal reflected light intensities occur on a conical surface around the reflection vector, as shown.

directions. As shown in Figure 7.8, a bell-shaped curve describes the light intensity as a function of the angle between the preferred reflected light direction, *r*, and the direction from which the reflected light is viewed, *v*. This angle is shown as ϕ in Figure 7.8. Since the angle ϕ is applied in three dimensions, specularly reflected light is contained in a cone centred around the direction vector *r* and is a strong function of the position of the viewer.

A physical explanation for specular reflection is that there are a large number of microscopic mirror surfaces randomly oriented in all directions at the surface of a shiny object. From each micro surface, the incident light is reflected with perfect specular reflection. The overall reflected light intensity is the combined effect of a very large number of these micro surfaces. Many physically based theories use statistics and distribution functions of the orientations of these small mirrors (or micro surfaces) to arrive at the specularly reflected light distribution. For computer graphics, an empirical formula suggested by Bui-Tuong Phong (1975) gained rapid acceptance. The strength of this formula lies in the fact that it is easy to calculate and that it produces reasonably realistic 3D images. The empirical formula for specular reflection is:

$$I_{\text{reflected}} = I_{\text{incident}} R_{\text{spec}} f(\theta) \cos^k(\phi) \tag{7.3}$$

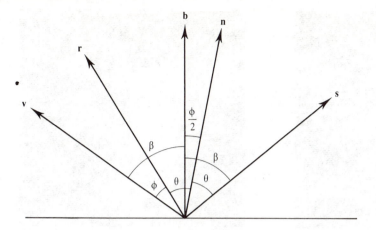

Figure 7.9
The cosine of the angle between the reflection vector and the normal can be calculated by the addition of the bisector that divides the angle between the light source vector, **s**, and the reflection vector, **r**, into two equal parts. Since the angle between **s** and **n** is equal to the angle between **r** and **n**, the angle between the bisector and the normal is one-half of that between the reflection vector and the normal.

The specular reflectivity R_{spec} indicates that some of the light may be absorbed by the surface. The function $\cos^k(\phi)$ provides the bell-shaped curve with a controllable parameter k, which determines how close the surface is to a perfect specular reflector. Values of k larger than 100 specify mirror-like surfaces while values around 1 are used for dull surfaces. The empirical function $f(\theta)$ is used to distinguish between materials like glass, plastic, metal or paper. This is a good example of a heuristic model that produces results that look good. Although it follows the general functional behaviour of real objects, it cannot be derived exactly. From the physical model, it can be concluded that the colour content of the specularly reflected light is the same as that of the incident light and that these reflectivity functions are not influenced by light wavelength.

As a first approximation, it may be assumed that the function $f(\theta)$ is a constant and that the $\cos(\phi)$ function may be calculated from the dot product between the reflection vector r and the vector v connecting the observed surface element to the viewer. Since all three vectors, s, n and r, are in one plane, planar geometry can be used to calculate a value for $\cos(\phi)$. One simple way is to use the method described in Section 4.2 to compute the reflected vector, r, and to use the fact that $\cos(\phi) = v \cdot r$. An alternative way is to use the bisector. As shown in Figure 7.9, the unit bisector vector, b, between s and v unit vectors makes an angle of $\phi/2$ with vector n. The bisector can be expressed as:

$$b = \frac{(s + v)}{|s + v|} \tag{7.4}$$

to give:

$$\cos(\phi) = 2\cos^2\left(\frac{\phi}{2}\right) - 1 = 2(b \cdot n)^2 - 1 \tag{7.5}$$

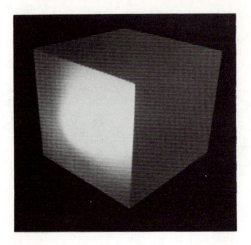 

Figure 7.10

Two cubes with surfaces producing purely specular reflection are illuminated with a point and distributed light source. The constant for the specular reflection curve is equal to 10.

Purely specular reflection for two cubes illuminated by a point and a uniform light source are shown in Figure 7.10. The parameter k in Equation (7.3), is equal to 10.

7.3.3   The complete illumination model

The ratio of R_{diff} to R_{spec} and the value of the specular parameter k provide a large range of surface characteristics from which to choose when both diffuse and specular reflections are used. The reflected light intensities depend only on these surface characteristics, the light source positions and the normal direction vector at the surface. There are, however, additional empirical factors that can add to the realism of portraying planar opaque surfaces. In an everyday scene, for example, multiple reflected light intensities illuminate those facets that would otherwise be in total darkness, because they face away from the light source. The background illumination of unlit surfaces may be included in the calculated illumination of an object by a constant called the **ambient light intensity**:

$$I_{\text{ambient}} = R_{\text{amb}} I_{\text{background}} \tag{7.6}$$

The background light intensity depends on the total intensity of the incident light from all sources. In real scenes, this will include the light sources and possibly a constant illumination arising from the environment which is independent of the light source. As shown in Equation (7.6), a separate reflectivity constant is used for ambient light.

Another factor that may influence the incident light intensity is the distance between the reflective surface element and the light source. Physically, the intensity is proportional to $1/d^2$, where d is the distance between

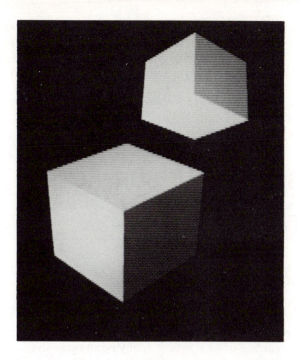

Figure 7.11
The results of using the complete illumination model for two cubes, one highly diffuse, the other highly specular, are shown. Both cubes are illuminated with two point light sources and depth cueing is also included in the calculations.

the light source and the surface. Similarly, the light intensity reaching the viewer can have an inverse dependency on the distance between the camera position and the object. Empirically, it has been found that pictures generated using the inverse square law do not appear realistic. The inverse function $1/(d_0+d)$ has been used in practice to obtain better results. Since this expression contains an extra parameter d_0, it can be adjusted for the most realistic effect. Two such functions may be used – one for the distance between the object and the light source, the other for the distance between the object and the camera – but in most cases the distance between the camera and the light source and that between the object and the light source are similar, and thus one inverse function suffices. In cases where the distance between the objects and the viewer varies widely, and a distance correction is applied, **depth cueing** results. Objects far away from the viewer then become faint, as compared to those closer to the viewer. By combining all these empirical illumination expressions, the total illumination of an object at a given point on its surface is given by:

$$
\begin{aligned}
I_{\text{reflected}} = R_{\text{amb}}I_{\text{background}} + \sum \left(\frac{I_{\text{incident}}}{d_0 + d}\right)&\big[R_{\text{amb}} + R_{\text{diff}}\cos(\theta) \\
&+ R_{\text{spec}}f(\theta)\cos^k(\phi)\big]
\end{aligned}
$$

where the summation is over light sources. Two cubes illuminated by two point light sources are rendered in Figure 7.11. Depth cueing has been used and d is calculated simply as the z co-ordinate. This is equivalent to the assumption that both the light sources and the camera are in the $z = 0$ plane.

7.4 SHADING OF SURFACES APPROXIMATED BY PLANAR FACETS

Once the reflected light intensity on a planar surface is known, a complicated solid object can be rendered by the collection of a large number of planar facets. As the simplest facet is a triangle, this will be used to demonstrate the basic techniques of shading. The objects that will be represented are the cone and the cylinder. In both cases, it is possible to determine the surface normal vector at any point by analytical means, and the way in which this can be done is described in Chapter 8. However, for the present, a piecewise approximation by triangles will be considered. The wire-frame models of these two objects with hidden lines eliminated are shown in Figure 7.12.

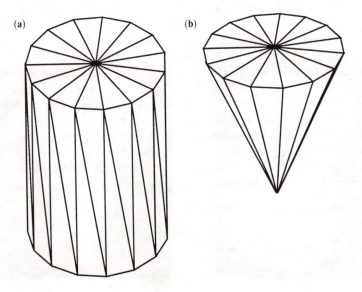

Figure 7.12
The wire-frame model of a cylinder and a cone with their surfaces approximated by a large number of triangular facets.

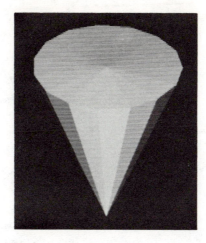

Figure 7.13
Constant shading for each triangular facet shows the discontinuous nature of the surfaces for both a cylinder and a cone. One distributed light and orthographic projection was used to create this diagram.

First, simple diffuse reflection with a single uniformly distributed light source and orthographic projection will be considered. In this case, each planar facet appears with constant illumination. The reflected light intensity is proportional to the cosine of the angle between the normal to the facet and the direction of the incident light. The resulting shaded objects are shown in Figure 7.13, illuminated by one light source, and in Figure 7.14, illuminated by two light sources. The planar facets are clearly visible as the eye psychologically accentuates the effect of a discontinuous jump in light intensity. This is called the **Mach band effect**. Adding the complete illumination model will not help, since the discontinuities in the surface normals are caused by the finite number of planar facets. Notice

Figure 7.14
When distributed light sources from two different directions are used, the facets are still clearly visible. Note the difference between shadings caused by the edges of the objects and edges due to the faceted representation of curved surfaces.

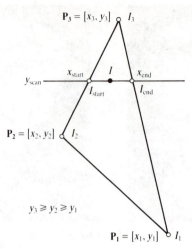

Figure 7.15
Gouraud shading is calculated by linear interpolation in the image plane. For triangular shapes, three intensities are given at the vertices and the intensities inside the triangle are determined by a linear combination of the three intensities.

that there is a very important difference between surface normal discontinuities inherent in the shape of the object – for example, where the side of the cylinder meets its top – and those caused by the faceted approximation.

7.4.1 Gouraud shading

One way to create the appearance of a smooth surface is to treat the vertices as knots and apply some kind of interpolation that produces continuous reflected light intensities at the facet boundaries. A simple form of interpolation was first used successfully by Gouraud (1971). An average intensity is calculated for each vertex – for example, by averaging the surface normals of all the facets that meet at that vertex. Then, linear interpolation is used in the image plane to determine the shaded intensities inside the facets. For triangles, the scan line method is particularly well suited for these calculations. As shown in Figure 7.15, there are three intensity values I_1, I_2, and I_3 for the three vertices of the triangle $\mathbf{P}_1 = [x_1, y_1]$, $\mathbf{P}_2 = [x_2, y_2]$ and $\mathbf{P}_3 = [x_3, y_3]$. The equation of a plane in parametric form is:

$$\mathbf{P} = \mathbf{P}_1 + \alpha(\mathbf{P}_2 - \mathbf{P}_1) + \beta(\mathbf{P}_3 - \mathbf{P}_1)$$

and if $0 \leq \alpha + \beta \leq 1$, $\alpha \geq 0$ and $\beta \geq 0$, then the locus of $\mathbf{P}$ is the triangular facet with vertices $\mathbf{P}_1$, $\mathbf{P}_2$ and $\mathbf{P}_3$. Projecting the vertices on to the image plane gives, in Cartesian form:

$$x = x_1 + \alpha(x_2 - x_1) + \beta(x_3 - x_1) \tag{7.7}$$

$$y = y_1 + \alpha(y_2 - y_1) + \beta(y_3 - y_1)$$

Hence, for given co-ordinates $[X, Y]$ in image space, it is possible to deduce values for α and β by solving Equation (7.7):

$$\alpha = \frac{(x - x_1)(y_3 - y_1) - (y - y_1)(x_3 - x_1)}{(y_3 - y_1)(x_2 - x_1) - (x_3 - x_1)(y_2 - y_1)}$$

$$\beta = \frac{(y - y_1)(x_2 - x_1) - (x - x_1)(y_2 - y_1)}{(y_3 - y_1)(x_2 - x_1) - (x_3 - x_1)(y_2 - y_1)} \tag{7.8}$$

The shading value can be found, for a given α and β, by linear interpolation of the intensities at the vertices:

$$I(\alpha, \beta) = I_1 + \alpha(I_2 - I_1) + \beta(I_3 - I_1) \tag{7.9}$$

When the scan line algorithm is used, great savings can be made by computing the change in intensity from one pixel to its neighbour. For a constant value of $y = y_{scan}$, the change in α and β from one pixel to the next is:

$$\Delta\alpha = \frac{\Delta x(y_3 - y_1)}{(y_3 - y_1)(x_2 - x_1) - (x_3 - x_1)(y_2 - y_1)}$$

$$\Delta\beta = \frac{-\Delta x(y_2 - y_1)}{(y_3 - y_1)(x_2 - x_1) - (x_3 - x_1)(y_2 - y_1)}$$

where Δx is the distance between adjacent pixels. Normally, all the co-ordinates will be in pixel units in which case Δx will be equal to 1. The change in intensity between adjacent pixels on the scan line in terms of a general Δx is given by:

$$\Delta I_x = \Delta\alpha(I_2 - I_1) + \Delta\beta(I_3 - I_1)$$

$$= \frac{\Delta x\left[(y_2 - y_3)I_1 + (y_3 - y_1)I_2 + (y_1 - y_2)I_3\right]}{(y_3 - y_1)(x_2 - x_1) - (x_3 - x_1)(y_2 - y_1)} \tag{7.10}$$

So, for each scan line, the left intersection between the scan line and the triangle is calculated and Equation (7.8) and Equation (7.9) can be used to

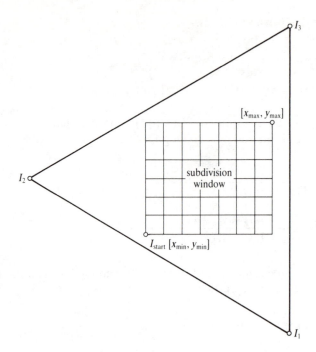

Figure 7.16
Gouraud shading can be used
for Warnock's subdivision
algorithm if the subdivided area
is completely inside the
triangular facet.

calculate the intensity at the first pixel on the scan line. Then, for each subsequent pixel, the difference ΔI_x is added to the intensity.

If Warnock's subdivision algorithm is used, then Gouraud shading is applied in a rectangular window and the differential algorithm can be applied in both x and y directions. As shown in Figure 7.16, the triangle must enclose the rectangular region completely. The intensity may be calculated at the lower left corner of the rectangular region by substituting the $x = x_{min}$ and $y = y_{min}$ values into Equation (7.8). The intensity values on one scan line are calculated by using the ΔI_x value given in Equation (7.10). When a new scan line is started, then a differential value in the y direction, ΔI_y, must be added to the intensity value at the start of the previous scan line. The differential is derived in the same way as in Equation (7.10) and is:

$$\Delta I_y = \frac{\Delta y \left[(x_3 - x_2)I_1 + (x_1 - x_3)I_2 + (x_2 - x_1)I_3 \right]}{(y_3 - y_1)(x_2 - x_1) - (x_3 - x_1)(y_2 - y_1)} \tag{7.11}$$

Consider now the question of calculating the intensity values at the vertices of the facets being shaded. If normals can be found at the vertices, then reflected light intensities can be found using the techniques specified

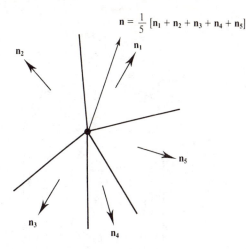

$$n = \frac{1}{5} \left[n_1 + n_2 + n_3 + n_4 + n_5 \right]$$

Figure 7.17
The normal vector associated with a vertex where many facets meet may be approximated by the average of normal vectors to the facets around the vertex.

in Section 7.3. There are two ways in which these normal vectors may be specified:

(1)   They may be calculated from the known shape of the object. In particular, if the object has a simple shape then these vectors can be determined exactly.

(2)   An average normal direction may be calculated from the surface normals of the facets meeting at the vertex, as shown in Figure 7.17. Surfaces with discontinuous derivatives must be handled carefully. For example, the cylinder shown in Figure 7.18 has discontinuous normal vectors at the top edge of the cylinder. For the two shaded triangular facets, the average normal vectors at vertex **V** must be calculated differently. In this case, the surface normals at the edges must be expressed for each facet – they cannot be calculated once only for each vertex.

A cylinder and a cone illuminated by two light sources are rendered in Figure 7.19. Perspective projection and Gouraud shading are used with triangular facets, as shown in Figure 7.12.

7.4.2   Phong shading

Gouraud shading can still produce visible streaks of intensity variations intensified by the Mach band effect, as the derivatives of the surface normals are discontinuous where the small planar facets meet. On examination of the interpolation method, it can be seen that the intensity has been assumed to be a linear function of distance in the projection plane.

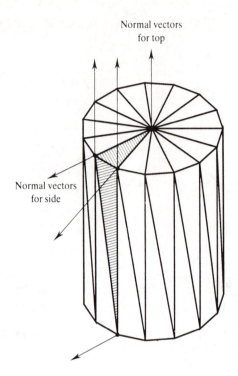

Normal vectors
for top

Normal vectors
for side

Figure 7.18

Normals at vertices where the
object has an edge must be
handled carefully. As shown,
the triangular facets meeting at
the top plane of a cylinder have
different normals depending on
whether they belong to the top
or the side of the cylinder.
Averaging the normals at these
vertices would introduce errors.

Because the reflected intensity depends on the surface normal through the
angles it makes with the light and the view vectors, the intensity cannot be
expected to be a linear function, even if the normal vector directions can be
expressed as linear functions of distance. An improved method, first

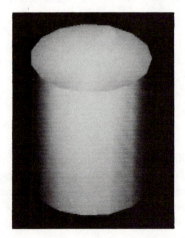
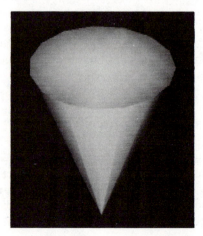

Figure 7.19

In this diagram, both specular
and diffuse reflections, two light
sources and Gouraud shading
are used for the rendering of a
solid cylinder and a cone. The
small triangular facets are still
visible.

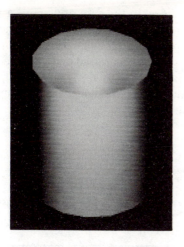

Figure 7.20
The same solid objects as shown in Figure 7.19 are rendered using Phong shading. When Phong shading is used, considerably more computing time is required but the appearance of the specular highlights is much closer to that produced by ray tracing.

developed by Bui-Tuong Phong (1975), linearly interpolates the three normal vectors at the vertices to arrive at a calculated normal vector for any point within the projected facet. The vector equation is similar to Equation (7.9):

$$\mathbf{n}(\alpha, \beta) = \mathbf{n}_1 + \alpha(\mathbf{n}_2 - \mathbf{n}_1) + \beta(\mathbf{n}_3 - \mathbf{n}_1) \qquad (7.12)$$

where, as before, α and β are given by Equation (7.8). The interpolation method is the same as for scalar intensities, except that the calculations have to be made three times, once for each component of the surface normal. After the normal vector has been calculated, the reflected intensity must be calculated for each pixel. Thus, the calculations will take much longer than for Gouraud shading. The same cylinder and cone rendered in Figure 7.19 are shown in Figure 7.20 recomputed using Phong shading.

It may be argued that an error is made when perspective projection is used and interpolation is carried out in the image plane. The foreshortening effect of the perspective projection does not linearly map a triangular facet in three dimensions into the projected triangular area. With additional computations, it is also possible to back project each pixel on to the 3D facet and execute the interpolation in three dimensions. This method of interpolation is similar to that for two dimensions. The only difference is that the values of the two scalar parameters, α and β, change when the pixel is back projected to the facet of the object, and so must be re-computed.

Shading methods that compute the back projection of pixels are similar to a much more general technique called **ray tracing**. Ray tracing for simple solid opaque objects uses a ray (view vector) passed through each pixel. Once the intersection between the ray and the surface closest to the viewer is determined, the actual normal at the surface can be calculated from the geometric description of the object. In the case of planar facets, the normal direction is equal to the outside normal of the intersected facet. Ray tracing is a very important general rendering technique since it can be used for more general scenes than those composed of solid opaque objects. Semi-transparent objects, refraction, diffusion, shadows and multiple reflections can all be calculated using ray tracing methods. Ray tracing is discussed as a separate subject in Chapter 8.

7.5 ILLUMINATED COLOURED OBJECTS AND COLOURED LIGHT SOURCES

Display devices that allow different colour and intensity levels at each pixel have the greatest flexibility for generating realistic graphics scenes. Most of these devices are based on the generation and mixing of the three primary colours, where the intensity levels for the three colours are specified. Hence, when a coloured picture is generated, the calculations must be made three times and three different intensity values must be determined.

When objects are illuminated, the surfaces reflect the three different colours with different reflection coefficients. White light contains equal intensities of each primary colour, while diffuse reflection of white light gives the object its colour. Other object colours result when scenes are illuminated using coloured light sources. The equations given for ambient, diffuse and specularly reflected lights must be calculated for each primary colour content of the light sources. As has been already mentioned in the previous section, ambient and diffuse light reflection coefficients are colour sensitive, while specularly reflected light has the colour content of the light source.

7.5.1 Colour vision and the definition of colour

One of the difficulties in specifying and generating colours is that colour is a part of everyday human experience as well as a scientifically defined property of light. Physicists specify colour by the wavelength (or frequency) of electromagnetic radiation. As shown in Figure 7.21, the visible spectrum is from around 400 nm (1 nm = 10^{-9} m) to 700 nm. A laser light with a wavelength close to 700 nm contains a very narrow band of frequencies, and so has a physically well-defined colour. It will have the colour red.

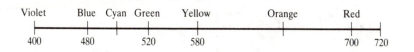

Light wavelength (nm)

Figure 7.21
The physical description of colour is based on wavelength measured in nanometers (10^{-9} m). The visible spectrum is from short wavelength violet to long wavelength red.

Radiation with wavelength of 400 nm will have the colour violet, while light of around 520 nm in wavelength will have the colour green. In addition to wavelength, the other easily measurable property of light is intensity, which expresses the energy per unit area carried by the electromagnetic wave.

The problem with using wavelength to characterize colour is that most coloured lights or objects radiate a band of frequencies – that is, a distribution of colours. White light includes all visible colours with approximately equal intensity, as shown in Figure 7.22, which also shows a light distribution for the colour red and a mixture of red and white, which is seen as pink. The human eye is extremely sensitive and can distinguish between an estimated 300 000 different shades of colour. It would be very difficult indeed to base a standard description of colours on the intensity distribution of electromagnetic radiation as a function of wavelength. Consequently, for practical applications, the physical description is abandoned in favour of an empirical description.

The empirical description of colours is based on colour mixing. It has been shown that with one red, one green and one blue light, called **primary colours**, any colour shade can be matched in the experimental arrangement shown in Figure 7.23. This experiment is based on the way colours are perceived; that is, the sensing of radiation intensities at three principal wavelengths – one short, one long and one in the middle. The process is assumed to be linear and the summation signs indicate that the intensities of different distributions are added together. To match a colour, either all three lights are added together with different intensities or, if matching is not possible by additive sources, two light sources are added and the third is added to the unknown light. If a linear model is assumed, then in this case the unknown light can be expressed as the weighed sum of two primary lights minus a portion of the third.

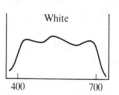
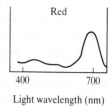
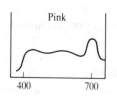

Light wavelength (nm)

Figure 7.22
Ordinary coloured light contains all visible wavelengths and can be characterized by a distribution of colours. If there is no dominant wavelength, the colour appears to be white (or gray). The combination of a dominant wavelength (red is shown) and white produces pastel colours, such as pink.

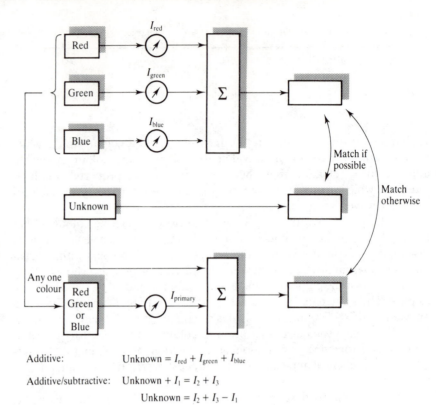

Figure 7.23
Colour may be defined by matching it to light produced by the sum of three primary colour sources: red, green and blue. A practical colour-matching experiment is shown schematically in this diagram. If matching with the sum of the three primary colours is not possible, then it is always possible to select one primary source, add it to the unknown colour and match the result with the sum of the two remaining primary sources.

Additive: $\qquad$ Unknown $= I_{red} + I_{green} + I_{blue}$

Additive/subtractive: $\quad$ Unknown $+ I_1 = I_2 + I_3$

$$\text{Unknown} = I_2 + I_3 - I_1$$

Surprisingly, not all colours can be matched by adding the three primary colours. A simple example will demonstrate the difficulty with a purely additive system. As shown in Figure 7.24, a colour distribution is to be matched that has approximately equal intensities at the red and green wavelengths, but contains very little blue component. Mixing the red and green lights produces the distribution shown in Figure 7.24(b), which closely matches the values at the red and green wavelengths, but because of the broad bandwidth of these two colours, the result contains too much blue. Adding blue to the unknown light solves this problem, as shown in the distribution in Figure 7.24(c).

Figure 7.24 also demonstrates why it would be very difficult to base colour definitions on intensity distributions. The mixing of red and green light gives the appearance of yellow, with the double hump distribution shown in Figure 7.25(b). On the other hand, pure yellow light should have the distribution shown in Figure 7.25(a), with a single maximum around 580 nm. These two distributions are perceived by the human eye as the same colour. Thus, colour that is defined empirically as it is perceived by the human eye must be matched to calibrated light sources to obtain a

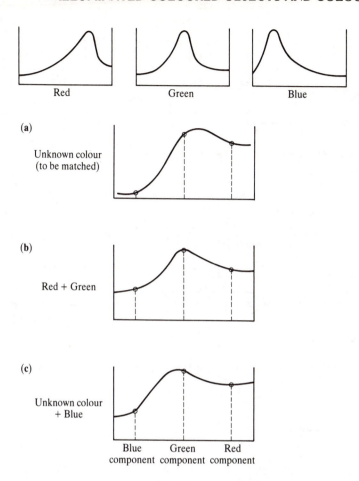

Figure 7.24
These diagrams show why matching one colour with the sum of three primaries is not always possible. The sum of red and green lights cannot match the required distribution because it has too much blue in it. Adding blue light to the colour to be matched solves this problem.

measurement of its equivalent wavelength. Once light sources are standardized and intensities are calibrated, the three-component, additive–subtractive system can form the basis of a standard description of colour. In this system, three numbers, all positive or one negative and two positive, specify any given colour.

A major simplification to this cumbersome colour system was made by the Commission Internationale de L'Eclairage (CIE) in 1931, when the standard CIE chromaticity diagram was created. Chromaticity defines colour ratios by a purely additive system in a normalized form. Since the system is assumed to be linear and purely additive, any colour may be specified as the mixture of three primary colour sources, which are expressed by three intensities:

$$I_{red}, I_{green}, I_{blue}$$

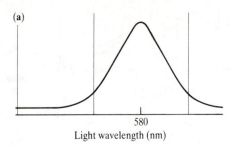

(a)

580

Light wavelength (nm)

Figure 7.25

Pure colour defined by a simple maximum, like yellow, may be matched by the sum of red and green lights which has quite different (double hump) distribution. These two diagrams illustrate the difference between the physical description of colour and the everyday experience of colour vision.

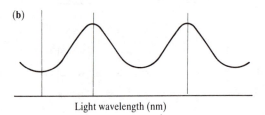

(b)

Light wavelength (nm)

From these absolute intensities, three normalized intensity ratios may be defined:

$$r = \frac{I_{red}}{I_{red} + I_{green} + I_{blue}}$$

$$g = \frac{I_{green}}{I_{red} + I_{green} + I_{blue}}$$

$$b = \frac{I_{blue}}{I_{red} + I_{green} + I_{blue}} = 1 - r - g$$

In some textbooks, the three variables are named x, y and z, but the letters r, g and b will be retained here for clarity. Since these normalized colour ratios always sum to 1, only two of them are independent. Therefore, a 2D diagram can be drawn, using the normal x and y axes, and can represent all colours within the triangle defined by the ranges:

$$0 \leqslant x \leqslant 1, \quad 0 \leqslant y \leqslant 1, \quad \text{and} \quad 0 \leqslant x + y \leqslant 1$$

The standard CIE chromaticity diagram developed defines a linear additive colour system based on three standard light sources, whose colour distribution curves are also defined. The light sources are mathematically

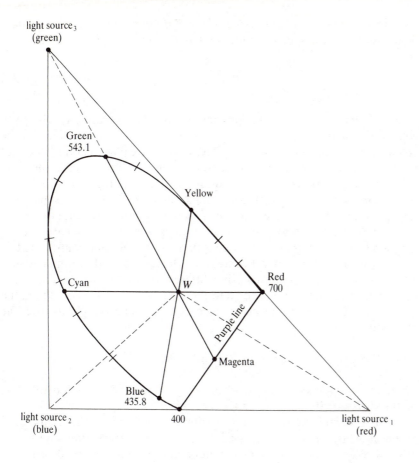

Figure 7.26

The standard chromaticity or CIE diagram represents all hue and saturation values with normalized intensity. The horse-shoe shaped curve represents empirically all the visible 100% saturated or pure colours. The point indicated with the letter W represents white light.

defined by $r = 1$ ($x = 1$, $y = 0$), $g = 1$ ($x = 0$, $y = 1$) and $b = 1$ ($x = y = 0$), as shown in Figure 7.26. The pure primary colours, red, green and blue, are defined by the following wavelengths:

Red light wavelength = 700 nm

Green light wavelength = 543.1 nm

Blue light wavelength = 435.8 nm

The empirically derived horse-shoe shaped curve represents all the visible pure colours, which are defined by their wavelengths and are shown on the curve in nanometers. The curve was produced using a colour-matching technique with calibrated light sources. The straight line completing the curve is called the **purple** line and it represents mixes of pure red and blue lights, for which there is no single frequency colour equivalent.

Since white light is defined as equal amounts of the three primary light intensities, the special point, point W, for pure white light is shown at:

$$r = g = b = \frac{1}{3}$$

'White' is defined as the best approximation for the 'average daylight'. Any colour within the visible spectrum may be defined as the sum of pure colour, called **hue**, and white light. Pure colours are placed at the border of the visible colour region. The purity of a colour is called its **saturation** and is expressed as a percentage. A saturation value of 1 (or 100%) indicates that there is no white light component; hence, the colour is pure. A saturation of 0 means there is no hue – that is, it indicates white or gray.

Any visible colour may be indicated by a point on the chromaticity diagram inside the horse-shoe shaped curve. A straight line connecting two points (two different colours) contains all those colours that can be generated by mixing the two colours using different ratios. Since the value of the normalized red intensity r is equal to the x distance and g is equal to y, the colour at any point on the line can be defined using the parametric line equation:

$$\text{Colour on line} = \alpha[r_1, g_1] + (1 - \alpha)[r_2, g_2]$$

where $\text{colour}_1 = [r_1, g_1]$ and $\text{colour}_2 = [r_2, g_2]$ are the endpoints of a line on the chromaticity diagram and α is between 0 and 1.

The complement of a given colour is defined as the colour that produces white light when it is added (with the correct intensity) to the original colour. Thus, the complement of a pure colour can be determined from the CIE diagram by drawing a straight line through the point representing the colour and the white point. As shown in Figure 7.26, the complement of red is cyan (turquoise) and the complement of blue is yellow. Both of these colours can be defined using a single frequency. The complement of green, however, is magenta, which is shown as a point on the purple line. Magenta cannot be defined by a single frequency, only as a mixture of red and blue.

Notice that from around 700 nm to 540 nm the pure colours are lying close to the $x = y$ (or $r = g$) line, which means that the blue component is very small. Thus, pure colours in this range can be produced by adding two primary colours only. For other pure colours, except the single point for 400 nm, all three colour sources are required. The standard CIE diagram with its indicated colour shades is shown in Colour Plate 3.

In Figure 7.27, a particular colour value C_1 is indicated on the CIE diagram. A straight line drawn through this colour point and W intersects the pure colour curve at two places. On the side of point C_1, the intersection point, C_1^0, defines the hue of colour C_1, its dominant colour. The line

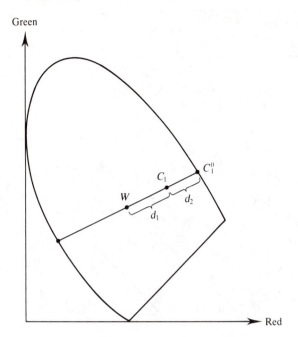

Green

C_1

C_1^0

W

d_2

d_1

Red

Figure 7.27

Any point inside the horse-shoe shaped curve represents a partially saturated colour. The colour represented by point C_1 has its dominant pure colour at C_1^0 which lies at the intersection of the pure colour curve and a straight line that passes through the W point. Saturation can be expressed by the ratio $d_1/(d_1 + d_2)$.

between W and C_1^0 represents the same hue with different saturation values. The saturation is given as the ratio of the distances between C_1 and W, and C_1^0 and W. Thus, for the colour example shown in Figure 7.27, the saturation value is equal to:

$$\text{Saturation} = \frac{d_1}{d_1 + d_2}$$

On the other side of point W, there are the complement colours of C_1. Any one of these may be used to produce white light when mixed with colour C_1.

A useful image-processing technique, known as **colour enhancement**, is based on changing the saturation of each point in an image. For each pixel, the saturation is increased, which is equivalent to moving the point C_1 in Figure 7.27 towards the point C_1^0. Thus, close points, near to the centre of the diagram, are separated. This makes it easier to distinguish those features in the image that are delineated by slight variation in colour. The technique is used in medical diagnosis.

7.5.2 Colour monitors

The advantage of using the chromaticity colour model for computer graphics is that colour monitors work on the three-colour additive principle.

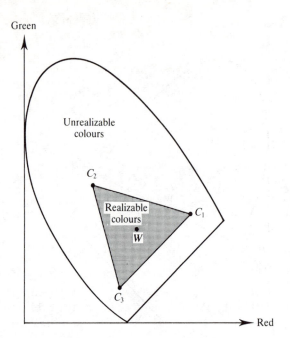

Figure 7.28
If the three primary sources of a colour monitor are mapped on the CIE diagram, then the triangle formed by them contains all the colours that can be produced by the monitor. As shown, a large number of colours are outside the triangle that cannot be produced by the monitor.

They also use red, green and blue for the three primary colours, although these would not be pure colours on the CIE diagram for a practical colour monitor. The primary colours of a monitor appear as points on the CIE diagram and the data for a typical colour monitor is as follows:

	r	g	b
RED	0.628	0.346	0.026
GREEN	0.268	0.588	0.144
BLUE	0.150	0.070	0.780

As shown in Figure 7.28, the three points define a triangle on the CIE chromaticity diagram. Only the colours represented by points inside this triangle may be reproduced by the display device and, as shown, there are a large number of colour shades that cannot be realized on such a colour display. Working with a given colour monitor, it is possible to change the frame of reference to realizable colours only and measure the normalized colour intensities $[r, g, b]$ in terms of the three given primary sources of the monitor. A CIE type of diagram, called here the red–green–blue (RGB) diagram, may be defined for a particular monitor using a right angle triangle with red normalized intensity along the x axis and green along the y axis. Such a diagram is shown in Colour Plate 4. The way in which this diagram was produced will be described later, after a discussion of the characteristics of a colour monitor.

Since both the CIE diagram and the RGB diagram for a colour monitor express linear relationships between colour and the $[x, y]$ co-ordinates, the data can be inter related by a matrix. The necessary transformation matrix can be derived simply from the definitions of the primary light sources:

$$[r, g, b]_{CIE} = [R, G, B]_{monitor} \begin{bmatrix} 0.628 & 0.346 & 0.026 \\ 0.268 & 0.588 & 0.144 \\ 0.150 & 0.070 & 0.780 \end{bmatrix}$$

The reverse transformation can be found by inverting the matrix.

Approximately 128 different hues may be distinguished by the human eye. For each hue, around 20 to 30 different saturations may be seen as different colours. The human eye is also capable of distinguishing between 60 to 100 different brightness, or intensity, levels. Therefore, the human eye can distinguish approximately 350 000 different colour shades.

Colours are generated in a monitor by the respective intensities of three signals, designated here as RED, GREEN and BLUE. In most display systems, a number of bits is designated to specify the intensities for the three colours. Medium-priced graphics systems usually allow this specification using 8 bits, or 256 levels, for each primary colour. Lower-priced devices may allow only 4 bits, or 16 intensity levels. The number of different colours that can be displayed at any one time will usually be less than the total number of colour shades the monitor can produce. The complete set of colours that a monitor can produce is called the **palette**. With 256 different intensities for each primary colour, $256 \times 256 \times 256$ different colour shades may be generated, giving the monitor a palette of over 16 million colours. This size of palette, which is commonly provided, therefore contains far more colour shades than can be actually seen by the human eye.

As already described in Chapter 1, medium-priced display systems contain a **colour lookup table**. This defines the subset of the palette that can be displayed at any one time. Typically, the colour lookup table would allow the selection of 256 unique colours. These colours are called **logical colours** and are indicated by integer numbers. The colour lookup table translates the logical colour number to an actual displayed colour. Each pixel is set using one of the logical colours. Changing an entry in the lookup table changes all the pixels set to the corresponding logical colour number.

Intensity is not shown in the CIE diagram and is used as a scaling factor for all three colours. For a given colour defined by absolute intensity values, denoted as RED, GREEN and BLUE, the normalized intensities in the RGB diagram for a particular monitor can be calculated as before:

$$R = \frac{RED}{RED + GREEN + BLUE}$$

$$G = \frac{GREEN}{RED + GREEN + BLUE}$$

$$B = \frac{BLUE}{RED + GREEN + BLUE} = 1 - R - G$$

which defines a colour. The range of intensity values that can be displayed for this colour can be expressed by a value parameter, V:

$$RED = VR$$
$$GREEN = VG$$
$$BLUE = V(1 - R - G)$$

where V ranges from 0 to V_{max}. The value of V_{max} depends on the hardware being used to display the picture.

In Colour Plate 5, the realizable portion of the CIE diagram has been generated by a relatively inexpensive system that has a palette of 16 million colours. The co-ordinates of the triangle are defined by the monitor's primary colour sources as they fall on the calibrated CIE diagram. Since two values, R and G, define each colour, the maximum achievable intensity is used and the displayed colour shades are given by:

$$RED = V_{max}R$$
$$GREEN = V_{max}G$$
$$BLUE = V_{max}(1 - R - G)$$

If the diagram is to be drawn on a system which can only display 256 colours simultaneously, there is an easy mapping between the R, G and B intensities and a logical colour number. This is computed using the following function:

```
function COLOUR_NUMBER(R, G : real) : integer;
begin
  (* R, G assumed to be positive *)
  if (R >= 1)
  then R := 0.999;
  if (G >= 1)
  then G := 0.999;
  COLOUR_NUMBER := trunc(16 * R) + 16 * trunc(16 * G);
end
```

In effect, the G and R values are scaled to be integers in the range $[0...15]$ and are packed into the top and bottom 4 bits of the 8-bit number indexing the colour lookup table. For each logical colour number found, the real colour, which is placed in the lookup table, is the maximum intensity colour that preserves the ratios between R, G and B. Since the system provides for 256 different levels for each primary component (0 to 255), the three values are:

$$255 \frac{R}{MAX(R, G, B)}$$

$$255 \frac{G}{MAX(R, G, B)}$$

$$255 \frac{B}{MAX(R, G, B)}$$

Although the given function fills all 256 places in the colour table, only 128 of the 256 colours will appear on the diagram. This is because the condition $R + G \leqslant 1$ must be satisfied within the displayed triangular area.

Assuming that the three vertices are located at positions $[x_1, y_1]$, $[x_2, y_2]$ and $[x_3, y_3]$ on the CIE diagram, the same method used for Phong shading can be applied to convert a pixel position to three colour intensities. In this case, however, the $[R, G, B]$ values are used instead of the $[n_x, n_y, n_z]$ normal vectors. At point $[x_1, y_1]$, the $[R, G, B]$ intensities are equal to $[1, 0, 0]$; at $[x_2, y_2]$ to $[0, 1, 0]$; and at $[x_3, y_3]$ to $[0, 0, 1]$. It can be shown that in this case the matrix equation for the intensities can be expressed as:

$$[R, G, B] = [x, y, 1] \begin{bmatrix} x_1 & y_1 & 1 \\ x_2 & y_2 & 1 \\ x_3 & y_3 & 1 \end{bmatrix}^{-1}$$

where $[X, Y]$ is the co-ordinate at any point inside the triangle and $[\,]^{-1}$ indicates the inverse of the matrix.

7.5.3 RGB model

One way of representing a complete set of colour shades, including intensities, is to use the 3D RGB cube, as shown in Figure 7.29. The cube is in the positive quadrant and the axes are labelled by the primary colours. The maximum intensities for all three primary colours can be normalized to the

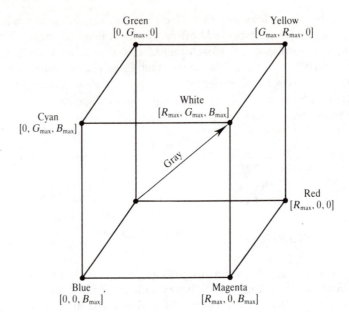

Figure 7.29
The RGB colour cube is an alternative representation of the additive model of a colour monitor. The intensities are not normalized and the cube contains all realizable colour. White or gray shades fall on the line connecting the origin with the farthest vertex of the cube.

range 0 to 1. Since intensity is now represented, the sum of the three primary colours at any point is not 1, as it was on the CIE diagram, and so the labels RED, GREEN and BLUE are used rather that r, g and b. The primary colours and their complements with maximum intensities are placed at the vertices of the cube. The diagonal connecting white and black represents grays that have equal intensities in the three primary colours.

The three facets adjoining the RED, GREEN and BLUE axes have points representing the maximum intensities that can be produced by the monitor. Thus, there is a one-to-one mapping between the colours on these faces and the two-dimensional RGB diagram. These three visible facets of the cube with the correct colours are shown in Colour Plate 6. The corresponding facets on any smaller cube will contain similar colours with less brightness and with their brightness parameter constant defined by:

Brightness = MAX(RED, GREEN, BLUE)

The possible range for the brightness is from 0 to 1, just as for the intensities RED, GREEN and BLUE. While the RGB cube is a good graphical representation for the colour monitor, it does not help the intuitive use of colour by an artist who relies on tints, shades and tone. Intuitive colour models try to imitate the mixing of pure pigments (hues) with white pigment (which decreases its saturation) and black pigment (which decreases its brightness). Although it is very difficult to match colours displayed on a colour monitor with colours produced on paper, a reasonably successful system based on three parameters, called hue, saturation and brightness (value), HSV, has been developed, which will now be discussed.

7.5.4 HSV model

To relate the RGB model with the more intuitive colour concepts of hue, saturation and brightness (value), it is necessary to realize that any three absolute intensities [RED, GREEN, BLUE] can be produced by the sum of a pure colour (hue) and white light. Saturation expresses the relative magnitudes of the pure colour and the white components. Since white light contains equal proportions of RED, GREEN and BLUE, a white component can be determined from the minimum of the three components of any colour:

$$RED_w = GREEN_w = BLUE_w = MIN(RED, GREEN, BLUE)$$

The pure colour is the mixture of at most two primary colours and can be calculated by the following expressions:

$$RED_h = RED - MIN(RED, GREEN, BLUE)$$
$$GREEN_h = GREEN - MIN(RED, GREEN, BLUE)$$
$$BLUE_h = BLUE - MIN(RED, GREEN, BLUE)$$

The index 'h' indicates pure hue and at least one of these components will be equal to 0.

The HSV model can be represented by a hexagonal cone, as shown in Figure 7.30. Colour, or hue, is defined by an angle with red being at angle 0°, yellow at 60°, green at 120°, and so on. A simple intuitive formula is used for the calculation of the hue angle for pure colours (which contain no more than two primaries). For example, between red and green:

$$\text{Hue angle} = \frac{120\,GREEN_h}{RED_h + GREEN_h} \quad \text{in degrees}$$

When $GREEN_h = 0$, red (hue = 0°) is obtained, when $RED_h = 0$, green (hue = 120°) is obtained and when $RED_h = GREEN_h$, yellow (hue = 60°) is obtained. Similar expressions are used for the five other sides of the hexagon.

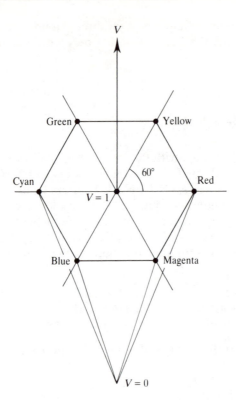

Figure 7.30
The HSV representation is closer to the everyday experience of colour described in terms of hue, saturation and value (brightness). This model may be represented by a hexagonal cone with the white or gray shades lying on the vertical axis. Colour is represented by an angle and constant value by a horizontal plane.

Although it would be possible to calculate the saturation value defined by the CIE curve, a much simpler formula is used for the value of the saturation in this intuitive model:

$$\text{Saturation} = \frac{\text{MAX(RED, GREEN, BLUE)} - \text{MIN(RED, GREEN, BLUE)}}{\text{MAX(RED, GREEN, BLUE)}}$$

Saturation in the HSV model is similar to colour purity, being equal to 1 for pure colours and 0 for white. However, its value is not exactly equivalent to the saturation values defined by the CIE diagram.

The brightness value, Value, is expressed simply by the intensity of the maximum component:

$$\text{Value} = \text{MAX(RED, GREEN, BLUE)}$$

There are similarities between the RGB colour cube and the HSV hexicube. For example, the top hexagonal facet of the hexicube is a mapping of the three facets of the cube that adjoin the axes (pure hues with maximum intensities) on to a planar hexagon. The colours generated by

---

Algorithm 7.1

Convert from RGB values to HSV values.

$MaxCol := MAX(Red, Green, Blue)$;
$MinCol := MIN(Red, Green, Blue)$;
$Value := MaxCol$;
if $(MaxCol = MinCol)$
then begin
      Saturation $:= 0$;
      { Hue is undefined, colour is white, gray or black }
   end
else begin
      $Saturation := (MaximumComponent - MinumumComponent)/MaximumComponent$;
      if $(MinCol = Blue)$ **then**
        $Hue := 120.0 * (Green - MinCol)/(Red + Green - 2.0 * MinCol)$
      else if $(MinCol = Red)$ **then**
        $Hue := 120.0 * (1.0 + (Blue - MinCol)/(Blue + Green - 2.0 * MinCol))$
      else
        $Hue := 120.0 * (2.0 + (Red - MinCol)/(Red + Blue - 2.0 * MinCol))$
   end;

---

the same graphics system for the top hexagonal facet of the hexicube are shown in Colour Plate 7.

The HSV hexicube also has similarities with the CIE diagram. The centre point is the white point and all the graphical relationships between colour points, mixing of colours and complement colours are similar to those in the CIE diagram. The intuitive indication of the saturation value is also the same as that on the CIE diagram. Points close to the centre have very small saturation values, whereas points on the border are pure hues. For a constant V value, the hexicube is cut by a plane perpendicular to the V axis, which yields a hexagon with size proportional to V. In fact, each hexagon produces a similar coloured diagram to Colour Plate 7, but with reduced intensity. The theoretical brightness value V is not exactly equal to an observed brightness, since the observed brightness of the colour is influenced by all three primary components, while the V value depends only on the maximum component. This demonstrates yet another difficulty when intuitive meanings are given to a mathematically derived colour model.

Algorithm 7.1 converts the RGB values, normalized to 1, to respective HSV values. Note, however, that efficiency is sacrificed for readability.

Algorithm 7.2

Convert from HSV values to RGB values.

```
if hue is undefined
then begin
        Red := Value;
        Green := Value;
        Blue := Value;
    end
else begin
        MinCol := Value * (1.0 − Saturation);
        if (Hue <= 120.0)
        then begin
                Blue := MinCol;
                if (Hue <= 60.0)
                then begin
                        Red := Value;
                        Green := MinCol + Hue * (Value − MinCol)/(120.0 − Hue)
                    end
                else begin
                        Green := Value;
                        Red := MinCol + (120.0 − Hue) * (Value − MinCol)/Hue
                    end
            end
        else if (Hue <= 240.0)
        then begin
                Red := MinCol;
                if (Hue <= 180.0)
                then begin
                        Green := Value;
                        Blue := MinCol + (Hue − 120.0) * (Value − MinCol)/(240.0 − Hue)
                    end
                else begin
                        Blue := Value;
                        Green := MinCol + (240.0 − Hue) * (Value − MinCol)/(Hue − 120.0)
                    end
            end
        else begin
                Green := MinCol;
                if (Hue <= 300.0)
                then begin
                        Blue := Value;
                        Red := MinCol + (Hue − 240.0) * (Value − MinCol)/(360.0 − Hue)
                    end
                else begin
                        Red := Value;
                        Blue := MinCol + (360.0 − Hue) * (Value − MinCol)/(Hue − 240.0)
                    end
            end
    end;
```

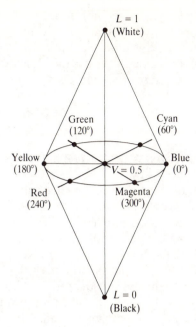

L = 1
(White)

Green
(120°)

Cyan
(60°)

Yellow
(180°)

V = 0.5

Blue
(0°)

Red
(240°)

Magenta
(300°)

L = 0
(Black)

Figure 7.31
The HLS system developed by Tektronix Incorporated uses a double cone to represent all the colours. Hue is again represented by angle, saturation by the closeness to the axis of the cones and lightness (value) by the distance along the *L* axis.

It is not difficult to invert Algorithm 7.1 and calculate the RGB values from the given HSV values. One version of this algorithm is given as Algorithm 7.2.

Tektronix developed yet another system called the HLS model, which is shown in Figure 7.31. This model is similar to the HSV model, but a double cone is used with the black and white points placed at the two apexes of the double cone. The pure hues are at the surface of the double cone and gray tones (saturation = 0) are along the *L* axis. The hue angle is calculated similarly to the HSV model, with angle 0° placed at the pure blue hue, but the other two parameters have somewhat different expressions. The lightness parameter is calculated by:

$$\text{Lightness} = \frac{\text{MAX}(\text{Red, Green, Blue}) + \text{MIN}(\text{Red, Green, Blue})}{2}$$

and if $L \leq 0.5$, then the saturation value is equal to:

$$\text{Saturation} = \frac{\text{MAX}(\text{Red, Green, Blue}) + \text{MIN}(\text{Red, Green, Blue})}{\text{MAX}(\text{Red, Green, Blue}) - \text{MIN}(\text{Red, Green, Blue})}$$

otherwise the expression is:

$$\text{Saturation} = \frac{\text{MAX}(\text{Red, Green, Blue}) - \text{MIN}(\text{Red, Green, Blue})}{2 - \text{MAX}(\text{Red, Green, Blue}) - \text{MIN}(\text{Red, Green, Blue})}$$

This and other models are combinations of the CIE, the RGB and the HSV models and do not add much new to the colour-generation concepts. Any usable model will have a one-to-one mapping between its parameters and the CIE diagram, which is the ultimate standard for colour comparison. Thus, the parameters can always be translated from one model to the other.

7.5.5 Anti-aliasing coloured images

One major problem still requiring an effective solution is the question of anti-aliasing colour images constructed with the RGB model. The same techniques that were discussed in Chapter 3 can be applied and will, in many instances, give reasonable results. Some examples are shown in Colour Plates 10, 11, 12 and 13. However, for cases where two contrasted colours are adjacent, the filtering algorithms will produce an averaged colour at the boundary, which is not the required effect. For example, a red polygon over a green background will be given some yellow pixels on the boundary. These may accentuate the alias frequency, rather than reduce it. Thus, the algorithm must first decide which pixels to include in the average and which to ignore. A similar problem exists when coloured images are converted from one resolution or aspect ratio to different ones.

7.5.6 Colour printers and paint mixing

When coloured pictures are produced on paper, it is the reflection of the light source that is observed. The apparent colour is created by absorption of some of its primary components. For this reason, the system is called **subtractive**. Thus, different paints applied to the paper absorb different proportions of the incident light and so produce different colours in the reflected light. White paint mixed with coloured paint reflects more white light, thereby decreasing the saturation of the reflected light. Black paint, on the other hand, absorbs all colours inherent in white light, so when black paint is mixed with coloured paint, it reduces all colour components equally. Hence, it reduces the brightness of the reflected light without changing its dominant wavelength.

Pure primary paints completely absorb a single primary colour. The three primary coloured paints are cyan (turquoise), which absorbs red; magenta, which absorbs green, and yellow, which absorbs blue. When coloured paints are added, the reflected light becomes darker. Cyan and magenta added together absorb both red and green, and the reflected light will be blue. The other possible combinations are shown in Figure 7.32.

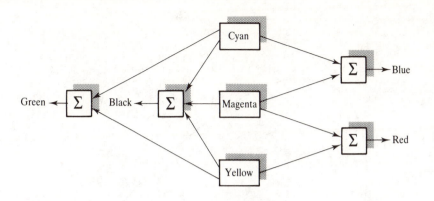

Figure 7.32
Paints or dyes follow the subtractive system because their colour is produced by absorption of selected wavelengths when illuminated by white light. The primary paint colours are cyan, magenta and yellow because they all absorb only one primary wavelength (red, green and blue). Mixing these primaries produces red, green, blue and black, as shown in the diagram.

Mixing the three primary paints will cause all incident light to be absorbed, producing black.

Knowledge of this subtractive system is important for programming hardcopy devices such as the ink jet printer, which can produce small ink dots on paper with any one of the seven colours shown in Figure 7.32. If white paper is used, then the lack of a coloured ink dot may be defined as the eighth colour (white). The problem is that neither the brightness nor the saturation of the dots may be changed. The only possible way to create more than eight colours with this system is to use simulated half-toning techniques, similar to those described in Chapter 3 for black and white pixels. Having seven different colour components, a variety of half-toning techniques and variable ratios between the densities of the coloured dots makes this technique extremely complicated. Empirical solutions to the problem of matching a given colour are currently being investigated.

7.5.7 Practical considerations

It has been amply demonstrated that working with colour is not a simple problem. In addition to all the different colour systems, the psychology of colour vision, ambient lighting conditions, physical characteristics of different monitors, and a large number of other physical and ergonomic factors all influence the final results. At the same time, however, colour adds an extremely important extra dimension to computer graphics which should not be ignored. Three main application areas can be distinguished.

Firstly, colour may be used as a tool for man–machine communication. For example, in business graphs, red may be used for debts while blue can indicate surpluses. Some colours may be used for highlighting messages or emphasizing some special icons. For this type of application, a few logical colours with set intensities may be quite sufficient. Since the emphasis in these cases is on contrast, the brightest possible colours of

Key

W	White	r	reddish
R	Red	b	bluish
B	Blue	g	greenish
G	Green	y	yellowish
Y	Yellow	o	orangish
O	Orange	p	purplish
P	Purple	pk	pinkish
PK	Pink		

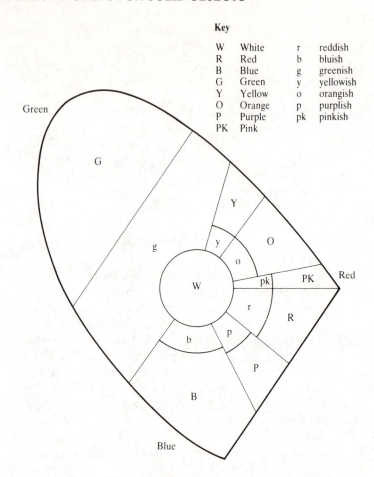

Figure 7.33

Areas of the CIE diagram that may be identified with a specific colour name like orange or orangish (orange with white added to it) are not equally spaced. The largest areas contain greens and blues, while yellows cover a relatively small area.

different hues and saturation are needed. The CIE diagram can be used for such a selection. It can be divided into different regions with 15 different named colours, as shown in Figure 7.33. Adding the possibility of no colour at all (black), gives 16 logical colours (4 bits per pixel), which can be found in most modern inexpensive colour systems. Figure 7.33 shows that equal steps in distance in, for example, the *pk* and *g* regions, do not produce equal contrast. The yellow and pink areas are very small, whereas the green, blue, or red areas are very large. This points towards empirical determination of 16 distinct colours that can be used to indicate different items.

The colour application areas at the other extreme are concerned with the rendering of realistic colour images using both colour monitors and high-quality colour printing systems. This is a very specialized area requiring as many colour shades as possible. Monitors providing 24 bits per pixel (16 million colours) will be sufficient for most applications, but they are very expensive. There are some coloured typesetting systems that will automatically transfer coloured images from a monitor to a high-quality printed image. One problem that such systems have to resolve is the large difference between the typesetter's resolution of 2000 dots per inch and that of the colour monitors, which is around 100 pixels per inch.

There are many applications between these two extremes where 8-bit systems allowing a choice of 256 colours out of a palette of 16 million may be sufficient. Applications include CAD/CAM, VLSI and modelling systems. Often, coloured solid objects are represented with Gouraud or Phong shading to show orientation, and depth cueing to show distance from the user. Since 8 bits per pixel is sufficient to produce a fully shaded monochrome image, a coloured shaded image can be produced on film by exposing the film three times, once for each primary colour component of the image. This will provide all 16 million colours on the film since, for each exposure, all 256 intensities of one primary colour can be used. Unfortunately, film exposure is not a linear process and the linear RGB model breaks down. Exposing film introduces a large number of new and unsolved problems in colour reproduction.

An added problem is that just as equal steps in chromaticity do not provide equal contrast in colour, equal steps in pixel intensity do not provide equal steps in perceived brightness. On a monochrome monitor, the eye observes brightness contrast by the ratio of intensities, rather than by the difference of intensities. For example, apparently equal steps of brightness will be produced by the normalized intensity values of 1, 0.9, 0.81, 0.721, and so on. For $(N + 1)$ different quantized levels, the brightness levels, V, providing equal intensity steps are given by the expression:

$$V_i = N^{\left(\frac{i}{N}\right)} \quad i = 0, 1, 2, ..., N$$

Unfortunately, another problem is that the light output produced by the screen phosphor is not linearly proportional to the pixel's given intensity value. Frequently, the relationship can be expressed by the exponential:

$$\text{Brightness} = kV^{\gamma}$$

where V is the intensity value set for each pixel. High-quality monitors provide automatic correction for this non-linearity which is called **gamma-correction**. For other monitors, values for k and γ can be experimentally determined, and for each desired brightness a good approximation for the V value calculated by inverting the above equation. These problems are further evidence of the difficulty of producing realistic computer-generated pictures.

7.6   COLOUR QUANTIZATION

As has already been mentioned, graphics systems that allow an unlimited choice of colours from a large palette (16 million) are expensive. On the other hand, systems that provide a large palette while limiting the number of colours that can be displayed simultaneously to typically 256 are comparatively inexpensive and widely used. These systems can produce rendered images whose quality can in many cases approach that of the expensive systems. The key to successful rendering is the selection of colours to be included in the lookup table. This section discusses some algorithms for making such a selection. For the purposes of this discussion, it is assumed that pictures have been generated using 24 bits for each pixel intensity, 8 for each primary colour, and that they are to be displayed on a system with 256 entries in the lookup table, each indexing a colour with 24 bits lookup table entries.

7.6.1   Uniform quantization

This is the simplest algorithm. The index to the table is treated as an 8-bit binary number divided into fields. For example, it may consist of a 3-bit field for red, a 3-bit field for green and a 2-bit field for blue, as shown in Figure 7.34. Thus, each index provides a value of red and green in the range 0 to 7 and a value of blue in the range 0 to 3. The associated lookup table entries may be found simply by scaling. So, red and green are multiplied by 32 and the blue by 64. The data in the image file is mapped into the table by inverse scaling. Thus, the red and green components are divided by 32 and the blue by 64. The choice of which colour is given a 2-bit representation and which a three, to produce the best result, depends on the image.

This method produces approximately six levels of intensity for each colour, which is not sufficient. Moreover, pronounced Mach band effects, sometimes called **contouring**, will be visible when the display is viewed. However, the method is very fast to compute, since the scaling can always be done by masking rather than dividing. For this reason, it can be used for previewing images, before more computationally demanding rendering techniques are applied.

Figure 7.34
Colour monitors allow only a limited number of bits for the specification of colours. Eight bits allow 256 different colours which may be divided equally among the three primaries, allowing four different intensity levels for red, green and blue.

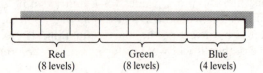

Red
(8 levels)   Green
(8 levels)   Blue
(4 levels)

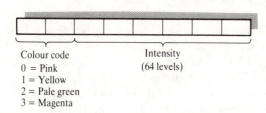

Colour code
0 = Pink
1 = Yellow
2 = Pale green
3 = Magenta

Intensity
(64 levels)

Figure 7.35
When only a few dominant colours are used, the limited number of bits may be separated between colour selection and intensity levels. Two bits allow the selection of four different hues leaving 6 bits for 64 different intensity levels for each hue.

7.6.2 Colour coding

Contouring is a direct result of there being too few intensity levels to produce the effect of a smooth shade gradient. It is possible to increase the number of different levels by restricting the number of colours used. This technique is applicable to molecular modelling, where only a few colours are required to distinguish the individual atoms, but smooth shading of each atom is required.

For colour coding, the index to the table is divided into two fields. One field is used to code the colour, while the other field stores the intensity level. For example, a four-colour table will have 2 bits to indicate the colour and a possible 64 levels of shade for each of the colours, as shown in Figure 7.35. The colours to be used must be defined by the user as a ratio of the three primaries. A simple way to generate the actual table entries for each colour is to set the largest primary to four times the indicated level of shade. Thus, it will range over the full 0 to 255 levels. The other two intensities are then computed according to the required ratios. As noted in Section 7.5.7, however, a better result can be obtained if a non-linear distribution is used, such that the ratio of the brightness of adjacent entries is a constant.

If colour coding is used, it is normal for the programs generating the scene to produce output in the correct form. However, an image file could be mapped into this table by first computing the ratios of RED : GREEN : BLUE, to identify the correct (or nearest) colour code, and then the intensity field found by dividing the maximum primary by four.

The method as described here cannot cope with specular highlights, since a highlight is produced by specular reflection and has the colour of the light source. If white light is used for the light source, then highlights will have bands of differing saturation, from pure white light at the centre to the defined colour at a small distance away. However, these effects can be simulated by reserving one table entry for white and using a half-toning technique, such as dithering, in the local area of the specular highlight.

7.6.3 Popularity algorithm

A method that does not require the user to specify a limited number of colours to be used involves preprocessing the image file to find the 256 most popular colours. These colours are then used as the entries to the colour table and all the colours in the image file are mapped on to their closest representative in the table. Although conceptually simple, this method has some drawbacks from a computational point of view. Firstly, there is a large memory requirement for pictures with a large number of different pixels. For a 512 × 512 image, a static implementation would require an array of 512 × 512 × 3 integers, which is about 1.5 Mbytes of store. Since data will be sparsely populated, some reduction can be made by using a list of pixels, but this will increase the computation time.

The second problem concerns the mapping of pixels in the real image to their nearest representative in the table. The distance between any two colours could be equated with the Cartesian distance between points in the RGB space. However, for this application, it is not the absolute distance that is of interest. It will be computationally cheaper to minimize:

$$|R_1 - R_2| + |G_1 - G_2| + |B_1 - B_2|$$

where $[R_1, G_1, B_1]$ are values for an image pixel and $[R_2, G_2, B_2]$ are intensities in the lookup table. The determination of the minimum distance can be done by exhaustive search. If the table members are sorted under one colour, say red, the entry with the closest agreement in red can be found and used as a first approximation to the table entry. The distance between this and the pixel being mapped can then be found and used to eliminate table entries whose distance along the red axis exceeds this minimum distance. The reduced table can then be sorted in blue. The entry with the closest agreement in blue can be checked and if it is closer it replaces the current estimate for the closest table entry. As before, the table entries can be reduced and the same process carried out on the green. At this stage, an exhaustive search of the remaining table entries would find the closest entry. Alternatively, to save computation time, the best entry found could be used.

As can be seen, this search, which is done on a per pixel basis, is computationally very expensive. Furthermore, this algorithm has the drawback that it misses small, but significant areas of colour. For example, a specular highlight of white light in an image without other white pixels will be incorrectly coloured.

7.6.4 Median-cut algorithm

Another type of algorithm uses subdivision of the RGB cube to ensure that each lookup table entry represents the same number of pixels. This division is always done by planes parallel to the axes. The initial division can be made along any of the axes. If red is chosen, a histogram of red values can be computed and used to determine the position of the subdividing plane. The image pixels are then split into two sets, depending on which subdivision of the cube they belong to, and the algorithm proceeds recursively, with the division of each volume being along its longest side. When 256 volumes have been generated, a table entry is assigned to each volume by computing the average of all the pixel values in the volume. Mapping of the pixels to the table entries can be simply achieved by comparing each of the pixel primary components with the bounding planes of the boxes.

The median-cut algorithm again requires a large volume of storage. For each volume in the subdivision, a record must be kept of all the pixels that belong to it. If duplicate values are not removed, at least twice the memory will be required to store the image: one block to store the image, the other to keep the same pixel values, but sorted into volumes. Some reduction can be made by eliminating duplicate pixels. However, this requires the sorting of image pixels in their full 24-bit representation.

7.6.5 Octree quantization algorithm

An ingenious method of quantization that reduces both the computing time and the memory requirement has been introduced by Gervautz and Purgathofer (1988). It is similar in principle to median cut quantization, except that a regular subdivision of the RGB cube into eight smaller cubes is used. This type of division of a cubic volume is called **octree decomposition**. The root of the octree represents the cube bounded by the planes $R = 0, R = 255, G = 0, G = 255, B = 0$ and $B = 255$. This cube contains all the image points. The root has eight children, made up by slicing the original cube with the planes $R = 127, G = 127$ and $B = 127$. Each of these children is a cube containing some, possibly none, of the image pixels. Continuing this form of subdivision as far as possible yields individual points in the RGB space as the leaves.

Conceptually, this method builds an octree with the image points. If the nodes that do not contain image points are not included, then the number of leaf nodes is equal to the number of different pixels in the image. The tree is then reduced by an averaging process. This involves taking in turn the nodes in the next level up from the leaves and calculating for each the average of the children. The children are then pruned from the tree and the reduction is continued at the next level. The average computed for a node should be the average of all the image pixels belonging to the corresponding cube. Thus, for correct computation of the average through successive reductions, it is necessary to keep a record of the number of image pixels in the averaged value of any reduced node. The reduction process is continued until there are exactly 256 leaf nodes, which are then used as the entries to the lookup table.

In practice, it is not necessary to build the complete octree, which will require considerable storage. Instead, the building and the reduction take place in one pass through the image data. The first 256 different pixels form the leaf nodes of a tree. If the tree has 256 nodes, then a reduction is made before adding the next pixel. Two possible strategies can be used for reduction. Either the deepest nodes are reduced, or the nodes containing the fewest pixels. These have slightly different effects on the final image quality. After a reduction, one or more further pixels can be added, either as leaf nodes or by inclusion in the average of a reduced node. In this way, the total number of leaf nodes and reduced nodes can be kept to 256, thereby reducing the memory requirement. Mapping of the image points to the lookup table entries is a simple search of the final octree.

Octree quantization, in addition to its advantages of speed and size, has the effect of preserving contrasting parts of the image. The problem of a specular highlight, which would be incorrectly rendered by the popularity algorithm, is overcome by octree quantization, since isolated branches of the tree are preserved. Visually, there is little difference in final image quality between median cut and octree quantization.

The CIE diagram is a severe test for colour quantization, since it contains a very large number of colours. Colour Plate 8 shows the CIE diagram generated for 300×300 pixels which originally contained $45\,000$ colours but was reduced to 256 colours by octree colour quantization. Colour Plates 9 and 15 show graphics scenes rendered using octree quantization.

The computer generation of realistic coloured objects is a vast subject that includes display technology, physics, human vision and psychology. Obviously, it is not possible to cover the whole field in one chapter of a general book on computer graphics. Rather, this chapter introduces the subject from the user's point of view, highlighting the basic principles of the models on which colour generation by computers is based. Readers interested in tackling this aspect of computer graphics should expect to spend a large amount of time and effort in the understanding and solving of problems in this field.

Exercises

7.1 Describe the differences between diffuse and specular reflection and demonstrate how these differences are expressed in the equations with which they are calculated.

7.2 Describe the physical reasons behind the inclusion of an ambient illumination term in the calculation of the light reflection intensity from opaque surfaces.

7.3 Show how the linearly interpolated intensity on a triangular facet is calculated when the 3D position vector representing the point on the facet is given by:

$$\mathbf{P} = \alpha\mathbf{P_1} + \beta\mathbf{P_2} + \gamma\mathbf{P_3}$$

Derive conditions on the parameters α, β and γ so that the point is located inside the triangle.

7.4 Show that accurate Phong shading without back projection can only be used for diffuse and not specular reflection. Can you suggest an approximate method for working entirely in the image plane which could be used for specular reflection as well?

7.5 The surface of a sphere with its centre at the origin and radius R is approximated by N triangles. Devise a method of subdivision so that the triangles have approximately the same area. Write down expressions for the vertices of the triangles.

7.6 A sphere with radius of 5 m is located at point $[0, 0, 10]$ and is viewed from the origin. Determine the $[X, Y, Z]$ co-ordinates of the points on the surface of the sphere which appear brightest to the viewer under the following conditions:

(a) A distributed light source is used with direction vector $[0, -1, 1]$ and the surface exhibits only diffuse reflection.

(b) A point light source is located at $[1, 1, 0]$ and the surface exhibits only diffuse reflection.

(c) A distributed light source is used with direction vector $[0, -1, 1]$ and the surface exhibits only specular reflection.

(d) A point light source is located at $[1, 1, 0]$ and the surface exhibits only specular reflection.

7.7 A colour point in the CIE diagram is defined by $r = 0.5$, $g = 0.4$. Determine the wavelength of its dominant colour, its complement pure colour and also its approximate saturation value. What colour names would be most appropriate for the original colour, its dominant and its complement?

7.8 Determine the colour point in the CIE diagram with the lowest possible saturation when two colours are mixed with one colour specified as $r = 0.2$, $g = 0.5$ and the other as $r = 0.3$, $g = 0.2$. Find the appropriate names for the two original colours and the mixture.

7.9 Develop an expression that relates the normalized r and g values of a colour in the CIE diagram to paint mixing. The amount of paints mixed together is characterized by variables c, m, y and w for cyan, magenta, yellow and white paints.

7.10 Discuss the relative advantages and disadvantages of the uniform quantization and the popularity algorithms and describe two practical situations so that for one the first method and for the other the second method would give clearly better results.

Problems

7.11 Express the vertex and the average surface normal vector co-ordinates at the vertices of the subdivided cylinder and cone shown in Figure 7.12 in terms of the number of subdivisions, the length of the cylinder or cone and the radius.

7.12 A plane parallel with the X and Y axis is located at $z = 4$ and is illuminated by a single point light source at $[2, 2, 0]$. For perspective projection, the centre of projection is at the origin and the equation of the projection plane is $z = 1$. The window through which the plane is viewed has corner co-ordinates $[1, -1, 1]$, $[1, 1, 1]$, $[-1, 1, 1]$ and $[-1, -1, 1]$. For each of the following conditions, determine the locations of the brightest and the darkest points of the projected image:

(a)   Orthographic projection and purely diffuse reflection.
(b)   Orthographic projection and purely specular reflection.
(c)   Perspective projection and purely diffuse reflection.
(d)   Perspective projection and purely specular reflection.

7.13 For each of the conditions described in Problem 7.12, determine the intensities at the brightest and darkest observed points with incident intensity and reflection coefficients equal to 1.0 and specular reflection proportional to $\cos^2(\phi)$.

7.14 Design an algorithm that applies Gouraud shading in a planar quadrilateral. The given data are the positions of the four projected vertices and the four intensities thereof.

7.15 Express the diffusely reflected intensity value of a perspectively projected point from the surface of a sphere with centre point $[x_0, y_0, z_0]$ and radius R for the following illuminations. As usual, the centre of projection is at the origin and the projection plane is at $z = 1$.

(a)   Distributed light with direction vector $[d_x, d_y, d_z]$.

(b)   Point light source located $[S_x, S_y, S_z]$.

7.16 Determine vector equations that may be used to determine the point on the surface of a sphere that appears to be the brightest for specular reflection when the sphere is viewed from the origin. Develop formulae for both distributed and point light sources. Discuss the nature of the arithmetic required to solve the equations for the $[X, Y, Z]$ co-ordinates. The sphere is specified by its centre (position vector **C**) and its radius R. The illumination is specified by the direction vector **d** or position of the light source **S**.

7.17 Write and test a program that draws the right-angle CIE triangle for your colour monitor. Each of the R, G and B intensities should be uniformly distributed, so that having $N + 1$ levels of intensities you should set:

$$I_i = (I_{max} + 1)^{i/N} - 1 \qquad i = 0, 1, 2, ..., N$$

where it is assumed that intensities range between 0 and I_{max}, and also that:

$$N^3 \leqslant \text{Number of displayable colours}$$

7.18 Design an algorithm that translates a point $[r, g]$ in the right-triangle CIE diagram for a colour monitor (see Colour Plate 4) to the $[X, Y, Z]$ co-ordinates of the corresponding point on the surface of the RGB colour cube.

Projects

7.19 Design a system that produces shaded colour images similar to Figures 7.19 and 7.20. Note that both a cylinder and a cone may be specified by two position vectors, C_1 and C_2, which represent the centre points of the two bounding planes, and two scalars, R_1 and R_2, which define the two radii ($R_1 = R_2$ specifies the cylinder and $R_2 = 0$ specifies the cone). Other variables are the position of point light sources S_i, direction vectors for distributed light sources d_i, incident light intensities, reflection coefficients, power factor for specular reflection and the number of divisions that define the number of triangles used for each object.

7.20 Design a colour demonstration system that indicates for a specified colour its normalized r, g, b intensities, its hue and saturation, and the actual R, G and B intensities used to display the colour on the terminal. Use a convenient interface so that the user could easily change any one of the five parameters (r, g, b, h or s). No brightness is considered, so always display the colour with its maximum possible brightness. If you have time, extend your project to include the subtractive cyan, magenta, yellow and white system, or the RGB cube and the HSV parameters as well.

8

Ray Tracing and Constructive Solid Geometry

Ray tracing has recently proved to be one of the most popular graphics techniques for rendering realistic scenes. The visual attributes of each pixel are determined by tracing the ray from the viewpoint, through the pixel until an intersection is found with one of the objects. Further tracing of rays that are reflected or refracted at the intersection with an object allows ray tracing to be used to create a large variety of optical effects.

Since there will usually be a large number of objects, coherence properties are used to reduce the number of intersecton calculations made. In the simplest case, these use bounding volumes. Object space subdivision and ray space subdivision offer more general solutions.

Some of the objects, such as spheres and cylinders, may be defined by simple mathematical means. To provide a greater variety, however, it is necessary to make use of procedural methods, such as sweeping or rotating, to define objects. In all cases, it is convenient to define an object in its own Cartesian axis system, and then relate this to the axis system of the whole scene through translation and rotation. Spline surfaces may also be ray traced.

One procedural method which offers a large number of possibilities is the CSG tree, where complex objects are defined in terms of simpler primitives.

8.1 INTRODUCTION

The algorithms that have been presented so far for rendering graphics scenes of opaque objects have processed the objects one at a time using techniques such as *z*-buffers to determine their visibility. A number of visible surface algorithms that could process faceted objects were discussed in Chapter 5. These algorithms, when combined with the methods outlined in Chapter 7 for calculating reflected light intensities, provide a practical method for calculating the intensity and colour for each pixel when a 3D scene is viewed. Such a scene can contain a number of faceted opaque objects and arbitrary light sources. It was previously mentioned that an alternative way of rendering a graphics scene is to process each pixel in turn and find the surface point in the 3D scene which determines its intensity and colour. This method is called 'ray tracing' since, in its simplest form, it is based on following a ray from the view point through the pixel until it meets a surface of an object.

Ray tracing is more than just an alternative method for rendering faceted opaque objects. It can cope with objects that have very complex surface shapes and can model optical phenomena such as shadows, reflections, transparency and translucency. No other rendering method has this flexibility.

Ray tracing will usually use considerable amounts of central processor time. Consequently, the definition of objects and the computation of intersections between rays and objects must be programmed with careful attention to computing time. The execution times are greatly influenced by object definition methods and by the use of optimizations.

8.2 RAY TRACING: AN OVERVIEW

The basic method of ray tracing is as follows. For each pixel, a ray is defined that is either the line joining the viewpoint to the pixel, for perspective projection, or the line through the pixel orthogonal to the raster screen, for orthographic projection. The intersection point of the ray with the primitive object that is nearest to the eye is found and the surface properties, orientation and incident light intensities at that point are used to determine the red-green-blue (RGB) intensities for the pixel.

The rays defined by the viewpoint and each pixel are known as primary rays. In the simplest case, when only dull, opaque objects are considered, the ray tracing process terminates when the nearest intersection is found. If other optical phenomena such as reflections or shadows

Algorithm 8.1

General ray tracing algorithm.

procedure *RAY_TRACE*(*r* : *Ray*, *Objects* : *ObjectSpace*,
                              var *RGB* : *IlluminationValue*);

var *NearestIntersection* : *NearestIntersectionRecord*;
     Illumination : *IlluminationValue*;
     SecondaryRay : *Ray*;

begin
  for each object **do**
  begin
    { Compute the intersection (if any) with the ray }
    { Update *NearestIntersection* }
  end;
  with *NearestIntersection* **do**
  begin
    if there are secondary intersections
    then repeat
            { Compute *SecondaryRay* }
            RAY_TRACE(*SecondaryRay*, *Objects*, *IlluminationValue*)
            { Compute RGB from returned *IlluminationValue* }
          until all secondary rays have been processed;
      else compute RGB from *NearestIntersection* surface properties;
  end
end.

are to be modelled, then one or more secondary rays must be traced, starting from the intersection point. For example, if a perfect mirror is to be represented, the secondary ray will start from the intersection point and travel in the direction reflecting the original ray about the surface normal. The intersection of this secondary ray with the first opaque object will then be used to determine the RGB intensity at the pixel of the primary ray. More complex still are objects made of semi-transparent material. For these, both reflection and transmission are possible and the primary ray originating at the viewpoint must be split at the surface into two secondary rays. The contribution to the pixel intensity will be a weighted sum of the contributions from the secondary rays. The process can be continued to allow multiple reflections.

The general ray tracing process is summarized by a recursive procedure Algorithm 8.1 which would be called once for each primary ray. It is relatively easy to implement. A ray is defined by a starting position **S** and a direction vector **d**. The parametric equation of a line is used for the position vector of the ray:

$$\mathbf{P_{ray}} = \mathbf{S} + \alpha \mathbf{d}$$

and the intersection calculations return a value (or values) for the scalar α. Since the ray is travelling in one direction, only positive values of α are used. The smallest positive value indicates the first intersection which, when substituted into the ray equation, determines the three Cartesian co-ordinates of the intersection point. If a negative value is returned for α, then the object is not intersected by the ray.

In principle at least, this algorithm is completely general and can be used for a wide variety of complex optical phenomena. Each object of the scene must have an associated algorithm for calculating intersection points and surface normal vectors, and, if appropriate, the secondary ray directions and the way in which the illumination values returned by the secondary ray trace are combined. In practice, however, there are limitations on memory and processing time. Multiple reflections must also be limited to prevent secondary rays getting locked into an infinite loop by bouncing back and forth between two reflecting surfaces.

Ray tracing using this simple algorithm will normally require excessive computing time, since the number of times the inner loop is executed is equal to the product of the total number of pixels and the number of objects. For a 1000×1000 grid of pixels and 1000 objects it will be repeated 10^9 times. If the objects themselves are defined by complex methods – surface patches, for example – each intersection calculation will also take a considerable amount of time. Obviously, even the largest super-computer would find this computing requirement hard to satisfy within a reasonable running time.

Decreasing computing time can be achieved both by software improvements and hardware additions. The next section discusses how software optimizations are made, while Chapter 10 considers the hardware optimization.

8.3 SOFTWARE OPTIMIZATION METHODS

The key to minimizing the ray tracing time is found in the inner loop, where the intersection calculation with each object is made. It is critically important to avoid wasting computation time on checking the ray against objects that have no intersection and which can be trivially eliminated. All the software optimization methods depend on eliminating such objects.

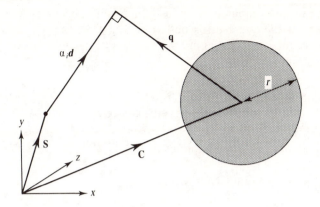

Figure 8.1
The simplest form of extent is the bounding sphere. It is necessary to test whether the ray **S** + $\alpha_i d$ will intersect the sphere. This is done by finding the vector **q**, and testing its magnitude against the scalar radius, *r*.

8.3.1 Extents

To treat all objects similarly in the algorithm that eliminates those without intersections, some simplification of the object's shape must be made. This is done by computing an **extent** or **bounding volume**. Normally, extents are one of two possible types: the bounding sphere or the bounding box. These are simply the smallest sphere, or smallest box, with sides parallel to the Cartesian axes that totally encloses the object. Extents can be computed prior to ray tracing a scene and stored in a database.

The bounding sphere provides a relatively simple test in 3D which can be applied to any ray. Suppose a bounding sphere for each object is defined with position vector **C** for the centre and scalar value *r* for its radius, then the parameter of interest is in the perpendicular distance from the centre of the sphere to the ray. If this is greater than the radius *r*, the object can be eliminated. If, as shown in Figure 8.1, the nearest point to the centre is at a distance α_i along the ray and **q** is the vector joining the centre to that point, the vector equation can be written as:

$$\mathbf{S} + \alpha_i d = \mathbf{C} + \mathbf{q}$$

Taking the dot product of *d* with both sides, noting that **q** is orthogonal to *d* and that *d* is a unit vector, gives:

$$\mathbf{S} \cdot d + \alpha_i = \mathbf{C} \cdot d$$

which can be rewritten as:

$$\alpha_i = (\mathbf{C} - \mathbf{S}) \cdot d \qquad\qquad (8.1)$$

Thus, α_i can be computed with just three multiplications and a vector subtraction. If the value turns out to be negative, the test may be concluded, since the object is behind the ray. If not, the modulus of $\mathbf{q}$ must be found and compared with r:

$$|\mathbf{q}|^2 = \mathbf{q} \cdot \mathbf{q} = (\mathbf{S} - \mathbf{C} + \alpha_i \mathbf{d}) \cdot (\mathbf{S} - \mathbf{C} + \alpha_i \mathbf{d})$$
$$= \alpha_i^2 + 2\alpha_i(\mathbf{S} - \mathbf{C}) \cdot \mathbf{d} + (\mathbf{S} - \mathbf{C}) \cdot (\mathbf{S} - \mathbf{C})$$

Using Equation (8.1), this simplifies to:

$$|\mathbf{q}|^2 = (\mathbf{S} - \mathbf{C}) \cdot (\mathbf{S} - \mathbf{C}) - \alpha_i^2$$

To avoid taking the square root, r^2, rather than r, can be stored in the database. So, the test to eliminate the object becomes:

$$(\mathbf{S} - \mathbf{C}) \cdot (\mathbf{S} - \mathbf{C}) - \alpha_i^2 > r^2 \tag{8.2}$$

which requires one vector subtraction, two dot products, one multiplication and one subtraction; that is, all in all, seven multiplications and eight additions/subtractions. This is the best that can be achieved in three dimensions.

Another approach to the bounding sphere test is to do the testing in two dimensions using three orthographic projections. If the ray intersects the bounding sphere, it will intersect the bounding circle in each orthographic projection. Hence, if any one projection is found where there is no intersection, the test can terminate and the object is eliminated. Thus, many objects will be eliminated after just one test.

For the orthographic projection in the x direction, the projected ray is defined by:

$$\mathbf{S_p} = [S_x, S_y]$$
$$\mathbf{d_p} = \left[\frac{d_x}{d_x^2 + d_y^2}, \frac{d_y}{d_x^2 + d_y^2} \right]$$

The bounding circle has radius r and:

$$\mathbf{C_p} = [C_x, C_y]$$

Computing the projections of the ray is done once for all the objects, and so does not appear in the inner loop. Since a vector formulation of the test has been used, Equation (8.1) and Equation (8.2) apply equally well to the 2D case. To evaluate them fully in two dimensions requires five multiplications and five additions/subtractions. If the test requires only the orthographic projections to be computed for the majority of the objects, then the two-dimensional test does provide some improvement, although it may be very marginal, considering all the other calculations that are required. Notice that the test works correctly for the special case when $d_p = [0, 0]$ and the projected ray becomes a point. In this case the test for no intersection is that the point is further away from the centre of the circle than r.

The bounding box is defined by six variables:

$$XMin \quad XMax \quad YMin \quad YMax \quad ZMin \quad ZMax$$

For primary rays generated by orthographic projection in the positive z direction, the ray is defined by the pixel position $[XPixel, YPixel]$. The two tests for a possible intersection with the ray are:

$$XMin < XPixel < XMax \quad \text{and} \quad YMin < YPixel < YMax$$

For perspective projection, the bounding box itself can be projected on to the view surface and the same test used.

These simple tests are, however, not available for secondary rays from reflections or refractions. The projection method described for the bounding sphere can be applied in these cases. In the orthographically projected plane, the already familiar problem of a line segment clipped by a rectangular window, which was covered in Section 5.2, arises. One endpoint of the line segment is given by the projection of its starting point, S_p. The other may be set by the limit when α becomes a very large positive number. Alternatively, the point where the ray leaves the bounding extent of the whole scene can be computed. In this case, it is only necessary to determine whether the line is totally clipped. Thus, the full Sutherland–Cohen algorithm need not be implemented. As before, the test should be applied to all three orthographic projections and it can terminate as soon as one view is found where the ray does not intersect the window.

The same test can also be applied in three dimensions, using a simple extension of the Sutherland–Cohen clipping algorithm. In this case, there will be six conditions and a 6-bit binary code will be generated. The determination of the condition for no intersection will be the same as before; that is, the bitwise AND of the codes for the two endpoints is not zero. Analogous to the 2D case, one of the endpoints is S, while the other is found by setting α to a very large positive number.

The 6-bit codes of the starting point and the endpoint determine which planes have to be intersected by the ray to perform the clipping. At best, there will be one plane and three in the worst case. To perform the intersection calculations in three dimensions, the intersection points between the ray and the infinite planes have to be found. These will be defined by equations of the type:

$$S_x + \alpha d_x = XMin$$
$$S_x + \alpha d_x = XMax$$
$$S_y + \alpha d_y = YMin$$

...

The values of α are used to determine the new endpoints for a further clipping test.

8.3.2 Coherence based on scan conversion

It seems reasonable to assume that the bounding spheres or boxes will eliminate a large number of objects, even for general rays. But, as has been seen before, another large saving of computer execution time may be made by making use of the fact that the order in which the pixels are processed during scan conversion is known. Thus, the objects can be sorted into order to reduce the number of extents that must be tested for each primary ray. This can be done similarly to the scan line algorithm discussed in Chapter 5, where active lists containing only a small portion of the total number of facets were maintained. In this case, for each primary ray, a small active list of objects may be rapidly determined, which includes only those objects that could intersect the ray.

Assuming that the scan is being carried out in the horizontal direction with increasing x and the scan lines are being processed in order of increasing y, the active list can be maintained as outlined in Algorithm 8.2. It is assumed that the list of objects is sorted in increasing order of the *YMin* of their bounding box. As this list may be very long, it is accessed by a pointer (*ListPointer*) indicating the current position. When moving from one scan line to the next, the Y active list can be updated by deleting all those objects for which $YMax < YPixel$ and adding all those objects in the complete list that become potentially visible. This reduced list is then sorted in increasing order of *XMin* and an X active list is created by taking all the objects for which $XMin < 0$ and $XMax > 0$. An identical algorithm is used to maintain the X active list as the ray tracing proceeds from pixel to adjacent pixel. Finally, the active list for the pixel is sorted into increasing order of *ZMin* so that if an intersection has been found for which the z value is less than the *ZMin* value of the next object on the list, the ray trace can stop.

The initial sorting of the objects by *YMin* can be viewed as a preprocessing step, since it is executed proportionally to the number of objects but is independent of the number of pixels. The sorting by *XMin*

Algorithm 8.2

Maintenance of the active object list for a scan line.

for each object on the Y active list **do**
if $YPixel > YMax$
then remove the object from the active list;
repeat
   with the current item on the object list sorted by $YMax$ **do**
   if $YPixel > ListPointer.YMin$
   then add the object to the active list
   $INCREMENT(ListPointer)$
until $YPixel < ListPointer.YMin$

required to create the X active list is an overhead that is traded against the large number of extents that must be tested if the list were not sorted. Similarly, the cost of sorting the final active list by $ZMin$ is offset by the reduced number of intersection calculations. Since the number of objects actually intersecting one ray is usually much smaller than the total number of objects, the savings obtained by sorting and using active object lists are very significant.

8.3.3 Object space subdivision

Object space subdivision methods are another way in which coherence can be established. The entire 3D object space is divided into a number of small regions and for each the set of objects whose extents intersect the region is found. In effect, space subdivision is a bucket sorting algorithm that associates each small region with a small number of objects and each object with a small number of neighbouring regions.

The simplest method uses rectangular boxes. Using the front projection and back clipping planes, a rectangular box can be defined for the entire object space. Suppose this box is divided into $N \times N \times N$ smaller regions, as shown in Figure 8.2 where $N = 8$ so that there are 512 such small boxes. A general ray may enter at any one of the six facets of a small box. For each small box, only a small number of objects have to be tested for intersection. If intersections are found, then the closest intersection to the starting point of the ray is the required first intersection, and no objects

Figure 8.2
Object space subdivision is
used to reduce the number of
intersection calculations. The
object space is divided regularly
into a number of volumes each
containing a small number of
objects, then the ray is traced
through each small volume.
Since a ray will only pass
through a small number of the
subdivided volumes, it follows
that intersection calculations
need only be made with a few
objects.

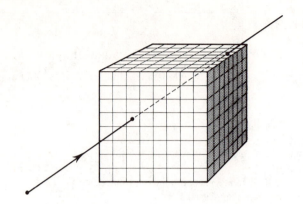

in other regions have to be tested. If no intersection is found, then the ray exits from the region and its direction and point of entry to the next small box can be calculated.

In fact, the space subdivision method determines an active object set for each small region and, because of their known location and the direction of the ray, the regions are, in effect, sorted according to the order in which they would be visited by an uninterrupted ray. This method allows drastic reductions in processing time and the efficiency improvement is a function of the number of objects and the number of subdivided regions, which is limited only by memory size. In fact, the space subdivision method is so effective that, for a given number of subdivided regions, the execution time of the ray tracing calculations is almost a constant, and does not increase significantly with an increasing number of objects. Of course, the execution time for determining the active object sets is proportional to the number of objects. However, the set calculations are done only once for each object, of which there may be thousands, while the ray tracing calculations are done for each pixel, of which there are a million.

The reason why the number of objects has no drastic effect on computation time can be understood by observing the effect of both a small number and a large number of objects on the calculations. If there are only a small number of objects, then many regions will be empty and very little testing will have to be done. On the other hand, if there are a large number of objects in a small region, then the probability of an intersection being found is high, so that the ray tracing for the given ray will be effectively terminated and only a few regions will be tested.

There are many details in the implementation of such a method where savings can be made. Since there are millions of rays in a general scene, each successful saving of time will be greatly multiplied. For example, the calculation time to determine the next region a ray enters after traversing one of the subdivided regions may be reduced by using optimized assembler code, integer arithmetic or lookup tables. This will speed up the processing of empty regions, while bounding sphere or box calculations can still be used for each object in the subdivided region.

A problem with object space subdivision is the difficulty involved in achieving a balanced distribution of objects to regions. If the majority of the objects of the scene are clustered together, then little saving is made when tracing the regions that are highly populated. However, it is possible for the regions to have differing sizes, so that, as far as possible, the number objects associated with each region is the same. The commonest data structure used for this purpose is the octree, which was discussed in Chapter 7. The subdivision of the scene by an octree can start from the bounding extent of the whole scene. For each node, a decision must be taken as to whether that node should be subdivided. The choice depends not only on the number of objects associated with the node, but also on their size and on the space available for storing the tree. The subdivision of a node requires the creation of its eight children and, for each child, a computation of which object extents have an intersection with it.

Although octrees neatly solve the object distribution problem, they complicate the calculation of the entry point into the successive small regions. Searching for the correct neighbour in the octree adds computational overheads. It is much simpler to preprocess a list of divided volumes when there are an equal number in the x, y and z directions. Depending on the starting point of the ray at the boundary of the entire octree volume, the tree is traversed from the root until the correct subdivided volume is found. If this is empty, then the next volume must be determined. If the volume contains objects, then the closest intersection point with one of the surfaces is established and the normal calculated. It is possible, of course, for the ray to miss all the objects, in which case the next subdivided volume must be determined. If a ray leaves a subdivided volume, then the tree must be traversed up, until the ray is contained within the combined volumes, and then down again to find the new terminal node. Obviously, a ray along the direction of one of the axes is easy to trace. A ray with general direction of travel requires much more processing.

8.3.4 Ray space divisions

In the foregoing discussion, only the subdivision of Cartesian space was considered, starting from some bounding volume that contains the whole scene being ray traced. An alternative method, proposed by Arvo and Kirk (1987), is to divide the space in which the rays are defined and then find the objects that belong to each such subdivision.

As before, each ray has a unique starting point, which is designated by the position vector symbol **S**, and a direction in which it travels, denoted by a unit direction vector d. Thus, a ray is completely specified by a 6-tuple:

$$[S_x, S_y, S_z, d_x, d_y, d_z]$$

Since a unit direction vector is specified, this may be written as:

$$d = \left[d_x, d_y, \pm \sqrt{(1 - d_x^2 - d_y^2)} \right]$$

meaning that only two parameters and a sense (the sign for the z component) are required to specify the direction. Thus, the specification of a ray can be reduced to a signed 5-tuple:

$$\pm[S_x, S_y, S_z, d_x, d_y]$$

Bounds can be placed on the individual ordinates of the 5-tuple so that only the rays that can penetrate the bounding volume of the scene are considered. For rays originating outside the scene bounding volume, the first intersection of the ray with the bounding volume can be used as the starting point. It follows that:

$$XMin \leq S_x \leq XMax$$
$$YMin \leq S_y \leq YMax$$
$$ZMin \leq S_z \leq ZMax$$

Since each ordinate must be in the range $[-1...1]$ for unit vectors, the following bounds apply to the rays appearing in the scene:

$$-1 \leq d_x \leq +1$$
$$-1 \leq d_y \leq +1$$

A volume in 5-space is called a **hypercube**. This is denoted here as a signed 5-tuple of subranges. Two such hypercubes contain all the possible rays that could exist in the scene under question:

$$+[\,\{XMin ... XMax\}, \{YMin ... YMax\}, \{ZMin ... ZMax\}, \{-1 ... 1\}, \{-1 ... 1\}\,]$$
$$-[\,\{XMin ... XMax\}, \{YMin ... YMax\}, \{ZMin ... ZMax\}, \{-1 ... 1\}, \{-1 ... 1\}\,]$$

These hypercubes can be subdivided by a binary division of each component, just like the Cartesian space division used in the octree. The hypercube in 5-space has 32 children of subdivision. Each of these children contains a proportion of the rays. Each child hypercube also defines a subdivision of the objects of the scene contained in the parent hypercube. The basis of the algorithm is therefore to build a tree of hypercubes, like an

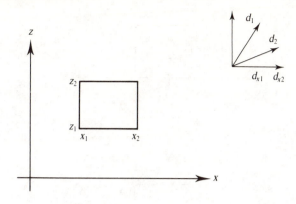

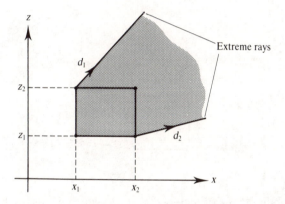

Figure 8.3
A ray is defined by a starting point and a direction. Hence, in two dimensions, an area and a range of directions specifies a set of rays. The space covered by such a set of rays is defined by projecting the extreme rays, and is shown shaded.

octree, continuing division until each leaf hypercube contains only a few objects. Then, when tracing a ray, the tree is searched for the hypercube containing that ray, and intersection calculations are only carried out with the objects in the hypercube. In practice, it is not feasible to create the complete tree. Therefore, subdivisions are only computed when required by the ray tracing process.

To find out which objects in the scene could be intersected by its rays, it is necessary to determine the volume defined by a hypercube. As this is hard to visualize, consider first an equivalent 2D problem. Taking the x–z plane as an example, an area can be defined by a square and two direction vectors. Figure 8.3 illustrates a possibility defined by:

$$+ [\{x_1, x_2\}, \{z_1, z_2\}, \{d_{x1}, d_{x2}\}]$$

The rays that belong to this area all start from within the box and all fall within the angle between d_1 and d_2. The area that they trace is shown

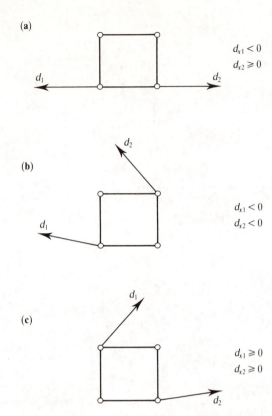

(a)

$d_{x1} < 0$
$d_{x2} \geq 0$

(b)

$d_{x1} < 0$
$d_{x2} < 0$

(c)

$d_{x1} \geq 0$
$d_{x2} \geq 0$

Figure 8.4
The extreme rays shown in Figure 8.3 may be found by inspection. For the case where $y > 0$ and $d_{x1} < d_{x2}$, there are only three possibilities, which are shown here.

shaded. To subdivide the objects according to which lie inside this area, the two extreme rays must be found. Since the data is such that $d_{x1} < d_{x2}$ and the sign of the two y components is always the same, there are only six possibilities to check for. The three of these for positive y directions are shown in Figure 8.4. From the position vectors of the vertices and the direction vectors, the functional form of the line equations of the extreme rays can be derived. The functional form of the edges of the square that bound the region can also be determined. They will be $x - x_1 = 0$, $x - x_2 = 0$, and so on. The list of objects belonging to the parent hypercube can be subdivided by checking which objects lie outside each half-space containing the square. This results in a list of objects that intersect the hypercube.

The 3D subdivision method follows the same principle. The first three subranges in the 5-tuple define a cube – or, in general, a rectangular volume. The last two define four limiting direction vectors. Each direction vector and cube edge define a plane, and it is the extreme planes that bound the set of rays emanating from the cube. Finding the extreme planes is difficult; however, one simple solution is to decompose the problem into

Algorithm 8.3

Ray space subdivision.

if the ray originates outside the scene bound box **then**
    { Compute the first intersection with the scene bound box }
{Go to the leaf node of the hypercube tree containing the ray }
while the node can be subdivided **do**
begin
    { Generate the 32 children of the node }
    { Go to the new leaf node containing the ray }
end
{ Compute all intersections with the objects belonging to the node }
{ Return the intersection and object attributes }

two orthogonal 2D cases. These are the orthographic projections in the x–z plane and the y–z plane. If an object's bounding box lies outside the area defined on either plane, then it may be eliminated from the list of objects belonging to the hypercube.

In summary, ray space subdivision is shown in Algorithm 8.3. The decision as to whether to subdivide a leaf node depends on the number of objects in its list and the minimum size that can be generated, which in turn depends on the memory available for the storage of the tree.

The objective of ray space subdivision is to capitalize on coherence between adjacent rays. If rays are generated for a local group of pixels, then it is likely that they will belong to the same hypercube. Thus, once the subdivision has been made, all other rays can be computed quickly. In this respect, ray space subdivision offers advantages over ray casting through Cartesian space division, where the relationship between neighbouring boxes and ray directions is more complex. Similar coherence is likely to be present in rays emanating from light sources but, unfortunately, is less likely to exist in the case of reflected or refracted rays.

This technique carries a large overhead in terms of computing time and memory requirements to build the tree. Depending on how the tree generation is limited, these overheads will not depend on the number of objects, and hence the saving in time will increase as the number of objects increases.

8.4 OBJECT DEFINITION METHODS

One of the major gains that can be made in a ray tracing system is to use object definitions that minimize object data and optimize intersection calculations. Wire frames are costly in that they carry no semantic information about the objects being represented. Hence every vertex and every edge must be accommodated in the data base. Intersections are then found by processing the ray with each facet. The use of splines provides one method of reducing the size of the database; however, bi-varate spline functions are not easy to invert and so are not readily adaptable for simple intersection calculations.

An alternative method is to let the graphics system handle a number of primitive objects that can be defined simply and with little data. For example, to define a sphere, it is only necessary to specify its centre and radius, and this will represent a large saving over any wire-frame representation where a large number of facets are required to produce a visually acceptable image. The gains made are not only in terms of database size, but also in computation time, if transformations are to be defined on the objects.

The study of object definition methods based on simple primitives is often termed **solid modelling**, although, as will be seen, this is not a very appropriate name, since in all cases of interest the primitives are defined by specifying their surfaces, rather than their solid volume. Scenes defined in terms of a number of primitive objects are suitable for ray tracing, and following sections discuss a small repertoire of such primitives and how to ray trace them.

8.4.1 Ray and object transformations

For all non-spherical objects there is a preferred co-ordinate system orientation for which the intersection calculations become simpler. For a rectangular box, for example, it is where the x, y and z axes are aligned with the edges of the box. For a cylinder, it is with the centre axis of the cylinder aligned with one of the Cartesian axes.

When graphical data structures were described in Section 2.5, a practical data structure, the hierarchical object data structure, was discussed as an example. It is well suited to ray tracing. Each object can be defined in its own preferred co-ordinate system. The names $[u, v, w]$ will be used here for the axes of this system. Once scaled, each object is related to the co-ordinate system of the whole scene, where the ray equations are defined, by a translation and a rotation.

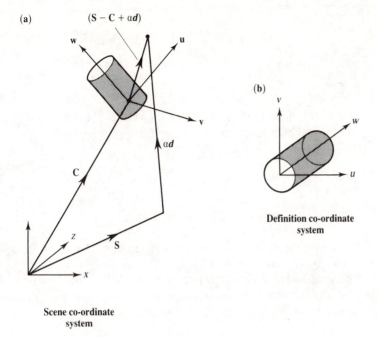

(a)

$(S - C + \alpha d)$

w

u

v

αd

C

z

S

x

**Scene co-ordinate
system**

(b)

v

w

u

**Definition co-ordinate
system**

Figure 8.5
Objects are defined in their
own definition space in which
the axes are labelled [u, v, w].
When they are placed in the
scene for drawing, the position
of the origin of the definition
co-ordinate system (position
vector **C**) must be specified, as
must the orientation, which is
defined by unit direction
vectors **u**, **v** and **w**. The ray
being traced is given by
S + α**d**.

Chapter 4 showed how such transformations can be constructed and combined into a 4×4 homogeneous matrix. Such a matrix could transform the object from its definition co-ordinate system into the scene co-ordinate system, after which the intersection and secondary ray computations could be made. Alternatively, the ray could be transformed by the inverse of the matrix, the intersection calculations performed in the object definition co-ordinate system and the results transformed back into the scene system. However, for the special case of ray tracing, a third possibility exists; that is, to create an instance of the definition co-ordinate system in the scene co-ordinate system. Although mathematically equivalent to transforming the ray, this approach is conceptually simpler. For each object, the position in the scene is selected by specifying the position of the origin of its definition co-ordinate system. This will be the point $C = [C_x, C_y, C_z]$, which is defined by position vector **C** in the scene co-ordinate system. The rotation, to ensure the correct alignment, is about point **C** and may be defined by a 3×3 (non-homogeneous) rotation matrix R.

For a given object instance in the scene co-ordinate system, three unit vectors **u**, **v** and **w** are calculated. These are the unit vectors along the three axes in the [u, v, w] co-ordinate system, rotated into the [x, y, z] system. Their spatial arrangement for a cylinder is shown in Figure 8.5.

Thus:

$$u = [1, 0, 0] \cdot R$$
$$v = [0, 1, 0] \cdot R$$
$$w = [0, 0, 1] \cdot R$$

These simple relations indicate that the rotation matrix can be expressed by the three unit row vectors as:

$$R = \begin{bmatrix} u \\ v \\ w \end{bmatrix}$$

If there is no rotation, ($R = I$), the respective definition co-ordinate axes line up with the x, y and z axis of the rays.

The w ordinate in the definition system, which is equivalent to the z ordinate of a point on the ray in the scene space, can be simply obtained by using the dot products with the unit vector w (Figure 8.5):

$$P_w = (\mathbf{S} - \mathbf{C} + \alpha d) \cdot w$$

Similar dot products with u and v yield the corresponding x and y co-ordinates for the transformed ray, which can be written as the position vector:

$$[(\mathbf{S} - \mathbf{C} + \alpha d) \cdot u, (\mathbf{S} - \mathbf{C} + \alpha d) \cdot v, (\mathbf{S} - \mathbf{C} + \alpha d) \cdot w]$$

As the resulting intersection point(s) will be expressed in terms of α, no further calculation is required to transform it to the $[x, y, z]$ co-ordinate system. However, the surface normal found must be transformed back using the rotation matrix R.

The intersections are determined for several types of object. For simple objects, the method of computation will be given in a general way, so that computation could be done in either co-ordinate system. For more complex objects, the intersection is usually computed in the definition co-ordinate space, as just shown.

8.4.2   Spheres

Spheres were treated in Section 8.3 when bounding spheres were described. However, for bounding spheres, it is only necessary to determine whether an intersection exists or not. The problem now is to find the

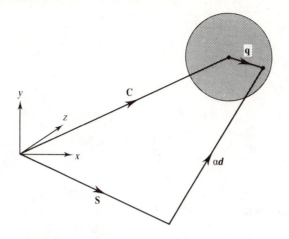

Figure 8.6
Calculating the intersection between a sphere and a ray in vector space. In the case of the sphere, symmetry makes it unnecessary to use a definition co-ordinate system.

exact position of the intersection point, if any. As before, the centre of the sphere is defined by the position vector $\mathbf{C}$ while its radius is given by the scalar r. The vector $\mathbf{q}$ will be taken from the centre to the point of intersection. This arrangement is shown in Figure 8.6. As before:

$$\mathbf{S} + \alpha d = \mathbf{C} + \mathbf{q} \qquad\qquad (8.3)$$

$$\mathbf{q} \cdot \mathbf{q} = (\mathbf{S} - \mathbf{C}) \cdot (\mathbf{S} - \mathbf{C}) + 2\alpha d \cdot (\mathbf{S} - \mathbf{C}) + \alpha^2$$

In this case, $|\mathbf{q}| = r$, which gives a quadratic in α:

$$(\mathbf{S} - \mathbf{C}) \cdot (\mathbf{S} - \mathbf{C}) - r^2 + 2\alpha d \cdot (\mathbf{S} - \mathbf{C}) + \alpha^2 = 0$$

The intersection points are given by the roots of the quadratic as:

$$\mathbf{S} + \alpha_i d \qquad i = 1, 2$$

and the corresponding unit surface normals are:

$$n_i = \frac{\mathbf{q}}{|\mathbf{q}|}$$

For a solid opaque sphere, only the closest intersection, the minimum of α_1 and α_2, is of interest, but for a transparent sphere or a concave hemispherical surface, the second intersection may be needed.

It is also possible to determine whether the intersection point is in the sphere's shadow or not. The test is similar to that for self-hidden surfaces, which was discussed in Chapter 3. If, as shown in Figure 8.7, the direction unit vector s, which is not to be confused with the ray starting position vector denoted by $\mathbf{S}$, points towards the light source, then the sign

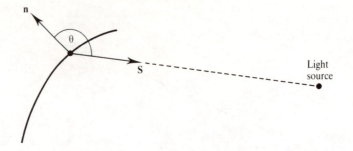

Figure 8.7
When an object intersection
has been found, it is necessary
to determine whether it is in
shadow. If the angle θ is
obtuse, then the intersection is
in the object's own shadow.

of the dot product between the normal and *s* indicates the cosine of the
angle between them. Thus, the intersection point in shadow is:

$$n \cdot s < 0$$

The direction vector *s* is a constant for parallel light rays and it is the vector
that starts at intersection points and points towards the light source for
local point light sources.

The other calculations to obtain the diffuse and specular reflection
components from each light source were described in Section 7.3 and can
be directly applied once *n* and *s* are known. The generation of secondary
rays will be discussed in Section 8.5.

8.4.3 Cylinders

The simplest case is to define a cylinder with open ends and with walls
infinitesimally thin, as depicted in Figure 8.8. To define such a cylinder,
the following must be specified in the database:

- C_1, the position vector of the centre of one end,
- C_2, the position vector of the centre of the other end,
- r, the scalar radius.

The vector along the cylinder axis is defined as:

$$l = C_2 - C_1$$

Using $S + \alpha d$ as the position of the intersection, as before, there are two
vector paths to the point of intersection:

$$C_1 + \varphi l + q = S + \alpha d$$
$$q + \varphi l = S + \alpha d - C_1 \tag{8.4}$$

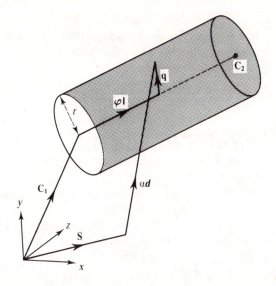

Figure 8.8
Calculating the intersection
between a cylinder and a ray in
vector space.

Since $\mathbf{q} \cdot \mathbf{l} = 0$:

$$\varphi\,(\mathbf{l} \cdot \mathbf{l}) = \mathbf{S} \cdot \mathbf{l} + \alpha d \cdot \mathbf{l} - \mathbf{C}_1 \cdot \mathbf{l}$$

$$\varphi = \frac{\mathbf{S} \cdot \mathbf{l} + \alpha d \cdot \mathbf{l} - \mathbf{C}_1 \cdot \mathbf{l}}{\mathbf{l} \cdot \mathbf{l}}$$

Substituting back into Equation (8.4) gives:

$$\mathbf{q} = \mathbf{S} + \alpha d - \mathbf{C}_1 - \left(\frac{\mathbf{S} \cdot \mathbf{l} + \alpha d \cdot \mathbf{l} - \mathbf{C}_1 \cdot \mathbf{l}}{\mathbf{l} \cdot \mathbf{l}}\right)\mathbf{l}$$

$$= \alpha\left[d - \left(\frac{d \cdot \mathbf{l}}{\mathbf{l} \cdot \mathbf{l}}\right)\mathbf{l}\right] + \mathbf{S} - \mathbf{C}_1 - \left(\frac{\mathbf{S} \cdot \mathbf{l} - \mathbf{C}_1 \cdot \mathbf{l}}{\mathbf{l} \cdot \mathbf{l}}\right)\mathbf{l}$$

This equation has exactly the same format as Equation (8.3), which
describes the intersections with a sphere. So, again, using the fact that:

$$\mathbf{q} \cdot \mathbf{q} = r^2$$

gives a quadratic with either two roots or no roots for α, indicating no
intersection.

It is still necessary, however, to identify whether the intersection
occurs between the points defined by $\mathbf{C}_1$ and $\mathbf{C}_2$. To do this, the foregoing
equations have to be solved for the value of φ. Let the roots for α be, as
before, α_1 and α_2. If α_1 is the smaller, then:

$$\varphi_1 = \frac{\mathbf{S} \cdot \mathbf{l} + \alpha_1 d \cdot \mathbf{l} - \mathbf{C}_1 \cdot \mathbf{l}}{\mathbf{l} \cdot \mathbf{l}}$$

is computed first. If this value is in the range 0 to 1, it follows that there is an intersection on the outside surface, which will be the visible point for ray tracing. Otherwise, it is necessary to compute:

$$\varphi_2 = \frac{\mathbf{S} \cdot \mathbf{l} + \alpha_2 \mathbf{d} \cdot \mathbf{l} - \mathbf{C_1} \cdot \mathbf{l}}{\mathbf{l} \cdot \mathbf{l}}$$

If φ_2 is in the range 0 to 1, then there is an intersection on the inside surface. In both cases, it is now possible to find the normal, and thus the illumination for the pixel.

Spheres and cylinders represent the simplest useful primitives that can be defined. However, there are other primitives that can be analyzed in this manner and which can be useful for solid modelling. These include the cone, taurus and ellipsoid. The analysis for these solids is not as easy as that for the sphere and cylinder, and more easily done using the procedural methods discussed later.

Further extension of the method of solid modelling can be achieved by considering objects made up from not one but several simpler primitives. For example, if a solid cylinder is to be one of the objects, this is dealt with as a hollow cylinder with two circularly bounded faces for the ends. Thus, further primitives are required, which may be combined into a large variety of objects. In addition to the two primitives already defined, the most useful primitives are bounded planes. Three examples of these will now be considered.

8.4.4   Planes bounded by circles

This primitive is quite similar to the sphere and is shown in Figure 8.9. The parameters that need to be specified are:

- r, the radius of the circle with centre at the origin,
- C, the position vector corresponding to the centre of the circle,
- n, the unit vector normal to the plane of the circle,
- q, the vector joining the centre to the point of intersection on the circle.

The position vector for the intersection point between the plane of the circle and the ray is again given by:

$$\mathbf{C} + \mathbf{q} = \mathbf{S} + \alpha d \qquad\qquad (8.5)$$

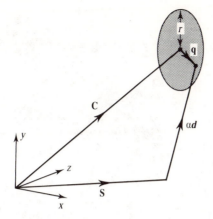

Figure 8.9
Calculating the intersection between a circularly bounded plane and a ray. The vector arrangement is identical to that for a sphere, but the conditions on $|\mathbf{q}|$ are different.

Since $\mathbf{n}$ is perpendicular to the plane of the circle:

$$\mathbf{q} \cdot \mathbf{n} = 0 = (\mathbf{S} - \mathbf{C}) \cdot \mathbf{n} + \alpha \mathbf{d} \cdot \mathbf{n}$$

from which α can be determined:

$$\alpha = - \frac{(\mathbf{S} - \mathbf{C}) \cdot \mathbf{n}}{\mathbf{d} \cdot \mathbf{n}}$$

To check whether the intersection is within the area of the circle, the solution for α is substituted back into Equation (8.5) to give a value for $\mathbf{q}$. The condition for a valid intersection is:

$$|\mathbf{q}| < r \quad \text{or} \quad \mathbf{q} \cdot \mathbf{q} < r^2$$

The sign of the surface normal, $\mathbf{n}$, has to be chosen to determine the illumination. Since the visible side of the surface is towards the origin of the ray, the sign of $\mathbf{n}$ must be chosen to satisfy:

$$\mathbf{n} \cdot \mathbf{d} \leqslant 0$$

Note that if the circle is defined in the object definition space, the centre will be at the origin and the normal will be along one of the axes, say w. In this case, the resulting equations will be identical to the above with the unit vector w replacing $\mathbf{n}$.

8.4.5 Planes bounded by triangles

The primitive defined by a triangle is very important since, as mentioned before, general surfaces may be approximated by triangular facets.

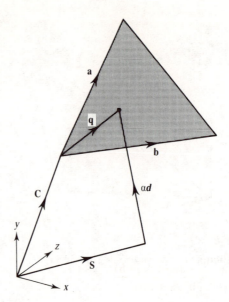

Figure 8.10

Calculating the intersection between a triangular facet and a ray. A triangular facet is defined by two direction vectors, **a** and **b**, and a position vector **C**.

Triangles were considered in Chapter 4. One vertex of the triangle is placed at the origin of the object co-ordinate system, and so appears in the scene at position **C**. As shown in Figure 8.10, the other two vertices are defined by vectors **a** and **b**, which are the edges of the triangle adjacent to the vertex at **C**.

The normal to the plane of the triangle can be constructed by using the cross-product:

$$n = \pm \frac{a \times b}{|a \times b|}$$

where the sign, as before, must be selected to ensure that $n \cdot d \leq 0$. If there is sufficient memory, it is more efficient to store the n unit vector with the object data, rather than evaluating the cross-product during the ray tracing process. It can be observed that if **a** is parallel to **b**, then the triangle is not well defined.

The calculation for α is exactly the same as for the plane bounded by the circle:

$$\alpha = -\frac{(S - C) \cdot n}{d \cdot n}$$

but the determination of a valid intersection is different. It was shown in Section 4.5 that any point inside a triangle defined by the two edge vectors

a and **b** can be expressed with two scalar multipliers, μ and ν:

$$\mathbf{q} = \mu\mathbf{a} + \nu\mathbf{b} \tag{8.6}$$

and the three conditions:

$$0 \leqslant \mu \leqslant 1$$
$$0 \leqslant \nu \leqslant 1$$
$$\mu + \nu \leqslant 1 \tag{8.7}$$

The intersection point, as before, is evaluated from the known value of α and Equation (8.5), yielding a value for **q**. Taking the dot products of both **a** and **b** with both sides of Equation (8.6), two equations in μ and ν can be obtained, from which μ can be calculated by the following expression:

$$\mu = \frac{(\mathbf{b} \cdot \mathbf{b})(\mathbf{q} \cdot \mathbf{a}) - (\mathbf{a} \cdot \mathbf{b})(\mathbf{q} \cdot \mathbf{b})}{(\mathbf{a} \cdot \mathbf{a})(\mathbf{b} \cdot \mathbf{b}) - (\mathbf{a} \cdot \mathbf{b})^2}$$

The scalar ν is given by a similar expression. Alternatively using the already known value of μ, it can be calculated by the simpler expression:

$$\nu = \frac{(\mathbf{q} \cdot \mathbf{b}) - \mu(\mathbf{a} \cdot \mathbf{b})}{\mathbf{b} \cdot \mathbf{b}}$$

The calculated values of μ and ν are then tested for the three conditions in Equation (8.7) for a valid intersection.

8.4.6 Planes bounded by parallelograms

A trivial extension of the analysis just given makes it possible to handle planes bounded by parallelograms. As shown in Figure 8.11, the equations are identical in all cases, except the boundary condition. This is looser than that for the triangle, requiring only that:

$$0 \leqslant \mu \leqslant 1 \quad \text{and} \quad 0 \leqslant \nu \leqslant 1$$

The vector representation of a parallelogram therefore requires less data to be stored than its Cartesian representation. There are many similar cases of more complex objects where it may not be necessary to keep a complete set of vectors for each set of bounded planes required. For example, a rectangular box can be defined by three mutually perpendicular vectors in the object definition co-ordinate system. If the box is correctly oriented in the definition co-ordinate space, then only the translation

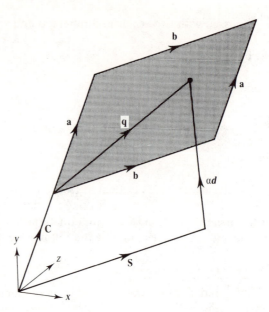

Figure 8.11
Calculating the intersection between a parallelogram and a ray. As in the case of the triangular facet, a parallelogram is defined by two direction vectors, **a** and **b**, and a position vector **C**.

vector **C** is required to complete a description of the box. Thus, only $4 \times 3 = 12$ numbers, instead of $8 \times 3 = 24$, are required for the vertices. Both the number of vectors requiring storage and transformation calculations are reduced by one-half in this case.

In practice, there seems to be a trade off between simplicity and applicability. The objects that offer the greatest savings, by virtue of the fact that they correspond to simple mathematical entities, are less applicable for drawing graphics scenes in all but a few specialized cases. However, most published complex computer-generated scenes use spheres whenever possible.

8.4.7   Swept surfaces

One way to improve the variety of objects available in a solid modelling system is to define a surface by a planar curve that is moved along the normal to the plane of the curve. If the curve is closed, then a volume may be generated by adding the two bounding planes at the start and end of the sweeping motion, as shown in Figure 8.12. This is an instance of a procedurally defined object and methods of tracing such objects have been the subject of considerable study – Kajiya (1983) and van Wijk (1984).

In this treatment, it is again assumed that the object is defined in its own co-ordinate system and that the curve is drawn in the $w = 0$ plane. The sweeping occurs from $w = 0$ to $w = l$, where the scalar l is the length

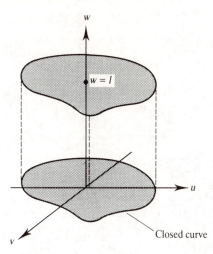

Figure 8.12
A swept surface can be defined by specifying a closed curve in the $u-v$ plane and a sweeping distance in the W direction.

of the volume. The cylinder, which was covered in an earlier section, could have been defined in this way, with a circle as the generating curve.

As before, the ray tracing process consists of finding the nearest intersection of the ray and the object. A bounding box can be easily constructed if a bounding rectangle for the planar curve is available.

The determination of the intersection point(s) and the surface normal(s) is divided into two parts. First, intersection points are determined in two dimensions, in the plane in which the curve is defined, and, second, their components are tested to see whether they are between 0 and l. Clearly, such computations are more easily carried out in the object definition co-ordinate system. For the first part, the ray is projected on to the object co-ordinate's $u–v$ ($w = 0$) plane. The 2D ray can be specified by its ordinates, which, as has been shown, are computed using the dot products:

$$[(\mathbf{S} - \mathbf{C}) \bullet \boldsymbol{u} + \alpha \boldsymbol{d} \bullet \boldsymbol{u}, (\mathbf{S} - \mathbf{C}) \bullet \boldsymbol{v} + \alpha \boldsymbol{d} \bullet \boldsymbol{v}] \qquad (8.8)$$

The same ordinates can be obtained by taking the 2D projection of the ray equation, ignoring the third ordinate.

The curve to be swept could be specified by a parametric form, which could be written as:

$$u = f_u(\mu) \quad \text{and} \quad v = f_v(\mu) \qquad (8.9)$$

Substituting the components of the 2D ray into Equation (8.9) gives:

$$(\mathbf{S} - \mathbf{C}) \bullet \boldsymbol{u} + \alpha \boldsymbol{d} \bullet \boldsymbol{u} = f_u(\mu)$$
$$(\mathbf{S} - \mathbf{C}) \bullet \boldsymbol{v} + \alpha \boldsymbol{d} \bullet \boldsymbol{v} = f_v(\mu) \qquad (8.10)$$

The parameter α may be eliminated from Equation (8.10) to yield one equation in μ:

$$d \cdot v[f_u(\mu) - (S - C) \cdot u] = d \cdot u[f_v(\mu) - (S - C) \cdot v] \tag{8.11}$$

The μ values that satisfy this equation indicate possible intersection points. For each solution for μ, say μ_i, using Equation (8.10), the corresponding α_i is calculated. Thus:

$$\alpha_i = \frac{f_u(\mu_i) - (S - C) \cdot u}{d \cdot u}$$

For a valid intersection, α_i has to be positive. The possible intersection points still have to be tested to ensure that their w component is between 0 and l. This test may be expressed as:

$$0 < (S - C) \cdot w + \alpha_i d \cdot w < l \tag{8.12}$$

Finally, once the nearest intersection point has been found, the surface normal can be determined from the 2D curve. This simplification can be made because the sweeping of the surface is equivalent to translating the curve in 3D space, and the normal direction vector is invariant to translation. For an intersection point, the normal vector may be obtained by differentiating the curve, to obtain the tangent, and then taking the orthogonal vector. Thus, the surface normal is given by:

$$n = \left[\frac{df_v(\mu)}{dv}, \frac{-df_u(\mu)}{du}, 0 \right]$$

A unit vector may be calculated in the usual way, by dividing the vector components by the magnitude of **n**. To determine the correct illumination, the normal vector must be rotated into the scene co-ordinate system by the rotation matrix R, defined earlier. The sign of the resulting normal must be adjusted, as for the circular plane, so that:

$$n \cdot d \leq 0$$

The advantage of using a parametric form is that the curve to be swept can be specified by any one of the splines studied in Chapter 6. The complexity of Equation (8.11), which is used for the calculation of intersection points, depends on the spline used. Thus, as long as the polynomials are no higher than third order in μ, the intersection calculations are exact and no iterative numerical methods are required. However, it should be noted that separate calculations need to be carried out for each inter-knot interval. Splines no higher than third order include B-splines, β-splines, cubic patches and patches made up of Bezier curves approximating no more than four knots.

The alternative method is to define the curve to be swept in its functional form:

$$f(u, v) = 0 \qquad\qquad\qquad\qquad\qquad\qquad \textbf{(8.13)}$$

As before, the intersection point(s) between the curve and the projected 2D ray equation have to be determined. The projected ray equation can be written as given in Equation (8.8).

Substituting the projected ray ordinates into Equation (8.13) gives:

$$f(\ ((\mathbf{S} - \mathbf{C}) \bullet \mathbf{u} + \alpha\mathbf{d} \bullet \mathbf{u}),\ ((\mathbf{S} - \mathbf{C}) \bullet \mathbf{v} + \alpha\mathbf{d} \bullet \mathbf{v})\ )$$

which can be solved for α. The positive solutions may be valid intersection points for which the w values have to be tested as described before.

An example will demonstrate the calculations. An elliptical cylinder may be generated by sweeping an ellipse. The parametric equations for the ellipse in their simplest form are:

$$u = a \cos (\theta)$$
$$v = b \sin (\theta)$$

A parameter μ could be defined by:

$$\mu = \cos (\theta)$$
$$\sin (\theta) = \sqrt{(1 - \mu^2)}$$

Thus:

$$u = a\mu \quad \text{and} \quad v = b\sqrt{(1 - \mu^2)}$$

Equation (8.11) then becomes:

$$\mathbf{d} \bullet \mathbf{v}\big[a\mu - (\mathbf{S} - \mathbf{C}) \bullet \mathbf{u}\big] = \mathbf{d} \bullet \mathbf{u}\big[b\sqrt{(1 - \mu^2)} - (\mathbf{S} - \mathbf{C}) \bullet \mathbf{v}\big]$$

As the scalar quantities $\mathbf{d} \bullet \mathbf{v}$, $\mathbf{d} \bullet \mathbf{u}$, $(\mathbf{S} - \mathbf{C}) \bullet \mathbf{u}$ and $(\mathbf{S} - \mathbf{C}) \bullet \mathbf{v}$ are known, a quadratic equation in μ has to be solved. After the solutions for the μ values have been found, they are substituted into Equation (8.10) and the α_i values calculated:

$$\alpha_i = \frac{a\mu_i - (\mathbf{S} - \mathbf{C}) \bullet \mathbf{u}}{\mathbf{d} \bullet \mathbf{u}}$$

For valid intersection(s), α must be greater than 0. However, to verify that these intersection points are actually on the surface, the w component must

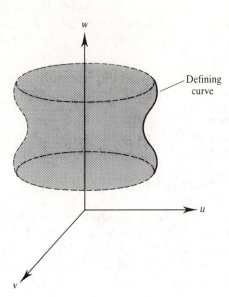

Figure 8.13

A surface of revolution can be specified by defining a curve on the u–w plane, and rotating it about the *W* axis.

be tested. This can be done using Equation (8.12) and the known α_i. If the functional form of the ellipse, $f(u, v) = 0$, is used then the equation is in the form:

$$\frac{u^2}{a^2} + \frac{v^2}{b^2} - 1 = 0$$

The components of the projected ray equation can now be substituted to give a quadratic equation for α, from which solutions, if any, for α can be determined.

8.4.8 Surfaces of revolution

A method similar to sweeping can be used to generate another class of surfaces by rotating a curve around a given axis. For surfaces of revolution, the curve is defined in the u–w ($v = 0$) plane and is rotated around the w axis as shown in Figure 8.13. The equations are simplest when the curve is defined in its functional form:

$$u = f(w)$$

Since the surface is rotated around the w axis, the radius of the circle of revolution for an intersection point given by w_i is $u = f(w_i)$. The radial distance, r, can be expressed by the sum of the squares of the u and v

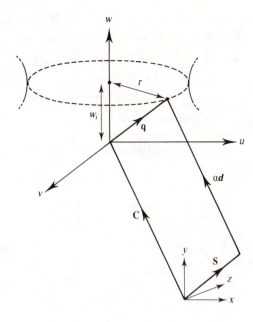

Figure 8.14
The vector arrangement for computing the point of intersection between a ray ($\mathbf{S}$ + $\alpha\mathbf{d}$) and a surface of revolution.

components of the intersection point. Referring to the arrangement in Figure 8.14, Pythagoras's theorem can be applied to the triangle defined by the vector $\mathbf{q}$, the radius, r, and the w axis:

$$|\mathbf{q}|^2 = w_i^2 + r^2$$

Because $r = f(w_i)$, since the point is on the surface of revolution, this can be written as:

$$\mathbf{q} \cdot \mathbf{q} = w_i^2 + f^2(w_i) \qquad\qquad (8.14)$$

As before, the w ordinate of the intersection point can be obtained using the dot product:

$$w_i = \mathbf{q} \cdot \mathbf{w} = (\mathbf{S} - \mathbf{C}) \cdot \mathbf{w} + \alpha\mathbf{d} \cdot \mathbf{w} \qquad\qquad (8.15)$$

Since:

$$\mathbf{q} = \mathbf{S} - \mathbf{C} + \alpha\mathbf{d}$$

it follows that:

$$\mathbf{q} \cdot \mathbf{q} = (\mathbf{S} - \mathbf{C}) \cdot (\mathbf{S} - \mathbf{C}) + 2\alpha(\mathbf{S} - \mathbf{C}) \cdot \mathbf{d} + \alpha^2 \qquad\qquad (8.16)$$

By substituting Equation (8.15) and Equation (8.16) into Equation (8.14), $\mathbf{q}$ and w_i can be eliminated to obtain one equation for α:

$$\alpha^2\{1 - (d \cdot w)^2\} + 2\alpha\{ (S - C) \cdot d - ((S - C) \cdot w(d \cdot w) \} \qquad \textbf{(8.17)}$$
$$+ (S - C) \cdot (S - C) - ((S - C) \cdot w)^2 = f^2((S - C) \cdot w + \alpha d \cdot w)$$

Depending on what the function f is, it may or may not be possible to solve Equation (8.17) for the roots α_i. If an exact solution is not possible, then iterative methods must be applied.

One simple solid of revolution is the cone which is defined by rotating the line:

$$u = kw$$

where k is a constant. Thus:

$$f(w) = kw$$

and so:

$$f^2[(S - C) \cdot w + \alpha d \cdot w] = k^2[(S - C) \cdot w + \alpha d \cdot w]^2$$

Substituting this into Equation (8.17) yields a quadratic in α, which can be solved for two roots. This is as would be expected since a ray, which is not parallel to the cone wall, will intersect a cone surface at most twice.

For the purposes of graphics, the cone would be considered to be bounded by a range of w – for example:

$$0 < w < 1$$

Thus, for each positive root α_i found, the corresponding value of w_i needs to be computed from Equation (8.15). If a valid intersection is found, then the normal vector must be obtained. For the defining line, $u = kw$, a normal vector is given by:

$$\mathbf{n_0} = [1, 0, -k]$$

This, however, is a normal vector in the u–w plane and must be rotated into the plane of the intersection before an illumination value can be deduced. Since the intersection is given by the vector $\mathbf{q}$, which is a position vector in the $[u, v, w]$ co-ordinate system, although not in the $[x, y, z]$ system), the rotation angle, θ, can be deduced from its ordinates. Referring to Figure 8.15, it can be seen that:

$$\cos(\theta) = \frac{\mathbf{q} \cdot u}{r}$$

$$\sin(\theta) = \frac{\mathbf{q} \cdot v}{r}$$

$$r^2 = (\mathbf{q} \cdot u)^2 + (\mathbf{q} \cdot v)^2$$

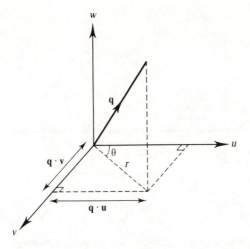

Figure 8.15
Calculating the rotation angle of an intersection with a solid of revolution.

So, performing rotation by the usual matrix method, the resulting surface normal in the $[u, v, w]$ co-ordinate system is:

$$\mathbf{n} = \left[\frac{\mathbf{q} \cdot u}{r}, \frac{\mathbf{q} \cdot v}{r}, -k \right]$$

As before, the unit normal vector is obtained by taking:

$$n = \frac{\mathbf{n}}{|\mathbf{n}|}$$

the sign of n being arranged so that $n \cdot d < 0$. The final normal vector is rotated back into the $[x, y, z]$ co-ordinate system, as before.

Another shape that can be generated by this method is the torus. In this case, it is a circle that is rotated around the w axis, as shown in Figure 8.16. Two scalar quantities are required in the object co-ordinate system:

- u_0, the u value of the centre of the small circle,
- r, the radius of the small circle.

The functional form of the generating curve is:

$$(u - u_0)^2 + w^2 = r^2$$

Rearranging this equation:

$$u^2 = f^2(w) = [\ \sqrt{(r^2 - w^2)} + u_0\ ]^2$$

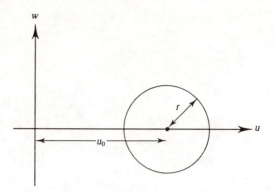

Figure 8.16

To define a torus, it is only necessary to specify a circle on the u–w plane. It is then rotated about the w axis.

Unfortunately, when this is substituted into Equation (8.17) to eliminate $f^2(w_i)$ for an intersection, the resulting equation in α is fourth order. Thus, an iterative method must be used to solve for α in this case. Once an intersection point is found, the normal direction vector can be expressed in the $v = 0$ plane as:

$$\mathbf{n_0} = \left[1, 0, -\frac{du}{dw}\right]$$

where the differential is evaluated at the point given by the value w_i. This may be computed by differentiating the equation of the circle to get:

$$2(u - u_0)\frac{du}{dw} = -2w$$

A wide variety of objects can be specified by using cubic curves in the form:

$$u^2 = k_0 + k_1w + k_2w^2 + k_3w^3 \tag{8.18}$$

This is a cubic curve which can be used to define a variety of smooth curves on the u–w plane. Writing this in functional notation gives:

$$f^2(w) = k_0 + k_1w + k_2w^2 + k_3w^3$$

For an intersection point, the value w_i defined by Equation (8.15) can be substituted, which will give a cubic polynominal in α for the term $f^2(w_i)$. If this term is substituted into Equation (8.17), then a cubic equation in α is obtained whose roots can be found analytically. The resulting roots are then processed as before.

The differential of Equation (8.18) is:

$$2u \frac{du}{dw} = k_1 + 2k_2 w + 3k_3 w^2 \tag{8.19}$$

and the normal vector on the defining plane can be written as:

$$\mathbf{n_0} = \left[1, 0, -\frac{du}{dw} \right]$$

Thus, the unit surface normal vector for the closest intersection can be found, as before.

For more complex curves, spline patches can be defined between adjacent pairs of knots. Following the method described for cubic patches in Chapter 6, if the differential is specified at each knot, then for an adjacent pair of knots, Equation (8.18) and Equation (8.19) can be used to provide four equations from which k_0, k_1, k_2 and k_3 can be computed. If spline patches are used, then the intersection computations must be carried out for each patch, before the closest intersection can be found. Colour Plate 14 shows a surface of revolution generated by this method.

An alternative method is to specify the curve in the u–w plane by using its parametric form. It is still possible to express one equation in μ, but because of its complicated form, for all practical applications, only an iterative solution will be possible. For the sake of completeness, the derivation is given here, but its practical importance is in great doubt.

The parametric equations of the curve in the u–w plane are:

$$u = f_u(\mu)$$
$$w = f_w(\mu)$$

As the analysis follows the method outlined for the functional form, the following equation, equivalent to Equation (8.17), is obtained:

$$\alpha^2 \{1 - (\mathbf{d} \cdot \mathbf{w})^2\} + 2\alpha\{ (\mathbf{S} - \mathbf{C}) \cdot \mathbf{d} - ((\mathbf{S} - \mathbf{C}) \cdot \mathbf{w}) (\mathbf{d} \cdot \mathbf{w}) \} \tag{8.20}$$
$$+ (\mathbf{S} - \mathbf{C}) \cdot (\mathbf{S} - \mathbf{C}) - ((\mathbf{S} - \mathbf{C}) \cdot \mathbf{w})^2 = f_u^2(\mu)$$

This time, however, it is necessary to solve for the value of the parameter μ before solutions can be obtained for α.

Since it is known that:

$$\mathbf{q} \cdot \mathbf{w} = f_w(\mu) = (\mathbf{S} - \mathbf{C} + \alpha \mathbf{d}) \cdot \mathbf{w}$$

then:

$$\alpha = \frac{f_w(\mu) - (\mathbf{S} - \mathbf{C}) \cdot w}{d \cdot w} \tag{8.21}$$

Substituting this equation into Equation (8.20) gives an equation in μ, from which it is possible to obtain roots for μ. Each value μ_i found can then be substituted into the parametric equation to find the w component of the intersection point, which can be checked for any limit on the w ordinate. The corresponding α_i can be obtained from Equation (8.20) and must also be checked, since it must be positive for a valid intersection point.

After the intersections have been found, it is necessary to compute the surface normal. As before, the normal in the u–w plane is used. This time it is found by differentiating the curve:

$$\mathbf{n_0} = \left[\frac{df_w(\mu)}{d\mu}, 0, -\frac{df_u(\mu)}{d\mu} \right]$$

As in the previous case, this is rotated to the correct position in the $[u, v, w]$ co-ordinate system giving:

$$\mathbf{n} = \left[\frac{\mathbf{q} \cdot u}{r} \frac{df_w(\mu)}{d\mu}, \frac{\mathbf{q} \cdot v}{r} \frac{df_w(\mu)}{d\mu}, -\frac{df_u(\mu)}{d\mu} \right]$$

where r is the radius of the circle of revolution at the point of intersection ($r^2 = (\mathbf{q} \cdot u)^2 + (\mathbf{q} \cdot v)^2$). From this, the sign and magnitude of the outward unit surface normal are computed as before.

The practical problem encountered here is that even the simplest functional or parametric curves produce equations that can be solved only by iterative methods. For example, if a B-spline is used, the parametric equations are of third order and Equation (8.18) yields a sixth-order polynomial in μ. In addition to the numerical difficulties in solving a sixth-order equation, all conditions need to be tested – in the worst case, six times. This may be a waste of time for practical solid objects for which only one or two intersection points exist.

8.4.9 Spline-generated surfaces

While ray tracing of swept surfaces and surfaces of revolution can be implemented in a reasonably straightforward manner, the complexities of the computations increase dramatically when arbitrary spline surfaces are considered. As was seen in Chapter 6, a point on a surface can be defined by two scalar parameters, μ and ν, and a double sum of the product of knots and blending functions:

$$\mathbf{P}(\mu, \nu) = [P_x, P_y, P_z] = \sum_{i=0}^{N} \sum_{j=0}^{M} \mathbf{P_{i,j}} B_i(\mu) B_j(\nu) \qquad (8.22)$$

For a reasonably smooth surface, for each four neighbouring knots $\mathbf{P_{i,j}}$, $\mathbf{P_{i+1,j}}$, $\mathbf{P_{i,j+1}}$ and $\mathbf{P_{i+1,j+1}}$, a bounding box should be determined which completely encloses the surface, so that if the ray misses the bounding box, then there could be no intersection. If the ray intersects the box, then there is a good chance of an intersection. The difficulty is determining whether the ray definitely intersects the surface inside an intersected bounding box, and if it does, then how many intersection points there are.

One possible way of finding an approximate solution is to start with initial trial values for μ and ν. Using Equation (8.22) and the values of μ and ν, the three components of the corresponding point on the surface, P_x, P_y and P_z, can be calculated. For an intersection, this must be equated with the ray equation, so:

$$\mathbf{P}(\mu, \nu) = \mathbf{S} - \mathbf{C} + \alpha d$$

One of the ordinates can then be used to compute the value of α. Using the x component gives:

$$\alpha = \frac{P_x - S_x + C_x}{d_x}$$

The other two components, Y_{ray} and Z_{ray}, can be determined from the known value of μ. These would have to be equal to P_y and P_z for a true intersection. Iteratively, the μ and ν values have to be changed until a solution is found. If the partial derivatives $\partial y/\partial \mu$, $\partial y/\partial \nu$, $\partial z/\partial \mu$ and $\partial z/\partial \nu$ are determined from the first differentials of Equation (8.22), as explained in Chapter 6, then a steepest descent search for the solution may be used. Since this procedure has to be repeated for many possible solutions, for a general surface and a very large number of rays, the computing requirements become very demanding.

An alternative is to use surface subdivision into small micro patches. The minimum size of the micro patches is chosen so that each projects into not more than one pixel. As it is easier to apply surface subdivision to triangles in the μ–ν space than quadrangles, the surface area between four knots is divided into two regions of three knots. This is illustrated in Figure 8.17 which shows three points on the surface, which will be called $\mathbf{P_1}$, $\mathbf{P_2}$ and $\mathbf{P_3}$. In parameter space, they have values $[\mu_1, \nu_1]$, $[\mu_2, \nu_2]$ and $[\mu_3, \nu_3]$. The aim is to compute the intersection point, shown as $\mathbf{P_4}$ in Figure 8.17,

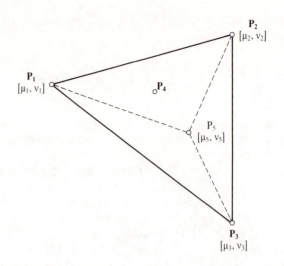

Figure 8.17

Computing the intersection between a spline surface and a ray may be done iteratively. For three points, $\mathbf{P_1}$, $\mathbf{P_2}$ and $\mathbf{P_3}$, the surface can be approximated as a triangle, and solved for the intersection with the triangle $\mathbf{P_4}$. This is then used to find the coefficients k in the equation $\mathbf{P_4} = k_1\mathbf{P_1} + k_2\mathbf{P_2} + k_3\mathbf{P_3}$. These are used to estimate the position of the point in parameter space, $\mu = k_1\mu_1 + k_2\mu2 + k_3\mu_3$ and $\nu = k_1\nu_1 + k_2\nu_2 + k_3\nu_3$.

which is between the ray and the triangle spanned by the three points $\mathbf{P_1}$ to $\mathbf{P_3}$. The calculation of the intersection between a ray and a triangle was discussed in Section 8.4.5.

If there is no intersection because the ray is parallel to the plane of the triangle or the intersection point is outside the triangle, then the average of the three vertices is taken to calculate $\mathbf{P_4}$:

$$\mathbf{P_4} = \frac{1}{3}(\mathbf{P_1} + \mathbf{P_2} + \mathbf{P_3})$$

In either case, the new point may be expressed as a vector sum:

$$\mathbf{P_4} = k_1\mathbf{P_1} + k_2\mathbf{P_2} + k_3\mathbf{P_3} \qquad (8.23)$$

and for an arbitrary intersection point the three coefficients k_1, k_2 and k_3 can be calculated from the three components of vector Equation (8.23). Now, linearly interpolated new values for μ and ν can be expressed as:

$$\mu_5 = k_1\mu_1 + k_2\mu_2 + k_3\mu_3$$
$$\nu_5 = k_1\nu_1 + k_2\nu_2 + k_3\nu_3$$

A new point on the surface, $\mathbf{P_5}$, can be calculated using the new parameter values $[\mu_5, \nu_5]$. The distance between $\mathbf{P_4}$ and $\mathbf{P_5}$ is found and, if it is sufficiently small, the search terminates. Otherwise, the original triangle is decomposed into three triangles, as shown in the Figure 8.17. If the ray has an intersection with one of the three triangles, the iteration can continue with that triangle; otherwise, all three triangles may have to be examined.

The difficulties in covering arbitrarily shaped surfaces militates against ray tracing spline surfaces, as does the fact that an iterative search is required, which must be carried out for each pixel.

8.5 MODELLING OPTICAL PHENOMENA

It has already been stated that ray tracing provides the only practical method of handling complex optical phenomena such as shadows, reflections, refraction and so on. A few of the most popular phenomena for which ray tracing has been successfully applied will now be discussed.

8.5.1 Multiple light sources and shadows

So far, only one light source has been considered. Having identified the nearest point of intersection, it is easy to compute the diffuse and specular reflections. Coping with multiple light sources presents no extra difficulties on its own, since the diffuse and specular reflection components can be added for each light source used.

Similarly, the fact that a reflected light for each additive colour component is computed separately means that different coloured sources present no further difficulties. The light source is completely specified by its position and its $[r, g, b]$ intensities. Similarly, each object of the scene will have separate reflectance constants for red, green and blue stored with it. Thus, the rendering of a coloured scene represents just a triplication of the monochrome case.

Better realism with multiple light sources is achieved by allowing objects to throw shadows on each other. This can be done by the application of the ray tracing procedure to light rays. For example, if the nearest intersection point has been identified, a check is then made to see if it is illuminated by each of the light sources in turn. To do this, a ray starting from the point of intersection and travelling in the direction towards the light source is used. If it intersects with any other object, then that light source is ignored; otherwise, the reflected light due to it is computed and added to the running total.

In formulating the ray tracing procedures for the primitive objects in Section 8.4, care was taken to ensure that no assumptions were made about the starting position of the ray. Hence, exactly the same equations, and indeed computer code, can be used to deal with shadows. Since the light position is constant and a single intersection is sufficient for determining shadows, space coherence of objects may be used for the order in which objects are examined. It should be noted that this analysis will not correctly model the shadows thrown by translucent objects.

8.5.2 Reflection

Opaque matt objects have the advantage that, after the nearest intersection point and its surface normal vector have been determined, only the illumination value of the corresponding pixel has to be calculated. However, some surfaces may be sufficiently shiny that reflections of other objects may be seen in them. In the most general case, the light intensity at a point of intersection will be a combination of the light due to reflection, that due to refraction (for transparent objects), plus the diffuse and specular intensities due to each light source.

Diffuse and specular reflections can be treated in exactly the same way as before, and their computation should be done first. In some cases – for example, those involving specular highlights – the contribution from specular reflection will be so large that the computation of reflected and refracted components becomes unnecessary. In such cases, a threshold must be defined, above which the contribution from the light sources is assumed to be sufficiently large that there is no need to compute a component for the transmitted or reflected light from other sources.

Having found the point of intersection between an incident ray and an object, the direction of a reflected ray can be expressed by a vector equation as shown in Section 4.2. In this case, it is the view vector d that is reflected, rather than the vector from the light source s. The point of intersection and the reflected direction are taken to define a new ray, which is then traced through the scene. The intersection point is given by position vector $\mathbf{I}$, and the new ray is:

$$\mathbf{I} + \alpha \left[d - 2(d \cdot n)n \right]$$

where d is the unit vector for the incident ray direction and n is the unit vector for the outside normal. The equation is also correct for the two limiting cases. These are when $d \cdot n = 0$ and so the incident ray is parallel to the surface, and when $d \cdot n = -1$, and the ray is perpendicular to the surface.

The code for a ray trace will return an intensity value for the reflected ray, which in the simplest case is used as the pixel intensity. The returned intensity values are simply treated as if produced by a light source and are combined with the other components additively, in the same manner as described for multiple light sources. Colour Plate 14 demonstrates multiple reflections in a complex scene, including a surface of revolution defined by 25 knots, and two spheres.

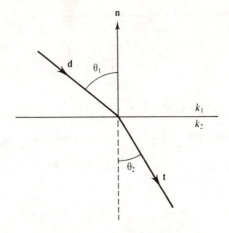

Figure 8.18
Calculating the bending of a ray when it crosses from one medium (for example, air) to another (for example, water) may be done using Snell's law, $k_1 \sin(\theta_1) = k_2 \sin(\theta_2)$. The original ray direction is **d** and the transmitted ray is **t**.

8.5.3 Refraction

The direction a ray takes when it crosses the boundary between one medium and another is governed by Snell's law, which states that:

$$k_1 \sin(\theta_1) = k_2 \sin(\theta_2)$$

where θ_1 is the angle between the incident ray and the surface normal, θ_2 is the angle between the refracted ray and the surface normal, k_1 is a constant for transmission medium 1 (for example, air) and k_2 is a constant for transmission medium 2 (glass). This physical model is illustrated by Figure 8.18. As shown, the incident and transmitted rays and the normal are co-planar. The direction vector for the refracted ray can be derived in several ways. The method described here is a direct derivation using vector algebra.

If the incident ray is characterized by the unit direction vector **d** and the refracted ray by **t**, Snell's law states that:

$$k_1(\boldsymbol{d} \times \boldsymbol{n}) = k_2(\boldsymbol{t} \times \boldsymbol{n}) \qquad (8.24)$$

This equation ensures that the sine of the angles are correctly related and that vectors **d**, **t** and **n** are co-planar. Because all three vectors are co-planar, it is also possible to write:

$$\boldsymbol{t} = \alpha\boldsymbol{n} + \beta\boldsymbol{d} \qquad (8.25)$$

where α and β are scalar constants. Taking the cross-product of both sides of this equation with **n** gives:

$$(\boldsymbol{t} \times \boldsymbol{n}) = \beta(\boldsymbol{d} \times \boldsymbol{n}) \qquad (8.26)$$

Equation (8.24) and Equation (8.26) determine the value for the scalar constant β which is equal to:

$$\beta = \frac{k_1}{k_2}$$

Since t is a unit vector, it is also known that:

$$t \cdot t = 1 = (\alpha n + \beta d) \cdot (\alpha n + \beta d) = \alpha^2 + 2\alpha\beta(n \cdot d) + \beta^2 \qquad (8.27)$$

This equation is a quadratic in the scalar constant α, which can be calculated. The two solutions are:

$$\alpha = -\beta(n \cdot d) \pm \sqrt{\beta^2(n \cdot d)^2 - \beta^2 + 1}$$

only one of which is correct. The second root appears since the sign of t is lost in Equation (8.27). By considering the case where the ray is perpendicular to the surface, $d = -n$ and $t = -n$, it is found that the positive sign of the square root is the correct one. Substituting the values of α and β into Equation (8.25) gives:

$$t = \frac{k_1}{k_2}\left(\left\{\sqrt{\left[(n \cdot d)^2 + \left(\frac{k_2}{k_1}\right)^2 - 1\right]} - n \cdot d\right\}n + d\right) \qquad (8.28)$$

The square root constrains the magnitude of the $n \cdot d$ dot product; that is:

$$(n \cdot d)^2 > 1 - \left(\frac{k_2}{k_1}\right)^2 \qquad (8.29)$$

which indicates the physical phenomenon of the limiting angle, after which total reflection occurs when the ray exits a denser material ($k_2 < k_1$). This limit must be tested if $k_2 < k_1$, and if the dot product magnitude does not satisfy Equation (8.29), then total reflection must be used.

Snell's law enables a new direction to be computed for the ray being traced every time an intersection with a transparent object occurs. When a ray enters a transparent object, this new direction is used, together with the point of entry, to determine the second intersection with the object; that is, the point where the ray leaves the object. At this point, Snell's law is again applied to obtain a new direction vector for the ray with the constants k_1 and k_2 interchanged. With the ray exiting from the transparent material, a new ray trace of the scene can begin.

Any light value computed for this new ray will be attenuated in the passage through the object to the eye. The attenuation depends on several factors, such as the ratio of reflected to refracted light at the boundary and the distance travelled through the object. The attenuation factor for transmission through the object must be specified in the database. There will be constants for red green and blue, and if these are unequal, then the transparent object will appear as having a colour.

When the ray trace algorithm has finally returned a value for the intensity arriving at the first intersection point with a transparent object, this value must then be combined with the computed value of diffuse and specular reflection, and the reflected ray. This is normally done by a linear combination:

$$I = \mu I_r + (1 - \mu)I_t \qquad\qquad (8.30)$$

where μ is a measure of the ratio of reflected light to transmitted light for the object and is in the range $[0...1]$, I_r is the total light intensity from diffuse, specular and reflected components, and I_t is the light intensity due to transmission.

Colour Plates 15 and 16 demonstrate refraction through a transparent solid of revolution created by parabolic splines.

8.5.4 Translucency

So far, it has been assumed that the refraction is perfect. This assumption provides an adequate model for clear glass and water. However, in practical cases, the transmitted ray is distributed in a small cone around the direction computed by Snell's law, as is illustrated in Figure 8.19. This

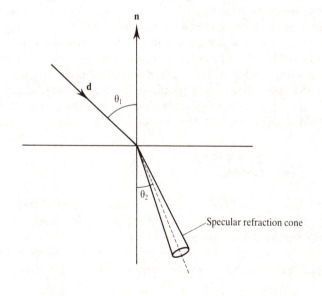

Figure 8.19

Modelling transmission through matt surfaces, such as ground glass, cannot be easily done by ray tracing since the rays disperse in a specular cone.

effect is known as **specular refraction**. Clearly, the ray tracing process cannot model this effect easily, since it now becomes necessary to trace several rays and make a representative selection from the specular cone. A model of frosted glass could, however, be created by using two or three refracted rays, selected at random according to the distribution of intensities in the cone.

The examples shown so far demonstrate the variety of optical phenomena that can be handled with ray tracing. Instead of getting lost in the details of the ray tracing of many more possible applications, the next section discusses a new and very important approach to surface definitions based on constructive solid geometry, which uses a general combination of primitive solid volumes.

8.6 CONSTRUCTIVE SOLID GEOMETRY

The preceding sections have dealt with simple primitive shapes, which although sufficient for certain purposes, such as molecular modelling, represent too limited a set for many applications. This is especially true of CAD systems used for mechanical design. Constructive solid geometry (CSG) provides a way in which primitives may be combined into complex shapes that are more widely applicable. The field of CSG is vast and complex and could occupy a large chapter of its own. This section therefore limits its coverage of CSG to its role in computer graphics. Since the rendering of objects defined by CSG is invariably done by some form of ray tracing, CSG is discussed in connection with ray tracing procedures.

Theoretically, CSG defines a combined solid volume from a number of solid volumes by the application of set operations such as union, intersection and complement. On the other hand, for many ray tracing procedures, individual surfaces are required. Hence, either the ray tracing procedures have to be modified or methods of determining surfaces from CSG-defined objects have to be developed.

8.6.1 CSG trees

The CSG procedure can be represented by a tree structure where the root of the tree defines an object. The terminal nodes are primitive volumes such as spheres, cones, boxes bounded by planes, and so on. The non-terminal nodes are combination operations, operating on their subtrees. The three basic combinators are intersection (I), union (U) and minus (M).

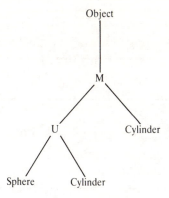

Figure 8.20
A CSG tree combines simple primitive objects into more complex ones using the operations union (U), intersection (I) and minus (M).

Minus can be replaced by complement and intersection, but it proves useful to include it as it corresponds to removing a solid volume of material. This often occurs in practice, for example, when a hole is drilled in a solid.

A simple tree is defined in Figure 8.20, while Figure 8.21 schematically shows how the primitive objects at the leaf nodes are combined into a complex shape by the tree. It can be seen from this example that complex shapes can be quickly and easily defined by this method. Clearly, the shape of the final object depends on the exact location and orientation of the individual primitives, and a large number of possible objects can be represented by the same tree. The tree shown in Figure 8.20 is a binary tree, but there is no limitation on the number of branches, since the combination operators are defined for an arbitrary number of elements.

8.6.2   Ray tracing a CSG tree

The method of ray tracing a CSG tree necessitates traversal in a depth-first manner, starting at the terminal nodes. What needs to be passed back up the tree from any node is a list of line segments of the ray that pass through

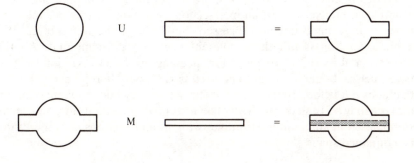

Figure 8.21
The object produced by a CSG tree depends critically on the definition of the leaf nodes. This is one possible instance of an object defined by the tree shown in Figure 8.20.

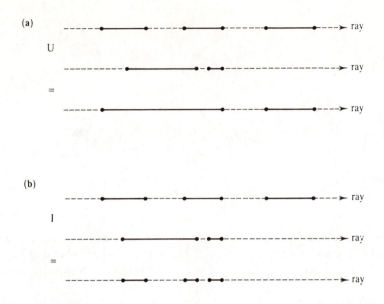

Figure 8.22

Ray tracing an object defined by a CSG tree requires that all the intersections with all the primitives be calculated and the results backed up the tree. At each non-terminal node, the intersections found on the two subtrees are combined. If the solid lines represent the parts of the ray that travel through the object defined by the subtree, then the union operator combines them as shown in (a) and the intersection operator as shown in (b).

the solid object. These are called **contained spans**, and may be characterized by the α values of the ray equation. For each span, it is necessary to keep a record of the object to which it belongs, since this will be required when the computation of the illumination value is made.

Values for α for the primitives at the terminal nodes are computed by applying the ray tracing methods described in Sections 8.4. Since the viewpoint must be placed outside the solid parts of the final object, a properly defined object will yield either an even number of intersections, which taken in order along the ray define the contained spans, or a *nil* list. At the non-terminal nodes, the contained spans are combined in a manner that depends on the operation. For example, two sets of spans that are joined by a union operation are shown in Figure 8.22(a). The combination of the same spans by an intersection node is show in Figure 8.22(b).

It will be observed that some pruning of the tree can take place. For example, if one subtree of an intersection operation returns *nil*, then the other subtree need not be processed. Similarly, if the left subtree of a minus operation is *nil*, then the right need not be computed. All the software and hardware methods for speeding up the intersection calculations such as bounding boxes and sorting can apply here. Each primitive that does not belong to the active object set of a ray and is a component of the tree may be replaced with *nil*. The sorting of the bounds in x and y may still be used in eliminating primitives with no intersections and, therefore, no contained spans.

One problem with the CSG tree is that, since the minus operation produces objects for which the primitives can define areas where there is a hole, it is not possible to use the *ZMin* of the bounding extents of the primitives to order the search for the nearest intersection.

8.6.3 Preprocessing a CSG tree

In some cases where objects are instanced many times in a scene, it may be advantageous to preprocess the CSG tree to return just one object that can be ray traced. In fact, this procedure transforms a volume into a collection of surface segments. A surface segment is defined by a simple surface – planar, spherical, conical – and a closed boundary curve on the surface. A valid intersection point between the ray and the surface segment must be contained within the closed boundary curve.

The preprocessing of the CSG tree is very difficult for many of the sets of primitives that have been used in this chapter. For example, mathematical functions that describe the boundary curve generated by the intersection of, say, a sphere and a cylinder are too intractable for rapid computer analysis. On the other hand, objects defined by planar facets produce planar polygons as boundary curves.

The union of two objects described as a list of facets is obtained simply by concatenating the lists. This is, in effect, what is done when a set of primitives are ray traced without a tree.

Intersection is harder to compute. Firstly, starting with one of the objects, each of its facets are processed in turn. Then, the lines of intersection with every facet in the second object are computed. These lines will typically divide the facet of the first object processed into a number of regions. For each of these regions, a containment test must be performed to discover whether a point in it is contained in the second object. If so, then that bounded region is a face of the intersection, and it is placed on the output list. When all the faces of *both* objects have been thus processed, the output list represents the boundary representation of the intersection. The detailed algorithm is highly complex.

The computation of minus can be similarly done. When processing the negative object, any part of a face found to be contained in the positive object is added to the output list. For the positive object, the parts of faces that are not contained in the negative object go to the output list.

Finally, a picture description is produced in which all the CSG trees have been reduced to lists of bounded planes. These can now be ordered to optimize the ray tracing algorithms, as previously described. As the operations that have been carried out are invariant to the usual transformations, it is possible to scale, translate or rotate the complex shape in the final picture.

8.6.4   Coherence in CSG trees

So far, little use has been made of the concept of coherence, as far as the structure of a single object is concerned. It has been shown how Cartesian space can be divided into smaller volumes to sort objects with the aim of speeding up ray tracing. In the context of single objects, coherence in its strictest form requires the identification of regions of space that belong to only one object or are empty. In general, the complexity of the shapes used does not allow the specification of coherent regions in any simple way; consequently, a search is made for areas of space that intersect the object in a simple way.

The simplest way of dividing up space is to use successive binary divisions on the smallest rectangular box containing the complex object. Algorithms for object representation and manipulation have been presented by Ayala, Brunet, Juan and Navazo (1985) and others.

There are two ways in which such a division is commonly implemented; namely, by means of bintrees or octrees. In the case of the bintree, the division is into two. Thus, the cube that contains the scene forms the root of a tree and has two children, each of which is a half-cube. Similarly, the children each have two children, and so on, until the leaf nodes are reached. The divisions alternate between the three principal axis directions. The octree, on the other hand, which was introduced in Section 7.6, uses division into eight subregions. Octrees maintain symmetry and all nodes represent volumes with the same shape.

The choice of which data structure to use is an implementation decision. For the purposes of this discussion, only the octree will be considered. Moreover, the convention that the sides of the box are aligned with the Cartesian axes will be adopted.

The coherence properties are described by allowing nodes to be of three types:

(1)   *black*, meaning that the volume is completely contained within a solid region of the object.

(2)   *white*, meaning that it is completely empty.

(3)   *gray*, meaning that one or more object boundaries are inside the subdivided volume.

These terms do not, of course, indicate anything about the shading of the final drawing. In practice, the leaf nodes will be either *black*, *white* or *gray*, but the non-terminal nodes must be *gray*, since black and white nodes are completely coherent, and therefore there is no reason to decompose them.

The depth to which space is decomposed can be limited in a number of ways. Clearly, since the discrete sampling is of a continuous space that will be ultimately represented in pixels, there is no need to go any deeper than the size of decomposition equivalent to one pixel. The volume elements (voxels) at this resolution can be thought of as 3D pixels. For drawing scenes in orthographic projection, voxels are very convenient, since, for some $[x, y]$ value, all that is required for each pixel is to find the voxel classified as *gray* or *black* whose z address is lowest. The problem with this approach is the vast memory requirement, although with current technology, voxel memories are becoming a reality.

Another way of limiting the tree is to further classify the gray nodes of the tree into types that can be simply processed. Without a subdivision of the gray nodes, the decomposition must extend to the smallest voxel size at every surface of every object in the scene, with the exception of the special case where objects are aligned with the axes at the cube boundaries. Considering only the case of objects made up of facets, this effect can be reduced by introducing the following new node types:

face, if the subdivided region includes exactly one facet.

edge, if it includes two facets forming exactly one edge.

vertex, if the region includes exactly one vertex formed by two or more edges.

These types progressively reduce the size of the tree. The simplest *face* nodes confine the areas requiring decomposition to voxel level only at the edges. Similarly, the introduction of *edge* nodes requires voxel decomposition only at the vertices, and so on. Similar node types can be introduced to deal with curved surfaces.

8.6.5   Combining octrees and CSG trees

Octrees can be used to combine the primitives of a CSG tree into one octree representation of the object. For two primitives that are to be combined, the first stage is to create an octree division of each within the whole scene volume, or possibly the bounding cube that surrounds both primitives. The creation of the octrees is done, as before, by recursive subdivision, terminating when nodes are *black*, *white*, *face* or possibly *edge* or *vertex* types. When a node is subdivided, the type of its children can be determined by computing their intersection with the primitive itself.

The two trees are traversed at the same time, generating an output tree. The rules used for determining the form of the output tree depend on the operator being used to combine the trees. For the case of intersection of two corresponding nodes the output is:

[*black*, *black*], output node is *black*.

[*white*, *any*], output node is *white*.

[*black*, *gray*], the *gray* node and its subtree are copied to the output.

Figure 8.23
If a node in an octree decomposition contains two non-intersecting faces, then either one object contains the other (a), or there is no intersection between the objects (b), or there is an intersection and further decomposition is required to obtain coherent nodes (c).

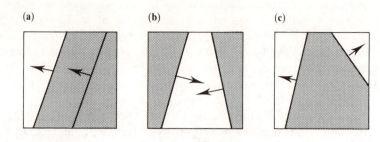

(a) (b) (c)

The processing of two terminal gray nodes presents problems. In such a case, two options are available, the choice of which is a trade off between the computation time in building the tree and the time taken to trace it. The first option is to create a special node on the output tree in which is stored the input nodes and an intersection operator. When ray tracing, the objects in that node are then processed as outlined in Section 8.3.2. The second option is to expand both nodes and process the subtrees until either one of the conditions listed is reached or the smallest voxel level is found. Some savings of space may be made if further information is available about the gray nodes themselves. For example, if dealing with *face* nodes, they are processed as follows: if the faces intersect, the node is expanded and the subtree is processed; otherwise, the normals of the two faces are examined to carry out what is, in effect, a containment test.

There are three possible cases for the normals of non-intersecting faces, which are illustrated in Figure 8.23. The three cases may be differentiated as follows. If the dot product of the two outer normals is positive, then it follows that the angle between them must be acute; thus, one object completely contains the other, as shown in Figure 8.23(a). In this case, the output tree receives the node from the tree describing the contained face. To determine which face is contained, one face is chosen and the intersection of a line from any point on that face within the node, in the direction of the outward normal, with the plane of the other face is computed. If the intersection yields a negative value for the parameter, then the other face is the contained one, and *vice versa*.

The two cases of the outward normals pointing in opposite directions must be distinguished by a similar test. For the case where they point towards each other, as shown in Figure 8.23(b), there is no intersection and the output tree node is *white*. For the case where they both point outwards, as shown in Figure 8.23(c), the node must be subdivided.

If *edge* nodes are used, the size of the tree will be reduced at the expense of further rules for the computation of the CSG tree. *vertex* nodes are a super-set of *edge* nodes, where rules are required depending on the number of edges used. As before, it may be possible to evolve rules for other types of node to prevent the tree growing to voxel level.

Octrees can be used very efficiently for simple preview models not requiring complex illumination calculations. For example, a CSG object can be previewed using single colours to indicate the primitives. Thus, the terminal nodes of the octree only contain a single colour of the primitive, rather than the surface normal and the light reflection properties of its surfaces. In such a model, it is possible to subdivide down into the smallest voxel level.

The fields of ray tracing and constructive solid geometry are vast. This is one area of computer graphics where the procedural and functional levels are inseparably intertwined. Constructive solid geometry is a functional concept; ray tracing is a procedural one. To produce an acceptable rendered image within a reasonable time, the two cannot be separated. The examples described in this chapter give an indication of the important features and problems associated with both fields.

Exercises

8.1   Explain what is meant by the term coherence. In what way could the use of extents be considered an example of coherence?

8.2   A ray being traced is given by the line $S + \alpha d$, where $S = [1, -3, 2]$ and $d = [-0.5, 0.8, 0.33]$. Check to see if it will intersect with the following three spheres:

(a)   Centre: $[-2, 2, 4]$; Radius: 1

(b)   Centre: $[-4, 1, 5]$; Radius: 2

(c)   Centre: $[2, 3, 3]$; Radius: 1

8.3   For the ray defined in Exercise 8.2, what are the values of α at the intersection points with the sphere that has centre $[-2.5, 2, 4]$ and radius 1?

8.4   A cylinder has radius 1, and centres at $[1, 1, 5]$ and $[2, -1, 6]$. Calculate what intersections, if any, it has with the ray; $S = [4, 20, 5]$ and $d = [0.23, -0.86, 0.45]$.

8.5   A triangular facet is defined by two vectors $\mathbf{a} = [1, 0, 5]$ and $\mathbf{b} = [0, -2, 6]$, and an apex $[1, 1, 10]$. Calculate the intersection point of its plane with the ray $S = [0, 0, -5]$ and $d = [0.1, -0.15, 0.98]$. Is the intersection point inside the facet?

8.6   For the sphere and ray of Exercise 8.3, calculate the secondary ray from the nearest intersection in the direction of a light source placed at $[10, 10, 5]$. Is this intersection illuminated by the light source?

8.7 If a shiny sphere is used in Exercise 8.3, calculate the reflected ray that will be traced. If the light source is at [0, 10, −10], what is the component of specular reflection?

8.8 A glass slab is to be incorporated in a graphics scene. Its front face is in the plane $z = 10$ and its back face is in the plane $z = 12$. A ray hits the front surface travelling in direction [0.2, 0.2, 0.96]. The refractive constants are $k_1 = 1$ for air and $k_2 = 1.2$ for the glass. In which direction does the ray travel through the glass, and at what point does it emerge?

8.9 Explain what is meant by the term specular refraction.

8.10 The sphere with centre [0, 0, 10] and radius 2, and the cylinder with ends [2, 1, 10] and [−2, 1, 10] and radius 3, are combined in a CSG tree. The scene is to be drawn in orthographic projection. For the ray with $x = 0$ and $y = 1$, parallel to the Z direction, compute the contained spans if the combination is by (a) intersection, (b) union or (c) cylinder minus sphere.

Problems

8.11 An object defined in its own [u, v, w] co-ordinate system is to be drawn in the [x,y,z] co-ordinate system at position $C = [2, -3, 5]$, and with its orientation changed by a rotation of 30° about the x axis. What are the unit vectors u, v and w indicating the definition axes expressed in the [x, y, z] co-ordinate system?

8.12 A cube is defined in a database as the position vector of an apex, C, and three orthogonal vectors, e_1, e_2 and e_3, of equal magnitude, which are along the edges that converge at that apex. Sketch out a pseudo-code implementation of a procedure that will compute the intersection of a ray $S + \mu d$ with the cube. To optimize the computation, an extent is to be used for each cube. Indicate how the extent is computed before the ray trace begins, and modify your procedure to use the extent.

8.13 A graphics scene is being defined and will contain several cylinders at different positions and orientations. If the computation time is to be minimized, which would be the best method of defining the cylinders: (a) directly using the method of Section 8.4.3, (b) as a swept surface or (c) as a surface of revolution.

8.14 A ray tracing system is to employ surfaces of revolution based on parabolic splines of the form $w = k_2 u^2 + k_0$. Using the method described in Section 8.4.8, write the pseudo-code of a procedure to determine the intersection between the surface and a ray $\mathbf{S} + \mu\mathbf{d}$.

8.15 A graphics scene is being drawn with the viewpoint under water. If the surface of the water is the plane $z = 10$, and the scene is viewed from the point $[0, 0, -5]$, what is the diameter of the circle in which the rays will pass through the water surface? The refractive constants are $k_1 = 1.2$ for water and $k_2 = 1$ for air.

8.16 Write a pseudo-code implementation for combining contained spans of a ray by (a) intersection and (b) union at a node in a CSG tree. Use the method outlined in Section 8.6.2.

Project

8.17 Write a ray tracing system in stages depending on the time available for the project.

Stage 1: The set of primitives is to include spheres and cylinders, with diffuse and specular reflections. The object data should be read from a file, and the raster image written to a file that preferably should be run-length encoded in the way described in Project 3.20.

Stage 2: Secondary rays should be included to provide reflections, refractions, multiple light sources and shadows. The object repertoire should be enhanced by the addition of bounded planes. The format of the file containing the object descriptions will need to be changed to accommodate this.

Stage 3: Procedurally defined objects, such as swept surfaces and solids of revolution, should be added to the system.

Stage 4: Optimization by space subdivision should be incorporated.

Stage 5: An interactive system should be provided for designing the scene. This should allow the creation of objects by means of CSG trees, and the code for tracing CSG trees included.

9 | Art, Special Effects and Animation

Computer artists work in a distinctly different way from engineers and scientists. They require systems that can be related to traditional methods, hence graphics interfaces have been developed to provide palettes and brushes. In increasing the visual realism of scenes generated by computer graphics, a large number of techniques have evolved. The simplest is the use of texture, which may be mapped on to polygons to produce real effects. Using a more detailed model of surface reflectance can produce the appearance of a wide variety of object materials, and the simulation of camera lens aperture effects can create the impression of looking at a real photograph.

Two-dimensional animation is now strongly supported by computer graphics. The main problem is to compute automatically the frames that fall between two specified key-frames, while preserving the correct position velocity and acceleration relations. Removal of temporal alias effects, such as car wheels apparently turning backwards, can be done automatically.

Three-dimensional animation is used in education and visualization of mathematical and scientific models. Real-time animation systems are of importance in teaching. The most significant example is flight simulation, where parallel processing is used to achieve the required frame rate.

9.1   INTRODUCTION

So far, the treatment of computer graphics has concentrated mainly on technological and scientific applications, but the techniques described are equally applicable to the generation of pictures for pure entertainment or for artistic expression. Systems to supply these classes of user are now becoming widespread, ranging from the cheapest raster system to fully comprehensive systems, which are used for the generation of commercial art.

9.2   GRAPHIC ART SYSTEMS

The way in which a creative artist would wish to use a computer is different from a scientist or technologist. The artist's primary concern is with aesthetics, not precision. It is therefore less important to expend large resources of computer time in accurate calculations of geometric properties. Instead, the artist's system must perform interactively with considerable capability for making alterations and adjustments to the primitives in the scene. Moreover, the computer system should operate in a way to which the artist can relate his or her skills and modes of thinking. It is largely unacceptable to expect the artist to set up a batch file containing a description of primitive objects. Instead, the systems should incorporate paints that can be mixed, brushes that apply the paints to an area of the raster screen canvas, or material that can be cut to shape and pasted at a set position to create a collage. These characteristic modes of interaction in paint systems need only be supplements to techniques such as ray tracing which may be of value to the artist who has the patience to wait for the computer to produce results. In some cases, artists deploy these techniques alongside brushes, as for example, in the Rodin system – see Nahas and Huitric (1982), and Huitric and Nahas (1985). However, the difficulty of describing and manipulating 3D space interactively has limited this approach.

9.2.1   Paintbox systems

In contrast the previous approach of maintaining a functional description of pictures till as late as possible in the rendering process, painting is usually accomplished in the frame memory or bitmap. This has the advantage that collage material can be included by the use of camera and frame grabber.

Creating line drawings presents no problems. If lines are confined to one pixel width, then all that is required is a locator to track the pixels to be set and a system for describing pixel attributes. Thicker lines may be used with little additional software. Fill areas can be processed in the bitmap simply by means of the seed-filling technique. A simple extension allows areas to be filled with different patterns of pixels, called **textures**, or with patterns that have already been drawn by the user. These may be selected from windows alongside the picture or from pop-up menus.

The introduction of brushes adds a new problem, however, since a real brush typically has a width that varies as it is turned or the pressure is changed, and the quantity of paint it delivers is dependent on how heavily it is loaded, the pressure applied and the speed of motion. The effect on the screen is not simply confined to the pixel identified by the locator, but involves its neighbourhood as well.

9.2.2   Brush trajectories

A brush is usually described by a closed convex curve in two dimensions. A brush trajectory consists of a centre line, together with a description of the brush orientation and pressure at each point. The area described at any point in the trajectory is bounded by the two points on the curve whose tangents are parallel to the slope of the centre line. For a closed convex curve, there are exactly two such points.

In an interactive paint system, the pressure and orientation of the brush can be read from special-purpose input devices. These may be processed in a variety of ways. For example, an elliptical brush can be specified as the ratio of the major and minor axes, and their angle to the Cartesian axes describing the pixel positions. A change in pressure changes the absolute values of the major and minor axes, while a change in orientation is reflected directly in the angle.

The computation of the trajectory at the raster level is complicated by the need to avoid unpleasant alias effects. For example, it is insufficient to approximate the gradient by considering the slope of the line joining adjacent pixels, since this allows only eight possible samples from the continuous space of 2π angles, which is too few. Thus, the computations must take place over a small region. For example, the trajectory could be computed at sample points, say, every fourth pixel along the centre line.

Since the computation is carried out as the brush is being moved, the slope of the centre line cannot be determined by applying the central difference method. Instead, an estimate must be made from the backwards difference – that is, the slope of the line joining the current position to the previous sample point. This, together with the brush orientation, allows a computation of the envelope pixels. Once the two envelope pixels have been computed, the trajectory can be drawn by also taking the previous envelope points and filling the area defined by the bounding quadrilateral. The resulting areas will need to be anti-aliased for the best effect.

This simple method may be improved by using a model of the distribution of paint in the brush. For example, the pixel intensity could fall off in a manner dependent on its distance from the centre line. This is just one of many techniques for modelling the distribution of paint. Other methods depend on more detailed modelling, such as accounting for the number and density of hairs in the brush, to create special effects such as streaks.

Brush trajectories need not necessarily be computed in the frame buffer. As an alternative, the brush centre line and orientation may be encoded as simple mathematical functions.

One possible application of brush trajectories outside the field of computer art is to store character fonts. This is an attractive method, since a brush trajectory requires far less storage than a bitmap and it can be scaled without the undesirable effects of pixel replication. The fonts can be initially defined interactively in a more natural way than is possible with simple spline curves. Further exploration of this idea will be found in Ghosh and Mudur (1984).

9.3   COMPUTER-GENERATED ART

Although most people regard aesthetic judgement as beyond the potential range of applications of the computer, it is still possible to use the computer to explore material that may either possess natural beauty or may be incorporated in a collage. Systems that do this may, or may not, contain aleatoric elements.

9.3.1   Chaotic functions

Much attention has been paid recently to certain classes of functions that, when iterated with particular initial values, neither converge or diverge. Treatments of these chaotic functions are found in Fischer and Smith (1985). The surprising properties of these functions are thought to model many natural or social systems that have proved intractable to conventional predictive modelling. Such modelling has, to date, proved unsuccessful due to the diversity of the functions. However, 2D functions have attracted the attention of computer artists. A picture can be generated simply by plotting the values of successive iterations of a two-argument chaotic function. Changing the colour every so often can produce a wide variety of different effects. An interesting example discovered by Martin (1986) is:

$$x_{n+1} = y_n - \text{sign}(x_n) \sqrt{(|Bx_n - C|)}$$
$$y_{n+1} = A - x_n$$

Depending on the initial conditions, this function gives a wide variety of patterns. A plot with $A = B = C = 0.3$, $x_0 = 0.8$, $y_0 = 0.003$ and over 50 000 iterations yields the attractive pattern of Colour Plate 18, which is nearly symmetric and could, for example, form the basis of a tile design.

Another famous example is the function discovered by Mandelbrodt:

$$t_{n+1} = st_n (1 - t_n) \qquad\qquad (9.1)$$

for complex numbers s and t. This function will partition the complex plane into two regions, one for which points diverge, the other for which the iterations remain bounded. The boundary points, called **fractals**, neither converge nor diverge. The boundary, which is infinitely long, may be drawn by iterating the inverse of the function:

$$t_{n+1} = \left(1 \pm \sqrt{1 - 4t_n/s}\right)/2$$

This locus presents new detail every time the resolution to which it is drawn is increased.

A more interesting way of viewing the fractals is to plot the points that remain bounded after a certain number of iterations. As the number is increased, the detail of the boundary also increases. Colour Plate 17 shows typical plots of the boundary region. The vertical axis is the imaginary one. Each pixel position on the complex plane is used as a starting point for the iteration by Equation (9.1). The colour that is plotted represents approximately the number of iterations made before Equation (9.1) diverged. A gradual increase in the complexity of the boundaries shape will be observed as the iteration continues.

9.3.2 Fractal landscapes

A more common application of chaotic functions is the creation of irregular terrain. This is achieved by a function that is best visualized geometrically. Starting with a triangle and moving the midpoint of each edge in some random direction by a small random amount, it is possible to

Figure 9.1

Creation of a fractal landscape can be done by division of a simple triangulated surface. The midpoint of each edge of the triangulation is displaced by a small random amount. The new midpoints, and the original vertices, are then used to form the vertices of four new triangles. Repeated application of the process yields an irregular surface which may be rendered to represent terrain.

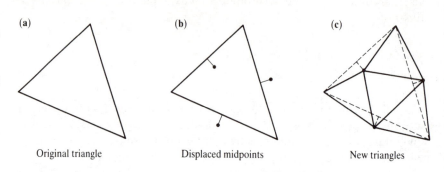

(a)   (b)   (c)

Original triangle   Displaced midpoints   New triangles

replace the original triangle by four successors, as shown in Figure 9.1. Repeated application of this process using a static random number generator yields a boundary that neither converges nor diverges.

Terrain can be generated by starting with a simple set of triangles in 3D space, which indicate a basic shape such as the rough outline of mountains. These basic triangles are then refined by the process just described. It is usual to restrict the midpoint displacement to one ordinate, say the vertical (y). The process continues recursively until a sufficiently small triangulation is achieved. The surface can then be rendered using rules to determine the illumination that creates the effect of mountains with snow on the peaks, forests, and so on. For example, triangles over a certain height could be coloured white and made reflective to give the impression of snow on the mountain peaks. The next height band could then be coloured dark gray and made less reflective to depict rock; and the next band green and non-reflective. Extra rules could be included to improve the realism – for example, very steep triangles would not be covered in snow, and so on.

If a non-random displacement of the midpoints is used, then the ray trace and the fractal decomposition can be done together; that is, the fractal decomposition is depth first, eliminating all triangles that do not contribute to a ray. This proves to be much more efficient computationally. The fact that it can be done can be deduced from the property that any point within a triangle must be bounded by the decomposition of that triangle or its immediate neighbours.

Recently, chaotic functions have been applied to image compression. The basic idea is to divide an image into regions that can be regenerated from iterating a chaotic function. Instead of storing the 250000 pixels, a few parameters are stored. The difficult parts of the technique are the division of the picture into regions and the selection of the chaotic functions that adequately describe each region. Although fractal compression greatly reduces the storage space and transmission time for images, it does so at the expense of large computer and human resources, which are required for compression and restoration. Moreover, images cannot usually be restored with complete accuracy. For this reason, analogue recording media, such as laser disks, are still the most popular means of mass storage of images.

9.3.3   Transformation techniques

Another way in which the computer can aid the artist is in computing the large number of shapes that result from applying one of a number of algorithmic transformations to a starting shape. Such a process can be carried out recursively to produce a tree of possibilities, and the artist can choose material from the tree and freely adapt it to produce the desired result. This approach has been used in sculpture by Latham (1986) and is also used in musical composition. From a computational viewpoint, it is difficult to make any generalizations about these systems, since, if they are to be effective, they must contain transformations that are specific to the artist's mode of working.

9.4   VISUAL REALISM

Except in a few cases, pictures generated by a computer do not appear as realistic as photographs or video images, and this lack of realism may be a severe limitation to the artist. The problem cannot be attributed to the display medium, since a low-resolution colour television is capable of producing a highly realistic image display. Rather, the reason is that the level of detail in a real picture is greater than could be programmed with the techniques discussed to date. Consequently, in the search for better realism, programmers have sought new models to cope with ever increasing levels of details, at the expense of computation time. Ultimately, such realism could be applied to areas such as flight simulation, or to entertainment or advertising.

9.4.1   Texture mapping

The simplest way to improve the appearance of an object is to add some texture to the surface. This could be either in the form of some design or a pattern whose intention is to deceive the viewer as to the regularity of the surface.

Texture is best thought of as a mapping between a texture space, where the surface properties required are defined, and the object space.

(a)

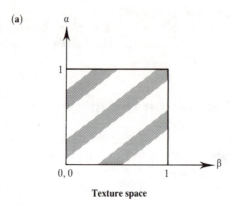

Texture space

Figure 9.2

Texture mapping can be performed between a defined texture space and any convex quadrilateral. The mapping of point **p** is computed by expressing it in terms of vectors **a**, **b** and **d**, and the scalar parameters α and β. The equivalent point in texture space is found by substituting the edge direction vector [1, 0] for **a**, [0, 1] for **b** and [1, 0] for **d**; that is, choosing the point with Cartesian co-ordinates [α, β] in texture space.

(b)

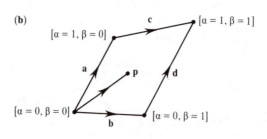

Vector space

This must be invertable if the object is to be rendered using ray tracing. Thus, when an intersection on a solid is found, the corresponding point in texture space is found, and is then used to determine the surface reflectance properties.

The most commonly found example is the texturing of quadrilateral polygons. The texture can be defined in the range [0...1, 0...1] in the parameter space [α, β] and mapped on to the Cartesian space. The mapping is best described using vector space. If the edge vectors of the quadrilateral to be textured are **a**, **b**, **c** and **d**, a mapping between texture space and vector space, illustrated in Figure 9.2, can be set up using the equation:

$$\mathbf{p} = \alpha[\,(1 - \beta)\mathbf{a} + \beta\mathbf{d}\,] + \beta\mathbf{b} \qquad (9.2)$$

If:

$$\mathbf{e} = (1 - \beta)\mathbf{a} + \beta\mathbf{d} \qquad (9.3)$$

then Equation (9.2) becomes simply:

$$\mathbf{p} = \alpha\mathbf{e} + \beta\mathbf{b}$$

meaning that $\mathbf{p}$ is the linear combination of the vectors $\mathbf{e}$ and $\mathbf{b}$. Now, since, as indicated by Equation (9.3), the vector $\mathbf{e}$ is made up by averaging vectors $\mathbf{a}$ and $\mathbf{d}$ over the range of β, it can be seen that Equation (9.2) gives an invertable one-to-one mapping between the texture and the object co-ordinate systems. Equation (9.2) simplifies to:

$$\mathbf{p} = \alpha\beta(\mathbf{c} - \mathbf{b}) + \beta\mathbf{b} + \alpha\mathbf{a} \qquad\qquad \textbf{(9.4)}$$

which, for any point $[\alpha, \beta]$ in texture space, can be used to calculate the corresponding point in Cartesian space.

The inversion is found as follows. Since it is assumed that the quadrilateral is in 3D space, Equation (9.4) can be thought of as a set of three equations. Eliminating the terms with the $\alpha\beta$ coefficient in the equations for the x and z ordinates gives the equation:

$$\alpha[a_z(c_x - b_x) - a_x(c_z - b_z)] + \beta[b_z(c_x - b_x) - b_x(c_z - b_z)]$$
$$- (c_x - b_x)p_z + (c_z - b_z)p_x = 0$$

Eliminating the $\alpha\beta$ terms from the equations for the y and z ordinates gives:

$$\alpha[a_z(c_y - b_y) - a_y(c_z - b_z)] + \beta[b_z(c_y - b_y) - b_y(c_z - b_z)]$$
$$- (c_y - b_y)p_z + (c_z - b_z)p_y = 0$$

These two equations will give a single solution for α and β, providing, as in the matrix formulation, the system is non-singular. It can be shown that the matrix is singular if the three direction vectors $\mathbf{a}$, $\mathbf{b}$ and $\mathbf{c}$ are in one plane. Thus this method can not be used for planar quadrilaterals.

The alternative approach is to map triangles. If, as shown in Figure 9.3, the quadrilateral is divided into two triangles, each triangle can be mapped separately into texture space. For the left-hand triangle:

$$\mathbf{p} = \alpha\mathbf{a} + \beta\mathbf{b}$$

and for the right-hand triangle:

$$\mathbf{q} = -\gamma\mathbf{d} - \delta\mathbf{c}$$

Clearly:

$$\gamma = 1 - \alpha$$
$$\delta = 1 - \beta$$

(a)

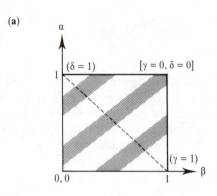

(b)

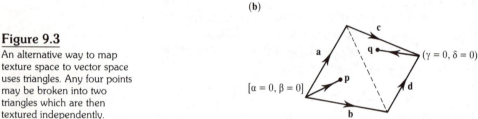

Figure 9.3

An alternative way to map texture space to vector space uses triangles. Any four points may be broken into two triangles which are then textured independently.

This way of mapping also works for non-convex quadrilaterals and, indeed, for any four non-planar points. However, it is necessary to identify which of the two triangles the point belongs to.

There is of course no need to confine texture mapping to planar objects. Any correspondence between object space and texture space can be used. For example, it is possible to map the unit square in texture space on to the surface of a cylinder, with the radial angle linearly related to one texture parameter and the axial length to the other. This mapping is easy to invert for the purposes of ray tracing. Mapping on to a sphere can be done in a similar way, once an axis has been chosen. The texture collapses into a point where the axis cuts the surface of the sphere. Parameterized spline surfaces are trivially mapped by setting the surface parameters $[\mu, \nu]$ equal to the texture parameters.

One important class of textures that are used in painting systems, and as part of flight simulators, are bitmaps. The texture space is quantized at some resolution and the mapping to the raster screen is on a pixel-to-pixel basis. In this case, the result is subject to alias frequencies appearing, due to the sampling in both the texture transformation and in the rasterization of the final scene. For this reason, some form of anti-aliasing is essential. This can be applied in exactly the same way as described in Chapter 3; however, better results will be obtained if some account is taken of the relative sizes of the texture map and the object being textured, in terms of the number of pixels with which it will be rendered. Thus, if one of the image pixels maps through the two transformations to an area in texture space of 3 × 3 pixels or less, the 3 × 3 convolution filter used in Chapter 3 will give adequate results. This filter is a 2D version of the third-order *B*-spline blending function introduced in Chapter 6. Higher-order blending functions become progressively wider and can therefore be used in cases where a larger number of pixels in texture space map into single image pixels. The effect of this is progressive blurring, which gives the right effect for distant objects. In cases where there are more image pixels than texture pixels, the effect is one of pixel replication. This will introduce unpleasant features in the image, and is best avoided.

Texture maps can also be used to specify reflectance properties in a ray tracing system. For example, an object may be made up of a number of planar facets. When a point on the surface is identified, its corresponding point can be found in the associated texture maps which specify not absolute pixel values, but rather the constants controlling diffuse and specular reflection. These maps can be chosen to create changes in colour and shine, or to create the impression of unevenness on the surface. The reflection and translucency properties can also be varied to create effects such as engraved mirrors or ground glass vessels. The tiles in Colour Plates 15 and 16 were created using this technique. They appear to have bevelled edges, but they were created with planar facets. A texture map was used to determine the surface normal, which was made to turn away at the edges.

Schemes have also been devised to map the illumination of an object. In this case, it is not the Cartesian co-ordinate that is mapped on to texture space, but the surface normal. The texture map, or illumination map as it is called in this case, is therefore best visualized as lying on the surface of a sphere surrounding the object being rendered. Such systems allow precomputation of illumination values and can be used to speed up image generation time.

Textures need not be confined to two dimensions. Systems that aim to model the cutting of materials such as wood or marble require a 3D texture map to describe the grain. Such maps are expensive to store, but can be simply generated using fractal techniques.

9.4.2 Reflectance models

The usual reflectance model, which was discussed in Chapter 7, owes its popularity to its relatively low computational demands. It is, however, a simplification of the normally accepted physical model, which requires greater parameterization. As pointed out by Cook and Torrance (1982), objects rendered in this manner have the appearance of plastic, and this is because a plastic has a substrate that is uncoloured, with pigment particles embedded into it. Thus, reflected light is not significantly altered in colour,

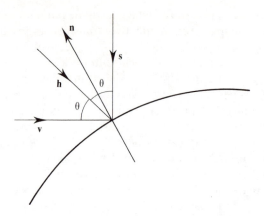

Figure 9.4
Computing the reflectance
properties of a surface using a
detailed physical model.

which is the usual assumption made when computing a specular highlight. Moreover, other physical effects, such as peaks that occur when the incident light is at a grazing angle – see Torrance and Sparrow (1967) – can be included in a more complex model.

A more detailed model of reflectance, used by Cook and Torrance, is described by the basic equation:

$$I_r = I_a K_a + \sum I_l (\boldsymbol{n} \cdot \boldsymbol{s}) \omega \, [t K_s + (1 - t) K_d]$$

The addition of the variable ω to account for the solid angle of the incident beam alters only the intensity of the reflected light. As before, the constants for diffuse and ambient reflection, K_d and K_a, are assumed constant for a given material. The specular component is, however, treated differently. Instead of computing the reflected vector, the unit vector bisecting the angle between the view vector and the vector to the light source, $\boldsymbol{h} = (\boldsymbol{v} + \boldsymbol{s})/2$, is used as shown in Figure 9.4. The specular constant is computed using:

$$K_s = \frac{FDG}{\pi(\boldsymbol{n} \cdot \boldsymbol{s})(\boldsymbol{n} \cdot \boldsymbol{v})}$$

G is a term that accounts for the masking of the reflected light due to unevenness in the surface. It is computed using:

$$G = \text{minimum}(1, \beta \boldsymbol{n} \cdot \boldsymbol{v}, \beta \boldsymbol{n} \cdot \boldsymbol{s})$$

where:

$$\beta = \frac{2\boldsymbol{n} \cdot \boldsymbol{h}}{\boldsymbol{v} \cdot \boldsymbol{h}}$$

D accounts for the local spread of the surface normals at a micro level. It is most simply computed using a Gaussian distribution, yielding:

$$D = n \exp\left(-\left(\frac{\alpha}{m}\right)^2\right)$$

where n and m are constants, and α is the angle between $\boldsymbol{n}$ and $\boldsymbol{h}$.

The greatest flexibility in the model comes from the inclusion of F, which is computed from a simplified version of the Fresnel equation:

$$F = \frac{\dfrac{p^2}{q^2}\left[1 + \dfrac{(cq - 1)^2}{(cp + 1)^2}\right]}{2}$$

where $c = \boldsymbol{v} \bullet \boldsymbol{h}$, $p = g - c$, $q = g + c$, $g = \sqrt{(n^2 + c^2 - 1)}$, $n = [1 + \sqrt{(F_0)}]/[1 - \sqrt{(F_0)}]$, and $F = F_0$ when $\theta = 0$.

The last effect that is taken into account is the shift in the wavelength of specularly reflected light with the incidence angle. As the angle approaches $\pi/2$, so the reflected wavelength tends towards that of the source. This effect may be accounted for by treating the computations of red, green and blue separately, and interpolating each between the value for an incidence angle of zero, where the reflection of a white light source approximates to the surface colour, and $\pi/2$, where the reflected light is white. The best results come not by interpolating linearly with angle, but with the constant F.

This model still represents a simplification of the true Fresnel equation, but clearly has greater flexibility in determining surface appearances. Cook and Torrance have obtained a variety of highly realistic surfaces using this form. Although computationally it is not very much more demanding than the conventional model, it suffers the disadvantage that a considerable number of parameters must be specified, and although these are obtainable from standards, they are not easily related to simple intuitive concepts, such as 'shine'. For this reason, such models are not widely adopted in commercial systems.

9.4.3   Camera aperture effects

Human visual perception has to some extent been conditioned by the large number of photographs that can be seen daily in books, magazines and papers. Because of the limitations of the optical system and the photographic process, these contain defects that are interpreted easily by the human eye, so much so that computer-generated images that include the degradation effects of photographs can look more realistic than those that do not. Thus, realism can be improved by incorporating the effect of the lens in a camera in computer-generated pictures.

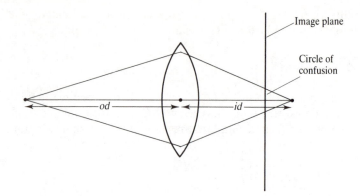

Figure 9.5

To create the effect of a lens projection, each point to be rendered must be focused at a point dependent on its distance from the lens. When the image point is not on the image plane, the visual attributes of the object point must be distributed within the circle of confusion.

In all the treatment to date, straight line projections between the object and the image have been used, which gives a result equivalent to the pinhole camera. In practice, however, a lens does not obey this law, but focuses an object point to an image point, whose distance from the lens is dependent on the object distance. The law that governs this is:

$$\frac{1}{od} + \frac{1}{id} = \frac{1}{f} \tag{9.5}$$

where od is the object distance, id is the image distance and f is the focal length, which is a constant for the lens. Figure 9.5 illustrates the situation where the view surface does not coincide with the image point. In this situation, an object point projects into a circle, called the **circle of confusion**, in the image. If the circle of confusion is sufficiently small, then the object is perceived as in focus. The range of distances for which this is true is called the **depth of focus**. The existence of this depth of focus is frequently exploited to create special effects in photography and film.

Depth of focus can be included in an image generated by ray tracing by computing the pinhole raster, as before, but with the addition that the object distance must be kept for each pixel. This distance is used to compute the diameter of the circle of confusion, and if its diameter is large enough, the returned pixel intensity is distributed among its neighbours. The computation of the diameter of the circle of confusion has been derived from geometric optics by Potmesil and Chakravarty (1982) and is:

$$C_d = \left| 1 - \frac{ip}{id} \right| \frac{f}{n}$$

where id may be computed from Equation (9.5), ip is the distance of the image plane from the lens and n is the aperture stop number.

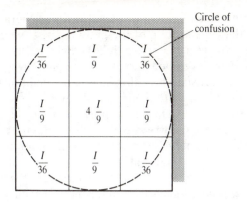

$$\begin{array}{|c|c|c|}
\hline
\dfrac{I}{36} & \dfrac{I}{9} & \dfrac{I}{36} \\
\hline
\dfrac{I}{9} & 4\dfrac{I}{9} & \dfrac{I}{9} \\
\hline
\dfrac{I}{36} & \dfrac{I}{9} & \dfrac{I}{36} \\
\hline
\end{array}$$

Circle of confusion

Figure 9.6
A simple way to distribute the visual attributes of an object point in the circle of confusion shown in Figure 9.5 is to use the 2D B-spline blending functions. For a circle of diameter n pixels, $B^{(n)}$ is used.

Having computed the diameter of the circle of confusion, the incident light intensity must be distributed within it. A simple way of doing this is to set up a number of filters, using, for example, 2D discrete B functions, as discussed in Section 6.7. These are then used as weights to distribute the computed intensities among the adjacent pixels. For example, a pixel where the circle of confusion is between three and four pixels in diameter would result in the intensities being added to nine neighbourhood pixels, as shown in Figure 9.6. Wider masks can be created using the higher-order B-spline blending functions discussed in Section 6.4. This heuristic method, although simple, does not fully model the physics. Better realism is available using a model that takes into account diffraction effects, which is derived by Potsmesil and Chakravarty. Plate 19 shows a picture with camera aperture effects.

9.5 TRADITIONAL METHODS FOR PRODUCING ANIMATED FILMS

The film industry has evolved an effective method of producing animated cartoon films, which is documented by several authors – Hales and Manvell (1968), and Hayward (1984). The methods and techniques will be briefly summarized before considering the question of their computerization.

The starting point for any animated film production is a **scenario**; that is, a textual description of the story detailing scenes and actions. Accompanying the scenario is the story board, which consists of a series of drawings of the most significant moments in the film. These together define a series of **sequences** of actions, corresponding to the acts of a play. Each sequence is divided into a number of scenes, characterized by a uniform location and certain groups of characters. Each scene has a predicted length, defined by the script, and this determines the number of individual frames or shots that are needed.

Thus, the organization of any animated film is hierarchical, and this is paralleled by the organization of the graphic artists who draw the film. The originators provide a few indicative sketches to accompany the scenario, which are then developed into the story board drawings by the most senior of the graphic artists. These drawings form the basic material, which is developed hierarchically into a number of key frames, which define the action of each scene. The last task is to draw the frames that go in between the key frames. These **in-betweens** will, in general, chart out the various stages of a simple movement, such as the raising of an arm, and drawing them is a matter of copying skill, rather than artistic ability.

Individual frames are made up of a number of component parts, which are drawn on cellophane sheets and hence are called **cells**. These are composed together to make the final frame. Thus, the sequence is essentially two-and-half dimensions and the use of opaque paint solves the hidden line removal problem. The use of cells cuts down the amount of drawing required in sequences involving repetition, such as a cartoon figure running. One set of cells can be created to depict one cycle of the body in motion and then used several times with cells depicting new backgrounds. Other effects, such as panning, or moving one cell horizontally relative to the others, may be easily incorporated.

The final stage of the process is filming the resulting frames. This is done on a rostrum camera, which is a device that allows accurate control of the camera position relative to the cells. Additional effects may be used at this stage, such as panning the whole image, tilting – a slightly misleading name for linear movement on the vertical axis – and spinning. Zoom can also be achieved by making adjustments to the camera lens. Other widely used effects are accomplished by altering the illumination levels. These include fade in and fade out, and cross-dissolve techniques whereby one image is changed into a different one. The simplest way of doing this is to optically mix two images, one being faded out while the next is faded in. Other cross-dissolve techniques that do not involve fading are popular. Before the advent of computer control, it was usually done by wiping the new image across the old. With raster processing, it is now possible to reduce the old image to any arbitrary area of the screen, and this is regularly done on normal television, as well as in animation.

Synchronization with the soundtrack is achieved by relying on the constant running speed of the film of 24 frames per second. The soundtrack must be recorded before the in-betweening takes place, since it determines the time span between key frames. Synchronization with speech causes particular problems and libraries of lip movements are available to match the individual phonemes making up a word. Synchronization with sound events, such as explosions or impacts, is less critical. Musical synchronization really need only be considered over a musical phrase, which typically takes the order of a few seconds. Even synchronization with a fast musical pulse does not present great problems. For example, the main beats of a

Viennese waltz do not occur more frequently than three per second, or one every eight-frame intervals. Hence, a synchronization error of two or three frames still produces acceptable results.

9.6 EVOLUTION OF COMPUTER-GENERATED ANIMATION

The idea of frame animation is almost certainly as old as drawing. However, the founder of today's industry is usually considered to be Joseph Antoine Plateau, who in 1831 produced a device called the phenakisto-scope. This consisted of a spinning disk with drawings that could be viewed through framing windows. Almost at the same time, Horner produced a device called the zoetrope, in which the drawings were produced on the inner surface of a drum. The individual frames could be viewed through slits in the inner rotating drum as they came past a fixed framing slit, through which the viewer looked. Devices of this sort became highly popular during the last half of the previous century, so much so that in 1892 Emile Reynaud opened the Theatre Optique in Paris. The popularity of such devices, especially the notorious 'what the butler saw' machines found at seaside resorts, continued well into the twentieth century.

Paralleling this development in frame animation, photography evolved fast in the last half of the nineteenth century. One major figure was Eduard Muybridge, who in 1874 produced a sequence of photographs showing the details of a horse galloping. His intention was to demonstrate that all four legs leave the ground together at one point in the cycle – his photographs were not intended as the basis of frame animation. However, they had an important influence on contemporary art and the perception of motion. Motion pictures themselves began just before the turn of the century and the first film using animation was drawn in negative to avoid reversal processing of the film. By 1909, the scale of animated films had expanded. 'Gertie the trained Dinosaur' made by Winsor McCay required 10 000 drawings. In 1915, Earl Hurd introduced the idea of cell animation. In 1928, the first synchronized sound/vision film was produced, introducing the most famous of cartoon figures, Mickey Mouse. In 1938, Walt Disney produced 'Snow White and the Seven Dwarfs'. This film, being of feature length, required over 100 000 frames to be constructed. The investment in terms of artists' time was so great that many people thought it would be a commercial failure. However, the box office success justified the expense and paved the way for other full-length cartoon films.

The animated film industry was well established when the computer made its first contributions. One of the early pioneers was Bell Laboratories in New Jersey, USA. Knowlton (1965) describes some of the work carried out there. The system used a raster image with 252×184 pixels, using eight levels of intensity – that is, only 3-bit planes. One important feature was the introduction of a simple language with statements to specify characters and fonts, lines and arcs, and fill areas. Although this simple system could not produce many of the appealing effects available with hand-drawn animation, it was used successfully to produce teaching films, including moving diagrams and visualization of an orbiting satellite. One movie, lasting about 20 minutes, contained 25 000 frames, of which 3000 were different. This film was specified by about 2000 lines of code and took two man-months to produce. This was therefore an important breakthrough, since the effort required to produce these somewhat limited animated films was far less than that required by conventional methods.

The work at Bell Laboratories was primarily directed at the scientific and education world. However, it was not long before the importance of the computer to the animation industry was realized. Advances in real-time systems allowed the computer to automate the control of the rostrum camera. Kallis (1971) describes a system capable of carrying out sequences of operations using pan, tilt, spin and zoom. Other non-graphical applications, such as documentation support, could be provided and early systems for drafting were used to produce some of the artwork.

At this stage, research turned to the area of the greatest potential gain. Could the computer do automatic in-betweening operations in cartoon animation? In the case of the Bell Laboratories work, the films were made using a computer model of the sequences to be described; hence, in-betweens could be easily constructed. However, in the cartoon industry, the model describing the motion was the property of the animator and difficult to describe algorithmically.

9.7 AUTOMATIC IN-BETWEENING

The first attempts at in-betweening used drawings that were divided into an ordered set of polylines called strokes. The two key frames used would be provided with a mapping of stroke into stroke, which could provide for points appearing and disappearing. Various methods of interpolating between the points defining the strokes were tried. To achieve a satisfactory result, both the path of motion and the dynamics must be correctly specified.

As far as the path is concerned, the key problem is to determine whether it is to be smooth or discontinuous. For example, consider a cartoon figure picking up an object. There may be five key frames depicting this movement, as shown in Figure 9.7. In this case, a smooth motion is

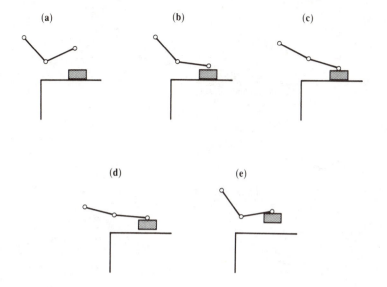

Figure 9.7
Interpolation between key frames to produce realistic animation must take into account the dynamics of motion. If an arm is picking up a weight, there will be a deceleration between key frames (a), (b) and (c), and an acceleration between (c), (d) and (e). The direction of motion changes at (c), and hence a single smooth spline cannot be used to interpolate the points.

required between frames (a), (b) and (c) as the arm comes down to the object. However, at frame (c) a change occurs in the muscular control, and hence a discontinuity should appear in the final film. Thus, the path of the three points of the stroke representing the arm should be defined by two smooth splines: one with knots as defined by frames (a), (b) and (c), the other whose knots are described by frames (c), (d) and (e). Linear interpolation or the use of a single spline would not give correct results in this case.

Creating the correct dynamics of motion is harder. Most natural movements contain a great deal of acceleration and deceleration; thus, the points that are chosen to define the strokes of the in-between frames cannot be placed equally along the spline joining the key frames. To do so would create the effect of a constant velocity. The simplest solution to this problem is to alter the ratio of in-betweens to key frames. Using fewer will give the impression of a faster movement; hence, the effect of an acceleration can be approximated by gradually reducing the number of in-betweens in a sequence of key frames. The degree to which this can be done is constrained by the requirement to synchronize with the sound track. An alternative approach, which is essentially the same, is to fix the number of in-betweens, but to choose the key frames to create the correct dynamic effect. Thus, for a slow movement, the key frames are close, while for a fast movement, they cover a greater Cartesian span. This method relies greatly on the skill of the animator.

Creation of dynamic effect by these methods is a stepwise approximation to what should be a continuous acceleration. The steps become

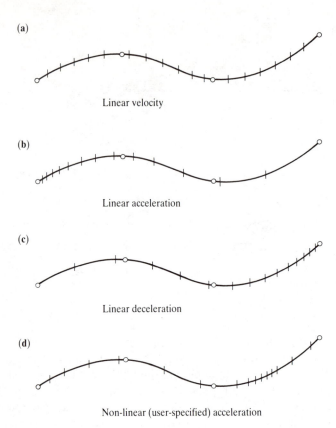

(a)

Linear velocity

(b)

Linear acceleration

(c)

Linear deceleration

(d)

Non-linear (user-specified) acceleration

Figure 9.8
Acceleration can be controlled by the animator by specifying the positions of the in-betweens along the interpolating spline. These may be simply represented by the parametric distances. The positions of the key frames are indicated by circles and the in-betweens by the straight lines.

more apparent as the number of key frames is decreased; hence, using these methods conflicts with the economic advantage that can be gained from automatic in-betweening. Consequently, systems have been written that allow the accelerations to be specified by the animator. Examples are described by Baecker (1969) and Reeves (1981). In essence, these systems allow the user to specify the parametric distances along the spline trajectory at which the in-between frames will occur. By this method, linear accelerations can be computed with little intervention from the animator. Non-linear acceleration effects can be produced with great flexibility. Figure 9.8 shows a typical spline trajectory. Four cases of different accelerations are shown by marking the position of each actual frame along the spline.

In some circumstances, it may be possible to model dynamic effects by recourse to physical laws. One example of this is the satellite model already discussed. These techniques are, however, usually not appropriate for 2D animation, where a complete dynamic model is not available.

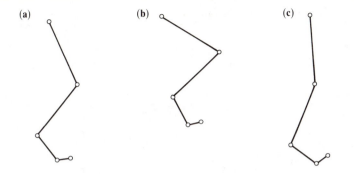

Figure 9.9
One technique used to create plausible movement is to give a skeleton to the figure being animated. Three key frames in a walking sequence could be represented by the the skeleton positions (a), (b) and (c).

Another problem facing the animator is how to maintain the movement of cartoon figures within plausible bounds. From time to time, humorous effects can be created by the stretching and contracting of particular limbs; however, for satisfactory results, these must be confined to highlights. To aid the animator, constraints can be applied by means of skeleton techniques, which were introduced by Burtnyk and Wein (1976). The idea is that many cartoon figures can be approximated by a jointed skeleton. Figure 9.9 shows how a leg could be approximated in key frames, which could be part of a walking movement. The point to observe is that the distance between adjacent joints in the skeleton is fixed. Hence, it is easy to devise an interactive animation system where adjacent points along a limb can be moved according to these constraints until the correct position is obtained. Using just a skeleton, a very fast interactive turnover is possible, since the compilations involved are shorter – less points are required and the interaction is governed by simple laws. Once the correct dynamic behaviour has been obtained with a skeleton, 'flesh' can be drawn about it to create the final image. This can be done automatically by defining a shape in one position. The method is similar to the mapping of texture, which was discussed in Section 9.4.

A point on the flesh may be defined by a scalar pair (μ, ν) where μ represents the distance along the bone and ν the distance away from the bone. Figure 9.10 shows how a point is computed. The unit vectors v_1 and v_2 are chosen so that they bisect the angle between the adjacent 'bone' sections. The unit vector v_3 interpolates v_1 and v_2. At a distance μ along v_4:

$$v_3 = (1 - \mu)v_1 + \mu v_2$$

So, within the segment, the position of the point (μ, ν) is given by:

$$\mu v_4 + \nu v_3 \quad \text{or} \quad \mu v_4 + \nu(1 - \mu)v_1 + \mu \nu v_2$$

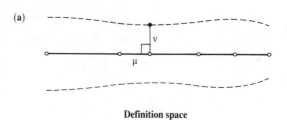

Definition space

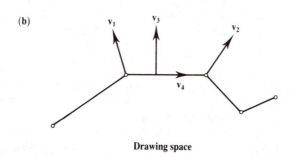

Drawing space

Figure 9.10
Flesh can be added to a skeleton in the same way that texture is mapped on to a quadrilateral. For each bone segment, the flesh position is described in a definition space in terms of scalar parameters μ and ν. In the drawing space these parameters are used to interpolate the bisector vectors at the joints.

and this relative position may be translated into an absolute position by adding the position vector of the second joint. Hence, for any set of co-ordinates for the joints, it is possible to determine the vectors v_1, v_2 and v_4, and from these compute a unique position for (μ, ν). Thus, the flesh can be added by selecting a number of characteristic points in each segment from one frame and computing the (μ, ν) values using these in subsequent frames. A simple continuity law applies at the joints; that is, the values in the adjacent segments must be the same.

This simple scheme implies a certain elasticity in that the volume is not preserved. Other more complex schemes could be devised to take that into account.

9.8 TEMPORAL ANTI-ALIASING

In Chapter 3, a discussion of alias frequencies, which create the unpleasant spatial effect of jagged lines on a raster display, was given. This phenomenon is essentially the result of presenting a continuous spatial image as a set of sampled points on the raster display.

Problems also occur when presenting a motion as a discrete set of frames sampling that motion. These are a result of sampling and occur in any film or television production. The essential characteristic is that

Algorithm 9.1

Continuous filter temporal anti-aliasing.

```
for each pixel of the image do
begin
    { Find all the sub-objects that project on to that pixel during the frame interval }
    for each sub-object found do
    begin
        { Determine the temporal span when it projects on to that pixel }
        { Add the start and finish times to an ordered list }
    end;
    { Find which object is visible between each pair of times on the ordered list }
    { Deduce the pixel intensity by combining the visible object attributes }
end
```

motion, especially at high speed, becomes jerky. This effect is very pronounced in pre-1914 films, which often used a low frame rate. Other
artefacts occur with repeated movements. These include wheels appearing
to spin backwards and rain appearing to fall upwards.

Temporal aliasing is more severe in the case of computer-generated
images, since in a film each frame represents an average sample taken over
about one-half the frame time. Typically, the shutter will open for $1/50^{th}$
second and, after it has shut, a further $1/50^{th}$ second will be taken up in
advancing the film one frame. The half-frame average creates the effect of
a motion blur, which is easily interpreted as part of a continuous movement. For conventional frame animation, there is no blurring. The figures
are created at one instant in time and filmed fixed on the rostrum camera.
Consequently, the effects of temporal alias frequencies become more
acute.

The main methods used for removing this problem correspond
directly to those used in the spatial case – that is, continuous filtering and
super-sampling. The continuous algorithm requires a function describing
the movement of each sub-object, and works on a pixel-by-pixel basis, as
shown in Algorithm 9.1.

Algorithm 9.1 is further illustrated by Figure 9.11. For the frame
interval shown, three objects are visible from the pixel whose intensity is
being computed. The objects and the temporal spans, when they project
on to the pixel, are depicted by the horizontal lines. The computation of
these spans must be done by the use of functions that describe the

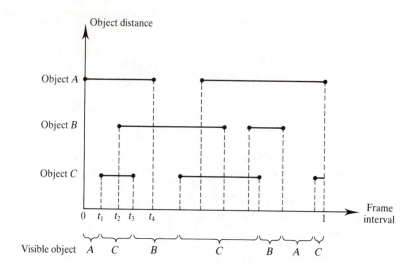

Figure 9.11
In temporal anti-aliasing, it is necessary to determine the times during a frame interval when an object is visible from a pixel. Here, three objects cover the pixel at different times, indicated by the solid lines. A depth test is then used to discover which objects are visible in which time interval.

movements of the objects. The ordered list of start and finish times is $[0, t_1, t_2, \ldots, 1]$. For a simple two-and-half dimensional system, the computation of which object is visible in each time interval is trivial, in the case shown, for $[0..t_1]$, object A is visible; for $[t_1..t_2]$, object C is visible, and so on. For a complex 3D animation, a depth test is required for each interval.

The simplest way of combining the attributes of the visible objects to arrive at a pixel intensity is to take their time average; however, a variety of other effects can be created by weighting the intensities with a suitable filter.

The weighting can be computed as an integral. If the time scale is chosen so that the inter-frame interval is one time unit, then the filter is a function $f(\tau)$ defined over $[0\ldots1]$ with the restriction that:

$$\int_0^1 f(\tau)\, d\tau = 1$$

If the pixel intensity is given by $s(\tau)$, which in the case of the continuous algorithm will be a piecewise function defined separately over each subinterval, then the resulting pixel intensity is given by:

$$\int_0^1 f(\tau)s(\tau)\, d\tau$$

The choice of filter function determines the effect created. For example, the wedge filter Figure 9.12(a) creates the effect of objects trailing away, somewhat like a comet. The box filter in Figure 9.12(b) represents a simple time average and so is the easiest to compute. Another

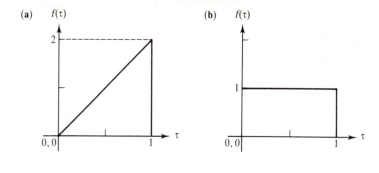

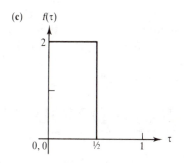

Figure 9.12
To determine the illumination of the pixel for the frame interval, the visible object attributes found by the method illustrated in Figure 9.11 are combined using a weighted average. Using filter (b), a simple average is used. Using (a), more prominence is given to later events, giving fast-moving objects a comet's tail. Using filter (c), the effect of a movie camera, whose aperture is shut for one-half of the frame interval while the film is advanced, is simulated.

filter, shown in Figure 9.12(c), would give an effect equivalent to the film motion blur.

This method suffers from computational problems; in particular, when computing the times at which a complex sub-object overlaps with a pixel. For this reason, it has been restricted to systems that use simple geometric shapes. For complex objects and movements, the super-sampling approach is normally adopted.

The super-sampling approach depends on generating further images at a fixed set of times through the frame interval. This can be done by computing many more in-betweens. The set of images is then combined, again using a filter function. Super-sampling is the basis of the technique used by conventional animators when conveying motion by means of 'speed lines'. The effect is shown in Figure 9.13, which also emphasizes the importance of filtering. The ball and foot appear at one position only; the images prior to that diminish with time.

Super-sampling can, however, cause unpleasant results, especially when objects are moving fast, due to the spaghetti effect, where several disparate images of the same object can be observed with equal intensities. The unpleasantness of this can be slightly ameliorated by using a higher sample rate.

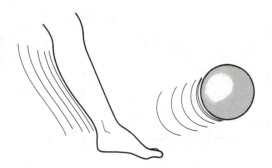

Figure 9.13
Super-sampling is a technique known to cartoonists who use speed lines to indicate motion. The speed lines are simply drawings of part of each super-sample.

Consideration of how the integral in the continuous method is computed in practice demonstrates that as the number of samples taken in the super-sampling method increases, the two methods become equivalent.

9.9   3D ANIMATED MODELS

Animation in three dimensions is analogous to the 2D case already studied and many of the methods discussed apply, at least in principle. Techniques already described for rendering 3D wire frames or solids can be directly applied to generate individual frames, with the apparent motion being created by the sequence of frames. Much of the difficulty that arises is how to specify the motion that is required. To avoid the use of mathematical functions, and extensive in-between calculations, track systems have been introduced for motion description by Gomez (1984) and others.

A track is specified for each object parameter that can change in the animation sequence. A track is simply a doubly linked list of events, each event being a discrete change of an object parameter. With this information, it is possible to compute all object parameters for each frame position without redundant calculations, and thus efficiently render successive frames. Sufficient flexibility is available to allow creation of continuous movement, and the method is suitable for temporal anti-aliasing by super-sampling.

As an alternative to the use of track systems, the method of key frames can be applied. This time, however, the interpolation between key frames is more complex, requiring careful attention. Restricting the treatment to rigid bodies, the first principle to be applied is that any 3D movement, which may be specified between two key frames, may be broken down into a translation of the object's centre of gravity and a single rotation about an axis through the centre of gravity. This fact can be used to separate the interpolation problem into two simpler problems.

The translation of the object's centre presents no further difficulties to those that have already been discussed for the 2D case. The interpolation methods using any spline curve are equally applicable to 3D space curves, and methods of specifying accelerations can be applied directly.

Rotation, on the other hand, is harder to interpolate. Adopting the matrix methods described in Chapter 4, any rotation must be broken into three rotations about the Cartesian axes, and these are then separately interpolated and recombined. This is not an easy process to visualize and, moreover, it is expensive in computing time. Accordingly, attention has recently been focused on the use of mathematical entities called **quaternions**, which can be used to describe rotations.

9.9.1 Quaternions

Quaternion algebra is not a new idea, but was worked out originally by Hamilton (1843) and Cayley (1845). A quaternion is a 4-tuple in which the atomic elements are real numbers. It will be represented here using the notation:

$$q = [w, x, y, z]$$

with:

$$|q| = \sqrt{(w^2 + x^2 + y^2 + z^2)}$$

The interpretation given to a quaternion is a scalar and a 3D vector, so it may be written as:

$$q = [\omega, \mathbf{v}]$$

where:

$$\mathbf{v} = [x, y, z] \quad \text{and} \quad \omega = w$$

Addition and multiplication operations over quaternions are defined as follows:

$$[\omega_1, \mathbf{v_1}] + [\omega_2, \mathbf{v_2}] = [\omega_1 + \omega_2, \mathbf{v_1} + \mathbf{v_2}]$$
$$[\omega_1, \mathbf{v_1}] * [\omega_2, \mathbf{v_2}] = [(\omega_1\omega_2 - \mathbf{v_1} \bullet \mathbf{v_2}), (\omega_1\mathbf{v_2} + \omega_2\mathbf{v_1} + \mathbf{v_1} \times \mathbf{v_2})]$$

The definition of multiplication will be seen to be similar to that for complex numbers, with the exception of the cross-product term.

The inverse of a quaternion is defined as:

$$q^{-1} = \frac{[\omega, -\mathbf{v}]}{|\mathbf{q}|^2}$$

and from this definition it follows that:

$$q * q^{-1} = [1, 0, 0, 0]$$

Many of the properties of quaternions are discussed in the original papers, as well as in subsequent applications, such as Brady (1982), Taylor (1982) and Shoemake (1985). In animation, their most useful property is in describing motion, and therefore it is possible to restrict further discussion to unit quaternions; that is, to those for which:

$$|q| = 1$$

To perform a rotation on a vector, using a quaternion, it is necessary to compute:

$$q^{-1} * [0, \mathbf{d}] * q$$

This will produce a quaternion with a zero scalar part. Its vector part represents a rotation of $\mathbf{d}$ about the direction $\mathbf{v}$ with angle θ given by the equation:

$$\omega = \cos\left(\frac{\theta}{2}\right)$$

This can be proved by expanding the quaternion multiplication and equating terms with the Cartesian matrix formulation. Note in passing that since unit quaternions are being used, the magnitude of $\mathbf{v}$ is given by $\sin(\theta/2)$.

Computationally, quaternions do not offer any real advantage over matrix methods, since a full evaluation of a quaternion product requires 22 real multiplications. Although all these multiplications are not required in the rotation formulation, in general 36 multiplications per rotation are necessary, as opposed to the 27 multiplications required for three orthogonal rotations in homogeneous co-ordinates.

The gain in using quaternions comes from the simple interpolation methods that they offer. Starting from some reference position, the orientation of a body in each successive key frame can be described by the quaternion effecting a rotation from the reference position to that new position. Interpolation between key frames then reduces to interpolating between associated quaternions, starting with the identity quaternion $\mathbf{i} = [1, 0, 0, 0]$, which produces a zero rotation, and is therefore associated with the reference position. The choice of interpolation method

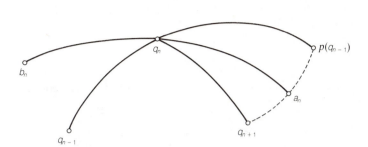

Figure 9.14
Quaternion interpolation is done by means of blending, akin to the Overhauser spline. The path leaving q_n is along the arc bisecting the arc from q_n to q_{n+1} and the arc from q_n to $p(q_{n-1})$, which is the projection of q_{n-1} through q_n. The approach to q_n is along the same path. In the interval between q_n and q_{n+1}, this path is blended with the corresponding path for q_{n+1}.

determines how the resulting motion appears. Linear interpolation between the individual atoms of two quaternions gives an effect of acceleration followed by deceleration, which is undesirable, except in a few cases.

A second scheme, which avoids this possibility, is to use spherical interpolation. In this case, the unit quaternions are thought of as forming a hyper-sphere in 4D space, analogous to the Gaussian sphere formed by the complete set of unit vectors in three dimensions. Then, the interpolation is taken along the great arc between the quaternions. The great arc is the shortest distance between two points on the surface of a sphere. Parametrically, this may be expressed as:

$$q(\mu) = \left[\frac{\sin((1-\mu)\phi)}{\sin(\phi)} \right] q_1 + \left[\frac{\sin(\mu\phi)}{\sin(\phi)} \right] q_2 \qquad (9.6)$$

where:

$$\cos(\phi) = q_1 \bullet q_2$$

(the 4D dot product).

This scheme is a viable one for practical animation systems. However, as with the simple interpolation schemes used in the 2D case, there can be an unpleasant visual effect caused by the first-order discontinuity at the key frames. This effect can be removed by a process of 'blending' the successive curve pieces between adjacent key frames. A technique for doing this has been proposed by Shoemake (1985). The principle is shown in Figure 9.14.

The point $p(q_{n-1})$ is defined by projecting the great arc from q_{n-1} to q_n and an equal distance beyond q_n. Thus, the path $q_{n-1} \rightarrow q_n \rightarrow p(q_{n-1})$ is a continuous great arc on the sphere. This arc is blended with the next segment by a simple averaging. Thus, at q_n, the movement is chosen to be along the arc from q_n to a_n, which bisects the arc between $p(q_{n-1})$ and q_{n+1}. To ensure that continuity is assured at q_n, it follows that the object must arrive at q_n along the arc from b_n to q_n, where b_n is defined as $p(a_n)$ that is, the projection of a_n through q_n. Similarly, the arrival at q_{n+1} must be along the arc from b_{n+1} to q_{n+1}. Thus, if:

$$q(\mu) = S(q_1, q_2, \mu)$$

is the spherical interpolant of Equation (9.6), the blended curve between q_n and q_{n+1} can be written as

$$q(\mu) = (1 - \mu)S(q_n, a_n, \mu) + \mu S(b_{n+1}, q_{n+1}, \mu)$$

This equation can be used to compute an arbitrary number of in-betweens and, as before, the parameter spacings can be used to create dynamic effects.

9.9.2 Soft objects

The restriction to rigid objects that has been so far used limits 3D animation in its realism. In practice, objects do deform and, as mentioned for the 2D case, many interesting effects arise from such deformations. Soft objects can be created by means of spline surfaces, with distortions created by moving the knots relative to each other. This is essentially the method used in the 2D skeleton case, which has the further restriction of maintaining the inter-knot distance. However, extending this case to three dimensions is difficult, since the relation between the knot positions and the surface is difficult to visualize, and, moreover, the rendering of such objects, if done by ray tracing, is expensive in computing time.

A simpler method of describing a class of soft objects has been introduced by Blinn (1982) and applied in animation by Wyvill *et al* (1986). The basis of the method is to consider objects to be made up from one or more point sources of charge, with the object surface being a field contour of fixed intensity. Since the aim is not to describe an accurate physical model, but to create visual effect, the equation describing the field may be chosen heuristically. Good results are available using:

$$F(\mathbf{P}) = \sum \alpha_i \exp(-\beta_i r_i^2)$$

where for point source i, α_i is the charge, r_i is the distance of the point source to the point $\mathbf{P}$ and β_i controls the rate at which the field decays. The surface is defined by the point where $F(\mathbf{P})$ is some threshold value T.

The rendering of objects defined in this way requires that the first point on the ray where the field exceeds the threshold is found. For multiple sources, this must be done iteratively. The search can be guided by computing the point where the distance between each point source and the ray is a minimum. These points will be local maxima and the first of these to exceed the threshold can be used as a starting point for the method of false position, or, alternatively, it could be used to produce an initial guess for a Newton Raphson iteration.

Having found the nearest intersection, the next problem is to determine the surface normal, which is simply the surface gradient defined by:

$$\left[\frac{\partial F}{\partial x}, \frac{\partial F}{\partial y}, \frac{\partial F}{\partial z}\right]$$

Here, the choice of field equation gives the advantage of a simple differential:

$$\frac{\partial F}{\partial x} = \sum -2\alpha_i(x - x_i) \exp(-\alpha_i r_i^2)$$

with similar equations for y and z.

This method has the advantage that object deformations may be specified by movements of the point sources. This can create effects such as objects breaking up and rejoining, which can be deployed for modelling fluids. Moreover, reflections and refractions require little extra computation, since the transformation of the scene into a new co-ordinate system requires transformation of the positions of the point sources only. Lastly, special effects can be created by assigning reflectance properties to each point source and combining these according to their distance from the point of intersection.

9.9.3 Particle systems

The creation of objects using pseudo-physical laws is becoming increasingly popular in computer graphics. One example is the use of particle systems, which can model objects with ill-defined boundaries such as clouds smoke and fire. The idea is to treat these objects as a collection of particles, each with specified dynamic properties. Accurate modelling of the physics of a particle system is not attempted, since extensive computation would be required. Instead, heuristic laws are used which will approximate the desired effect. Ultimately, the choice of these laws will be a compromise between physical, and therefore visual, accuracy, and computation time.

Depending on the desired effect, between 10000 and 100000 particles are used. The behaviour is created by computing the position of each particle at a frame instant. The image is then rendered using ray tracing, summing the effect of all particles projecting on to each pixel.

In computer terms, each particle will have a record that includes position, velocity, direction of movement, size, shape, colour, transparency and lifetime. In most cases, this record can be compacted by fixing the size and shape, typically to a small sphere, and considering the particles as opaque. Even so, at least seven real numbers and 7 bytes (35 bytes) will be required. So, the full system could require 3.5 Mbytes to store.

The choice of initial position of particles depends on the effect to be created. For example, to model smoke emanating from a chimney, new particles would need to be created in the mouth of the chimney, randomly distributed. Similarly, the initial direction of movement would be along the axis of the stack. The initial velocity would probably be best modelled conforming to a uniform distribution. Thus:

$$v_0 = v_m + r\,var$$

where v_m is the required mean velocity, var is the required variance, and r is a random number between -1 and 1.

Since smoke attenuates the light, it would not need a specified colour, but a transparency factor would be required to determine the final pixel intensity, and the particles would themselves reflect a gray intensity from the sources. The reflected light can be treated as a constant for each particle, since the notion of a normal vector from a particle is inappropriate. The lifetime, in frames, and the number of particles created in a time interval would be selected to determine the volume of the smoke.

The dynamics of the system are computed according to the effect to be created. The velocity, for example, could be computed by a vector addition of the particle velocity and the wind velocity. Similarly, diffusion forces, whose intensity depends on the particle density, could be incorporated to make the smoke disperse. This effect to some extent depends on the temperature gradient above the chimney. The computation of the dynamic properties of each particle must be carried out once for every frame, or twice if motion blur is required.

Lastly, the ray trace algorithm may need some modification if the particles are so small that several must be summed at a pixel. Specifically, it would be necessary to define a pixel as a rectangular area of the screen. Thus, the ray becomes a thin pyramid for perspective projection or a rectangular section box for orthographic and the problem is to find all particles whose centres fall within that shape, up to the first real object intersection, if any, that is found. The pixel value is found by summing the particle intensities and the transmitted intensity.

Particle systems were successfully used to model fire and explosions for the film 'The Wrath of Khan'. The use is described by Reeves (1983). The sequence in question depicted a bomb exploding on a barren planet, which was subsequently surrounded by a fire wall. Several particle systems were employed, each emanating particles from a circular area on the planet surface, whose direction of motion was distributed about the normal. The particle motion was described entirely by the initial velocity and a gravitational force. One large system, with a short lifetime, was used to depict the initial explosion. Subsequent spreading of the fire wall was created by smaller systems, which began producing particles at subsequent frame intervals. These were distributed in concentric rings around the system depicting the explosion.

Since the velocity was fairly high, and the particles were emitting light, rather than reflecting and attenuating as in the case of smoke, the scene was not drawn by ray tracing, but by following each particle trajectory over a half-frame interval and updating the pixels it covered. This could not be done by summing the values, and since a maximum intensity is available at each pixel, an exponential method of updating was required. The scene, although effective, falls short of realistic fire, since the individual movements of particles remain visible at the resolution generated.

Although at first sight it may be thought that very expensive equipment is required to produce this type of scene, this is not true. A particle system could be readily computed on a 32-bit machine. The ray tracing of a 512×512 scene requires 250K intersection computations for each potentially visible object, whereas the genesis bomb required only 100K. So, the order of time to compute a particle system is comparable to a ray trace.

9.10 REAL-TIME ANIMATION

Systems that successfully create animation in real time have generally done so by either making use of specific features of the machine or by increasing the available computer power – for example, by means of pipelined computation. The former class of system is often found in computer games, which can be created around special operations performed on the frame buffer. The latter class result from systems that aim to solve a real-world problem where the computer's functionality may not match the problem. This is usually the case where animation systems are required for teaching specific skills, such as flight simulation.

9.10.1 Frame buffer techniques

Movement of a small object in the foreground of a scene is one example of a frame buffer technique widely used in arcade video games. Such objects are sometimes termed **sprites**. The required operations are, firstly, saving the area of the screen where the sprite is to be written, then writing the sprite and, finally, restoring the background, before repeating the

Figure 9.15

Animating flow in pipes can be done without addressing the raster at all. Instead, the colour lookup table is changed. The vertical rows of pixels are allocated to successive entries in the lookup table as shown. Each cycle, the lookup table entries are copied to the next higher index, with entry 9 being copied to entry 0. Thus, in 10 short operations, the pixels appear to move one step to the right.

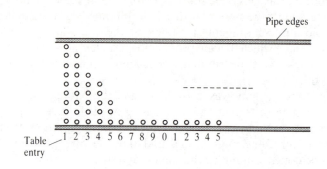

operations with the sprite in its next position. Thus, the movement only requires the updating of a small portion of the raster. The availability of raster operations in modern graphics systems makes this type of animation very fast.

Another technique that can be used in specific cases is to change the entries in the colour lookup table. This table, for a low-price system, has 256 colours, and apparent movement can be created by permuting these. A good example of where this could be used is for simulating movement along pipes in chemical process plant diagrams. For example, if a section of horizontal pipe is defined by the repeating pixel patterns shown in Figure 9.15, where each vertical line of pixels has the same colour table entry, then movement can be achieved by permuting the table entries such that one is copied to two, two to three, and so on. The last entry in position nine is copied to zero. By performing these few operations, movement can be created at any position on the screen. For piping diagrams, the 10 entries used can be different shades of one colour, ranging from dark to light for best effect.

9.10.2 Flight simulation

Flight simulators are systems that belong to the second class; namely, those where there is no special property of the computer that can be exploited. A flight simulator contains a geometric model of the terrain over which it is to fly, an image processor to draw a current view and a mathematical model to describe the dynamic behaviour of the aircraft. The latter reads the cockpit controls and computes a current viewpoint to pass to the image generation system. It also provides outputs to a set of hydraulic rams, which give an appropriate change of movement to the cockpit. The displays are raster graphic and require that the total computation be achieved in the standard frame time of 1/25th second.

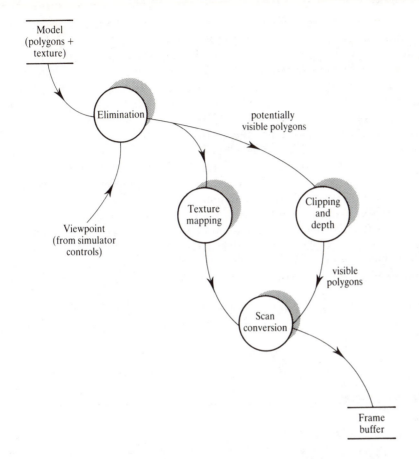

Figure 9.16

Flight simulation is one example where calculations are carried out in a pipeline. Here, three stages are used, allowing three processors to work in parallel.

The cost of building a flight simulator is very high, and as a consequence the computer hardware is itself a trivial part of the cost. Thus, simulators aim to utilize as much parallelism as is possible. Even so, the rendering times required by standard techniques such as fractals, particles or translucency models make them inapplicable. Consequently, a compromise is required between realism and response, and, in practice, current systems only use textured polygons to generate the image.

The simplest way of achieving parallelism is to break the raster image into several parts that can be computed and displayed separately. This is indeed done, with the resulting images being joined together by a projection system that merges the images by fading in and out at the edges. There is a limit to how far this technique can be applied, since the projectors need mechanical alignment, which is time consuming and costly in that it reduces the availability of the simulator. Consequently, three to five independent images are generated. A panorama effect is created by generating the images at different view directions.

The software follows in outline Figure 9.16. The first process, elimination, is used to remove any polygons that cannot be seen. This can be done in a variety of ways. For example, an object space subdivision by octrees can be intersected with a cone of view, yielding a list of potentially visible volumes, which can be easily converted to a polygon list. Further removal can be done on a depth basis. The potentially visible polygons can be processed to return the correct depth information and to clip to the cone of view. At the same time, the textures associated with the potentially visible polygons can be adjusted to compensate for the depth and view angle. This information can then be processed by a scan conversion system, based on a *z*-buffer type algorithm, suitably modified to compensate for translucent textures. This must eliminate the invisible polygons, then draw the others in reverse depth order with appropriate textures.

Effects such as changing illumination intensity are produced at scan conversion time, using a simple flat shading model, without specular reflection. Shadows are included as fixed polygons in the database or as moving polygons at a fixed position relative to any moving objects included in the simulation.

The scheme shown in Figure 9.16 may be computed in a parallel pipeline employing four processors. The way in which this can be done is discussed in the next chapter.

Exercises

9.1 Devise a possible menu structure for a paintbox system. Indicate which items on your menus would also be available in a CAD drafting system.

9.2 List the effects that you could create by mapping the unit surface normal vector on to a planar facet.

9.3 For a camera projection model, a lens of focal length 50 units is chosen. The image plane is 55 units from the lens. The aperture stop number is 2.8 and an object point is 300 units from the lens. What is the diameter of the circle of confusion on the image plane?

9.4 Is there any difference between the texture-mapping scheme given in Section 9.3 and the method given for fleshing out skeletons in Section 9.6?

9.5 What is the difference between spatial and temporal anti-aliasing? What are the common features?

9.6 What is a sprite? Make a list of possible applications.

Problems

9.7 A brush in a paint system is defined as an ellipse with major axis a and minor axis b. During brush strokes, it is always aligned so that the major axis is parallel to the x axis. If a brush trajectory is defined by the equation $y = f(x)$ for the centre of the ellipse, derive an equation for the envelopes of the trajectory.

9.8 Using the texture mapping of Section 9.3, will a straight line in texture space map into a straight line on a planar quadrilateral in object space? Under what conditions will the map of the line be contained within the quadrilateral?

9.9 For a camera projection model, a lens of focal length 135 units is chosen. The image plane is 145 units from the lens. The image being created is in the square with corners $[-50, -50]$ and $[50, 50]$ on the image plane, and a 512×512 raster screen is being used. Find the depth of focus for apertures of 2.8 and 16. The depth of focus is the range over which the circle of confusion projects into one pixel.

9.10 Prove that the vector part of the result of quaternion multiplication:

$$q_{-1} * [0, \mathbf{d}] * q$$

where $q = [\omega, \mathbf{v}]$ represents a rotation of $\mathbf{d}$ by $2 \arccos(\omega)$ about $\mathbf{v}$.

9.11 Discuss the role of heuristics in producing realistic images. Give several examples of their use and indicate what advantages they have over full physical models, and in what way they fall short.

Projects

9.12 Write a system to support skeleton animation. Your system should include a key frame editor, automatic in-betweening and some means of specifying the dynamics of motion. Initially, linear interpolation can be used for computing the in-betweens, but if time permits, try the effect of cubic splines for continuous movement. A further extension of the system is to include fleshing out the skeletons and introducing cells into the data structure to create a full two-and-half dimensional animation system.

9.13 Write a system to demonstrate the effects of temporal anti-aliasing. Use coloured circles as the main primitive and some simple mechanism for specifying their motion. Try out both the continuous and super-sampled methods, using a range of different filters.

9.14 Write a particle system for describing the movement of smoke from a chimney. Try experimenting with the heuristic rules suggested in this chapter, as well as any others you think appropriate.

10 | Hardware for Interactive Graphics

Currently, the field of specialized hardware for graphics is experiencing a dramatic change and expansion with new hardware devices and systems appearing practically every month. An entire textbook would be needed to cover all aspects of this field. This chapter presents the salient features of the 'hardware solution' to graphics which, no doubt, will play a very significant role in the field of interactive graphics in the near future. The 'classical' hardware solutions, such as graphics engines, parallel processing and pipelining, are discussed along with other more novel schemes under development, such as pixel planes and data flow machines. The hardware structure is divided into hierarchical levels similar to the functional, procedural and device levels of the software. The lowest – that is, pixel driver hardware level exists because of the structure of the frame buffer; therefore, no similar level exists in software. Direct operations on the frame buffer, such as hardware zooming, windowing, character generation, BitBlt and PixelBlt operations, provide at least a two orders of magnitude improvement in execution speed as compared to executing these operations by software. Parallel processing and pipelining on the lowest hardware levels provide further improvements in speed. Finally, as an example of a practical system, the hardware instruction set of a small inexpensive system used by the authors to produce most of the illustrations in this book are described. No doubt, by the time this textbook is published, there will be more advanced graphics systems in use; however, many of the features of this simple system will stand up to the test of time and will survive in the future.

10.1   INTRODUCTION

In Chapter 1, it was shown that the computational requirements of interactive graphics applications for realistic coloured images at an acceptable resolution are extremely high. To date, the chapters have presented mainly software methods to satisfy these requirements. Ultimately, the designer of a truly interactive complex graphics system must face reality and accept that the only option for satisfying interactive requirements may be a **hardware solution**. Such a solution would combine integrated graphics workstations, which are popularly referred to as **graphics engines**, and special-purpose electronics implementing graphics algorithms. In fact, the latter can now be created with little overhead by means of customized VLSI chips. Thus, it seems only a matter of time before many of the algorithms discussed in the foregoing chapters will be executed by special hardware in the ordinary equipment of computer graphics users.

Progress in solving graphics processing functions by hardware has been governed by economics and technology. The main areas where very expensive graphics systems are accepted are aircraft simulation, entertainment and advertising. The progress in these well-funded fields has been substantial, although very specific to the applications in question. Thus, these hardware solutions have not been very useful to the majority of computer graphics users, since they require special hardware to run on, which most people cannot afford.

The rapid development of VLSI memory and small processor technology has been closing the gap between the unaffordable and realistic hardware solutions. There is a large number of users who require high performance, non-specialized interactive graphics and who can afford medium-priced systems. Engineers using CAD and architects belong to this class. In the past five years, a substantial effort has been made by many large manufacturers to develop the ultimate engineering graphics workstation, which could become an industry standard in these fields. Even though the cited performance of these modern graphics workstations, like the rendering of the visible surfaces of 100 000 Gouraud-shaded polygons in one second, is very impressive, they have not yet been accepted by industry as a standard tool of design. There are many reasons for this: either the price is still too high, the systems are not easy to use for an engineer or architect with little computer background, or the workstations are too specialized and inflexible for special customer requirements.

There are a large number of computer graphics enthusiasts, especially in universities, who have access to ordinary computer equipment with the minimum of specialized graphics hardware. Those in this group that are interested in hardware advancement can do simulation studies to predict improved performance of new hardware equipment. The rest will still work mainly with software and will have to accept that truly interactive systems are out of their reach.

It is very difficult to do justice to computer hardware development, because at the time this book is being written it is in a state of change. Therefore, this chapter describes only a few principal ideas that probably are going to survive the test of time. As far as other current work is concerned, the reader can study some of the many recent conference proceedings and review papers on graphics hardware. A good place to start is the Tutorial published by IEEE (Reghbati and Lee 1988) and the hardware section of the NATO publication on Fundamental Algorithms for Computer Graphics (Earnshaw, 1985).

10.2 GRAPHICS SYSTEM REQUIREMENTS AND SYSTEM STRUCTURE

In a satisfactory interactive system it should not take longer than a second to update the graphics scene after an operator has given a command. Thus, *real time* in the context of most interactive applications means that a response time of the order of a second is required. In systems that require animation, such as aircraft simulators, the requirements are more severe. For a flicker-free display, a minimum of 25 frames per second is required; hence, a full frame must be generated every 40 ms.

On examination of the computing requirements for a high-quality display system that can respond this quickly, it immediately becomes obvious that solely software solutions to the graphics display problem are not possible. A reasonably good resolution display has 1024×1024, or approximately a million pixels, with at least 3 bytes of information per pixel for full colour. Assuming that 1/6th of the total number of pixels is updated for each frame, 500 000 bytes must be prepared per frame, or approximately fifteen million bytes per second must be processed. This speed just about equals the performance of the fastest single processor for its simplest operation. If the application requires a simple 2D transformation to be computed for each point, then the requirement becomes 400 megaflops (400 million floating-point operations per seconds). This is about two orders of magnitude larger than the performance of a high-performance floating-point processor.

Since most modern display systems are raster based, vector displays will not be considered in these discussions. Figure 10.1 is a schematic diagram of a raster scan graphics system built mainly from hardware. Note that distinction is still made here between 'hardware' and 'software'

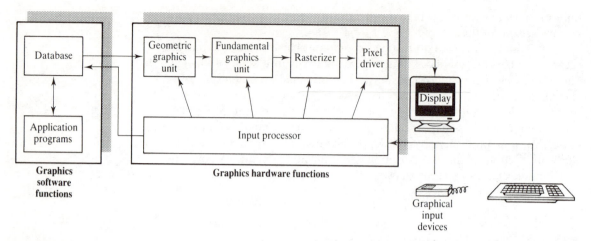

Figure 10.1

Functionally, graphics hardware can be divided into five major subsystems. Four of these, which ultimately control the displayed picture, are hierarchically connected and translate the descriptions of the graphical scene from the highest (functional) to the lowest (pixel) level. The fifth subsystem controls input devices.

components. This distinction is made on a functional basis. Unchangeable graphics facilities provided by the system are accepted as hardware, while the database and the application programs, which are the changeable portion of the system, constitute the software. In small systems, the word 'hardware' is used in a very loose sense, since many of the lower level functions are implemented within the kernel of the operating system. Of course, the operating system may be in a ROM, in which case it becomes true hardware.

The database and application programs have been separated from the hardware elements of the graphics system because it is felt that this will provide the most generally applicable hardware-driven system. Some manufacturers selected the GKS approach, where GKS workstations provide both segment storage and GKS functionality. Such workstations, according to the definition adopted here, become hardware as far as the total system is concerned. In fact, little more can be said about a system peripheral that executes a standard set of graphical functions, except that the application programmer must learn the functionality of the workstation and bend his or her application to its efficient utilization.

As shown in Figure 10.1, the hardware functions are divided into five modules. The output functions are shown to consist of four functional units and three of these can be directly related to the three levels of graphics software: functional, procedural and device levels. There is an additional block called the **pixel driver**, which is unique to graphics hardware, since it operates only on pixel data stored in the frame buffer.

The three hierarchical levels of software are related to three functional units called **geometric graphics**, **fundamental graphics** and **rasterizer**. These functional units can be viewed as data translators (like language processors); they transform the data from a high-level description to the low-level pixel intensities.

The input to the geometric graphics unit is given in terms of functional object definitions. For example, the CSG tree is a well-defined application-oriented database. Individual solid objects with their own attributes, transformations and surface characteristics constitute another well-defined application database. Note that the interactive graphical input devices act directly on the application database, while the graphics hardware system is driven at all times by the current state of the database. This structure is compatible with the evolving PHIGS standard described in Chapter 1.

The output from the geometric graphics unit and the input to the fundamental graphics unit are given in terms of convenient and uniform graphical primitives. For example, shaded planar polygons are currently very popular. For comprehensive graphics systems, more complex primitives such as surface patches, splines or conic sections could be used. Normally, the number of primitives is much larger than the number of geometrically described objects in the application database, but the characteristics of the primitives are much simpler than those of the original objects. There could also be a large loss of semantic information, such as which primitive belongs to which object, or which primitives share a common boundary.

The fundamental graphics unit executes all the necessary calculations that occur before rasterization. These include viewing transformations, clipping, hidden line and visible surface calculations, and determination of diffuse and specular reflection components. So far, all data may be retained in its high precision (floating-point) form. This ensures the device independence of the hardware up to this level. The output of the fundamental graphics unit is in a form that can be directly converted to pixel intensities. This may be lines, curves, surfaces and textual information. However, as before, there may be a loss of semantic information; for example, only visible line segments are kept and the original complete wire-frame model is lost. Also, there is a loss of information due to the projection of 3D objects into the 2D surface of the viewing screen.

The rasterizer produces the RGB intensities that are stored in the frame buffer. This process may be very time consuming, since millions of pixels have to be updated. Again, there is a large loss of semantic information, since what used to be a line, curve or smooth surface becomes three intensities per pixel stored in the frame buffer. In general, it is impossible to reconstruct the geometrical data from the pixel intensities. Computer vision researchers have been battling with this problem for decades. There is also a loss of precision, since the assumed infinite precision of the application data is reduced to a finite precision governed by the resolution of the frame buffer. This may not only occur for Cartesian variables but in some cases may severely affect colour information. If the frame buffer can accommodate only a relatively few colours, say 256, then a non-trivial problem arises as to the mapping of calculated colour intensities to available colours (see Chapter 7).

Finally, the lowest hardware level is represented by the pixel driver, whose most important function is to set each pixel to the required RGB intensities. As will be shown shortly, it is still possible to execute graphical functions on the pixel data itself; hence, the pixel driver is more than a simple passive scan converter between the frame buffer and the display device.

Some geometric algorithms, such as clipping or 2D transformations, may be executed by more than one hardware unit. Indeed, they can be incorporated in each unit where they are needed, thus causing some redundancy in hardware. On the other hand, a more complex hardware structure could organize hardware functions according to the algorithms they perform, in which case the simple hierarchical model of Figure 10.1 would break down. Breaking down the structure even further, the hardware could also supply generic processor blocks, all optimized to some often-needed functions, such as matrix multiplication, convolution or the solution of a set of linear equations. This leads to the popular pipeline architectures, which will be discussed later.

It is difficult to justify the hierarchical hardware structure presented in Figure 10.1 if the method of rendering is ray tracing. It is quite conceivable, as was shown in Chapter 8, that pixel intensities are generated in one logical step from the application data, as in the case of ray tracing a CSG tree. Obviously, ray tracing is not possible in a device-independent manner, since the technique relies on the fact that there are a finite number of screen locations where the RGB intensities must be defined. Thus, hardware solutions to ray tracing may have to be examined in addition to the proposed hardware structure of Figure 10.1.

In addition to picture generation in an interactive system, graphics hardware must include facilities for graphical input and event generation. The input module has to be connected to each output function module, since some interaction between them is required. For example, if the geometric graphics unit produces a circle, then the same unit must be used to determine whether a pointing device points to the circle. Similarly, the visible marker for the mouse must be handled by the hardware pixel driver so that it is always visible, regardless of the pixel intensities assigned by the fundamental graphics unit.

The following sections discuss how modern devices have been used to execute these hardware functions at rapidly increasing speeds.

10.3 GEOMETRIC GRAPHICS UNIT

The function of this block is to break down the objects defined by the application database into easily manageable graphics primitives.

Obviously, the specific functions of this block depend on the organization of the database and the form of the primitives. Normally, its operation is governed by the viewing parameters, such as the position of view, direction of view, projection type, window location and size, and the back clipping plane. However, it is not necessarily true that the window size, and the clipping of the objects in world co-ordinates needs to be considered at this high level of the functional model. Consider the advantage of translating the entire scene all the way to the pixel driver without regard to the current window settings. In this case, the pixel driver could provide zooming (change window size) and panning (change window location) instantaneously, as long as the frame buffer could accommodate both the visible and invisible (clipped) data. However, working with realistic processors and very large user databases, it is assumed that the processors are unable to transform all the data within the required time interval; hence, clipping is necessary.

Currently there are two main hardware methods by which the speed of the geometric graphics functions can be substantially increased. One relies on processors working in parallel, while the other is based on pipelining of processors. A third method, data flow machines, can be considered a hybrid between these two methods.

10.3.1 Parallel processing

Many graphics computations are inherently parallel and do not suffer from the unsolved difficult problem of breaking down a complex general process into independent parallel processes. As defined, the geometric graphics unit processes objects, which, for most applications, are independent entities; hence, they can be processed in parallel. An assumption often made when processing in parallel is that the limit is reached when one processor per object is provided, but this is not necessarily the case. For example, object primitives like spheres, cylinders or conical surfaces can be converted into polygons or, more simply a cylinder could be divided into two half-cylinders and given to two processors. In fact, the theoretical limit is reached when the number of processors is equal to the number of primitive polygons. It is not clear, however, how the correct division of geometric objects to processors would occur in this case. Also, it is unrealistic to expect that this theoretical limit could be ever achieved in practice.

The importance of the fact that the theoretical improvement in processing speed is not limited is that the speeding up can be proportional to the number of processors. However, to be proportional, all processors must be kept busy at all times, which is not a trivial task, since some calculations, like the breaking down of Bezier surface patches into small

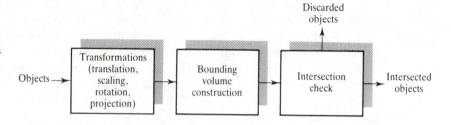

planar polygons, is much more time consuming than the breaking down of simple cylindrical surfaces.

There is another possibility for parallel processing when the application data is defined in terms of a CSG tree. In the case where ray tracing is used, the geometric graphics unit could pass only those primitives that are intersected by the ray to the fundamental graphics unit. The processing would require the traversing of the CSG tree to process the intersection and minus operators, and the testing of bounding volumes for the elimination of non-intersecting objects. Testing could be done in parallel for each object, but, more importantly, it could be a completely independent parallel calculation as far as each pixel is concerned. Thus, the theoretical limit on the number of processors in this case is equal to the product of the number of pixels and the number of objects. This is an absurdly large number, of course, which ensures that adding more processors will improve performance.

Parallel processing has found a fertile field in computer graphics applications. As shown by these few examples, it is relatively easy to improve graphics processing speeds by adding independent processors to the system.

10.3.2   Pipelining

Pipelining is the arrangement of successive processing functions in serial. The motor car manufacturer's production line is a good example. Each car is assembled in a number of stages, where each stage is kept busy all the time. Thus, although new cars appear in sequence, many are being manufactured in parallel. The same concept is applied to computations in a graphics system. For example, clipping can be done by the pipeline shown in Figure 10.2. Each object enters the pipeline and is first transformed according to the combined object co-ordinate system and projection transformations, after which the bounding box or sphere is constructed. Finally, the objects that are totally clipped by the current window are discarded. If the three successive phases take the same amount of time, with objects being continuously fed into the pipeline, there will be a speed up factor of three.

It is more difficult to use pipelines to their full capacity than parallel processors, since once an object enters the pipe, its progression is determined by the required calculations. This means that pipelined systems are liable to perform exceptionally well for problems with an even decomposition into processes, but may falter for general applications.

It is possible to combine parallel processing with pipelines and provide a number of parallel pipes. Also, it is possible to decouple the stages of a pipe and feed work independently into each stage according to its capacity. However, this scheme moves away from a traditional pipeline and towards the idea of data flow machines.

The usefulness of pipelines for the fundamental graphics unit is easier to demonstrate and will be covered in a later section.

10.3.3   Data flow machines

The basic idea behind data flow machines is that there are a number of processors (servers) and a number of job packets that carry the necessary data and instructions for processing. Each packet also contains synchronizing information, indicating when the packet can be processed. These architectures are well suited to graphics applications due to the inherent parallel nature of the rendering process. Because of the general structure of this hardware scheme, data flow machines eliminate the distinction between the geometric, the fundamental graphics units and the rasterizer. The pixel driver is still considered as a separate unit.

As an example, consider how ray tracing a number of solid objects may be implemented using the data flow architecture. As mentioned before, it is possible to arrive at the pixel intensity values directly from the application database when ray tracing is used. The ray tracing algorithm can be divided into independent parallel processes as far as the rays are concerned. The schematic diagram in Figure 10.3 describes the operation of the data flow machine, for which execution time is an inverse function of the number of processors used. There is a pool of ray packets. Each packet contains the ray starting point, its direction, the closest intersection found for the ray and the pixel co-ordinates to which it belongs. The object packets contain algorithms for intersection and reflected light intensity calculations for each type of solid object that may be copied by the processors into their private memory. The inner loop of the algorithm is executed by each processor for a different ray. The objects are tested by the object algorithms with data provided by the starting point and the direction of the ray. Once the object algorithm is copied into the processor's private memory, the intersection calculations run completely independently for each ray without interference from the other processors.

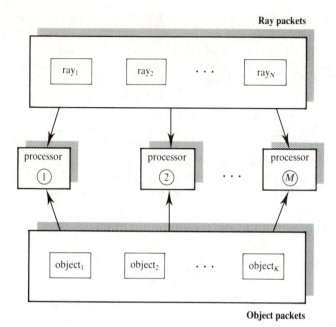

Ray packets

Object packets

Figure 10.3
Data flow machine may be used for the parallel processing of ray tracing. Since there is very little interaction between processors, the overall execution speed of the computer is proportional to the number of processors used.

In the limit of one processor per ray packet, there is very little interaction between processors. Interaction only occurs when two rays try to access the same object packet at the same time. Even this can be remedied with multiple copies of the object algorithms, which can be provided with increased main memory capacity.

Parallelism can also be exploited as far as objects are concerned. The intersections for each object may be calculated in parallel by a separate processor and when all of the calculations are completed, the closest intersection can be selected. Thus, in the limit of one processor per object, the execution time will be equal to the slowest intersection calculations for one object and will not be a function of the number of objects.

As before, whatever improvements have been made in the software algorithms (bounding box tests, for example), further improvements can be made by adding parallel processors until the number of processors reaches the limit of the number of rays times the number of objects. In the case of opaque objects, full parallelism can be exploited. In the case of specular objects (reflection) or semi-transparent objects (refraction), rays have to be traced from intersection to intersection, which is inherently a serial process, and the execution time is linearly related to the number of reflections (or refractions) a ray is subjected to.

Data flow machines are experimental hardware structures at present, but may become practical devices, especially in the field of graphics, in the future.

10.4   FUNDAMENTAL GRAPHICS UNIT

While hardware solutions for the geometric graphics unit are still experimental, hardware solutions for at least some of the fundamental graphics functions have become a practical reality. Some of these functions will appear again in the rasterizer and in the pixel driver. The main difference between the fundamental graphics unit and the pixel driver is that, for the former, data is still in a geometrical, 3D, high-precision form. Thus, graphics drivers, the agents of the fundamental graphics functions, are portable over display systems with different resolutions. The geometric functions of curve generation, clipping, area filling, and so on can be executed using normalized floating-point co-ordinates. The data is then transferred to the rasterizer which, with the knowledge of the resolution of the frame buffer, transforms the data to pixel co-ordinates.

Windows, viewports and clipping are good examples of fundamental graphics driver functions. Since setting a window viewport pair creates a transformation between user co-ordinates and normalized viewing co-ordinates, both the transformation and the clipping can be done at the hardware level. In addition to increasing processing speed, such a hardware facility is very convenient for the application programmer.

The use of viewports is very important for modern graphical human–computer interface design. Pop-up menus, dialogue boxes and windows all appear ultimately as viewports and graphical transformations at the lowest levels of implementation. The advantage of handling all these fundamental graphical entities at the lowest possible level is speed, portability and flexibility, since no code is required within the application package for these functions. For example, the automatic saving of that portion of the frame buffer data that is overlaid by a new menu and the subsequent redrawing of the overlaid screen area after the menu disappears are two very important functions that should be provided by the hardware. The input hardware drivers must also be integrated at this level. For example, the limits of motion and speed of a mouse should be governed by the currently active viewport dimensions.

With the continuing decrease in hardware costs and rapid increase in the use of graphics in all aspects of computing the migration of many basic fundamental graphics facilities towards low-level functions will continue. It is quite feasible that 3D transformations, clipping and viewing will become basic functions provided by future graphics systems.

10.4.1   Fundamental graphics pipeline

As has been seen, processing speed can be increased by parallel processing and pipelining at the highest hierarchical function level. Also, as

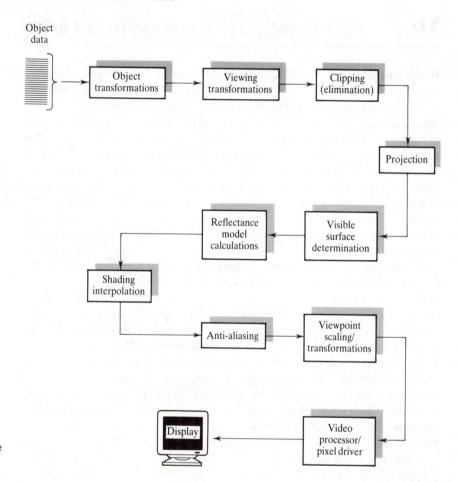

Figure 10.4

This is the main processing pipeline for the rendering of graphics scenes for 3D opaque objects.

mentioned before, pipelining can be effectively used at the fundamental graphics level as well. The main processing pipeline for 3D opaque objects is shown in Figure 10.4. Most of the blocks shown in the pipeline are applied to each geometric element in sequence and can be implemented by individual processors. The basic processor of the earliest successful system built on these principles is called the **geometry engine** (Clark, 1982). The geometry engine is a general floating-point matrix processor that can rapidly evaluate 3D transformations, clipping and scaling. The first models included twelve of these processors, while recent models use as many as twenty six.

Many of the pipeline functions may be incorporated into one stage. The visible surface determination function is performed with the help of a z-buffer. As before, the pipeline is fed continuously with object data and may have a large number of geometric objects (polygons, for example) being processed in parallel, each at a different stage. Many of the processing blocks contain arithmetic processors for floating-point numbers. Most calculations can be expressed as matrix multiplications of 4×4 homogeneous matrices or 4D vectors multiplied by matrices.

In the 1980s, many major manufacturers developed graphical workstations based on the pipeline hardware structure. As the speed of such a pipeline is limited by its slowest element, the most important design consideration is to match the different stages along the pipeline so that they provide the highest possible throughput when most processors are fully employed. For the slower stages, more basic processor elements are used, until the pipeline is finely tuned. Current geometric pipelines report throughputs of 100 000 polygons/s, which allows the real-time rendering of 4000 polygons.

To increase the speed further, parallel pipelines may be built. Since most of the geometric processing involves only one object, a number of pipelines may be supplied with different object data, increasing the parallelism of the calculations. Interaction does occur for the visible surface determination block, since all these processors must access the same z-buffer; however, by carefully selecting classes of objects whose projected images do not overlap, the parallel pipelines can be run with minimal interference.

Anti-aliasing for the geometric model involves only one object at a time, since the occluding boundaries or edges of the object must be anti-aliased. Thus, there is no interaction between the anti-aliasing blocks of different pipelines. The rasterizer, on the other hand, receives data from all active pipelines and may be responsible for the worst bottleneck. In this case, parallelism for the rasterizer or the pixel driver may be introduced, which is discussed in the next two sections.

The worst feature of the pipeline architecture is its inflexibility. For a different application, where, for example, ray tracing is required, the pipeline must be reconfigured. This may even mean hardware changes and additions. This criticism could be made for most hardware solutions. They are excellent for the applications they were designed for, but it is difficult to obtain the same level of performance for different applications. Conversely, parallel processors have less structure and it is therefore easier to reconfigure them.

10.5 RASTERIZER

The main function of the rasterizer is to set bytes in the frame buffer according to the required RGB intensities of the picture. Since the

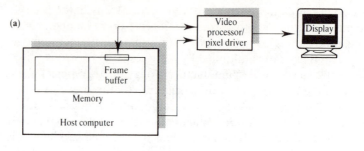

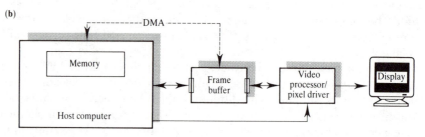

Figure 10.5
Two practical implementations of a graphics system. In system (a), the frame buffer is memory mapped and is directly available to the host computer's processor(s). In system (b), the frame buffer is external to the host computer.

processing of up to three million bytes is involved in the full colour case, this is a very time consuming and computing intensive operation.

From the rasterization point of view, the best hardware arrangement is shown in Figure 10.5(a), where the frame buffer is memory mapped. This allows the setting of the pixel bytes at full processing bandwidth and allows the host computer to access the frame buffer directly. Some memory-mapped frame buffers reduce the advantages of this closely coupled processor/frame buffer arrangement by providing an irregular bitmapping between pixel bits and computer memory. This will be discussed further in the section on the pixel driver.

Close coupling between the processor and the frame buffer may not be available in many low-priced systems. The frame buffer is attached to a graphical subsystem, which is connected to the main processor through a low-speed serial link. For example, if the transmission speed is around 2000 bytes per second (19 600 Baud), it takes more than 25 minutes to down load a 1024 × 1024 shaded picture, which can be hardly regarded as an interactive speed. A **direct memory access** (**DMA**) channel may speed up the data transfer between the computer's memory and the frame buffer.

The hardware processing capabilities of a loosely coupled system are usually provided by a special hardware processor tightly coupled to the frame buffer, as shown in Figure 10.5(b). This means that the processor has a set of machine-level graphics instructions. There are three types of instructions at the fundamental graphics level: line, curve and character generation instructions, area fill and shading instructions, and, finally, windowing, transformations, projections and clipping instructions.

One specialized graphics hardware function is the line generator. The input to this processor consists of four pixel numbers (x_1, y_1, x_2, y_2), possibly a line style (solid, dotted), a thickness indicator, colour and/or intensity. Again, the processor, on its own, sets all the necessary pixels to their required values. Similar curve generators may be constructed for circles, ellipses or even splines. A convenient feature of hardware line or curve generators is the writing mode. This can be defined most easily for bi-level displays. It is a special attribute that allows the pixels to be set, cleared or complemented, instead of simply replaced. Once set, the writing mode governs all rasterizer functions, such as character generation, area fill and so on. It is more difficult to define writing mode for shaded displays, as will be seen in the section on the pixel driver.

There is a considerable increase in processing speed when hardware components execute the rasterizing functions, since the video processor operates in parallel with the host computer, which provides the geometric data. Since the generation of a number of curves may also be executed in parallel, further increases in the speed of processing can be achieved by using more than one curve or character generator in the system. This assumes that the hidden portions of the curves have already been determined by the computer and only visible graphics elements are sent for rasterization.

It is worth re-emphasizing that although hardware solutions increase speed, they often restrict flexibility. For example, it has been shown that while a differential line or curve generator algorithm is executed, the decision as to which pixels to turn on is made by the magnitude of an error term. This same error term may be used for anti-aliasing, since it is indicative of the distance between the pixel turned on and the correct location of the geometric line or curve. A hardware curve generator may provide this anti-aliasing facility. But, if it does not provide it, there is no method by which the curve anti-aliasing can be added to the system, since there is no direct knowledge of the pixels chosen by the hardware curve generator. Thus, if anti-aliasing is required, a software curve-generation algorithm must be used, making the hardware generator completely useless.

A simple character generator, which is an integral part of all display systems, is another example of a specialized graphics processor. It is shown schematically in Figure 10.6. The input data to the character generator is an ASCII byte value and the upper left corner co-ordinates of the character. The processor then turns ON all bits within a given rectangular area that correspond to the required character pattern. The processor has access to a ROM that contains the patterns. If, say, the character is generated within a 10×10 area of pixels, one byte of information transmitted to the processor handles $10 \times 10 = 100$ pixels. This may provide a 100-fold speed increase when it is compared to software-generated characters.

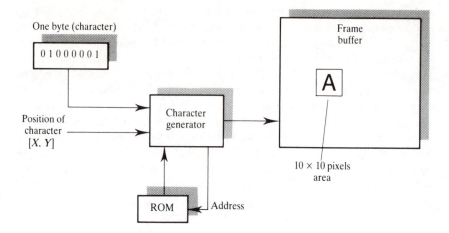

Figure 10.6

Schematic diagram of a hardware character generator, which has been an integral part of computer graphics output devices for a long time.

Area fill is another commonly used graphical function. Scan line fill algorithms belong to the geometric function block and seed fill algorithms to the pixel driver, but both will be discussed here since the geometric function and pixel driver functions operate very similarly for area fill functions. The seed fill algorithm can be easily executed by a video processor.

The simplest form of area fill sets all pixels to a given colour value within a bounded region. It requires as input data one pair of co-ordinates (the seed position), a colour intensity value and the colour value at the borders. A more complex area fill algorithm may provide simple texture mapping, which copies a predefined pattern over the required area. It is also possible to provide more complex functions like Gouraud shading by the video processor. In its simplest form, Gouraud shading may be applied to a triangle, when only three pairs of co-ordinates for the three vertices of the triangle are needed. The processor reads the intensities at the three vertices and sets the pixels within the triangle with the linearly interpolated intensity values. This works in general, only for monochrome shaded images, since the linear interpolation of colour intensities may produce unexpected colour effects. Anti-aliasing may be added to the borders of the Gouraud-shaded triangles similarly to the curve generator.

To produce Phong or more complicated shading models, 3D data must be supplied to the graphics driver. Until now, mainly 2D graphics processors have been used, especially for the lower-priced systems; however, it is very likely that with the new emerging GKS-3D and PHIGS standards, 3D graphics hardware will be more readily available.

There is not much more to add to what has already been said as far as the additional parallel processing capabilities are concerned at these fundamental geometric and rasterization levels. The same rules apply as for the higher geometric graphics level. The exploitation of the parallel nature of the pixels will be discussed in Section 10.6.

10.5.1   Partial regeneration

There is one more major concern that affects the interactive performance of graphics systems. In a truly interactive system, when the application database changes, the screen should ideally be updated within one frame, or a maximum of 40 ms. If the hardware functions can produce the entire transformation from application data to pixel intensities, the interactive requirement has been satisfied. However, as has been seen from the requirements of realistic computer-generated pictures, the state of the art is far from being able to provide a true hardware solution to the general graphics problem. Even if the rest of the system could complete all the required calculations, the rasterizer would have difficulty in coping. The only realistic approach is to try to do the best with the available hardware.

One specialized change of scene that happens often in interactive systems, particularly in computer animation, is the change of only a very small number of pixels in a complex scene. This is **frame coherence** in animation. If it is known which pixels change their intensities and how to recalculate them, it is quite possible that the interactive hardware solution could be applied to this specialized problem, which may be called **partial regeneration**.

Partial regeneration is required when one object is moved in a complex scene containing a large number of objects. It is relatively easy to determine the visible portions of the moving object as well as those pixels that were covered by the object in the previous frame but are not covered in the new one. However, it is much more difficult to determine the pixel intensities at the uncovered pixels, since the entire scene must be regenerated for those pixels. A simple hardware solution called **tiling** can solve this problem.

Tiling is similar to space division and could be called an image space division method. The screen is divided into a reasonable number of small rectangles, or tiles, and during rendering and rasterization the list of objects that would affect the pixels within each tile if they were visible are assembled. Similarly, each object record stores the set of tiles that are affected by the extent of the projected object on the screen. When an object is moved or removed, then it is only necessary to update a small number of tiles. Because of area coherence, the list of objects to be redrawn is in general only a very small portion of the application database.

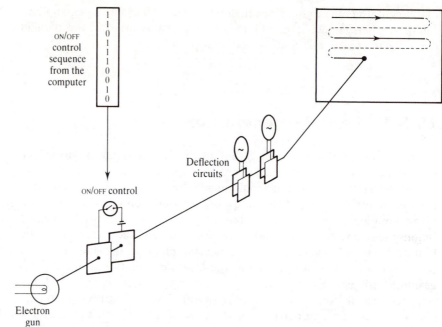

Figure 10.7
Schematic diagram of the
simplest hardware structure for
a raster scan output device.

10.6   PIXEL DRIVER

The previous sections have already covered the entire translation process
from application data to pixel intensities. What is left is the pixel driver
function. There are two main areas that need to be looked at. First, the
hardware scan conversion process, which translates pixel intensities into
brightness and colour on the screen. Second, the possibility of carrying out
meaningful picture processing at the pixel level only.

A simple, bi-level raster scan display system has already been
described in Chapter 1, but is shown again in Figure 10.7. The electron
beam is directed by the horizontal and vertical deflection circuits and is
modulated (turned ON or OFF) by an incoming bit sequence during its
travel across the display tube. The beam is swept horizontally while the
ON/OFF information is displayed and is blanked while it is being retraced.
Assuming that the display consists of a thousand horizontal lines and
provides 25 pictures per second, the line rate is equal to 25 KHz. The
television line rate is equal to 16.5 KHz at present.

The simplest way of providing data for the ON/OFF sequencer is by
using a shift register and a hardware buffer, as shown in Figure 10.8.
During the horizontal sweep, the shift register provides the ON/OFF data

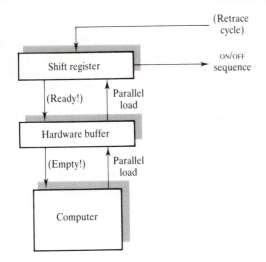

Figure 10.8

The simplest hardware solution for driving a raster scan output device is by the use of shift registers. In this case the output is created 'on the fly', which means that the host computer must provide video data in real time.

stream to the electron beam control and the computer updates the hardware buffer with data for the next horizontal line. During the retracing of the beam, the contents of the hardware buffer are loaded into the shift register. For this simple system, a data rate of 25000/8, or approximately 3200 bytes per second, is required from the computer to keep up with the display. This hardware arrangement generates the picture on the fly and is well suited to scan line-based graphics algorithms. Generating one byte of information in 250 ms seems to be within the capability of today's small microprocessors, even when executing a fair number of computations. The obvious disadvantage is that the processor is constantly occupied with the picture-generation function and may have very little time for other computations. This was the way the very earliest graphics systems were built when hardware was still very expensive.

With the advent of large and inexpensive random access memory (RAM), and the increased requirements for shaded colour displays, the use of frame buffers has become universally accepted. A **frame buffer**, also often referred to as a **video RAM** or **VRAM**, is a large block of memory with two ports. As shown in Figure 10.9, one port is 'read only' and is used to refresh the display similarly as before. The other port may be bi-directional and can be updated by a number of bits in parallel (bytes, 16 or 32 bits words are often used). Since the data rate required by the display may be very high (90 million bytes per second for the full colour system), this is not a simple system and, depending on its price and technology, the maximum data rate at the port connected to the computer may have to be severely restricted.

Selecting available VLSI memory devices for a high-performance VRAM application is not a simple task. For example, the currently popular 64K-bit memory chips do not provide 16-bit addresses. First, an 8-bit

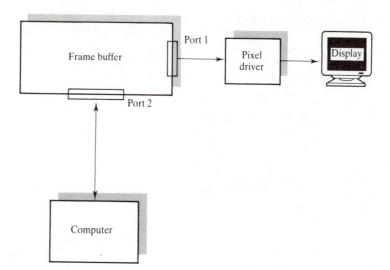

Figure 10.9

The conventional 'modern' solution of driving raster scan output devices employs a frame buffer which is a large, dual-ported, high-speed semiconductor memory, sometimes called a video RAM or VRAM.

row and then an 8-bit column address is clocked and latched into the chip, after which a read/write cycle can take place. In this case, the 8-bit chip organization has to be matched to the row/column organization of the video display for maximum performance. The frame buffer has many advantages over calculation on the fly. The most obvious one is that when frames are calculated in sequence, only those pixels that change from frame to frame have to be updated. If there is frame-to-frame coherence, as would be expected in computer animation, the number of pixels updated for each frame may only be a very small fraction of the total number of pixels in the frame buffer. This problem of partial regeneration has already been discussed in Section 10.5.1.

The other advantage is that once a frame buffer has been used, two distinct representations are available for a graphics scene. The starting representation is a geometric description. After projection and rasterization, a bitmap is produced. This new representation allows new processing functions, called **raster operations** or **RasterOps**, which work directly on the bitmap. The operations on the bitmap may be executed independently and in parallel with the operation of the computer.

There are basically two ways of incorporating a frame buffer into a computer system. First, as was shown in Figure 10.5(a), the frame buffer may be part of the computer's memory; in other words, it is memory mapped. The video processor that drives the video display must have access to the main memory of the computer as well. The advantage of this arrangement has already been mentioned; that is, all processing functions of the computer can be applied to the pixel intensities. The disadvantage is that the video processor may interfere with the operation of the computer and slow it down considerably, since it must have priority of access for its raster scanning operation. It is difficult to achieve fully parallel operation between the computer and the video processor with such an arrangement of the frame buffer. The other problem is that the video processor and the frame buffer must be integrated into the computer system, which will make future modifications and expansions difficult.

The alternative way of connecting the frame buffer to a computer system is shown in Figure 10.5(b). In this case, the video processor and the frame buffer form an integrated graphics system that is added to the computer system. The two important factors determining the performance of such a dual system are the speed of data transmission between the computer and the graphics system, and the set of available graphics functions the video processor can execute on the frame buffer. There is a clear distinction between the computer, which processes geometric data, and the video processor, which operates on pixel data. Normally, in a medium-priced dual system of this kind, the data transmission between the graphics system and the computer is orders of magnitude slower than the read/write cycle of the computer. Thus, if such a system is used for the execution of a scan line algorithm which updates all pixels of the display for each frame, performance will be poor. On the other hand, if the video processor can draw lines and fill areas, then the transmission of a few bytes, say the co-ordinates of the vertices of a polygon and a command 'fill area', could generate shaded facets that involve the processing of a very large number of pixels. Obviously, the graphics system with the best performance will have both a high-performance video processor, with a rich set of available RasterOps, and a high-speed link between the computer's memory and the external frame buffer, a DMA system, for example.

Before discussing some useful RasterOps in detail, the reader should note that rasterization is not a reversible operation. Geometric data is usually prescribed with much higher accuracy than the integer data that define the rasterized picture. For example, a straight line segment as a geometric identity may be defined by four values and may be assumed to be infinitely thin. When this line segment is rasterized, the best approxima-tion to the straight line becomes a number of pixels turned ON. Since the pixel area is finite, the line acquires a width that is proportional to the width of one pixel, which is inversely proportional to the resolution of the display. The same line will appear thinner when it is displayed on a high-resolution display system. This loss of accuracy and device dependence causes many problems when relying only on direct operations on the frame buffer.

10.6.1 Operations on the frame buffer

The zoom function is a good example of a function used to process the rasterized bitmap directly. Chapter 1 showed that to look at a graphics

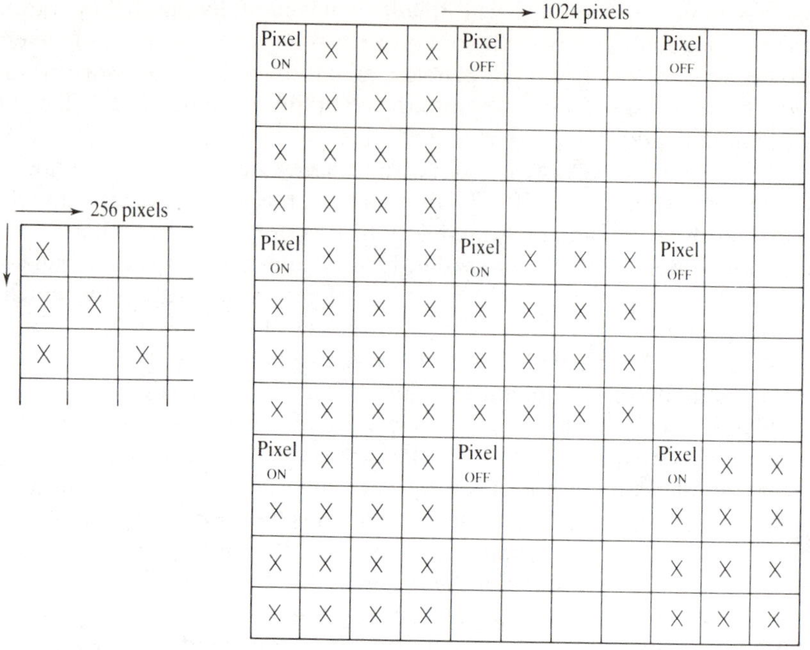

1024 pixels

256 pixels

Figure 10.10

Zooming in may be executed directly by hardware when a small area of pixel data is spread over a large area of pixels. The diagram shows a magnification of four. The original five ON pixels shown cause 90 pixels to be turned ON over the full screen area of 1024 × 1024 pixels.

scene in more detail, the window size is reduced. Since the window area is mapped to the entire display surface, reducing the window size is equivalent to magnifying (or zooming in) the image. Reducing the window size involves recalculation of the whole transformation–projection–clipping sequence for each object. The same magnification may be achieved by reducing the resolution of the display. Assume that a display of 10 × 10 inches has an area of 1000 × 1000 pixels. Hardware zooming may be achieved by selecting an area of 250 × 250 pixels that is mapped on to the display surface so that every fourth pixel is replaced by the original pixel value. Then, the entire 4 × 4 = 16 pixels are turned ON or OFF according to the pixel value in the upper left corner, as shown in Figure 10.10. This procedure has achieved a magnification of four, all done by hardware, and the zoom function can be executed instantaneously (within 1/25th of a second), regardless of the complexity of the scene the display represents.

The two types of magnification procedures are different. When zooming in is executed by windowing, lines and sharp edges of objects retain their fine definition. In this case, magnification may be defined by a floating-point number and there is no limit to the size of magnification. When processing is done directly on the bitmap, magnification may be done only by an integer number and, because line widths are increased as well, the definition of sharp edges disappears and the displayed image becomes useless beyond some magnification factor.

Conversely, increasing the window size makes the displayed image smaller and smaller. In practice, this means that a large number of objects are projected to the same small area of the screen and a complex object may appear in an area of a few pixels that produce only a small dot on the screen. Zooming out by hardware can be achieved only if the frame buffer is larger than the displayed image. This is the accepted practice for large graphics workstations. Unfortunately, the required frame buffer becomes too large to allow the implementation of a comprehensive zoom facility. For example, a frame buffer may be defined with the size of 16-bit addresses for each horizontal and vertical dimension. The displayed area is still 1024×1024 pixels and the frame buffer contains $64 \times 64 = 4096$ displayable pages, or about 1.2×10^{13} bytes. In such a system, the whole frame buffer could be mapped on to the screen by displaying the average intensity of each 64×64 square at each pixel. In this case, zooming in may be made by a factor of 64 without loss of definition. A practical system can be built with zooming factors of up to 8 without loss of definition and an additional zooming in of 4 to 8 with the duplication of pixel values. Such a system can combine RasterOps with geometric functions (GKS primitives, for example) to provide an integrated graphics workstation.

10.6.2   Frame buffer conversion

Picture data is often stored in the frame buffer format, where there is no geometric and semantic information. A problem occurs, however, if a picture in this device-dependent format is to be displayed on a variety of different display devices. This is not really a computer graphics problem but rather an image processing one. Nevertheless, it is frequently encountered in computer graphics applications. The information required for the translation is the horizontal and vertical number of pixels, the physical size and the number of RGB intensity levels to be displayed. It is safe to predict that this problem will never be solved satisfactorily for all devices and all picture types. To be able to suggest some form of satisfactory solution, only monochrome pictures will be considered here. Colour mapping was discussed in Chapter 7.

The first step is to normalize both the first and the second picture areas to the range of 0 to 1 in both the horizontal and vertical directions. It is assumed that the aspect ratios of the two display devices are the same. If this is not true, then either only a portion of the target display scene can be used, or the picture will be distorted because the horizontal and vertical distances will be scaled differently. If the source picture has NX_1 pixels in the horizontal direction and NY_1 in the vertical direction, and the target picture has similarly NX_2 and NY_2 pixels, then the middle of the pixel area

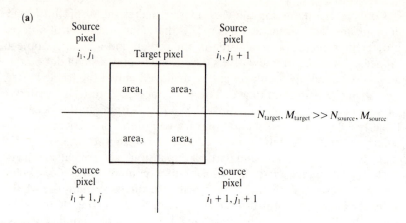

Figure 10.11

Conversion of data from the frame buffer of one resolution to that of another may be executed by averaging the overlapping pixel areas. The two extreme cases are shown. In (a), the normalized source pixel areas are much larger than those of the target pixels. In (b), the reverse is the case.

for the ith row and jth column in normalized distances is given by:

$$\left(\frac{i_1 + 0.5}{NX_1}, \frac{j_1 + 0.5}{NY_1}\right)$$

for the source picture and:

$$\left(\frac{i_2 + 0.5}{NX_2}, \frac{j_2 + 0.5}{NY_2}\right)$$

for the target picture. The two extreme cases are shown in Figure 10.11: when the target pixel is much smaller and when it is much larger than the source pixel. Both cases can be handled by a general algorithm that adds up all the contributions to the intensity of the target pixel of those source pixels found to be within the area of the target pixel. The conditions for the source pixel (i_1, j_1) to be partially covering a target pixel (i_2, j_2) are:

$$\frac{i_1 + 1}{NX_1} > \frac{i_2}{NX_2} \quad \text{and} \quad \frac{i_1}{NX_1} < \frac{i_2 + 1}{NX_2}$$

$$\frac{j_1 + 1}{NY_1} > \frac{j_2}{NY_2} \quad \text{and} \quad \frac{j_1}{NY_1} < \frac{j_2 + 1}{NY_2}$$

(10.1)

The source intensity levels are also normalized. If the minimum intensity for the source picture is $IMin_1$ and the maximum is equal to $IMax_1$, then the normalized intensity is equal to:

$$INorm_1 = \frac{I_1 - IMin_1}{IMax_1 - IMin_1}$$

The next step is to calculate the average intensity for each target pixel. This is a sum of weighted intensities where the weight is equal to the relative area that each source pixel covers:

$$IAverage_2(i, j) = \sum \text{Area}[i, j] \, INorm_1[i, j]$$

(10.2)

where i, j are those source pixels that satisfy Equation (10.1). The average intensity may be used directly for setting the target picture intensities. If the minimum intensity used for the target picture is equal to $IMin_2$ and the maximum is $IMax_2$, then the required target intensity is equal to:

$$I_2 = IMin_2 + (IMax_2 - IMin_2) IAverage_2$$

(10.3)

Even though Equation (10.3) is a fair assessment of target intensity, it does have the effect of reducing contrast and of blurring edges. In effect, some anti-aliasing is being provided with this method.

Thresholding may be used to keep the contrast of the source picture. A simple thresholding scheme providing the maximum contrast can be applied. During the evaluation of the sum in Equation (10.2), the local maximum and minimum intensities of the source pixels are recorded, designated here as $LocalMax_1$ and $LocalMin_1$. A target intensity is evaluated by the following thresholding operations:

```
if IAverage₂ >= (LocalMax₁ - LocalMin₁)/2
then IThreshold₂ := LocalMax₁
else IThreshold₂ := LocalMin₁
```

Then, similarly to Equation (10.3) the actual intensity is calculated by the expression:

$$I_2 = IMin_2 + (IMax_2 - IMin_2) IThreshold_2$$

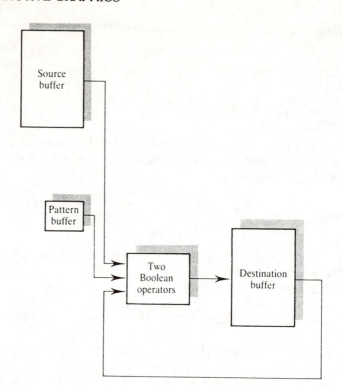

Figure 10.12
Schematic diagram showing
how the BitBlt operations are
executed. The resulting pixel
intensities that replace the
contents of the destination
buffer are calculated by a
Boolean expression using two
logical functions (AND, OR, XOR)
operating on the original
contents of the destination
buffer, a source buffer of similar
size and a small pattern buffer.
The pattern buffer is applied
periodically over the larger
surfaces of the other two
buffers using the **mod**( )
function.

Histogram equalization may be also used to increase the contrast of the
target picture, but this leads too far in the direction of image processing,
which is beyond the scope of this text.

10.6.3   BitBlt and PixelBlt operations

A general class of pixel driver functions, called **BitBlt** (bit block transfer)
or **PixelBlt** (pixel block transfer) **operations**, have become integral parts of
currently available advanced video processors. The difference between the
BitBlt and PixelBlt operations is that the BitBlt operations are applied to
bi-level display systems whereas the PixelBlt operations are extended to
shaded and colour displays.

BitBlt operations operate on rectangular areas of pixels and should
be viewed as an enhanced set of machine instructions that are specialized
for graphics. Since the frame buffer is a 2D array of pixels, machine
operations that work on a 2D data structure are much better suited to
graphics than the conventional machine instructions, which operate on a
1D (linear) memory.

Algorithm 10.1

BitBlt operations.

var *Result* : **Boolean**;

(* Source and destination buffers have side lengths *DX* and *DY* *)
(* The pattern buffer has side length *PX* and *PY* *)

for *XPixel* := 0 **to** *DX* − 1 **do**
  for *YPixel* := 0 **to** *DY* − 1 **do**
  begin
    Result := *Operator*1(*DestinationBuffer*[*XPixel*, *YPixel*] , *PatternBuffer*[*XPixel* **mod** *PX*, *YPixel* **mod** *PY*]);
    DestinationBuffer[*XPixel*, *YPixel*] := *Operator*2(*Result*, *SourceBuffer*[*XPixel*, *YPixel*]);
  end

BitBlt operations have three different operands called source, destination and pattern. The source, destination and pattern operands are rectangular arrays of pixels, and the operations are bitwise logical ones on all three operands, as shown in Figure 10.12. In the most general case, the source and destination operands can extend to the whole frame buffer, while the pattern operand is usually a smaller rectangular array that is used periodically over the entire frame buffer. The most general form of the BitBlt operation is as outlined in Algorithm 10.1, where *Operator*1 and *Operator*2 may be any one of the possible 16 logical operations between two Boolean variables. Thus, this algorithm represents $16 \times 16 = 256$ distinct operations. The location of each rectangular region is quite arbitrary for all three operands and, because of the **mod** operation, the pattern operand can be viewed as if it was repeated periodically in both *X* and *Y* directions.

The significant speed reduction of the BitBlt operations occurs because a large number of pixels are processed in parallel. There is a large number of useful functions that can be executed by BitBlt operations. Characters or patterns can be easily transferred from a pattern buffer to the destination frame buffer in one operation. Lines or curves may also be drawn by pre-storing a number of rasterized line segments in a pattern buffer and then transferring them to the destination buffer using BitBlt operations. Two BitBlt operations may be used to dither between two frame buffers. First, a pattern is used to blank out (turn OFF) pixels in the destination buffer and then the inverse of the pattern is logically ANDed with the source buffer, with the result ORed into the modified destination buffer. Schematically:

$$DestinationBuffer = Pattern \textbf{ and } DestinationBuffer;$$
$$DestinationBuffer = DestinationBuffer \textbf{ or } (InversePattern \textbf{ and } SourceBuffer);$$

With this hardware-dithering technique, a large number of colours may be generated from a relatively few basic colour shades. In this case, the different patterns are rectangular areas filled with the dithering matrix. With the dithering technique, two pictures may be mixed together in a traditional cross-dissolve animation sequence.

Animation of two-and-half dimensional scenes is another obvious application for BitBlt operations. One frame buffer contains the unchanging background scene while pattern buffers contain moving objects which are copied into the final scene at various pixel locations.

It is also possible to extend the traditional BitBlt operations to other useful functions like rotation, but the hardware structure and organization of the graphics system could limit the usefulness of such operations. If the distances between pixels in the horizontal and vertical directions are the same, then 90°, 180°, and 270° rotations are possible. Other angles of rotation, or non uniform aspect ratios in the X and Y directions, do not allow simple pixel-to-pixel transformations between the source and the destination buffers, and the usefulness of these extended hardware operations is much diminished.

In the case of shaded displays, each pixel data is expressed by a number of bits and simple Boolean operations on them may be meaningless. If the pixel data references logical colours, bit parallel Boolean operations may still be used. For example, in a 16-colour system (four bits per pixel), the colours may be arranged such that the values indicate complement colours. Value 0 (binary 0000) means black, value 15 (binary 1111) white; value 1 is assigned to red, value 14 to cyan, and so on. In this case, complementing the pixel value would be meaningful because the complement colour would be displayed.

When pixel values represent gray intensities, arithmetic functions between frame buffers may become useful. Thus, systems that provide PixelBlt operations include arithmetic functions in addition to the Boolean ones. The situation becomes very complex when the pixel values are RGB intensities and a useful set of PixelBlt operations for shaded coloured displays are yet to be developed.

BitBlt implementation

The last section presented BitBlt operations in their most general form. Unfortunately, hardware restrictions will make it very difficult to implement the most general form of these operations. Obviously, the 2D nature

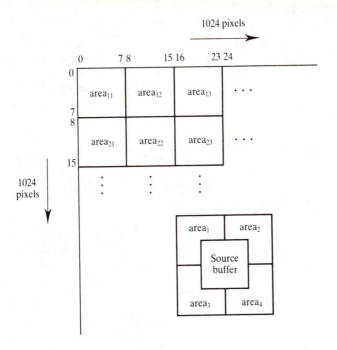

Figure 10.13
The usual implementation of BitBlt operations assigns fixed rectangular pixel areas for the destination buffer but allows the source area to have an arbitrary position. In the most general case, the rectangular source area covers four destination areas.

of the operations must also be used in the structure of the hardware for efficient implementations. This is possible for a fixed size BitBlt operation, but is virtually impossible for variable-sized rectangular areas. It has already been mentioned that many RAM devices are organized around 8-bit addresses; therefore, it seems reasonable to use 8×8 square areas for the BitBlt operations.

To demonstrate the types of difficulties encountered in hardware design of 2D graphics processors, we will now consider a high-performance pixel driver. A 1024×1024 display is divided into 128×128 or sixteen-thousand 8×8 areas of pixels, as shown in Figure 10.13. Any one of the 8×8 areas of pixels in the destination buffer can be updated in parallel – this is easily achievable by the 8-bit addresses of the RAM chips. However, to preserve the usefulness of the BitBlt operations, the 8×8 pixel area in the source buffer should be at any position. As shown in Figure 10.13, the 8×8 source buffer involves four 8×8 areas. Figure 10.14 shows a possible hardware structure that can perform this BitBlt operation in four cycles. Since the four small rectangles of the source data are located at different positions from where they must be in the destination buffer, some shifting operations must be carried out, as follows. First, $area_1$ is used as the source buffer. Circular shifts are used to move the the small 3×2 area at its lower right corner to the upper left corner. The shift requires a movement of five bits in the horizontal direction and six bits in the vertical

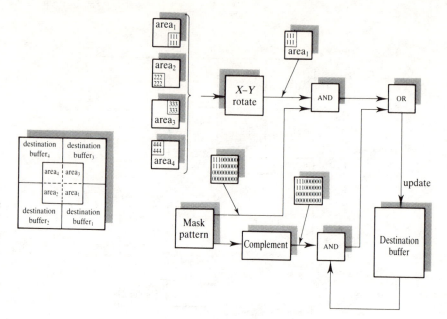

Figure 10.14
The hardware implementation of a simple 'transfer the rectangular source area into the destination buffer' requires four clock cycles. For each, one portion of the source buffer is transferred. As shown, both rotation and masking are required for the correct execution of the transfer operation.

direction. A mask pattern is set up and $area_1$ is masked for the small 3×2 area using the AND operation. Then, the destination buffer is ANDed with the complement of the mask and finally ORed to the prepared source data. Three similar operations, using the other three 8×8 areas as the source buffer, complete the transfer. For such a general BitBlt operation, the parallelism is 64/4 or sixteen, since in four cycles, 64 pixels are updated simultaneously.

The use of BitBlt and PixelBlt operations is one way that hardware can speed up graphical processing. Another way, as mentioned earlier, is to employ parallel processing techniques.

10.6.4 Parallel pixel processing

It is well known that when the limit of the processing speed for one processor has been reached, further improvements in speed can be made by using a number of processors. In cases when processes can be divided into independent parallel streams, an n-fold increase in speed can be expected when n processors are used. Similar improvements cannot be expected when the parallel processes are inter-dependent, since they may have to wait for each other's results or could slow down each other by trying to access the same resources at the same time.

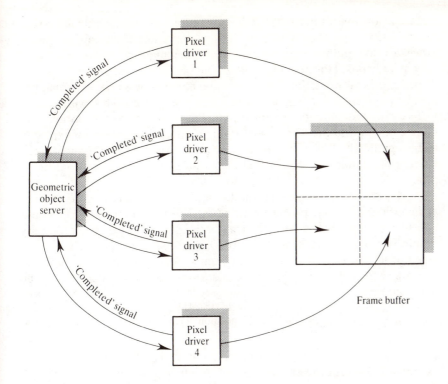

Figure 10.15

Schematic diagram of a
graphics system using four
parallel pixel processors.
Parallel processing may be
extended to the limiting case of
one processor per pixel.

One possible parallel hardware structure is shown in Figure 10.15. The display area is divided into four regions and is served by four similar pixel drivers. The four regions represent four independent memory blocks of the frame buffer where four simultaneous read/write cycles may be executed concurrently. The object server hardware must feed all the geometric objects to all four pixel drivers asynchronously; that is, it must be able to send a new object to any one of the pixel drivers after the completion signal has been received from it. There are two reasons why there is considerable improvement in speed over the single processor.

(1)   For large objects that extend to all four regions, all four processors are executing the rasterization task.

(2)   For small objects that are entirely within one region, three processors return the completion signal immediately and will start work on different objects.

Consequently, it is possible that at any one time four different objects are being rasterized.

The physical arrangement in Figure 10.15, shows the inherent parallel nature of pixel drivers. The z-buffer, which provides the easiest visible surface algorithm for hardware execution, allows all surface calculations to be executed in parallel. Dithering and spatial anti-aliasing are graphical processes that require interaction between neighbouring pixels; thus, they cannot be handled entirely in parallel. The pixels that are at or near to the dividing lines between the regions must be handled by a processor that has access to pixels belonging to more than one region. This will lead to memory access contentions, but the number of pixels at the borders are small compared to the total number, and the loss in speed is not expected to be significant. When the number of processors, and consequently the number of regions, are increased, then anti-aliasing may become a difficult problem.

It is possible to take the subdivision of the display area to its limit and consider using one processor per pixel. This may seem impractical, but it has been shown by Fuchs (1981) that if the processor has just a few very simple instructions, it is possible to construct such a massively parallel video processor by using VLSI components. As an example of a practical one-processor-per-pixel scheme, consider each processor calculating the function:

$$f(x, y) = Ax + By + C \qquad\qquad (10.4)$$

where x and y are the pixel co-ordinates, and A, B and C are constants. For example, the pixel processors in the lower left corner calculate values:

$$f(0, 0) = C$$
$$f(1, 0) = A + C$$
$$f(0, 1) = B + C$$
$$f(1, 1) = A + B + C$$
$$f(2, 1) = 2A + B + C$$
$$...$$

It is possible to arrange the hardware so that these calculations are made in parallel and the pixel processors are updated at the same time. Once the function value has been calculated, it is compared to 0 or the value stored in the z-buffer. On the basis of some of these comparisons, the pixel processor may turn itself OFF, in which case it will not take part in subsequent calculations until it is restarted. The pixel processor can update the z-buffer as well. If the processor is still active at the end of the calculations, then it may set the intensity of the pixel to the last calculated function value.

It is remarkable how many graphics functions can be calculated using the simple linear equation in Equation (10.4) in this way. Containment or clipping using a convex polygon can be calculated by sending the line equations of the edges to the pixel processors. The linear expressions evaluate to a positive number if the pixel is contained inside the polygon, otherwise become negative. Pixels that are outside the polygon are turned OFF by their respective pixel processors.

Gouraud shading also requires a linear formula. In this case, the equations for the colour intensities are sent to the pixel processors. When the coefficients represent a plane equation, then Equation (10.4) can be used to calculate the Z co-ordinate of a facet. Comparison of this Z value with the value stored in the z-buffer determines the visibility of the plane.

When a large number of pixel processors are used, the processing time becomes proportional to the number of geometric objects and remains independent of the number of pixels. For example, if this one-processor-per-pixel system is used for the processing of a large number of planar facets, the entire picture is rasterized for each facet, including visible surface determination. Thousands of facets could be handled in real time if the processing time per facet could be reduced to the order of 50 µs. Since the calculations are simple, this hardware system may become practical in the near future.

10.7   PRACTICAL EXAMPLES

To conclude this chapter on hardware developments, some of the hardware that was available to the authors for generating the illustrations and colour plates in this book is described. There is a danger of becoming out of date when describing state-of-the-art examples in such a rapidly developing field. However, the following examples demonstrate some of the currently available low-cost, graphics hardware facilities and should at least illuminate the gap between what has been presented as possible or desirable and what actually is available.

10.7.1   Extended graphics adapter

The extended graphics adapter (EGA) is supplied for IBM PC/AT and compatible systems. When the frame buffer memory is fully expanded, it can display 16 colours (four bits per pixel) at each of the 224 000, or 640 (horizontal) by 350 (vertical), pixels. The palette has 64 colours (six bits) which are generated by four discrete levels of the RGB intensities. The maximum system has two full frame buffers which can be switched for animation.

Unfortunately, the pixel bits are not simply mapped to memory bits. Machine instructions set different control registers which allow three different memory write schemes. With some of these, it is possible to XOR the bits stored in the frame buffer, whereas with others a number of pixels can be written in parallel and thus increase the pixel writing speed. The irregularity of the mapping between host memory and pixel bits makes it difficult in general to take advantage of the closed coupling between the frame store and the processor. However, considering that the EGA is a very low-priced device, it provides an excellent performance.

The main use of the EGA display system is as a medium-resolution bi-level or business-type display device. Logical colours are used for highlighting and improved man–machine communication. In fact, with the four possible gray levels (black, dark gray, light gray, white), it is possible to supply a minimal form of shading and anti-aliasing.

In summary, the EGA is a minimal closely coupled display system with only a minimum of hardware facilities. Its basic instruction set may be summarized as:

SET_EGA_TO_GRAPHICS_MODE;
RESET_EGA_TO_ASCII_MODE;
SET_PIXEL(*X*: *XRes*; *Y*: *YRes*; *Colour*: *FourBits*);
XOR_PIXEL(*X*: *XRes*; *Y*: *YRes*; *Colour*: *FourBits*);
READ_PIXEL(*X*: *XRes*; *Y*: *YRes*; **var** *Colour*: *FourBits*);
SET_PALETTE(*Colour*: *FourBits*; *ColourType*: *SixBits*);

where:

type *XRes* = 0..639;
 YRes = 0..349;
 FourBits = 0..15;
 SixBits = 0..63;

All other functions of the pixel driver or rasterizer have to be provided by software. For maximum speed, assembler language should be used, but using C has given satisfactory results.

10.7.2 PLUTO System

The PLUTO graphics system manufactured by i-Research Computer Graphics Limited is a loosely coupled graphics system using an Intel 8088 processor dedicated to graphics alone. The display frame buffer in its highest resolution mode has 442 368 or 768 × 576 pixels and normally 256 colours (8 bits per pixel). The palette provides over 16 million (8 bits for each RGB) colours and it is possible to connect three PLUTO systems to provide a full 24-bit shaded colour system.

The 8088 processor runs a local microcode that provides a very large number of rasterizer hardware functions. Only the main features of the instruction set will be described here.

The PLUTO system has four types of output operation:

(1)   Line and circular arc generator.

(2)   Rectangular fill and write pixel operations.

(3)   Block transfer (RasterOp).

(4)   Miscellaneous output operations.

For the first three types, a large number of writing modes can be set, which includes the usual set, clear, XOR, logical OR and logical AND operations. There is a current colour attribute and for the logical functions the current colour value is used. For example, if the current colour number is set to 255 (all 1s) and the XOR operation is selected, then the simple complementing function is achieved. There are additional functions for the three groups which work with any one of the four writing modes.

The line and circular arc generator (or rasterizer) allows a pattern mask that is a sequence of 1s and 0s and controls the generator action. When the pattern mask bit is 1, the function is executed; when it is zero, it is ignored. By application of the pattern mask, dotted or dashed lines, or arcs may be drawn. The line and circular arc generator also includes the skipping of the first point. This is very useful for the complementing function since connected lines (like polylines) will draw the vertices correctly. Otherwise, the point at the vertex would be complemented twice and therefore not drawn. The same problem would occur for a full circle.

The rectangle fill and write pixel operations include the same four drawing functions but no additional features. The complement function for a rectangular area is often used for highlighting menu options, a useful graphical interface feature.

The block transfer operations have only two operands: the source and the destination rectangular areas in the frame buffer. In addition to the four logical functions mentioned, it has a paint mode. This is similar to a copy source mode, except that one specific colour, called the transparent colour, is not copied to the destination but is used as an inhibit function, so that the destination pixel remains unchanged. If the copying of only colour number 255 (all 1s) is needed, then the paint function may also be executed by the logical OR function using colour 0 as the transparent colour. The paint function in general will copy any non-rectangular shape from the source to the destination buffer.

The lack of a third operand for the BitBlt is compensated somewhat by additional functions that allow the complementing and rotation (by either 90°, 180° or 270°) of the source block before the block operation is executed. There is also a special mode available, when the source block is used only as a mask, which determines which one of two designated colours (called foreground and background colours) are used. This mode is useful for writing text on the screen at any position using stored font masks, because the masks do not have to be changed for the changing of the colour of the copied text.

The block transfer operations also include a write protect mask that disables the writing of any one of the eight pixel bits for all BitBlt operations. This feature is helpful in situations where text and graphics are combined and the updating of the two types of information is separated.

Miscellaneous output functions include boundary, flood fill and polygon fill commands. The system also generates Gouraud shaded polygons. An interesting feature of these commands is that the vertex data is scaled by 16; that is, the processor divides the supplied data by 16 before the polygons are rasterized. This improves accuracy without slowing down the operation, since the unscaled pixel locations require two bytes per co-ordinates anyway. The system also provides hardware zooming (up to a factor of 16) and panning facilities, since the actual maximum frame buffer is larger than the area displayed, even at the highest resolution.

The usual commands for setting up the colour lookup table are also available. In fact, two lookup tables are allowed and the active one can be switched between two frame refresh times (during the retrace of the electron beam). This provides another dimension for animation since parts of the display can appear and disappear without the necessity to rewrite the pixel bits. Of course, when the colour lookup table is used to change the images, the number of usable colours is reduced.

Finally, there is a macro facility that allows the storing and execution of a list of graphics instructions without the need to supply each instruction to the PLUTO system one by one. This is a convenient feature for 'customizing' the system for specific applications when standard sequences of instructions can be collected into macro operations and executed by a single macro call. In addition to PLUTO instructions, the macro code can include Intel 8088 assembler code as well. Thus, it is possible to expand the PLUTO microcode by customer supplied code and macro operations.

The main features of the PLUTO system have been described to show that a currently low-priced, medium-resolution graphics system includes many of the hardware features discussed in this chapter. Although it is only a single processor, non-pipelined system, with the decreasing cost of hardware and improving VLSI technology, it can be expected that in a short time many more features and substantially faster speeds will be available for the average graphics user.

Exercises

10.1   For both software-controlled and hardware-generated area fill algorithms, estimate the time it would take to fill in K rectangles of area $A_{\text{rectangle}}$ for a bi-level display with $N \times M$ pixels in the frame buffer and total display area of A_{display}. Use realistic instruction execution times and the hardware structure of a computer you are currently using.

10.2   Describe the functions of the geometric graphics, fundamental graphics and rasterizer units. Relate them to the three software levels: functional, procedural and device.

10.3   Explain why the pixel driver is presented as a separate functional unit and not as part of the rasterizer function.

10.4   Discuss why the input processor unit must be functionally connected to all other hardware units in Figure 10.1. Give specific examples for which these connections are required.

10.5   Discuss how parallel processing and pipelining techniques can be used at the geometric graphics unit level. Quoting specific examples, such as CSG trees and hierarchical object descriptions, discuss whether a large number of similar processors or a number of specifically designed processor types could give better results.

10.6   Discuss the respective advantages and disadvantages of hardware and software curve generation.

10.7   Write a program using your favourite computer language to implement a general frame buffer converter for bi-level (ON/OFF) pixel data. Test your program with line segments at various angles which show up aliasing effects.

10.8   Identify combinations of logical operators *Operator1*( ) and *Operator2*( ) and describe the data stored in the pattern buffer in Algorithm 10.1 with which useful BitBlt operations can be executed. For example, consider operations such as data transfer, character write, area fill with a pattern and pixel complementing.

10.9   Design the processing hardware similar to that shown in Figure 10.14 which includes rotation of the pixel block by 90°, 180°, and 270°.

10.10 Find graphical applications for the one processor per pixel computing scheme and Equation (10.4) which have not been mentioned in the text.

Problems

10.11 Using each of the following rendering techniques, estimate the time it requires to render K coloured (not shaded), randomly distributed spheres with an average projected area of $A/50$ for an $N \times M$ frame buffer covering area A. Use realistic execution times from the hardware manual of a computer you are using.

(a) Painter's algorithm.

(b) Line scan algorithm.

(c) Ray tracing with volume subdivision.

(d) Warnock's area subdivision algorithm.

10.12 Suggest a practical hardware design, using already available processor elements such as transputers or RISCs, which could implement the data flow machine scheme suggested in Figure 10.3. Identify areas where processor interactions occur and estimate the maximum number of processors that could be most likely used without seriously degrading the expected linear dependence of speed on the number of processors.

10.13 Identify 'generic' arithmetic and logical processing functions that may be used as processing units in large numbers in the fundamental graphics pipeline shown in Figure 10.4. Also, identify units that serve specialized functions used once only. From these units, construct the pipeline and estimate the speed increase you would expect under the most optimistic conditions. How could the performance deteriorate under the most pessimistic assumptions?

10.14 Using an available hardware processor (transputer, RISC, microprocessor), design a hardware line generator using Bresenham's line-generating algorithm. If time allows, include features like writing modes, line thickness and line type selection. Estimate the ratio of execution times for hardware and software line generation.

10.15 Repeat the design as described in Problem 10.14 for the differential ellipse generator discussed in Section 3.4.

Project

10.16 Develop a hardware simulator program that uses either the fundamental graphics pipeline or ray tracing algorithms as a basis for the realistic assessment of the computing requirements for graphics problems. Then, study performance by the indicated parallel processing, pipelining and data flow schemes discussed in this chapter. Try to provide realistic simulation to the elements of the system where contention is likely to occur, such as the frame buffer or VRAM, channels between the host computer and the graphics processing elements, and so on.

A | Fundamentals of Vector and Matrix Algebra

The simplest way of describing a vector is as a 1D array of real numbers; hence:

$$[2, 3.1] \qquad [5, 923.8, 665, -1, 1/3] \qquad [\pi, 22, 5]$$

are all vectors. However, for the purposes here, attention will be restricted to two or three dimensions. A geometric interpretation can be given to a 3D vector by associating each element of the vector with distances along the three Cartesian co-ordinate axes. This yields, starting from any point, a line with magnitude and direction, but of no fixed position, as shown in Figure A.1. The convention used here is that **boldface**, lower-case letters represent such vectors, which may be placed anywhere. From Figure A.1, for a vector:

$$\mathbf{p} = [p_x, p_y, p_z]$$

the application of Pythagoras's theorem gives the magnitude of the vector as:

$$|\mathbf{p}| = \sqrt{(p_x^2 + p_y^2 + p_z^2)}$$

The direction of the same vector may be expressed by the cosine of the three angles it makes with the X, Y and Z axes. These can be expressed by:

$$\cos(\theta_x) = \frac{p_x}{|\mathbf{p}|} \qquad \cos(\theta_y) = \frac{p_y}{|\mathbf{p}|} \qquad \cos(\theta_z) = \frac{p_z}{|\mathbf{p}|}$$

It is convenient to distinguish a special type of vector, called a unit vector, whose magnitude is equal to unity. These will be designated by

483

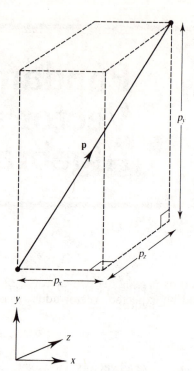

Figure A.1
The three components of a vector define its magnitude and direction but usually no fixed position in space is assigned to the vector.

boldface italic script. From the expressions of the cosines just given, it can be seen that for a unit vector **d**, the components of the vector are equal to:

$$d = [d_x, d_y, d_z] = [\cos(\theta_x), \cos(\theta_y), \cos(\theta_z)]$$

Unit vectors are also called direction cosines, because of the relationships between their components and the cosines of the angles.

As unit vectors in the directions of the three co-ordinate axes will be frequently encountered, it will prove convenient to reserve standard letters for them; namely, *i*, *j* and *k*, where:

$$i = [1, 0, 0] \quad j = [0, 1, 0] \quad \text{and} \quad k = [0, 0, 1]$$

Vector addition is achieved simply by adding up the individual elements of the vectors:

$$s = \mathbf{p} + \mathbf{q} = [p_x, p_y, p_z] + [q_x, p_y, q_z] = [p_x + q_x, p_y + q_y, p_z + q_z]$$

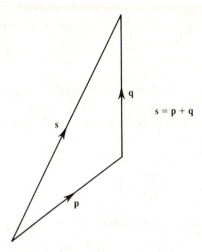

$s = p + q$

Figure A.2
The addition of two vectors can
be geometrically constructed by
drawing a triangle with vector **s**
defined as the sum of vectors **p**
and **q**.

This may be visualized by placing the two vectors end to end, as shown in Figure A.2. As would be expected, vector addition is both commutative and associative; so:

$$p + q = q + p \quad \text{and} \quad p + (q + s) = (p + q) + s$$

Subtraction of two vectors is done similarly:

$$p = s - q = [s_x, s_y, s_z] - [q_x, p_y, q_z] = [s_x - q_x, s_y - q_y, s_z - q_z]$$

where the geometric interpretation gives a vector that extends from the end point of **q** to the end point of **s**.

There are three ways of multiplying vectors. These are multiplication by a real number, and the dot and cross products. Multiplication by a constant real number, a (called a scalar in this context), is defined by:

$$a p = [a p_x, a p_y, a p_z]$$

where as long as $a > 0$ only the magnitude of the vector changes – its direction remains constant. If $a < 0$, then the vector is rotated 180°; if $a = 0$, then the result is equal to [0, 0, 0], which is a special case of a vector that has zero magnitude and an undefined direction. Multiplication by a scalar is distributive with respect to addition or subtraction:

$$a(p + q) = a p + a q \quad \text{or} \quad a(p - q) = a p - a q$$

The dot or scalar product of two vectors is defined as:

$$p \cdot q = p_x q_x + p_y q_y + p_z q_z$$

which produces a single real number and it can be easily verified that:

$$\mathbf{p} \cdot \mathbf{q} = |\mathbf{p}| |\mathbf{q}| \cos(\theta)$$

where θ is the angle between the two vectors. From this definition, it can be seen that orthogonal vectors have a zero dot product, a property that is very useful for using vectors in the analysis of 3D Cartesian space. The dot product is commutative and distributive with respect to addition (or subtraction) of vectors:

$$\mathbf{p} \cdot (\mathbf{q} + \mathbf{s}) = \mathbf{p} \cdot \mathbf{q} + \mathbf{p} \cdot \mathbf{s} \quad \text{and} \quad \mathbf{p} \cdot (\mathbf{q} - \mathbf{s}) = \mathbf{p} \cdot \mathbf{q} - \mathbf{p} \cdot \mathbf{s}$$

From the definition of the dot product, it can be easily shown that:

$$a\mathbf{p} \cdot b\mathbf{q} = ab(\mathbf{p} \cdot \mathbf{q})$$

The cross, or vector, product is defined by:

$$\mathbf{p} \times \mathbf{q} = (p_y q_z - p_z q_y)\mathbf{i} + (p_z q_x - p_x q_z)\mathbf{j} + (p_x q_y - p_y q_x)\mathbf{k} \qquad \textbf{(A.1)}$$

The cross-product of two vectors is a vector whose direction is orthogonal to the plane in which they lie. The magnitude can be shown to be equal to:

$$|\mathbf{p} \times \mathbf{q}| = |\mathbf{p}| |\mathbf{q}| \sin(\theta)$$

where θ is the angle between $\mathbf{p}$ and $\mathbf{q}$.

If, for example, $\mathbf{p} = i$ and $\mathbf{q} = j$, then the cross-product becomes:

$$i \times j = (0 \times 0 - 0 \times 1)i + (0 \times 0 - 1 \times 0)j + (1 \times 1 - 0 \times 0)k = k$$

which is a unit vector along the z axis. The direction of the resulting vector is into the plane, as shown in Figure A.3, which sets up a left-handed co-ordinate system with the x axis pointing to the right, the y axis upwards and the z axis into the plane of the page. This left-handed co-ordinate system is used throughout this book.

The cross-product is not commutative because:

$$\mathbf{p} \times \mathbf{q} = -(\mathbf{q} \times \mathbf{p})$$

The exchange of the order in which the vectors are cross-multiplied rotates the resulting vector by 180°. Also, it is not associative, so that:

$$\mathbf{p} \times (\mathbf{q} \times \mathbf{s}) \neq (\mathbf{p} \times \mathbf{q}) \times \mathbf{s}$$

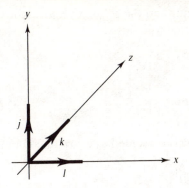

Figure A.3
The left-handed co-ordinate system is characterized by three mutually perpendicular unit vectors *i*, *j*, and *k* where *k* = *i* × *j* and the directions of the unit vectors are as shown in the diagram.

The cross-product is distributive with respect to addition and subtraction of vectors, thus:

$$\mathbf{p} \times (\mathbf{q} + \mathbf{s}) = \mathbf{p} \times \mathbf{q} + \mathbf{p} \times \mathbf{s}$$

and a similar relationship holds for subtraction. From the definition of the cross-product, it is also possible to show that:

$$(a\mathbf{p}) \times (b\mathbf{q}) = ab(\mathbf{p} \times \mathbf{q})$$

If the cross-product of two vectors is equal to 0, then the directions of the two vectors are equal or one is rotated by 180° with respect to the other.

A matrix is constructed as a vector of vectors; that is, as a vector whose components are vectors themselves. A 3 × 3 matrix M may be shown as:

$$M = [\mathbf{m_1}, \mathbf{m_2}, \mathbf{m_3}]$$

where $\mathbf{m_1}$, $\mathbf{m_2}$ and $\mathbf{m_3}$ are 3D vectors. The elements of a matrix can be indicated by two indices, such as m_{11} and m_{12}, and can be laid out as a 2D array of real numbers:

$$M = \begin{bmatrix} m_{11} & m_{12} & m_{13} \\ m_{21} & m_{22} & m_{23} \\ m_{31} & m_{32} & m_{33} \end{bmatrix}$$

The normal convention is that the first index refers to the row, while the second refers to the column number of the matrix. To draw a parallel between the elements of a matrix and its representation as a vector of vectors, two different graphical representations of a vector are needed –

namely, the row vector and the column vector. Row vector $\mathbf{r}$ and column vector $\mathbf{c}$ are represented as follows:

$$\mathbf{r} = [r_1, r_2, r_3] \qquad \mathbf{c} = \begin{bmatrix} c_1 \\ c_2 \\ c_3 \end{bmatrix}$$

Thus, a matrix can be represented as a row of column vectors:

$$M = [\mathbf{m_1}, \mathbf{m_2}, \mathbf{m_3}]$$

where:

$$\mathbf{m_1} = \begin{bmatrix} m_{11} \\ m_{21} \\ m_{31} \end{bmatrix} \qquad \mathbf{m_2} = \begin{bmatrix} m_{12} \\ m_{22} \\ m_{32} \end{bmatrix} \qquad \mathbf{m_3} = \begin{bmatrix} m_{13} \\ m_{23} \\ m_{33} \end{bmatrix}$$

or as a column of row vectors:

$$M = \begin{bmatrix} \mathbf{m_1} \\ \mathbf{m_2} \\ \mathbf{m_3} \end{bmatrix}$$

where:

$$\mathbf{m_1} = [m_{11}, m_{12}, m_{13}]$$
$$\mathbf{m_2} = [m_{21}, m_{22}, m_{23}]$$
$$\mathbf{m_3} = [m_{31}, m_{32}, m_{33}]$$

With the introduction of row and column vectors, the dot product of two vectors is redefined by the requirement that the vector on the left must be a row vector and that on the right a column vector:

$$\mathbf{p} \cdot \mathbf{q} = [p_1, p_2, p_3] \cdot \begin{bmatrix} q_1 \\ q_2 \\ q_3 \end{bmatrix} = [p_1 q_1 + p_2 q_2 + p_3 q_3]$$

In this way, two types of multiplication of a vector by a matrix are defined. When the vector is on the left, then it is a row vector and the matrix is expressed as a row of column vectors. The product results in a vector whose components are dot products of the row vector on the left and the three column vectors on the right:

$$\mathbf{r} = \mathbf{p} \cdot M = \mathbf{p} \cdot [\mathbf{m_1}, \mathbf{m_2}, \mathbf{m_3}] = [\mathbf{p} \cdot \mathbf{m_1}, \mathbf{p} \cdot \mathbf{m_2}, \mathbf{p} \cdot \mathbf{m_3}]$$

where the components of $\mathbf{r}$ are given by:

$$r_1 = p_1 m_{11} + p_2 m_{21} + p_3 m_{31}$$
$$r_2 = p_1 m_{12} + p_2 m_{22} + p_3 m_{32}$$
$$r_3 = p_1 m_{13} + p_2 m_{23} + p_3 m_{33}$$

A matrix–vector product is also defined with the matrix on the left and the vector on the right, in which case the vector must be a column vector and the matrix is expressed as a column of row vectors. In this case:

$$\mathbf{r} = M \cdot \mathbf{p} = \begin{bmatrix} \mathbf{m_1} \\ \mathbf{m_2} \\ \mathbf{m_3} \end{bmatrix} \cdot \mathbf{p} = \begin{bmatrix} \mathbf{m_1} \cdot \mathbf{p} \\ \mathbf{m_2} \cdot \mathbf{p} \\ \mathbf{m_3} \cdot \mathbf{p} \end{bmatrix}$$

and the components of the product vector are:

$$r_1 = p_1 m_{11} + p_2 m_{12} + p_3 m_{13}$$
$$r_2 = p_1 m_{21} + p_2 m_{22} + p_3 m_{23}$$
$$r_3 = p_1 m_{31} + p_2 m_{32} + p_3 m_{33}$$

which are not the same as those of the first product; therefore, the vector–matrix multiplication is not commutative.

Similarly, the product of two matrices can be defined by expressing the matrix on the left as a column of row vectors:

$$R = M \cdot T = \begin{bmatrix} \mathbf{m_1} \\ \mathbf{m_2} \\ \mathbf{m_3} \end{bmatrix} \cdot T = \begin{bmatrix} \mathbf{m_1} \cdot T \\ \mathbf{m_2} \cdot T \\ \mathbf{m_3} \cdot T \end{bmatrix}$$

or expressing the matrix on the right as a row of column vectors:

$$R = M \cdot T = M \cdot [\mathbf{t_1}, \mathbf{t_2}, \mathbf{t_3}] = [M \cdot \mathbf{t_1}, M \cdot \mathbf{t_2}, M \cdot \mathbf{t_3}]$$

In both cases, the result is a matrix and the elements of the matrix are the same and can be expressed as:

$$r_{ij} = \sum_{k=1}^{3} m_{ik} t_{kj}$$

So far, 3×3 matrices and 3D vectors have been used for the demonstration of vector–matrix and matrix–matrix products. For a general matrix having M rows and N columns, the row–vector multiplying it from the left must have M components, while the column–vector multiplying it from the right must have N components. If such a general $M \times N$ matrix is multiplied from the left by another matrix, it must have M columns, while a matrix multiplying it from the right must have N rows. This can be seen from the expression given for the components of the product matrix. In fact, the expression given for r_{ij} is applicable for a vector–matrix product when i has the value of one only, or for a matrix–vector product when j is equal to one.

As might be expected, the matrix–matrix product is not commutative. However, either the matrix–matrix, the matrix–vector or the matrix–vector products are associative with respect to matrix–matrix multiplication, so that:

$$\mathbf{p} \cdot (M1 \cdot M2) = (\mathbf{p} \cdot M1) \cdot M2$$

or

$$(M1 \cdot M2) \cdot \mathbf{p} = M1 \cdot (M2 \cdot \mathbf{p})$$

or

$$(M1 \cdot M2) \cdot M3 = M1 \cdot (M2 \cdot M3)$$

The vector–matrix product may be interpreted as a linear transformation, since the vector–matrix product of a 3D vector $\mathbf{p}$ and a 3×3 matrix A is equal to a 3D vector $\mathbf{q}$:

$$\mathbf{p} \cdot A = \mathbf{q}$$

Given the vector $\mathbf{q}$, this equation is interpreted as three linear equations with three unknowns:

$$a_{11}p_x + a_{21}p_y + a_{31}p_z = q_x$$
$$a_{12}p_x + a_{22}p_y + a_{32}p_z = q_y$$
$$a_{13}p_x + a_{23}p_y + a_{33}p_z = q_z$$

where p_x, p_y and p_z are unknowns. This vector–matrix equation can be solved symbolically by multiplying both sides of the equation by a matrix that is the inverse of matrix A, for which the symbol A^{-1} is used:

$$(\mathbf{p} \cdot A) \cdot A^{-1} = \mathbf{p} \cdot (A \cdot A^{-1}) = \mathbf{p}I = \mathbf{p} = \mathbf{q} \cdot A^{-1}$$

where **I** is the identity matrix, an $N \times N$ matrix whose main diagonal elements are all equal to 1 ($a_{ii} = 1$) and all other elements are equal to 0 ($a_{ij} = 0$ for $i \neq j$). For the 3D case:

$$A \cdot A^{-1} = I = \begin{bmatrix} 1 & 0 & 0 \\ 0 & 1 & 0 \\ 0 & 0 & 1 \end{bmatrix}$$

if the inverse of matrix A exists. A matrix whose inverse exists is called non-singular. A matrix is non-singular if its determinant is not equal to 0, which means that the foregoing vector–matrix equation represents a proper linear transformation and the system of equations can be solved for its unknowns. If the determinant of a matrix is equal to 0, then the matrix is singular, which means that any one row (or column) vector in the matrix can be expressed as a linear combination of the other row (or column) vectors of the matrix.

The determinant of a square matrix of dimension $N \times N$ is a number associated with that matrix that can be computed recursively from the equation:

$$\mathrm{Det}(M) = m_{1,1} \qquad \qquad \text{if } N = 1$$

$$= \sum_{j=1}^{N} (-1)^{j-1} m_{1,j} \, \mathrm{Det}(M_{(-j)}) \qquad \text{if } N > 1$$

where $M_{(-j)}$ is the matrix formed by deleting row 1 and column j from matrix M.

The determinant is used in methods of inverting matrices. It is also a convenient notation for expressing certain equations. For example, the cross-product of two vectors can be conveniently written as the determinant:

$$\mathbf{p} \times \mathbf{q} = \begin{bmatrix} p_x & p_y & p_z \\ q_x & q_y & q_z \\ i & j & k \end{bmatrix}$$

The reader may care to verify that evaluation of this determinant yields the result given in Equation (A.1).

The only other matrix operation used in the book is called the transpose of a matrix (or a vector). The transpose of matrix A is indicated by the symbol A^t. For a square matrix, it is the reflection of the elements of the matrix through the main diagonal. For example, if B is the transpose of A, then:

$$B = A^t \quad \text{and} \quad b_{ij} = a_{ji}$$

The transpose of a vector changes its type from a row vector to a column vector and vice versa. The identity:

$$(A^t)^t = A$$

holds for all matrices. The transpose of an $N \times M$ matrix is equal to an $M \times N$ matrix, and can also be expressed by the equation $b_{ij} = a_{ji}$. Using the transpose, it can be shown that for vector $\mathbf{p}$ and matrix M the vector–matrix product is equal to the matrix–vector product of the transpose, or:

$$\mathbf{p} \cdot M = M^t \cdot \mathbf{p^t}$$

The Cartesian co-ordinate system is defined by three unit vectors i, j and k. If another co-ordinate system is defined by three mutually perpendicular unit vectors, say u, v and w, then the dot product is very useful for expressing the co-ordinates of any vector in the new co-ordinate system. A vector $\mathbf{p}$ has components:

$$\mathbf{p} = [p_x, p_y, p_z]$$

in the $[x, y, z]$ co-ordinate system. The unit vectors u, v and w can also be expressed in the $[x, y, z]$ co-ordinate system having components:

$$
\begin{aligned}
u &= [u_x, u_y, u_z] & u_x^2 + u_y^2 + u_z^2 = 1 \\
v &= [v_x, v_y, v_z] & v_x^2 + v_y^2 + v_z^2 = 1 \\
w &= [w_x, w_y, w_z] & w_x^2 + w_y^2 + w_z^2 = 1
\end{aligned}
$$

Since the vectors are perpendicular:

$$u \cdot v = v \cdot w = u \cdot w = 0$$

The components of the $\mathbf{p}$ vector in the $[u, v, w]$ co-ordinate system satisfy the following vector equation:

$$\mathbf{p} = p_u u + p_v v + p_w w$$

where dot products yield the scalar component values:

$$p_u = \mathbf{p} \cdot u = p_x u_x + p_y u_y + p_z u_z$$

and, similarly:

$$
\begin{aligned}
p_v &= \mathbf{p} \cdot v = p_x v_x + p_y v_y + p_z v_z \\
p_w &= \mathbf{p} \cdot w = p_x w_x + p_y w_y + p_z w_z
\end{aligned}
$$

References

Arvo J. and Kirk D. (1987). Fast ray tracing by ray classification. *ACM Computer Graphics*, **21**(4), 55–63.

Ayala D., Brunet O., Juan R. and Navazo I. (1985). Object representation by non-minimal division of quadtrees and octrees. *ACM Trans. Graphics*, **4**, 41–59.

Baecker R. M. (1969). Picture driven animation. *Proc. AFIPS SJCC*, **34**, 273–88.

Barsky B. B. and Beatty J. C. (1983). Local control of tension in Beta-splines. *ACM Trans. Graphics*, **2**(2), 109–34.

Blinn J. F. (1982). A generalisation of algebraic surface drawing. *ACM Trans. Graphics*, **1**(3), 235–56.

Brady M. (1982). Trajectory planning. In *Robot Motion: Planning and Control* (M. Brady, J. M. Hollerbach, T. L. Hohnson, T. Lozano-Perez and M. T. Mason, eds.). The MIT Press.

Bresenham J. E. (1965). Algorithm for computer control of a digital plotter. *IBM Syst. J.*, **4**(1), 25–30.

Bui-Tuong Phong (1975). Illumination for computer generated pictures. *CACM*, **18**(6), 311–17.

Burtnyk N. and Wein M. (1976). Interactive skeleton techniques for enhancing motion dynamics in key frame animation. *CACM*, **19**(10).

Cayley A. (1845). On certain results relating to quaternions. *Philosophical Magazine*, **26**, 141–5.

Chazelle B. and Incerpi J. (1984). Triangulation and shape complexity. *ACM Trans. Graphics*, **3**, 135–52.

Clark J. H. (1982). The geometry engine: A VLSI geometry system for graphics. *Computer Graphics*, **16**(3), 127–33.

Cook R. L. and Torrance K. E. (1982). A reflectance model for computer graphics. *ACM Trans. Computer Graphics*, **1**(1), 7–24.

493

Earnshaw R. A., ed. (1985). Fundamental algorithms for computer graphics. *NATO ASI Series* Vol. F17. Springer-Verlag.

Fischer P. and Smith W. R. (1985). *Chaos, Fractals and Dynamics*. Marcel Dekker.

Fournier A. and Montuna D. Y. (1984). Triangulating simple polygons and equivalent problems. *ACM Trans. Graphics*, **3**, 153–74.

Fuchs H. and Poulton J. (1981). Pixel planes: A VLSI-oriented design for a raster graphics engine. *VLSI Design*, **2**(3), 20–8.

Ghosh P. K. and Mudur S. P. (1984). The brush trajectory approach to figure specification: Some algebraic solutions. *ACM Trans. Graphics*, **3**, 110–34.

Floyd R. W. and Steinberg L. (1975). An adaptive algorithm for spatial grey scale. *SID 1975 Int. Symp. Dig. Tech. Papers*, **36**.

Gervautz M. and Purgathofer W. (1988). A simple method for colour quantisation: Octree quantisation. In *New Trends in Computer Graphics* (Magnenat-Thalmann and Thalmann, eds.), pp. 219–31. Springer-Verlag.

Gomez J. E. (1984). Twixt: A 3D animation system. In *EUROGRAPHICS 84* (Bo and Tucker, eds.), pp. 121–33. Elsevier Science Publishers.

Gouraud H. (1971). Computer display of curved surfaces. *IEEE Trans.*, **C20**(6), 623.

Griffiths J. G. (1987). Rendering with space filling curves. *Proc. CG87*. ONLINE Publications: London.

Halas J. and Manvell R. (1968). *The Technique of Film Animation*. Hastings House: New York.

Hamilton W. R. (1844). On quaternions: Or on a new system of imaginaries in algebra. *Philosophical Magazine*, **25**, 10–13.

Hayward S. (1984). *Computers for Animation*. Focal Press: London and Boston.

Huitric H. and Nahas M. (1985). Realistic effects with Rodin. In *Frontiers of Computer Graphics, Proceedings of Computer Graphics Tokyo 84* (Kunii, ed.). Springer-Verlag.

Kajiya J. T. (1983). New techniques for ray tracing procedurally defined objects. *Computer Graphics*, **17**(3), 91–102 (SIGGRAPH 1983).

Kallis S. A. (1971). Computer animation techniques. *J. Soc. Motion Pictures and Television Engineers*, **80**(3), 145–8.

Knowlton K. C. (1965). Computer produced movies. *Science*, **150**, 1116–20.

Latham W. (1986). Form Synth, the rule based evolution of complex forms from geometric primitives. In *Computer Graphics in Art Animation and Design* (J. Landsdown and R. A. Earnshaw, eds.). Springer-Verlag (in press).

Martin B. (1986). Graphic potential of recursive functions. In *Computer Graphics in Art Animation and Design* (J. Landsdown and R. A. Earnshaw, eds.). Springer-Verlag (in press).

Nahas M. and Huitric H. (1982). Computer painting with Rodin. *IEEE Symposium on Small Computers in the Arts*, pp. 95–103.

Potmesil M. and Chakravarty I. (1982). Synthetic image generation with a lens and aperture camera model. *ACM Trans. Graphics*, **1**, 85–108.

Reeves W. T. (1981). In-betweening for computer animation using moving point constants. *Computer Graphics*, **15**(3), 263–9.

Reeves W. T. (1983). Particle systems – A technique for modelling a class of fuzzy objects. *ACM Trans. Graphics*, **2**, 91–108.

Reghbati H. K. and Lee A. Y. C., eds. (1988). *Tutorial: Computer Graphics Hardware, Image Generation and Display*. IEEE Computer Society Press.

Roberts L. G. (1964). Machine perception of three dimensional solids. In *Optical and Electro-optical Information Processing* (J. T. Tippet, ed.), pp. 159–97. The MIT Press.

Shoemake K. (1985). Animating rotation with quaternion curves. *Computer Graphics*, **19**(3), 245–54 (SIGGRAPH 1985).

Sutherland I. E., Sproull R. F. and Schumacker R. A. (1974). A characterisation of ten hidden surface algorithms. *Computing Surveys*, **8**, 1–55.

Taylor R. H. (1982). Planning and execution of straight line manipulator Trajectories. In *Robot Motion: Planning and Control* (M. Brady, J. M. Hollerbach, T. L. Hohnson, T. Lozano-Perez and M. T. Mason, eds.). The MIT Press.

Torrance K. E. and Sparrow E. M. (1967). A theory for off-specular reflection from roughened surfaces. *J. Opt. Soc. Am.*, **57**, 1105–14.

van Aken J. and Novak M. (1985). Curve drawing algorithms for raster displays. *ACM Trans. Graphics*, **4**(2), 147–69.

van Wijk J. J. (1984). Ray tracing objects defined by sweeping planar cubic splines. *ACM Trans. Graphics*, **3**, 223–37.

Warnock J. E. (1968). *A Hidden Line Algorithm for Half-tone Picture Representation*. University of Utah Computer Science Report TR 4–5 (NTIS AD 761 995).

Warnock J. E. (1969). *A Hidden Surface Algorithm for Computer Generated Half-tone Pictures*. University of Utah Computer Science Report TR 4–15 (NTIS AD 753 671).

Wyvill B., McPheeters C. and Wyvill G. (1986). Animating soft objects. *The Visual Computer*, **2**, 235–42.

Index

497